(12)
15
35382
B4

The Measurement
of Economic and Social Performance

NATIONAL BUREAU OF ECONOMIC RESEARCH

*CONFERENCE ON RESEARCH IN INCOME
AND WEALTH*

The Measurement
of Economic and Social
Performance

MILTON MOSS, Editor

NATIONAL PLANNING ASSOCIATION
AND NATIONAL BUREAU OF ECONOMIC RESEARCH

Studies in Income and Wealth
VOLUME THIRTY-EIGHT
*by the Conference on Research
in Income and Wealth*

NATIONAL BUREAU OF ECONOMIC RESEARCH
NEW YORK 1973

Distributed by COLUMBIA UNIVERSITY PRESS
NEW YORK AND LONDON

Printed in the United States of America

Prefatory Note

THIS volume of *Studies in Income and Wealth* contains the papers presented at the Conference on the Measurement of Economic and Social Performance held November 4–5, 1971, at Princeton University, under the joint sponsorship of the university's Department of Economics and the NBER's Conference on Research in Income and Wealth. We are indebted to the National Science Foundation for its support and to the Program Committee which consisted of Dale W. Jorgenson, F. Thomas Juster, and Milton Moss, who also served as program chairman and conference editor.

We acknowledge with gratitude the preparation of this volume for publication by Ester Moskowitz, and preliminary editorial work by Virginia Meltzer. H. Irving Forman drew the charts with his customary skill.

Funds for the economic research conference program of the National Bureau of Economic Research are supplied by the National Science Foundation.

Contents

The Measurement
of Economic and Social Performance

Introduction

MILTON MOSS

WHEN this conference was first planned, in late 1969, the national economic accounts were being subjected to considerable challenge. Gross national product, the principal output of the accounts, was under attack both as a goal of national effort and as a measuring rod of economic performance.

Some have deplored the pursuit of high growth in GNP as a goal, asserting that it distorts national priorities, does not improve or may even worsen the distribution of income, and irreparably damages the environment. Critics have asserted that countries with the highest levels of GNP are not necessarily the ones with the highest life expectancy, lowest crime rate, or cleanest air.

Critics have charged that as a measuring rod GNP gives incorrect indications of changes in welfare mainly because it fails to allow for the disamenities associated with industrial growth, particularly pollution of air and water. Some have also argued that even apart from not serving as an adequate index of welfare, which it was not designed to do, GNP fails to serve as an accurate index of economic growth, in large part because it does not include appropriate measures of economic performance of households and governments.

While these charges are not new, their recent intensification has come, interestingly enough, at a time when the U.S. national accounts have been enjoying the widest acceptance here and abroad by nearly all classes of users—and when the publication each quarter of the latest figures has continued to be prime news in the major newspapers and broadcast media in this country. These attacks, moreover, may have appeared to be crudely lacking in appreciation for the very substantial advances achieved by the U.S. Department of Commerce in recent years to widen the scope of the accounts and improve their detail and timeliness.

The present conference, held at Princeton in November 1971, brought together divergent points of view, including the professional users of the accounts and those responsible for their compilation. Thus, the conference helped sharpen some of the issues and, it was hoped, pointed the way toward resolution of some of them.

Measurement problems were the direct concern of this conference, with policy goals only an indirect concern. As such it was reminiscent of an earlier Income and Wealth Conference held in November 1955.[1] Indeed, as Simon Kuznets observes in his "Concluding Remarks" to this volume, many of the problems raised in the conference are of long standing, having been brought to light, as we all know, in good part by Simon Kuznets himself. Both conferences were concerned with probing "truer" appraisals of performance, i.e., with improved definitions of *final* product, and both were concerned with seeking more useful and comprehensive accounting designs, i.e., with better modes of arrangement, sectoring, and classification. Nevertheless, the present conference differed in certain significant respects.

Indeed, the present conference reflected in good part the emergence of issues which were given relatively little attention in 1955. Thus, because of the greatly heightened concern with pollution, it gave far more explicit attention than the earlier one to the problem of assessing the impact of production and consumption on the physical environment. The subject of the allocation of time was new compared to the earlier conference, and so were some of the suggestions for and attempts at bold new imputations to measure nonmarket activities.

Generally speaking, by its emphasis on the welfare implications of the accounts, particularly nonmarket amenities and disamenities and on the possibility and consequences of capitalizing human capabilities, this conference gave far more attention than the earlier one did to the personal and household sector. Notwithstanding this concern with persons and households, little attention was given to the distribution of personal income and wealth.[2]

The present accounts seek to measure and summarize transactions for the entire economy, covering income and expenditures of businesses, households, governments, and other groups. In arriving at a measure of economic performance or net output of all of these transactions, the accounts total the final sales made mainly by the enterprise economy to other groups, principally households and governments for their consumption and to enterprises themselves for capital formation. Thus,

---

[1] The proceedings of that conference were published as *A Critique of the United States Income and Product Accounts*, Studies in Income and Wealth 22, Princeton University Press for the National Bureau of Economic Research, 1958.

[2] Two conferences on distribution have been scheduled to follow this one.

the scope of the measure of economic performance is confined in broad terms mainly to production for sale by enterprises.

Largely because this net output sum can be and is measured in "quantity" or constant price terms, the national accounts have a significant welfare dimension. The accounts can be used, for example, to determine whether the physical volume of goods purchased by consumers in one year is larger than in another year, and very importantly whether that increased volume has been obtained by working more hours or by achieving more output per hour. A determination can also be made of whether the added output as presently measured is currently more widely distributed among households than before. Finally, the accounts permit the determination of whether the stock of capital required by enterprises to produce this volume of goods has increased or not after allowance for capital consumption. Net national product (NNP) in constant prices rather than GNP thus becomes the measure of net economic performance in the present conceptual framework of the national economic accounts. In these respects, GNP and NNP do provide highly consequential measures of economic welfare and performance. But the conference sought to go beyond these measures. In seeking to broaden the scope of measurement of economic performance and possibly welfare, the conference raised essentially two sets of questions.

1. Should the measurement of economic performance extend significantly beyond the enterprise economy? For example, should it include households—their capital formation and their production? Should it also include an evaluation of environmental resources that reflects both their deterioration and improvement? And finally should the measure include the services supplied by government and not merely, as at present, the wages it pays?

2. Should the measurement of economic performance of enterprises themselves be re-examined? For example, should the measure of business capital formation and depreciation be modified in significant ways?

The importance of these questions stems not so much from matters of conceptual curiosity as from reactions to major changes in the patterns and consequences of economic growth. Over a measurable period of several decades, households have undergone considerable change, as married women have increasingly devoted more time to paid work in enterprises and government and less in the home. Investment by persons and families in tangible capital equipment and in education has risen greatly, changing the pattern of time and expenditure allocated to work both in the market and at home and to investment and consumption.

The increase in the volume and variety of government services and in related capital investment has been a major feature of economic change in recent decades.

The changed distribution of effort among households, government, and enterprises devoted to satisfying wants has raised the question of whether sales of goods and services by enterprises per se can serve as an adequate measure of total economic output and income. Also, the marked shift in investment from enterprises to households and government has raised a similar question: whether a full measure of capital formation by society is adequately comprehended in a measure restricted largely to capital formation by enterprises.

Associated with such questions as the scope of production and of capital formation are the matters of cost and of final consumption. If costs or payments for using up resources are restricted to those paid for by enterprises, what then of losses of resources which everyone uses but no one individual or firm owns—such as the losses from using up clean air and clean water?

And what about enterprises themselves? With marked changes in tax laws permitting charge-offs on buildings and machinery that bear little relation to the rate of their economic usages; with enormous increases in outlays by business on research and development; with increasing expenditures devoted to abating pollution and to services typically provided by government such as education or job training, health plans, and police services—should not the costs of production, capital formation, and net output of the enterprise sector itself be reexamined?

GENERAL PROPOSALS FOR NEW FRAMEWORKS

Most of the main measurement issues are covered in a general way in the challenging paper by Thomas Juster and the forceful reactions by George Jaszi.

Juster's most important proposals are to include a capital account for the tangible or physical capital of households and government and for the intangible capital of households and enterprises; to develop a new accounting for environmental pollution and its abatement; and to undertake a major extension in the accounts for the nonmarket activities of households organized around the allocation and evaluation of householders' time.

The proposal to establish an account for tangible capital held by households and governments met little opposition, at least on conceptual grounds. Jaszi points out that official work has been underway to establish such accounts, particularly for autos and household durables. He warns, however, that serious problems, especially for government capital, still remain unsolved, such as what items of equipment and construction should be covered, how to value and depreciate them and what service lives to assume.

Among the most intensively discussed questions were those that pertained to control of the environment, in part because this was also the most prominent public issue for the conference. The issue is of considerable consequence for measurement of economic performance since expenditures for pollution control are expected to become a large portion of total national expenditures,[3] and to exert a substantial influence on prices, real output, and productivity.

Juster argues that recognition should be given in economic measurement to the fact that air and water are assets, and that the benefits from them have been seriously diminished by economic production and consumption. But he recognizes that solving the difficulties of calculating a regular measure of these benefits or damages seems highly remote if not impossible. Most of the discussion on the environment is concerned with how to treat expenditures for pollution abatement. The question at issue is: do these expenditures add to net output or do they simply offset a deterioration that otherwise would have occurred? In Juster's view, they are simply an offset and should not be included in a measure of real output, at least in a measure which is welfare-oriented. In Denison's view, which Jaszi favors, they should be considered as an addition to real output.[4] They should certainly be added in according to Jaszi if the expenditure is by consumers—and they are so added presently in the accounts. If the expenditure is by business they are now counted as intermediate but Jaszi suggests that this treatment might need to be reconsidered.

In Denison's view, the subtraction or deflation of a consumer expenditure for an antipollution device, say an emission filter in an automobile, implies, falsely, that we would be no better off with the antipollution device than without it. The expenditure should therefore be counted as final rather than intermediate product. Robert Solow, in his comments, however, makes the point that essentially the same argument

[3] See the paper by Herfindahl and Kneese, Table 1, in this volume.
[4] See Edward Denison, "Welfare Measurement and the GNP," *Survey of Current Business,* January 1971. A reprint of the article was distributed to conference participants as a background paper because of its direct pertinence to the subject of the conference.

can be made about any intermediate product. Replacing or repairing worn-out machinery, for example, makes us better off than if we did not make such replacements.

The idea of excluding from GNP expenditures the so-called regrettable necessities drew considerable debate. Most of the controversy arose because of opposition to attempts to orient GNP toward a measure of welfare. But it also stemmed conceptually from the proposal to extend the concept of production to include household production and of capital to include human capital. So long as expenditures could be identified as inputs to production (whether in households or business) or as serving only to maintain capital intact rather than to augment the capital, Juster argues that such expenditures should be treated as intermediate rather than final output. For example, time and money spent to travel to work or expenditures for drugs to combat illness serve respectively as inputs to production or to maintain human health intact.

In this view such expenditures are analogous to business expenditures on current account, say, either for fuel or supplies, or for repair and maintenance of physical equipment and plant. Their only difference, it might be argued, is that they pertain to human or household production or capital rather than to business production or capital.

Jaszi turns a good deal of his fire against the concept of "regrettable necessities" and against the proposal for a major extension of the accounts to include imputations for the nonmarket activity of households. No meaningful line can be drawn, in his view, between expenditures that are for their own sake and those which are means, inputs, or regrettable costs to achieving direct satisfaction. Jaszi raises similar objections to Juster's suggestion that the allocation of household time be classified so as to separate hours which are truly outputs from those which represent inputs. He also questions whether a meaningful value can be placed on nonmarket time, most particularly leisure time.

Robert Eisner in commenting on the Jaszi-Juster exchange sides with the view that the present classification of outlays by households, governments, and business firms should be re-examined to determine which more precisely reflect expenditures on current and which on capital account, i.e., to delineate more sharply those which contribute to future income and those which contribute to present consumption. Thus, Eisner would have business firms capitalize R and D expenditures, and not count them as current costs. He urges that the reckoning of depreciation of business plant and equipment be made on an "economic" rather than internal-revenue basis as at present, and also favors counting consumer durables as investment, since the stream of services they yield over time is as much consumption if provided in the home as by the business establishment.

Jaszi reminds participants that efforts have been underway in his office to incorporate several proposals to modify the accounts, including: the aforementioned estimation of stocks of consumer durables, the substitution of a measure of "economic" rather than tax-related depreciation of business capital, and the planning for development of an information base for identifying the major sources of environmental pollution and of expenditures to abate such pollution.

Nancy and Richard Ruggles, in addition to proposing changes in the conceptual design of the accounts, reaffirm their steadfast interest in greatly increasing the detail of economic information for the study of consumer and business behavior at the level of the decisionmaking units. For several years they have actively pursued their mission to win support for developing this detail from much of the economic and social information gathered in the various record-keeping practices of society.

There is a growing recognition that all sorts of information now gathered for government administration or statistical purposes for individuals, households, and governments could be utilized much more efficiently. In their paper, the Ruggleses recommend, first, extending further the efforts to merge data from different record sets and surveys, for example, income data from tax returns with demographic data from Census surveys. This need not be done for all individuals or even for an identifiable sample. It could be done "synthetically" or statistically by creating a synthetic record for each unit in the combined data set. The term "synthetic" is used because it would be done for a statistically created unit rather than by matching records for the same individuals.[5] With this procedure the identity of individual reporting units cannot be disclosed.

The Ruggleses also recommend, second, aggregating these microdata sets within a consistent national accounting framework. Among other gains, this would provide a much improved basis for simulation of the effects of government policies. For example, the integrated microrecords, by allowing for the differing responses by different individuals and firms to changes in tax laws or social security legislation, could enable

---

[5] See, for example, Edward C. Budd, "The Creation of a Microdata File for Estimating the Size Distribution of Income," *Review of Income and Wealth,* December 1971. Budd explains the techniques of *statistical* matching he used in merging microdata files from various sources to improve income data by type of income and income recipient.

an estimation of effects on federal revenues and expenditures or national consumption and savings which could be much more accurate than if the simulation were done on the basis of national accounting aggregates alone. Fairly detailed simulations are of course now being made with the IRS Tax Model or with the Current Population Survey. But the Ruggleses recommend a fairly extensive merging of such files with other records and an integration with the National Income Accounts.

After aggregation to national totals, and in order to keep the household sector as identifiable as possible, the Ruggleses recommend that households be set up as a separate sector apart from nonprofit institutions, and that these institutions, plus the business and government enterprises, be combined into a new enterprise sector.

Their third recommendation is to provide, to the extent feasible in the microdata sets and at aggregate levels, information on household and government capital formation, capital gains, investment in education, and research and development outlays by business. These data would provide the basis for new capital accounts for business, households, and governments as recommended by Juster, and by others, principally Kendrick and Eisner.

In commenting on the Ruggleses' paper, Edward Denison agrees on the importance of developing synthetic microdata sets for economic analysis, but he seriously questions whether the microdata sets will aggregate to the national economic accounts as readily as the Ruggleses seem to suggest. As Denison states, totals from the former are on a combined basis while those from the latter are on a consolidated basis. Denison also disagrees on the desirability of separating nonprofit institutions from households, and "diluting" the analysis of productivity change by including these institutions with business enterprises. Perhaps the ideal solution is to attempt to have a separate sector entirely for nonprofit institutions.

Douglas Hartle in his comments requests a clearer conceptual framework for deciding what, besides national accounting-type data, should be recorded in microdata sets. Hartle seeks a microrecord which might embody the concept of maximizing an individual's net worth, broadly defined. Toward this end, Hartle proposes a balance sheet and net worth statement for each person, presumably on a sample basis, showing the present value of expected lifetime benefits and costs which might be estimated as associated with certain assets and liabilities. The assets would include, in addition to marketable assets, human capital and claims specific to the person and to his group or community. The categories proposed require a wide range of imputations concerned with social advantage and disadvantage. They extend well beyond the measurement of economic performance per se, into that of society as a whole. Hartle's highly imaginative proposal contains no clear clues, however, for implementation.

Abraham Aidenoff in his general comments describes the exploratory attempts by the United Nations to integrate social and economic statistics by combining social indicators on the conditions of the population, say health and education, with data on the resources expended by establishments providing the services of health, education, etc., to the population, and with information on the distribution of income and wealth.

HOUSEHOLD AND BUSINESS SECTORS

Subsequent papers contain more intensive examinations of certain of the issues discussed earlier. In regard to the household sector, the papers deal with highly specialized issues, rather than with the sector as a whole. One such issue, and a major one in the conference, relates to the valuation of nonmarket time of households. How are the activities of housewives, students, and social service volunteers to be valued? Many hours of many people are devoted to such nonmarket activities, the time devoted to such activities has changed markedly, and these activities more often than not represent substitutes for services performed by enterprises and other organizations that pay wages. As evident in the Nordhaus-Tobin paper, discussed later, the calculation of the level and change of total economic effort is substantially altered if nonmarket activities are included.

Two problems need to be solved in this reckoning: how many person-hours are devoted to such activities and what price per hour should be used in the different nonmarket activities? Is the average wage rate, for example, a useful basis for such an evaluation?

Reuben Gronau addresses himself to the latter question. In one of the few empirical studies in the conference, he attempts to deal with the problem of estimating the value of housewives' time based on a survey of labor force participation of Israeli women. By comparing married women who do and do not work in the market (standardized for income of husband, age and education of wife, and presence of children under three years of age), Gronau derived estimates of the value of time of housewives that turned out to be approximately the same as the average wage rate of women who worked.

Gronau basically sought to determine why some married women work for market pay and others stay at home. Are the ones who work for wages poorer homemakers, on the average, than those who stay at home, or are they simply better wage earners? The women who remain housewives have a higher value of time than the average wage of working women with similar market qualifications if the first assumption is true and lower if the second. The two alternative assumptions give rise in Gronau's paper to two estimates, an upper one based on the first assumption and a lower one based on the second. Using the Israeli data on labor force participation of women and their wage rates Gronau found that the two estimates did not differ markedly, a finding which suggested to him that the average wage rate was a reasonable proxy for the value of a housewife's time.

Gilbert Ghez applauds Gronau's ingenious attempt to obtain estimates of the value of time of married women who stay at home, using essentially only data on labor force participation and the average wage rate to accomplish this. Ghez's comments on Gronau's paper should be viewed mainly as suggestions for future research rather than as complaints, given the limitations Gronau faced of inferring from the sample survey of Israeli conditions. Ghez does suggest, however, a number of interesting and sometimes rather subtle factors which might be further researched and which could influence the choice married women face between working at home and working for wages. Ghez's own research on the allocation of time and consumption over the life cycle, for example, leads him to suggest that the choice between working now or later in life or spending time at home now or later could be affected by "a positive rate of interest . . . [and] changes in nonmarket productivity" with age. These factors, according to Ghez, can give rise to variations in the price of time independently of the presence or absence of children.

Dan Usher's paper is concerned with how to go about giving economic recognition to what he believes to be one of the most important dimensions of individual welfare: life expectancy. He grants that a value for increased life expectancy should not be imputed in the standard economic accounts, which are concerned largely with marketed output. In a welfare-oriented measure, however, Usher believes that such an imputation makes a good deal of sense.

Usher calls attention to large increases in life expectancy in recent years in most countries, particularly for the developing countries. In consequence of these increases in longevity per se, individuals have been given the prospect of an increase in total permanent or lifetime income and consumption.

Under the present reckoning of economic performance, a decline in welfare occurs if per capita GNP falls because of an increase in population relative to GNP. Suppose, however, that the relative increase in population occurred solely because of a decline in the death rate. Would the decline in per capita GNP resulting from increased longevity give the correct welfare indication? Common sense would suggest that the individuals concerned would feel better off because of the increased prospect of longer life per se. How should this increased longevity per se be valued? Usher is careful to distinguish the concept he seeks from others which, for this purpose, should not be used. He narrows the concept down to the question: "How much would I pay to avoid a small probability of my death?"

Usher discusses the acute difficulties of imputing a value of life, considering the great variation among persons as to the amount they would be willing to pay for avoiding a small probability of death. While this variation raises philosophic questions about putting a higher value on the life of a rich versus a poor man, Usher nevertheless does suppose there is a unique price corresponding to a set of national mortality rates and a level of total permanent consumption, as there would be if society were "one individual writ large." This price would only apply at an aggregate level.

Usher finds that the rate of growth of real income in Canada from 1926 to 1968 is significantly increased if it is inclusive of an imputation for the average increase in life expectancy. On the basis of his preferred estimates, the effect of the imputation for increased life expectancy is to raise the annual growth rate by about half a per cent per year—from about 2.3 per cent without the imputation to 2.8 per cent.

Robert Willis presents an illuminating discussion of the complex questions of income and utility raised in Usher's paper. He contrasts Usher's concept with the more conventional one and shows how Usher's emphasis on *lifetime* utility could help deepen the conventional one. Willis is impressed with the sizable effect the longevity imputation has on the Canadian growth rate and suggests that it may be too high.

Willis points out that Usher began his theoretical model with the injunction, "Ignore the fact that men live in families and that families are imbedded in communities of people who are concerned with each other's being." Since the increase in life expectancy—particularly pronounced for underdeveloped countries—has been mainly in the decrease in infant mortality, shouldn't this increase in utility be assigned to the parents rather than, as Usher does, to their offspring? If so, the imputation for increased longevity would be reduced since this gain in lifetime consumption would be less for parents than for their offspring.

Usher's paper may not in the first instance result in the widespread development of a major new imputation in present economic accounting, but it does raise one of the more profound philosophic questions concerning the meaning of income to the individual and to society. It gives pause to any easy answer to the question of a possible trade-off between increasing per capita GNP and lengthening the life span.

In moving from the household to the private sector as a whole, Laurits Christensen and Dale Jorgenson present a major proposal for developing a new simplified system of accounts for both flows and stocks. Their paper provides for a consistent set of accounts for production, income, and expenditure, and for capital accumulation and its period-to-period revaluation, all in current and constant prices for the period 1929–69. Estimates are presented for the private sector including households by extending their "enterprise" activities from investment in housing, as presently treated in the accounts, to investment in consumer durables. In their concluding section Christensen and Jorgenson propose extensions of the capital accounts to include investment in human capital and in research and development. A number of other major extensions are also suggested in their presentation.

Several key measures of economic performance are derived from the authors' presentation of the data: output in constant prices, output per unit of capital and labor input, and an interesting new concept which Christensen and Jorgenson call "standard of living," and which they calculate as the ratio of expenditures to factor income, each in constant prices. This ratio is equivalent to a ratio of the price of total factor income to the price of expenditures. If the price of income of both capital and labor rises relative to those of commodities and services, then the purchasing power of that income rises, and, by definition, so does the "standard of living." It is a broader concept of standard of living than one based solely on real wages.

In his comments on the Christensen and Jorgenson paper, John Kendrick particularly commends them for presenting both income *and* wealth accounts consistent with one another, and providing such consistency in current and constant dollars. He encourages them to extend their system beyond the private economy, suggesting also that for purposes of productivity analysis a clearer separation would be desirable between businesses on the one hand and households and nonprofit institutions on the other. In this way, productivity analysis of the business sector could be kept "clean" of the imputations needed for the household and institutional sectors. In connection with the accounts in constant prices, however, Kendrick questions the deflators at a number of points.

Robert Eisner raises the question of what formula to use in measuring the decline in value of a given capital good, a perennial question. In Eisner's view, the long-run solution to this vexing problem is to undertake major empirical work to illuminate the actual path of depreciation. In the meantime, he advocates the use of a straight-line depreciation path, not a geometric one, as he alleges Christensen and Jorgenson have used. The authors reject Eisner's criticism on the ground that what was employed in the paper was a geometric decline in a *cross section* ("across vintages") not "over time," as Eisner assumed was done.

It is hoped that this technical question, which has important implications for how the U.S. capital stock should be valued, can be further illuminated by showing how in fact the behavior of a geometric decline "across vintages" differs from that "over time."

THE PUBLIC SECTOR

If the welfare dimension of a national measure of economic and social performance is to have any substance, a major portion will perforce relate to our capability for appraising the quantity and quality of services provided by governments. But nowhere is measurement of performance more difficult than for services and especially the services of the public sector. The cost of welfare-oriented public sector services including those for income support, education, health, housing and community development, and manpower training—the so-called "human resource" programs —have risen dramatically in the last decade to approximately $110 billion or 45 per cent of the total federal budget for fiscal 1973. Some believe this allocation of funds is far too small; others, that it is excessive. Most agree that we cannot be sure which of these judgments is correct since we cannot in fact measure its real value. The same argument goes for other public outlays, whether for defense, the largest part of the budget, space, general government, or various international programs. What is the fundamental difficulty—lack of a measure of "prices," or lack of a measure of the "physical" content of the service?

Mancur Olson in his paper argues that the main difficulty lies in the inability of government to determine what the physical output of the service really is. It is this difficulty, in Olson's view, which results in the alleged inherent inefficiency in government. Olson dismisses various other explanations for alleged inefficiency, for example, that government decisions are not "governed" by competitive markets. To Olson the clue to the difficulty lies in the "collective" nature of public goods where the physical aspects cannot readily be divisible into measurable units and where the distribution of benefits and costs are exceedingly difficult to trace. The solution in his view lies in developing "social indicators." In that way a move toward "output-type" measures of social conditions would get started. Olson also recommends conducting experiments to determine consumer demand functions as a means of obtaining "market" evaluation of public services.

Charles Schultze argues that the problem is not in our inability to identify the physical content of the particular government service to be rendered but in the price per unit to assign to it. From his perspective as former director of the Bureau of the Budget he probably could recall that the acute difficulty in allocation decisions was not in understanding what a given service was intended to do but whether that service or some other "equally persuasive" one represented a better buy for the Budget dollar. In fact, the problem of defining benefits has both a physical volume and price dimension, inextricably related, and elusive for society to appraise. Olson and Schultze in their exchange of views serve to indicate the great difficulties involved in quantifying these dimensions.

The difficulties of determining real output of the educational system are surveyed by Alice Rivlin. Rivlin discusses six alternative approaches and finds them all wanting, mainly for two reasons: first, the quality of education varies greatly from school to school, which lessens the usefulness of measures such as those based on years of schooling, on number and types of courses taken, degrees obtained, etc.; second, as has been often noted, the students and their family background may play a large role in student performance, which belies in good part the significance of measures based on test scores. Differences in such scores over time or among schools may significantly reflect changes in the school population or in the way that population is mixed rather than in the improved use of resources by the schools themselves. Rivlin concludes that the search for performance measures is worthwhile but should not necessarily be done in the context of the national economic accounts, given the present state of the arts. She implies that we should "live with" input measures, but with more provision for differences in various classes of manpower in the schools, recognizing that no input measure, however detailed by class of input, can by itself measure productivity of education.

Burton Weisbrod, in commenting on both the Olson and Rivlin papers, suggests that in many service areas, such as Medicare and recreation, governments are often not so much concerned with the efficiency with which resources are allocated for the given activity as a whole as with "distributional efficiency." The government in some cases will set a zero price in order to insure equality of access—at least as far as price effects can provide such equality. He then raises the interesting point that a given output in the aggregate differently distributed may in fact imply a different aggregate value. He does not, however, indicate how different values may be placed on different distributions of a given aggregate.

Ernest Grove in his characteristic style takes issue sharply with Olson and suggests that the problems of government inefficiency lie in the inherent nature of bureaucratic organization itself. He argues for more individual responsibility and, with Ralph Nader, urges that the professional employee should feel a "duty to dissent" but be "protected by an organization of his peers, by his professional society, and by law that requires due process and substantial justice."

Zvi Griliches raises the general question of the difficulty of measuring the contribution of investment in research to economic growth, particularly the calculation of the *social* rate of return of such investment.

Nestor Terleckyj calls attention to the joint character of public and private inputs in contributing to varied outputs, and of various outputs contributing differently to social welfare goals. Based on studies he is undertaking in goals analyses he urges the use of a matrix both of public and private inputs (represented by the quantities of specific goods and services) and of outputs (represented by the change in selected indicators of well-being). For example, if the data were available, such a matrix might show the marginal contribution to longevity associated with given activities aimed at curtailing smoking or reducing obesity, contingent on the existence of other activities.

AMENITIES AND DISAMENITIES OF ECONOMIC GROWTH

While positions differed markedly on whether GNP should or should not measure welfare there seemed broader agreement that some attempts should be made to provide some measures of the positive and negative consequences of economic production and consumption. Such a measure need not seek to put plus or minus values on every economic activity.

It could attempt to deal with a few major matters of social concern such as the costs of environmental control or of urban congestion on the negative side and, say, of leisure presumably on the positive side. The paper by Orris Herfindahl and Allen Kneese and that by Wassily Leontief analyze in greater detail than discussed in the earlier papers the measurement issues connected with environmental control. William Nordhaus and James Tobin present a bold attempt to put values on several positive and negative consequences of economic growth in their measure of economic welfare.

Herfindahl and Kneese in a highly comprehensive paper examine three problem areas: the possibility of modifying GNP or NNP to measure the benefits and costs associated with pollution and its abatement; models specifically designed to measure the effects of alternative strategies of production, consumption, and pollution control; and information systems of a highly specialized nature which would help in the design and detailed administration of pollution control schemes.[6]

In reviewing the problems of measurement within a national accounts framework, Herfindahl and Kneese conclude with others that the comprehensive evaluation of changes in the flow of services of clean air, water, and space seems to present a hopeless task, even though that calculation might appear to be necessary for welfare determination. However, some systematic accounting of expenditures to control or defend against pollution appears to be mandatory considering the prospect of huge and rising outlays for this purpose. While no one disputes this accounting need, the question is: how should this accounting be done?

The authors concede, perhaps with some reluctance, that the official definitions in the national accounts should not be changed. They recommend nevertheless the regular preparation and publication of series showing the expenditures for control of waste products arising from production and consumption by industry, government, and consumers. This information could be used, according to the authors, to interpret changes in GNP or NNP associated with expenditures for environmental control. They could provide the basis for supplementary adjustments to GNP and NNP, listed by the authors, to satisfy different points of view on whether pollution control does or does not contribute to the output of final product.

[6] Orris Herfindahl died on December 16, 1972, in Nepal, while on a hiking expedition in the Himalayas. The paper reflects the keen interest and concern he had for the natural environment.

Herfindahl and Kneese warn, however, that accurate information on these expenditures may be exceedingly difficult to obtain. The separate identification of abatement expenditures, they indicate, cannot be very precise in such cases as when a new plant or process is introduced which among many other innovations also happens to cut down on pollution emissions.

The authors then proceed to examine in considerable detail four types of models designed to measure the benefits and costs of environmental control: a national input-output model, as formulated by Leontief; regional and interregional input-output models; a materials-balance model; and the Russell-Spofford model.

They discuss in some depth the limitations of each approach, partly conceptual and partly lack of data. They point to the present lack of detailed information on such matters as the marginal response (often nonlinear) of costs—direct and indirect—and of various benefits sought; the damages, say to health, of different degrees of pollution; the effect that the control of emissions to one environmental medium may have at the expense of increased discharge to another; and the features of pollution abatement often unique to small geographic areas. National models by definition cannot cope with unique regional problems; input-output models which are regional do not encompass all materials flows within the complexities of ecological systems; while the materials-balance model, although it seeks to account for all materials flows has not yet been fully linked to economic models. The Russell-Spofford model seeks the widest applicability in scope and concreteness of all the ones described.

In a final section, Herfindahl and Kneese highlight the fact that the development of an information system needed to integrate environmental aspects (physical, chemical, biological, medical aspects) with economic ones—all for purposes of monitoring, analyzing, and administering pollution control programs—is bound to entail an extraordinary effort. Nevertheless, they recommend that such efforts be undertaken presumably because their cost is still likely to be small compared to the great urgency and magnitude of the environmental pollution problem.

William Vickrey, among the first to advocate use of the price system to further welfare objectives in controlling socially undesirable effects of production and consumption, suggests that pollution control per se need not always be very costly when such control helps also to check other diseconomies. This appears possible, at least in the case of the automobile, if the imposition of user charges to reduce the cost of traffic congestion and of accidents were also to be coupled with the imposition of charges to reduce the pollution resulting from such congestion.

Wassily Leontief, who in recent years has introduced applications of input-output to the analysis of environmental pollution and its abatement, presents a schematic and instructive table of interindustrial flows expanded to include the generation and elimination of pollution. With such a table, adequately detailed, it should be possible to compute the costs of an additional unit of output of any good and of any eliminated unit of the net output of each major pollutant. Basic features of this approach are appraised in the Herfindahl-Kneese paper.

One of the main questions of the conference was how a reasonably broad assessment of the amenities and disamenities of economic growth would compare with actual GNP or NNP? Would the nation show the same growth rate?

To arrive at an answer, Nordhaus and Tobin seek a comprehensive measure of the annual real consumption of households, or a "measure of economic welfare" (MEW). This is in contrast to GNP or NNP which, in their view, are measures of *output,* and are the relevant measures both for short-run stabilization policy and for assessing the economy's long-run performance as a productive machine. In aiming at a *consumption* measure, MEW also differs from an index of happiness, since it does not attempt to say whether today's U.S. consumer with all his goods and services is any happier than his less affluent counterpart of years past or of some other country.

The authors aim at a more modest measure of welfare, though bold enough, by making the following main adjustments to GNP or NNP: they include values for what in their judgments are major contributions to direct consumption, not now counted, chief of which are imputations for leisure and for nonmarket activities, and exclude values which do not contribute to direct consumption, the most important of which are expenditures for national defense, and a "disamenity" correction for the "costs of urbanization"—or the added costs associated with the crowded and other unpleasant conditions of city living.

Since MEW is calculated on a per capita basis, a quantitatively significant and subtle adjustment is also made to GNP for what the authors term the "growth requirement." The explanation for this starts with NNP. By allowing for capital consumption, NNP should indicate that level of consumption which could be extended indefinitely into the future. But Nordhaus and Tobin assert that NNP fails to do so. They seek to prove that in order to maintain consumption at a constant level on a per capita basis the capital stock must grow at a rate equal to that of the population. The "growth requirement" then is an estimate of the cost, over and above capital consumption as presently calculated for NNP, necessary to maintain a rate of growth in the capital stock equal to the rate of growth in population. This is a difficult concept and dependent upon restrictive assumptions concerning technological change but it results in a sizable adjustment, amounting in 1965 to 16 per cent of GNP.

Nordhaus and Tobin find that with their admittedly tentative numbers the corrections in level are very substantial—more than twice the official level of NNP. The annual rate of growth of MEW, however, is slower, 1.1 per cent for MEW as against 1.7 per cent for NNP per capita over the period 1929–65. These figures are based on their preferred variant of MEW.

Perhaps the most interesting inference drawn by the authors is their answer to the question posed by the title to their paper, that growth is not obsolete, that zero economic growth is far too crude a response to removing the disamenities of positive economic growth, and that better solutions lie in developing economic incentives to innovate and utilize more salubrious technologies.

Largely because the imputation for leisure dwarfs all other imputations in the Nordhaus-Tobin paper (it is one-half of total MEW or exceeds total NNP in 1965) the discussion focused largely on the imputation for leisure.

Edward Denison questions the fundamental approach to valuing leisure time at a price equal to the hourly wage: either that of the base year, as in variant A of the Nordhaus-Tobin paper, or the wage rate in each year adjusted for changes in commodity prices, as in variant C.

Denison argues that the conceptually appropriate hourly wage for valuing leisure time should equal the difference between the utility of that hour of free time which a person would be most willing to give up (his hour with least utility) and the disutility of the most onerous hour passed in gainful work (the hour with the greatest disutility). Hence, one approach for arriving at a value of the marginal nonworking hour would be to *subtract* from the hourly market wage the disutility of the marginal working hour. That resulting value might of course be only a very small fraction of the hourly market wage.

Denison directs other criticisms to the "correction" for leisure time.

He also alerts future imputers to the fact that the large variance in working time—from zero to more than 45 hours per week—requires recognition of the nonlinear change in the value of time in relation to a given decrease in working hours. The value of one hour of nonworking time will differ, he warns, if obtained with a decrease from 45 to 44 as compared to a drop from say 10 to 9 hours per week.

John Meyer calls attention to interesting differences in direction between MEW and NNP, expressing his "feeling" that on the whole when the two diverge MEW is not necessarily superior as a welfare indicator to NNP. In particular, he believes that the decline in NNP in the 1929–35 period gives a more accurate measure of change in welfare than MEW, which is stable or slightly rising over that time span. An improved measure of human capital, indicating more of its deterioration during the early 1930s and its improvement after 1947, would in Meyer's view strengthen MEW for measurement of economic welfare. Meyer also makes a number of suggestions for refining the calculation of MEW, especially the adjustments for the disamenities of urbanization. This latter suggestion is also stressed in the comments by Fred Singer.

Nordhaus and Tobin agree on the need to refine the calculations regarding urbanization. On the matter of leisure, they concur that many unanswered questions are involved in determining the number of hours and their value—both empirical and conceptual. Questions of fact concerning the number and composition of hours of leisure and nonmarket activities remain to be determined in future studies of the allocation of time. These points as well as a number of highly intricate questions of concept are examined in the closely reasoned replies by Nordhaus and Tobin.

CONCLUDING REMARKS

Simon Kuznets in his concluding remarks reminds us all that many of the issues raised in this conference—of the dividing line between economic and noneconomic, productive and unproductive, of distinguishing between costs and returns—have been the foci of discussions in various forms for some two centuries.

For Kuznets this re-emergence in new guise of some of the perennial problems of economics relates in good part to the effects of and concern with economic growth. The high rates of growth obtained in recent years in many countries have brought about deep changes in the condition of life in the home, in industry, and in the cities and towns. To comprehend these enormous shifts, Kuznets calls for new experimental scholarly research, as exemplified by the Nordhaus-Tobin exploratory effort. He sees research efforts such as those on human capital, on deeper analyses of real income distribution, on measures of the long-run sustainable growth path, and on the "final" goals of economic output as best done outside of government. With this characteristic forward look from Simon Kuznets the conference was brought to an end.

Proposals for New Frameworks for the Measurement of Economic and Social Performance

A Framework for the Measurement of
Economic and Social Performance

F. THOMAS JUSTER

NATIONAL BUREAU OF ECONOMIC RESEARCH

INTRODUCTION

THE present system of U.S. national income and product accounts has, in recent years, been subjected to mounting criticism relating to conceptual framework, what is included and excluded from measured final output and income, the adequacy with which the accounts carry out their intended purposes, and whether they can and should be more specifically designed to measure changes in economic welfare. The criticism has been as diverse in its sources as in its content: social accountants have pointed to deficiencies in the capital accounts, in the treatment of household economic activity, and in the treatment of consumption provided directly by business enterprises; [1] those in the forefront of the ecology movement, including a number of physical scientists, have issued scathing and often ill-informed critical comment about the degree to which the present accounts overstate the gain in real income because of the way in which environmental deterioration and the unwanted byproducts of economic

NOTE: With minor changes in language, the text of this paper is identical to the draft discussed at the Princeton conference, thus enabling the reader to see what the discussants were reacting to rather than what I might have written with the benefit of the discussion. A few clarifying footnotes have been added, and these are identified by asterisks.

In addition, I have appended several supplementary notes to the paper, and have prepared a brief reply to George Jaszi's comments. The supplementary notes are designed to clarify issues which were raised at the conference and which were not discussed adequately in the original paper.

[1] See N. Ruggles and R. Ruggles, *The Design of Economic Accounts,* New York, NBER, 1970; J. W. Kendrick, "The Treatment of Intangible Resources as Capital," paper presented to the Twelfth General Conference of the International Association for Research in Income and Wealth, Ronneby, Sweden, September 1971; F. T. Juster, *Household Capital Formation and Financing, 1897–1962,* New York, NBER, 1966; R. Eisner, "Measurement and Analysis of National Income (Non-income Income)" in NBER, *51st Annual Report,* New York, 1971, pp. 79–80.

activity are handled; and even the "man in the street," as represented by the popular literature produced by journalists and other writers, has been sufficiently aroused to add an occasional voice to the chorus.

Although a fair amount of the more extreme critical comment is based either on misinformation or superficial analysis of what the accounts do and do not measure, a cogent argument can be made for the view that the present set of national accounts provides an increasingly deficient representation of the substantive economic activities taking place within the system, and that many of these deficiencies are capable of being remedied by using available data within a broadened framework of what might best be termed Economic and Social Accounts. The fact that this conference was held is itself a clear indication of discontent with the existing system of accounts, as well as a reflection of recent conceptual and empirical developments that could form the basis for a restructuring of the system.

In examining the relation between a system of social accounts and the measurement of economic and social performance, the question of what constitute feasible objectives of an accounting system must be kept in mind. We want the accounts to record changes in the material wellbeing of the community. That evidently means that the accounts must register changes in the flow of goods and services going through the market mechanism, where the bulk of economic activity takes place, but it does not preclude the accounts from registering nonmarket activity to the extent that it bears directly and measurably on material wellbeing. In addition, we want the accounts to say something about the efficiency with which flows of goods and services accomplish their economic objectives, that is, whether the community is doing better or worse as reflected by what the economic and social system is accomplishing and not by recording effort or costs that represent inputs into the system. That is a thorny and complicated question, and a good bit of attention is devoted to it in the paper.

Finally, economists generally have no desire to turn the accounts into some sort of happiness index, in which one's ability to get along with one's wife or children, or to find an appropriate mate, or to realize the more fundamental philosophical purposes of human existence constitute potential measures of performance. These may well be more important considerations than mere material goods and services, but they are not within the purview of the economist or the social accountant. Thus the system of social accounts is inherently limited in what it does and ought to try and measure, but within these limits there are wide differences of view as to what activities should be included and what measurements can or should be made.

A system of economic and social accounts must be designed to serve the needs of at least two broad groups of actual or potential users. One is the scientific community, including economists and other social scientists as well. Social scientists need a system of accounts which illuminates the problem they are investigating. The objectives, broadly speaking, are to describe, understand, explain, and ultimately predict significant economic and social phenomena. The accounts have long been used for this purpose by economists with an interest in the macroeconomic problems of cyclical fluctuations in output, employment, and prices, and in the macroeconomic problems of economic growth. For reasons discussed in more detail below, I would argue that the present accounts are better adapted to analysis of cyclical problems than real economic growth problems.

A second important group of users are those concerned with the formulation of public policy. To identify and establish the quantitative significance of social and economic problems and priorities, policy makers need, among other types of information, a set or sets of accounts which describe the significant dimensions of the system for which they are responsible. Also, a system of comprehensive performance measures is clearly indispensable both for any evaluation of changes in policy and for the analysis of policy alternatives.

In an important sense, it is probably true that the demand of policy makers for economic and social performance accounting systems is really derived from the demands of social scientists. Without the aid of the latter in building and testing models with behavioral content and demonstrated predictive value, little effective use can be made of the system by policy makers. Thus, the major policy uses of the present accounts have been for the range of problems where social scientists have found the accounts most useful, that is, for the analysis of macroeconomic problems of cyclical variability in output, employment, and prices. To see this, one need only ask how much of our present rather substantial (though still far from satisfactory, as witness the last several years) progress in understanding and forecasting economic aggregates would have been possible without the present set of National Income and Product Accounts.

The Present Accounts: Background and Framework

The present U.S. economic accounts have their roots in the conceptual and empirical work undertaken in the early part of the century by King and culminating in the much more fully articulated system devised by

Kuznets,[2] along with the conceptual modification and extensive operational work done by Gilbert, Jaszi, and their associates at the Office of Business Economics during the 1940's and continuing up to the present.[3] The current version of the Accounts is, except for the treatment of government, basically consistent with the Kuznets framework developed in the 1930's. Of course, there have been a great many changes in methods and sources of measurement, and some rather more modest changes in the conceptual treatment of various types of both actual and imputed transactions. In addition, the analysis of National Accounts aggregates has, during recent decades, tended to focus much more on gross rather than net output concepts, which represents a marked departure from the emphasis found in Kuznets. But that is largely a consequence of the kind of uses to which accounts have been put rather than any change in conceptual treatment; the more net measures of economic output still continue, and are still used by those concerned with economic growth.

The boundary line for activities considered to be economic in the present system of accounts, and considered as resulting in a flow of output and income, can be broadly characterized as being drawn to include virtually all market activities and to exclude virtually all nonmarket ones. This boundary results from the distinctions in the accounts between the activities of business enterprises and those of households. When a product or service leaves the enterprise sector and comes into the possession of a household unit, neither its durability, its requirements for complementary inputs of time and other goods owned by the household in producing satisfactions, nor its substitutability for goods or services provided within the household itself are considered to be of interest to the social accountant. The only exception to this generalization is the treatment of owner-occupied housing, where the account adopts the convenient fiction of supposing that households are really small firms

[2] See W. I. King, *The National Income and Its Purchasing Power,* New York, NBER, 1930; and S. Kuznets, *National Income and Its Composition, 1919–1938,* New York, NBER, 1941; Kuznets, *National Product in Wartime,* New York, NBER, 1945; Kuznets, *National Product Since 1869,* New York, NBER, 1946; and Kuznets, *National Income: A Summary of Findings,* New York, NBER, 1946.

[3] See M. Gilbert, "Statistical Sources and Methods in National Accounts Estimates and the Problem of Reliability," in *International Association for Research in Income and Wealth,* Series III, 1951; G. Jaszi, "The Conceptual Basis of the Accounts: A Re-examination" in *A Critique of the United States Income and Product Accounts:* Studies in Income and Wealth, Vol. 22, Princeton University Press for NBER, 1958; and G. Jaszi, "The Statistical Foundations of the Gross National Product," *Review of Economics and Statistics* Vol. 38, 1956, pp. 205–214.

selling the services of housing to themselves at values commensurate with that of housing rented in the market.

A second important boundary relates to the treatment of capital formation. The only capital assets recognized as having the capacity to yield future services consist of tangible structures and equipment owned by business enterprises, including the fictional owner-occupied housing owned by the "household" enterprise. All other forms of investment, whether they be tangible assets owned by households and governments, intangible capital assets (knowledge acquired through research and development outlays) owned by business firms or governments, or increases in the stock of skills and knowledge embodied in humans and acquired through investment in some form of education or training, are considered to be current consumption flows if they are included in the accounts at all.

These boundaries, especially the first, are not of course fully observed even in the present accounts. It has been useful to estimate implicit prices for various kinds of activities which clearly represent market-type activity even if no actual market transaction takes place. Cases in point are the treatment of food consumed on farms by the owner, and the value of financial services rendered by banks in situations where legal prohibitions prevent a market price from emerging of its own accord. But a basic premise of the present accounts is that valuation of activities that lack explicit market prices is justifiable only in cases where a simple, objective, and easily identified basis for the valuation is available.[4]

To understand the framework of our present accounts, it is helpful to recall the economic background during the period of their development. The system was formulated during the 1930's and 1940's, when the main forces affecting the level and movement of economic activity were initially cyclical, subsequently the national defense effort. During major cyclical swings in the level of economic activity, focusing on market output produced a measure whose welfare implications were probably very similar to those that would have resulted from focusing on a much broader range of activities. And during a major war, the emphasis was naturally on productive capacity for military output, for which a measure like GNP is well suited—better suited, for example, than a measure like

---

[4] As pointed out many years ago by Kuznets, the presence of an apparently comparable valuation base does not necessarily solve the problem: for example, farm families probably consume more food of the type they grow themselves than if they sold the crop and purchased food in the open market—in effect, food consumed by farm families is overvalued.

NNP. In consequence, given the catastrophic decline in market activity during the Great Depression and the subsequent recovery when World War II erupted, many of the welfare-oriented conceptual problems gradually came to be regarded as of little practical or analytical importance, even though these problems had undergone extensive discussion during the formative period of the account. Hence, the account came de facto to be largely a reflection of economic "activity," regardless of the purposes to which the activity was directed.

The National Income and Product Accounts of the U.S. are thus basically designed to provide an efficient measure of cyclical changes in total activity. In such a framework, the focus is on flows of inputs and outputs; stocks of assets are important only insofar as they cause cyclical movements in the related flows. A similar rationale can be adduced for the concentration in the accounts on the amount of time allocated to market activities: if cyclical variability is the major concern, the critical labor-time variable is the amount of market employment and unemployment, not the amount of time people choose to allocate to nonmarket activities, leisure, etc. Hence, the allocation of labor-time has always been viewed as a simple flow of inputs yielding market income, with no attention paid to the fact that time allocated to the market is only one of many possible uses.

Given this background, it was natural for the emphasis to be on a system of accounts designed to trace variations in output, employment, and productivity in the market sector, where performance during the 1930's had been so unsatisfactory. Moreover, it was entirely reasonable to equate changes in output thus measured with changes in economic and social welfare, since changes in the one dominated changes in the other. But during the past few decades, both empirical and analytical developments suggest that the present framework needs to be modified, perhaps substantially so, if it is to provide a satisfactory basis for gauging either performance or material wellbeing.

Recent Empirical and Analytical Developments

The degree to which a set of economic accounts serves both the scientific and policy needs of potential users depends in part on the nature of the problems that have the highest priority. As argued above, the present accounts are basically designed to be effective in the analysis of cyclical variability in the market sector—a purpose which they serve reasonably well. But recent developments have tended to generate a different set of priorities and opportunities.

Of the empirical developments that have resulted in changed priorities, one can note the marked reduction in the amount of cyclical variability manifested by the economic system.[5] Since the end of World War II, there has been a persistent tendency for periods of economic recession and underutilization of resources to be milder than before.[6] The change appears due in part to changes in the structural characteristics of the economy (toward the production of relatively stable services and away from the production of relatively unstable goods),[7] and in part to the impact of specific policies designed to mitigate the effect of economic declines and to prevent their cumulating into periods of serious recession or depression. It may also be true that the better over-all performance on the cyclical side is in part a consequence of the present set of economic accounts themselves, which have provided an indispensable data base from which models of cyclical behavior have been constructed— models which may have played no small role in the formulation of policies designed to moderate periods of economic decline and extend periods of expansion. That question is unclear, and I do no more than note the possibility.

The structural shift toward services and away from goods is not only true of the economy over-all but also of the capital formation sector of the economy. Since the end of World War II there has been a dramatic rise in outlays for research and development on the part of both corporations and governments, as well as a relatively rapid rise in resources devoted to investment in humans as measured by schooling outlays, and those changes have highlighted the inadequacy of the pres-

[5] *It has been objected that the current concern with inflation and unemployment problems is evidence that there really has not been any shift in priorities away from cyclical problems. In the sense of relative concern with different types of problems, I think the shift is real: after all, concern with urban and environmental problems did not disappear during the recent recession, but simply took up a lower visibility than before. But concern with cyclical problems is itself clearly a cyclical variable, regardless of the severity of a current cyclical episode.

On the other hand, I think it probably is correct that our standards of tolerance for recessions may have lessened almost as much as our ability to modify their economic and social consequences. If so, declining cyclical variability may not result in a lower social priority being accorded to cyclical problems.

[6] See S. Fabricant, "The 'Recession' of 1969–1970," in *The Business Cycle Today,* Fiftieth Anniversary Colloquium I, New York, NBER, 1972; and Fabricant, "Recent Economic Changes and the Agenda of Business-Cycle Research," in *National Bureau Report 8, Supplement,* New York, May 1971. See also Juster, *Household Capital Formation.*

[7] See V. Fuchs, *The Service Economy,* New York, NBER, 1969; and Fuchs, ed., *Production and Productivity in the Service Industries,* Studies in Income and Wealth 34, New York. NBER, 1969.

ent capital accounts for analysis of economic growth.[8] Capital in the form of knowledge or human skills is just as much capital in the production function sense as machinery and structures, and the growing quantitative import of capital in these intangible forms provides a compelling reason to undertake a major modification in the capital accounts structure of the present system.

Also on the structural side, the rapid growth in female labor-force participation over the last several decades has reemphasized the fact that our accounts measure solely activity in the marketplace and not in the household.[9] During periods when the proportions of market and home work remain relatively constant, it makes little difference to growth rates of real income and output whether activity within the household is systematically incorporated into the accounts or not, but this is clearly not the case when the proportions are changing systematically.

Another and somewhat different empirical change concerns the rapid growth of output in sectors, especially services, where existing output measures are seriously deficient because they are essentially measures of inputs and not outputs. With the service sector now comprising roughly half of constant dollar total output and service industry employment comprising well over half of total employment, we can no longer be satisfied with a measurement which says that output grows at the same rate as employment with an arbitrary (usually zero) assumption about productivity growth. Understandably, there is a growing demand for direct measures of changes in the quantity of output in these areas.

Finally, we should note the relatively recent change in apparent social priorities toward a concern with environmental and ecological problems, which are generally interpreted as reflecting negative external byproducts of the way in which our economic and social system is

---

[8] See below, "Implementing the Proposed Framework," where Kendrick's data and findings are discussed. Also see T. W. Schultz' initial article "Capital Formation by Education," *Journal of Political Economy,* Vol. 68, 1960, and his most recent book, *Investment in Human Capital: The Role of Education and of Research,* New York, The Free Press, 1971. Also see G. Hanoch, "An Economic Analysis of Earnings and Schooling," *Journal of Human Resources,* Vol. II, No. 3, Summer 1967; and *Education, Income, and Human Capital,* Studies in Income and Wealth 35, New York, NBER, 1970.

[9] See J. Mincer, "Labor Force Participation of Married Women," in *Aspects of Labor Economics,* New York, NBER, 1962; W. Bowen and T. A. Finegan, *The Economics of Labor Force Participation,* Princeton, N.J., Princeton University Press, 1969; G. S. Becker, "A Theory of Time Allocation," *Economic Journal,* September 1965; and R. Gronau, "The Measurement of Output of the Nonmarket Sector," in this volume.

organized. The mounting concern with environmental and ecological problems probably reflects the highly nonlinear nature of the economic and social loss function from these externalities, coupled with the relatively high income elasticity of the supply of negative byproducts in industrialized societies as well as a high income elasticity of the demand for ecology per se.

Byproduct wastes and disamenities have always been part of the process of economic growth and development. But water, air, noise, etc., pollution have certain nonlinear characteristics which clearly relate to the economic costs of the process as well as to the process itself. Thus, for example, as noted in Denison's recent SCB article,[10] a trivial amount of air pollution will not even be noticed, a moderate amount will cause minor inconvenience and negligible welfare loss, while a substantial amount will cause major inconvenience and impose very high welfare costs. Thus, both the visibility and the costs of environmental deterioration are nonlinear, and we have apparently passed over the visibility threshold in a number of areas although not necessarily to the point of imposing significant economic costs. And lastly, environmental and ecological considerations seem to be of much greater concern to the relatively vocal and high income residents of suburban and exurban areas than to the less vocal and relatively low income residents of urban areas, despite the fact that the major impact of environmental deterioration is on the latter and not on the former. In short, residents of urban ghettos are likely to be much more concerned with employment opportunities and the educational system than with environmental problems, while the reverse is often true for residents of high income suburban areas.

Along with, and in part a consequence of, changes in observable economic phenomena has been a series of theoretical developments that provide both the framework and the justification for expanding the scope and content of the accounts. Foremost among these changes in our understanding of economic phenomena is the burgeoning field of human capital analysis, focused on the costs of investment in schooling and the returns to that investment in the form of higher lifetime earnings in the market.[11] Most economists probably now agree that

[10] E. F. Denison, "Welfare Measurement and the GNP," in *Survey of Current Business*, January 1971.

[11] G. S. Becker, *Human Capital: A Theoretical and Empirical Analysis, with Special Reference to Education*, New York, NBER, 1964; F. Thomas Juster, ed., *Education, Income, and Human Behavior*, Carnegie Commission on Higher

humans do undertake investment in their own skills, that these investments involve costs on both the private and the social side, and that such investments have economic consequences in the form of differentials in lifetime earnings streams. Whether schooling involves more than investment in skills is a more difficult question, certainly to quantify, but it does not have to be answered in order to incorporate some of the investment insights from human capital theory into economic and social accounts.

Moreover, the human capital investment analysis is now being extended well beyond the domain of formal schooling, in recognition of the fact that the acquisition of marketable skills is a process that takes place throughout the entire lifetime of the individual and not just while attending school.[12] Analysis of investment that takes the form of foregone earnings on the job, with the promise of future returns from a learning or training experience, suggests that a quantitatively important investment-in-learning component is involved in labor market decisions. And we are just beginning to make progress on the quantification of investment that takes the form of both preschool and during-school learning and training in the home.[13] This development has the prospect of providing, among other benefits, an explanation for the common empirical finding that rates of return to females from investment in formal schooling are much lower than those observed for males, and also of explicating one of the links in the intergenerational transmission of earnings.

A related but distinctly different theoretical development is in the economics of the household itself. It can be argued that one of the most cogent reasons for distinguishing between economic activity and "active life," as Kuznets termed it, was the existence of a well-defined framework for the analysis of business enterprise decisions within which output and income could be measured with objectivity and consistency. A similar theory of household decision making as it relates to the production of goods and services within the household did not exist when

Education, forthcoming; B. Chiswick, "Income Inequality and Schooling: A Cross-Sectional Study," New York, NBER, 1973, processed; J. Mincer, *Schooling, Experience, and Earnings,* New York, NBER, forthcoming; and T. W. Schultz, in *Human Resources,* Fiftieth Anniversary Colloquium VI, New York, NBER, 1972.

[12] J. Mincer, "On the Job Training," *Journal of Political Economy, Supplement,* October 1961; and Mincer, *Schooling, Experience, and Earnings.*

[13] See, for example, A. Leibowitz, "Home and Market Work in the Life-Cycle of Women by Education," Ph.D. dissertation, Columbia University, 1971; and R. Hill and F. Stafford, "The Allocation of Time to Children and to Educational Opportunity," University of Michigan, 1971, mimeo.

the present accounts were formed, but it exists now in the theory of within-household allocation of goods and time developed by Becker, and the related theory of consumer demand for goods and services as a derived demand for particular combinations of performance characteristics developed by Lancaster.[14] The theory treats households as small firms producing a flow of utilities or satisfactions, with a production function whose arguments are the time of family members allocated to intrahousehold activities and the command over purchased goods and services reflected by the money income earned by family members via allocation of time to the market. Thus, household time enters explicitly into the production of goods and services, and is substitutable for the household's money income as reflected in the goods they can acquire. As a consequence, we now have an analytical framework in which the time of family members can be valued, although we are still a good way from being able to make quantitative value imputations for a specified set of activities. Nonetheless, it is one thing to argue for the inclusion of household activity in a social and economic accounts framework when no economic model for such activities has been developed but another to suggest the possibility of their systematic inclusion within a framework in which market-based valuations begin to be feasible.

I should note one important distinction between the economic activity of firms and households, which does have implications for the economic and social accounts treatment of the household. In a market system, firms can and do cease to exist if they fail to provide an adequate return to their owners because they have proved unable to compete in the market place. Families do not need to meet the same test.[15] The prices at which firms sell goods and services is clearly the appropriate price at which to value output. Inefficient firms, which can produce a given output only at higher costs than other firms, will not be

[14] Becker, *Human Capital;* Becker, "A Theory of the Allocation of Time," *Economic Journal,* Vol. 75, September 1965, pp. 493–517. See also Gronau, "Measurement of Output"; G. Ghez, "Life Cycle Consumption and the Price of Time," in Juster, ed., *Education, Income, and Human Behavior;* and a study by M. Landsberger, to be published by the National Bureau of Economic Research. For a somewhat different theoretical approach, see K. Lancaster, "A New Approach to Consumer Theory," *Journal of Political Economy,* April 1966.

[15] See the discussion in Wesley C. Mitchell, "The Backward Art of Spending Money," in his *The Backward Art of Spending Money and Other Essays,* New York, McGraw-Hill, 1937.

The parallel between households and small family enterprises should be noted. Proper social accounting would treat many family firms as showing losses instead of profits, because the alternative labor income for the proprietor is greater than the profits realized from the firm.

around for long because competition forces them to sell their output at the market-determined price and thus at a loss. But families can produce services at very different levels of costs and efficiency without being faced with a market constraint. Thus, the same product or service will have a different value for families who differ in their respective valuations of time or in the efficiency with which they utilize time and purchase goods.[16]

A third development has been the growth of methods for replacing input measures of economic activity with measures that come closer to being true output measures. I have in mind here both the growth of the PPB systems in some of the service industries, especially government, as well as the use of hedonic price indexes to measure quality change. The former has the capacity to develop activity measures which are at least a step closer to output measures than simply costing the inputs, as we now do.[17] Thus, although pages of computer printout or numbers of statistics issued do not really measure the contribution of the Commerce Department to final output, they are a lot closer to that measure than the sum of salary payments and computer rentals would be. Similarly, numbers of patients treated (successfully?) is a lot better measure of output in the medical industry than the cost of doctors, nurses, and X-ray equipment. While I do not think that we yet have an adequate basis for substituting estimated flows of output services for input costs in these and other areas, it may be possible to substitute indexes of output that are both independent of input costs and better proxies for what one would like to measure.

A somewhat similar development is the use of hedonic price indexes to measure output in sectors where quality change is pervasive and not uniquely associated with changes in costs. On the whole, our present system of accounts recognizes a change in quality only when it is associated with an identifiable difference in cost relative to the displaced type of output. An alternative way to handle the problem, which has been extensively explored for various types of durable goods, is to recognize that quality change can be described in terms of dif-

[16] Note that families can, to some extent, effectively sell time to other families through different allocations of market and nonmarket time. One family can choose to repair its own appliances, while another can choose to increase market work and use the proceeds to buy appliance repair services in the market.

[17] See N. E. Terleckyj, "Measuring Output of Government Activities," paper presented at the International Conference on Income and Wealth, Ronneby, Sweden, August 1971; and A. M. Rivlin, *Systematic Thinking for Social Action,* Washington, D.C., Brookings Institution, 1971.

ferent dimensions of performance for which the product is better suited than its predecessors, and that an output measure can be obtained by pricing these performance dimensions with weights obtained via regressions of the prices of various products on particular performance characteristics.[18]

Social Accounting Systems Versus Social Indicators

Two general types of solutions, by no means mutually exclusive, have been advanced as a way to remedy the real or alleged deficiencies in our current system of economic accounts. The first, which forms the main subject of this paper, is to expand the content and coverage of the accounts to incorporate activities that are now excluded, to recognize the intermediate product nature of many expenditures now classified as final output, and in general to incorporate, within a bounded double-entry accounting system, as many of the significant dimensions of welfare as can be conceptualized and measured. An alternative is to devise supplementary indicators which attempt to identify dimensions of welfare which either are not or cannot be fitted within a system of accounts that require a homogeneous unit of measure such as dollars. For example, average years of schooling, crimes of specified types per capita, average number of hospital bed-days per unit of population or per specified type of illness, average carbon monoxide content of the air over major industrial cities, etc., clearly have something to do with economic welfare and at the moment are not accommodated within the economic accounts.[19] The question is whether one should attempt to accommodate such measures within an expanded accounting framework, or whether one should recognize the serious valuation and comparability problems and settle for a supplementary list of social indicators.

Let me start by noting some significant dimensions of welfare that cannot, for the foreseeable future and perhaps forever, be accommodated within an accounting framework that requires a single unit of measure. Of the activities just mentioned, all could in principle be accommodated within a meaningful general framework of economic and

---

[18] See Price Statistics Committee, Federal Reserve Board, *Price Indexes and Quality Change,* ed. Zvi Griliches, Cambridge, Harvard University Press, 1971.

[19] See "Toward a Social Report," U.S. Department of Health, Education and Welfare, Washington, D.C., 1969; E. B. Shelden and W. E. Moore, *Indicators of Social Change: Concepts and Measurements,* New York, Russell Sage Foundation, 1968; and M. Olson, Jr., "The Plan and Purpose of a Social Report," *Public Interest,* no. 15, Spring 1969.

social accounts: years of education is already implicitly included via expenditures for formal schooling, and an even more appropriate measure—gains in educational achievement for those in school—would be a better output measure than costs of teachers and school buildings if we could agree on a way to measure achievement gains; crimes per capita have measurable economic and social consequences in terms of losses through mortality or temporary disability, destroyed or damaged assets, etc.; hospital bed-days per unit of population represent losses of productive time; and even the carbon monoxide content of the air over major industrial cities could in principle be represented by the economic losses it causes rather than by description of a physical fact.

There are, however, dimensions of welfare that are not easily, even in principle, represented in a set of social accounts. As a nation we are concerned not only with the aggregate output of the economic and social system but with its distribution among persons and families. A more rapid growth of real income coupled with a relative lack of progress on the part of low-income families does not necessarily represent an overall improvement in welfare. The distribution of the gains in educational achievement is not irrelevant to an evaluation of the returns from a better educated population. And it is difficult to see how one can find a place in economic and social accounts for subjective perceptions of wellbeing as distinct from the objective facts. Thus, there is always a need for information, relevant to an evaluation of the economic and social performance of the systems on the whole, which cannot neatly or easily be fitted into a uniform social accounting framework, even one that is greatly augmented relative to the present one. And even if such measures could in principle, and ultimately in fact, be fitted into a unified framework, there is a very long interim period during which comprehensive social accounts could not possibly exist and where social indicator measures represent the only feasible alternative.

A quite different argument is one with an appreciable following in the economics profession, namely, that an attempt to convert the present economic accounts to a much more extensive system of economic and social accounts would accomplish little more than destroying the usefulness of the existing system. The argument deserves careful examination, since the present system of accounts clearly serves a number of useful purposes that can be served in no other way.

The argument seems to have two main strands. One is that government social accountants should not be put in the position of having to make arbitrary judgments about the value of nonmarket activities that are deemed to have sufficient economic content to warrant their inclusion in a measure of total output or income. Since the valuations of these activities would probably show more variance among social accountants than the comparatively objective or purely descriptive measures contained in the present accounts, it is thought that expansion of the accounts to cover a great many imputations would tend to make the resulting system a more arbitrary and, hence, less widely accepted and useful measure. The second strand is that mixing a greater proportion of nonmarket imputations with the existing collection of transaction-based measures would make the resulting set of accounts less viable as a tool for the analysis of production, productivity, and cyclical variability, where the main focus is clearly on market activity.[20]

My reaction to the first point is that the appropriate coverage and content of economic and social accounts should be determined by their usefulness for understanding and explaining the behavior and performance of the system, and if that imposes a greater burden on social accountants, so be it. On the second point, while I recognize the considerable utility of the existing accounts framework for the measurement of cyclical variability in the market sector, I do not see that expansion of the accounting framework, even a considerable expansion, need result in reduced usefulness for that purpose. The simplest answer to that objection is that economic and social accounts can clearly have subaccounts which deal solely with market transactions. Alternatively, economic and social accounts can have nonmarket supplements that provide additional information which can be easily integrated into the market accounts for those who wish to do so.

Another consideration, which has always seemed highly relevant to me, is that the extension and restructuring of the accounts suggested here might actually increase their usefulness for the analysis of cyclical fluctuations. To cite the obvious case, inclusion in personal consumption expenditures of the large and relatively stable lump represented by the imputed services of owner-occupied housing clearly does nothing to improve the usefulness of the accounts for cyclical analysis. The same is probably true of all the other imputations now made in the economic accounts. Hence, setting up an accounting framework with clearly defined market and nonmarket or imputed sectors has much to recommend it as a way of improving the accounts for analysis of the market or monetary part of the economic system.

[20] *See Supplementary Note A for additional discussion on this point.

In the same vein, splitting out households as a separate sector with its own capital account seems to me a considerable improvement, for purposes of analyzing investment and consumption behavior, over the present structure in which one must work with residential housing as a whole and not the owner-occupied and rental portion of the total, and where such untidy anomalies as the classification of mobile homes under "automobile parts" makes it difficult to analyze the demand for durables without taking special pains to eliminate that particularly expensive automobile part. Of course, anyone who builds cyclical behavior models from the accounts has to deal with these things as a matter of course, but it seems clearly desirable that the accounts set out household investment outlays in a way that makes it unnecessary for everyone to "roll his own," so to speak. Thus, I would reverse the argument completely, and suggest that expansion and restructuring of the existing accounts would improve their usefulness for the major purpose they are now called on to serve—a framework for the analysis of aggregate demand, output, and employment.

Finally, let me note the crucial distinction between social indicators measured in heterogeneous units and economic and social accounts covering a wide range of phenomena and measured in homogeneous units of output like dollars of constant purchasing power. In the formulation of public policy, the second has clear advantages over the first. Let me illustrate with a typical ecology problem. Assume we know that the quality of air and water resources has deteriorated by a specified level in physical terms, or more precisely, by a combination of different physical dimensions. How are we to evaluate the impact of this deterioration? The appropriate policy question surely involves a comparison of the economic and social costs of the deterioration relative to the cost of full or partial restoration. But the physical unit measures tell us nothing about economic and social loss, and before a rational policy can be formulated, someone has to translate these physical unit measures into a loss function. I would rather see that translation process carried out within the framework of an economic and social accounting system than carried out piecemeal and ad hoc by whoever has a particular ax to grind.

A SUGGESTED FRAMEWORK FOR ECONOMIC AND SOCIAL ACCOUNTS

It is not my purpose in this paper to set out a detailed accounting framework in which some parts can be measured currently and others would have to await future developments on the data or analytical side. Rather, I propose to sketch out the broad outlines of what such a framework might consist of and the conceptual principles on which it would be based. In a later section of the paper, I take up some of the detailed questions and present some quantitative evidence on the changes implied by the proposed accounting framework relative to the present one, but these excursions are best regarded as illustrative.

I also discuss below the question of possible timetables for altering the structure of our present accounts. Some of the suggested changes could easily be implemented and many of them have in fact been implemented in existing studies.[21] Others represent changes within a well-defined framework where the empirical ingredients to implement the framework are lacking, while still others represent situations where a satisfactory analytical framework for the activity and the data required for implementation are both lacking at present. And in some cases in the last category, it is by no means clear that either the conceptual or empirical problems can be solved in a way compatible with the needs of a quantitative social accounting system.

The basic principle that ought to underline economic and social accounts is that the income (output) of the system is derived in one way or another from an implicit set of wealth accounts. Irving Fisher pointed out many years ago that all income is derived from wealth. Although few would follow Fisher in equating social income with consumption (most of us tending to follow the Haig-Marshall tradition of defining income as consumption plus net additions to wealth), the most sensible concept of income is perhaps Samuelson's suggestion of income as the discounted value of all future consumption—clearly a wealth rather than an income concept, and one that recognizes both the future consumption potential of present investment and the inherent arbitrariness of defining income in relation to a particular slice of chronological time.[22]

Although I do not suggest that it is possible or necessary to set up specific wealth accounts corresponding to the economic and social income accounts, I do suggest that the proper interpretation of various types of economic activity can always be derived from a wealth framework, and is often derived improperly if one ignores the basic propo-

[21] See note 1, above.
[22] See I. Fisher, *The Nature of Capital and Income,* New York, 1930; and P. A. Samuelson, "The Evaluation of Social Income: Capital Formation and Wealth," in F. A. Lutz and D. C. Haig, eds., *The Theory of Capital,* London, 1961.

sition that income comes from wealth and from no other source. I should note in passing that, for measurement purposes, it is often true that the only way we have to estimate the value of wealth is by capitalizing an observable income flow, but that is simply the reason why I would not argue for the necessity of a set of wealth accounts per se. The fact that wealth cannot be measured independently of income does not bear on the question of the desirability and usefulness of a wealth framework.

An implicit set of wealth accounts has two general principles of classification—type and ownership. A possible classification by type, which is not without certain ambiguities, would be:

1. Reproducible tangible wealth (structures and durable equipment).
2. Reproducible intangible wealth (the stock of disembodied socially useful knowledge).
3. Human wealth (the stock of skills and knowledge embodied in persons).
4. Natural physical resource wealth (the stock of mineral, forest, water, climate, etc., assets).
5. Sociopolitical wealth (the stock of personal and national security, freedom, equity, privacy, etc.).

The classification by ownership is the familiar one:

1. Enterprise wealth including nonprofit organizations.
2. Personal and family wealth.
3. Common property (government) wealth.

Reproducible Tangible Wealth

Of the classifications of income-producing wealth, only parts of the first, second, and fourth are currently treated in the accounts in a way that is fully consistent with the suggested framework. To the extent that reproducible tangible assets are owned by enterprises (or by the fictional enterprise that owns single-family housing), the income generated by these assets is counted as part of income and output as currently measured. However, if such assets are owned by households or governments, they are not now counted as part of the wealth and are not viewed as producing income to the owners or to society.

Any number of studies have provided empirical estimates of the stock of both household and government-owned capital assets, and many have provided quantitative estimates of the imputed income obtained from these sources; hence, the difficulty is not our inability to quantify the relevant measure.[23] The most questionable aspect of developing the necessary imputation is that of an appropriate rate of return on these assets in both household and government sectors. For enterprise capital, implicit rates of return are obtained from an impersonal market in which competition insures (it is hoped) that resources are used to their maximum marginal social product and that the return on capital assets represents a competitive equilibrium price. That this is certainly untrue in the short run, and probably in the long run as well in many areas, does not deter social accountants from assuming that it is a good enough approximation to reality to warrant use of the available data on profits.

I do not see how it can be disputed that household capital as well as government capital also yields a return to its owners, although I can see a great deal of legitimate dispute over what an appropriate measure of that return is. For consumers, we have to face up to the analytical problem that rates of return to capital assets almost certainly differ among households: some consumers acquire capital assets by borrowing from the market at rates like 12–30 per cent per year, while others acquire assets by foregoing the income from savings accounts or other liquid assets. Viewed as investment decisions, it therefore seems that some household assets have only to yield a 5 per cent or so return to justify their acquisition, while for other households a return in excess of 20–30 per cent is needed to justify acquiring the asset. Even worse, one often finds that the same household will acquire different assets at very different borrowing costs, suggesting that returns vary among types of assets for the same household as well as among households. For example, the same household will often own a house acquired at a 6–7 per cent borrowing cost, a car acquired at a 12 per cent cost, and a refrigerator acquired at an 18 per cent or 20 per cent borrowing cost. My own preference would be to register these market borrowing costs in the imputed gross income from assets, which in practice means that aggregate gross income from household durables would be a function of the distribution of cash and credit purchases among households. Total interest costs then represent part of the flow of services, and would be subtracted from gross yields in arriving at imputed net income. This seems to me no more difficult than other procedures for estimating imputed returns, and as being closer to the market valua-

---

[23] See Ruggles and Ruggles, *op. cit.;* Kendrick, *op. cit.;* Juster, *op. cit.;* and R. W. Goldsmith, *The National Wealth of the United States in the Postwar Period,* Princeton University Press for NBER, 1962

tion basis than any alternative.[24] For government assets, the same general principle can be adopted; its application would suggest substantially lower rates of return for government-owned assets than for either household or enterprise assets.

Human Wealth

At present we treat human wealth in the accounts only to the extent that participation in the labor market measures the yield from human capital assets, and that resources spent on formal schooling measure some of the costs of investment in human capital. That treatment strikes me as a long way from being satisfactory, since it not only fails to recognize significant dimensions of human capital investment (in the home and in learning on the job) but also mixes together capital and current account transactions which can and should be disentangled. It is possible to consider changes in the treatment of human capital in the accounts that range all the way from full-scale integration involving the full sweep of both investment and consumption types of nonmarket activity, along with allowance for the appropriate depreciation and maintenance requirements, to a rather modest adjustment of the consumption-investment distribution that simply recognizes the investment nature of direct schooling costs. Getting better measurement of changes in the stock of human capital into the economic and social accounts seems to me of paramount importance to the development of a set of accounts that would substantially expedite analysis of the distribution of economic effort between present and future, the distribution of total wealth among families, and the process of economic growth and development.

An important aspect of the treatment of human wealth in the accounts is the appropriate treatment of nonmarket activity generally. For the most part, these activities are unmeasured simply because they represent uncompensated uses of time on the part of individuals and families. Some of these uses of time involve activities which differ little if at all from those recorded in the accounts because compensation is received —i.e., volunteer help vs. paid nurses' aides in hospitals. Others represent allocations of time which are probably best viewed as maintenance requirements of the human capital stock—sleeping, eating, some personal

---

[24] Enterprises as well as households borrow at different rates from the market, depending on the characteristics of the loan. Thus, inventory carrying costs or trade credit may be associated with relatively high borrowing costs, fixed investment with substantially lower ones. The accounts faithfully record these differences.

care, and possibly a good bit of what is ordinarily described as leisure. Still others represent activities with an investment implication—rearing and training one's children, job-oriented activities done on a person's own time and not at work, etc. Still others represent pure consumption —watching television, reading, and attending baseball games or concerts. Many of these activities probably represent joint outputs; raising children probably involves a consumption as well as an investment component, and television viewing is often conducted simultaneously with activities such as taking care of the ironing and washing. And finally there are the relatively straightforward, for accounting purposes, activities that simply represent unavoidable job-related costs—regrettable necessities like commuting time and costs. Some of these problems are explored in greater detail below.

Reproducible Intangible Wealth

The next asset category, reproducible intangible wealth, is meant to be coterminous with business and government outlays for research and development. These are currently treated as intermediate products in the accounts except to the limited extent that they are capitalized rather than expensed by business. But the market mechanism surely tells us that these are capital assets with an expected future return— how else does one explain the fact that firms in industries with rapid technological growth and heavy R&D outlays are apt to sell at stock market price-earning multiples of 20 or 30, while other firms in industries with stagnant technology and little or no R&D outlays are apt to sell at multiples of 8 or 10?

While one does not have to regard the stock market as a reliable barometer of all relevant economic activities, the persistence of these relationships over long periods of time suggests that firms with a heavy technological orientation somehow have more assets than show up on the balance sheet in terms of equipment and structures. These considerations also suggest, incidentally, that real profits have been growing at something in excess of reported profits, since research and development outlays have (until recently) had a much more rapid growth rate than other types of investment outlays.

The appropriate treatment here is relatively straightforward. The social accountant does have to decide which outlays can appropriately be viewed as oriented toward future rather than immediate returns, and he has to assign a depreciation rate to the accumulated stock of such outlays. But that decision is no more troublesome than the one currently faced and resolved (pragmatically) in regard to the distinction between investment and maintenance outlay and the associated decision to use the reported data on capital depreciation.

Environmental Wealth

The final two wealth categories present, in some respects, the most difficult conceptual and measurement problems. Most of us would probably agree that both the physical and sociopolitical environment constitute some kind of asset from which the community derives benefits. In our normal business accounting procedures, which are reflected to some degree in the present economic accounts, depletion of certain types of natural resources is explicitly recognized: oil that is no longer in the ground makes us poorer in the future, as do trees that have been cut for railroad ties or house construction and even clam shells whose innards are no longer available to satisfy gourmet palates. We also recognize that natural resources which exist but are unknown or at least inaccessible have no economic and social value until resources are expended to locate and develop them for future use. But these are, of course, within the framework of a set of accounts that register resource use and change entirely within the context of enterprises that produce for sale on the market.

Other natural resources, such as temperature, precipitation, etc., do not explicitly enter any system of accounts except insofar as they are reflected in a higher or lower level of productivity in industries which find them advantageous, such as agriculture. Thus, even the business use of the asset "a warm and sunny climate" tends to be reflected in services of rental housing or owner-occupied housing in resort areas, in the yield of agricultural crops which benefit from that particular climate, and so on. Again, we appear to have an adequate social accounting representation of the benefits (or lack of them) which accrue to the operations of business firms from the use of even free natural resources. And even to the extent that the current concern over deterioration of the physical environment through misuse of natural resources is reflected in one way or other in the costs of ongoing business enterprises, our present accounts tend to recognize that fact: environmental deterioration which imposes costs on business firms will show up as higher prices of goods and services produced and sold, and even investment outlays to restrain or reverse environmental deterioration will show up as higher current investment but lower future net output as depreciation allowances result in lower earnings or higher prices or both.

There is some current dispute about the appropriate treatment of business investments in environmental control, and I will comment on that in detail below.

On the whole, to the extent that changes in stocks of physical wealth have an impact on the operations of business firms within the system, our present accounts are more or less adequate to handle the situation. The major gap is in regard to the effects of changes in physical environmental assets on the flow of direct consumption benefits to ultimate users. In principle, most of these effects could be quantified although we are a long way from being able to do so. If changes in the level and composition of water resources impose direct costs in the form of foregone recreational activities by consumers, one in principle could regard this as imposing an economic and social cost equal to the (unobservable) cost of using less convenient or desirable recreational facilities or of foregoing their use altogether. The fact that consumers cannot individually decide whether or not to buy adequate water resources for recreational needs does impose measurement and valuation problems of a kind that other consumption flows do not. But that is not clearly much different from the valuation problem arising from the fact that some consumption or investment flows result from legislative decree, such as the requirement for all children to have a minimum number of years of formal schooling to be paid for from the public treasury if necessary; the measurement problem is of course more complicated.

This subject is discussed extensively in other conference papers and elsewhere in this paper.[25] At this point I wish to argue only the straightforward proposition that environmental changes can and do have an impact on direct consumption flows as well as on business enterprises, and that these costs can, in principle, be approximated by estimates that are more difficult to make but not more arbitrary than some now included in the accounts. Thus, the differences seem to be in difficulty of measurement, not in differences of concept. The point simply is that there are physical environmental assets that provide flows of direct consumption benefits to final users, and that deterioration (or improvement) in these environmental assets will result in a reduction (or increase) in the flow of such benefits and in economic and social welfare appropriately defined. I would also note that the question whether environmental assets

[25] See the following articles in this volume: M. Olson, Jr., "Evaluating Performance in the Public Sector"; O. C. Herfindahl and A. V. Kneese, "Measuring Social and Economic Change: Benefits and Costs of Environmental Pollution"; and A. M. Rivlin, "Measuring Performance in Education."

are depreciating or appreciating is one that is capable of being answered, in principle and in fact. If air quality in New York City is less good than five years ago, or if it has improved this year over last year, the flow of benefits from environmental assets can be assumed to change in the same direction as air quality. How to measure the costs or benefits of these changes is another question, but to record the fact that benefit levels have changed is not beyond our present state of knowledge or technical competence. Similarly, we know whether use of water resources for recreational purposes is inhibited by an increasing level of pollution and whether that situation has reversed. Thus, it is possible to measure the direction of change, and the quantitative dimensions (in physical terms) of that change, in a number of significant benefit-yielding natural environmental resources.

Although the fact that directions of change in physical environmental assets can be ascertained in physical terms may not seem to create much possibility for measuring the economic and social consequences of the change, we are still better off there than in many aspects of the sociopolitical environment. I do not think that there will be much agreement, if any, on propositions such as "the United States contains more personal freedom today than ten years ago" or "real income is more (or less) equitably distributed today than ten years ago," or "the United States has more (or less) to fear from external aggression today than it had ten years ago," and so on. Sociopolitical environmental assets consist of highly subjective intangibles and in some cases they really involve subjective perceptions of reality. Nonetheless, as social accountants we have to recognize that a society which spends 10 per cent of its total output to provide for defense against potential external enemies, and another several per cent to protect itself against domestic violence, is less well off than a comparable society which can achieve the same level of national and personal security without the need to incur such costs.

This is not to say that expenditures for national or personal security reduce economic and social welfare: indeed, the usual presumption of rational political decisions is that the decline in security that would result from failure to spend these resources would more than offset the costs, and welfare would decline rather than rise.

Sectoring to Include Households and Governments

Before proceeding to discuss some of the substantive implications of this broad framework of social and economic accounts in greater detail, including some specifics as to which parts of the framework can be implemented with existing knowledge and which clearly need to be deferred until later if implemented at all, let me comment briefly on sectoring.

The principal point that needs to be made is that it is high time we recognized the existence of household units as economic enterprises that purchase goods and services in the market and produce services for their own members. One can have serious reservations about the degree to which household activities can or should be recognized in the accounts, but I do not see how we can gain in understanding economic behavior by continuing to assume that households do nothing but consume and that what goes on inside the household is of total noninterest to economists. I have made the point before [26] that even for purposes of cyclical analysis, the fluctuations in household decisions to acquire tangible capital assets is of at least as great import as business decisions to acquire equipment and structures. Hence, I do not see how we can any longer justify a system of accounts which ignores both the tangible asset accumulations within households as sources of future income as well as the human capital producing operations in which individual households are a major source of inputs. Thus, regardless of how one feels about such matters as imputation of nonmarket activities involving the time of household members in the accounts, I do think that recognition of a capital account in the household sector has significant analytical benefits and no serious drawbacks either on the conceptual or empirical side.[27]

The same seems to me basically correct so far as community-owned or government assets are concerned. As I recall the history of government capital accounting in the U.S., its earlier adoption was vetoed largely on the grounds that it was considered to be a subterfuge by which the incumbent administration was attempting to hide the existence of a sizable deficit in the national budget. Since virtually all shades of opinion have learned to live comfortably with sizable budget deficits (only the monetary economists seem to be much concerned about budget deficits these days), there really seems no practical or analytical reason for continuing to regard the construction of particle accelerators, airports, and super highways as the economic equivalent of putting another GS-12 on the HEW payroll. (I recognize that this is an inept

[26] See Juster, *Household Capital Formation.*
[27] The sectoring problem bears directly on the crucial question of distinguishing between intermediate and final output. See Supplementary Note B, below.

illustration, since someone is sure to point out the major function of the additional GS-12 is to assist in putting together a report on community health programs, which will have a longer life than the particle accelerator, and that in this paper I have stressed the importance of measuring output rather than input!)

As regards the enterprise sector, one issue is whether business firms do or don't provide direct consumption services in addition to the goods or services they sell in the market. In its broadest aspects, the question involves nonmonetary compensation to employees in the form of benefits ranging from more pleasant working conditions to expense-paid business conferences that are 90 per cent tax-free consumption and 10 per cent business. Growth in these benefits is of course encouraged both by employee preference for some income gains in this form rather than in the form of straight compensation, as well as by their nontaxable nature.

Another less pervasive but quantitatively important type of business consumption is that provided by the structure of the advertising business in the United States. Business firms interested in persuading people to buy their product purchase space or time on various communications media like newspapers and television stations, and hope to persuade people to notice their product by providing free information or entertainment. The costs of the information or entertainment are fully charged off as business expenses and presumably show up in higher product prices, while the associated free benefits that go along with the advertising messages are not counted as consumption because they are given away free.[28] And of course a negative side of the same coin is the decline in consumption benefits from observing the local scenery while driving along roads heavily encumbered with pleas to purchase Brand X or Brand Y or to stay awake. In any event, the issue is whether business firms can in principle provide direct consumption benefits, and it would seem that the answer is yes.

IMPLEMENTING THE PROPOSED FRAMEWORK

The first part of this paper has been concerned with the broad outlines of a framework in which economic and social performance would be more effectively measured than at present. In this part I examine in greater detail some of the areas in which marked changes in treatment seem both desirable and, at last in principle, feasible. The final

[28] For empirical estimates, see Ruggles and Ruggles, *op. cit.*

section of the paper discusses the question of an appropriate time-table for implementation of the system, recognizing that some changes are presently feasible and could be accomplished immediately while others that might be equally desirable can only be implemented after substantial additional work on both the analytical and empirical side.

Revised Capital Accounts

The proposition that the treatment of capital formation in the present accounts seriously distorts the distribution of economic output between present and future cannot be seriously disputed. In a study done during the mid-1960's, I examined the consequences of treating durable goods expenditures by consumers as part of gross capital formation, and of distributing residential construction into household (owner-occupied) and rental investment. The disparity in long-term trends in the investment-GNP ratio between the business enterprise and the household sector, using these definitions, is striking. For example, the ratio of business investment in structures and equipment to GNP goes from around 12–14 per cent in the early part of the century to around 7–9 per cent in the 1960's, measured in constant (1929) prices (Chart 1). While the marked cyclical variability of these expenditures shows up strongly, the virtual uninterrupted secular decline since 1900 shows up equally strongly. For the household sector, in contrast, the ratio of gross investment to GNP shows exactly the reverse trend: from a level of 5–6 per cent around the beginning of the century, household gross investment had moved to levels of 10–12 per cent by the late 1950's and early 1960's. Both cyclical fluctuations and a powerful secular trend are equally evident in the data.

Measured in current prices (Chart 2), the same trend appears, although the decline in the business investment-output ratio is not quite so pronounced while the rise in the household ratio is a bit larger. The difference in trend is unaffected, in that enterprise investment goes from about 14 per cent to about 9–10 per cent, while household investment goes from 3–4 per cent in 1900 to about 10–12 in the 1960's.

A more detailed treatment of a wider range of investment activity has been undertaken recently by Kendrick in a project still under way at the National Bureau. Kendrick's data cover the period 1929 through 1969, and provide estimates of net and gross investment in a variety of intangible capital assets as well as the more traditional tangible asset forms. Investment in intangibles includes direct schooling costs, foregone earnings of students, business and government out-

CHART 1

Business Enterprise, Household, and Public Gross Fixed Capital Formation as Ratios to GNP, 1929 Prices, 1897–1966

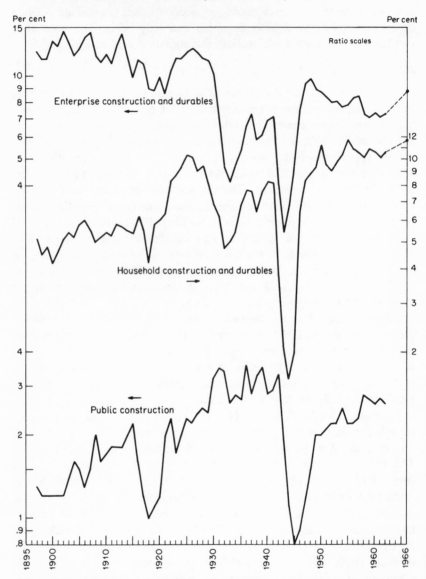

NOTE: Household capital formation includes owner-occupied residential structures and expenditures on consumer durables. Business enterprise capital formation includes capital equipment, commercial structures, and the rental part of residential structures. Public construction excludes military.

SOURCE: Data from Chart 10 in F. T. Juster, *Household Capital Formation, and Financing, 1897–1962,* New York, NBER, 1966; figures for 1966 estimated from Kendrick's data.

CHART 2

Business Enterprise, Household, and Public Gross Fixed Capital Formation as Ratios to GNP, Current Prices, 1897–1966

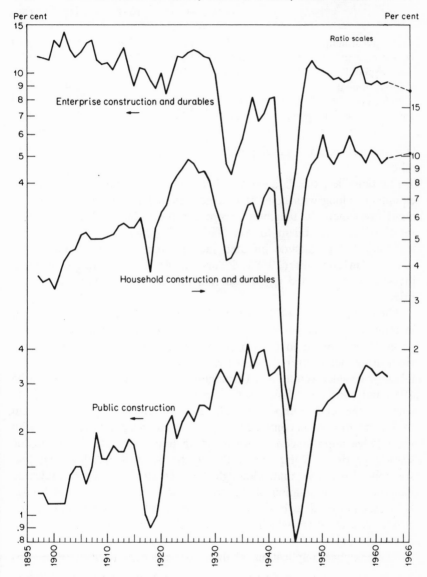

NOTE: See Note to Chart 1.

SOURCE: Data from Juster, *Household Capital Formation,* Chart 9; figures for 1966 estimated from Kendrick's data.

TABLE 1

Ratios of Net Investment to Net National Product, 1958 Dollars

	1929	1937	1948	1957	1966
Total investment	20.7	17.1	22.8	19.0	26.3
Investment in tangibles	11.9	10.1	12.6	8.4	13.1
Household	3.5	1.5	5.7	3.7	5.0
Government	2.3	3.8	0.2	1.4	1.7
Business	6.1	4.8	6.7	3.3	6.4
Investment in intangibles	8.8	7.0	10.2	10.6	13.2

lays for research and development, and investments in health and mobility.

For tangibles, the data shown above include business structures and
equipment along with household structures and equipment and government investment in tangibles except for the military. Table 1 shows
ratios of net investment to Net National Product, with the NNP figures adjusted to include imputed income from all capital assets; the
data are in constant (1958) dollars. Table 2 shows ratios of gross
investment to adjusted Gross National Product figures, both in current
prices.[29]

The striking aspect of the Kendrick data is the behavior of investment
in intangibles. Whether measured by net investment in constant prices
or gross investment in current prices, investments in intangibles have
risen dramatically over the past four decades. Much of this growth has
taken place since World War II, judging from the difference between the
1948 and 1966 data shown in the tables. Thus, it seems unquestionably
true that the relative importance of different forms of capital investment
in the economy have continued to show pronounced secular shifts, with
the relative importance of investments in human capital and intangible
knowledge rising in importance during the last few decades (and presumably also before that, although data are lacking). There may also
have been a continuation of the growing relative importance of household as contrasted to business enterprise investment in equipment and
structure, a tendency which was clearly observable during the first half
of the century.

The analytical implications of these data are considerable. In the first

[29] The data in Tables 1 and 2 below do not include Kendrick's estimates of the
investment in children represented by rearing costs up to working age.

TABLE 2

Ratios of Gross Investment to Gross National Product,
Current Dollars

	1929	1937	1948	1957	1966
Total investment	35.9	34.1	37.0	38.5	43.5
Investment in tangibles	23.0	21.2	22.7	21.6	23.0
Household	10.2	7.8	10.4	10.3	10.1
Government	2.1	3.3	1.8	2.4	2.7
Business	10.7	10.0	10.4	8.9	10.2
Investment in intangibles	12.9	12.9	14.3	16.9	20.5

place, the fraction of total U.S. economic effort devoted to future uses has not, as is often stated, tended to decline; if anything, it appears to have increased substantially. Secondly, it is probably not true that either household or total saving is characterized by secular stability relative to income; rather, there appears to be a pronounced upward trend in the saving-income ratio, providing that savings are defined appropriately. Finally, the use of capital-output ratios, and inferences drawn from them, will evidently show a quite different conclusion depending on how capital is defined.

Households as Output Producing Firms

In his definitive *National Income and Its Composition* volume, Simon Kuznets remarked about his suggested dividing line between included and excluded economic activities in the national income concept:

Exclusion of the products of the family economy characteristic of all national income estimates, seriously limits their validity as measures of all scarce and disposable goods produced by the nation. . . . Over long periods distinct secular shifts occur in the relative contributions of the business and the family economy to the total of economic goods, most broadly defined. One must, therefore, guard against the common tendency to consider national income totals as all conclusive summaries of the scarce and disposable sources of satisfaction produced by the nation. Such summaries would become practicable only if the data improved substantially or if the family disappeared entirely as a producer of goods.[30]

Kuznets' decision to exclude intrahousehold activity as part of the output of goods and services, which has become the conventional divid-

[30] Kuznets, *National Income and Its Composition*, p. 10.

ing line, was based in part on lack of available data to implement the needed accounts and in part on a desire to limit the scope of the accounts to activities that would be generally viewed as having economic content and (implicitly) as being explainable within the traditional framework of market-based valuations.

Since Kuznets wrote, the possibility of implementing a set of household accounts has clearly improved substantially in regard to data availability; the desirability of implementing such accounts has, in my judgment, also moved in the same direction. Our present accounts ignore a great deal of purposive activity that is not only a consequence of market forces but also has strongly influenced the way in which the market has developed. Over the past several decades there has been a dramatic growth in labor-force participation on the part of females, with a resulting substitution of time spent in the market for time spent elsewhere; there has been an equally dramatic growth in the stock of household owned capital goods (durables, appliances, etc.) which has presumably increased the efficiency with which intrahousehold activities are conducted; there has been a transfer from the household to largely public institutions of functions like caring for the elderly and the permanently disabled; there have been dramatic shifts in the production function for retail trade services, away from time intensive and locationally convenient outlets toward more concentration among less time intensive and relatively less accessible locations that can be reached only by automobile, and an associated shift of storage costs from the firm to the household; and the growth of home ownership plus very rapid rises in costs for skilled craftsmen like carpenters, plumbers, electricians, etc., has probably meant that maintenance and investment activities in real property have been increasingly carried out within the household rather than in the market. We do not know what the net impact of all these changes has been on the rates of growth of market and nonmarket produced goods and services over time, but it seems increasingly important that we begin to find out.

Perhaps most important of all, analytical developments over the past decade or so have now provided us with a framework in which household activities can be systematically incorporated into economic and social accounts. Here I have in mind both the extensive development of human capital analysis with the work of Schultz, Becker, Mincer, and their associates, and the very promising beginnings of household production function analysis using a framework in which households produce utilities by combining goods purchased on the market with inputs of their own time. The key to both the conceptual appropriateness and the empirical feasibility of implementing household accounts into a system of economic and social accounts clearly lies in the analysis and measurement of the allocation of time. To the extent that we can impute broadly agreed on valuations to the use of time outside the market, and to the extent that we can identify analytically appropriate uses of time, the complete articulation of household accounts is both appropriate and feasible.

Before examining some of the problems that would need to be resolved in the process of full implementation of household accounts, it might be well to state explicitly how our present accounts treat household activities. It is one thing to point to the difficulties and arbitrary valuation procedures that would inevitably be involved in a fully articulated set of household accounts; it is quite another to argue that our present treatment is satisfactory and that any change would make it worse. To quote an admittedly biased observer:

At present, the accounts essentially specify that only the application of human skills to activities that result in money earnings are to be counted as output, and no adjustment is made for either positive or negative net investment in the stock of human capital. Hence, students, housewives, hospital volunteers, unpaid members of civic or social agencies, vacationers, and Wednesday afternoon golfers are all presumed to be engaged in unproductive activity.

The possibilities for anomalies are boundless. . . . For example, according to the present system, output is increased if a woman stops putting in ten hours a week at a remedial reading clinic for ghetto youngsters and begins to work ten hours a week as a dental technician; output will be increased if a clinical health program manned by volunteers becomes funded through a government grant and the volunteers thus receive pay; output is increased if a man who ordinarily takes off one afternoon a week to relax is coerced into earning income during that afternoon; output is reduced if, to cite the traditional case, a man marries his housekeeper. . . .[31]

In short, our present set of accounts recognizes that human capital produces an output only when its services are purchased in the market. Nonmarket uses of such capital, whether it consists of organized and purposeful activities with a close counterpart to compensated market activities, pure leisure activities which yield direct consumption benefits like going to the opera, to a baseball game, or watching TV, activities

[31] F. T. Juster, "On the Measurement of Economic and Social Performance," NBER, *50th Annual Report,* New York, 1970.

like eating and sleeping designed to maintain the stock of human capital, activities oriented toward future market productivity and earnings such as going to school or teaching one's children, and activities like being unemployed or underemployed and thus allowing one's skill to depreciate and deteriorate are all regarded as a homogeneous collection of activities with a common value equal to zero.

Yet the first produces net output by the usual standards of market imputation, the second certainly has a positive effect on welfare although it is admittedly difficult to value, the third is a necessary cost which one would like to minimize, the fourth is an investment which will show up as future income, and the last has a net value which is at best zero and at worst substantially negative. Hence, if the choice is between staying with our current treatment or moving to implement a comprehensive treatment in which households are viewed as firms producing output with a twenty-four-hour time input to be allocated and valued, I would opt for the latter despite the formidable difficulties involved. However, there appear to be alternative and reasonably sensible way stations between these two extremes, and these may represent an intermediate target worth aiming at and capable of being reached.

Let me begin by sketching out the analytical and empirical requirements for full implementation of household accounts, then note some of the more serious difficulties. Implementation of a complete household sector account basically involves recognition of the fact that households produce output by using the services of stocks of tangible reproducible assets like houses, cars, and appliances, stocks of financial assets, and stocks of human capital assets. The latter can be used either for earning money income in the market or for a variety of activities outside the market. The present accounts incorporate the influence of household ownership of financial assets and housing; extension to other household tangible capital goods is a relatively straightforward matter and has been discussed above. Except for the underestimate of output associated with earnings that reflect a combination of market output and learning geared to future market productivity and earnings, the part of human capital allocated to the market already shows up in the accounts as the earnings of labor.

Hence, the major subject of discussion is the extension of outputs to cover the allocation of human capital to activities outside the market. These cover a wide range of activities with different conceptual content. Thus the basic problem is: How do we value the output and income associated with the use of human capital in nonmarket activities, i.e., what value do we place on time allocated outside the market?

In one sense, the measurement and valuation problem is trivial: if we are willing to assume that all human activities are adjusted so as to yield equalized returns at the margin, all nonmarket activities can be valued at market wage rates. Thus, the gross output of human capital is an hourly wage rate multiplied by 24; for measuring net output we simply subtract the amount of time associated with human capital maintenance activities.

There is something to be said for this view on both the theoretical and empirical level. Individuals can generally allocate their time between market and nonmarket activities as they see fit, and families can do so with even greater ease than individuals because they have more flexibility in the alternative ways of allocating the total available time of all family members. The market provides us with a great many illustrations of the flexibility with which individuals and families do allocate time. Families can and do substitute purchased services (housekeeping, child care, home maintenance, etc.) for inputs of their own time, and the higher the value of time as reflected by market wage rates the more likely the substitution of purchased services for own time. Similarly, families can and do substitute market earnings for leisure or nonmarket activities, either by varying hours of time via overtime and multiple job holdings or by moving into or out of the labor force as the demands for household time vary with number and age of children, etc. A good first approximation, therefore, is that available time is allocated so as to equalize its value in all activity at the margin. If one of these activities is involvement in the market, we have a price at which time can be valued. This is essentially the approach adopted by Nordhaus and Tobin in their recent paper,[32] and it is clear that available data are sufficient to enable us to develop a broad quantification of that framework. There are, of course, some problems.

The first and most important is whether it is reasonable to assign what is usually an average observed wage rate to an allocation of time that evidently ought to be based on marginal wage rates. Except in those cases where individuals are on the margin of expanding or contracting their labor supply to the market, we cannot observe marginal wage rates. In the clearest such cases, people holding second jobs in order to augment money income, marginal wage rates are generally lower than

[32] See W. D. Nordhaus and J. Tobin, "Is Growth Obsolete?", below.

average wage rates on principal jobs, not equal to or higher than such rates. In general, however, we cannot tell whether individuals or families are at the margin on substitution of market for nonmarket activity, or whether during any given observation period they tend to have too little or too much market activity. The reason we cannot tell is the existence of conventional rigidities in time schedules in the job market. There may be a presumption that disequilibrium on the side of too little market activity, hence a marginal wage rate lower than observed wage rates, is more common than the opposite: for those whose normal schedule requires more market activity than they wish, intermittent absenteeism seems a fairly common way to make the adjustment. But for those in the opposite situation, ability to put in small additional increments of hours is less easily accomplished. Finally, nonmarket time should clearly be valued at earnings after tax rather than pre-tax, since the tax laws do not recognize nonmarket activity as generating taxable income.

We can define a number of analytically useful categories to describe the way in which human agents of production allocate time. The relevant distinctions have to do with types of activities where the appropriate valuation criteria might be different, and where imputed time values might thus vary. Candidates for the most relevant categories would be:

1. Time allocated to maintenance of the stock of human capital itself.
2. Time that represents a cost of engaging in job-market activity.
3. Time that represents a cost of maintaining the flow of intrafamily maintenance activities.
4. Time allocated to "pure" leisure or consumption.
5. Time devoted to investment in future job-market productivity.
6. Time devoted to investment in other family members (children).
7. Time devoted to purposeful activities for which some job-market counterpart exists.

To make the intended distinction a bit clearer, the kind of activities I have in mind under each of these categories are as follows: For human capital maintenance, eating, sleeping, and probably some part of leisure; for costs of job-market activity, commuting time; for intrafamily maintenance activities, housework, food preparation, etc.; for pure leisure, any activity carried on for its own sake rather than because it serves as an input into some other activity; for investment in market productivity, job search, school attendance, general skill-upgrading; for investment in other family members, primarily rearing and training children; and for purposeful market-related activities, most volunteer work like helping in hospitals, running the boy scouts, and attending PTA executive committee meetings.

Simply running down the list of activities suggests the nature of some of the valuation problems, and they are both numerous and difficult to resolve—some, probably impossible to resolve because questions of motivation are basically at issue. Just illustrating some of the problems may seem discouraging, but my view is that many of them can be handled with just as reasonable valuation assumptions as underlie the ones we now make all the time. To pose some of the problems: How much apparent leisure is really a cost of maintaining job-market productivity, or at least a mixture of maintenance and pure consumption activity? How do we handle joint activity, such as commuting to work and reading the newspaper or having a pleasant chat with fellow commuters? Does time spent in maintaining household services like meals available on time, orderliness, cleanliness, etc., represent time spent in maintaining a *fixed* level of intrafamily household services or does the level of final output itself increase as, for example, more capital is mixed with the same or a lesser amount of labor time? Is the leisure time of a $100,000 a year man worth more than the leisure time of a $10,000 a year man? It obviously costs more, but does it have more ultimate consumption value? How do we differentiate between activities that represent both investment in future earnings on the market and also contain a significant element of final consumption because individuals enjoy learning things and improving their skills? How do we value the quality of time, as distinct from its amount, spent on rearing and training children? By market wage rates? By level of formal schooling of the parents? By the perception of an unseen observer psychologist who is an expert at child rearing? And, perhaps trivial but still important, should volunteer activities be valued at the market wage rates of their closest market counterpart or at the market wage rate of the individual volunteer in his customary pursuit? That is, is a college trained person a more effective hospital volunteer than a high school trained person?

While I do not regard any of these questions as yielding simple, unambiguous, and generally agreed upon answers at the present state of our knowledge, I also do not regard exclusions of this range of activities as being particularly helpful when it comes to evaluating economic and social performance over time. In general terms, my feeling is that many of these distinctions can be made in a reasonably objective way, and that the resulting information will on balance improve the way in which the accounts record economic activity and output flows. The valuation problems are both interesting and treacherous, and deserve a good bit of study and research before one moves much beyond a rather simple and relatively arbitrary distinction among types of activities. But it does seem to me that such distinctions can now be made, and that the above list of activity types is a reasonable initial framework.

Let me make two final points on the question of using marginal market wage rates to value activities on the assumption that time has been allocated at the margin so as to equate its value in all uses. I do not think that recognizing different valuation bases for different types of activities is necessarily inconsistent with that view. For example, the relevant marginal wage rate in a great many of the nonmarket activities discussed above may be much below the observed average wage rate for market activity. If the choice is to work an extra two hours a week in the market or to spend that time in pure leisure activities, the relevant wage rate is what could be earned in the extra two hours divided by the total amount of time it would take to expand market activities by two hours of paid work. Counting the time involved in locating a way to spend an extra two hours a week working, and adding the cost of getting to and from the additional work activity, the after-tax earning from expanding market activity could wind up being a rather small fraction of an observable market wage rate. It could well be low enough to make it worthwhile for a $50,000 a year earner to cut the grass himself, even though he could hire a teen-ager for $1.50 an hour to do so. In short, the efficient use of blocks of time for different types of activities may tend to make it difficult, though not impossible, to expand market activity by small amounts. As a result, the relevant marginal wage rates may not only be quite a bit lower than observed wage rates for many families and individuals, but may vary with the type of activity because of the transition costs of changing activities.

The second point concerns the economic and social cost of unemployment or underemployment. Evidently, a person who is unable to find market work does something with the available time; hence, we would necessarily find that such an individual undertook a number of definable activities which were presumably of less value to him than the market work he is unable to locate. In some such cases, counting unemployment or underemployment as something akin to leisure may not be inappropriate at all. Workers whose job patterns call for seasonally intensive activity combined with a Florida vacation and unemployment compensation during the off-months may be relatively rare or relatively frequent, but their unemployment does not involve much if any social cost. On the other hand, those unable to find gainful employment for long periods of time ought to be represented in the accounts not only as enjoying "leisure" with a very small or zero value, but also as suffering declines in marketable skills as their unemployment period lengthens and their competitive position in the labor market deteriorates. While these distinctions may be difficult to draw in particular cases, I do not see them as being unmeasurable. Finally, the fact that human skills can be eroded by persistent unemployment surely warrants recognition in an accounting framework whose purpose is to measure changes in present and future wellbeing.

Environmental Assets and Returns

The question of how to treat outlays for environmental control is a major one for this conference, and is discussed in the Herfindahl-Kneese paper as well as in the background article by Denison. If I understand the discussions in both these papers, there are conceptual difficulties with either suggested treatment.

Viewing the returns from environmental assets as a flow of ultimate consumption services seems to me to provide the right framework for analysis of expenditures on environmental control equipment. Let us consider several alternative states of the world. In the first, environmental assets are never permitted to deteriorate and the flow of benefits remains unchanged at a fixed level. That is, water and air resources are maintained at a given state of physical purity corresponding to some happy condition existing in agrarian society. Through time, the growth of industrial output and changes in technology result in an increasingly serious waste disposal problem, since negative byproducts are likely to rise more sharply than the volume of output. But none of this potential emission problem is ever permitted to appear because stringent regulations require that business enterprises and households undertake defensive expenditures to filter out any possible rise in the unwanted byproducts of industrial growth. Since the by-product problem grows more rapidly than output, the implication is that defensive expenditures also grow more rapidly than output. The question is: How should we treat these defensive expenditures by enterprises and households, given that a rigid level of control is constantly maintained?

The answer seems unambiguous and straightforward. Emission filters on automobiles, tall stacks on factories, and water treatment facilities at industrial plants add nothing to the flow of economic or social benefits produced by the system. They simply represent costs of maintaining the constant level of environmental benefits from which society is presumed to have started. To the extent that these costs are incurred by business enterprises who have larger capital stocks and depreciation allowances to show for it, the lower-than-potential rate of growth of real output which these control measures impose is appropriately measured and no adjustment needs to be made. To the extent that these costs are incurred directly by households, adjustment of price indexes to record emission control devices as a quality improvement clearly gives the wrong answer —the car does not run any better or more efficiently, and it simply costs more to get the same combination of vehicle services plus constant environmental benefits. Thus, it is not appropriate to count consumer defensive outlays as part of net output, nor is it desirable to add back in industrial defensive outlays as a part of net output.[33]

But let us be clear about the assumptions that justify these conclusions. This result follows only because it has been assumed that the flow of environmental benefits (which is, unfortunately, unobservable) remains at a fixed level and does not change over time. While the environment is not being improved by these defensive outlays, it is not being permitted to deteriorate either and thus we can avoid the difficult and possibly unmanageable problem of what to do if environmental quality is altered by defensive outlays.

The second state of the world bears a closer resemblance to what we have today, although still not (probably) a perfect one. Here, let us assume that industrial growth with its undesired byproducts is allowed to result in a deterioration of environmental assets, thus reducing the flow of environmental benefits, and that environmental quality approaches an asymptotic floor fixed by law. That is, society at some point decides that environmental deterioration has gone far enough, and imposes a set of constraints in physical terms which fixes the level of environmental benefits at something less than it was in "the good old days." At this new fixed level, environmental assets and benefit flows are maintained by defensive outlays on the part of both enterprises and households. As before, the presumption is that the level of defensive outlays necessary to maintain the given level of environmental qualities will grow through time because byproducts grow more rapidly than output.

Even in this case we still get unambiguous and defensible criteria for handling environmental control outlays. All such outlays, by assumption, fail to result in environmental improvement and are designed solely to

---

[33] *See Supplementary Note A for amplification of this point.

maintain a specified level of environmental quality. Thus, at no point do we have a combination of increased defensive outlays and net improvement in environmental quality; we do observe that increasingly larger outlays are needed to maintain the fixed (but lower than original) quality level. As in the first case, all the control outlays have done is to maintain a fixed level of environmental assets and benefit flows; the increasingly higher costs incurred to do so do not warrant inclusion in net output.

The only difference between case two and case one is that economic and social welfare is overstated by net output in case two, because the level of environmental benefits to consumers is less than it was before the age of industrial growth and nothing in the accounts records this fact. But from the time we begin making defensive outlays, the accounts properly register changes in the flow of final output if enterprise outlays are not counted as part of net output and if direct consumer outlays are counted as a price and cost increase but not as a quality improvement.

Before proceeding to discuss the third case, which I think looks much like what we are actually experiencing, a serious difficulty with cases one and two should be noted. The problem is that neither can represent (on any reasonable assumptions that I can think of) an optimum level of economic welfare given the resources available to society. When changing technology and growing wealth result in a rising flow of undesired byproducts which deteriorate environmental assets and benefit flows, it cannot be right to maintain environmental assets at any fixed level of quality. A slightly lower quality can always be purchased with some reduction in defensive outlays, thus making more resources available for the production of goods and services. Since the cost of maintaining constant quality is assumed to rise constantly, at some point the benefits of permitting a bit more deterioration must outweigh the costs, and an optimally ordered society would move in that direction. To put it in extreme form, it cannot be worth paying any price to maintain the stock of American eagles so that eagle connoisseurs can enjoy the benefits of bird-watching, nor can it be worth any cost to maintain all streams and rivers at sufficient levels of purity to enable anyone to drink from them without harm, etc. Thus, no society should actually adopt the kind of standards which would make welfare measurement relatively simple and straightforward. While that is unfortunate for the social accountant, it seems a modest price to pay for an improvement in welfare.

The third case supposes that society allows environmental assets and benefit flows to deteriorate until the cost of that deterioration becomes sufficiently noticeable to arouse a public outcry, then takes steps to enforce environmental control outlays which initially result in a net improvement in environmental quality and subsequently in a more or less constantly maintained level of environmental quality. In effect, the system overshoots the eventual target by a bit in the process of getting geared up to fight environmental deterioration, then returns to a target level which is itself a variable and not a constant.

This case provides the justification for Denison's proposed treatment, which would count defensive outlays by consumers as net output and would add back into net output defensive outlays by enterprises. The justification for so doing is that these defensive measures have resulted in a clear welfare improvement (the improvement in environmental benefit flows) or else the legislation would not have been passed, and in this situation one does not want to have the national accounts recording that output growth rates have declined as a consequence of defensive expenditures.

The difficulty with this argument is that one may get the right answer (at least in terms of direction) in comparing one quarter with the previous one or one year with the previous one, but one almost certainly gets the wrong answer comparing output today with output a decade or two ago.

The case for treating defensive outlays of firms and households as part of net output and thus welfare increasing activities is that they have in fact improved environmental quality and the accounts should register that improvement. The argument against such treatment is that the environment is clearly worse today than it was in the mid-1950's, and comparison of real output between these two periods is already overstated because environmental deterioration has been permitted to occur —and the suggested treatment of defensive outlays would make the comparison even worse, not better. For the social accountant, the key to what is the appropriate measurement clearly lies in recording direct changes in the flow of environmental benefits. Welfare producing activity can be thought of as consisting of the combination of environmental benefits plus goods and services produced from available resources. If available resources are used to combat environmental deterioration, welfare must be assumed to be higher. But higher than what? The answer is that it is higher than it would have been if such outlays had not been undertaken, not higher than last quarter or last year.

Thus, we cannot tell whether welfare is improved over some past period simply by noting that defensive outlays that yield a net return have been increased. If the outlays have been sufficient to cause a net improvement in environmental quality, welfare broadly considered may have gone up; if all the outlays have done is prevent the environment from deteriorating even further, welfare broadly considered has gone down, but not as much as it would have without the defensive outlays.

Hence, there is no solution to the treatment of environmental control outlays unless we can also quantify the change in direct consumption benefits from the environment. If such quantification were possible, environmental control outlays would represent a cost of maintaining a given quality level, but the outlays themselves are not part of net output while the direct benefit flows are.

Without quantification of direct benefit flows, I see no way to handle environmental outlays to be correct both for comparing this quarter with last quarter or this year with last year and for comparing this year with ten or twenty years ago. I take for granted that the environment, now or after national policy has succeeded in establishing higher standards than at present, will still be worse than in the simpler agrarian society from which long-term trends in output are being measured.[34] If forced to choose between alternative treatments, my own preference is to subtract defensive outlays by consumers and not to add defensive outlays by enterprises. The reason is that all defensive outlays are geared to specific aspects of environmental quality, not to the problem in its broadest prospectives, and I think it is a reasonable assumption that defensive outlays will only result in eliminating particularly apparent sources of damage and will not in general provide an improved over-all level of environmental benefits. That is, the single most reasonable assumption to make is that society recognizes that environmental quality can only be purchased at a cost, and that it is willing to live with a non-improving level of environmental benefits provided the most troublesome problems are eliminated. Thus, on the whole, outlays for environmental control tend not to result in over-all improvement, but only keep the deterioration within tolerable bounds—an assumption that amounts to no more than supposing that the political judgments underlying environmental legislation reflect a cost-benefit calculus which tends to be a reasonable approximation to optimal allocation. Different assumptions will of course produce different conclusions about appropriate treatment.

[34] That is, it will be worse considering that the benefits yielded by such environmental improvements as paved streets are considered to be counted already in the stock of government capital.

One implication of this argument, which bears on the general question of how to treat nonmarket activities in economic and social accounting systems, concerns the relevant time dimension for welfare oriented accounts and market transaction accounts. A case can be made for the proposition that cyclical variability in economic welfare is reasonably well measured by something like our existing accounts. Secular changes in economic welfare, in contrast, seem to me not necessarily well measured, and the measurement would be greatly improved by making serious attempts to account for the kinds of economic and social phenomena discussed at this conference. The treatment of environmental investment just discussed might well provide the wrong answer in terms of changes in social and economic welfare if comparisons are made between one quarter and the previous one or even one year with the previous one. The analysis would, it seems to me, provide the correct answer when comparing longer spans of time, and is thus entirely appropriate for measuring long-term rates of change. Thus, one might argue for a set of accounts which measures market phenomena on a monthly or quarterly basis, and a wide range of market-related phenomena on a less frequent basis.

The second set of environmental assets, the sociopolitical ones, is in one sense simpler to handle and in another present more conceptual problems. The reason they are simpler is that we have more of the appropriate kinds of data readily available, and the question is how to use the data rather than how to obtain it. The conceptual problems are typified by that rather ancient chestnut: how do we treat national defense outlays.

The basic difficulty with defense outlays, as I see it, is that we have no present or foreseeable way to determine, directly or indirectly, whether the asset "security from external aggression" is higher or lower as a consequence of different levels of defense outlays. It is perfectly clear that the effectiveness of any given volume of resources devoted to defense against external aggression depends entirely upon the volume of resources similarly devoted by potential external enemies. Thus, $10 billion of U.S. defense outlays buys as much security as $100 billion if Soviet and Chinese defense outlays were one-tenth their present size. It is this interaction of domestic and foreign outlays for national security that makes it impossible to decide whether the community is more or less secure than in previous years or in previous decades. Obviously, one is always more secure, given the level of foreign outlays, if one's own outlays are higher; but the mutual escalation that seems inherent in this process ultimately seems to end up providing about the same level of security at a much higher cost.

The basic issue here as elsewhere turns on whether expanded outlays for national security have in fact resulted in net investment in the sociopolitical asset, national security.

The only clear-cut case I can think of where a rise in national defense outlays can be thought of as adding to assets rather than simply maintaining them is the case of an aggressor nation that builds up its military establishment in order to expand its territorial coverage and (presumably) derive some economic benefits by conquest. Although there are plenty of critics who regard the United States as an aggressive nation, I know of none who are willing to argue that our recent military involvements have been based on the hope that investments in military outlays would produce an economic return. The acquisition of Texas after the Mexican War may have produced an economic return and the war itself may have been motivated partly by the hope of such return, but it seems a little difficult to argue that, for example, either the Korean War or the Vietnam involvement was either motivated by, or can be sensibly analyzed in terms of, the returns to investment in aggression.

There is, incidentally, an interesting difference between the case in which defense needs (real or imagined) result in a country spending x per cent of its resources for military purposes, and the case where deterioration of the physical environment results in a country deciding to use the same x per cent of resources to control or abate pollution. In the latter case, there is a strong presumption that deterioration of the environment is a direct consequence of a normal functioning and growth of the economy; if so, the accounts clearly overstate the flow of benefits from economic growth unless they include an allowance for the negative by-products of growth. In the former case, however, aside from the military aggression case noted above, deterioration of the sociopolitical environment as manifested by the need to maintain a large or growing defense establishment is unrelated to the normal functioning and growth of the economic and social system.

If so, and if the size of the military establishment is simply an exogenous event, should one penalize the system by registering defense outlays as a cost of maintaining the sociopolitical environment? If the objective is to measure economic and social welfare, the answer seems to be yes: Resources used for defense cannot be used elsewhere, and I cannot see that it matters *for purposes of measurement* whether defense needs are a cause of one's own actions, are real but exogenous to one's own actions, or are wholly imaginary. It does, however, make a great deal of difference *for purposes of policy decisions* whether or not the system has caused its own defense needs. If this is the case, there is a large hidden cost to a change in social policy that increases the optimum size of the defense establishment, just as there is a large hidden cost to a growth policy that produces deterioration in the physical environment as an inevitable concomitant of growth.

One solution is to make the explicit assumption that the level of the asset "national security" is entirely invariant with respect to expenditures for that purpose. That is, national security is always the same, and the only thing that varies is the cost of maintaining security at a fixed level. According to that view, all expenditures on goods and services for national defense represent maintenance costs of one aspect of the sociopolitical environment, and never represent net investment or disinvestment in that asset. Thus, it would be misleading for the social accountant to regard national wealth as increasing simply because more airplanes, tanks, etc., are being produced, or to regard stocks of military capital as depreciating because those same airplanes, tanks, etc., are wearing out. Stocks of military capital are built up when it is necessary to do so in order to maintain a given level of security, and they are allowed to depreciate when it is no longer necessary to do so in order to maintain the same level of security.

On the whole, that seems to me a sensible and justifiable treatment of the problem, and it has the added merit of being no more arbitrary than any other assumption and involving the least cost in terms of resources needed to make the calculation.

Other aspects of the sociopolitical environment, to the extent that they are measurable at all, present problems that are little different from the physical environmental ones discussed above. Freedom from violence against persons or property is a sociopolitical environmental asset that has deteriorated somewhat in recent years. The deterioration manifests itself in explicit costs that are observable and measurable—crime rates, property damage, etc. The costs of containing the deterioration within tolerable bounds are also identifiable and measurable and they comprise outlays for police and fire protection, safety locks, night watchmen, private guards, etc. All such outlays are simply costs of maintaining personal security, and if they have done nothing more than keep deterioration within limits the decline in total wellbeing is underestimated simply by removing such outlays from measured final output: the true decline would also register the amount of deterioration in the flow of benefits in addition to the higher maintenance costs of keeping the deterioration at its present level.

Substitution of Output for Input Measures

For purposes of measuring performance, a major shortcoming of the present accounts is their orientation toward measuring outputs by the cost of inputs in areas where the measurement of true output is difficult or impossible.[35] All social accountants are well aware of these areas, and of the fact that they comprise an increasingly important portion of total output as conventionally measured. In education, health, police protection, fire protection, the administration of justice in the courts, in national defense industries, in much of construction, to cite just the obvious cases, what is recorded as output in the accounts is really some kind of cost of inputs index without any adjustment for productivity gains. These conventions have not been adopted because social accountants are lazy or incompetent or lack an innovative spirit. Rather, they have been forced on the social accountant by a general inability to devise satisfactory and independent measures of the outputs produced in these sectors. We would all like to do better than measuring the value of education output by the cost of teachers' salaries and materials plus (or often not plus) the value of buildings used for instructional purposes, but it is not yet clear that we can.

The real question is not whether we should undertake a wholesale revamping of economic and social accounts to substitute clearly superior output measures for the obviously unsatisfactory input measures now in use. Rather, the question is: Can we devise some index of output that is a closer approximation to what is wanted than the input index now in use? Put that way, it should be possible to improve on present practice in at least a number of areas. Data are becoming available which, while not directly reflecting output, at least come much closer to it than input costs. For example, there are a lot more pupil achievement scores available than used to be the case, and what the schools are supposed to be doing, among other things, is improving on those scores through time; there are data on days lost through illness and lives lost through the incidence of disease; we know a good bit about crime rates, and how

---

[35] This discussion refers to the measurement of changes in output in constant dollars. In current dollars, changes in input costs and output values are obviously identical by definition. Thus, we are talking about what is essentially a deflation problem.

they have changed over time; there are data on fire losses through the records of fire insurance companies; and so on. While I do not suggest that these are readily convertible into output measures, it does seem reasonable that these and similar kinds of information could be used to construct what are essentially intermediate output indexes, with the characteristic of being no worse than input indexes and, if carefully constructed, a step closer to the objective of measuring final output. That is, I would simply argue that we can do better than we have in devising proxies for the effectiveness of services where the market does not provide us with much information on output, and that it is worthwhile to spend some effort in trying to devise output proxies that could be considered candidates for an index of real output over time.

A similar argument can be made with respect to those product areas where quality change is pervasive and not generally caught in the procedures for measuring output change now in use. In general terms, a quality change is not captured in present deflation procedures unless it can be represented by an identifiable change in cost. But much quality change is not of that nature, and simply consists of the replacement of products that yield more services for the same price and cost. Such measurement is possible only if we can identify and quantify the dimensions of quality improvement, e.g., by the construction of hedonic price indexes.[36] While I am no more sanguine than the rest of the profession about the operational feasibility of being able to construct hedonic price indexes that are analytically and empirically satisfactory, it does seem that efforts along this line have at least a modest payoff in terms of measuring what the system is doing rather than what it costs to do it.

Intermediate Versus Final Output

Much of the disagreement between defenders and critics of our present system of accounts really comes down to what is a sensible definition of final and intermediate output. At present we classify everything purchased by households as final consumption, everything purchased by government as final consumption, and most of the things purchased by business enterprise as intermediate products because they later appear in different form for sale to ultimate household, government, or business users. We all recognize that this is a convenient and useful fiction, in that most of what we now call final product is really intermediate in the more

---

[36] For studies about both the construction of hedonic price indexes as well as the application of such quality indexes to specific industries, see Griliches, ed., *Price Indexes.*

fundamental sense. The question is: Can we devise a different set of convenient fictions that comes closer to measuring what would be generally agreed on as final product? This is a very old problem in economic and social accounts, and has been the subject of much discussion and controversy in the past. There are really no fresh analytical insights, so far as I can tell, that can be brought to bear on the question. But that does not mean that there might not be general agreement on a different set of conventions than the one embedded in our present system of accounts.

The problem is best illustrated by asking how to measure final consumption by households. At present everything purchased by households from enterprises is so classified. By the most rigid definition, only the surplus of satisfaction-yielding output over all requirements for maintenance of both tangible and human capital stock would be so classified. But what is necessary, for example, to maintain the stock of human capital is very probably a function of what people have gotten accustomed to rather than some absolute physically determined maintenance requirement. And if we further recognize that what is essential for maintenance probably depends on the degree to which it yields satisfactions comparable to those obtained by associates and neighbors, the entire concept of final output dissolves into the proposition that what is needed keeps pace with what is available and that final output is neither worth discussing or trying to measure.

One does not have to go to quite that extreme, and that is why conventional treatments are useful and analytically helpful. For example, it seems clear (at least to me) that few people prefer to commute to work if they can avoid it. In a simpler society many people walked to work because their work was very close to their home, and if they lived further away they walked because there was no choice. In our society, people locate themselves with reference to the advantages and disadvantages of distance from work place, and the fact that they choose a location from which they must ride to work and pay for it means only that any location has both positive and negative aspects, not that commuting costs are any less a cost.

In a similar vein, it can be argued that washing machines and clothes dryers are not final output, except for those few families who realize a consumption benefit from ownership per se.[37] People want washing

---

[37] Lancaster's approach to consumer demand theory contains an implicit analytical distinction between the intermediate and final output components of consumption goods and services.

machines and clothes dryers to wash and dry clothes, and the alternative is to wash them by hand and dry them on the line. But the output is washed and dried clothes, not the equipment or the time, which clearly represent inputs. Nor do I think families buy vacuum cleaners, dust mops, and other cleaning supplies because they derive direct consumption benefits from their ownership. Rather, what people want are houses free from dust and dirt and the stains from leftover food, and a specified level of such benefits clearly represents final output while the cleaning implements required to produce it do not.

How far one wants to push this argument is another question. Do people go on picnics because it relaxes them and therefore enables them to work more efficiently or because they like to go on picnics? I suppose the answer must differ from one family to the next, and I am not sure we can ever hope to find out whether picnics are a maintenance cost or a final output. Do families buy furniture because they need a place to sit or because they like what the furniture does to the appearance of their house? I think this is different from vacuum cleaners and dishwashers, since people do derive pleasure from contemplating a new couch and I doubt that many people derive pleasure from contemplating their new vacuum cleaner. On the other hand, it does seem to me that people go to hospitals because they are sick (or need reassurance that they are not sick), not because the food is good and the room is airy and bright. I doubt that people collectively spend money on national defense because they enjoy watching tanks and planes in the annual Army or Navy parades. I doubt that people collectively decide to put filters on their automobiles because it improves the performance of the car or produces more vehicle-services per mile; nor do I think that people pay for the services of policemen, armored cars, personal weapons, and improved locks on their cars and houses because they derive consumption benefits from these activities. So far as I am concerned, these are pure and simple costs of maintaining a flow of services from assets, and they represent final output only to the degree that they increase the flow of services from those capital assets via net investment.

Regrettable Necessities and Progress

Some recent discussions have suggested that any attempt to differentiate between final output and intermediate product in the form of regrettable necessities is incapable of improving on the current "convenient fiction" that all products sold to households and governments are homogeneous with respect to their ultimate consumption value. Essentially that point is made in both Edward Denison's recent article and in Arthur Okun's note.[38] The argument is that treating commuting costs or the costs of heating and air conditioning as regrettable necessities (maintenance costs, in the terminology generally used in this paper) basically amounts to saying that it makes no difference whether people walk or ride to work or whether they do or do not have air conditioning, and that what is a regrettable necessity for those who ride to work and have air conditioned homes is surely at least as regrettable for those who do not.

The real issue seems to me somewhat different, and in fact the issue is different in the two illustrations. If I choose to locate at a fair distance from my place of work, I presumably do so with full cognizance of the fact that commuting time and costs are involved in enabling me to get to and from work. Whether commuting costs are high or low is determined by a locational decision with multiple arguments—the gains and losses associated with choosing to live at greater or lesser distances from the work place. I do not see any way out of the proposition that if the same gains could be obtained by living next door to the work place, everybody would prefer it and commuting costs would decline. Thus, I am not better off by having a car in which to ride to work; more precisely, I am not better off than if the same locational advantages could be obtained without the need to commute.

On whether expenditures on goods like air conditioning and heating are regrettable necessities, it matters greatly for the analysis whether we are comparing welfare in the same country at two different points in time or comparing it at the same point in time between two different countries with rather different natural environments. Expenditures for air conditioning and heating are essentially a way of buying reduced temperature variability. That reduction in variability has a cost, and the national income statistician would presumably judge, along with others, that the cost is worthwhile if it is incurred. But the real output obtained—more stable and comfortable temperature and humidity—is clearly higher in the case of families who purchase air conditioning and heating than for those who cannot, and the cost of the purchased inputs is a fair reflection of that difference in benefit flow.

In contrast, if one is comparing welfare in a country like the United States with welfare in the Virgin Islands, a good case can be made for saying that expenditures by U.S. residents on heating and air condition-

[38] See Denison, "Welfare Measurement and the GNP"; and A. M. Okun, "Should GNP Measure Social Welfare?" Brookings *Bulletin,* Summer 1971.

ing do not provide any more benefits than Virgin Islanders get by simply living where they do. The real output is still mean level and variability of temperature, and if it can be bought with no cost in the Virgin Islands that is surely at least as good from a welfare viewpoint as obtaining it by purchasing air conditioning and heating equipment in the United States. Thus, national accounts cannot be used to compare welfare between countries with different levels of natural resource benefit flows, although it is still true that expenditures on temperature and humidity control devices yield significant benefits for those in climates where such expenditures reduce undesired variability.

In any event, keeping a firm eye on flows of net consumption benefits yields the correct answer in both cases, while ad hoc arguments about whether one is better or worse off with air conditioning do not. Within the environmental wealth-income framework, a pleasant and relatively invariant temperature is clearly an asset which costs nothing to get in some parts of the world and a good deal to get in others. Over time, countries where this is not a natural phenomenon can acquire more of the desired good, but only at a cost. Thus, if the United States spends enough on heating and air conditioning, it can eventually attain the level of environmental benefit of the sort the Virgin Islands residents have always had with no costs at all. Appropriate welfare accounts should register that dichotomy.

It should be recognized that distinctions between final and intermediate product will inevitably have some element of arbitrariness surrounding them. That seems to me unavoidable, and I do not suggest that there are ways to get around it. Nonetheless, there are degrees of arbitrariness just like anything else, and I would argue that we can provide a better set of distinctions between intermediate and final product than the ones now embedded in the conventions underlying our existing accounts. Nothing compels us to go the complete route of intermediating virtually all of output because one could think of arguments for doing so. Converting some but not all of our present final outputs to intermediate outputs should represent an improvement in what we now measure as net output, and there is no need either to decry the fact that all such conversions that could be made were not made or that the conversions are based on the judgments of social accountants.[39] Our present accounts are partly based on that, and I simply sug-

[39] To quote Kuznets (*National Income*, p. 3): "The statistician who supposes that he can make a purely objective estimate of national income, not influenced by preconceptions concerning the 'facts,' is deluding himself, for whenever he

gest that those judgments can be significantly improved with a wide degree of consensus that the change represents an improvement.

Possible Timetables for Implementation

So far this paper has been addressed almost exclusively to examination of an economic and social accounting framework that represents an objective to aim at, not necessarily or even probably one that represents an achievable goal next year or in the next five years or even in the next decade. The pragmatic question is: Given agreement about the broad outlines of the framework, what if anything should be done immediately? Within a few years? Within the next decade?

Immediate Objectives. The suggested framework contains a number of separable changes which differ as to difficulty of implementation, agreement about the desirability of implementation, and the availability of the data with which implementation can be achieved. These changes might be categorized as follows, in roughly descending order of feasible implementation:

1. Sectoring to include households and governments as enterprises.
2. Capital accounts to include tangible consumer and government capital, intangible business capital, and some dimensions of human capital (e.g., outlays for formal schooling).
3. Provision for direct consumption benefits provided by enterprises.
4. Provision for those costs associated with maintenance of physical and sociopolitical environmental assets where the costs can easily be measured or are measured now.
5. Inclusion of the major categories of time allocated to nonmarket activities by households.
6. Substitution of output measures for input costs.
7. Improvement of present output measures for quality change not associated with distinct cost differences.
8. Provision for complete human capital accounts, going beyond schooling costs to include foregone earnings, learning and training at home, and learning and training in the job market.

includes one item or excludes another he is implicitly accepting some standard of judgment, either his own or that of the compilers of his data. There is no escaping this subjective element in the work, or freeing the results from its effects. In consequence, all national income estimates are appraisals of the end products of the economic system rather than colorless statements of fact; and, like all appraisals, they are predetermined by criteria that are at worst a matter of chance, at best a matter of deliberate choice."

9. Measurement of the direct environmental benefit flows to consumers.

As far as the first two items are concerned, there is no question that economic accounts incorporating these activities can be implemented; they already have been in several published and in-process studies. Including a household sector that does more than consume owner-occupied housing, along with a counterpart government sector that makes investments as well as provides services, and expanding the capital accounts to register investment by business in intangibles and by governments and households in formal schooling does no more than rearrange existing transaction flows in a more analytically useful framework. The only real questions involve imputations for the return on consumer and government owned capital assets, and in both cases there are available market yardsticks. In fact, there are alternative market yardsticks available, which complicates the problem somewhat. Since many of these suggested changes have regularly been advocated by virtually all critics of the present accounts since the time the accounts were framed, and since the necessary empirical measurements are available in abundance, the case for implementation as soon as resources permit seems to me entirely persuasive.

Recognition that business firms provide direct consumption benefits to households (generally but not exclusively employees) seems to have a slightly lower priority both on the data side and on the conceptual appropriateness side. One aspect of the problem is a purely institutional difference in the financing of news and entertainment; significant differences in the treatment of identical activities are created between countries where communications media are nationalized and those where they are private. The argument here rests in part on the desirability of uniform treatment, and since most developed countries have nationalized communications media, the U.S. accounts might appropriately yield to the common denominator. But the analytical arguments are compelling: one cannot question the simple fact that the news media provide information, entertainment, and opinion which is costly to produce and for which no direct charge is made. It does not seem less arbitrary to impute interest income to the owners of checking deposits for services rendered than to impute entertainment income to the viewers of television programs. In the latter case it is not even necessary to buy a joint product, since one does not have to suffer through the advertising.

Intermediate Range Implementation. The situation is perceptibly different for the next four areas on the list. There is no general agreement among social accountants on how to handle either national defense outlays or defensive expenditures for environmental control—although perhaps that situation might be different at the conclusion of this conference. There are serious and perhaps insoluble measurement problems involved in the latter, since there is no way to identify changes in output that are a consequence of environmental quality legislation or requirements, as pointed out in the Herfindahl-Kneese paper. For those environmental control outlays that can be identified and measured, it appears desirable as a minimum to start collecting and tabulating information in order to have a better data base for whatever decisions eventually emerge.

On the nonmarket activity sector, the problems are both unavailability of adequate data and the need for conceptual clarification of how these activities should be valued. Both require time as well as research inputs to overcome, and we can expect that the implementation of nonmarket activities in economic and social accounting systems will have a much broader base, on both the data and the analytical side, within the next several years. Needless to say, any emerging agreement does not necessarily involve inclusion of the full range of nonmarket activities, or even of any such activities, in a fully integrated system of accounts.

Longer-Range Implementation. The last two changes are subject to much more serious difficulties than the others both in terms of available data and agreement on appropriate conceptual structures. Both lend themselves to being better understood and quantified by research efforts, of which several are reported on later in this conference. One appears more likely than the other to emerge with operationally useful concepts and available data with which to measure them—for example, full implementation of the human capital concept is probably both feasible and desirable, given research under way or in prospect. Prospects for direct measurement of environmental benefits seem a bit further off if not totally unmanageable with our present techniques, although an interesting alternative way of handling the problem was recently suggested in the Nordhaus-Tobin paper prepared for the NBER's economic growth colloquium.[40] Their approach abstracts entirely from the need to measure either physical environmental changes or the consequence of changes in flows of economic benefits, since they rely on the

---

[40] William Nordhaus and James Tobin, "Is Growth Obsolete?" *Economic Growth,* Fiftieth Anniversary Colloquium V, New York, NBER, 1972; the text, excluding the appendixes, is reprinted in this volume.

market to have provided equalizing wage differentials between areas with differential flows of direct environmental benefits. While physical flows on the environmental side can certainly be measured in principle with enough resources, and while the economic consequences of these flows can in principle be approximated (how much would you pay to clean up the X river so that you could swim in it?), these possibilities seem further away and more difficult to achieve.

SUPPLEMENTARY NOTE A:
Production Accounts and Output Measures

One distinction that needs to be made clear concerns the use of the accounts to measure changes in production or productivity, and their use to measure changes in economic welfare. This difference appears to be at the root of the disagreement about the proper treatment of pollution control investments. Perhaps the best way to structure this problem is to recognize that there are different levels at which the distinction between intermediate and final product can be made. Let me illustrate with the treatment of emission control devices on automobiles.

From the point of view of production and productivity analysis, equipping vehicles with emission control devices clearly represents an addition to final output. One can consider this either as the production of two separate goods—the vehicle and the emission control device —or as the production of one good with an additional dimension of performance, similar in many ways to the addition of automatic transmissions on vehicles. Thus, the accounts should record that production of goods is increased by the addition of emission filters, and if such filters are produced more efficiently and become available at lower real cost, that ought to show up in analysis of productivity in the market sector.

From a broader point of view, however, emission control devices may represent an intermediate or instrumental product rather than a final product. They clearly do nothing to increase the consumption benefits obtained from automobile services, and they may or may not expand other types of consumption benefit flows. Whether or not they do depends on whether the filter has increased the flow of environmental benefits, managed to hold the flow constant by preventing deterioration, or served only to keep deterioration within tolerable bounds. Taking a long-term view of the productivity of emission control devices suggests that either of the latter two conditions probably holds; environmental quality is presumably less good than ten years ago, and automobile filters have succeeded only in making deterioration less than it otherwise would have been. While filters constitute gross investment in environmental assets, they would not result in net investment unless they have more than offset the natural forces making for environmental degradation.

Thus, vehicular emission control devices are clearly part of gross national product in current prices, and for production account purposes they are also part of gross national product in constant prices and should not be deflated out. But they would not be part of net (welfare-oriented) output in constant prices, and would appear only as an offset against the depreciation of environmental assets.

If we had direct measurements of environmental benefit flows, the capitalized value of any change in benefit flows would appear as depreciation or appreciation. The investment cost of the filters would not show up directly in this case, but would be reflected indirectly in the net amount of depreciation or appreciation. That is, in the absence of investment in filters, the implication is that there would have been either a greater amount of depreciation or a smaller amount of appreciation. If the filters have simply prevented deterioration from taking place and thus maintained environmental assets intact, the accounts should simply register the absence of any change from previous periods in environmental benefit flows. An equivalent way to produce the same result is to show depreciation on environmental assets as the precise quantitative equivalent to gross investment in such assets in the form of filters, thus having gross investment and depreciation accounts of equal size with net investment of zero.

The main point is that, for purposes of analyzing production and productivity the gross national product accounts would continue to serve their current very useful purpose of incorporating goods that are not further processed within the enterprise sector of the economy, and in valuing these goods at their costs of production. But for describing consumption and net investment flows with a welfare-orientation, a substantial range of products which make no contribution to welfare but simply prevent welfare producing assets from deteriorating should be subtracted out as representing gross but not net investment.

SUPPLEMENTARY NOTE B:
Economic Accounts and the Organization of Economic Activity

The difference in treatment in the present accounts between activities carried out in the enterprise sector and those carried out in households, as well as between activities carried out by private firms and by governments, might be regarded as analytically justifiable if the characteristics of activities were uniquely associated with their production in a particular type of economic organization. It is one thing to argue that housework or television viewing or child-rearing does not constitute economic output, while police and fire protection do, if all of the former activities are carried out solely by households and not by firms or governments while all the latter are carried out solely by governments and not by firms or households. But that argument is less persuasive if activities are carried out simultaneously within households, enterprises, and governments, with their location being determined by considerations of demand, efficiency, and cost.

The kinds of anomalous situations that most tend to irritate critics of our present accounts are precisely those in which a given activity is usually carried out by households but is, in fact, sometimes carried out by firms or governments, and where the activity is counted as output in the latter two cases but not in the former. In such situations, the valuation of total output depends on the location of particular activities, and one can get quantitatively important shifts in measured output where nothing has really changed except that production has shifted from the household to the firm or vice versa.

One way to decide whether or not a given activity should be considered as output is to ask how the activity would be handled in the accounts if it were carried out by business firms and sold for a price. Application of this criteria would exclude consideration of some types of welfare-producing activities which could not conceivably be organized by business firms and sold to consumers or government, and these turn out to be precisely the cases where the most disagreement exists with regard to inclusion or exclusion of the activity in measured output. For example, business firms can hardly sell leisure time to individuals, although they obviously sell products that are complementary to leisure time.

Let me illustrate the problem with two typical cases. The present accounts classify most activities involving protection against fire and theft as final output; these are predominantly but not exclusively activities organized by governments. Yet they can be organized by business firms, and where this is the case the costs of protection show up as intermediate rather than final product. This is true whether each firm buys its own protection or whether specialized firms produce protection and sell it to other firms. As a consequence, the services of alarm systems or Pinkerton guards used in business are not final output, but the same services provided by municipal employees are. Moreover, alarm systems or private guards hired by individuals rather than firms are considered to be final output, just as much as the services of municipally employed policemen and patrol cars. The reason for the coexistence of private and governmental protection systems presumably is that people want different amounts of protection, and some of them choose to supplement what the government provides. But that does not make one output and the other not.

Next, educational services are produced in all three sectors. In very early childhood years, households typically produce their own education and training services for their own children. But in later years, households typically purchase educational services from either private firms or governments. The reason for this division of labor presumably has something to do with relative efficiency in the respective producing units. In early childhood years, rearing and training children is a highly unspecialized and time-intensive activity; buying the service would cost a large fraction of the earnings of a typical family, and that's why it's done by families themselves except those rich enough to afford a full-time nurse or governess. As children mature, rearing and training activities require somewhat more specialized skills but can be carried out at considerably lower unit cost, since the typical pupil-teacher ratio is a lot higher than the typical nurse-baby ratio. Hence, we have organized schools from which parents buy education services.

Moreover, one of the reasons for the relative inefficiency of market produced nursery care is that the necessary time-inputs cover most of the day but are heavily concentrated in small segments of the day. Thus, a mother taking care of her own children can do a great many other things while the children are sleeping or playing alone, while a business producing the same services cannot efficiently do any of the complementary things that mothers of young children do when not immediately occupied with the children. The pattern of time-use in the rearing and training process changes as the child matures, and that is presumably why organized schools become more efficient at some stage of the child's development. But none of this constitutes a reason to count formal schooling as output and training at home as not. The measurement problems are obviously more serious for training at home, but that seems to be the only real difference.

In measuring changes in output and income with a given set of rules about what is to be counted as output and what is not, technical change that alters the relative efficiencies of production among different types of organizations may thus introduce essentially arbitrary changes in the measurement of output. For example, the advent of the safety razor drastically changed the distribution of barber services—toward the household and away from the business sector. Increased social frictions associated with urbanization, along with the development of sophisticated protection devices, have probably altered the mix of protective services toward the firm and away from government. Neither these nor similar changes ought to influence the measurement of output.

COMMENT
GEORGE JASZI, Department of Commerce

Although he does not say so explicitly, Juster deals with the core of the work of the Office of Business Economics. He proposes a basic restructuring of the national accounts as we prepare them currently. I am uncertain whether this response to him is a "defensive" use of my time, in Juster's sense of the term, or a use of my time that generates positive delight.

I am quite anxious because I know that I shall be excluded from the restructured measure of U.S. output if I am judged defensive. Should I be offensive to escape such ignominy?

Given the nature of my involvement, I shall not engage in intensive analysis of some of his proposals, but address myself to all of them. I shall state which of them I should like to implement and to which I am opposed. I shall give my reasons in each case, but I shall have to be brief—much briefer than desirable—because the story is long and the time I have to tell it, short.

SPECIFICS

Accounts for Tangible Consumer and Government Capital

Juster proposes the establishment of capital accounts for tangible capital held by consumers and government. I associate myself with this proposal, even though I would be more inclined than he to stress the difficulties surrounding its implementation especially in the case of government capital. Difficult decisions relating to coverage, service lives, depreciation, and valuation will have to be made.

Even though there is no real disagreement here, I should like to provide some perspective. These capital accounts are on the blueprints of the full-fledged systems that some of the most conservative national accountants would like to implement. It would be wrong to believe that we are faced here with a novel proposition with which national economic accountants, as distinguished from the broader minded race of sociologically inclined investigators, would tend to disagree. Far from it, we at OBE, who can certainly be thought of as belonging to the former stick-in-the-mud type, have almost completed estimates of the stock of consumer capital, as I believe Juster knows, and shall proceed to estimate government capital if budgetary resources permit.

Juster mentions that in the OBE accounts mobile homes are classified with automobiles in personal consumption expenditures instead of as part of housing investment. Judging from the context, I must assume that he considers this as evidence of the shortcomings of the broader aspects of our method of dealing with consumer capital accounts. I would have to disagree with such reasoning. It would be about as cogent as reasoning that his plan for capital accounts is defective because in his paper he inadvertently omits inventories from his itemization of wealth.

If present practice is to be adduced as evidence of basic flaws, Juster could have cited a more convincing case. He could have drawn attention to the fact that we have not yet integrated our estimates of business capital with the regular publications of the accounts, and he could have pressed us about using Internal Revenue Service-based depreciation charges in lieu of economically meaningful estimates in the latter.

It is convenient here to correct Juster's interpretation of our preference for gross over net output measures. Our use of gross measures stems largely from our caution in introducing economic measures of depreciation. We do not feature the gross measures, as Juster seems to think, primarily because we believe that they are superior in economic analysis. The concepts and methods underlying economically meaningful depreciation estimates are subject to considerable controversy within the economic and accounting professions, and we also know from experience that business is quite sensitive to the measurement of depreciation because it affects corporate profits. We want to be as sure as we can about the theoretical and statistical foundation of our estimates before we incorporate them into the official accounts.

Imputed Returns on Tangible Assets

I turn to imputed rates of return on tangible assets. As far as I know, Juster has wide support for his proposition "that household capital as well as government capital also yields a return to its owners. . . ." I certainly subscribe to it. My view that no imputation of a net rate of return to either form of capital should be made in the foreseeable future has somewhat different roots. It stems from the proposition that in some cases no estimate is preferable to a poor estimate.

I do not agree with Juster that estimating such imputed rates of return involves no greater shortfall from the ideal than do our present estimates of corporate profits. He seems to believe that we would like to measure profits as they would be in a competitive economy that is in equilibrium and in which private and social marginal products are equal; and that we settle for the profits of the actual world only because we cannot reach this goal. I have always thought that we want to measure profits of the actual world and that in measuring them we are not settling for a second-best.

I must disagree also with Juster's statement that many usable estimates of imputed net returns have actually been made. Finally, I do not think that the procedure which he suggests for consumer capital is encouraging. If I understand it correctly, it results in a zero net rate of return.

In sum, I am skeptical about prospects in this area of measurement. If any progress is to be made, the first step will have to be a clarification of what concept of a net rate of return would be useful in economic analysis. Would a variable or a fixed rate of return fit the underlying concept? And what pattern of variability, or what level of fixedness, would provide useful empirical approximations to whatever our analytical aim turns out to be?

Intangible Investment and Capital

I have difficulties in evaluating Juster's proposal to extend the measurement of investment to intangibles, because he does not provide a definition of investment. Let those who are inclined to react to this comment by saying that it is pedantic because the concept of investment is self-evident hold their fire, and try their hands at penning a definition that is satisfactory. I think they will be surprised.

Setting this handicap aside, I believe that the calculation of intangible investment and capital stocks presents problems of coverage, service life, depreciation formula, and valuation procedure that are much more difficult than the ones that are encountered in the preparation of estimates of tangible capital. I regret that lack of time compels me to let this statement stand as assertion, but expect that many who hear it will agree.

I may note in passing that Juster's statement, to the effect that it would not be more difficult to calculate depreciation charges on intangibles than it is to calculate the IRS-based depreciation charges now embedded in the accounts, leaves me aghast. As I have just noted, the IRS-based charges are practically useless in economic analysis (although they have some claim to existence because they summarize actual calculations performed by business). Also, I cannot see how, even if one wanted to, the IRS-based methodology could be transferred or adapted to the measurement of depreciation on intangible capital.

I am receptive to work on intangible investment in spite of these caveats. I am fairly ignorant on this subject, but I sense that many important kinds of specific analysis (and not just the yearning to measure welfare) require such estimates. It would seem to me that progress in this area will have to be based upon a specification of the conceptual tools that are required for the solution of problems of analysis and decisionmaking that we face. It may turn out that in the course of such a specification certain segments of the work will turn out to be more important and feasible than others and that a sensible research strategy will emerge.

Household Production

Juster proposes extensive imputations for household activities. My philosophy about imputations is that incursions into the nonmarket economy should be permitted only with stringent safeguards. In each case, the investigator should be in possession of a search warrant that is issued to him only if he can prove that he is looking for information he requires to analyze significant specific problems for the solution of which there is realistic concern; and that a search warrant should not be issued to him just because he wants to go on a fishing expedition to measure welfare. Given this predisposition, I was initially somewhat skeptical of Juster's proposed time and motion study of households, but I have come to the conclusion that the type of study he suggests might be of great interest if it were based upon the insights of individuals or groups who are sensitive to the sociological processes that are fundamental to our society, and not on the fancies of isolated research subcultures.

However, I cannot go with Juster all the way. I cannot follow him in his attempt to measure hours spent that are truly outputs and to eliminate hours that represent inputs: The reference I made at the beginning of these comments to one way in which he tries to formulate the distinction was not purely facetious. Nor can I follow him further in his attempt to value the hours so obtained. I think that the full imagery associated with will-o'-the-wisps and quagmires is fitly displayed in connection with his attempt, and that I need do little more than to refer the reader to Juster's own discussion to document this view.

I do, however, go one step further to formulate my own bewilderment. I take it that Juster does not want to value the time spent in various types of household production by imputing to them the price of the closest market analogue. For instance, he would not want to value the time I spend doing homework with my children at the wage rate that a school teacher earns. Instead, he proposes to use the wage rate I earn. This would result in estimates in which my fumbling attempts to teach new math to my children would be valued much higher than the instruction provided to her own child by a competent school teacher. Also, it would provide no basis for valuing the time of rentiers and retired people and of preschool and school children. Surely, the welfare of these groups must be a large chunk of total welfare.

But perhaps most disturbing, I cannot see why the value of an hour of leisure should be equated to the wage rate of the person enjoying the leisure. The hourly wage rate I earn in a job that combines fatigue and boredom does not seem to have anything to do with the value of the hour I spend watching my favorite TV program. What relevance does the sum I would require to do an oven-roast for an hour have for the value I should put on an hour I spend rocking on the porch? I cannot think this through. The only thing that comes to my mind is the story of another Tom. That Tom was forced to whitewash a fence by his Aunt Polly and managed not only to get his friends to do the chore for him but also to get them to pay him for being allowed to do so. Perhaps what our Tom suggests is feasible also, especially because he is willing to settle for imputed dollars. I should add that the puzzle was suggested to me by my friend Denison; the association was mine only.

Let me note finally that Juster seems willing to put up with input measures in his proposals for household production, instead of pressing for output measures as elsewhere in his paper. I suspect that he is motivated by the biblical recognition that "sufficient unto the day is the evil thereof."

Evidently, this is an area that is full of booby traps. But even if we were successful in valuing the time spent by consumers during nonwork hours, I should like to see these estimates as supplementary information integrated into the accounting system rather than as a part of the measure of production. This is so because I cannot be shaken of the common sense view that there is a distinction between production and leisure and that for most purposes it is useful to keep the two apart.

Miscellaneous Points

Before I turn to the environment and to other matters dealt with later in Juster's paper, I want to be sure that I have addressed myself to all the major alterations he has proposed so far. I take note of his suggestion to impute a value to the services of TV (upon further thought, other news media, including newspapers, would also be involved) and to a limited range of services provided by business to its employees. I see no objection to extending the measure of production in these two ways, although I am a little surprised that Juster is in favor of the latter extension. However, if Juster were to advocate—what to the best of my understanding he does not—measuring the "conditions of work" broadly defined, I would have to question the feasibility of such a project.

I am not sure that I have commented on everything that Juster wants us to do by way of restructuring the accounts of households (and government). In particular, I am not sure whether I have caught the full significance of his statement that the "sectoring [is] to include households and government *as enterprises*" (my italics); and I am not sure whether Juster has fully transmitted the lessons for national accounting of the burgeoning theories of human capital and household economics which we have neglected so far.

I should like also to register some skepticism about Juster's generalization that "the basic principle that ought to underlie economic and social accounts is that the income (output) of the system is derived in one way or another from an implicit set of wealth accounts." The establishment of a human wealth account leads *prima facie* to the proposition that human consumption is an intermediate product, like pig fodder. Far from being heuristically useful, the new approach which a human wealth account opens for income and output measurements is planted with snares and delusions which the national accountant will have to dodge assiduously and ingeniously if he is to reach an output concept that is worth reaching.

Environment

The management of the environment has become an important public issue and, even though the current burst of concern may not be fully sustained, it is likely to remain one in years to come. Accordingly, the national accountant should lend all the aid and assistance he can to the analysis of environmental problems even if he is not particularly interested in the measurement of welfare. The measurement of the environment is a difficult problem and Juster does not improve the clarity of our view of it by implying that a somewhat related problem, the accounting for the depletion of natural resources, has been solved. It has not. Because of insurmountable difficulties in dealing with natural resources in a manner useful for economic analysis, the discovery value of natural resources and charges for their depletion are left out of the accounts.

If I understand him correctly, Juster believes that no wholly satisfactory way of accounting for environmental change is possible unless both the value of environmental damage and of the costs of abating it can be quantified. He also seems to see that a valuation of environmental damage is not in the cards. He is less explicit about this, however, and there are passages in his paper that point to a contrary view. But in his suggested solution for the measurement of environmental change he does not contemplate the valuation of damage, and works with antipollution expenditures only. I shall follow him in this respect and not argue that the valuation of environmental damage is indeed impossible. This is an extremely interesting and complex problem about which it is difficult to reason and which should be clarified further. But it is just as well that I need not concern myself with it in these comments which threaten to become overlong.

With the problem and its solution set in terms of the use of information relating to antipollution expenditures only, Juster advocates the omission of such expenditures when incurred by consumers and government from real output (in which they are now included). He rejects the solution advocated by Denison to the effect that antipollution costs incurred by business (now excluded from real output) should be quantified and used to interpret changes in output as now measured or, conceivably, added to it. I cannot go much further here in describing the background. But I want to note that the anomalous behavior of the present measure of output which Denison's proposal is designed to deal with is this: Real output as currently measured declines if there is a shift of factors of production to the abatement of pollution from the production of items (say automobiles) sold to consumers or government, if the abatement activities are paid for by business.

Juster presents illustrations showing that in cases in which the increase in pollution that would have occurred in the absence of antipollution expenditures by consumers (or government) is exactly offset by these expenditures, their omission will give the correct welfare answer for the change of output whereas Denison's measure will result in an overstatement. (Because of his belief in the priority of wealth concepts, Juster would state the same condition by saying that net environmental assets are not changed by the antipollution expenditures.) Denison's measure will give a correct welfare answer in cases in which the antipollution expenditures are associated with corresponding improvements in the environment. Juster chooses the former solution on the ground, I believe, that as compared with the past, environment is not likely to improve in the long run as a result of antipollution expenditures.

I am strongly inclined toward Denison's solution on the following ground, even though it also is beset with difficulties which I shall not discuss here. I am not willing to base a general solution of the problem on the particular assumption that the increase in pollution that would have occurred in the absence of antipollution expenditures is exactly offset by them, any more than on the alternative assumption under which Denison's proposal happens to work. My disinclination to follow Juster has to do with the kind of output measure toward which his solution points. Juster's solution is based on the assumption that we can identify in the national product certain kinds of expenditures which are "defensive" (and proceed to exclude them from output).

I believe that "defensive expenditures" is a disabled veteran among output concepts which cannot be relied upon to provide effective support in output measurement. It suggests that food expenditures defend against hunger, that clothing and housing expenditures defend against cold and rain, that medical expenditures defend against sickness, and religious outlays against the fires of hell. The concept then demands that these expenditures be left out altogether, or that they be recognized only to the extent that they are not offset by a change in needs. For instance, an increase in bread production should be counted only to the extent that it is not offset by healthier appetites; an increase in the output of galoshes, to the extent it is not offset by increased rain; increase in the number of aspirin tablets, to the extent it is not offset by an increase in the number of headaches (perhaps of national income estimators who have followed Juster's advice).

I am stopping at the gates of hell. I think that it is a basic mistake to try to construct a measure of national output that attempts to exclude items on the basis of the indefensible distinction that they are "defensive," and to roll into one "needs" and "production," two concepts that should be kept apart. I should like to be able to say that bread production has increased if the number of loaves of bread produced has increased, without further investigation of the state of human appetites. I prefer Denison's solution because it does not rely heavily on feeble concepts, and keeps distinct distinctions that should be kept distinct.

Output vs. Input, Intermediate vs. Final Output,
and Regrettable Necessities

In the final sections of his paper, Juster discusses many important issues that are not as disparate as their titles would indicate. They have much in common and are closely related to Juster's discussion of the environment. From a heuristic standpoint it would be extremely useful to find their common factor. I shall make an incomplete attempt to do so in the following comments.

Output vs. Input Indexes. Substitution of output for input measures, for instance in measuring the services rendered by government, is obviously a worthwhile objective if it can be achieved, because, to put it most broadly, it is an essential condition for cost-benefit analysis. My only objection to Juster's approach is that he seems to associate the problem particularly with government. He does not realize in a systematic way that measurement of household consumption is beset by exactly the same problem. I am not referring to the trivial case of domestic service, but to a more general phenomenon that can be illustrated by the observation that we measure the flour, spices, butter, sugar, etc., purchased by housewives and not the cakes she bakes with these ingredients (or perhaps something even further removed). This is no different from the present treatment of government expenditures which is being criticized. We measure the labor, pencils, pens, writing pads, etc., OBE buys, and not the national accounts that some think it cooks. Or should these accounts not be counted because they are misleading indicators of welfare? Or should we try to measure an event that is even further down the line? I am not drawing the household analogy facetiously. Juster, in particular, should not think so. After all, he regards households as producing enterprises whose activity should be analyzed instead of letting them live in the benign neglect that is now granted to them as passive consumers. Incidentally, the neglect is not as complete as Juster implies. Reading his paper, one might think that we are not interested in classifications of consumer expenditures. In fact, we prepare one of the most elaborate classifications which exists.

The consumer analogy is helpful, I believe, because it brings out the generality and full complexity of this problem. I do believe that further search for improved output measures should be undertaken in spite of the very disappointing return that research of this type has yielded to date. I am not hopeful at all that the conventions now used in the accounts can be superseded, but the work undertaken should prove useful in various kinds of specific cost-benefit analysis.

Hedonic Output Measures. Juster suggests the wider use of "hedonic" indexes based on regression techniques as an improvement over the conventional method for measuring quality change that takes into account only the quality improvement that is accompanied by an increase in real cost. When I last surveyed this territory, I came to the conclusion that the hedonic method was in principle identical to the conventional method, and best regarded as an alternative technique of implementing it. I did so in a note, in the *Review of Economics and Statistics,* which received wide neglect but, to the best of my knowledge, was not shown to be wrong.

Service vs. Goods Output. I should like to question another generalization that Juster makes about real output measurement, one that is by no means unique to him. It is that the volume of service output as a class is harder to determine than the volume of output of tangible commodities as a class. I find it easier to quantify the output of shoeshines than that of automobiles. This is not intended as a capricious example; I do not believe that the frequently voiced generalization about the relatively greater difficulty of satisfactorily measuring service than commodity output holds.

Defense and Other Defensive Government Outlays. Juster revives the hoary proposition that national defense outlays (and other "defensive" government outlays) should be excluded from the measure of national output. The argument he conducts is essentially the same as he makes for the amputation of antipollution expenditures: He claims that defense expenditures are "defensive" and therefore should be excluded from output if we assume that they offset the increase in insecurity from aggression which would have occurred in their absence, an assumption which he is willing to make. In the course of his argument he states that he doubts "that people collectively spend money on national defense because they enjoy watching tanks and planes in the annual Army or Navy parades." I believe he is somewhat short of sociological insight in making this remark. Certainly in some European countries military pomp is an important form of collective conspicuous consumption. Should not this be taken into account in comparing the welfare of nations? Also, there have been and are warlike nations to whom war is a form of production, just as hunting is production to tribes of hunters. But I should not really be drawn into these murky speculations. I reject Juster's recommendation to amputate military production on the same ground that I reject his proposal for the treatment of the environment: The concept of "defensive outlays" is too feeble to back him up.

"Defensive outlays" is not the only concept which Juster uses in his argument. The concept of "regrettable necessities" is also introduced. This seems to be an identical twin of "defensive outlays." A third in his platoon of tottering veterans is "expenditures that are made not for their own sakes but for the sake of obtaining something else." It would be interesting to explore the relation of this concept to the other two. I know that it is at least their first cousin, but I would not be surprised if upon further analysis we would find that we are dealing with triplets. These concepts are not new. They are the Eternal Jews of national income measurement. They do not die and, unlike some other old soldiers, they do not even fade away.

In connection with the controversy about the government, I note that Juster considers our current treatment a major miscarriage. It is tantalizing therefore to read in an earlier part of his paper that our system represents only a "conceptual modification" of Kuznets in the treatment of government. In the words of Auden "the mouse we banished yesterday is an enraged rhinoceros today."

My sadness about this vicious transformation was alleviated only by an old story. A scientific congress was being harangued by a speaker who insisted that, after all, the anatomical difference between the sexes was very small. The audience listened patiently for a long time, but finally one of its members cried out: "Long live the small difference."

Commuting and Air Conditioning. In the last part of his paper Juster returns to the application of the concept of "regrettable necessities" (alias "defensive outlays") to components of consumer spending, specifically commuting and air conditioning. I do not think that he adds any new point. He comes to the conclusion, which I expected, that commuting expenditures should be omitted from the GNP. To my surprise, however, he favors the inclusion of expenditures for air conditioning. I cannot follow him in his argument in either case. In the case of commuting, for instance, it might be argued that larger expenditures for commuting buy additional environmental comfort: We buy the clean air and quiet of the suburb instead of putting up with the smoke and noise of downtown. This would seem, in Juster's own conceptual framework, to call for the inclusion of commuting expenditures. As regards air conditioning, we might argue for its exclusion on the ground that the need for it is to a large extent the result of the rise of urban civilization in which masses of humanity are crowded together like ants in a heap. Compare the oppressiveness of the heat that threatens urban slums with that associated with rural surroundings. Thus, one might argue that an increase in air conditioning is not a sign of increased welfare. Quite to the contrary, it is a "defensive" outlay to offset a deterioration in our welfare which would be even larger if we would not defend ourselves against it.

GENERAL CONSIDERATIONS

Before I summarize the main points of my argument, I should like to mention two differences in style of thinking and working that separate me from Juster.

Differences in Styles of Research

The first of these can be illustrated by reference to the often heard proposition "It makes sense in theory but it cannot be done in practice." This proposition has some validity; undoubtedly there is some antithesis between theory and practice that results in a synthesis that is nearer to truth. But I do believe that the proposition should be kept on a short leash lest it promote empty theorizing on the one hand and mindless empiricism on the other. By and large, I like to believe that good theory works in practice. Juster's style of thinking admits a larger gulf between theory and practice than mine.

This difference is camouflaged by a second one: I have a much narrower view of what can be done in practice than he. Reading his paper, I never ceased to be amazed as to what he considers feasible: the imputation of net rates of return to intangible capital, the valuation of time spent outside work, the implementation of the concept of defensive outlays, to mention only a few examples at random. Suppose I look out of the window and decide that a good imputed rate of return on capital is 9 per cent because a much lower rate would compete with Treasury bills and a much higher rate would smack of usury. Does this act of mine prove that imputation of net rates of return is feasible? It is hard to analyze our difference. But I sense that it may be due to the fact that Juster is willing to put up with much more subjective judgment than I am, and that he is less eager than I to make sure that a solution which is dubbed feasible is also useful for the analysis of some specific problem.

In support of his contention that certain procedures are feasible, Juster often contends that procedures now used in economic accounting are just as "arbitrary" as his. But there is a great difference between the two kinds of arbitrariness. By and large, the national accounts depict trans-actions in the way the transactors see them. This picture is modified only at the margin, in the interest of hardheaded economic analysis. It can be called arbitrary only if one looks at it from the vantage point of an undefined concept of welfare. As we have seen, Juster's procedures are arbitrary in quite another sense.

Impossibility of Welfare Measures

As to substance, the basic difference between Juster and myself is that he believes in the usefulness and possibility of constructing measures of welfare; I do not. Such measures are not possible because they have no boundaries; because they try to quantify what cannot be quantified; to value what cannot be valued; and to roll into one, aspects of human activity that should be kept apart. These comments have spelled out the reasons for my disbelief. In this summary I want to repeat only that it is due mainly to the fact that we cannot rely on our trio of faltering output concepts: defensive outlays, regrettable necessities, and expenditures not made for their own sakes.

I hasten to add that I am not among those who say that a measure of production is unnecessary, or that a measure of production can be de-fined without reference to welfare. This is the other extreme. What I do believe is that it is the art and responsibility of the national accountant to steer his ship firmly between the two extremes without veering to port or starboard.

The Need for Welfare Measures

It is often said that welfare measures are needed for economic and social analysis and for the decision-making, mostly by government, which should be based on such analysis. This argument seems weighty, but upon closer examination there is less to it than appears at first sight. One important approach to the measurement of welfare is to value ele-ments of welfare that are not now valued, in prices at which consumers would value them in case they did value them. The other approach is to admit the value judgment of the estimator on a broad front.

As to the first approach, I cannot discuss here the great difficulties that arise in obtaining realistic consumer valuations under these con-ditions. The consumer is not likely to have a realistic evaluation of what he is asked to evaluate, because he does not have the daily practice of market transactions through which he learns to evaluate the things he buys and sells. In addition, he is not likely, in giving his answers, to take his budget constraint into account. I am reminded of the story in which a customer is charged one dollar for a widget in a hardware store and protests angrily that the same widget is being sold for ten cents in the store across the street. Upon being asked by the store owner why he did not buy it across the street, he says that it was out of stock. "On days I am out of stock, I also sell it for ten cents," the store owner replies.

Even if a realistic consumer evaluation could be elicited, it is very questionable whether this evaluation would have much relevance for major government decisions. As I see it, such government decisions are made in areas in which there are important externalities and/or in which the existing distribution of income does not result in a just allocation of purchasing power. Inasmuch as the expression of subjective preferences in the market place fails to equate private and social marginal product when externalities are present, and inasmuch as these market expressions are tainted by an unjust distribution of income, I doubt very much whether measures of welfare based upon a reconstruction of individual preferences would be as useful as they are generally said to be.

Alternatively, the proposed measure of welfare could eschew a reconstruction of consumer preferences and use the judgments of the national accountant who constructs it. This would put the national accountant in an impossible position, and the results he produces would be of no use to the policymaker. Juster walks away from this issue when he says, "if that imposes a greater burden on the social accountant, so be it." If we are looking for pithy statements to summarize the essence of the situation, I prefer Okun's remark that in national accounting there is no room for philosopher-kings.

An Alternative Approach

The focus on the measurement of welfare is a snare and delusion to the national accountant. It is more fruitful to look upon his task in another way. It is his task to construct a comprehensive description of the economic process that is disciplined and realistic and, as such, useful in the analysis of problems that call for decision-making in our society. Obviously, output must be in the center of this picture, and the process that is depicted must be the production, distribution, and use of that output, because that is what our economy is all about.

In the description of this process, let him use imputations sparingly— only when they are dictated by the needs of analysis and decision-making. But even more important, let him shun amputations like hell, because they result in loss of vital information about the process.

This view of the task of the national accountant will provide tools that are feasible and useful. It does not preclude better approximations to economic welfare than are available at present, and, inasmuch as it is unnecessary to be pedantic about the delineation of what aspect of human activity is economic, the view provides for the integration of a wider range of phenomena into the accounts, more likely as supplementary information, but conceivably also as changes in the present definition of output. This view has the signal advantage over the welfare approach of putting the horse before the cart.

Usefulness of Alternative Approach

Juster admits that the present accounting framework is useful for the analysis of cyclical fluctuations, but says that this framework is becoming obsolete, because interest in cyclical problems is becoming passé. We in Washington do not share this observation—perhaps we are too provincial—and feel that Juster's position is as exaggerated as the reports of Mark Twain's death.

Moreover, Juster's emphasis on the cyclical uses of the present accounts is lopsided. His discussion would imply that the heyday of the accounts was during the Great Depression of the thirties. He seems to forget that these accounts did not see the light of day until the forties, and that the period of their most intensive use was in the postwar period in which the economy became less cycle-prone, according to Juster because of several structural changes which he enumerates in his paper.

The accounting system we now produce would be of interest also if cyclical problems were really a matter of the past. Employers and employees would remain interested in wages and profits; sales managers would want to monitor the markets in which they sell; concern with our balance of payments would continue; and government would always want to know about tax bases and tax yields—to mention only part of the intelligence that is revealed by the accounts.

Moreover, it is not true that the changes Juster proposes would not impair, but on the contrary improve, the usefulness of the accounts in their present function. In putting forward this view in the earlier part of his paper, Juster illustrates it by reference to a more careful separation of cash and imputed items, a better separation between consumption and investment, and other features that are quite compatible with the entelechy of the present accounts. He does not mention at this stage certain of his most basic proposals, for instance, his treatment of environment and national defense expenditures: all major amputations which, unlike his imputations, would mutilate the measure of output to an extent that would make it useless in the uses to which it is now put.

Juster argues further that the reconstruction of the accounts would make them more useful for long-term economic analysis. I am not an expert on growth, and I have overdrawn the time that has been allotted to me, but permit me one more doubt: In a long-term analysis of the productivity of textile workers, would it be really advantageous to have productivity rise if these workers produce civilian suits and to set productivity at zero if they produce military uniforms?

ROBERT EISNER, Northwestern University and
National Bureau of Economic Research

George Jaszi's critique of the paper by Tom Juster may seem to presage a Holy War. The battle cry of the Office of Business Economics would appear to be, "No measure is better than a poor measure." The appeal is to the great majority of us who are economists, not psychologists, and have little taste for measures of "welfare" that stem more readily from the psychiatrist's couch than the market place.

But wars are costly and it would be good to avoid this one, all the more so because on the real issues there should be no division. Rather, these issues should unite all economists in the further pursuit of more consistent and more useful measures of economic income and output, a path on which we were well and boldly started by Simon Kuznets more than a third of a century ago.

For the real issues go back to the central economic concept of income: the sum of consumption and the accumulation of capital. We may make many accommodations to institutional arrangements, and stress for convenience transactions that take place in the market. Our measures are most exact (though not necessarily most correct) for economic activity in the carefully accounted business sector. But we should never lose sight of that central concept of income, which has nothing to do with markets or business, which would exist in a socialist economy without the latter and a Crusoe economy without the former.

Income is consumption plus capital accumulation. And consumption involves services to individuals—I was about to say final services, but perhaps I should say services rendering final utility. While problems of measurement may vary, as far as that central concept goes it should not matter whether the consumption services are purchased by the household, business, or government, whether they are sold in the market or not, or even whether they have readily observable market counterparts. And capital accumulation, or investment, is part of income no matter the form or the institution in which it is accomplished, whether in the physical capital of plant and equipment and inventories measured by the OBE and the development of our wealth of natural resources which the OBE does not usually measure, or in the human or intangible capital of knowledge, training, and skills, social or individual.

If we commit ourselves firmly to that central concept, we see that the research and development expenditures of the firm may constitute just as significant investment, contributing to the flow or "growth" of future output as the firm's expenditures for plant and equipment. Similarly, the training of the worker on the job and the education of the future worker in home and school constitute investment. But also, of course, the clotheswasher acquired in the home is just as much investment as the clotheswasher acquired in the commercial laundry or laundermat. And the clotheswashing services are just as much consumption in the home as in the commercial establishment.

If we recognize that we accumulate wealth in developing our natural resources then we may not find it strange to note the decumulation of wealth in the despoiling of these resources and in the destruction of our environment. All of the environmental investment of so much current interest is then indeed clearly investment, but to be matched, or more than matched, by the disinvestment or capital consumption which takes place when we destroy the value of our air, our water, and our land.

Further, if we keep our eye on the economic activity taking place and not only on the market transaction to which it relates, there is no more— or less—reason to consider the services to business by a private detective agency as intermediate than similar services provided by municipal police. All security forces may be seen to constitute current maintenance expenditures to protect or preserve intact human and physical capital, or investment in their future preservation. But that same argument may well be extended to national defense expenditures. These too are presumably devoted to protection of the nation's human and physical capital— or to acquisition of that of another nation. They are either akin to maintenance expenditures or to gross investment, with a comparable but not necessarily equal allowance for capital consumption as weapons systems or armed forces, or their purposes become obsolete.

With the argument that the supplementary accounting called for by the revisionists among us would be arbitrary and inaccurate, the matter of capital consumption allowances and rates of return is a good place to linger. Can there be anything more economically arbitrary than the present measures of business capital consumption allowances? They are overwhelmingly at the whim of tax considerations, and change rapidly over time as accounting depreciation in very considerable part conforms to allowable tax depreciation. The OBE's *Survey of Current Business* has itself reported the results of substantial studies documenting the vast differences in capital consumption allowances that relate to differences in depreciation methods. Would allowances for capital consumption of household and government capital have to be any more arbitrary than those currently offered for business? Freed from the tax-motivated constraints that have affected business accounting, they might more easily be permitted to correspond to a meaningful and consistent measure of economic depreciation. And if only because of the vagaries of depreciation charges but also for many other reasons relating to the arbitrariness of estimation and allocation of costs over time, there is hardly much more cause for satisfaction with the Department of Commerce estimates of earnings on business capital than with the series we outsiders would project for earnings on capital in the household and government.

The OBE is not after all universally opposed to estimating what seems conceptually important even where the record of market transactions or the figures of business accountants are not available. Most conspicuous, within the business sector itself, are inventory valuation adjustments, again "arbitrary" but accepted in the service of a central concept.

The growing band of economists devoted to innovation and expansion in our national income and product accounts does not comprise alien psychologists and other social scientists aiming to measure some mythical concept of happiness or welfare. We are concerned with the usefulness and integrity of our own economic accounts. We want our measures of income and output to permit reasonable comparisons across countries and economic systems and over time. We want measures of outputs and factor inputs to be just those and not arbitrary aggregates of activities which at a particular time and place happen to fit our quite institutionally determined categories of "final products" and the "costs" of their production. We want to be able to perceive the paths of output and input in a way that will be most useful to ascertaining the extent and factors in economic growth, for our own nation and the world.

If battle lines must be drawn I must certainly here be on the side of Tom Juster—and Richard and Nancy Ruggles, John Kendrick, William Nordhaus, and James Tobin and most of the participants in this conference, including Simon Kuznets, who see no vice in boldness in the pursuit of theoretical consistency and social and economic relevance. I am hopeful and confident that George Jaszi and his able band in the government will aid us in that pursuit and, where appropriate, join us. We want no Holy War.

ROBERT M. SOLOW, Massachusetts Institute of Technology

I suppose I ought to take some kind of position on this hassle. Do I join the standpatters like Denison and Okun, who remind one of the unforgettable words spoken by Senator James K. Jones on the floor of the Senate: "Change the name of Arkansas? Never!" Or do I support the deviationists like Juster, who believe that the best things in life are imputed? Actually, the differences between them are not very important in a practical way. Denison and Okun only want their GNP; they can hardly complain if someone, possibly even the OBE, processes the figures further, rearranges them, adds and subtracts some things, and calls the result MEW, or measure of economic welfare, to use the Nordhaus-Tobin phrase. On the other side, Juster would presumably have no objection to publishing the quarterly MEW tables in such a way that anyone can recover the old-fashioned GNP from the data given.

This is very important. One hundred quarters of more or less comparable national income and product accounts constitute an environmental resource of some significance, at least to economists. I don't care what Tom Juster does to the figures, as long as twenty-five years from now there are two hundred quarters of comparable data available.

Actually I do care what Tom Juster does to the figures and, with some minor reservations, I think he suggests doing right and interesting things. I don't see how any reader of the Nordhaus-Tobin paper can fail to find the results fascinating and to want to know what a more extensive approach to a MEW would show. It will be done, in any case, even if only by private research workers. It will be done for the obvious reason: Just as Okun wants his GNP so that he can study the effects of stabilization policies on production and employment, so many others will want their MEW so that they can analyze and evaluate the effects of other kinds of policies on economic well-being. Exactly as with the national accounts, if the thing can be done seriously, it will eventually have to be done by the federal government—if not in OBE and Commerce, then elsewhere—because no one else has the resources. Before that can happen, however, professional economists and others will have to reach some agreement on a compromise framework that is both sensible and feasible. Juster's paper, and indeed this whole conference, are part of that process.

In that spirit, I suppose the proper thing for me to do is to raise questions where Juster's analysis and recommendations are least convincing.

For example, I confess that I have never been entirely happy with the "human capital" approach to education. I don't doubt at all that there is an investment-like element in education, with the return coming in subsequent higher productivity and wages. But I have deliberately said "investment-like" because it is not precisely clear to me that what education creates is properly a stock. It is even less clear to me that it is appropriate to add the stocks belonging to different people. I have the impression that the human capital theorists have tended to ignore—and therefore to underestimate—the consumption component of education. It has seemed to me also that they have failed to analyze the consequences for the social valuation of education of the possibility that diplomas and degrees function in part as a kind of signaling or screening device for certain traits and habits, and not simply as a scale measuring the volume of a stock accumulated. So I would have to be convinced that the right thing to do is to treat all educational expenditures as gross investment.

If I am suspicious of the stock concept as applied to human wealth, I am obviously going to be suspicious of the concept of "sociopolitical wealth." This is at best a metaphor, and not a very useful metaphor. The main trouble with it, as Juster says himself, is that it is hopelessly subjective. Am I entitled to deduct from the MEW some allowance for the activities of the Vice-President and the Attorney General if I am convinced that they are subtracting from the sociopolitical wealth of the United States? In the case of the Vice-President, can I allow for his exports of negative sociopolitical wealth to other countries? Must the figures be revised when someone with different political opinions begins to compile them? Once again, I am arguing against the superstructure, not the probable practical outcome. The main effect of adopting Juster's point of view is that, say, defense and police expenditures would be excluded from MEW unless there were independent evidence that they had done something over and above offsetting potential deterioration of national security and internal peace from other causes. That seems sensible to me.

Here, by the way, I think Denison is wrong in arguing the contrary.

He says that this procedure "yields the false result that we are equally well off whether, in the same circumstances, we . . . provide or do not provide for national security." This argument appears to be a confusion of gross and net concepts. Denison earlier agrees that NNP is in principle a better measure than GNP of the output available to satisfy needs. I could equally claim that it is not, because it makes the false claim that we are equally well off whether, in the same circumstances, we replace or do not replace worn-out machinery and buildings. Defense spending may be part of GMEW, but only that part of it that does more than off-set wear and tear on the national security belongs in NMEW. (The analogue to a "worsening international situation"—assuming it were true and not mere lies as it no doubt often is—is a natural disaster that destroys a lot of existing plant and equipment. In both cases net spending is reduced for given gross spending.)

On an interesting but minor point, I think that Juster is probably wrong in arguing for the exclusion of all commuting expense from MEW. As a matter of casual observation, I am not so sure that people would really rather live near their work. Of course nobody enjoys commuting, but it is not very useful to take this view to mean that people would like to live near their work provided that the neighborhood had none of the characteristics of a neighborhood near which people work. As a matter of theoretical analysis, I think it can be shown that part of an increase in commuter expense does represent increase in welfare: loosely speaking, that part which is not offset by falling rents as you move further from the workplace.

I guess I am somewhere between the standpatters and the deviationists, but with a definite leaning toward the latter. I would like to see much more experimentation along the lines mapped out by Juster and actually followed for some distance by Nordhaus and Tobin. The experimentation needs to be both analytical and practical, with a view to finding out what can actually be done with available data, and how it can be interpreted rationally. The analytical and the practical come together on the key problem of the valuation of nonmarket activity or, more broadly, of noninternalized market activity as well. Okun seems to take it for granted that if you cannot observe a market price—hard money in the act of changing hands—that's the end of it. More adventurous souls might be willing to take a flyer on inferring valuations from a combination of theory and indirect observation.

I think it has to be kept in mind that the object of experimentation is not the definition of a perfect measure of economic welfare. Any major step in that direction, starting from the income and product accounts, would be an achievement. What is absolutely indispensable is the evolution of some sort of professional consensus on a concept that is feasible, analytically sensible, and interpretable. Otherwise one can hardly expect the federal government to make the major investment necessary to launch a statistical enterprise against which, as in the case of the national accounts, its own performance will eventually be judged. It is enough if that concept is only an imperfect measure of economic welfare, as long as we understand what it means. I am not much impressed with the argument that others will incorrectly interpret it as a complete and perfect measure of economic welfare. Half the people who talk about the GNP every quarter don't understand what it means either.

I make my final remark with diffidence, because I ought to have thought it through myself instead of asking it as a question. One of the useful things about the income and product accounts is suggested in the name: the relation between the product side and the income side. This is not a trivial piece of good fortune. I think the main reason why the notion of social accounts has dwindled into the much more limited idea of a collection of social indicators is that there is no double-entry framework of this kind that could serve as the definitional scaffolding of theory. Now neither Juster nor Nordhaus-Tobin makes any comment about the income side of their expanded welfare accounts. They talk entirely in terms of the product side. Well, what does happen to the income side? Is there a meaningful total? Is there a meaningful breakdown? Will the traditional income categories have to be supplemented by some transpersonal account that collects benefits not imputable to any person in particular? Under ideal conditions, one can interpret the wage as the value of the marginal private product of an hour of labor. It is natural to wonder if, hidden on the income side of an ideal set of MEW accounts, is a number that could, under ideal conditions, be interpreted as the value of the marginal social product of an hour of labor.

REPLY BY JUSTER

Jaszi's comments can be grouped into three categories: First, those where he is in essential agreement with my paper; second, those where he is unhappy with my suggestions but where the differences can probably be resolved by a more careful statement of our respective positions;

third, areas where we are quite far apart on substantive issues. In quantitative terms, I would judge that despite the generally critical tone of his comments, each of the above categories contains roughly a third of the points discussed (weighted, of course). Let me make a few specific comments where I think we have no real disagreement but where misunderstanding apparently exists. I will also comment briefly on the points where substantive differences seem to be important

Jaszi notes that my suggested procedure for estimating net returns to consumer capital results in a zero estimate, presumably because I suggested that the returns be estimated from interest charges or foregone returns on liquid assets, depending on whether the purchase was financed with borrowed funds or equity funds. If all consumer capital were purchased with borrowed funds, and if the life expectancy of the capital asset coincided with the term of the loan, Jaszi would be correct. But neither condition holds. For capital assets purchased with equity funds, I do not see how the presently estimated actual or imputed interest returns to households would be affected in any way, and there would be an additional imputed interest return to households that acquired capital assets for cash. For those who borrow, the expected life of the capital assets is greatly in excess of the typical loan repayment period, and the assets would presumably continue to yield a return after the loan has been repaid. Thus, there would be some net income created by the imputation.

On the question whether one should be aghast at my suggestion that estimation of depreciation charges on intangibles present problems which are no worse than for tangible capital assets, I think there is simply a misunderstanding. I had in mind that the calculation of economic depreciation on intangibles was no worse than the calculation of economic depreciation on tangibles, not that there existed IRS data from which one could calculate intangibles depreciation as is currently done for tangibles. My assumption was that economic depreciation estimates were preferable to IRS based estimates, and that a change from the tax basis to an economic basis would be made for tangibles. The source of the misunderstanding is my own imprecise language, not the quite normal interpretation given to it by Jaszi.

On the very complicated question of how to value time spent in nonmarket activities, I did not really suggest a preferred solution but instead pointed out the range of alternative solutions and noted some of the problems arising with each. Along with Jaszi, I agree that this is a very knotty question, and I am not now prepared to argue strongly for any one solution. Let me be a bit more specific about the alternatives. Jaszi asks whether it makes sense to value his "fumbling efforts to teach new math to his children" at his own wage rate rather than the wage rate of a professional teacher. I think he should not be so modest. My guess is that George Jaszi is substantially more productive in his "fumbling" efforts to teach new math to his own children than his child's teacher is—but that's because he is a person with a very high degree of quantitative sophistication and his child's teacher is probably not. Another way to put the question is: Why do the George Jaszi's of this world spend time in supplementing the formal training of their children by their own efforts? In part, it's because they are like any other parent and enjoy spending time with their children; helping to teach their children represents one way of spending time that they view as useful. But in part, I suggest that Jaszi's reference to teaching his children new math is not independent of the fact that he is George Jaszi rather than Alfred Kazin or Arthur Schlesinger, and that similar references by the latter two would probably be in the context of teaching their children an appreciation of literature or an understanding of political philosophy, not new math.

To put the matter more generally, I make the assumption that people generally allocate their time in a rational and systematic way, and that choices about particular activities reflect not only their own comparative advantage in different activities but also the choice between using their own time or buying the equivalent product in the market. We all do a bit of both when it comes to training children, since we buy the services of full-time teachers when the child gets to be a certain age (but not before). And it could be argued that if a person spends time in a particular activity rather than other activities, or if he buys the equivalent service where possible, the reason is that marginal products in all activities are being equalized.

The other alternative, while different, seems to me not less arbitrary; one could value nonmarket time at the wage rate of the closest market counterpart. If I teach my children new math, I get the imputed wage rate of a mathematics teacher. If I spend time shaving myself, I get the imputed wage rate of the barber. If I spend time driving my family on a Sunday afternoon outing, I get the imputed wage rate of a chauffeur. And if I spend my time watching the Monday evening football game, I get the imputed wage rate of???

In general, I do not presently see any perfectly satisfactory solution to this problem, and I do not suggest one in the paper. On the other hand, I do not see how we can ignore the fact that nonmarket uses of time are just as productive, although harder to value, as market uses of time.

Jaszi notes that the proposal advanced by Edward Denison to deal with outlays for pollution control is really designed to deal with the problem that at present sectoral shifts in the location of pollution control outlays have an influence on the measurement of output. The reason, as Jaszi points out, is that pollution abatement activities paid for by business show up as a higher cost of producing an unchanged real output, while if the abatement activities are represented by consumer or government purchases of products, they show up as final output.

I agree that the present treatment is an anomaly, but I would point out that this anomaly is very pervasive and is, in fact, one of the considerations underlying the suggested treatment in my paper. It doesn't just apply to pollution control devices, as is surely evident. For example, if protection against theft and violence is represented by business outlays for guards, watchmen, machine guns, and pistols, it does not enter final output as presently defined; but it does enter final output if these same activities are engaged in by governments who hire policemen or consumers who purchase weapons and locks. The same is true for national defense outlays. If all of the business firms in the community got together and decided to form a private army to defend their property against external aggression, the national accounts would faithfully register the fact that national defense outlays were intermediate product and not final product. But if the citizens of the community band together through their government and decide to hire a public army, it's final output.

Finally, let me try once more to persuade the critics that the notions of "defensive outlays," "regrettable necessities," and "instrumental" outlays are neither so devoid of empirical content nor so analytically intractable as Jaszi's comments would suggest. It is certainly true, as Jaszi suggests, that defensive expenditures are not easily identified: food expenditures do defend against hunger, clothing and housing outlays do defend against cold and rain, medical expenditures do defend against illness, and so forth. But it does not follow that the defensive character of food against hunger requires that food expenditures be left out of final output. One can defend against hunger with sirloin steaks and asparagus tips followed by an after-dinner brandy; one can also defend against hunger by purchasing the appropriate mixture of soybean meal and water. The difference between the two is that the first costs a lot and the second costs a little, and that the first goes substantially beyond defending against hunger in the direction of providing final consumption benefits net of expenditures required to maintain the stock of human capital. That really seems to be the issue here. Virtually all of my suggested defensive outlays can be characterized as outlays required to maintain a given flow of benefits from one or another type of asset, while Jaszi's objections to the concept are all illustrated by activities that go well beyond the maintenance cost of assets and thus provide net consumption benefits.

Thus, while I do not question the proposition that implementation of the defensive outlay concept is neither simple nor easy, I do insist that meaningful distinctions can be made between outlays required to maintain benefit flows from assets and outlays which are not. That is what I mean by defensive, and perhaps a better term is instrumental, or the one I use most consistently, which is simply "maintenance."

A Proposal for a System of Economic

and Social Accounts

NANCY RUGGLES

AND

RICHARD RUGGLES

NATIONAL BUREAU OF ECONOMIC RESEARCH
AND YALE UNIVERSITY

IN recent years, the measurement of economic and social performance
has been the topic of many conferences, governmental committees, and
special studies. On the one hand, there has been a growing feeling that
the national economic accounts are deficient in many dimensions, that
the traditional concepts are inadequate for dealing with the types of
economic and social problem with which we are now confronted, and
that considerable extension of the accounts is required in order to make
them relevant to today's problems. On the other hand, the relative success of national economic accounts in providing a framework for analysis of the behavior of the economic system has been held up as a
model of the kind of systematic framework needed for noneconomic
information about our society and it is argued that we should get on
with the task of developing social indicators and social accounts independently of the economic accounts.

These two approaches to the development of social information are
more closely related than might at first appear. It is now being realized
that the extension of the economic accounts to make them more relevant cannot stop with the adjustment of the economic accounting framework to cover imputed transactions or social costs in the deterioration
of the environment, and other monetary measures. The extended accounts must by their very nature grapple with the demographic and
social characteristics of the population. Problems relating to health
care, education, income of the aged, and discrimination require the introduction of nontransactions information rather than merely more comprehensive coverage of actual and imputed transactions. Furthermore,

those who are concerned with the development of social indicators and social accounts recognize the importance and relevance of related economic information. Thus, poverty as a social condition is directly related to income received. The level and change in government expenditures on education and health and the distribution of these benefits over the population are relevant to social as well as economic analysis. It thus becomes obvious that social accounts cannot be conceived of as sets of information distinct from the economic accounts, but must be highly intertwined with the economic accounts.

It is in this context then that we propose to examine current developments in economic and social measurement, and to propose an economic and social accounting system which can serve as a tool of both economic and social research and can provide the basis for monitoring the behavior of the social as well as the economic system.

CURRENT DEVELOPMENTS IN ECONOMIC AND SOCIAL MEASUREMENT

The Extension of Economic Accounts

During the past 35 years, national income measurement has developed from the estimation of a summary measure of the nation's income to a comprehensive reporting of the transaction flows among the different sectors of the economy. In this process, the economic constructs have themselves become broader. The framework has been expanded to take into account the role of government in the economy, and the concept of gross national product has replaced that of national income as the central measurement of the system. By and large, however, the present economic accounts record—and are intended to record—market transactions. The imputations which are made for nonmarket transactions such as owner-occupied housing, imputed interest, and produce grown and consumed on farms are relatively minor elements, introduced into the accounts for the sake of symmetry and completeness. Nonmarket activity, even when of a productive nature, has been largely disregarded. Kendrick [1] has challenged this basic procedure, and has made estimates which extend the accounts to include such things as the services of housewives, compensation for students, imputed rentals on capital goods held by households, institutions, and governments, and intangible investment including such things as education and training, research and development, and costs of rearing children. Such imputations, Kendrick maintains, are needed if we are to analyze the growth which has taken place in a given economy, or compare the levels, structures, and rates of growth of different economies. The broader concept of economic production including nonmarket activity is needed, he argues, since the boundary between nonmarket and market activity changes with the development of society. Thus, if only market activities are taken into account the movement of women from housework into the labor force would overstate the amount of growth taking place. Conversely, an increase in the educational activity of a society would dampen its growth if students are removed from the labor force and their activities as students are not counted as having value.

Another study in extending the traditional economic accounts is being undertaken by Robert Eisner and his associates [2] in their estimation of nonincome income—i.e., transaction flows which individuals consider to be income, but which are not reflected in the present national accounts measures. One of the major elements on which Eisner is focusing is the income generated by changes in capital values. Capital gains provide a substantial amount of unearned income, but this is not included in either business or personal income in the national accounts. Any understanding of the income distribution or measurement of income inequality should take into account this major source of unearned income. In the business sector, Eisner focuses on the difference between the depreciation which is charged and the economic depreciation which actually takes place. Since it is of benefit for businessmen to charge off depreciation as fast as they are allowed to for tax purposes, the estimates in the national accounts are substantially higher than the economic depreciation which is taking place. Finally, Eisner, like Kendrick, is interested in measuring the contribution of consumer durables such as automobiles to the flow of services available in the economy. In principle, these extensions are very worthwhile indeed, and conceptually they can be introduced quite easily into a national economic accounting framework. Recently, we have proposed that the present U.S. national income accounts should be revised to recognize some of these imputations explicitly [3]. How far one wishes to go in the inclusion of nonmarket activity through imputed transactions depends in part on the degree of confidence one has in the possibility of valuing nonmarket activities.

It has been proposed by Thomas Juster [4] that the deterioration of the physical and social environment be measured and entered into the accounts to yield more significant measures of economic and social welfare. Logically this is an extension of the type of estimation undertaken by Kendrick, but obtaining the type of information required to introduce meaningful valuations poses considerable problems. It remains to be seen how such measurements can be made.

However, even if such extensions of the macroeconomic accounts were successful and relatively complete, the resulting set of information would still fall short of what is required for a comprehensive economic and social accounting system. All of these proposed extensions rely upon stating everything in terms of dollar valuations, thus insisting that the transactions formulation appropriate to economic activity is the relevant one for all social and economic problems. This approach gives relatively little explicit consideration to social and demographic characteristics, or to differential behavior of different groups in society. Thus, questions of discrimination, provision of economic opportunity, crime, and health are left relatively untouched except insofar as they are reflected in the monetary estimation of social gain or loss.

The Development of Social Indicators

Concern with domestic social problems and social unrest in recent years has stimulated a widespread interest in social indicators among both academic social scientists and government statisticians. In the United States a plan was proposed to prepare a social report parallel to the Economic Report of the President, produced by the Council of Economic Advisers. For a number of reasons this publication did not materialize, but there is still in the planning stage a publication on social indicators intended to cover the fields of income distribution, employment, education, health, housing, public safety, and recreation and leisure. It is too early to say precisely what this publication will contain, but it is likely to be quite similar to *Social Trends* [5], published by the Central Statistical Office of the United Kingdom.

As Claus Moser of the CSO [6] points out, strictly speaking such collections of tables are social statistics, rather than social indicators; and there is, unfortunately, no clear indication in the literature as to precisely how the term "social indicators" should be defined. A number of characteristics have been suggested. Thus, for example, it is sometimes suggested that a social indicator should be a weighted composite index number—an aggregate of many subseries, much in the way the gross national product represents many different transactions flows. Others view social indicators as a normative concept, not dissimilar, perhaps to the sort of temperature-humidity comfort index used by weather forecasters—a measure that would reflect the quality of life. Still others feel that social indicators should reflect the outputs of societies rather than merely the inputs in different social areas. Thus, for example, in the case of education and health services social indicators should evaluate the accomplishment, rather than merely show the resources utilized. Most of the discussion of social indicators assumes that they should be comprehensive in coverage, and to the extent that they are based upon partial information such partial information is considered to be a proxy for the more general concepts. Finally, those who are most concerned with social accounts would maintain that the social indicators must be part of a structure or system of social statistics, much in the same way that the economic constructs such as national income are an integral part of the structure of economic accounts.

Moser recognizes that at the present time social indicators and social accounts are not parallel with the economic indicators and economic accounts. He argues that economic accounts and indicators were developed in parallel, with feedback between the theory and the measurement resulting in the present close interconnection. In his view, the same process may be expected to evolve with social accounts and social indicators, and sociological theories about society relating to specific fields and sectors, occupational mobility, education, mental health, etc., can gradually be built up. Such theories would give insight into social change and suggest how to manipulate policy instruments for the improvement of social conditions.

It cannot be denied that the interaction between empirical research and the development of theory is important. However, it does not follow that such an interaction will lead naturally from social indicators to social accounts. Economic indicators were developed separately from the national economic accounts, and in fact had little if any impact upon them. Thus, freight car loadings, bank clearings, retail sales, pig iron production, cattle slaughtered, and electric power generated existed as time series data to indicate changes in specific kinds of economic activities long before the national economic accounts, or any of the national income aggregates, were developed, and they still exist today, in a form unrelated to the national economic accounts. The development of the national economic accounts reflected an attempt to generate a unified treatment of transactions flows in an accounting framework. The statistical work was greatly influenced by the Keynesian model, and the development of macroeconometric models was in turn greatly influenced by the statistical estimation processes. The economic constructs that emerged from this process were the product of both theoretical and empirical research, but they bore little or no relation to the pre-existing economic indicators. Unfortunately, most of the social indicators which have been suggested are more nearly parallel to the economic indicators than they are to the economic constructs of the national accounts. Like the economic indicators, their units of measure are widely different; some may be in tons, others in dollars, others in percentages. There does not seem to be at the present time any systematic set of indicators which are related to a formal underlying structure of social accounts.

Social Matrices as Social Accounts

Richard Stone has proposed an integrated system of demographic, manpower, and social statistics which can be linked with the national economic accounts [7]. The basic framework of the system consists of a standard matrix, the marginal vectors of which contain the opening and closing stocks, and the entries in which show the flows connecting them. For the purposes of analysis, Stone uses a life sequence approach, tracing changes of state from birth to death in different aspects of life. In particular, he concerns himself with education, employment, social mobility, health, delinquency, family relationships, and migration and tourism. The social matrix for a given sequence provides information on how a beginning population changes during a period and what its state is at the end of the period. Thus, for example, a social matrix concerned with education can show for each age group the educational status of individuals, how that status changes, and what the final result is at the end of the period. To a limited extent, additional characteristics can be entered into the table. For example, it is quite possible to provide additional information in a social matrix on education to take into consideration the effect of grades received by students on their progression through the educational system. Similarly, information can be entered on the socioeconomic background of individuals to see its effect on progression through the education matrix.

As Stone himself points out, however, there is a severe limitation on the number of variables and classifications which can conveniently be handled in a social matrix. If, for example, one wishes to study the interaction of 10 variables in a sociodemographic matrix, and each of these variables contains 10 classifications (both very small numbers to characterize the sociodemographic system), the number of cells in the matrix is 10^{10}, or 10 billion. Given the size of the populations of most countries and the natural clusterings, most of these cells would of course be empty. Stone trims his problem down to manageable size by allowing variables to interact only on a pair-wise basis. This is, of course, a severe restriction for any multivariate analysis.

Integration of the social matrices with each other and with the national economic accounts is achieved by linkages through common classification systems or through subdivision of a total in one system in another system. Thus, the linkage between different tables may be quite close in some cases, where the elements of one matrix correspond quite closely to the elements in another matrix, and in other cases may be very loose, the two matrices merely dealing with the same population.

The matrix form for subsystems appeals to Stone in large degree because he conceives of his analytic models in terms of regular or absorbing Markov chains. In other words, he analyzes the change in the structure of a subsystem over time by applying transition coefficients to the various cells in the matrix. Subsystems which are linked but are not fully integrated with each other must be so drawn up that for most purposes they do not need to interact. As Stone suggests, it may be useful to combine a number of subsystems into a sequence: for instance, learning activities, earning activities, and inactivities can be combined to form an active sequence tracing human progression from birth through education and employment to retirement and finally death.

How well does such a statistical system meet the general needs for analyzing social and economic problems? The design of Stone's proposed integration of social and economic accounts is highly dependent on the uses to which the accounts are expected to be put. These uses in turn are a direct reflection of the context within which a particular analyst views the social and economic problems which confront a society. As social and economic problems shift or different analysts view these problems differently, the design of the statistical system will be affected. Different classifications, pair-wise subsystems, and linkages will be required. Just as no single set of cross tabulations of a census is satisfactory for all users, it is difficult to envisage a single system of economic and social matrices and submatrices which would meet the data requirements relevant to the wide range of existing social and economic problems. Movement toward any significant degree of generality would result in explosion of the matrix approach. In this sense, thus, Stone has not really provided a general solution for the integration of social and economic data, but rather a specific solution for a particular analytic use.

Balance Tables and Social Accounts

A somewhat related concept of social accounts utilizing balance tables has been suggested by Margaret Mod [8]. In her view, social accounts should be drawn up to cover such things as the level and distribution of the population's earnings and incomes, the level and pattern of the population's consumption, traditional social care, e.g., care for children, the aged, mothers, infants, and other forms of social security, health, education, the training of manpower, and housing conditions. In her view the system should be open-ended, to draw in other areas of special importance. The essential characteristic of the social accounts is that although they are still macro, they go deeper into detail than the national accounts in the same fields. Social accounts are thus more disaggregated than the national accounts according to object, purpose, institutional form, and strata of the population. Mod's social accounts, unlike Stone's social matrices, are not conceived as a technique of analyzing social change; rather they are more akin to Moser's social indicators which attempt to depict current social conditions. Unlike both Stone and Moser, however, Mod feels that there should be an underlying social statistical system of a micro nature containing detailed information on individuals and households. In such a context, of course, it becomes extremely debatable whether the macro social accounts or the micro statistical system is the basic element. On the one hand, the macro social accounts define the scope and elements of information required in the basic statistical system. On the other hand, the micro statistical system once defined would be capable of generating many different macro systems of aggregate accounts, and in a substantive sense is more basic and unchanging than the macro accounts. What Mod does point out is that some crystallization of the micro statistical system into an aggregated form is required if the basic information is to be applicable to the depiction of social circumstances.

Microdata Sets

In the early 1960s the Norwegian Central Bureau of Statistics initiated the development of a system of personal data files. In 1964 an identification number was assigned to each inhabitant covered by the 1960 population census, and the assignment of such numbers has been continuously maintained since 1964 as part of the current population registration. The number comprises eleven digits. The first six refer to date of birth, and the following three digits distinguish persons born on the same date and at the same time specify sex. The last two digits are check digits. These personal identification numbers are used for almost all Norwegian statistical surveys and censuses of persons. In addition, the identification number system has been adopted by administrative agencies such as the tax authorities, national social insurance, health administration, school administration, the courts, etc. The existence of the personal identification number permits the linkage of individual records over time and from different sources.

The original impetus to the creation of the personal file system was the need to satisfy general and special requests for tailor-made statistics. By maintaining the original data in micro form, special tabulations could be made as needed. In particular, the need for regional information for such things as planning, communication, transportation, and pollution control required recasting the data in different forms and the flexibility of the files of individual data meant that these needs could be met. By accumulating information for the same individual over time, longitudinal studies were made possible. The main application to date has been in the estimation of the structure of demographic models. Given the development of a personal data file system, Aukrust and Nordbotten [9] point out that it can be useful for the development of sociodemographic models in a wide variety of fields, such as demography, economics, education, labor relations, social medicine, consumer behavior, criminology, election research, economic geography, etc. In other words, a single general file containing information on individuals and households can be used for a wide variety of problems. As hospital files, social security files, and criminal records, as well as specialized statistical surveys are folded into the information base, more and more types of information become available.

Given such a microdata base, it would always be possible to generate the social matrices suggested by Richard Stone. Conversely, however, given Stone's social matrices it would not be possible to generate the microdata base which underlay it. Stone [10] recognizes that if a continuously updated comprehensive system of individualized data were available, his social matrices and the necessity for dividing life into sequences and the subsequent restrictions they impose would be irrelevant. In terms of practical reality Stone argues, however, that most countries are a long way from such a system, and any system of this type would be expensive, technically difficult, and not without its political dangers.

At first blush, this line of reasoning is very persuasive. In a country such as the United States, with a population of over 200 million, the maintenance of individualized files for every aspect of an individual's life is not a practical alternative. The cost of developing and maintaining such a system would be very substantial, and the technical problems of getting cooperation and coordination from all of the statistical agencies and administrative organizations in a highly decentralized statistical system are formidable. The fact that many of the statistics in large countries are based upon sample data would further reduce the value of linking information for the same individual, since in most cases different individuals are covered by different samples, and thus the information contained in the different samples cannot be directly linked through personal file identifiers. Finally, the privacy issue which Stone implicitly raises is already a major difficulty, and would surely in the case of the United States make the development of a personal file system politically unattainable.

The impracticability of a comprehensive personal file system for large countries does not, however, vitiate the usefulness of microdata sets per se for analytic uses. In any specific area, it is possible to use an appropriate sample of data precisely as Aukrust and Nordbotten propose to use the Norwegian personal file system. Sampling theory permits the use of relatively small bodies of information to achieve the same analytic results as would be obtained using complete sets. Besides reducing costs, furthermore, sampling can be used to solve the privacy question, since identification of specific individuals can generally be omitted from the sampling records.

Using different samples which were developed for different purposes does have the disadvantage that, unlike the personal file system, information for a specific individual from different sources and time periods cannot be brought together. There are, however, techniques for getting around this problem. Where there is a substantial overlap of the same type of information in different samples, a synthetic matching of data can be carried out, in which the data for individuals from one sample are imputed to similar individuals in a second sample, upon the basis of relationships observed in the first sample. Generally speaking such imputation should be done on a stochastic basis, so that the means and variances of the imputed information will match those in the original data. What is in effect being done by such a procedure is to map information from one sample onto the data of another sample to derive a new synthetic data set that is a union of the information in the two original samples, in such a way that the resulting data set will have the same statistical characteristics as each sample independently.

The development of synthetic data sets will often be difficult, since the information reported in different samples will be different and inconsistent. Decisions will then have to be made about which information should dominate under what conditions in the new synthetic data set. But such problems are not new to national accountants. In making estimates for various segments and components of the national accounts, a variety of different sources are used. Many sources conflict with each other, and the task of the national accountant to a major extent is that of resolving the inconsistencies in the sources and integrating the information into a single consistent set of figures.

The major question which needs to be faced is not whether a complete personal file system is desirable or feasible, but whether microdata sets can provide the necessary conceptual and analytical basis for a system of social and economic accounts. As already suggested, unless it is possible to link the basic social information with the economic information in the context of the economic system as a whole, the objective of developing a satisfactory framework for the study of economic and social problems will not be met, and we may be forced to continue to use a separate system of national economic accounts, ad hoc social indicators, cross tabulations of data, Stone social matrices, and various kinds of unrelated microdata sets. This then is the question we try to examine.

A PROPOSAL FOR A SYSTEM OF ECONOMIC AND SOCIAL ACCOUNTS

In the evolution of national economic accounting, there has always been an implicit recognition that the macroeconomic accounts were an aggregation of the income accounts of decision-making units in the economy. The national income originating in the enterprise sector was conceived of as an aggregate of the wages, salaries, dividends, and profits recorded in the income statement for each enterprise. Personal income reflected income received by households, and thus included not only the wages, salaries, and dividends received, but also the transfer payments such as social security benefits, welfare, veterans benefits, etc., which the household received. Thus, each sector viewed income as it appeared in terms of the accounts of its own decision-making units.

Although conceptually the national economic accounts reflect this view of the accounts of enterprises and households, they traditionally have been more concerned with the development of the economic constructs rather than with providing systematic accounts for the different sectors of the economy. Thus, for instance there is no explicit enterprise sector in the present form of the U.S. accounts. The information for the enterprise sector is contained in the national income and product account, along with information for other sectors. The personal income account, while largely composed of information relating to individual households, also contains the income and outlay of nonprofit institutions. The government sector is perhaps the only sector in which the accounts do actually reflect the income and outlay recorded for the different levels of government.

The explicit recognition of enterprises, households, and government as decision-making units with income accounts and saving and investment accounts would not require major changes in the form of the national economic accounts. An outline of a set of national income accounts which present sector accounts and provide some of the extensions proposed by Kendrick and others is shown in the appendix to this paper. What is involved in these accounts is the setting up of an income and outlay account for the enterprise sector, the transfer of nonprofit institutions from the household sector to this new enterprise sector, and the provision of saving and investment accounts for each sector.

The reorganization of the national economic accounts along these lines permits the development of a new type of information base. Once it is recognized that an account for a sector represents an aggregation of the accounts for reporting units composing that sector, it is possible to focus attention on the individual reporting unit. At the level of the individual reporting unit, new types of information can be introduced. Thus, for a given household, demographic information on the age, race, and sex of each of the members of the family, together with social information such as education, occupation, health, place of residence, and place of work can all be recorded, as well as the economic information on the household's income and expenditures and their assets and liabilities. Although it is true that the economic accounts of the household sector aggregate only the transactions information, the nontransactions information is not irrelevant for analytic purposes, and can be used in conjunction with the economic information in a variety of ways. If the social and demographic information described above were available for each household in the nation, it would be possible, for example, to obtain distributions of income by size for specific socioeconomic groups. Thus, the differential in income by race and age could be studied for different regions of the country. Such an analysis requires the integration of economic and social data and is capable of producing information of an aggregated nature which is directly pertinent to the problem of racial discrimination.

As was pointed out in the discussion of personal files, it would, of course, not be possible to obtain an income statement and balance sheet, together with a rather complete set of demographic and social information, for every household in the nation. The size of the data set would be appallingly large. However, the same analytic results can be achieved with a sample of households rather than complete coverage. If the sample is sufficiently large and representative, analyses performed on it will give approximately the same results as would analyses with the full set of all households. What is in fact being proposed is that the economic and social accountant develop a microdata set of households which when appropriately weighted will generate the accounts for the household sector of the national economic accounts and at the same time will have attached to each household unit in the microdata set the important demographic and social characteristics that are needed for social accounts. The microdata set for households thus would become the basic statistical system underlying the national economic accounts, and would permit the utilization of interrelated demographic and social information for households.

For the enterprise sector, many different kinds of enterprises need to be recognized. Corporations, noncorporate farm and nonfarm enterprises, government enterprises, and nonprofit institutions all play a very different role in the producing sector. Yet they all have income statements and balance sheets, together with other characteristics such as industry, location, ownership characteristics, kind of production facility, etc. One level of disaggregation below the enterprise also needs to be recognized. Many enterprises have more than one establishment, and the operating statements for each establishment should be an integral part of the microdata set underlying the enterprise sector. This data structure is well recognized in the *Annual Survey of Manufactures,* for example, where operating information is collected for each establishment, each establishment is linked with the enterprise owning it, and headquarters information is provided for each enterprise. Although in the case of enterprises social information is considerably less important than for households, there are questions of pollution and environment to be considered, and to the extent that information can be obtained on the nature and characteristics of the labor force of different enterprises or establishments, such questions as discrimination could be analyzed. Much of the benefit of having microdata available at the establishment level, however, would lie in the economic, rather than social, analysis which could be carried out. For example, the analysis of prices, costs, and productivity at the establishment level can provide considerable insight into the mechanism of inflation and growth. Establishment and enterprise microdata can also provide the basis for the study of mergers and industrial concentration.

Regional Information

The need for regional information is increasing substantially with the growth of governments' concern with economic and social conditions within specific regional areas and the need for administration of economic and social policy affecting these areas. Unfortunately, there is no single system of regional classification that can satisfy all users. For a great many problems, the definition of a regional unit must depend upon economic, demographic, social, or environmental criteria. The Standard Metropolitan Statistical Area (SMSA), used for much of the federal statistical system, is based on density and population size. But in many cases more homogeneous groupings are needed. Thus, for example, a Standard Metropolitan Area may contain both high income areas and low income areas. The latter might be eligible for federal assistance programs if it were independently defined, but cannot receive aid when it is averaged with a high income area. In other cases, broader areas are required. Thus, a river basin which is being considered for economic development must encompass a broader area, based on geographical proximity. Market areas are still another regional grouping desired by business groups interested in the establishment of plants or retail outlets. Those in charge of administering political units such as school districts, cities, and states, need yet different sets of regional information. They are properly concerned with knowing the economic and social characteristics of their constituencies so that they can make realistic budget estimates and evaluate the impact of their policies.

This substantial and highly diverse demand for different kinds of regional information can only be met if it is possible to generate the large variety of regional information needed through different aggregations drawn from a detailed data base. At the level of the individual reporting unit, address information provides the basis for geocoding systems which can map individual data into any desired regional boundaries. Both the U.S. and Canadian governments have been preparing such geocoding systems, but even without such sophisticated codes the zip codes contained in addresses provide an extremely useful basis for locational aggregation. If adequate microdata sets exist for households, enterprises, establishments and governmental units, each of which is geographically located, it would be possible to develop any required regional aggregations. The microdata sets required to yield satisfactory regional information will need to be very much larger than what would be needed on a purely national level. Nevertheless, given the capabilities of modern computers and the kind of information available, this locational dimension is feasible. Furthermore, the kinds of problem with which we are faced demand such information. Certainly problems relating to environment and pollution cannot be considered except in terms of their regional dimension. But similarly the wide difference in the economic and social condition of the population in different regions has important consequences for the governmental activity needed. The adequacy of schools, the availability of employment, health, the condition of housing, and crime all have important regional and locational dimensions which need to be considered.

THE DEVELOPMENT OF SYNTHETIC MICRODATA SETS FOR ECONOMIC AND SOCIAL ACCOUNTS

The development of synthetic microdata sets has already been undertaken by a number of different research workers independently. The impetus to such developments has arisen usually because of the inadequacy of existing aggregated data for a specific problem in which the researcher was involved. Although this type of research is still in its early stages, there has been sufficient experience and research output to indicate the basic methodology involved and the potentiality of the data files for analyzing economic and social problems.

Data Files of the Household Sector

The Office of Business Economics of the Department of Commerce is now engaged in creating a microdata file for the household sector of the national accounts, specifically designed for estimating the size distribution of income. Edward C. Budd [11] has reported on the progress of this work, and described in some detail the technique used to create a synthetic microdata set for the household sector. The project was undertaken because the methodology previously used for estimating the size distribution of family personal income could not provide the kind of social and demographic breakdowns needed for the evaluation of economic and social policy. The old methodology relied upon published tabulations and cross tabulations of different kinds of information from a large variety of sources. Further disaggregation or alternative break-downs were not possible, given the basic data. The decision to develop a synthetic microdata set for households stemmed from the realization that such a data set once created could be used to provide any desired form of income distribution. Four basic sets of microdata files were used. These were the March 1965 Current Population Survey, the 1964 Sample of Personal Income Tax Returns, the 1962 Federal Reserve Board Survey of Financial Characteristics of Consumers, and the Internal Revenue Service Audit Study for 1963. The first step in the process was to match statistically, record by record, information for similar households in the Current Population Survey and the sample of personal income tax records. Corrections were made to this file using the IRS audit file. After this, the merged file was matched, record by record, with the FRB Survey of Financial Characteristics. At various stages in the process, comparisons with the national income control totals were made, so that the degree of underreporting or other biases could be estimated. The need for corrections to insure consistency between the macro and micro data does not, of course, always mean that the error is in the micro file. In some instances the development of the microdata sets may well lead to an improvement in the aggregate figures.

A similar effort in creating a microdata set for households has been undertaken by Benjamin Okner [12] of Brookings, in order to obtain an improved data base for the Brookings Tax Model. The original Brookings Tax Model had used a microdata set of personal income tax returns, but this of course contained only households that file tax returns, and the omission of data for people not required to file distorts the distribution at the low end of the income scale. In 1967, the Office of Economic Opportunity conducted through the U.S. Bureau of the Census a sample survey of 30,000 households with income information for the year 1966 and supplemental financial and demographic data. Okner used this sample as a frame, and constructed a new merged data file adding information on individual tax returns from the 1966 tax file for 87,000 individuals. The first step in the process was to analyze the SEO (Survey of Economic Opportunity) file to determine the characteristics of the household which could be used as a basis for selecting an actual return from the tax file to link with an individual in the SEO family. The characteristics which were used were (1) the marital status under which the return was filed, (2) whether the head or spouse of the tax unit was 65 or over, (3) the number of dependent exemptions in the unit, and (4) the reported pattern of income. In almost all cases the actual selection of a tax file return was done by the computer using tightly prescribed rules for defining an acceptable match. The resulting merged data file thus provided each SEO household with an income tax return which was consistent with the data in the SEO file about that household. Furthermore, since the tax returns were selected from the actual tax file, the new merged file contained all the information in the original tax file, except that the sampling frame of the SEO file was accepted instead of that of the original tax file.

Although both the OBE and the Brookings microdata sets for households have emphasized the income dimension, they were both created because of the need to link the income of the household to its other social and demographic characteristics. They represent attempts to switch from an income classification of reporting units to a demographic classification. The principles involved in the creation of these synthetic data sets can equally well be applied to other bodies of information about households. Data on the spending patterns of households contained in the Survey of Consumer Expenditures collected by the Bureau of Labor Statistics are prime candidates for integration into the microdata set for households. On a more regular basis, the monthly Current Population Survey collected by the Bureau of the Census can provide current updating of information on households at the microdata level. These samples are an extremely valuable statistical source of information on what has taken place in the immediately past period. Over the longer term, matched sets of data in the Social Security files contain information on the mobility of individuals in terms of both residence and employment, together with changes in wages. Recently, in order to obtain a longer longitudinal perspective, the Office of Economic Opportunity has initiated a special panel survey which reports exhaustively on a sample of 5,000 households over a period of five years.

The increasing demand for microdata files for individuals and households has been explicitly recognized by the Bureau of the Census in connection with the 1970 census. The Census Bureau is making available a series of six Public Use Samples, each containing individual records for 2 million people (a 1 in 100 sample). In order to prevent disclosure, different kinds of information have been suppressed in the different samples, since obviously if the exact address and full set of family characteristics were given for a household its identification would be complete. Such comprehensive samples of the population, however, provide the necessary basis for establishing microdata sets on individuals and households in 1970.

Since in the United States different samples of households do not contain the same individuals, synthetic matching must be the general practice. As already noted, this procedure avoids the question of privacy of the household, since by definition the synthetically matched records do not refer to any actual household. The major question which remains, however, is whether microdata sets derived by synthetic matching will be satisfactory for the analytic uses for which they are designed.

Synthetic matching is essentially imputation, and the validity of imputation depends on how the imputed information is related to information already known about a particular case. If there is no relation between the information which is being imputed and the known characteristics of the individual, a stochastic imputation which relates information from two files on a random basis would be satisfactory in the sense that the means and variances of the imputed information would correspond to those of the original files, and the lack of correlation among the various characteristics would be preserved. For most characteristics, however, there are major interrelationships which must be preserved in the imputation process. Thus, in the Brookings and OBE studies, the income and family composition information contained in the one file had to be closely matched with income and dependency information in the second file. To disregard these common elements of information would do violence to the matching procedure. Thus, overlapping relevant characteristics between files are needed to insure valid imputation. Where these are lacking there may be no adequate basis for merging the files. The problem of determining what information is relevant, i.e., how specific information in one file is correlated with information in another file, may not be soluble solely on the basis of internal evidence in the files themselves. In such cases separate studies can be developed to provide such linkages. At the present time the federal government has under way a special link project that is attempting for a given sample to match identical individuals in tax data, social security data, and census data. Such exact matching projects can serve as a basis for synthetically matching data from these three files. In other cases, it may be necessary to collect a special sample which does cover for each observation in the sample all the items of information contained in the various files to be merged.

Data Files for Enterprises and Establishments

With respect to the enterprise sector, the situation is somewhat paradoxical. On the one hand, large corporate enterprises are required to file public reports relating to their income and balance sheets, and this information is made available to the public as part of the services of the Securities and Exchange Commission. On the other hand, Census data relating to enterprises and establishments is considered extremely confidential, and is not available either to the general public or to the rest of the government except in a tabulated form which does not divulge identifiable information on any single establishment or enterprise. Nevertheless, within the Census Bureau the potentiality for creating extremely useful microdata sets on establishments exists, and some work has been done in this area.

As part of the Census monograph program, research workers have been allowed to analyze the basic census records. In this connection, a microdata set of the manufacturing establishments covered by the *Annual Survey of Manufactures* was created which showed their year by year change over an extended period [13]. Because the data are available at the individual establishment level, it has been possible to compute for each individual establishment the changes in real value added, deflating both inputs and outputs, to analyze such factors as productivity and price-cost behavior, in relation to other factors during various periods of inflation and recession. The technical problems caused by changes in the computers and procedures used by the Bureau of the Census, and the need to insure confidentiality throughout the entire project have caused this type of research to go very slowly indeed. However, other studies involving the analysis of industrial concentration, regional and industry growth, mergers, and research and development have all made good use of the microdata files available in the Bureau of the Census.

There are in addition related files on enterprises and establishments in other government agencies. The Bureau of Labor Statistics, the Internal Revenue Service, the Federal Trade Commission, and the Federal Reserve Board all have extremely valuable sets of information. Although some exact matching of these files has been done, for example the Internal Revenue files with Bureau of the Census files, for the most part these sets of data remain unrelated.

In addition to the data held by the government, there are private sources of microdata files. The Compustat tapes of Standard Statistics Corporation embody much of the income statement and balance sheet information filed with the SEC, in addition to other related data. These files provide quarterly information for each major corporation going back as far as 1948. Dun and Bradstreet provides credit and other information on individual establishments, and links these individual establishments with their parent firms. The Compustat tapes have furnished corporate data for many Ph.D. dissertations and some use has also been made of establishment data from various sources. For example, Robert Leone [14] of the NBER has studied the mobility of manufacturing establishments in the New York area, and Charles Berry [15] has studied the changing composition of firms and establishments (birth, death, merger, etc.) based on a Fortune sample. Michael Gort [16] is studying diversification and integration using both firm and establishment data.

All this activity suggests a need for bringing together known public information about individual firms and establishments. This process will be facilitated by the government's proposed register of firms and establishments. This register presumably will be comprehensive, and will indicate the name, location, and type of activity of each firm and establishment in the economy.

Other Bodies of Microdata

Various other major sets of microdata exist. Some of these fit directly into the national economic accounts, and others form special subsets delineating areas of special interest for social and economic policy. The Census of Governments contains information on the budgets and activities of state and local governments. This is a substantial microdata set, involving over 80,000 governmental units, as well as reports on other specific groups in the fields of health and education. Institutions of higher learning, hospitals, and medical programs, both public and private, generate large bodies of microdata. Some of these sets of data relate to the institutions that enter the national economic accounts as enterprises or government units; others relate to individual households. Finally, there are large bodies of data which relate to international trade and the balance of payments. While these data even at their most disaggregated level usually do not refer to decision-making units and do not constitute microdata sets in the same sense, the highly detailed information on imports and exports by commodity and country collected by the United Nations represents a valuable body of highly detailed information.

Implementation of Integrated Economic and Social Accounts

The task of implementing an integrated system of economic and social accounts cannot be left to individual research workers. To do so would mean leaving major statistical gaps because of limited resources, and continuation of the fragmentation that characterizes much of the present situation in the area of social information. What is needed is the same sort of development that occurred with the macroeconomic accounts. Although the national income estimates were initially developed by private researchers, the federal government has assumed full responsibility for implementing the national economic accounts and keeping them up to date. It was not until this happened that the comprehensive accounting framework was devised, and over time, the quality and the amount of information provided by the national economic accounts has increased substantially. It would indeed be unthinkable to turn the task back to private organizations.

If the government is to undertake the responsibility for developing and maintaining an integrated system of economic and social accounts, however, several major changes will need to be made. First, the macroeconomic framework will have to be modified to be consistent with synthetic microdata sets for households, enterprises, and other units. This would be quite possible without significantly disrupting the present national economic accounts or other types of macro information. Second, the government must be empowered to use its own information for statistical purposes. The present decentralized federal statistical system makes the creation of synthetic data sets difficult, since the different agencies responsible for different portions of the data guard their own portions zealously on the ground of preserving confidentiality and privacy. It is highly debatable whether any minor modification in the present organization of the statistical system will be sufficient to achieve the needed access to information. Nevertheless, even within the bounds of the present situation much could be done, if modest cooperation could be obtained among the Bureau of the Census, the Office of Business Economics, the Bureau of Labor Statistics, the Social Security Administration, and the Internal Revenue Service. In other countries, where central statistical offices exist, progress is being made in unifying the statistical system in terms of economic and social data.

The privacy question with respect to household information can be handled by the development of synthetic data sets. In other areas where disclosure is a problem, e.g., establishment and enterprise data, other techniques may have to be used to provide access to important microdata sets and at the same time preserve confidentiality. One promising approach has been suggested by both the Bureau of the Census and the Social Security Administration. Once the basic microdata files containing confidential information are created within the appropriate government agency, test samples with dummy information having statistical characteristics similar to the actual data could be provided to users, so that they could develop and test computer programs which could then be run on the actual files. The agency would undertake to run the programs for the private researcher, and give him the results after examining them for disclosure. For many types of research, this would give the individual researcher access to information sufficient to test hypotheses or to carry out simulations. This does, of course, presuppose that the microdata set exists in clean, consistent, and edited form, and that the computer facilities in the federal government can be made available to private users on a reasonable basis with respect to both timing and cost.

Although the discussion of implementation so far has been in terms of the accounts for the United States, the proposed system of economic and social accounts utilizing synthetic microdata sets is, of course, relevant to other countries as well. The acceptance of such a system does imply, however, that central statistical offices must change their approach to place primary emphasis on maintaining in usable machine readable form the micro information which they receive on households and enterprises. As has been noted, the Norwegian Central Statistical Office has already taken this view in the development of their statistical file system for individuals. Ivan Fellegi and Simon Goldberg [17] of Statistics Canada have recognized that the storage of the most detailed microdata provides a capacity for retrieval of an almost infinite variety of unanticipated cross-classifications and aggregations consistent with confidentiality requirements, and consequently they recommend basing the development of the nation's statistical system on microdata. Within the confidentiality restriction, they also recognize the value of record linkage, and are interested in experimenting with "pseudo-linkage" of different microdata sets. This view of the statistical data base is in contrast with the older approach taken in many statistical offices that certain designated cross-tabulations of data constitute the primary basis of the statistical system.

The development and use of microdata depends upon the existence of a computer which makes the storage and processing of large amounts of data feasible. Even with punched card technology, the retention and use of large bodies of data were not feasible due to the cost of storage and handling. Cross-tabulation and aggregation were necessary to reduce the data to a manageable form.

The proposed system of economic and social accounts is not solely pertinent to those highly industrial countries that already have extensive statistical systems. Even in countries with large nonmarket sectors and inadequate statistical coverage, using microdata sets to develop economic and social accounts is a valid technique. Almost every country in the world now has computers available to it, and it is of benefit to use the computer to handle those areas of government activity which involve substantial data processing. Thus, tax returns, social security records, census records, and foreign trade statistics will be among the first records to be computerized. In addition, sample surveys of consumer budgets, agricultural production, and unemployment may be made from time to time. Given these kinds of information there is considerable value in creating and maintaining microdata sets in machine readable form. With such sets of microdata available, it becomes more feasible to create satisfactory macroeconomic accounts for the nation, and at the same time to relate these economic accounts to important demographic and social data.

IMPLICATIONS OF THE SYSTEM FOR
ECONOMIC AND SOCIAL RESEARCH

It is quite reasonable to ask how the proposed system of economic and social accounts can be used. This sort of question has been a constant embarrassment to national economic accountants with respect to national economic accounts. Unfortunately, there is no magic process by which a given set of information can be used to produce answers to major problems. While it is true that macroeconometric models abound which make use of the information in the national economic accounts, few national economic accountants would wish to claim that this use is the major justification for the existence of national accounts. The record of success in this area has been too slim to justify the tremendous expenditure on the development of the basic data. Instead, the ultimate justification is that the national economic accounts provide a systematic record of what takes place in the economy in much the same way as records for the firm indicate what is happening within the firm, and although there is no magic way of processing business accounts to forecast the future of the firm or to automatically provide solutions to all of the firm's problems, the information in the accounts is essential to the operation of the business.

It is not enough, however, merely to state that the system of economic and social accounts provides comprehensive and systematic information on the operation of the economy and the society. One wishes to know just what fruits can be expected from the new type of information which were not available heretofore. For this purpose, it will be useful to look at some of the studies which have already been mentioned to see precisely what they have produced or can be expected to yield.

The work on the distribution of income being carried out by the Office of Business Economics will when completed provide extremely valuable information on the distribution of income for different demographic and social groups. Although Roosevelt's one-third of a nation was a dramatic and politically satisfying social indicator, a much clearer delineation of the nature of poverty and the injustice of inequality is needed for the development of social policy designed to change these conditions. We have fragmentary evidence from tax returns, from poverty samples, and from census data about different aspects of the distribution of income, but these different sets of information have not been successfully brought together and matched against the control totals for the nation as a whole. Until this is done, considerable confusion will exist as to what the situation actually is since we will be able to get different answers from what appear to be contradictory sets of information, and thus will be unable to resolve the central questions regarding poverty and inequality.

The Brookings Tax Model has already proven itself to be of major value. The Internal Revenue Service now uses a related tax model to determine the impact of changes in the tax laws and the effect of different economic conditions on tax payments. The recent merging of non-taxpayers into the tax file will greatly improve the usefulness of the model for examining broader changes in the tax law [18].

A related use of microdata sets for evaluating transfer income programs was undertaken by the Commission on Income Maintenance Programs, and this work is being further extended at the Urban Institute by Nelson McClung [19] and his associates. Much of the work on evaluating transfer incomes has been done on the samples derived from the Survey of Economic Opportunity, but this work is now being extended through the use of Current Population Survey files, National Health Interview Surveys, personal income tax returns, Federal estate tax returns, and longitudinal panel surveys. The purpose of these studies is to determine how different transfer income proposals would work out both in terms of the people they would benefit and the costs they would entail. The technique used is simulation, in which each individual case is examined in terms of the criteria of the proposal which is being evaluated. This sort of research is extremely valuable in enabling the policy maker to compare the costs and benefits of different proposals. Although past results have been very useful indeed, a considerable improvement can be expected in the future as the data base expands and the sophistication of the simulation models increases.

A somewhat related area of concern is the simulation of social security systems and the projection of the distribution of income of the aged. James Schulz of Brandeis University has undertaken research in this area in conjunction with the Social Security Administration. Schulz's initial models [20] were concerned with aging the population in 1960 to the year 1980, and examining the implications of present private pensions combined with the social security system in relation to the distribution of income of the aged in 1980. Schulz was particularly interested in how changes in vesting of pensions and in provisions of the social security law would affect the income distribution twenty years hence. More recently, Schulz has used his basic model to compare the performance of different social security systems [21], specifically the West German and Swedish, to indicate for the same population how these systems would perform relative to the U.S. system. Such analyses as these are very useful in trying to evaluate how substantially different social security systems compare with one another under ceteris paribus assumptions.

A more ambitious general purpose microanalytic simulation is being undertaken by Guy Orcutt [22] and his associates at the Urban Institute. This model is more comprehensive and exhaustive than anything undertaken previously. The basic information is a microdata set of households, but considerable attention is focused on the demographic aspects of the household, i.e., birth, family formation, marriage, divorce, intergenerational transfers, and death. Furthermore, the micro model is being embedded in an auxiliary macro model concerned with such things as aggregate unemployment rates, changes in price levels, and growth rates. Unlike the analyses discussed above, Orcutt's microanalytic model is conceived of as a general economic tool which can be used for a wide variety of purposes, both for simulating the effect of economic policy and for analyzing economic and social conditions. This work is a logical extension of the development of an integrated economic and social accounting system.

The Role of the Computer in Economic and Social Research

The need for computers in the creation of the microdata base has already been discussed. It is equally true that the use of the data base for economic and social research would not be possible without the advances which have been made in computer technology. The simulations described above require substantial data processing and computing capacity. The increase in the power of computers and the sharp decline in computational costs are having a major impact on economic and social research. Unfortunately, these changes are so recent that research methodology has not had time to adapt to them fully. Most graduate students in the major universities have some programming experience, but it is still true that a predominant number rely solely on regression packages and time series analysis of aggregated data to carry out their research. The increasing availability of microdata sets within the past few years coupled with the improvement in computers, however, is having a major influence, and new Ph.D. theses are increasingly using microanalytic models and simulation techniques.

The Function of Social Indicators

The discussion in this paper has concentrated for the most part on the macroeconomic accounting system and its relation to microdata sets containing both economic and social data. Little has been said about the place of social indicators in the system. Unfortunately, no one to date has devised a convincing set of social indicators which has a formal, cohesive structure.

The discussion of social indicators in the first part of this paper pointed up the unsatisfactory nature of ad hoc and conceptually unrelated social indicators. Nevertheless, social indicators of some sort are very much needed. Information in highly disaggregated form such as microdata sets is of little direct use to the policy maker without the intermediation of the research worker. The solution to this problem is to develop macro social indicators which are systematically based on aggregation of the data in the microdata sets of the economic and social accounts. Such social indicators need to do more than present a summary of the raw information; they must also provide a context for the information. Thus, for example, with regard to poverty, the percentage of poverty households in different cities or regions, or in terms of different races, can show the relative importance of the problem in different situations. Similarly, changes over time in poverty can show whether poverty is being successfully reduced in different places or among different groups. Most of such social indicators will not have the kind of short run interest which economic indicators possess. Monthly and quarterly economic data are needed because economic fluctuations can be significant in the short run. Social indicators, on the other hand, tend for the most part to reflect structural conditions in the society, and usually cannot be expected to show significant month to month change. But their breakdown in terms of regions and demographic and social groups is substantially more important.

In summary, it is useful to view social indicators as derived from the economic and social accounts. To the extent that there is a macro structure among the social indicators, it will exist mainly because different social indicators are based on the same or related microdata sets, and thus are consistent with each other. Social indicators will also have a role in shaping the content of the economic and social accounts. The need for specific macro social indicators will logically lead to the inclusion of the relevant information in the microdata base. Conversely, the availability of specific microdata can suggest types of social indicators which might otherwise not be thought of. In this manner the joint evolution of social indicators and of economic and social accounts can take place and provide for monitoring the society and carrying out basic research on economic and social problems.

TABLE 1

The Proposed System: National Income and Product Account for the US, 1966

(billions of dollars)

INCOME ORIGINATING		FINAL EXPENDITURES	
1.1 Enterprise Sector	529.0	1.13 Consumption	590.0
a. Employee compensation	359.1	a. Households	435.7
b. Self-employed compensa-		1. Market	339.4
tion	40.0	2. Nonmarket	96.3
c. Imputed interest on plant		b. Government	125.1
and equipment	50.0	1. Market	73.1
d. Net operating surplus	79.9	2. Nonmarket	52.0
		c. Enterprises	29.2
1.2 Government Sector	92.6		
a. Employee compensation	76.6	1.14 Gross Capital Forma-	
b. Imputed income from de-		tion	308.2
velopment and durables	16.0	a. Households	100.2
		1. Development	12.7
1.3 Household Sector	38.4	2. Housing	17.2
a. Nonmarket production	.9	3. Other durables	70.3
b. Imputed income from de-		b. Government	81.2
velopment and durables	37.5	1. Development	40.0
		2. Structures	24.2
1.4 National Income	660.0	3. Other durables	17.0
		c. Enterprises	126.8
1.5 Capital Consumption	165.5	1. Development	26.0
a. Depreciation	122.5	2. Structures	35.1
1. Enterprises	55.6	3. Other durables	52.3
2. Government	16.0	4. Change in inventories	13.4
3. Households	50.9		
b. Amortization	43.0	1.15 Exports	37.3
1. Enterprises	16.0		
2. Government	20.0	1.16 *Minus:* Imports	36.4
3. Households	7.0	1.17 Gross Domestic Product	
		at Market Prices	899.1
1.6 Gross National Product			
at Factor Cost	825.5	1.18 Factor Income From	
		Abroad	5.7
1.7 Business Transfers	2.7		
		1.19 *Minus:* Factor Income	
1.8 Business Consumption	18.0	Sent Abroad	1.5
1.9 Indirect Taxes	65.1		
1.10 *Minus:* Subsidies	5.4		
1.11 Statistical Discrepancy	−2.6		
1.12 GROSS NATIONAL PRODUCT AT MARKET PRICES	903.3	1.20 GROSS NATIONAL PRODUCT AT MARKET PRICES	903.3

TABLE 2a

The Proposed System: Enterprise Income and Outlay Account for the US, 1966

(billions of dollars)

2.1	Enterprise Consumption	29.2	2.6	Enterprise Income	529.0
	a. Business consumption	18.7		a. Corporate	360.4
	1. Mass media support	13.0		1. Employee compensation	275.9
	2. Provision of consumption goods	5.7		2. Net interest paid	−2.4
	b. Nonprofit consumption	10.5		3. Imputed interest on corporate net assets	40.0
	1. Religious	5.0		4. Corporate net profits	46.8
	2. Health, education, welfare	3.5		b. Noncorporate	139.2
	3. Other	2.0		1. Employee compensation	59.2
2.2	Payments to Households	489.3		2. Net interest paid	11.2
	a. Employee compensation	359.1		3. Self-employed compensation	40.0
	b. Interest paid	40.9		4. Imputed interest on noncorporate net assets	15.0
	c. Dividends	20.5		5. Noncorporate net profits	13.8
	Plus: (d + e)			c. Government enterprises	11.3
	d. Proprietor and rental income	79.1		1. Employee compensation	8.0
	e. Adjustments	−10.3		2. Surplus	3.3
	Or *plus:* (f + g + h)			d. Nonprofit institutions	14.0
	f. Self-employed compensation	40.0		1. Employee compensation	16.0
	g. Imputed interest on noncorporate assets	15.0		2. Net interest paid	−2.0
	h. Net noncorporate profits	13.8		e. Rest of the world	4.2
2.3	Direct Taxes and Other Payments	41.8		1. Corporate profits	3.3
	a. Corporate profits tax	34.5		2. Net interest	.9
	b. Government enterprise surplus	3.3	2.7	Transfers to Nonprofit Institutions From Households	6.5
	c. Interest paid to government	4.0			
2.4	Retained Enterprise Income	35.2	2.8	Enterprise Receipts Expensed	20.7
	a. Undistributed corporate profits	27.7		a. Business consumption	18.0
	b. Corporate profits adjustments	6.4		b. Business transfers to nonprofit institutions and consumer bad debts	2.7
	c. Retained nonprofit income	1.0	2.9	Interest Paid by Consumers	25.3
			3.0	Interest Paid by Government	13.9
2.5	PAYMENTS AND RETAINED INCOME OF ENTERPRISES	595.4	3.1	RECEIPTS OF ENTERPRISES	595.4

TABLE 2b

The Proposed System: Enterprise Capital Formation Account for the US, 1966

(billions of dollars)

2.10 Development Expenditures	26.0	2.15 Enterprise Capital Consumption	71.6
a. Research and development	18.0	a. Depreciation	55.6
		1. Corporate	39.0
b. Education and training	8.0	2. Noncorporate	15.6
		3. Nonprofit institutions	1.0
2.11 Durables Expenditures	87.4	b. Amortization	16.0
a. Structures	35.1	1. Corporate	12.0
b. Other durables	52.3	2. Noncorporate	4.0
2.12 Change in Inventories	13.4	2.16 Retained Income	35.1
		a. Corporate	34.1
2.13 Net Foreign Investment	2.2	b. Nonprofit	1.0
		2.17 Net Borrowing From (+) or Lending to (−) Other Sectors	+24.9
		a. Households	+17.7
		b. Government	+ 7.2
		2.18 Statistical Discrepancy	−2.6
2.14 GROSS ENTERPRISE CAPITAL FORMATION	129.0	2.19 GROSS SAVING AND NET BORROWING OR LENDING BY ENTERPRISES	129.0

TABLE 3a

The Proposed System: Government Income and Outlay Account for the US, 1966

(billions of dollars)

3.1	Consumption	125.1	3.7	Indirect Taxes	65.1
	a. Current expenditures	73.1		a. Sales	17.7
	b. Imputed services of de-			b. Excise	13.2
	velopment and durables	52.0		c. Property	24.3
	1. Imputed interest	16.0		d. Other	9.9
	2. Capital consumption	16.0			
	3. Amortization	20.0	3.8	Direct Taxes and Other	
				Payments by Enterprises	41.8
3.2	Subsidies	5.4		a. Corporate profits tax	34.5
				b. Surplus of government	
3.3	Transfers to Households	41.2		enterprises	3.3
	a. Social insurance	29.1		c. Interest	4.0
	b. Other insurance and pen-				
	sions	5.6	3.9	Tax Payments by	
	c. Public assistance	4.3		Households	113.4
	d. Other	2.2		a. Social insurance contri-	
				butions	38.2
3.4	Transfers to Abroad	2.3		b. Income taxes	75.2
3.5	Current Surplus	48.4	3.10	Transfers From Abroad	*
			3.11	Imputed Income From	
				Development and	
				Durables	16.0
				a. Development	6.0
				b. Durables	10.0
			3.12	*Minus:* Interest Paid	13.9
3.6	GOVERNMENT				
	CURRENT OUTLAYS		3.13	GOVERNMENT	
	AND SURPLUS	222.4		RECEIPTS	222.4

NOTE: An asterisk denotes less than 0.05.

TABLE 3b

The Proposed System: Government Capital Formation Account for the US, 1966

(billions of dollars)

3.13 Development Expenditures	40.0	3.17 Capital Consumption		36.0
a. Research and development	10.0	a. Depreciation		16.0
b. Education	20.0	b. Amortization		20.0
c. Health	10.0			
		3.18 Current Surplus		48.4
3.14 Structures Expenditures	24.2	3.19 Net Borrowing From (+) or Lending to (−) Other Sectors		−3.2
a. Buildings	8.9			
b. Highways and streets	8.3	a. Households		4.0
c. Other	7.0	b. Enterprises		−7.2
3.15 Other Durables Expenditures	17.0			
3.16 GROSS GOVERNMENT CAPITAL FORMATION	81.2	3.20 GROSS SAVING AND NET BORROWING OR LENDING BY GOVERNMENT		81.2

TABLE 4a

The Proposed System: Household Income and Outlay Account for the US, 1966

(billions of dollars)

4.1	Tax Payments	113.4	4.8	Payments by Enterprises	489.3
	a. Social security	38.2		a. Employee compensation	359.1
	b. Income taxes	75.2		b. Interest payments	40.9
				c. Dividends	20.5
4.2	DISPOSABLE INCOME	506.8		d. Self-employed compensation	40.0
				e. Imputed interest on proprietor net assets	15.0
4.3	Consumption	435.7		f. Proprietor net profits	13.8
	a. Current expenditures	339.4			
	b. Nonmarket production	.9	4.9	Compensation of Government Employees	76.6
	c. Services of development and durable goods	95.4			
	1. Imputed interest	37.5	4.10	Transfers From Government	41.2
	2. Capital consumption	50.9		a. Social insurance	29.1
	3. Amortization	7.0		b. Other insurance and pensions	5.6
				c. Public assistance	4.3
4.4	Transfers to Nonprofit Institutions	6.5		d. Other	2.2
4.5	Transfers to Abroad	.6	4.11	Transfers From Abroad	*
4.6	Current Saving	64.0	4.12	Income Originating in Households	38.4
				a. Nonmarket production	.9
				b. Net imputed income	37.5
				1. Owner-occupied housing	23.5
				2. Automobiles	5.0
				3. Other durables	7.0
				4. Development outlays	2.0
			4.13	*Minus:* Interest Paid	25.3
4.7	PERSONAL CURRENT OUTLAY AND SAVING	620.2	4.14	PERSONAL INCOME	620.2

NOTE: An asterisk denotes less than 0.05.

TABLE 4b

The Proposed System: Household Capital Formation Account for the US, 1966

(billions of dollars)

4.14 Development Expenditures	12.7	4.17 Capital Consumption	57.9
a. Health	5.0	a. Depreciation	50.9
b. Education	6.7	1. Owner-occupied housing	7.9
c. Other	1.0	2. Automobiles	18.0
		3. Other	25.0
4.15 Durables Expenditures	87.5	b. Amortization	7.0
a. Owner-occupied housing	17.2	1. Health	3.5
b. Automobiles	29.9	2. Education	3.0
c. Other	40.4	3. Other	.5
		4.18 Current Saving	64.0
		4.19 Net Borrowing From (+) or Lending to (−) Other Sectors	−21.7
		a. Enterprises	−17.7
		b. Government	− 4.0
4.16 Gross Capital Formation by Households	100.2	4.20 Gross Saving and Net Borrowing or Lending by Households	100.2

TABLE 5

The Proposed System: External Transactions Account for the US, 1966

(billions of dollars)

5.1 Exports	37.3	5.6 Imports	36.4
5.2 Factor income from abroad	5.7	5.7 Factor income to abroad	1.5
5.3 Transfers to households	*	5.8 Transfers from households	.6
5.4 Transfers to government	*	5.9 Transfers from government	2.3
		5.10 Net foreign investment	2.2
5.5 Receipts From Abroad	43.0	5.11 Payments to Abroad and Net Foreign Investment	43.0

NOTE: An asterisk denotes less than 0.05.

REFERENCES

1. Kendrick, John W. "Studies in the National Income Accounts." In National Bureau of Economic Research, *47th Annual Report,* June 1967, p. 9.
2. Eisner, Robert. "Measurement and Analysis of National Income (Nonincome Income)." In National Bureau of Economic Research, *50th Annual Report,* September 1970, p. 44.
3. Ruggles, Nancy, and Richard Ruggles. *The Design of Economic Accounts.* New York, National Bureau of Economic Research, 1970.
4. Juster, F. Thomas. "On the Measurement of Economic and Social Performance." In National Bureau of Economic Research, *50th Annual Report,* September 1970, p. 8.
5. U.K. Central Statistical Office. *Social Trends.* London, Her Majesty's Stationery Office, 1970.
6. Moser, Claus A. "Social Indicators—Systems, Methods and Problems." *Review of Income and Wealth,* Series 19, No. 2, June 1973.
7. Stone, Richard. "An Integrated System of Demographic, Manpower and Social Statistics and Its Links with the System of National Economic Accounts." New York, United Nations, May 28, 1970.
8. Mod, Margaret A. "Manpower Balances in Socio-Economic Statistical Systems." *Review of Income and Wealth,* Series 19, No. 2, June 1973.
9. Aukrust, Odd, and Svein Nordbotten. "Files of Individual Data and Their Potentials for Social Research." *Review of Income and Wealth,* Series 19, No. 2, June 1973.
10. Stone, Richard. "A System of Social Matrices." Paper presented at 12th General Conference of the International Association for Research in Income and Wealth, Ronneby, Sweden, 1971.
11. Budd, Edward C. "The Creation of a Microdata File for Estimating the Size Distribution of Income." *Review of Income and Wealth,* Series 17, No. 4, December 1971.
12. Okner, Benjamin A. "Constructing a New Data Base from Existing Microdata Sets: the 1966 Merge File." *Annals of Economic and Social Measurement,* Vol. 1, No. 3, July 1972, pp. 323–362.
13. Ruggles, Nancy, and Richard Ruggles. "Data Description, Price-Cost Behavior of Manufacturing Establishments." January 1971. Mimeographed.
14. Leone, Robert. "Location of Manufacturing Activity in the New York Metropolitan Area." Ph.D. thesis, Yale University, December 1970.
15. Berry, Charles H. "Industrial Diversification and Corporate Growth." In Brookings Institution, *Biennial Report 1968–69.* Washington, 1970.
16. Gort, Michael, and Robert McGuckin. "Firm Data and Industry Aggregates in the Analysis of Diversification and Integration." Paper presented at Workshop on the Use of Microdata in Economic Analysis sponsored by the National Bureau of Economic Research, October 1970.
17. Fellegi, Ivan P., and Simon A. Goldberg. "The Computer and Government Statistics." Paper presented at Conference on the Role of the Computer in Economic and Social Research in Latin America, Cuernavaca, Mexico, October 1971.
18. Okner, Benjamin, and Joseph Pechman. "Uses of Tax Files Combined with Field Surveys." Paper presented at Conference on the Role of the Computer in Economic and Social Research in Latin America, Cuernavaca, Mexico, October 1971.

19. McClung, Nelson, John Moeller, and Eduardo Siguel. "Transfer Income Program Evaluation." The Urban Institute, Working Paper 950–3, September 2, 1970.
20. Schulz, James H. *The Economic Status of the Retired Aged in 1980: Simulation Projections.* Office of Research and Statistics, Social Security Administration, Research Report No. 24. Washington, D.C., Government Printing Office, 1968.
21. ———. "Simulation of Social Security Systems." Paper presented at Conference on the Role of the Computer in Economic and Social Research in Latin America, Cuernavaca, Mexico, October 1971.
22. Orcutt, Guy H., Harold W. Guthrie, Steven B. Caldwell, Gerald E. Peabody, and George Sadowsky. "Microanalytic Simulation of Household Behavior." The Urban Institute, Working Paper 504–5, September 9, 1971.

COMMENT

DOUGLAS G. HARTLE, Treasury Board, Canada

Those responsible for the program probably made a mistake in choosing me to discuss the Ruggles' paper. Interesting discussion is engendered by dissent rather than accord, and I find myself in substantial agreement with their approach. Indeed, when I read the paper I found myself becoming impatient with an attempt to explain the virtues of synthetic microdata sets when I was already persuaded.

I have been associated with three major research projects that have used synthetic microdata sets to simulate the direct effects at the individual level of three proposed policy changes—tax reform, a revision of the unemployment insurance system, and an evaluation of alternative negative income tax systems. In each case the analysis was greatly strengthened by the simulations. In each case the simulations would not have been possible without the use of synthetic microdata sets. There is no doubt in my mind that many issues can only be approached at the micro level and that micro analysis can be greatly advanced by creating microdata sets either by merging data pertaining to the same individual unit from several sources or by inferring data about that unit from other sources.

Having given this testimonial to the general approach, I would like, however, to point out that in some respects the Ruggles' paper does not go very far. They are, of course, on firm ground when they suggest that the units for which microdata sets should be created are the basic decision-making units in each of the major sectors of the economy—the household, the business establishment, and governments. (It is not so obvious what should be done about "the rest of the world.") And as long as one adheres to the concept of income used in the formulation of the national accounts there would seem to be no reason in principle why it should not be possible to make estimates at the micro level that are reconcilable with the macro level estimates with which everyone is familiar. If each of the units had a detailed descriptive code, and if the same data were accumulated for the same units over time, microdata sets that did nothing more than encompass the national accounts concepts of income would be enormously valuable for analytic purposes.

What makes me uneasy about the Ruggles' proposal is that it is not clear on what basis they would discriminate between the data to be included and the data to be excluded from their proposed microdata sets. There is, in short, no conceptual framework beyond that of the national accounts. Yet they describe their proposal as a "system of economic and social accounts." Just what does this phrase mean? To me, what they have described is a system of micro income and expenditure accounts that would be supplemented by any other microdata that could be obtained—demographic, health, education, social security, credit, labor force, crime, and so on. To call this potpourri a system of economic and social accounts seems to me to be going rather far. Just what is a "social account"?

While the modern computer makes it technically feasible to store, retrieve, and process enormous quantities of data, and the cost of doing so continues to fall dramatically, these operations are still not free goods. Some hard choices are going to have to be made between the information to be retained and the information to be discarded. Without some conceptual framework how are we to decide?

A conceptual framework that appeals to me is shown in Table 1. This pro forma balance sheet includes not only marketable assets and financial liabilities but the present values of all expected lifetime flows of benefits and costs. I would suggest that the microdata base for individuals and families should, in principle, include the *flows* of dollars and the imputed dollar values of the flows of tangible goods and services.

The flows of psychic costs and benefits and the flows of benefits derived from collective consumption obviously cannot be valued objectively. It is here that so-called social indicators have a role. Changes in certain indicators can be used as proxies for changes in benefits and costs that cannot be valued directly. If we assume that the individual adjusts his portfolio over time in order to maximize his *perceived* net worth, changes in individual behavior are attributable either to changes in tastes and preferences or changes in perceived relative prices. If, on

TABLE 1

Individual Wealth: A Comprehensive Formulation

Assets and Claims [present value (p.v.) of expected lifetime benefits]	Liabilities and Obligations [present value (p.v.) of expected lifetime costs]

Marketable assets
  Dollar value of current holdings
  P.v. of expected imputed income in kind
  P.v. of expected imputed psychic benefits derived from perceived prestige based on conspicuous wealth or market power [a]
Human capital
  Gross return
    P.v. of expected earnings
      Dollar amounts
      Imputed income in kind
      Imputed psychic benefits derived from prestige, esteem, and pride associated with the individual's occupation [b]
    P.v. of expected "leisure"
      Imputed earnings foregone
      Imputed psychic benefits derived from prestige associated with conspicuous indolence
  Deduct
    P.v. of expected "subsistence"
      Dollar costs
	Financial liabilities, not elsewhere stated
	
	Other obligations
	  To relatives and other individuals
	    P.v. of expected dollar outlays
	    P.v. of expected imputed outlays in kind
	    P.v. of expected imputed earnings or leisure foregone
	    P.v. of expected imputed psychic costs in conforming to behavioral standards of others, less psychic benefits (pride) in conforming to own behavioral standards
	  To governments (local, provincial, and federal)
	    P.v. of expected dollar amounts of taxes and losses resulting from expropriations
	    P.v. of expected imputed earnings or leisure foregone under conscription
	    P.v. of expected imputed psychic costs in conforming to law, less psychic benefits (pride) in conforming to own behavioral standards
	  To voluntary associations
	    P.v. of expected dollar outlays

Imputed outlays in kind

Imputed earnings or leisure foregone

P.v. of expected education costs

Dollar costs

Imputed outlays in kind

Imputed earnings or leisure foregone

Imputed psychic costs in conforming to educational standards

P.v. of expected health costs

Dollar costs

Imputed outlays in kind

Imputed earnings or leisure foregone

Imputed psychic costs of pain and suffering

Claims to transferred benefits specific to the individual

From relatives and other individuals

P.v. of expected dollar receipts

P.v. of expected imputed receipts in kind

P.v. of expected imputed psychic benefits derived from prestige, esteem, or affection accorded the individual by relatives or other individuals

From governments (local, provincial, and federal)

P.v. of expected dollar receipts

P.v. of expected imputed receipts in kind

P.v. of expected imputed psychic benefits derived from prestige or esteem accorded the individual by governments

P.v. of expected imputed outlays in kind

P.v. of expected imputed earnings or leisure foregone

P.v. of expected imputed psychic costs in conforming to behavioral standards of the associations, less psychic benefits (pride) in conforming to own behavioral standards

Net worth

149

(continued)

TABLE 1 (concluded)

Assets and Claims [present value (p.v.) of expected lifetime benefits]	Liabilities and Obligations [present value (p.v.) of expected lifetime costs]

Claims to transferred benefits specific to the individual (cont.)

From voluntary associations

P.v. of expected dollar receipts

P.v. of expected imputed value of receipts in kind

P.v. of expected imputed value of psychic benefits derived from the prestige or esteem accorded the individual by the other members of each group of which he is a member

Claims to share in collective benefits

P.v. of expected imputed benefits derived from the common property of each of the groups of which the individual is a member: family, neighborhood, community, region, nation, world, voluntary associations, racial-ethnic-linguistic

Common property includes:

Quantity and quality of unappropriated natural resources including air, water

Access to stock of knowledge and the quantity and quality of that stock

Access to social, cultural, and recreational activities and the quantity and quality of such activities

Availability of privacy

Prestige of the group in the eyes of nonmembers, based on the power of the group to influence the decisions of other groups

Esteem of the group in the eyes of nonmembers, based on conformity of its behavior to their standards

Pride of the members of the group in the group, based on conformity of its behavior to the standards of the group

NOTE: In principle, all dollar values are deflated by the expected prices of the basket of goods and services the individual would purchase. Wealth is expressed, therefore, in terms of real purchasing power.

[a] Psychic benefits and costs are subjective and not capable of objective evaluation. Psychic benefits from prestige or esteem depend upon the perceptions of the individual about the perceptions of others and are doubly subjective.

[b] Prestige is defined as the perceived favorable attitude of others arising from the perceived influence of the individual in allocating rewards and punishments to others. Esteem is defined as the perceived favorable attitude of others derived from the perceived conformity of the behavior of the individual to their standards. Pride is defined as the sense of satisfaction enjoyed by the individual, achieved through conforming to his own behavioral standards.

151

the basis of attitudinal information we can ascertain that preferences have not changed it is possible to infer that perceived changes in relative prices have occurred even though these prices may be intangible benefits and costs.

This suggests that microdata sets should encompass not only the behavioral information associated with portfolio adjustments involving assets and liabilities with intangible benefits and costs (e.g., political activity) but also attitudinal data that would make it possible to infer whether a change in such activity was attributable to changes in preferences (e.g., a change in group standards) or a change in perceived relative prices (e.g., a change in the expected payoff from political activity relative to that of other activities).

This framework is, of course, only one of many possible alternatives. It may well be that superior approaches either exist or can be devised. But the point I want to make is that without some framework it will be impossible to select the information to be included in the microdata sets on a rational basis. We might well end up with much information that is relatively trivial *and* major gaps that could have been filled had the resources been used to better purpose.

Let me conclude with a few comments on Tom Juster's paper. Here I generally agree with the conceptual framework he espouses but question the uses to which he puts it. Surely he is correct in claiming that changes in the national income as estimated in the national accounts are hopelessly inadequate as *the* measure of changes in national welfare. The fact that changes in the interpersonal distribution of income are ignored would seem to me to be a decisive argument even if no other limitations were to prevail—and Juster has shown that there are many others. But I do not believe that the way to reduce the errors involved in a misinterpretation of the national accounts is to adjust the accounts to make them more closely reflect a concept of welfare.

Even if all of Juster's proposed changes were implemented, the changes in "his" national income estimates would not be a valid indicator of changes in welfare either *and* the degree of subjectivity required to formulate them would have risen perceptibly. I would have thought that the best way to avoid the misuse of the national income estimates would be to provide separate series on other dimensions of welfare to which the user could apply his own weights. While one can argue at the margin about the reliability of certain imputations (e.g., leisure), at the far end of the continuum there are some components of welfare that everyone would agree cannot be valued objectively—e.g., national pride in an equitable distribution of income.

If a scalar measure of welfare is impossible—except for individuals who have identical normative values—is it wise to "improve" the national accounts so that they become a "better," but still hopelessly inadequate, welfare indicator?

ABRAHAM AIDENOFF, Statistical Office, United Nations

I propose to comment on Juster's and the Ruggles' papers in terms of the work of the United Nations on economic and social accounts.

TWO SYSTEMS OF ACCOUNTS

The United Nations has recommended a System of National Accounts (SNA) for use by countries in improving their economic accounts and the international reporting of data; and we are working on a System of Demographic, Manpower, and Social Statistics (SDMS) in order to assist countries to organize, coordinate, and expand these statistics. The two systems will complement one another and cover all the data dealt with by Juster and the Ruggleses. The SNA accounts relate to all economic transactions and stocks of a country; the SDMS is to incorporate data on the welfare of the population and the catering social services—public and private—in a coherent accounting framework. The two accounting systems are to be coupled through the ties between the activities and accomplishments of the social services and their economic costs and resources and through the links between social conditions of the population and their economic situation.

Thus, unlike Juster and the Ruggleses, who propose to construct a single set of economic and social accounts, the United Nations Statistical Office has decided on two distinct, but coupled, systems. We have adopted this approach for two reasons: First, while Juster believes that money values are the most appropriate unit of measurement in social accounts, we find that unlike economic transactions and stocks, a number of important aspects of social conditions are not amenable to objective, meaningful measurement in money units. Second, contrary to Juster, we consider that it is necessary to look at production in a different light in the case of social accounts than in the case of economic accounts.

MULTIPLE UNITS OF MEASUREMENT AND VALUATIONS

Natural (physical) units of measurement are needed—and are used in the SDMS—in order to furnish useful data on such topics as educational attainment and the state of educational institutions, the health of the population and the available medical facilities, the frequency, incidence, and severity of crime, or on how persons use their time and leisure. Certain facets of social conditions and social services may be usefully and objectively measured in money values—and are so measured in the SDMS. However, it would be necessary to impute questionable unit values for this purpose in other instances; and money values would not yield relevant data in a number of still other cases. While the use of natural units of measurement restricts the ability to aggregate the series of the SDMS and to combine the series of the SDMS and the SNA, it does not significantly diminish the usefulness of the data for purposes of dealing with social problems. In the case of the welfare of the population, the major interests are in the circumstances of particular groups of the population and in problems of the distribution of services, benefits, etc., among them. Furthermore, the structure, definitions, and classifications of the SDMS are so designed that the series on the various dimensions of welfare and on the pertinent social services, whether in natural or monetary units, may be correlated, one with the other, and with the data of the SNA.

Social accounts like the SDMS are concerned with the contribution of people's activities to their economic and social welfare, whereas economic accounts like the SNA focus on the production of goods and services for the society. Not only is the scope of the activities covered much wider in the case of the former system (for example, the inclusion of the housekeeping or the recreation of the family members), but the mode and basis of valuation may be different in the case of items covered in both systems. In the social accounts, values are based on the net addition to social welfare (benefits) derived from the production of goods and services, while in the economic accounts, values reflect the activities and costs at the margin of producing the goods and services as well as their utility to consumers. The two sets of values not infrequently differ in the case of such government services as universal education. They may even be different in the case of marketed goods and services because of the differences in horizon between social welfare and individual utility.

SOCIAL INDICATORS

I should like to make an additional general observation before turning to specific aspects of the papers by Juster and the Ruggles. Contrary to the Ruggles' statement that at present there is no systematic set of social indicators which are related to an underlying system of social accounts, social indicators are integrated into the SDMS. They summarize the various series of the accounts of each subsystem in the light of the social concerns attended to in each.

NONPROFIT PRODUCERS

As Juster recommends, the SNA includes full production and capital accounts for government and private nonprofit bodies. The production accounts focus attention on the social and community services these bodies produce and their associated costs. They also furnish a structure for estimating production in constant prices in terms of outputs rather than inputs. We are working on the question of constant-price estimates in the context of both the SDMS and the SNA. In the former case, we find it essential to distinguish between the output of the government and private nonprofit services and the benefits accruing to the recipients of the services because of the considerations I mentioned earlier.

EDUCATION AND RESEARCH AND DEVELOPMENT

As government and private nonprofit bodies furnish substantial educational and research and development services, it is convenient to comment now on the recommendations in the papers under discussion concerning the classification of the output of these services as intangible capital formation.

Educational services are designed to serve social and economic objectives; they contribute partly to human capital formation and partly to final consumption. Valuation of the flow in terms of income foregone by the recipients bears little, if any, relationship to the output of the services and is even unrealistic from the recipients' point of view. It may be appropriate to value the capital formation involved in higher than compulsory education in the light of the expected stream of greater future earnings but these estimates are difficult to make. Furthermore, still more intractable problems would arise in making the correlated estimates of the obsolescence in the acquired knowledge and skills.

Research and development is treated as capital formation in the SNA only when embodied in tangible capital goods. While the other outputs from research and development expenditures should be part of capital formation, it is very difficult to identify and value them. In the case of the outputs that are not embodied in capital goods, it would be inappropriate to include the research and development expenditures themselves in capital formation because not infrequently the output is not commensurate with the expenditure. When the results of research and development are patented or licensed, valuation in terms of the expected streams of income becomes possible. We propose to include these results of research and development expenditures in the balance-sheet accounts of the SNA.

HOUSEHOLDS ACCOUNTS

Juster considers that the boundary of production in the national accounts should be extended to include a number of intrafamily activities and that households should therefore have production and capital accounts.

The housekeeping, tutoring, recreational, etc., activities carried on by family members for themselves no doubt make important additions to their welfare. And, with economic development, more of these services are furnished through the market. Nonetheless the intrafamily services are not included in production in the SNA. These activities and the relevant decisions of family members are essentially noneconomic in character; and when the activities become matters of public concern, the questions and policies involved differ greatly from those concerning production for the market. Moreover, the inclusion in national accounting aggregates of the questionable and large imputations for intrafamily activities would significantly alter the meaning and attenuate the analytical uses of these aggregates.

Because intrafamily activities are important for the welfare of the population and are often matters of social concern, data on these activities are included in the SDMS. The data will be primarily included in a subsystem on how much time individuals spend on their various social and economic activities.

The SNA furnishes a capital account for households but the only consumer durables covered are owner-occupied dwellings. In the course of preparing the present SNA, the proposal to classify all consumer durables as capital goods was rejected in view of the serious difficulties of imputing values to the involved flow of services and the resulting alteration in the meaning of the aggregate on gross fixed capital formation.

INTERMEDIATE AND FINAL CONSUMPTION

It is recommended in the papers under discussion that business expenditures which contribute to the population's welfare—for example, health and recreational services that employers render to their employees and television and radio programs—should be treated as final consumption instead of intermediate consumption. On the other hand, Juster argues that the outlays on "regrettable necessities," on items made not for their own sake but for the sake of obtaining others and on "defensive measures"—for example, on commuting to work, on a hospital stay, on a strong door lock, on the police—should be classed as intermediate consumption instead of final consumption.

Intermediate consumption in the SNA includes the employers' outlays on health, recreational, and social services which they furnish collectively to their employees, because in most cases these outlays bring important direct benefits to the employers as well as to the employees. However, as these outlays do contribute to the employees' welfare, they are covered in the concept "total final consumption" that is used in the SDMS. The same approach would be appropriate in the case of television and radio programs.

The main reason that Juster gives for classing outlays on "regrettable necessities" and the like as intermediate consumption is that no benefits are derived directly from these items themselves. In the case of commuting to work, for example, he points out that people do not derive pleasure from this activity and would generally prefer to live within walking distance of their place of work. However, commuters, in residing a considerable distance from their work, have revealed their preferences in the light of the alternatives open to them. And the outlays on commuting are as much a part of the costs of obtaining the benefits of residing where they do as are the rents, or the equivalent, that they pay. The argument that the outlays should be treated as intermediate expenses because commuting is an instrumentality of residing far from work does not hold water. Almost any consumer outlay may be considered to be an instrumentality for satisfying some other, usually more basic, need. In fact, Juster considers outlays on air conditioning or heating to be final expenditures as they are costs of maintaining comfortable temperatures in climates where the temperature would otherwise be uncomfortable.

Juster's reasons for classing the "defensive expenditures" of persons or government as intermediate rather than final are also questionable. Surely, receiving medical attention or police protection or adding a door lock when needed contributes to people's welfare when they are faced with these situations. I believe that the reasons for treating these and other defensive outlays, for example, on pollution control devices, as final are essentially the same as those in the case of expenditures on air conditioning or heating.

I might note in passing that the SDMS is designed to furnish data on the aspects of welfare mentioned above, namely, commuting, the state of health and of public safety, housing, conditions of the physical environment, and on measures adopted in order to improve these conditions and their costs and benefits.

MICRODATA SETS

The Ruggles' paper stresses the values of microdata sets in economic and social accounting. I am in complete agreement with them concerning the usefulness of microdata sets as a source of basic data for these purposes. Microdata sets furnish an efficient and flexible means of assembling a wide range of disaggregated series of data that are nonetheless coordinated and linked; they are also an effective and practicable way of compiling longitudinal data.

The availability of detailed, consistent, and linked data greatly facilitates the compilation of interrelated economic and social accounts at various levels of aggregation and the carrying out of correlation and factor analyses. In fact, disaggregated, linked basic data on the various aspects of a population's welfare and the relevant social services are essential to building an integrated system of social accounts. And it is generally not feasible to gather all these series of data on the population at the same time or through the same agency. It is necessary to divide up the series over a number of phases or agencies that are tied together either through the use of an identical sample of households or individuals or preferably through the use of samples drawn from the same strata. The strata of households or individuals should be defined in terms of the characteristics which are strategic in the variance of the various aspects of the population's welfare.

Detailed longitudinal data are wanted in economic and social accounting for purposes of studying the sequences of experience and behavior of people, enterprises, and institutions over time. Synthetic microdata sets offer a means of gathering longitudinal data which avoids the difficulties of gathering data on identical respondents over a long period of time and the serious response errors that are involved in retrospective queries.

However, building and maintaining microdata sets is probably more costly and raises more complex statistical and administrative problems than the traditional methods of compiling data for broader groups of a population. This is so because, for example, a larger number of respondents is needed in the microdata approach, and they must be matched from phase to phase. The choice between the two approaches should depend on evaluating their relative benefits and costs in the light of the circumstances of a country. For example, I believe that many developing countries would find it advantageous to use microdata sets in order to gather and compile economic and social data on households.

EDWARD F. DENISON, The Brookings Institution

I share with Nancy and Richard Ruggles the expectation that synthetic microdata sets will contribute importantly to future economic analysis and wish only to express one comment on their presentation and one dissent.

It will be more difficult than they imply to integrate microdata sets with macroeconomic accounts because totals from the former are necessarily on a combined basis whereas the latter are and should be on a consolidated basis. The difference is fundamental and poses difficult problems for integration.

I disagree with the recommendation to transfer nonprofit institutions from the personal to the business sector. This recommendation doubtless stems from the authors' observation that if one wishes to analyze individual behavior the inclusion of nonprofit organizations is inconvenient. My objection stems from the observation that inclusion of nonprofit institutions in business is inconvenient if one wishes to analyze business, and that I do this much more often. We could both be satisfied by transferring nonprofit institutions to government (which the treatment of institutions in the national accounts most closely parallels) but this would inconvenience another group of users.

One possible expedient is to make nonprofit organizations a separate sector. This is feasible if low standards of statistical accuracy are acceptable; the necessary annual estimates would be weak and hardly any information would be available on a more frequent basis. This solution requires (1) data on all transactions between nonprofit institutions and other "persons" (mostly families and individuals) and (2) the segregation of purchases of goods and services by these institutions from purchases by other persons. I once made annual estimates for most of the required series of the first type for the 1929–41 period.[1] The most important single statistical source, the decennial *Census of Religious Bodies,* unfortunately last appeared for 1936, but no doubt rough annual estimates could still be made. Most of the required information of the second type is provided in the present annual personal consumption expenditures tables or the worksheets from which they are derived.

To make nonprofit organizations a separate sector is not a good idea even though it may be feasible if one accepts wide margins of error. It would greatly complicate the presentation of the annual and quarterly national income and product data without providing the aggregate combined income and outlays of families and single individuals to which one would expect microdata to aggregate. To obtain such series, far more adjustments than elimination of nonprofit institutions must be made to personal income and to personal consumption expenditures, consumer interest, and personal taxes. A more constructive request would be to ask OBE to try to provide such series on an annual basis without disturbing the accounts. I presume that something close to the income series so defined will necessarily emerge as a byproduct of the resumed publication by the OBE of size distributions of family and individual income.

[1] Edward F. Denison, "Consumer Expenditures for Selected Groups of Services, 1929–41," *Survey of Current Business,* October 1942, pp. 23–30.

The Household and Business Sectors

The Measurement of Output of the

Nonmarket Sector: The Evaluation

of Housewives' Time

REUBEN GRONAU

HEBREW UNIVERSITY

ONE may agree with the group of economists calling for a drastic revision of the set of social accounts so as to reflect social welfare, or one may adopt a more conservative approach, designing the national accounts to yield merely a measure of output of all goods and services produced during a given period, but foremost on the agenda of both camps is the broadening of the current definition of the national accounts to include nonmarket production.

Very few economists ventured to estimate the importance of the nonmarket sector relative to the over-all economic activity, but those who tried are united in their claim that even in the most advanced economies the nonmarket sector contributes a considerable share of total output. Reconstructing the social accounts to generate a measure of economic welfare (MEW), Nordhaus and Tobin figured that the value of leisure and nonmarket work constituted in 1965 three-quarters of their measured MEW (the value of leisure accounting for about one-half and the value of labor inputs in home production accounting for one-quarter of MEW [15]). Morgan estimated [13, p. 5] that the inclusion of unpaid work in the national accounts would have increased gross national product in 1964 by 38 per cent.[1] Sirageldin, using the

NOTE: The empirical part of this paper is from my study, "The Labor Force Participation of Israeli Women," carried out at the Maurice Falk Institute for Economic Research, Jerusalem. I am indebted to Gary Becker, Giora Hanoch, Ruth Klinov, David Levhari, and Shlomo Yitzhaki for their comments, and to Jacob Ish-Shalom for the data he made available to me.

[1] Nordhaus and Tobin's MEW is almost twice the GNP in 1965. Thus, Morgan's estimate and the Nordhaus and Tobin estimate of the ratio of nonmarket work to GNP (38 and 48 per cent, respectively) are not too far apart.

same data as Morgan, states that had we measured the value of housework and home production, the average family's disposable income would have increased by 43 per cent [16, p. 55].

Given the large fraction of resources devoted to nonmarket production and given differences in this fraction among countries and changes in this fraction over time, it is difficult to make any meaningful international comparison of the level of economic activity or to make any accurate statement about national economic growth, ignoring the unmeasured economic activity taking place at home.

The measurement of this activity is hampered by both conceptual and technical difficulties. The large heterogeneity in the quality of the various home services (e.g., child care, meals, home decoration, etc.) produced by different households makes it difficult to provide a clear definition of the physical units of output in this sector. Moreover, the absence of an open market for these outputs outside the household impedes the evaluation of this product.

One would like to resort to a method applied in national accounting in some other cases where the outputs are nonmarketable (e.g., government services) and evaluate the output of the nonmarket sector according to its costs of production. However, even this method runs into two major stumbling blocks: the absence of data on physical inputs and the difficulty in assigning them a price. While the difficulties in the measurement and evaluation of the capital input in the nonmarket sector do not exceed those encountered in the case of their market counterparts, it is hard to overcome the obstacles imposed by the lack of data on physical inputs and prices of the labor services used in the home sector. The cure for the absence of information on time inputs in nonmarket activities lies in an intensive effort to collect time budget data. The difficulty in assigning these inputs a price is of a more conceptual character.

A common practice in pricing the time inputs in the nonmarket sector is to place on them the price they could charge if they were sold in the market. This criterion, however, is hard to apply when the person does not sell any of his time in the market. For one, it is difficult to know what is the price the market would have offered this person for his time, and secondly, it is just because this person found this price inadequate that he declined to sell any of his time in the market. Since over forty per cent of all the adult population do not participate in the labor force, and given that these nonemployed provide over 60 per cent of all time inputs in the home sector, and since labor's share in total nonmarket output is about 75 per cent,[2] it is important to generate some more accurate measures of the value of time for this population group.

The evaluation of the price of time of the unemployed and its comparison with the price of time of the employed are of particular importance when one attempts to measure the change in over-all economic activity over time or to compare the economic activity in two different economies at a point of time. For example, Denison estimated that over one-fourth of the annual growth in real GNP in the period 1929–59 can be explained by the growth of labor inputs [3, p. 41]. However, at least part of the increase of the labor inputs in the market was at the expense of the nonmarket sector, due to the increase in the labor force participation rates of women, and, in particular, of married women.[3] To obtain a measure of the rate of growth of the total U.S.

[2] The capital-labor ratio is obtained by dividing Nordhaus and Tobin's estimate of the value of consumer and government capital services by their estimate of the value of labor in home production (had we included in the denominator the value of labor in home production plus the value of leisure, the capital-labor ratio would have shrunk from 1:4 to 1:11). The estimate of the share of the not employed in the home-sector labor inputs is based on the following table:

| | Male | | Female | | | |
| | Employed | Not Employed | Employed | | Not Employed | |
			Married	Single	Married	Single
Adults 14+ (1,000)	51,705	13,445	16,154	9,798	29,037	15,703
Daily hours of work at home per adult	1.9	1.9	4.8	3.7	7.8	6.1

SOURCE: Line 1: [18, pp. 31, 228], line 2: [17, Table 2.10]. It is assumed that employed and not employed males spend the same amount of time in home production.

[3] The data presented in note 2 and Table 1 indicate that employed women tend to spend less time in home production than housewives. However, it seems that at least part of the increased market supply of labor is at the expense of leisure. The increased labor force participation of women was therefore accompanied by a relative decline in time inputs in both home production and leisure. Over the past forty years, this tendency may have been accentuated by a reallocation of time of housewives and working men and women.

The only extensive time budget study in the United States in the thirties is the one reported by Lundberg *et al.* [11]. This study is based on a sample of 2,460 people reporting on 4,460 days and was conducted in Westchester County, New York, in 1932. The surprising aspect of the Lundberg results is the relatively economic activity one has to know the extent to which the increase in the labor force participation of married women affected home production, the extent to which this possible decline in labor inputs was compensated for by capital input increases in the nonmarket sector, and the rate of increase of labor productivity in the nonmarket sector relative to the market sector.

Another example, one which seems to be popular with politicians, is the comparison of U.S. and U.S.S.R. economic activity. Clearly, the focusing on GNP yields only a partial picture. However, to obtain a full account of the goods and services produced by the two nations it is not sufficient to know the amount of time spent in home production and males' and females' productivity in the market, but one has to take into account also the different degrees of specialization in home production in the two countries. Table 1 indicates that there is no great difference in the adult's average time inputs in home production in the two countries, but there is a significant difference in the way this production is distributed among the various members of the household. In the United States, the major burden of home production is borne by women not employed in the market, while in the U.S.S.R. this production is much more equally distributed among all adults. The lower incidence of unemployed married women in the U.S.S.R. is offset by the fact that on the average every Russian male and female (employed and not employed) spends 15–20 per cent more time in home production than his or her American counterpart. Thus, unless one knows the relationship between the productivities of the not employed in the market and nonmarket sectors one cannot produce an accurate answer to this beguiling question.

This paper addresses itself to the estimation of the price of time of a group that constitutes one-half of the not employed and contributes about 40 per cent of the time spent in home production,[4] namely, the housewives. As indicated earlier, the wife's rejection of the proposal

small amounts of time spent in home production. Employed women were reported to spend only 1.2–1.4 hours a day on household duties, child care, and shopping, while the corresponding figure for housewives was 4.2 hours. These figures are substantially below the 1965 figures presented in Table 1. Another striking feature of this report is the large amounts of time spent on physiological needs and free time. For most population groups it exceeded the corresponding 1965 figures by almost 2 hours (in the case of housewives the difference is almost 3 hours). It is difficult to believe that this difference can be fully explained by the admittedly biased nature of the sample.

[4] See note 2.

TABLE 1

Comparison of U.S. and U.S.S.R. Daily Time Budgets,
Males and Females
(hours)

	Market-related Work	Work at Home	Free Time and Physiological Needs	Physiological Needs	Free Time
All adults [a]					
U.S.	4.80	4.20	15.00	9.90	5.10
U.S.S.R.	6.50	4.10	13.40	9.20	4.20
U.S./U.S.S.R.	0.74	1.02	1.11	1.08	1.21
Married men, employed					
U.S.	7.55	1.90	14.55	9.70	4.85
U.S.S.R.	7.70	2.30	14.00	9.40	4.60
U.S./U.S.S.R.	0.98	0.83	1.04	1.03	1.04
All women [a]					
U.S.	2.65	6.15	15.20	10.10	5.10
U.S.S.R.	6.10	5.30	12.60	9.20	3.40
U.S./U.S.S.R.	0.43	1.16	1.21	1.10	1.50
Married women, employed					
U.S.	5.45	4.80	13.75	9.85	3.90
U.S.S.R.	6.80	5.50	11.70	9.10	2.60
U.S./U.S.S.R.	0.80	0.87	1.18	1.08	1.50
Married women, not employed					
U.S.	0.10	7.80	16.10	10.20	5.90
U.S.S.R.	0.10	8.90	15.00	10.30	4.70
U.S./U.S.S.R.	1.00	0.87	1.07	0.99	1.25

SOURCE: [17, Tables 2.9–2.11] The figures for the United States are a simple average of the data in Tables 2.10 and 2.11.

[a] Including single persons.

to enter the labor force indicates that the wage offer facing the woman falls short of the value that she places on her time. However, it is unknown whether the source of this discrepancy lies in a low wage offer or in her high valuation of her time. We do not know the value assigned to a person's time and if this person happens not to work we do not know the wage offers he rejected. This leaves the door open to two interpretations: according to the first, the fraction of those women who do not work are those who are the most efficient in the home sector (i.e., those who have the highest value of time), while according to the second, those who abstain from entering the labor force are those who are the least efficient in the market sector (i.e., those who face the lowest wage offers). If one adopts the first interpretation, one tends to conclude that the value of time of housewives exceeds the average wage of working women with similar market qualifications. The second assumption leads, on the other hand, to the conclusion that the average price of time of housewives falls short of the average wage of women who work in the market. The two alternative hypotheses give rise, naturally, to two alternative estimates of the housewives' average price of time.

The paper opens with a brief discussion of the factors affecting the wife's price of time. This discussion is followed by a description of a method to estimate this price of time and the paper ends with a report on the data and the results. It is found that under the first assumption the housewives' average value of time exceeds the average wage rate of working women by no more than 5 per cent. Given the second assumption, the lower limit of the housewives' average price of time is about 80 per cent of women's average wage rate. The housewives' mean price of time increases with the husbands' income, the elasticity of the price of time with respect to income ranging between 0.30 and 0.50. Differences in income tend to offset the effect of the existence of young children. Thus, we could not find any evidence that in the aggregate the price of time of housewives with young children exceeds that of housewives without young children.

THE VALUE OF TIME OF MARRIED WOMEN

The analysis of the factors affecting the price of time of a single person is well established in economic literature (see [1], [9], [14]). The incorporation of this analysis within a model of multiperson households calls for only minor modifications.

Let us assume, for simplicity, a two-person household trying to maximize family welfare:

$$U = U(Z_1^c, \ldots, Z_n^c, Z_1^W, Z_2^W), \tag{1.1}$$

where U denotes utility, Z_i^c denotes the ith consumption activity, and Z_j^W denotes the activity work in the market by person j.[5] Using the terminology developed by Becker [1] and Lancaster [10], a consumption activity is a combination of goods (X^c) and consumption time of the husband and/or his wife (T_1^c and T_2^c, respectively)

$$Z_i^c = F_i(X_i^c, T_{1i}^c, T_{2i}^c); \qquad (i = 1, \ldots, n); \tag{1.2}$$

where X and T_j are vectors of different goods and different units of time (e.g., different hours of the day).[6] Similarly, the activity work in the market by person j consists of a combination of goods (X_j^W), e.g., commuting services, and jth working time (T_j^W)

$$Z_j^W = G_j(X_j^W, T_j^W); \qquad (j = 1, 2). \tag{1.3}$$

The maximization of utility is subject to two kinds of constraints. The first (a) is the budget constraint, which states that expenditures on goods cannot exceed total income:[7]

$$\sum_{i=1}^{n} P_i^c X_i^c + \sum_{j=1}^{2} P_j^W X_j^W \leqslant W_1(Z_1^W) + W_2(Z_2^W) + V, \tag{1.4}$$

where P is a price vector, $W_j(Z_j^W)$ are the earnings of person j, and V denotes other sources of income. The second (b) contains two separate time constraints,

$$\sum_{i=1}^{n} T_{ji}^c + T_j^W \leqslant T_0; \qquad (j = 1, 2); \tag{1.5}$$

where T_0 is a vector of all the time units available. The maximization of the welfare function (1.1) subject to the budget and time constraints

---

[5] For simplicity we ignore the multidimensions of Z_j^W. Work is a heterogeneous activity, and the utility derived from work depends not only on the amount of work performed but also on the occupation the person is in. This topic has been discussed recently by Diewart [4].

[6] This paper does not distinguish between leisure time and time spent in work at home. This distinction is discussed in more detail in [7].

[7] This is a one-period model. One can easily adapt the discussion to an intertemporal model by defining one of the consumption activities as saving. For a discussion of the allocation of time and goods over time, see [5].

[(1.4) and (1.5)] yields the values placed by the family on its members' time, i.e., the optimal trade-off between time and goods.

Analyzing the price of a specific unit of time (i.e., a specific element of T_j) one has to distinguish between two cases: (a) the case where some units of this element of time are traded in the market (i.e., the corresponding elements in T_j^W are positive); and (b) the case where no unit of this element is sold by the family in the market (i.e., the corresponding element in T_j^W equals zero). In the first case, the price of this unit of time is determined by the marginal wage rate, in the second by the time scarcity.

Formally, the optimum combination of goods and time of person j in the production of activity Z_i^c is determined by the equality,

$$\frac{\partial Z_i^c / \partial T_{ji}^c}{\partial Z_i^c / \partial X_i^c} = \frac{\mu_j / \lambda}{P_i^c} = \frac{K_j}{P_i^c}; \qquad (j = 1, 2); \qquad (1.6)$$

where μ_j is the marginal utility of the time of j, λ is the marginal utility of income, and K_j is the price placed by the family on the time of j. For those units of time for which the elements of $T_j^W > 0$

$$K_j = \left[\frac{\partial W_j(Z_j^W)}{\partial T_j^W} - P_j^W \frac{\partial Z_j^W / \partial T_j^W}{\partial Z_j^W / \partial X_j^W} \right] + \frac{\partial U / \partial T_j^W}{\lambda} = W_j + (U_j^W / \lambda), \quad (1.7)$$

where W_j is the net marginal wage rate (i.e., the remuneration person j receives for selling the marginal unit of time in the market minus any money costs involved), and U_j^W is the marginal utility the family derives from a unit of j's time in work in the market. For those units of time which are freely substitutable for work in the market the value of time depends on the net marginal wage rate. It equals W_j to the extent that work does not yield any direct marginal utility or disutility.

If a person does not sell any amount of a specific unit of time in the market, and in particular if he does not sell any time in the market (e.g., a housewife), the wage rate he could have received in the market constitutes merely a lower boundary for his value of time. The shadow price assigned to his time depends on the demand and supply of time in the nonmarket sector. The supply of time for nonmarket uses is in this case completely inelastic and the price of time is demand determined. The demand for time can be considered as a derived demand for an input. Any change that affects the final demand for activities, such as a change in income or a change in tastes due to the acquisition of children, and any change that affects the productivity of time, such as the acquisition of home durables, would change the value placed by the family on its members' time.[8]

ESTIMATION OF THE PRICE OF HOUSEWIVES' TIME

It has been shown in the previous section that if one ignores the marginal utility (or disutility) and the cost incurred as the result of work and if one assumes that the marginal wage rate does not change with the amount of time spent in the market then the average wage rate (net of taxes) can serve as a close approximation for the value of those elements of time sold in the market. However, if certain elements of time are not sold in the market or as in the case of housewives when no unit of time is sold in the market, the potential wage rate can serve only as a lower limit for the estimate of the price of time. The evaluation of the price of time depends in this case on the answer to two questions: (a) by how much does the price of time of people not employed exceed their potential wage rate, and (b) to what extent does the potential wage rate of those not employed differ from the actual wage rate of those employed. It will be shown in this section that at least partial answers to these questions can be obtained by comparing the rates of participation and the average wage rates of married women belonging to different age-education-income groups.

If the wife's price of time were determined solely by her family income, and if all women in, say, a given age-education group expected the same potential wage rate, one would expect all women in the given age-education-income group to act in the same way. Thus, one should observe that either all the wives in a given age-education-income group participate in the labor force, or that none of them do. The dispersion in the working habits of women belonging to the same group indicates that the women either differ in terms of their potential wage rate or in terms of their value of time or both.[9]

Let us assume that the potential wage rate W and the housewife's price of time W^* are jointly distributed within an age-education-income group with a joint density function $f(W, W^*)$. The percentage (P) of wives participating in the labor force in a given group equals the per-

[8] For a more formal discussion of this case, see [7]. Note that a change in income may affect one's price of time even if one works and the wage stays constant, inasmuch as it leads to a change of the money equivalent of the marginal (dis)utility of work (u_j^W/λ).

[9] Ben-Porath [2] reaches somewhat similar conclusions. However, his analysis is carried out in the framework of a single-person household and in terms of "taste for work" rather than the value of time.

centage of wives whose value of time falls short of their potential wage rate [10]

$$P = \text{Prob } (W > W^*) = \int_{-\infty}^{\infty} \int_{W*}^{\infty} f(W, W^*) dW dW^*. \qquad (2.1)$$

The average wage rate of the women who work ($\bar{W}$) equals the conditional expectation of W where W exceeds W^*:

$$\bar{W} = E(W|W > W^*) = \frac{1}{P} \int_{-\infty}^{\infty} \int_{W*}^{\infty} Wf(W, W^*) dW dW^*; \qquad (2.2)$$

and the average price of time of women who do not work ($\bar{W}^*$) equals the conditional expectation of W^* where W^* exceeds W:

$$\bar{W}^* = E(W^*|W^* > W) = \frac{1}{1-P} \int_{-\infty}^{\infty} \int_{W}^{\infty} W^*f(W, W^*) dW^* dW. \qquad (2.3)$$

In particular, if one assumes that the potential wage rate and the price of time within each group are independent and have a bivariate normal distribution,[11] then

$$f(W, W^*) = \frac{1}{2\Pi\sigma_W\sigma_{W*}} \exp\left\{ -\frac{1}{2} \left[\left(\frac{W - \mu_W}{\sigma_W} \right)^2 + \left(\frac{W^* - \mu_{W*}}{\sigma_{W*}} \right)^2 \right] \right\} \qquad (2.4)$$

$$= \frac{1}{2\Pi\sigma_W\sigma_{W*}} \exp\left[-\frac{1}{2} (x^2 + y^2) \right],$$

where μ_W and μ_{W*} are the mean values, and σ_W and σ_{W*} are the standard deviations of the marginal distribution of W and W^*, respectively, and where $x = (W - \mu_W)/\sigma_W$ and $y = (W^* - \mu_{W*})/\sigma_{W*}$ are standardized normal variables. The women's labor force participation rate is

$$\text{Prob } (W = \mu_W + x\sigma_W > \mu_{W*} + y\sigma_{W*} = W^*) \qquad (2.5)$$

$$= \text{Prob } (x > A + By = y^*)$$

$$= \frac{1}{2\Pi} \int_{-\infty}^{\infty} \int_{y*}^{\infty} e^{-(1/2)(x^2+y^2)} dxdy,$$

where $A = (\mu_{W*} - \mu_W)/\sigma_W$ and $B = \sigma_{W*}/\sigma_W$. The average wage rate $\bar{W}$ is

$$\bar{W} = \mu_W + \bar{x}\sigma_W, \qquad (2.6)$$

[10] This analysis assumes implicitly that the wives react to actual wage offers rather than to expected ones as suggested by the theory of search (see for example [6]). The incorporation of the theory of information in our framework may not change the major conclusions but would have complicated the estimation procedure considerably.

[11] This assumption rules out any intragroup dependence of the value of time on age and education. Thus, we ignore the possible positive correlation between the price of time and the potential wage rate due to natural ability.

FIGURE 1

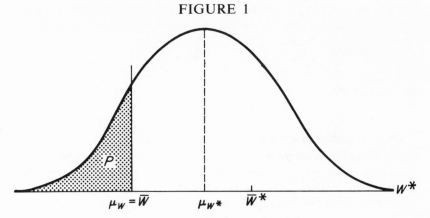

where

$$\bar{x} = E(x|x > y^*) = \frac{1}{2\Pi P} \int_{-\infty}^{\infty} \int_{y^*}^{\infty} x e^{-(x^2+y^2)/2} dx dy \qquad (2.7)$$

$$= \frac{1}{P} \left(2\Pi \frac{\sigma_W^2 + \sigma_{W*}^2}{\sigma_W^2} \right)^{-1/2} \exp\left[-\frac{1}{2} \frac{(\mu_{W*} - \mu_W)^2}{\sigma_W^2 + \sigma_{W*}^2} \right].$$

Finally, the average price of time of housewives equals

$$\bar{W}^* = \mu_W^* + \bar{y}\sigma_{W*}, \qquad (2.8)$$

where [12]

$$\bar{y} = E(y|y^* > x) = \frac{P}{1-P} \frac{\sigma_{W*}}{\sigma_W} \bar{x}. \qquad (2.9)$$

Given the above assumptions, the participation rate and the average wage rate of a given group are a function of the mean values and the dispersions of the price of time and wage offer (i.e., potential wage) distributions. To estimate the mean value of time of housewives one has to reduce the number of parameters of the joint distribution.

Assuming that the standard deviation of the wage offer distribution is zero ($\sigma_W = 0$), i.e., that all women in a given age-education group expect the same wage rate μ_W, differences in participation behavior reflect differences in the price of time (see Figure 1). The rate of participation P within a given age-education-income group equals

$$P = \text{Prob } (W^* < \mu_W) \qquad (2.10)$$

$$= \text{Prob } \left(y = \frac{W^* - \mu_{W*}}{\sigma_{W*}} < \frac{\mu_W - \mu_{W*}}{\sigma_{W*}} = -\frac{A}{B} = Z \right).$$

[12] For a fuller explanation of (2.7) and (2.9), see the mathematical appendix.

Moreover, since $\sigma_W = 0$, the average wage rate of working women equals the mean value of the wage offer distribution $\bar{W} = \mu_W$. Thus

$$Z = -\frac{A}{B} = \frac{\mu_W - \mu_{W*}}{\sigma_{W*}} = \frac{\bar{W} - \mu_{W*}}{\sigma_{W*}}$$

or alternatively

$$\bar{W} = \mu_{W*} + Z\sigma_{W*}. \tag{2.11}$$

Observing that in income group i, P_{ij} per cent of the women belonging to potential wage group j (i.e., age-education group j) participate in the labor force, one can (using the tables of the normal distribution) generate the values of Z_{ij} satisfying Prob $(y < Z_{ij}) = P_{ij}$. Given a sufficient number of potential wage groups and assuming that the mean value of the price of time μ_{W*} and the standard deviation σ_{W*} do not vary with age and education [13] one can estimate within each group i

$$\bar{W}_{ij} = a_i + b_i Z_{ij}, \tag{2.12}$$

the constant a_i serving as the estimate of the mean value of time $\mu_{W_i^*}$ in this income group and the regression coefficient b_i serving as an estimate of the standard deviation $\sigma_{W_i^*}$.

Inserting (2.7) in (2.9) and assuming $\sigma_W = 0$,

$$\bar{y} = \frac{1}{(1 - P)\sqrt{2\Pi}} \exp\left[-\frac{1}{2}\left(\frac{\mu_{W*} - \mu_W}{\sigma_{W*}}\right)^2\right] \tag{2.13}$$

$$= \frac{1}{(1 - P)\sqrt{2\Pi}} \exp\left(-\frac{1}{2} Z^2\right).$$

Given the values of P_{ij} and Z_{ij} one can generate the value of $\bar{y}_{ij}$, and given the estimated values of $\mu_{W_i^*}$ and $\sigma_{W_i^*}$ one can estimate the average value of the housewives' time

$$\bar{W}_{ij}^* = \mu_{W_i^*} + \bar{y}_{ij}\sigma_{W_i^*} = a_i + b_i\bar{y}_{ij}. \tag{2.14}$$

Alternatively, one can assume that differences in participation behavior originate in differences in wage offers, i.e., the standard deviation of the value of time distribution within a given income group

---

[13] The assumption of intergroup independence of W and W^* is a much stronger assumption than the assumption of intragroup independence, ignoring the effect of education on the wife's nonmarket productivity (an effect discussed by [12]). Fortunately, it is not necessary for the estimation procedure. Its removal is discussed in the concluding section.

$\sigma_{W*} = 0$ (see Figure 2). The rate of participation within a given age-education-income group is

$$P = \text{Prob } (W > \mu_{W*}) = \text{Prob } \left(x = \frac{W - \mu_W}{\sigma_W} > \frac{\mu_{W*} - \mu_W}{\sigma_W} = A \right). \quad (2.15)$$

By equations (2.6) and (2.7) the average wage of working women is $\bar{W} = \mu_W + \bar{x}\sigma_W$ where

$$\bar{x} = E(x|x > y^* = A) \quad (2.16)$$

$$= \frac{1}{P\sqrt{2\Pi}} \int_A^\infty x e^{-x^2/2} \, dx = \frac{1}{P\sqrt{2\Pi}} e^{-A^2/2}$$

since $B = 0$.

Given the value of P_{ij}, one can generate the value of A_{ij} and compute the value of $\bar{x}_{ij}$. Since $\mu_W = \mu_{W*} - A\sigma_W$

$$\bar{W}_{ij} = \mu_{W_j} + \bar{x}_{ij}\sigma_{W_j} \quad (2.17)$$

$$= \mu_{W_i^*} + (\bar{x}_{ij} - A_{ij}) \sigma_{W_j} = \mu_{W_i^*} + Z_{ij}^* \sigma_{W_j}.$$

Assuming that the standard deviation of the wage offer distribution does not vary among potential wage groups, one can estimate within each income group

$$\bar{W}_{ij} = a_i + bZ_{ij}^*, \quad (2.18)$$

again, the constant is an estimate of the mean value of time μ_{W*} and the regression coefficient b is an estimate of the standard deviation of the wage offer distribution σ_W. Since it is assumed that all women within a given group have the same price of time the average price of time of housewives equals the mean price of time $\bar{W}^* = \mu_{W*}$.

FIGURE 2

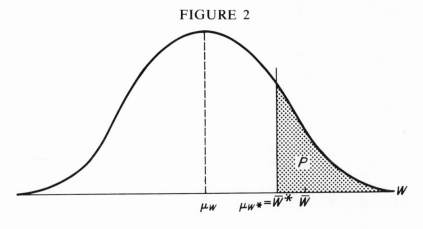

It is worth noting the difference between our two assumptions. According to the first assumption ($\sigma_W = 0$), women who work are those who have the lowest price of time, i.e., are the least productive at home, while by the second assumption ($\sigma_{W*} = 0$), women who work are those who have received the highest wage offers, i.e., are the most productive in the market. This difference carries over to the relationship between housewives' average price of time and the average market wage rate. According to the first assumption one would expect the housewives' average value of time to exceed the average wage rate of working women belonging to the same age-education-income group [$\bar{W}* = E(W*|W* > \mu_W = \bar{W}) > \bar{W}$], while by the second assumption $\bar{W}*$ falls short of $\bar{W}[\bar{W} = E(W|W > \mu_{W*} = \bar{W}*) > \bar{W}*]$. Actually it can be shown at least in the second case that it yields a lower limit for the mean value of time.

Finally, if the size of the sample does not allow a very detailed classification of potential wage groups, the number of observations might be too small to allow reliable estimates of equations (2.12) and (2.18). In this case the relationship between the mean value of time μ_{W*} and income I [i.e., $\mu_{W_i^*} = g(I_i)$] must be prespecified. Thus, if, for example, one assumes that there exists a linear relationship

$$\mu_{W_i^*} = \alpha_0 + \alpha_1 I, \tag{2.19}$$

one can estimate

$$\bar{W}_{ij} = a + b_1 I_i + b_2 Z_{ij} \tag{2.20}$$

$$\bar{W}_{ij} = a + b_1 I_i + b_3 Z_{ij}^*,$$

where $a = \text{est} (\alpha_0)$, $b_1 = \text{est} (\alpha_1)$, $b_2 = \text{est} (\sigma_{W*})$, and $b_3 = \text{est} (\sigma_W)$.

Furthermore, if one assumes that the standard deviation of the price of time varies linearly among income groups

$$\sigma_{W_i^*} = \beta_0 + \beta_1 I_i, \tag{2.21}$$

one can estimate

$$\bar{W}_{ij} = a + b_1 I_i + b_4 Z_{ij} + b_5 (Z_{ij} I_i), \tag{2.22}$$

where $a = \text{est} (\alpha_0)$, $b_1 = \text{est} (\alpha_1)$, $b_4 = \text{est} (\beta_0)$, and $b_5 = \text{est} (\beta_1)$.

THE DATA AND THE RESULTS

The data used to estimate the value of time of housewives consists of a sample survey conducted during the months January–March 1969 by the Manpower Planning Authority of the Israeli Ministry of Labor. The purpose of the study was to investigate the labor force participation of Israeli married women and the sample contained about 1,200 observations of Jewish married women aged 18–65 living in urban areas.

The sample was investigated by Ish-Shalom [8] who fitted a linear probability function to the disaggregated observations. Ish-Shalom reports that among all the variables examined he found only four that played a significant role in explaining participation. These are (in descending order of importance): wife's potential wage rate, husband's income, monthly debt payments, and the presence in the household of a child less than three years old.[14] As expected, husband's income and the presence of a young child had a discouraging effect on women's labor force participation, and participation increases with the potential wage rate and the burden of debt repayment.

To estimate the price of time, the data were classified according to 12 age-education groups [four ages (18–30, 31–40, 41–50, 50+) by three education groups (primary, secondary, and higher)][15] and six income groups (husband's regular monthly income in Israeli pounds, IL: 0–200, 201–400, 401–600, 601–800, 801–1,000, 1,001+).[16]

Finally, since the presence of young children seems to have a significant bearing on the wife's productivity at home and the value assigned to her time, the data were subdivided into two additional groups according to whether the household did or did not include children below the age of three.

There were too few potential wage groups and income groups to allow definite conclusions from the results of regressions (2.12) and (2.18). Thus equation (2.20) was estimated by adopting two alternative assumptions: (a) that the mean price of time (μ_{W*}) varies linearly with income (I), and (b) that the mean price of time varies linearly with the natural logarithm of income (ln I). A weighted regression was estimated separately for all married women, for women with a child less than three years old, and for women with no child below three (the weights being the number of working women in each cell). The results are reported in Tables 2 and 3.

[14] Ish-Shalom defined the potential wage rate as the expected wage rate of women belonging to a given age-education group. He did not attempt, however, to include in his regression both the potential wage variable and the age-education variable. Thus, part of the estimated wage effect may be attributable to tastes.

[15] It was found that age and education explain 42 per cent of the dispersion of wage rates among women who work full time. This classification of age-education groups differs somewhat from that used by Ish-Shalom.

[16] Increasing the number of income groups from six to eight (0–200, 201–400, 401–600, 601–800, 801–1,000, 1,001–1,200, 1,201–1,400, 1,400+) did not affect the results.

TABLE 2

Estimate of the Relationship Between Housewives' Value of Time and Income, Where $\mu_{W*} = \alpha_0 + \alpha_1 I$

	Adj. R^2	Constant		Income I		$Z(Z^*)$	
		a	t	b_1	t	b_2	t
Assumption I ($\sigma_W = 0$): $\bar{W} = a + b_1 I + b_2 Z$							
Total	.55	337.0	9.10	.261	5.70	75.79	4.63
Child <3	.41	379.8	6.07	.209	2.73	65.00	4.14
No child <3	.50	303.5	7.14	.287	5.44	61.99	3.11
Assumption II ($\sigma_{W*} = 0$): $\bar{W} = a + b_1 I + b_2 Z^*$							
Total	.48	234.9	5.08	.278	5.71	103.72	3.62
Child <3	.38	288.7	4.11	.215	2.74	96.86	3.89
No child <3	.45	232.0	4.34	.298	5.41	76.70	2.27

$\bar{W}$ = average monthly gross earnings of women who worked full time.
I = average monthly gross earnings of the husband.
Z and Z^* — see text (it is assumed that $Z = Z^* = 3$ when $P = 1$).

TABLE 3

Estimate of the Relationship Between Housewives' Value of Time and Income, Where $\mu_{W*} = \alpha_0 + \alpha_1 \ln I$

	Adj. R^2	Constant		Log of Income ($\ln I$)		$Z(Z^*)$	
		a	t	b_1	t	b_2	t
Assumption I ($\sigma_W = 0$): $\bar{W} = a + b_1 \ln I + b_2 Z$							
Total	.47	−280.8	−1.59 [a]	125.23	4.62	75.90	4.29
Child <3	.44	−286.7	−1.05 [a]	126.13	3.04	64.39	4.20
No child <3	.39	−326.1	−1.57 [a]	130.14	4.05	62.54	2.82
Assumption II ($\sigma_{W*} = 0$): $\bar{W} = a + b_1 \ln I + b_2 Z^*$							
Total	.39	−414.6	−2.21	132.66	4.60	99.12	3.19
Child <3	.40	−365.4	−1.29 [a]	125.33	2.92	94.24	3.84
No child <3	.33	−427.4	−1.97 [a]	136.45	4.09	74.26	1.98 [a]

[a] Not significant at the 5 per cent level.

The results of Table 2 confirm our expectations. The coefficients of I, Z, and Z^* are all positive and significant. An increase of 1 Israeli pound in the husband's gross earnings increases the value of his wife's time (if she does not work) by IL 0.2–0.3.[17] The standard deviation of the value of time, σ_{W*}, is about IL 60–75 while that of the wage offer distribution, σ_W, is about IL 75–100. The assumption that the mean value of time changes linearly with the logarithm of income (Table 3) yields estimates which are somewhat inferior in terms of explanatory power (i.e., adjusted R^2). However, the estimates of the standard deviation (σ_{W*} and σ_W) are almost identical to the ones obtained assuming a linear relationship between the mean price of time (μ_{W*}) and income (I).[18]

Relaxing the assumption that the standard deviation of the price of time σ_{W*} is constant, and allowing it to vary with income, I tried to estimate equation (2.22). Unfortunately, the results are somewhat ambiguous due to multicollinearity (the coefficient of correlation between Z and ZI exceeds 0.93). In all cases the coefficient of Z is found to be nonsignificant. Thus, assuming that the standard deviation σ_{W*} varies proportionately with income, $\sigma_{W*} = \beta_1 I$, we estimated

$$\bar{W} = a + b_1 I + b_2 ZI, \tag{3.1}$$

b_2 being an estimator of β_1. The results reported in Table 4 give some support to the hypothesis that the dispersion of the price of time within each income group increases with income, but leave intact the estimates of the effect of income on the mean price of time.

The discussion in the previous section asserts that if one assumes that all women belonging to a given age-education-income cell are homogeneous with respect to their potential wage rate (i.e., $\sigma_W = 0$) then the average price of time of housewives $\bar{W}^*$ exceeds the average wage rate of working women ($\bar{W}$) belonging to the same group. On the other hand, if all women belonging to the same group have the same price of time (i.e., $\sigma_{W*} = 0$) then W exceeds W^*. The mean price of time in the absence of market opportunities (μ_{W*}) exceeds the group's average wage rate ($\bar{W}$) if one adopts the first assumption for all those

---

[17] There exists almost no correlation between income (I) and both Z and Z^* (the correlation coefficients being about 0.1). Thus, one obtains the same income coefficient whether Z or Z^* are used in the regression.

[18] This is again an outcome of the small correlation between ln I and both Z and Z^*. Since $Z(Z^*)$ is uncorrelated with both I and ln I the coefficient of $Z(Z^*)$ should be the same whether I or ln I are included in the regressions. Thus, one obtains the same estimates (b_2) of the standard deviations.

TABLE 4

Estimate of the Relationship Between Housewives' Value of Time and Income, Where $\sigma_W = 0$ and $\sigma_{W*} = \beta_1 I$

	Adj. R^2	Constant		Income		$Z \cdot I$	
		a	t	b_1	t	b_2	t
$W = a + b_1 I + b_2(Z \cdot I)$							
Total	.57	328.9	9.13	0.267	6.00	.110	4.99
Child <3	.39	391.7	6.18	0.195	2.50	.082	3.95
No child <3	.53	306.3	7.40	0.278	5.39	.091	3.51
$\bar{W} = a + b_1 \ln I + b_2(Z \cdot I)$							
Total	.49	−311.8	−1.82 [a]	129.44	4.91	.111	4.64
Child <3	.41	−224.5	−0.80 [a]	116.84	2.74	.080	3.94
No child <3	.43	−313.3	−1.56 [a]	127.53	4.11	.095	3.35

[a] Not significant at the 5 per cent level.

groups where the rate of participation is less than 50 per cent. It falls short of $\bar{W}$ if the second assumption is used. These relationships, however, need not necessarily hold if one estimates $\bar{W}$, $\bar{W}^*$, and μ_{W*} for the population as a whole.

The average wage rate of all working women is obtained by averaging the wage rates of each group, where the weight given to the group is proportional to the number of working women in that group. To obtain an estimate of the mean price of time (μ_{W*}) one has to estimate for each group

$$\hat{\mu}_{W*} = a + b_1 I \tag{3.2}$$

and to average over all groups, where the weights are the number of women belonging to each group. To obtain an estimate of the housewives' average price of time one has to compute

$$\hat{\bar{W}}^* = \hat{\mu}_{W*} + b_2 \hat{y} \tag{3.3}$$

if one adopts the first assumption, or uses the estimate of $\hat{\mu}_{W*}$ [equation (3.2)] in the second case and averages over all groups where the weights are the number of women not participating in the labor force. The relationship between $\bar{W}$, $\bar{W}^*$, and μ_{W*} in the population is affected by the relationship within each individual group[19] as well as by the difference in the weighting schemes.

[19] The estimated relationship between $\bar{W}$, $\bar{W}^*$, and μ_{W*} may deviate from the theoretical one because of misspecifications in the assumed relationship between the mean price of time (μ_{W*}) and income [i.e., equation (2.20)].

TABLE 5

Estimates of the Value of Housewives' Time
(pounds Israeli)

	Total	Child Younger than 3	No Child Younger than 3
Labor force participation rate, P	0.357	0.307	0.380
Average wage of working women, $\bar{W}_W$	536.2	562.6	524.8
Average potential wage, $\bar{W}_T$	489.3	499.0	486.9
Housewives' potential wage, $\bar{W}_H$	470.1	470.1	468.1
Assumption I ($\sigma_W = 0$):			
Mean price of time, $\hat{\mu}_{W*}$	529.7	527.9	518.6
Price of time elasticity, $\hat{\epsilon}_{W*I}$	0.36	0.28	0.41
Price of housewives' time, $\hat{W}^*$	564.5	549.5	548.9
Price of time/wage rate ratio:			
$\hat{W}^*/\bar{W}_H$	1.20	1.17	1.17
$\hat{W}^*/\bar{W}_W$	1.05	0.98	1.05
Assumption II ($\sigma_{W*} = 0$):			
Mean price of time, $\hat{\mu}_{W*}$	441.0	440.3	457.2
Price of time elasticity, $\hat{\epsilon}_{W*I}$	0.46	0.35	0.48
Price of housewives' time, $\hat{W}^*$	438.2	437.2	455.4
Price of time/wage rate ratio:			
$\hat{W}^*/\bar{W}_H$	0.93	0.93	0.97
$\hat{W}^*/\bar{W}_W$	0.81	0.78	0.87

The estimates of $\bar{W}$, $\bar{W}^*$, and μ_{W*} are presented in Table 5.[20] Comparing the average potential wage rate (using as the weights the number of women belonging to each group) with the estimates of the mean price of time in the absence of market opportunities ($\hat{\mu}_{W*}$), it is found that the first assumption yields an estimate of $\hat{\mu}_{W*}$ that exceeds the average potential wage rate by less than 10 per cent, while the second assumption yields an estimate that falls short of the average potential wage by a similar margin (these relationships are only slightly different if one estimates $\hat{\mu}_{W*}$ separately for wives with young children and wives without young children).

Applying these estimates of the mean price of time to estimate the elasticity of the price of time with respect to income,

[20] The estimates in Table 5 are based on the assumption that the mean price of time is a linear function of income (i.e., the regression estimates presented in Table 2). Had I adopted any of the other assumptions the results would have been almost identical.

$$\epsilon_{W*I} = b_1(\bar{I}/ \mu_{W*}), \tag{3.4}$$

it is found that an increase in the husband's income by 1 per cent increases his wife's value of time (if she does not work) by 0.30–0.40 per cent. A somewhat higher estimate of the elasticity is obtained (0.35–0.50) if one adopts the second assumption ($\sigma_{W*} = 0$).

Comparing the housewives' average price of time with their potential wage rate ($\bar{W}_H$), it is found that under the first assumption ($\sigma_W = 0$) the price of time exceeds the wage rate by 20 per cent. Adopting the second assumption ($\sigma_{W*} = 0$), the price of time falls short of the potential wage by 7 per cent.

The comparison of the housewives' average price of time with the average wage of working women is affected by the two different weighting schemes used in their computation. If one assumes $\sigma_W = 0$, $\bar{W}^*$ exceeds $\bar{W}$ by no more than 5 per cent ($\bar{W}^*$ falls short of $\bar{W}$ in the case of wives with young children). On the other hand, if it is assumed that $\sigma_{W*} = 0$, then the estimated price of time of housewives falls short of the women's average wage rate by 13–22 per cent.

The income of wives with a young child is less than IL 710 while that of wives without a young child is IL 750 (the average for the population being about IL 740). These differences in income tend to offset the effect young children may have on housewives' price of time. Thus, there is almost no difference in our estimates of the average price of time of housewives with and without young children.

SOME CONCLUDING REMARKS

The results presented in the preceding section proved to be quite robust, not being much affected by changes in the assumptions about the relationships between the mean and the standard deviation of the price of time distribution (μ_{W*} and σ_{W*}) and income (I). However, one would like the estimates to pass some additional sensitivity tests before they are accepted at face value. For one, it seems advisable to remove the assumption of intergroup independence between the wage offers and the value of time (W and W^*, respectively). Allowing for an additive effect of age and education on the mean price of time, one can rewrite equation (2.19)

$$\mu_{W^*_{ij}} = \alpha_{0j} + \alpha_1 I_i \tag{4.1}$$

and estimate

$$\bar{W}_{ij} = \sum_{j=1}^{12} a_j D_j + b_1 I_i + b_2 Z_{ij} \tag{4.2}$$

and

$$\bar{W}_{ij} = \sum_{j=1}^{12} a_j D_j + b_1 I_i + b_3 Z_{ij}^*,$$

where D_j is a dummy variable presenting potential wage group j, $b_1 =$ est (α_1), $b_2 =$ est (σ_{W*}), $b_3 =$ est (σ_W), and $a_j =$ est (α_{0j}) measures the effect of age and education on the mean price of time. Secondly, one may wish to replace the normality assumption by some alternative form of distribution of W and W^* (say, the log normal).[21]

Even if the estimates passed all these sensitivity tests one would place more confidence in them if they could be compared with some other estimates in this field. Unfortunately, there are as yet no comparable studies against which the validity of the results can be tested. There is no remedy to this situation but further research.

The same procedure can of course be applied to other bodies of data. The kind of data investigated here is easily available (e.g., the 1/1,000 sample of the U.S. Bureau of the Census), and a more detailed classification should yield further insight into the factors determining the price of time. I used only the information on the rate of participation P and the average wage rate $\bar{W}$ to derive an interval estimate of the mean price of time. Additional information about the wage dispersion and the relationship between the average wage rate and income may narrow the range in which the mean price of time is to be found.

As mentioned, the housewife's price of time has considerable bearing on her purchasing, traveling, and recreational habits. One should therefore be able to find supporting evidence from studies of these areas. In evaluating such evidence, one limitation of the study must, however, be borne in mind. Throughout the study, I have ignored differences in the marginal utilities of work in the market and work at home. The possible effect of any such difference on labor force participation was attributed to the price of time. Thus, one would expect the estimates of the price of time obtained when the labor force participation decision is investigated to differ from those obtained when the investigation focuses on other decisions relating to the allocation of the housewife's time.

In summary, it is quite encouraging that the two estimates of the

---

[21] Note, however, that the assumption that within an age-education-income group W and W^* are independently normally distributed does not imply that the observed distribution of wages of working women (or the unobserved distribution of the price of time of housewives) within a group is normal (or even symmetrical). The distribution of W among working women (and the distribution of W^* among housewives within each group) are truncated distributions and hence positively skewed. Furthermore, clearly, the assumption of within-group normality does not imply over-all normality (or symmetry).

price of time of housewives did not differ too much from the average wage rate. Given our estimates, the average price of time of housewives should be found within a range of −20 to +5 per cent of the average wage of working women. The average wage rate of working women can, therefore, serve as a first approximation to the value of labor inputs in home production. However, given the importance of housewives in home production, and the share of nonmarket production in total output, one has to improve this estimate considerably to obtain reliable estimates of the imputed total economic activity. It is hoped that this paper can serve as a first step. Certain further improvements were suggested in this section. Admittedly, there is still a long way to go.

MATHEMATICAL APPENDIX

Assuming that the price of time and the potential wage rate are independently distributed with a bivariate normal distribution, the percentage of women participating in the labor force is

$$P = \text{Prob} (W > W^*) = \text{Prob} (x > A + By = y^*) \qquad (A.1)$$

$$= \frac{1}{2\Pi} \int_{-\infty}^{\infty} \int_{y*}^{\infty} e^{-(x^2+y^2)/2} dx\,dy$$

where

$$x = (W - \mu_W)/\sigma_W,$$

$$y = (W^* - \mu_{W*})/\sigma_{W*},$$

$$A = (\mu_{W*} - \mu_W)/\sigma_W,$$

$$B = (\sigma_{W*}/\sigma_W).$$

The average wage of working women equals $\bar{W} = \mu_W + \bar{x}\sigma_W$ where

$$\bar{x} = E(x|x > y^*) = \frac{1}{2\Pi P} \int_{-\infty}^{\infty} \int_{y*}^{\infty} xe^{-(x^2+y^2)/2} dx\,dy \qquad (A.2)$$

$$= \frac{1}{2\Pi P} \int_{-\infty}^{\infty} e^{-(y^2+y^{*2})/2} dy$$

$$= \frac{1}{2\Pi P} \int_{-\infty}^{\infty} \exp\left\{ -\frac{1}{2} [A^2 + 2ABy + (B^2 + 1)y^2] \right\} dy$$

$$= \frac{1}{2\Pi P} \int_{-\infty}^{\infty} \exp\left\{ -\frac{1}{2} \left[(B^2 + 1) \left(y + \frac{AB}{B^2 + 1} \right)^2 + \frac{A^2}{B^2 + 1} \right] \right\} dy$$

$$= \frac{1}{2\Pi P} \left(\frac{2\Pi}{B^2+1}\right)^{1/2} \exp\left\{-\frac{1}{2} [A^2/(B^2+1)]\right\}$$

$$= \frac{1}{P} [2\Pi(B^2+1)]^{-(1/2)} \exp\left\{-\frac{1}{2} [A^2/(B^2+1)]\right\}$$

$$= \frac{1}{P} \left[2\Pi \frac{\sigma_W^2 + \sigma_{W*}^2}{\sigma_W^2}\right]^{-(1/2)} \exp\left[-\frac{1}{2} (\mu_{W*} - \mu_W)^2/(\sigma_W^2 + \sigma_{W*}^2)\right].$$

The average price of time of housewives equals $\bar{W}^* = \mu_{W*} + \bar{y}\sigma_{W*}$ where

$$\bar{y} = E(y|y^* > x) = E\left[y\Big|y > \frac{1}{B}(x-A) = x^*\right] \tag{A.3}$$

$$= \frac{1}{2\Pi(1-P)} \int_{-\infty}^{\infty} \int_{x^*}^{\infty} y e^{-(x^2+y^2)/2} dy dx$$

$$= \frac{1}{2\Pi(1-P)} \int_{-\infty}^{\infty} e^{-(x^2+x^{*2})/2} dx$$

$$= \frac{1}{2\Pi(1-P)} \int_{-\infty}^{\infty} \exp\left\{-\frac{1}{2B^2} [A^2 - 2Ax + (B^2+1)x^2]\right\} dx$$

$$= \frac{1}{2\Pi(1-P)} \int_{-\infty}^{\infty} \exp\left\{-\frac{1}{2B^2} \left[(B^2+1)\left(x - \frac{A}{B^2+1}\right)^2 + \frac{A^2 B^2}{B^2+1}\right]\right\} dx$$

$$= \frac{1}{2\Pi(1-P)} \left(\frac{2\Pi B^2}{B^2+1}\right)^{1/2} \exp\left(-\frac{1}{2} \frac{A^2}{B^2+1}\right)$$

$$= \frac{B}{1-P} [2\Pi(B^2+1)]^{-1/2} \exp\left[-\frac{A^2}{2(B^2+1)}\right]$$

$$= \frac{1}{1-P} \left(2\Pi \frac{\sigma_W^2 + \sigma_{W*}^2}{\sigma_{W*}^2}\right)^{-1/2} \exp\left[-\frac{1}{2} \frac{(\mu_{W*} - \mu_W)^2}{\sigma_W^2 + \sigma_{W*}^2}\right]$$

$$= \frac{P}{1-P} \frac{\sigma_{W*}}{\sigma_W} \bar{x} = \frac{P}{1-P} B\bar{x}.$$

P is a function of A and B. An increase in A results in a decrease in P:

$$\frac{\partial P}{\partial A} = \frac{\partial}{\partial A} \left[\frac{1}{2\Pi} \int_{-\infty}^{\infty} \int_{A+By}^{\infty} e^{-(x^2+y^2)/2} dx dy\right] \tag{A.4}$$

$$= -\frac{1}{2\Pi} \int_{-\infty}^{\infty} e^{-[(A+By)^2 + y^2]/2} dy = -P\bar{x} < 0,$$

since $\bar{x} > 0$. An increase in B results in an increase in P:

$$\frac{\partial P}{\partial B} = \frac{\partial}{\partial B}\left[\frac{1}{2\Pi}\int_{-\infty}^{\infty}\int_{A+By}^{\infty} e^{-(x^2+y^2)/2}dxdy\right] \tag{A.5}$$

$$= -\frac{1}{2\Pi}\int_{-\infty}^{\infty} ye^{-[(A+By)^2+y^2]/2}dy$$

$$= \frac{1}{(B^2+1)2\Pi}\ e^{-[(A+By)^2+y^2]/2}\ \Big|_{-\infty}^{\infty}$$

$$+ \frac{AB}{(B^2+1)2\Pi}\int_{-\infty}^{\infty} e^{-[(A+By)^2+y^2]/2}dy = \frac{AB}{B^2+1}\ P\bar{x} > 0,$$

since in general $A > 0$, P being smaller than 50 per cent.

Similarly, one can compute the changes of $\bar{x}$ with respect to A and B

$$\frac{\partial \bar{x}}{\partial A} = -\bar{x}\left(\frac{\partial P/\partial A}{P} + \frac{A}{B^2+1}\right) = \bar{x}\left(\bar{x} - \frac{A}{B^2+1}\right) \tag{A.6}$$

and

$$\frac{\partial \bar{x}}{\partial B} = -\bar{x}\left[\frac{\partial P/\partial B}{P} + \frac{B}{B^2+1} - \frac{A^2B}{(B^2+1)^2}\right]$$

$$= \frac{B\bar{x}}{B^2+1}\left(\frac{A^2}{B^2+1} - A\bar{x} - 1\right).$$

Finally, changes in A and B affect also $\bar{y}$:

$$d\bar{y} = \bar{y}\left[\frac{dP}{P(1-P)} + \frac{dB}{B} + \frac{d\bar{x}}{\bar{x}}\right]. \tag{A.7}$$

Given the values of P and $\bar{W}$, a change in the assumptions about B calls for a compensating change in the assumptions about A. For example, let us assume that σ_W is given and that the value of σ_{W*} is overestimated by $d\sigma_{W*}$. Since P is given,

$$dP = \frac{\partial P}{\partial \sigma_{W*}}\ d\sigma_{W*} + \frac{\partial P}{\partial(\mu_{W*} - \mu_W)}\ d(\mu_{W*} - \mu_W) \tag{A.8}$$

$$= \frac{\partial P}{\partial B}\frac{\partial B}{\partial \sigma_{W*}}\ d\sigma_{W*} + \frac{\partial P}{\partial A}\frac{\partial A}{\partial(\mu_{W*} - \mu_W)}\ d(\mu_{W*} - \mu_W) = 0.$$

Thus,

$$d(\mu_{W*} - \mu_W) = -\frac{\dfrac{\partial P}{\partial B}\dfrac{\partial B}{\partial \sigma_{W*}}}{\dfrac{\partial P}{\partial A}\dfrac{\partial A}{(\mu_{W*} - \mu_W)}} d\sigma_{W*} \qquad \text{(A.9)}$$

$$= -\frac{\dfrac{AB}{B^2+1}\dfrac{P\bar{x}}{\sigma_W}}{-\dfrac{P\bar{x}}{\sigma_W}} d\sigma_{W*} = \frac{AB}{B^2+1} d\sigma_{W*}.$$

Given the overestimate in $d\sigma_{W*}$ and the compensating overestimate in $d(\mu_{W*} - \mu_W)$ the estimate of $\bar{x}$ should change by

$$d\bar{x} = \frac{\partial \bar{x}}{\partial \sigma_{W*}} d\sigma_{W*} + \frac{\partial \bar{x}}{\partial(\mu_{W*} - \mu_W)} d(\mu_{W*} - \mu_W) \qquad \text{(A.10)}$$

$$= \left[\frac{\partial \bar{x}}{\partial B}\frac{\partial B}{\partial \sigma_{W*}} + \frac{\partial \bar{x}}{\partial A}\frac{\partial A}{\partial(\mu_{W*} - \mu_W)}\frac{d(\mu_{W*} - \mu_W)}{d\sigma_{W*}}\right] d\sigma_{W*}$$

$$= \frac{d\sigma_{W*}}{\sigma_W}\left[\frac{B\bar{x}}{B^2+1}\left(\frac{A^2}{B^2+1} - A\bar{x} - 1\right) + \frac{AB}{B^2+1}\bar{x}\left(\bar{x} - \frac{A}{B^2+1}\right)\right]$$

$$= -\frac{B\bar{x}}{B^2+1}\frac{d\sigma_{W*}}{\sigma_W}.$$

Since $\bar{W}$ is given:

$$d\bar{W} = d\mu_W + \sigma_W d\bar{x} + \bar{x}d\sigma_W = d\mu_W + \sigma_W d\bar{x} = 0. \qquad \text{(A.11)}$$

Hence an overestimate of σ_{W*} by $d\sigma_{W*}$ results in an overestimate of μ_W by

$$d\mu_W = -\sigma_W d\bar{x} = \frac{B\bar{x}}{B^2+1} d\sigma_{W*} > 0, \qquad \text{(A.12)}$$

and an overestimate of μ_{W*} by

$$d\mu_{W*} = d\mu_W + d(\mu_{W*} - \mu_W) = \left(\frac{B\bar{x}}{B^2+1} + \frac{AB}{B^2+1}\right) d\sigma_{W*} \qquad \text{(A.13)}$$

$$= \frac{B}{B^2+1}(A + \bar{x})d\sigma_{W*} > 0.$$

The same change affects the average price of time of housewives by

$$d\bar{W}^* = d\mu_{W*} + \sigma_{W*}d\bar{y} + \bar{y}d\sigma_{W*}. \qquad \text{(A.14)}$$

By equations (A.3), (A.7), and (A.9),

$$d\bar{y} = \bar{y}\left(\frac{\partial B/\partial\sigma_{W*}}{B} + \frac{\partial\bar{x}/\partial\sigma_{W*}}{\bar{x}}\right)d\sigma_{W*} = \frac{P}{1-P}\frac{B\bar{x}}{B^2+1}\frac{d\sigma_{W*}}{\sigma_{W*}}, \quad \text{(A.15)}$$

and hence

$$d\bar{W}^* = \left[\frac{B}{B^2+1}\left(A + \frac{\bar{x}}{1-P}\right) + \bar{y}\right]d\sigma_{W*} > 0. \quad \text{(A.16)}$$

Thus, an underestimate of σ_{W*}, yields an underestimate of both μ_{W*} and $\bar{W}^*$. In particular, the assumption $\sigma_{W*} = 0$ yields an underestimate of the mean price of time and housewives' average price of time.

Assuming that σ_{W*} is given and that the value of σ_W is overestimated by $d\sigma_W$, and since P is given

$$dP = \frac{\partial P}{\partial\sigma_W}d\sigma_W + \frac{\partial P}{\partial(\mu_{W*} - \mu_W)}d(\mu_{W*} - \mu_W) \quad \text{(A.17)}$$

$$= \left(\frac{\partial P}{\partial A}\frac{\partial A}{\partial\sigma_W} + \frac{\partial P}{\partial B}\frac{\partial B}{\partial\sigma_W}\right)d\sigma_W + \frac{\partial P}{\partial A}\frac{\partial A}{\partial(\mu_{W*} - \mu_W)}d(\mu_{W*} - \mu_W) = 0.$$

Thus,

$$d(\mu_{W*} - \mu_W) = -\frac{\dfrac{\partial P}{\partial A}\dfrac{\partial A}{\partial\sigma_W} + \dfrac{\partial P}{\partial B}\dfrac{\partial B}{\partial\sigma_W}}{\dfrac{\partial P}{\partial A}\dfrac{\partial A}{\partial(\mu_{W*} - \mu_W)}}d\sigma_W \quad \text{(A.18)}$$

$$= -\frac{\dfrac{P\bar{x}}{\sigma_W}\left(A - \dfrac{AB^2}{B^2+1}\right)}{-\dfrac{P\bar{x}}{\sigma_W}}d\sigma_W = \frac{A}{B^2+1}d\sigma_W.$$

Given the overestimate in $d\sigma_{W*}$ and the compensating overestimate in $d(\mu_{W*} - \mu_W)$ the estimate of $\bar{x}$ should change by

$$d\bar{x} = \frac{\partial\bar{x}}{\partial\sigma_W}d\sigma_W + \frac{\partial\bar{x}}{\partial(\mu_{W*} - \mu_W)}d(\mu_{W*} - \mu_W) \quad \text{(A.19)}$$

$$= \left\{\frac{\partial\bar{x}}{\partial A}\left[\frac{\partial A}{\partial\sigma_W} + \frac{\partial A}{\partial(\mu_{W*} - \mu_W)}\frac{d(\mu_{W*} - \mu_W)}{d\sigma_W}\right] + \frac{\partial\bar{x}}{\partial B}\frac{\partial B}{\partial\sigma_W}\right\}d\sigma_W$$

$$= \left[\bar{x}\left(\bar{x} - \frac{A}{B^2+1}\right)\left(\frac{A}{B^2+1} - A\right) - \frac{B^2\bar{x}}{B^2+1}\left(\frac{A^2}{B^2+1} - A\bar{x} - 1\right)\right]\frac{d\sigma_W}{\sigma_W}$$

$$= \frac{B^2\bar{x}}{B^2+1}\frac{d\sigma_W}{\sigma_W}.$$

Since $\bar{W}$ is given,

$$d\bar{W} = d\mu_W + \sigma_W d\bar{x} + \bar{x}d\sigma_W = 0.$$

Hence, an overestimate of σ_W by $d\sigma_W$ results in an underestimate of μ_W by

$$d\mu_W = -(\sigma_W d\bar{x} + \bar{x}d\sigma_W) = -\bar{x}\left(\frac{B^2}{B^2+1}+1\right)d\sigma_W < 0 \quad \text{(A.20)}$$

and a change of μ_{W*} of

$$d\mu_{W*} = d\mu_W + d(\mu_{W*} - \mu_W) \quad\quad\quad\quad\quad \text{(A.21)}$$

$$= \left[-\bar{x}\left(\frac{B^2}{B^2+1}+1\right) + \frac{A}{B^2+1}\right]d\sigma_W$$

$$= [A - (2B^2+1)\bar{x}]\frac{d\sigma_W}{B^2+1}.$$

$$d\bar{y} = \bar{y}\left(\frac{\partial B/\partial \sigma_W}{B} + \frac{\partial\bar{x}/\partial\sigma_W}{\bar{x}}\right)d\sigma_W = -\frac{\bar{y}}{B^2+1}\frac{d\sigma_W}{\sigma_W}. \quad \text{(A.22)}$$

Hence,

$$d\bar{W}^* = d\mu_{W*} + \sigma_{W*}d\bar{y} = [A - (2B^2+1)\bar{x} - B\bar{y}]\frac{d\sigma_W}{B^2+1}. \quad \text{(A.23)}$$

It seems to me that the terms in (A.21) and (A.23) are always negative and, hence, the estimates based on the assumption $\sigma_{W*} = 0$ are upper limits of σ_{W*} and $\bar{W}^*$, but I cannot prove it. Note, however, that when $\sigma_W = 0$

$$d\mu_{W*} = d\bar{W}^* = -2\bar{x}d\sigma_W < 0, \quad\quad\quad \text{(A.24)}$$

i.e., μ_{W*} and $\bar{W}^*$ are local maximums.

REFERENCES

1. Becker, G. S. "A Theory of the Allocation of Time." *Economic Journal,* September 1965, pp. 493–517.
2. Ben-Porath, Y. "Labor Force Participation Rates and the Supply of Labor." Harvard Institute of Economic Research, Discussion Paper No. 206, September 1971.
3. Denison, E. F. *The Sources of Economic Growth in the United States and the Alternatives Before Us.* Committee for Economic Development, Supplementary Paper No. 13, January 1962.
4. Diewert, H. E. "Choice of Labor Markets and the Theory of the Allocation of Time." 1971. Mimeograph.

5. Ghez, G. R. *A Theory of Life Cycle Consumption.* Ph.D. dissertation, Columbia University, 1970.
6. Gronau, R. "Information and Frictional Unemployment." *American Economic Review,* June 1971.
7. ———. "The Intra Family Allocation of Time: The Value of the Housewives' Time." *American Economic Review,* forthcoming.
8. Ish-Shalom, J. *Married Women's Participation in the Labor Force.* Manpower Planning Authority of the Ministry of Labour, Jerusalem, 1970.
9. Johnson, M. B. "Travel Time and the Price of Leisure." *Western Economic Journal,* Spring 1966, pp. 135–145.
10. Lancaster, K. J. "A New Approach to Consumer Theory." *Journal of Political Economy,* April 1966, pp. 132–157.
11. Lundberg, G. A., M. Komarovsky, and M. A. McInerny. *Leisure, A Suburban Study.* New York, Columbia University Press, 1934.
12. Michael, R. *Education and Consumption Patterns.* New York, NBER, forthcoming.
13. Morgan, J. N., I. A. Sirageldin, and N. Barewaldt. *Productive Americans.* Ann Arbor, University of Michigan Press, 1966.
14. Moses, L. N., and H. F. Williamson Jr. "Value of Time, Choice of Mode, and the Subsidy Issue in Urban Transportation." *Journal of Political Economy,* June 1963.
15. Nordhaus, W., and J. Tobin. "Is Growth Obsolete?"—in this volume; see below.
16. Sirageldin, I. A. *Non-Market Components of National Income.* Ann Arbor, University of Michigan Press, 1969.
17. Szalai, A. "Multinational Comparative Social Research." *American Behavioral Scientist,* December 1966.
18. U.S. Bureau of the Census. *Statistical Abstract of the United States, 1966.*

COMMENT

GILBERT R. GHEZ, University of Chicago and National Bureau of Economic Research

Gronau offers an ingenious and promising procedure for estimating an important but essentially unobservable variable, namely, the value of time of housewives. I applaud this attempt, and hope that in time the procedure will be implemented more widely, with different data sets, for other groups (for instance, teen-agers and retired persons) and with additional refinements.

Gronau proposes a procedure such that with only two data sets—data on labor force participation and the average wage rate—he can get estimates of the mean value of time of those who do not work.

Quite correctly, he calls to our attention that wives who work are either those who are the most productive in the market or those who are the least productive at home. According to the first interpretation, the mean price of time of housewives would be smaller than the average wage rate of working women, while according to the second, the mean price of time would exceed the average wage rate.

Structurally, the problem is the same as the following. Consider an industry producing a given product. For any given demand conditions, are those firms in the industry those which are the most efficient at producing this good, or are they the firms which are the least efficient at producing other goods?

There are several problems connected with the particulars of Gronau's application. In the first place, the sole income variable entered in the regressions to explain the price of time of housewives is the regular income of the husband. Presumably, this variable includes both his earnings and his portion of family nonwage income. These two components have, however, rather different effects on the price of time of housewives. Leaving aside intertemporal planning considerations, to which I will return in a moment, a 1 per cent difference in property income may have very different effects from a 1 per cent difference in the wage rate. Indeed, while a rise in property income would raise her price of time (as long as her home time were normal), a rise in his wage rate, aside from the income effect, would induce substitution toward or against her time depending on whether her home time and his were substitutes or complements. With a sufficient degree of complementarity between these nonmarket times, a rise in the husband's wage rate could even produce a negative effect on the price of time of the wife. The estimates produced by Gronau mix both the effect of changes in nonwage income and that of changes in the husband's wage rate. It would be desirable if in future work these effects could be disentangled.

My second comment relates to the need to embed the model in a general intertemporal planning framework. From that point of view, one would expect variations in the price of time independent of variations in the husband's wage rate or of the presence of children. Indeed, as long as all productivities and income streams were perfectly anticipated, a positive rate of interest (net of time preference) would in itself induce substitution toward future consumption, thereby raising the demand for future home time relative to present home time. In other words, it would have been appropriate to have an age variable in the regression to capture the effect of a positive rate of interest (net of time preference), as well as the effect of changes in nonmarket productivity which are not correlated with the presence of young children. Alternatively, it would have been better if the estimation was done for a given age group rather than over the whole population.

My third comment addresses itself to the treatment of children. The children variable is introduced as a control, and yet children themselves are not exogenous, but rather are produced by parents with a certain degree of control. In fertility studies we take the price of time (the wage rate) as exogenous, while in this study, as in labor force studies, one takes children as exogenous. Some day, I hope, a fully integrated model will be developed.

Fourth comment. The empirical procedure rules out all fixed costs resulting from engaging in market activities. There are no commuting costs, no time "lost" in switching activities. Were these incorporated into the analysis, the condition $W > W^*$ (with W^* evaluated at an income net of the fixed costs) would still be a necessary condition but would no longer be a sufficient condition for entry into the market. Sufficiently high transaction costs could make a potential participant better off by staying at home. Since these fixed costs vary in a systematic way across income groups, the estimates produced by Gronau are biased on this account. I hope this difficulty can be remedied in future work.

Finally, I find little comfort that ". . . the two estimates of the price of time of housewives did not differ too much from the average wage rate . . . ; the average price of time of housewives should be found within a range of −20 to +5 per cent of the average wage of working women," as Gronau puts it. That range in itself is not so narrow, and moreover the estimates were obtained under the implausible assumption that the price of time of a housewife is independent of her age and education. Although the evidence is still scanty, one may presume that investment in education by women raises not only their potential earnings but also their nonmarket efficiency. Some work has been done to estimate the nonmarket returns to males' education. Robert Michael estimates that the elasticity of real full income with respect to the education of males is positive, and may be as high as 0.5. Presumably, the effects are even stronger for housewives since they spend more time in the home than men do. May we soon have Gronau's revised estimates.

An Imputation to the Measure of Economic
Growth for Changes in Life Expectancy

DAN USHER

QUEEN'S UNIVERSITY

ONE of the principal uses of national income statistics is to determine whether and to what extent people are becoming better off over time. For instance, the central piece of evidence cited by Pearson in *Partners in Development* [1] to support his case that poor countries need more aid than they are getting is a table showing growth rates of real GNP per head of rich and poor countries to be 3.6 and 2.5 per cent, respectively, over the years 1960–67. The argument is that the disparity in growth rates, if it continues, will in time prove detrimental to rich and poor countries alike, and that aid is a means of reducing the disparity.

I am not concerned in this paper with Pearson's argument per se but with the role of statistics in that argument. To serve as evidence in the kind of case Pearson is making, income statistics must reflect well-being, and it must be at least approximately true that people are better off in countries where incomes are high than in countries where incomes are low. From this it follows that the scope of income should be comprehensive, for if a substantial component of well-being is excluded from income and if that component of well-being grows at different rates in different countries, then it may happen that income as conventionally measured grows faster in country A than in country B despite the fact that people in country B are becoming relatively better off.

The aspect of well-being that is to be examined in this paper is longevity. If you ask a man whether he prefers economic conditions as they are today to those of fifty or a hundred years ago, he would prob-

NOTE: I am grateful to Ruth Simonton of Statistics Canada and to Philip Smith, a graduate student at Queen's University, for developing the computer program. Philip Smith also assisted me ably in searching for and processing data. This study has been financed in part by the Canada Council and in part by Statistics Canada.

[1] L. B. Pearson, *Partners in Development,* Pall Mall Press, 1969, p. 55.

ably answer that he prefers conditions as they are today, and his preference might well have less to do with the material things we possess than
with the fact that we live longer. He may add that he might not have
survived to his present age had his date of birth been pushed back fifty
or a hundred years to a time when mortality rates in infancy and childhood were very much higher than they are now. In Canada, from 1926
to 1968, the infant mortality rate fell from about 1 in 10 to about 1 in 50
and the mortality rate of children aged 1 to 4 fell from 1 in 100 to 1 in
1,000. It is possible that no increase in goods and services would induce
us to accept a return of mortality rates as they were as recently as 1926.

One can understand why the increase in life expectancy is not normally included as an element in the measure of economic growth. Life
expectancy, or the mortality rates from which it is composed, is a peculiar
commodity. Mortality rates are partly private goods and partly public
goods, partly purchased and partly free, and some expenditures tending
to increase life expectancy are already included in the accounts so that
an imputation for increased life expectancy would result in double counting if the rest of the national accounts were left unchanged. The imputation would constitute a major departure from the convention that only
marketable or potentially marketable items be included in the national
accounts. That convention is appropriate for statistics designed as an aid
in determining fiscal or monetary policy, and the decision to impute for
increased life expectancy would involve us in having to keep two time
series of income statistics, one for stabilization policy and another as a
social indicator.

The first step in the development of an imputation for increased life
expectancy is to make life expectancy commensurate with the rest of the
data in the national accounts. Like any value, the value of increased life
expectancy must be amenable to representation as the product of a
quantity and a price. Quantities present no difficulty because age-specific
mortality rates may be looked upon as though they were quantities, and
we have adequate historical data on age-specific mortality rates for many
countries.

The difficulty is in determining price. The price data do not come
ready-made from the national statistical offices as do the data on mortality
rates, but we may draw on a fairly extensive and growing body of
economic literature on the value of life; for the price that is required
to construct an imputation in the accounts is the same price that is appropriate in cost-benefit analysis of medical expenditure, road safety, and
the like.

At the outset of this discussion, it is important to distinguish between three questions which are perhaps related but which are nonetheless distinct. The first of these, which might be called the insurance question, is "What is my life worth to my wife and children?"; and the expected answer is "A sum of money that would enable my wife and children to be as well off financially in the event of my death as they would be if I remained alive." The second, which might be called the birth control question, is "How much better or worse off would the community at large be if I ceased to exist or if I had never been born?" The answer to this question might well be that the rest of you would be better off financially without me. The third question, which is the true "valuation-of-life question," is "How much would I pay to avoid a small probability of my death?" If I were prepared to pay $500 to avoid a 1 in 1,000 probability of death through disease or accident, then it might be said that my valuation of my life is $500,000. The valuation of life in the community is some average of the valuations of individuals. Whatever the answer to the valuation-of-life question, that answer is distinct from the answers to the insurance question and the birth control question.

Dublin and Lotka,[2] though by no means the first to examine these issues, are generally taken as the starting point for modern work. It is significant that they were employees of an insurance company. Their problem was to determine the amount of insurance a man ought to carry. They computed the difference between the present value of a man's earnings and the present value of his consumption and called that difference the value of his life. Given their purpose, their procedure was correct to the best of my knowledge.

Recently, Dublin and Lotka's methods have been used for an altogether different purpose. Weisbrod, Klarman, Fein, Rice, and others[3] have dealt with the problem of determining the cost of disease. The cost of a disease is the sum of direct cost, including medical expenditures and loss of a man's earnings while he is alive, and indirect cost, which these authors take to be the present value of the forgone earnings of the men who die of the disease.[4] The general principle in these computations

[2] Louis I. Dublin and Alfred J. Lotka, *The Money Value of a Man,* Ronald Press, 1946.

[3] The recent history of attempts to evaluate the costs of disease is presented in J. A. Dowie, "Valuing the Benefits of Health Improvement," *Australian Economic Papers,* June 1970, pp. 21–41. A useful bibliography is included.

[4] There is an interesting discussion in Dowie's article of whether the present value of a man's consumption should be deducted from the present value of his income in computing the value of his life, a problem which is symptomatic of the confusion over the interpretation of the phrase "value of life."

is that declines in mortality rates can be evaluated according to the forgone earnings of the dead. The principle, if correct, would provide us with a simple way of evaluating the historical decline in mortality rates. In my opinion the principle is incorrect, because it supplies the right answer to the wrong question. It answers the insurance question in place of the value-of-life question. The present value of the forgone earnings of the dead is the right amount of insurance for a man to carry, but it is not indicative of the amount of money he would pay to avoid a small risk of losing his life, and it is not indicative of the amount of money rational men would be prepared to pay to eradicate a disease.[5]

A man who has insured his life for the full value that Dublin and Lotka have put upon it is not indifferent to whether he lives or dies, and the value he puts on his life in forestalling risks of losing it may be greater or less than the amount of his insurance.

The use of discounted future income as a measure of the value of one's life is sometimes justified on the grounds that one's earnings are a measure of one's value to the rest of the community. This is a confusion between the valuation of life question and the birth control question. A consensus has emerged in the literature on the cost-benefit analysis of birth control that the benefits derived from preventing a birth are very great and that the eventual per capita income of the community is a decreasing function of the birth rate. The reason is the Malthusian one that the smaller the population, the greater the capital-labor ratio. This argument applies with less force to adults than to unborn children, but it applies nonetheless. Imagine a family complete with children and all heirs destroyed in an automobile accident. Notwithstanding the loss of forgone earnings, this event makes the rest of us better off because we acquire title to all the family's assets including their rights to use schools and other public property. By definition, if the family is typical, any excess of its earnings over its consumption would accrue to its heirs and not to the rest of us. There is some dislocation in the economy if a departure is less orderly, but there is no reason to suppose that the costs to the survivors of having people go separately rather than in families outweighs the effect of a man's death

---

[5] My views on this issue are very close to those of Thomas Schelling, "The Life You Save May Be Your Own," in S. Chase, ed., *Problems in Public Expenditure Analysis,* Brookings, 1968, pp. 127–161. A more complete exposition of this approach to life saving is contained in E. J. Mishan, "Evaluation of Life and Limb: A Theoretical Approach," *Journal of Political Economy,* July–August 1971, pp. 687–705. Mishan evaluates the saving of lives by means of the concept of consumer surplus and, formally at least, incorporates externalities into the analysis, but he makes no attempt to specify functional forms of his curves or to produce numerical estimates.

on the capital-labor ratio. Certainly we are concerned as a community to keep each other alive but that concern is based on something other than the maximization of GNP, in total or per head.

To equate the value of life to discounted earnings forgone is to suppose that the lives of housewives and old people are worthless. In one sense this is quite true. Dublin and Lotka's calculations would imply that old people and wives ought not to carry insurance, and this may well be the case. It is not the case that old people and wives place no value on prolonging their lives or that society as a whole is unconcerned with the matter.

The present value of earnings is not a measure of the value of a man's life, in the sense of reflecting the amount of money a man would spend to reduce age-specific mortality rates. To find a value of life for converting reductions in age-specific mortality rates into an imputation in the national accounts, we need to consider carefully what it is that is maximized in expenditures to reduce age-specific mortality rates and to seek evidence on what people actually pay for this purpose. We begin with an examination of utility maximization in circumstances where the length of life is variable. Then we attempt to generalize the concept of income to incorporate changes in mortality rates as benefits. Finally, on the strength of some very crude assumptions, we construct an imputation for the increase in life expectancy, and compare growth rates of income with that imputation and without it.

MAXIMIZATION OF UTILITY WITH A LENGTH-OF-LIFE VARIABLE

Ignore the fact that men live in families and that families are imbedded in communities of people who are concerned with each other's well-being. Suppose instead that each man seeks to maximize his own welfare represented by the function

$$U = U(U_0, P_0, U_1, P_1, \ldots, U_n, P_n), \tag{1}$$

where U is his welfare in the present circumstances, P_i is the probability of his living for exactly i years, U_i is his welfare if he lives for exactly i years, and n is the postulated upper limit to the length of his life. The probabilities must sum to 1.

$$\sum_{i=0}^{n} P_i = 1. \tag{2}$$

Values of the terms U_t, P_t, and n depend on a man's age. If the maximum length of life is assumed to be 90 years, the n relevant to a 50-year-old man is 40. The value of P_{10} for a 50-year-old man depends on mortality rates between age 50 and age 60; the value of P_{10} for a 60-year-old man depends on mortality rates between age 60 and age 70, and so on. In deriving an imputation for the national accounts, values of U will have to be averaged over the age distribution of the population.

The utility function, U_t, corresponding to a life of t years depends on consumption in each of those years

$$U_t = U_t (C_0, C_1, C_2, \ldots, C_{t-1}), \tag{3}$$

where C_0 is consumption in the current year, and C_i is consumption in the year i.

The functions (1), (2), and (3) form a discrete representation of what is in reality a continuous process. It is convenient to think of consumption C_i as evenly spread out over the year i, and of death occurring if at all on the first day of the year. It is as though the whole risk of dying in a year were concentrated on one's birthday. A man alive in the year 0 is presumed safe until the first day of the year 1, and if he survives that day he is safe again until the first day of the year 2, and so on.

It is useful to define two additional mortality variables: D_t is the mortality rate t years hence, and S_t is the probability of surviving up to the year t. The variables P_t, D_t, and S_t are related by the formulas

$$S_t = \prod_{j=0}^{t-1} (1 - D_j); \tag{4}$$

$$P_t = D_t S_t = D_t \left[\prod_{j=0}^{t-1} (1 - D_j) \right]. \tag{5}$$

Obviously, $0 < D_t < 1$, $0 < P_t < 1$, and $0 < S_t < 1$, and $D_n = 1$ if n is the maximum length of life.[6]

---

[6] Equations (2) and (5) are consistent as long as $D_n = 1$. From equation (4) it follows that $S_t = S_{t-1} - D_{t-1} S_{t-1}$ for all values of t.

$$\sum_{t=0}^{n} P_t = \sum_{t=0}^{n} D_t S_t = D_n S_n + \sum_{t=0}^{n-1} D_t S_t$$

$$= S_{n-1} - D_{n-1} S_{n-1} + \sum_{t=0}^{n-1} D_t S_t$$

$$= S_{n-1} + \sum_{t=0}^{n-2} D_t S_t$$

$$= S_{n-2} + \sum_{t=0}^{n-3} D_t S_t$$

$$= S_1 + D_0 S_0 = S_0 = 1.$$

The utility functions can be expected to have the following properties:

$$\frac{\partial U_t}{\partial C_i} > 0 \text{ for all } i < t \tag{6}$$

$$\frac{\partial U}{\partial U_t} > 0 \tag{7}$$

$$\frac{\partial U}{\partial D_t} < 0. \tag{8}$$

These properties jointly imply that a man thinks himself better off if consumption in any year is increased or if his probability of dying in any given year is reduced. For simplicity we are also assuming that the consumption C_t takes on the same value in every utility function U_j in which it appears.

The assumptions represented by the inequalities (6), (7), and (8) are reasonable and for the most part innocuous, but they are not strong enough to connect the theory to the available data so as to permit us to incorporate an imputation for increased life expectancy into the statistics of economic growth. As a first step toward constructing this imputation, let it be assumed that the utility function of equation (1) takes the special form

$$U = \sum_{t=0}^{n} P_t U_t. \tag{1'}$$

This specification which we shall refer to as "the expected utility assumption" fits exactly into the terms of reference of the "states of the world" approach to the theory of choice under uncertainty. All possible lengths of life t correspond to mutually exclusive states of the world and the P_t are probabilities of their occurrence.[7] It is a well-known property of utility functions of this sort that they are cardinal rather than ordinal and may be defined up to a linear transformation;[8] given values of any two utility functions U_i and U_j for the years i and j and for any given time paths of consumption, all values of all utility functions U_t for all years t and all time paths of consumption could be determined by a conceptual experiment of the sort used to determine the shape of an ordinary indifference curve.

[7] See J. Hirshleifer, "Investment Decisions Under Uncertainty," *Quarterly Journal of Economics*, November 1965 and May 1966.

[8] For a justification of this assertion see Robert D. Luce and H. Raiffa, *Games and Decisions*, Wiley, 1957, Chap. 2.

The price a man would pay for a reduction in any age-specific mortality rate may be derived from his utility function. Taking current consumption as the numeraire, the value of a reduction in the mortality rate of the year t is[9]

$$-\frac{\partial C_0}{\partial D_t} = \frac{\sum_{j=t}^{n} \frac{P_j}{1 - D_t} (U_j - U_t)}{\sum_{j=1}^{n} P_j \frac{\partial U_j}{\partial C_0}}, \tag{9}$$

which is independent of the two arbitrary values used to establish a scale for the utility function U, because these values cancel out between the numerator and the denominator of equation (9).

In principle, the value of a reduction in any age-specific mortality rate could be determined from equation (9) if the right conceptual experiment were performed to determine the shape of U. No attempt at such an experiment is made in this paper.[10] Instead we postulate the general shape of the function U_t and endow the function with a parameter the value of which may be determined from independent evidence on, or

[9]
$$\frac{\partial C_0}{\partial D_t}\bigg|_U = \frac{\partial U}{\partial D_t} \div \frac{\partial U}{\partial C_0}$$

$$\frac{\partial U}{\partial C_0} = \sum_{j=0}^{n} \frac{\partial U}{\partial U_j} \frac{\partial U_j}{\partial C_0} = \sum_{j=0}^{n} P_j \frac{\partial U_j}{\partial C_0}$$

$$\frac{\partial U}{\partial D_t} = \sum_{j=0}^{n} \frac{\partial U}{\partial P_j} \frac{\partial P_j}{\partial D_t}$$

$$= \sum_{j=t}^{n} U_j \frac{\partial P_j}{\partial D_t} \left(\text{because } \frac{\partial P_j}{\partial D_t} = 0 \text{ if } j < t \right)$$

$$= U_t \frac{P_t}{D_t} - \sum_{j=t+1}^{n} \frac{P_j}{(1 - D_t)} U_j$$

$$= \sum_{j=t}^{n} \frac{P_j}{(1 - D_j)} (U_t - U_j).$$

The final step in this derivation follows from the fact that

$$\frac{P_t}{D_t} - \sum_{j=t+1}^{n} \frac{P_j}{1 - D_t} = S_t - S_t \left[\sum_{j=t+1}^{n} D_j \prod_{i=t+1}^{j-1} (1 - D_i) \right] = 0.$$

The proof in note 6 can be extended to show that the expression in square brackets is equal to 1.

[10] At least one attempt has been made to derive by questionnaire a utility function encompassing income, risks of death, and various states of ill health. See G. Torrance, *A Generalized Cost-Effectiveness Model for the Evaluation of Health Programs*, Faculty of Business, McMaster University, Research Series No. 101, 1970.

subjective feelings about, the value of life. Assume that the contributions of each C_i to the function U_t are separable and that all utility functions U_t take the special form

$$U_t = \sum_{i=0}^{t-1} \frac{C_i^\beta}{(1+r)^i},$$ (3')

where r is a rate of discount connecting "annual utility" accruing at different periods of time and β is the elasticity of annual utility with respect to consumption.

Given this assumption, the price of a reduction in the mortality rate at time t becomes[11]

$$\frac{-\partial C_0}{\partial D_t} = \frac{1}{\beta} C_0 \left[\sum_{j=t}^{n} \frac{\left(\frac{C_j}{C_0}\right)^\beta S_j}{(1+r)^j} \right] \frac{1}{(1-D_0)(1-D_t)}.$$ (10)

If we make the additional assumption, an assumption which is reasonable in the context of national accounting, that $C_i = C_j = C$ for all i and j, then the price of an instantaneous reduction in today's mortality rate becomes

$$\frac{-\partial C_0}{\partial D_0} = \frac{1}{\beta} C \sum_{j=0}^{n} \frac{S_j}{(1+r)^j} \frac{1}{(1-D_0)^2}.$$ (11)

[11] Equation (10) is derived by substituting equation (3') into equation (9). The numerator of equation (9) becomes

$$\sum_{j=t}^{n} \frac{P_j}{(1-D_t)} (U_j - U_t) = \sum_{j=t}^{n} \frac{P_j}{(1-D_t)} \left[\sum_{i=0}^{j-1} \frac{C_i^\beta}{(1+r)^i} - \sum_{i=0}^{t-1} \frac{C_i^\beta}{(1+r)^i} \right]$$

$$= \sum_{j=t}^{n} \frac{P_j}{(1-D_t)} \left[\sum_{i=t}^{j-1} \frac{C_i^\beta}{(1+r)^i} \right]$$

$$= \frac{1}{(1-D_t)} \sum_{j=t}^{n-1} \left[\frac{C_j^\beta}{(1+r)^j} \left(\sum_{i=j+1}^{n} P_i \right) \right]$$

$$= \frac{1}{(1-D_t)} \sum_{j=t}^{n-1} \frac{C_j^\beta S_{j+1}}{(1+r)^j}.$$

The denominator becomes

$$\sum_{j=0}^{n} P_j \frac{\partial U_j}{\partial C_0} = \sum_{j=1}^{n} \beta P_j C_0^{\beta-1} = (1-D_0)\beta C_0^{\beta-1}.$$

Consequently,

$$\frac{-\partial C_0}{\partial D_t} = \frac{1}{\beta} C_0 \left[\sum_{j=t}^{n} \frac{\left(\frac{C_j}{C_0}\right)^\beta S_j}{(1+r)^j} \right] \frac{1}{(1-D_0)(1-D_t)}.$$

The term $1/(1 - D_0)^2$ enters equation (11) as a consequence of our assumption that consumption and risk of death enter the utility function as discrete units instead of as flows over time. The term could be eliminated from equation (11) by shortening the time periods enough that the probability of dying in any period is effectively zero. Instead of graduating time in years, we might graduate it in weeks, days, or seconds.

The parameter r in equations (3′) and (11) is different from and as a rule less than the real rate of interest on riskless assets. A lender of money faces two types of risk. The first is that the borrower does not repay the loan. The second is that the lender himself dies before the date of repayment. Normally, when we speak of a loan as being riskless we are referring to the absence of only the first type of risk whereas r is a rate of discount riskless in both respects. An individual in a competitive market arranges his time pattern of work and consumption to equate his rate of substitution in use between present and future consumption to the discount factor in the market. To be precise,

$$\left.\frac{-\partial C_0}{\partial C_t}\right|_U = \frac{1}{(1 + i_t)^t}, \tag{12}$$

where i_t is the market's real rate of interest on riskless t year loans. On the other hand, it is a consequence of equation (3′) that for any $j > t$,

$$\left.-\frac{\partial C_0}{\partial C_t}\right|_{U_j} = \frac{1}{(1 + r)^t}. \tag{13}$$

It is easily shown that

$$\frac{1}{(1 + i_t)^t} = \left.-\frac{\partial C_0}{\partial C_t}\right|_U = \frac{S_t}{S_1}\left(\frac{C_0}{C_t}\right)^{1\beta}\frac{1}{(1 + r)^t}, \tag{14}$$

which implies that $r < i_t$ as long as $C_0 \le C_t$. The term S_t/S_1 in equation (14) is like a second discount factor, for it is the product of annual components, all of which are less than 1.

The separability assumption (3′) is a much stronger assumption and a much less theoretically acceptable one than the expected utility hypothesis (1′). It is a discrete version of an assumption used widely in the theory of economic growth, and its advantages and disadvantages in that context are well-known.[12] The advantage of equation (3′) in our context is that it can accommodate any observed market price of life through an appropriate choice of r and β. If, for instance, a man of age 30 pays $100 to

---

[12] See H. Wan, *Economic Growth*, Harcourt Brace Jovanovich, 1971, pp. 267–285.

avoid a 1 in 1,000 chance of losing his life, his value of $-\dfrac{\partial C_0}{\partial D_0}$ is \$100,000 and values of the parameters of r and β can be chosen to equate the two sides of equation (11). The principal disadvantage of equation (3') is that no value is placed on longevity itself independently of the level of consumption. Instead of assuming that U_t takes the form (3'), we might have assumed that

$$U_t = t^\alpha \sum_{j=0}^{t-1} \frac{C_j{}^\beta}{(1+r)^j}, \qquad (3'')$$

which would imply, if $\alpha > 1$, that a man would accept a reduction in the present value of the timestream of $C_j{}^\beta$ in order to prolong his life. The consequences of assumptions like (3'') will not be investigated.

GROWTH OF WHAT?

Economic growth is usually defined as the rate of appreciation of real income per head. Though the customary measure of income in this context is gross national product, we recognize that net national product is the more appropriate concept and would use it as the measure of income but for certain difficulties in measuring depreciation. Our problem is to expand the concept of real income per head to impute for the fall in mortality rates.

One's first instinct is to go back to Hicks's definition of income as the amount that a man may consume in a year without impoverishing himself. This is usually interpreted by the formula,

$$Y(t) = C(t) + W(t+1) - W(t), \qquad (15)$$

where $Y(t)$ is income in the year t, $C(t)$ is consumption in the year t, and $W(t)$ is wealth at the outset of the year t.[13] Presumably anticipated improvement in mortality rates would be incorporated in wealth which in turn is closely related to utility as defined by equations (1), (2), and (3) above. If during the course of a year, a man comes to believe that the mortality rates facing him in the rest of his life will be lower than he had anticipated at the beginning of the year, then $W(t+1)$ will be that much greater than $W(t)$ and income will have increased accordingly.

There are several reasons why this framework is not appropriate for imputing a value for the fall in mortality rates. First, a national account-

---

[13] We shall use a term of the form $X(t)$ to refer to the value of the variable X in the year t. This usage should be distinguished from X_t, which refers to an event that may or may not occur t years in the future.

ant measuring growth cannot be expected to predict future mortality rates, any more than he can be expected to predict future consumption. The most the national accountant can be expected to observe is current consumption, current age-specific mortality rates, current investment, and that part of current wealth that is actually evaluated in the market. Second, anticipated reductions in age-specific mortality rates appear to individuals as windfall gains that accrue not in the present year but in the future. Such windfall gains could play havoc with measures of growth of income as defined by equation (15), for they could cause income to decline steadily from the base year even though people are becoming steadily better off. Suppose C is constant forever and mortality rates are improving at a decreasing rate, so that $W(t + 1) > W(t)$ for all t, but $[W(2) - W(1)] > [W(3) - W(2)] > [W(4) - W(3)]$ and so on. Clearly, Y is declining over time and economic growth is negative. Whatever it is to which we impute a value for increased life expectancy, it cannot be income as defined by equation (15).

I suggest that what we are seeking to observe is the growth rate of a surrogate for U as defined in equation (1). We wish to record the improvement in well-being inclusive of current consumption and prospects for the future. This statement must be qualified in an important respect. As has already been said, the national accountant cannot presume to know what people expect for the future. He designs measures to reflect, not welfare given current expectations for the future, but welfare as it would be if current conditions persisted indefinitely into the future. Measures of economic growth should be designed to reflect the growth of U of equation (1), as it would be if all C_j were equal to current income per head and all D_j were equal to age-specific mortality rates in the current year. The C_j are measured by current income rather than by current consumption on the assumption that income is the maximum consumption that can be sustained indefinitely with present technology and resources.[14]

Our statistics of economic growth are to reflect the improvement in U, but they cannot record the growth of U itself because, at best, U is only defined up to a linear transformation and the growth rate of U is not defined at all. We must find a variable which is a surrogate for U and for which a growth rate is well-defined. Fortunately this problem is fundamentally the same as that of measuring real consumption in circum-

---

[14] This interpretation of real income is compared with other interpretations in Dan Usher, "The Concept of Real Income," Queen's Discussion Papers, No. 99, 1973.

stances where prices are changing over time. In that case, we choose a base year and define real consumption in any other year to be the amount of money needed to make one as well off in the base year as one was in the other year.

By analogy, we define a term $\hat{C}(t)$ to be the value of net national product at which one would be as well off with mortality rates of the base year as one was in the year t with actual net national product, $C(t)$, and actual mortality rates, $D_j(t)$, of that year. If the base year is 1961, $\hat{C}(t)$ is defined by the equation

$$U[\hat{C}(t), D(1961)] = U[C(t), D(t)], \tag{16}$$

where $D(t)$ is a vector of age-specific mortality rates in the year t. As conventionally measured, economic growth is the growth of $C(t)$. When an imputation is made for increased life expectancy, economic growth becomes the growth of $\hat{C}(t)$. The effect of the improvement in mortality rates on growth is the difference between the growth rate of $\hat{C}(t)$ and the growth rate of $C(t)$.

These measures are illustrated in Figure 1. Imagine three men, one living in 1926, one living in 1961, and one living in 1968. They can

FIGURE 1

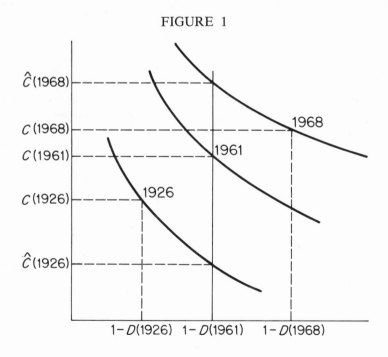

live for at most two periods, they face probabilities $D(t)$ of dying at the start of the second period, their consumption, $C(t)$, is the same in both periods, and their utility functions are identical.

$$U(t) = U[C(t), D(t)]. \tag{17}$$

Three indifference curves, one containing the C and D of 1926, another containing the C and D of 1961, and a third containing the C and D of 1968 are shown in Figure 1. Points representing values of C and D in the years 1926, 1961, and 1968 are labeled accordingly. Consumption as conventionally measured is indicated by the points $C(1926)$, $C(1961)$, and $C(1968)$ on the vertical axis. Consumption inclusive of a premium for the improvement in mortality rates is indicated by the points $\hat{C}(1926)$, $\hat{C}(1961)$, and $\hat{C}(1968)$ where each $\hat{C}(t)$ is defined in accordance with equation (16) as the amount of consumption one would need in 1961 to be as well off as a man living in the year t.

Finally there is the question of whose utility we are considering in estimating values of U or its surrogate $\hat{C}$. In accordance with accounting conventions, we would want to measure the average value of $\hat{C}$ in the population as a whole, taking young and old into account. Other things being equal, the $\hat{C}$ of a young man would be greater than the $\hat{C}$ of an old man, and these would have to be averaged according to the proportions of young men and old men in the population. This averaging procedure would have to be conducted with respect to a standard age distribution (for instance, the age distribution in the base year), for we would not want our statistics to imply that people are becoming better off over time if all that is happening is that the proportion of young people in the population is increasing.

MEASURING ECONOMIC GROWTH WITH AN IMPUTATION FOR THE INCREASE IN LIFE EXPECTANCY

The development of the argument so far is that economic growth inclusive of an imputation for increased life expectancy is the growth of a variable $\hat{C}(t)$ where

$$U[\hat{C}(t), D(1961)] = U[C(t), D(t)] \tag{16}$$

where the utility function in equation (16) is of the form

$$U = \sum_{j=0}^{n} P_j \left(\sum_{i=0}^{j-1} \frac{C_i^{\beta}}{(1+r)^i} \right) = \sum_{j=0}^{n} \frac{C_j^{\beta} S_j}{(1+r)^j}, \tag{18}$$

and U is measured as if all C_i were equal to the current net national product, and all D_i were current age-specific mortality rates. Designate the common value of C_j by $C(t)$ and the value in the year t of

$$\sum_{j=0}^{n} \frac{S_{j+1}}{(1+r)^j}$$

by $L(t)$. Hence, equations (18) and (16) become

$$U(t) = C(t)^\beta L(t) \tag{19}$$

and

$$\hat{C}(t) = C(t)[L(t)/L(1961)]^{1/\beta}. \tag{20}$$

The significant feature of equation (20) is that the terms on the right-hand side of the equation representing conventional income, $C(t)$, and increased life expectancy, $[L(t)/L(1961)]^{1/\beta}$, are multiplicative; so the rates of growth of the two terms cumulate rather than average out in the formation of the final rate.

$$G_{\hat{C}} = G_C + (G_L/\beta). \tag{21}$$

Normally imputations to the accounts are added in rather than multiplied in, so that the effect of an imputation is to reduce the rate of growth whenever the growth of the imputed item is less than the growth of the rest of the accounts. It follows from the assumptions we have made about the form of utility function and the concept of income that the effect of the imputation for increased life expectancy is necessarily to increase the rate of growth, and that the increase is normally greater than the rate of growth of life expectancy itself.

If we ignore the term $1/(1 - D_0)^2$ in equation (11), the value of life becomes

$$\frac{-\partial C_0}{\partial D_0} = \frac{1}{\beta} CL. \tag{22}$$

Equations (21) and (22) are the basis for all of the estimates which we will derive.

Time series of $\hat{C}(t)$ can be computed from observed values of income and mortality rates for given values of the parameters r and β. Recall that the parameter r is defined in equation (3′) as a rate of discount on annual utility for a given length of life. It is different from and as a rule less than the market rate of interest. It seems reasonable to suppose that this rate lies between zero and 5 per cent.

The choice of a value for β is more critical and we have less a priori information to guide us in our judgment. A case can be made for supposing that $\beta = 1$. This would imply that in all decisions affecting values of C_j and D_j, people act to maximize their wealth, W, defined as

$$W = \sum_{j=0}^{n} P_j \sum_{i=0}^{j-1} \frac{C_i}{(1 + r)^i}. \tag{23}$$

A man would pay a $\frac{1}{1,000}$ part of the present value of his expected lifetime consumption. He would be indifferent to whether he lives a long life or a short life if consumption per year in the short life is sufficiently higher than consumption per year in the long life that the present values of consumption are the same. It is possible for taste to have this form but there is no good reason to suppose that it does, and a man might well be willing to exchange some present value for a longer life. Nevertheless, the maximization of wealth assumption has the right qualitative implications: the value of life is an increasing function of consumption and of the expected length of life, but the marginal valuation of an extra year of life at any given value of consumption is a decreasing function of life expectancy. One might argue that the growth over time of the expected present value of lifetime consumption as it would be if current income and current mortality rates persisted indefinitely is a useful statistic to observe even though it is a poor surrogate for utility.

The alternative to supposing that $\beta = 1$ is to estimate β from equation (22). For this purpose we need an observation on the value of the life of a man of whom we know his age, his expected consumption, and his mortality rates in every future year because all of these characteristics affect the value of $-\partial C_0 / \partial D_0$. In principle, one could get this information from questionnaires. One might ask, "Suppose there is a 1 in 1,000 chance that the cup in front of you contains hemlock rather than coffee. What would you pay to avoid having to drink the contents of the cup?" The answer, multiplied by 1,000, would be the value the respondent places on his life, and, by questioning people of different ages and with different incomes, one could obtain some notion of how the response is affected by these variables. Of course, no serious statistician would ever pose this question because the respondent cannot be expected to answer it truthfully. The reason for mentioning it in this context is to keep in mind the sort of information we would like to obtain if we could.

There are situations where this question has to be answered. Decisions have to be made in circumstances where lives are at stake, and where valuations of changes in mortality rates are implicit in public and private decisions.

a. We place values on life-saving in our decisions to engage or not to engage in medical expenditures. If the cost per patient of a kidney transplant is $72,000, and if we decide that those who need kidney transplants will get them, and if the expected life of a person with a kidney transplant is 17 years, we are deciding that a 17-year extension of life is worth at least $72,000.

b. Similarly, a valuation of life-saving is implicit in expenditures to prevent road accidents.

c. A valuation of changes of mortality rates reflecting private as opposed to public decisionmaking is implicit in rates of hazard pay. If a carpenter who works at the top of a high building runs a 1 in 1,000 risk per year of falling off, and if he accepts a premium of $100 for taking that risk, he values his life at $100,000.

d. If the amount of armor on an airplane affects the chances of its being shot down, a valuation of life is implicit in decisions as to how much armor the plane should have.

Though the pricing of life is implicit in many public and private decisions, it is difficult to find prices and to extricate valuation of life from other considerations. I have only been able to find a few prices and these are shown in Table 1. In interpreting these prices an in using them to impute values of decreases in mortality rates, several considerations should be kept in mind.

First, by value of life, I mean nothing more than $\partial C_0 / \partial D_0$, the amount one would pay per unit for a decrease in one's mortality rate in the current year. The statement that the price of life is $20,000 in this sense does not mean that a man would sacrifice his life for $20,000, any more than the statement that the price of butter is $0.25 per pound means that a man would pay $20,000 for the pleasure of consuming 40 tons of butter.

Second, the valuation of life implicit in decisions affecting mortality rates is different from the valuation society puts on saving the lives of identifiable people. Thedie and Abraham [15] have expressed this point as follows: "If a miner is imprisoned at the bottom of a pit, if a mountaineer is in danger up in the mountains, if a vessel is in danger of shipwreck on

[15] J. Thedie and C. Abraham, "Economic Aspect of Road Accidents," *Traffic Engineering and Control,* 1961, p. 590.

TABLE 1

Scraps of Evidence on the Value of Life
(implicit or explicit value of the life of a man about 30 years old)

	Dollars (thousands)
1. Hazard pay	
premium miners accept for working underground	34–159
test pilot	161
2. Medical expenditure	
kidney transplant	72
dialysis in hospital	270
dialysis at home	99
3. Valuation of the cost of disease	75
4. Valuation of the cost of airplane accidents	472
5. Traffic safety	
recommended for cost-benefit analysis by the National Safety Council	37.5
value of life in a cost-benefit study of highways	100
6. Military decision-making	
instructions to pilots on when to crash-land airplanes	270
decision to produce a special ejector seat in a jet plane	4,500

SOURCE: Line 1. Hazard pay: Three collective bargaining agreements in the mining industry contain premiums for working underground of 14, 5, and 3 cents per hour. These were respectively: Opemiska Copper Mines (Quebec) Ltd., and Le Syndicates Travailleurs des Mines de Chibougamou-Chapais (1965), Lake Shore Mines Ltd. and International Union of Mine, Mill, and Smelter Workers Local 240 (1958), and Hollinger Consolidated Gold Mines Ltd. and United Steelworkers of America Local 4305 (1961). In the United States, the risk of a fatal accident is 0.49 per million man-hours in coal mining and is 0.05 in all industries combined (*Accident Facts 1970*, the National Safety Council, Chicago). Suppose that half of the premium for working underground is compensation for the risk of a fatal accident and the other half is compensation for the risk of nonfatal accidents and for inconvenience, and that, in the mines to which the agreements refer, the risk of a fatal accident above ground is 0.05 per million hours and the risk of an accident underground, in mining proper, is 0.49 per million hours, so that the extra risk of working underground is 0.44. The value of life implicit in the three agreements is therefore $159,000, $57,000 and $34,000, respectively. The questionable aspects of this calculation need neither emphasis nor elaboration. Note however that in principle hazard pay yields a true value of life in that, like all wage rates, it reflects valuations at the margin. If the hazard pay were set too low, the miners would be disinclined to work underground and if hazard pay were set too high they would be disinclined to work above ground. A United States air force pilot whose basic salary was $12,012 was paid a premium of $2,280 for engaging in especially dangerous test flights that raised his chance of losing his life from 0.1348 to 1.695 per cent per year. The

(Notes continued on next page)

Notes to Table 1 (continued)

value of life implicit in that contract was $167,000 [$2,280 ÷ (.01695 − .001348)]. (J. W. Carlson, "Valuation of Life-Saving," Ph.D. dissertation, Harvard University, 1963.)

Line 2. Medical expenditure: These figures are based on data from H. E. Klarman, J. O'S. Francis, and G. D. Rosenthal, "Cost Effectiveness Analysis Applied to the Treatment of Chronic Renal Disease," *Medical Care*, 1968, pp. 48–54. Discounting at 6 per cent, they find the present values of the costs of hospital dialysis, home dialysis, and transplantation to be $104,000, $38,000 and $44,500, respectively, and that the years gained in the three treatments are 9, 9, and 17. The figures in our table are not the costs of the treatments but the implications of these numbers about the value of the life of an average man of 30 years of age whose life expectancy is 45 years. The value of life of a 30-year-old man that would make hospital dialysis, for instance, a marginal life-saving expenditure is $104,000 × (18/7), where 18 and 7 are the approximate discounted life expectancies at 5 per cent of 45 and 9 years of life. The discounted life expectancy of 17 years is 11 years. In principle, all of these medical estimates may reflect intramarginal situations in that many people who have to pay their full share of the extra taxes required to finance these treatments would willingly vote to have these treatments made available for everyone even if the treatments were more expensive than they are now. Nevertheless, one gets the impression from the literature that the cost of hospital dialysis is, if anything, extramarginal in that the expenditure on hospital dialysis is often said to be more than society "can afford."

Line 3. The source of this estimate is Dorothy P. Rice, *Estimating the Cost of Illness*, Health Economics Series 6, U.S. Department of Health, Education, and Welfare, 1966, p. 93. The figure in Table 1 is an average of the discounted earnings of a man and a woman of age 25–29 when the discount rate is 6 per cent. For reasons discussed at the outset of this paper, I believe that this type of calculation is inappropriate in principle for determining the value of life. I include it together with the valuation of loss of life in airplane accidents because endorsement of this calculation by the U.S. government puts a certain weight on the estimate of the value of life independently of the validity of the method by which the estimate was arrived at, and signifies that the estimate itself is deemed reasonable.

Line 4. Gary Fromm measures the cost of a fatality in an air crash as the present value of the lifetime earnings of the typical passenger ("Civil Aviation Expenditures," in R. Dorfman, ed., *Measuring Benefits of Government Investments*). Assuming the average age of a passenger to be 40 years, and setting the discount rate at 6 per cent, he estimates the cost per fatality in 1960 to be $373,000. I increase this number to $472,000 in Table 1 to approximate the present value of the earnings of an airline passenger whose income is typical of incomes of all airline passengers but who is only 30 years old. Fromm thinks of his calculation as representing a lower limit to the true value of life. Leaving aside the question of the suitability of the present value of earnings calculation for evaluating the cost of loss of life, the contrast between Fromm's estimate of the value of life of an airline passenger who tends to be rich and Rice's estimate of the value of life of an average American raises the interesting issue of whether a public decision-maker ought to accept private valuations in cost-benefit analysis where life-saving is one of the benefits or costs. This would seem to be a case in which each dollar of benefit ought not to be counted as equal to every other dollar of benefit "to whomsoever the benefits may accrue."

Line 5. Traffic safety: A figure of $37,500 was recommended as the value of life for cost-benefit analysis of traffic safety by J. L. Recht, *How to Do a Cost-Benefit Analysis of Motor Vehicle Accidents*, National Safety Council, September 1966. This figure also seems to have been arrived at by discounting somebody's lifetime earnings. The figure

(Notes continued on next page)

of $100,000 is presented, without justification or explanation other than that it is alleged to be customary, in a study conducted for the National Highway Safety Bureau of the U.S. Department of Highways, No. FH-11-6495.

Line 6. Military decision-making: The pilot of a F-86L jet fighter plane occasionally finds himself in a position where he might either eject himself from the plane, allowing it to crash, or attempt a landing. Instructions to the pilot as to when to eject himself from the airplane imply a value of life of at least $270,000, when consideration is given to his probability of survival if he abandons the plane, to his probability of survival if he tries to land the plane, to the cost of the plane, to the probability of losing it in the event of an attempted landing, and to the damage that might be caused by a crashing plane. This figure is not very instructive because the cost of training a pilot for a F-86L jet is $300,000 (Carlson, *op. cit.*). Carlson also cited a case in which the Air Force spent $9 million designing and producing an ejector seat which would save between one and three lives.

Table 1 is a collection of numbers which are not obviously intramarginal. In my cursory examination of cost-benefit analysis in circumstances where the lengthening of lives is one of the benefits, I encountered many examples of projects which had to be intramarginal in the sense that no rational decision-maker could refuse to undertake such projects when the possibility of doing so is recognized. For instance, G. Torrance (*A Generalized Cost-Effectiveness Model for the Evaluation of Health Programs,* Faculty of Business, McMaster University, Research Series No. 101) found that the cost per newborn child saved in a program of preventing hemolytic disease was $932.00. I would hope that this fact conveys no information about the value of life.

---

the high seas, it would be criminal to reckon efforts and money according to the number of human lives to be saved. It would be vain to inquire whether the sum spent on saving these few lives if invested elsewhere (on roads for instance) might not have enabled more lives to be saved. It is impossible to weigh in the balance certain deaths and probable deaths, even if the latter are in greater number."

Thirdly, the price of life is different from the price of butter in that the price of butter is the same to everyone who buys butter while the price of reductions in mortality rates may vary from one man to the next within the same market. Mortality rates are private commodities, by which I mean that they are not and cannot be traded in the market because they are produced in the household from ordinary commodities. Other private commodities are risk and capital as components of stocks and bonds, the consumption activities in Lancaster's formulation of the theory of demand,[16] leisure, and the components of a hedonic price index. Ordinary commodities like pounds of butter or hours of the services of a carpenter cost the same to a rich man and a poor man alike. The price of a private commodity like leisure is different to a rich man than to a poor man, for each man values leisure as the marginal product

[16] K. Lancaster, "A New Approach to Consumer Theory," *Journal of Political Economy,* 1966, pp. 132–157.

of an hour of work, and the marginal product of a poor man is different from the marginal product of a rich man insofar as productivity of labor is the source of the difference in their incomes. If the price of butter were lower to the poor man than to the rich man, the poor man in a competitive economy would sell butter to the rich man and cause prices to equalize. No comparable mechanism equalizes the price of leisure. Leisure cannot be detached from its owner in the way that butter can be detached from its owner, and arbitrage fails to equalize prices in this market.

Precisely the same is true of the price of a reduction in mortality rates. Suppose, as illustrated in Figure 2, that a man is confronted with a number of ways of reducing his mortality rate, listed here in order of cost; wearing a safety belt in his car, visiting his doctor for an annual check-up, fire-proofing his house, having a special test for cancer, installing a radio transmitter in his yacht, reinforcing his automobile, keeping a co-pilot at all times in his private jet plane. These options constitute a supply curve to the individual of reductions in his mortality rate, and corresponding to this supply curve is a demand curve for reductions in mortality rates which could be derived in the usual way as the locus of all combinations of $\partial C_0 / \partial D_0$ and D_0 consistent with the utility function of equation (1) when other parameters are held constant or varied in some systematic way with D_0. The position of the demand curve would depend on the tastes of the individual and on his income, and the wealthier he is, the more he would pay to reduce mortality rates and the higher would be his demand curve. Each man's supply curve of reduction of mortality rates is also unique as it depends on the circumstances of his life, in particular, on the nature of his work. In Figure 3 the supply curves facing a rich man and a poor man are presumed to be identical. Their demand curves differ, and the value of life of a rich man (in our special sense of the term "value of life") is higher in equilibrium than the value of life of a poor man.

Evidence on shadow prices of mortality rates is of limited use in constructing an imputation to economic growth, because mortality rates are private commodities. Even in perfect markets, values of reductions in mortality rates differ from one man to the next so that prices implicit in given transactions are relevant only to people who actually engage in those transactions and not to the population as a whole. Furthermore, private commodities are typically indivisible; so their costs need not be shadow prices at all. The value of a reduction of the mortality rate implicit in the decision to have an annual medical check-up need not

FIGURE 2

Supply Curve of Mortality Rate Reduction to a Rich Man

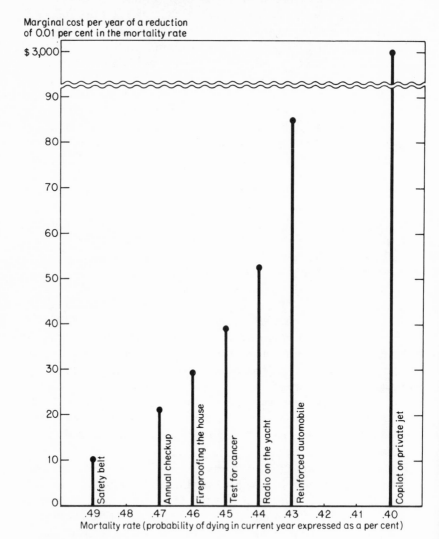

Marginal cost per year of a reduction
of 0.01 per cent in the mortality rate

FIGURE 3

Choice of Mortality Rates of a Rich Man and a Poor Man, Assuming
Their Supply Curves Are the Same

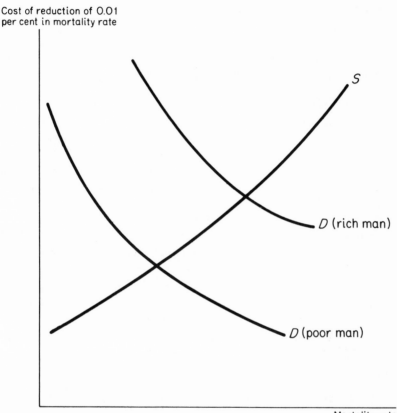

Cost of reduction of 0.01
per cent in mortality rate

S

D (rich man)

D (poor man)

Mortality rate

reflect a man's valuation of his life if his demand curve cuts his supply
curve at a higher value.

The issue is complicated still further by the fact that reductions in
mortality rates have externalities. We are prepared to sacrifice to prolong our neighbor's life even though we are relatively unconcerned
about the size of our neighbor's income. Evidence of public and private behavior in circumstances where decreases in mortality rates can
be bought conveys some useful information and gives hints of what
might be a reasonable valuation of life in cost-benefit analysis and in our

imputation for increased life expectancy. This evidence does not point to a unique price or to a unique range of prices depending on a man's age and his mortality rates in each future year. Reductions in mortality rates differ from ordinary commodities in that unique prices do not exist.

Having said this, we shall suppose that there is a unique price $\partial C_0/\partial D_0$ corresponding to a set of mortality rates D_j and a level of permanent consumption C, as there would be if society were one individual writ large, and we shall use this information to impute a value for the increase in life expectancy in the national accounts.

AN IMPUTATION TO THE CANADIAN ACCOUNTS

Both the value of life and the corresponding growth rate of income inclusive of an imputation for the increase in life expectancy are computed in accordance with equations (21) and (22) with several values of the parameters r and β and with Canadian data for the years 1926 to 1968. The data required are time series of real net national product per head to measure $C(t)$ and age-specific mortality rates to measure $D_j(t)$. In each year, the value of L for the population as a whole was taken to be a weighted average value of L in that year for all ages, with weights reflecting the age distribution of the population in 1961. The rate of interest, r, was given values of 1, 3, and 5 per cent, and β, which is the more critical variable, was given all values between .05 and 1.0 in steps of .05. The growth rate of real net national product per head over the years 1926 to 1968 was 2.25 per cent. For all combinations of r and β, the computed values of life and growth rates of net national product inclusive of the imputation for increased life expectancy are presented in Table 2. The effect of the imputation for increased life expectancy depends very much on the values chosen for the parameters β and r. For $r = 1$ per cent, the rate of economic growth inclusive of the imputation for increased life expectancy varies from 2.48 per cent when $\beta = 1$ up to 6.98 per cent when $\beta = 0.05$. From among these growth rates, we choose the one corresponding to a computed value of life that approximates values of life recorded in Table 1.

If one sets a value of life at, say, $150,000, the effect of the imputation for increased life expectancy is to raise the growth rate by about one-half of 1 per cent a year, from 2.25 per cent without the imputation to about 2.8 per cent. This result holds for all three interest rates; if $r = 1$ per cent, then, to the nearest 0.05, $\beta = 0.45$ and the growth rate is 2.77 per cent; if $r = 3$ per cent, then $\beta = 0.30$ and the growth rate is 2.84 per cent; if $r = 5$ per cent, then $\beta = 0.25$ and the growth rate is 2.80 per cent.

TABLE 2

Growth Rates, 1926–68, and the Value of Life

β	$r = 1$ Per Cent		$r = 3$ Per Cent		$r = 5$ Per Cent	
	Av. Value of Life, 1961 [a] (000 omitted)	Growth Rate of Income [b]	Av. Value of Life, 1961 [a] (000 omitted)	Growth Rate of Income [b]	Av. Value of Life, 1961 [a] (000 omitted)	Growth Rate of Income [b]
5%	$1,331	6.98%	$910	5.78%	$671	5.00%
10	666	4.61	455	4.01	336	3.63
15	444	3.83	303	3.42	224	3.17
20	333	3.43	228	3.13	168	2.94
25	226	3.19	182	2.95	134	2.80
30	222	3.04	152	2.84	112	2.71
35	190	2.92	130	2.75	96	2.64
40	166	2.84	114	2.69	84	2.59
45	147	2.77	101	2.64	75	2.55
50	133	2.72	91	2.60	67	2.52
55	121	2.68	83	2.57	61	2.50
60	111	2.64	76	2.54	56	2.48
65	102	2.61	70	2.52	52	2.46
70	95	2.59	65	2.50	48	2.45
75	89	2.56	61	2.48	44	2.43
80	83	2.54	57	2.47	42	2.42
85	78	2.53	54	2.46	40	2.41
90	74	2.51	51	2.44	37	2.40
95	70	2.50	48	2.43	35	2.39
100	67	2.48	46	2.42	33	2.39

NOTE: The growth rate of income without the imputation for increased life expectancy is 2.25 per cent. Values of the variable $C(t)$ from 1926 to 1968 are taken from the national accounts. The appropriate concept is net national product in 1961 dollars which is not provided directly by the accounts but which may be estimated as [gross national expenditure in constant (1961) dollars × (gross national expenditure − capital consumption allowance)] ÷ (gross national expenditure), all the terms of which are contained in *National Income and Expenditure Accounts, 1926–1968*, Dominion Bureau of Statistics, August 1968.

Time series of age-specific mortality rates for the first year of life, for the next four years, and for five-year intervals thereafter up to age 84, and with a final category of age 85 and above, were obtained from various issues of *Vital Statistics*, Dominion Bureau of

(Notes continued on next page)

Notes to Table 2 (concluded)

Statistics, pp. 84–101. Annual mortality rates were constructed on the assumptions that the rate for any grouping of ages applies equally to all ages within that group and that ninety years is the maximum length of life. These annual mortality rates do not correspond exactly to the terms D_j because D_j is the probability of dying on the first day of the year j on the special assumption that all deaths occurring in any year are concentrated on the first day. Consequently the estimate of L differs slightly from that implied by equations (16) and (19). In the calculations leading to Table 2, the discounted life expectancy of a man who is now j years is measured as

$$L_j = \sum_{i=j}^{90-j} \frac{\left[\prod_{k=j}^{i-1}(1 - \bar{D}_k)(1 - \bar{D}_i/2)\right]}{(1 + r)^{i-j}},$$

where the $\bar{D}_j$ are age-specific mortality rates obtained from vital statistics data. The term in square brackets is the sum of the probability of a man of age j completing at least $i - j$ man years of life

$$\left[\prod_{k=j}^{i}(1 - \bar{D}_k)\right]$$

and half the probability of his dying $i - j$ years from now

$$\left[\prod_{k=j}^{i-1}(1 - \bar{D}_k)(\bar{D}_i/2)\right].$$

The factor 2 is included in the expression above because a man who will die i years from now has an expectation of remaining alive for half of that year.

The term $L(t)$ in equation (23) is estimated as

$$L(t) = \left[\sum_{j=0}^{89} P_j(1961)L_j(t)\right] \div \left[\sum_{j=0}^{89} P_j(1961)\right]$$

where $L_j(t)$ is the value of L_j in the year t and $P_j(1961)$ is the Canadian population of age j in the year 1961.

  [a] Defined as $(1/\beta)C(1961)L(1961)$.
  [b] Inclusive of an imputation for increased life expectancy: growth rate of $C(t)[L(t)/L(1961)]^\beta$.

The estimated increase of one-half of 1 per cent in the growth rate attributable to the improvement in life expectancy is by no means insignificant but seems to me to be rather low. The reason may be that I have underemphasized the importance of the fall in mortality rates in infants and children. The first hypothesis in the calculation is that each man is concerned with his own mortality rate exclusively, and since the great majority of people have passed infancy, the decline in the infant mortality rates cannot have a great effect on the final estimate. The decline in the infant mortality rate would have had a greater impact on the imputation if the interest of parents and prospective parents had been taken into account explicitly.

I have criticized the use of present value of earnings as a measure of the value of life, arguing that the present value of earnings does not reflect what a government responsive to the preferences of its citizens would pay to reduce mortality rates. However, the alternative concept of the value of life gives rise to measurements that have a good deal in common with the present value of earnings measurements they are intended to replace, for both are variants of expected discounted income. An important empirical difference between the two measures is in the age distribution of the value of life, illustrated in Charts 1 and 2. Chart 1 is based on our calculations and Chart 2 shows present values of earnings as estimated by Rice [17] in a study under the auspices of the U.S. Department of Health, Education, and Welfare. It turns out that both calculations put a value of about $130,000 on the life of a 30-year-old man, but the graph of the present value of earnings is an inverted U that peaks sharply at about age 30, while the value of life attains its maximum at about age 2, implying that society would spend more to preserve the life of a child than it would spend to preserve the life of an adult. Disease occurs chiefly in infancy and in old age when the present value of earnings is quite low relative to our calculation of the value of life. Rice assessed the cost per death from tuberculosis to be $31,000 and the cost per death from diseases of infancy and early childhood to be only $25,000, despite the fact that she valued the life of an adult at prime earning capacity at over $100,000. An implication of the calculation in this paper is that the value of the life of a child is on the order of $150,000: a government representing people whose preferences are described by equations (1′) and (3′) with $r = 5$ per cent and $\beta = 0.25$ would be prepared to spend up to $150,000 to save the life of a randomly selected child in 1961. Another difference between the present value of earnings calculation and the value of life calculation in this paper is that the former values men more than women while the latter puts the same value on the lives of men and women.

The final test of these two contrasting age distributions of the value of life is whether they reflect preferences in the community at large. I have no hesitation in saying that my preferences as to the comparative values of children and adults, and of men and women, are more nearly represented by the calculation in this paper than by the present value of earnings calculation. Unfortunately, the very plausible age distribution of the value of life in Chart 1 emerges in part for the wrong reasons. The value of a child's life is high not because concern of parents for children is

[17] Dorothy P. Rice, *Estimating the Cost of Illness,* Health Economics Series 6, U.S. Dept. of Health, Education, and Welfare, 1966.

CHART 1

Value of Life by Age in 1961, $r = 5$ Per Cent, $\beta = 0.25$
(Canadian dollars)

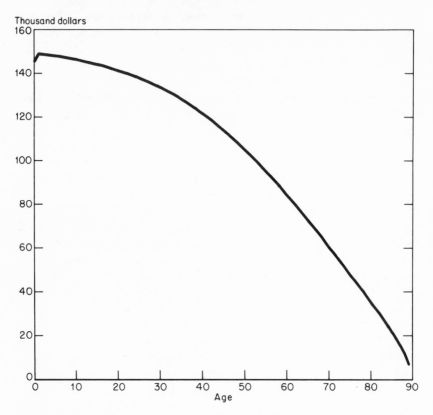

Thousand dollars

built into the utility function but because the expected discounted consumption is higher for children than for adults. The year to year change in discounted life expectancy, L, is shown in Chart 3.

As mentioned briefly at the outset of this paper, the addition of an imputation to the accounts for the improvement in life expectancy involves an element of double-counting if the rest of the accounts are left unchanged because the maintenance or increase of life expectancy is part of the benefit of medical and other expenditures already included in the accounts. I have chosen to ignore this issue and to add, or rather multiply, the improvement in life expectancy to the conventional measure of income without additional adjustments. My reasons for doing so are these: First, a substantial part of medical expenditure must surely be attributable to the attainment of comfort rather than increased life expectancy. Second, medical expenditures are not the only ones that increase life expectancy. If the expenditures that increase life expectancy are scattered among the major categories in the accounts, and if these expenditures grow at about the same rate as the rest of the accounts, it makes no difference to the final estimate of the rate of growth whether the mix of expenditures that increase life expectancy is included or not. Third, in strict logic there is really no end to the list of expenditures that may affect life expectancy. Food, clothing, and housing are all on the list in the sense that without any of these our lives would be shortened con-

CHART 2

Present Value of Lifetime Earnings: Amount by Sex and Discount Rate

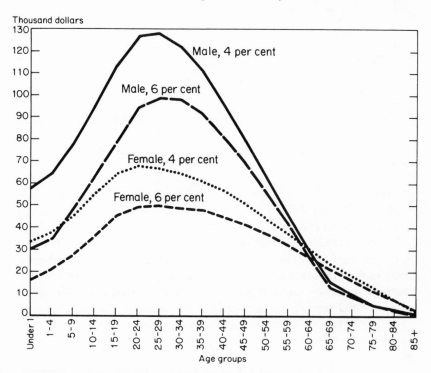

NOTE: The chart is based on data for the year 1963.
SOURCE: D. P. Rice, *Estimating the Cost of Illness*, U.S. Department of Health, Education and Welfare, 1966, p. 94.

CHART 3

Average Discounted Life Expectancy, 5 Per Cent, All Ages, 1961 Weights

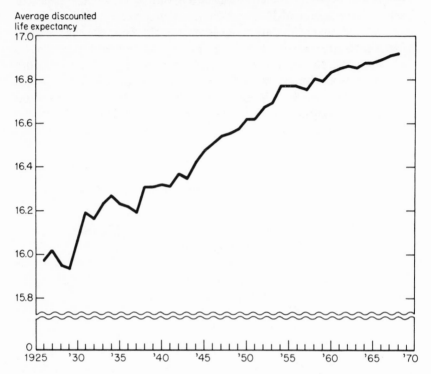

siderably. But as a rule, the marginal dollar of expenditure in these categories has little to do with life expectancy and what connection there is had best be overlooked.

Closely related to the problem of double-counting is the fact that most of the change in mortality rates from one period of time to another appears to the individual as a free good. The imputation we have been discussing is to the expenditure side of the accounts exclusively—to the list of goods and services we obtain from the economy in any year—and there do not appear to be comparable items that may be attached to the income side of the accounts to restore the balance.

IMPUTATIONS FOR OTHER COUNTRIES

I have no direct intuition about the value of life in countries outside of North America, and no information with which to determine reasonable values of r and β. What can be done is to suppose that their tastes are the same as ours. In that case combinations of r and β which are plausible for Canada are plausible for other countries as well. Calculations on these lines are set out in Table 3. The numbers in the table are derived in exactly the same way as the Canadian numbers were derived, and the table should be self-explanatory. The reader who is uncomfortable with the assumption that shapes of indifference curves and values of β and r are the same elsewhere as in Canada may interpret the statistics in Table 3 as indicating the growth of income of Ceylon, for instance, as it would be assessed by a Canadian in the circumstances of the Ceylonese economy.

The interesting feature of Table 3 is the magnitude of some of the imputations for some of the underdeveloped countries. The growth rate of Ceylon is more than doubled, and the growth rate of Chile is almost doubled. If one may generalize from these scanty bits of information, it seems that in the period since World War II the underdeveloped countries, alleged by Pearson and many other authors to have prospered less on average than the rich countries, have in fact done no such thing. It was in this period that many poor countries enjoyed an improvement in life expectancy greater than that enjoyed by rich countries in this or any other period of time, an improvement that more than compensates for the difference between rich and poor countries in growth rates of GNP as conventionally measured.

COMMENTS

Though the coverage of the national accounts may be satisfactory for the purpose of designing and evaluating short-run economic policy, it is generally believed to be too narrow for the purpose of monitoring the progress of the economy as a whole. In the last few years there has developed an interest in social indicators, which are time series of significant aspects of life—justice, health, progress in the arts—outside the normal coverage of the national accounts. (Expenditures on these items are included in the national accounts, but it is input to these items rather than outputs that is reflected in measures of real income.)

An imporant constraint on the use of social indicators is that there does not seem to be a natural and appealing way of aggregating them into a single measure of the progress of the economy. Of course, weights can always be chosen, but there is normally no basis for preferring one set of weights to another, no way of finding weights that reflect common rates of trade-off in use between social indicators, and no assurance that

TABLE 3

Imputations for Increased Life Expectancy in Other Countries

Country	Period	Growth Rate of GNP [a]			
		Without Imputation for Life-Expectancy Increase	$r = 1\%$, $\beta = .45$	$r = 3\%$, $\beta = .30$	$r = 5\%$, $\beta = .25$
Ceylon	1946–63	1.65%	3.81%	4.22%	4.14%
Chile	1931–65	1.57	2.77	2.94	2.89
France	1911–64	1.82	2.47	2.56	2.53
Japan	1930–60	3.13	4.49	4.67	4.58
Taiwan	1952–66	4.15	5.09	5.25	5.22

SOURCE: The principal sources of data were various issues of the U.N. *Yearbook of National Accounts Statistics* and the U.N. *Demographic Yearbook.* These sources were supplemented by (a) for France, *Annuaire Statistique de la France,* 1966; C. Kindelberger, *Economic Growth in France and Britain, 1851–1950,* and *Long-Term Economic Growth, 1860–1965,* U.S. Department of Commerce, 1966; (b) for Japan, *Japan Statistical Yearbook,* 1964; (c) for Taiwan, *National Accounts of the Less-Developed Countries, 1950–1966,* Organization for Economic Cooperation and Development, and *China Yearbook, 1966–1967,* China Publishing Company, Taiwan; (d) for Ceylon, *Statistical Abstract of Ceylon,* various issues; (e) for Chile, M. Mamalakis and C. W. Reynolds, *Essays on the Chilean Economy,* Irwin, 1965, statistical appendix, p. 384.

Gross national product was used instead of net national product to represent $C(t)$ because the information needed to estimate the latter is frequently unavailable. Quite a bit of crude estimating was required to derive annual mortality rates from the available data. As with the Canadian data, mortality rates in five-year intervals had to be attributed to each year separately, but in addition some even larger time intervals had to be dealt with, and sometimes the time intervals differed from one year to the next. The higher age-groups were particularly troublesome. Two methods were used to derive mortality rates in five-year intervals from data on mortality rates in ten- or fifteen-year intervals. If data were available for five-year intervals in another year, I would normally assume proportionality between mortality rates in the five-year intervals in the two years. Otherwise mortality rates in intervals longer than five years would be attributed to each year in the interval. The maximum age was assumed to be 90. Sometimes when the final open-ended time interval, intervals such as "mortality rates for people over 70 years of age," began well short of age 85, mortality rates in five-year intervals were estimated by postulating that they rose in a systematic manner consistent with available data on population and mortality rates in the larger time intervals. For each country, data on income and mortality rates were collected for the first year, the last year, and selected years in between.

[a] Inclusive of an imputation for increased life expectancy.

the coverage of the different series is mutually exclusive. Confronted with a set of social indicators, one finds oneself in a position such as one would be in if faced with innumerable time series of ordinary quantities —chicken soup, can openers, light bulbs, ties, spark plugs, telephones— without prices and with no way of aggregating the series into a single index. The emergence of social indicators gives rise to a search for a way of combining them with each other and with the economic information in the national accounts.

The task of this paper has been to find a natural way of combining two social indicators, the GNP and mortality rates, into a single, comprehensive index. Weights were constructed from information about the value of life, from assumptions about the form of utility functions, and on the strength of a somewhat unfamiliar concept of real income. The resulting system of weights for comparing the conventional measure of income and mortality rates on the same scale, while not wholly arbitrary, is less well-grounded in observed behavior in the market than the price weights used to combine quantities in the national income; there is every reason to believe that people differ in their assessments of the relative importance of growth of national income and the decline in mortality rates, for arbitrage does not equalize values of life among people in the way it equalizes prices of butter. In the final analysis, the weighting of the growth of conventional income and decline of mortality rates for cost-benefit analysis or in a unified measure of economic growth is a political problem.

Despite this intrinsic lack of precision, the imputation for the decline in mortality rates is worth making because of its magnitude. A large part of the answer to the question "How are we doing?" depends on whether life expectancy is increasing or not. An imputation of an extra half per cent to the rate of economic growth in Canada is too large to be ignored. To exclude the imputation for increased life expectancy in measuring the rate of economic growth of certain poor countries is to overlook half of the economic growth and to misrepresent economic history on a very large scale.

The imputation of a value to the accounts for the increase in life expectancy casts a wider net among the social indicators than may be evident at first glance. The worst effects of pollution are eventually manifest in mortality rates. Admittedly there are aspects of pollution, such as noise and congestion, that probably do not affect mortality rates significantly. But the major concern with pollution is with its lethal aspects, and these are accounted for in the imputation. Any attempt to impute a negative value to the national accounts for the ill effects of pollution will have to be done in the context of the complete matrix of causes of changes in mortality rates. One might well want to show that pollution causes income, in some sense of the term, to be less than it might otherwise be, but one would not want to show a reduction of income as a consequence of the lethal aspects of pollution unless one also shows that the potential decline is overbalanced by the over-all rise in life expectancy. The general rule is that one ought not to impute for a part of any category, such as life expectancy or leisure, if the trend of growth of the part is opposite to the trend of growth of the category as a whole.

The aspect of the analysis in this paper that I find least satisfactory is the mechanical and arbitrary nature of the separability assumption (3') used in deriving the utility assumption. The main point made in the introduction is that value of life is essentially a matter of taste. The inclusion in the utility function of the parameter β, which may be set in accordance with real or imagined evidence about behavior, gives considerably more scope for taste than is incorporated into the present value of earnings calculation. The relation between a person's age and the value of his life seems reasonable in that high values are placed on the lives of children. Unfortunately, this very plausible result emerges from the wrong reason. It ought to reflect externalities in the utility function, particularly the concern of parents for children. Instead it is based on the fiction that children, who have longer to live than adults, place higher values on their lives. Though the implications of our utility function are plausible, we really have no assurance that anybody's tastes are actually reflected in it.

COMMENT

ROBERT J. WILLIS, City University of New York and National Bureau of Economic Research

Perhaps no single factor has so altered the prospects of the individual as the historically unprecedented decline of mortality which began in the mid-nineteenth century in the West and in this century in the less developed countries. In northern Europe, the expectation of life at birth, which averaged about 40 years in 1850, rose to about 70 years by 1950. Even more dramatic is the estimate that one-fourth of a cohort of births in the 1840's would be dead by age 2.5 while in the 1940's the first quarter of a cohort would not be dead until age

62.5. As Stolnitz [3, p. 28] put it, "the number that could expect to survive the childhood years a century ago was substantially smaller than the number reaching old age today." The decline of mortality, facilitated by the transfer of Western medical and public health technology, has been even more rapid in the less developed countries although, of course, their mortality rates remain well above those in the advanced countries.

Common sense would suggest that such changes in longevity should be a major source of increased individual welfare; yet the national income accounts which provide the main statistical basis for judging changes in welfare omit altogether any direct consideration of changes in mortality rates. At the very least, Dan Usher in his attempt to remedy this difficulty has provided us with an imaginative, tightly argued and intriguing way of looking at the problem of imputing value to changes in longevity and has, as well, illustrated a number of ways in which it should not be done. If this method is accepted, the paper also takes on major substantive importance because of the magnitude of the adjustment to conventionally computed growth rates when imputations for the value of changes in age-specific mortality rates are made. For instance, he finds that under certain assumptions the growth rate of Canadian per capita income from 1926 to 1968 was increased by one-half of 1 per cent—from 2.25 to 2.8 per cent—by the imputation while the growth rates of some less developed countries which have recently experienced very rapid declines in mortality were doubled, becoming higher than growth rates in more developed countries rather than lower, as the conventional measure would have it. I believe that Usher's work points in the right direction and that this direction is important to explore further, but, for theoretical reasons I shall elaborate shortly, I think his imputations overstate the contribution of increases in life expectancy to the growth in welfare.

The need for a new approach to the economic valuation of human life has been amply illustrated, sometimes in grisly fashion, from examples drawn from existing approaches in a recent paper by Mishan [2] and by Usher in this paper. For example, using per capita income or consumption as a standard, most neoclassical growth models imply that a decrease in mortality rates would generally imply a reduction in economic welfare. In these models, the impact of declining mortality on national economies is usually considered, following the Malthusian tradition, to be exerted mainly through its impact on the rate of population growth which, in turn, determines the rate of growth of the labor force and, sometimes, the savings rate. It is almost always concluded that in steady state growth, the level of per capita income or consumption at any moment in time will be inversely related to the rate of population growth. Furthermore, in some models excessive rates of population growth induced by income growth (or transfer of medical technology) may prevent an economy from escaping a "low level equilibrium trap" to reach a higher level of living in which population growth is smaller. These implications are frequently invoked to support policies to reduce birth rates but, in logic, they may equally well be used to support policies to raise death rates.

The question being answered by such models, which Usher terms the "birth control question," is: "How much better or worse off would the community at large be if I ceased to exist or if I had never been born?" The thrust of this question is that, because of the law of variable proportions, a marginal increase in the labor force caused by population growth will reduce the average income of others. This will cause a decrease in welfare if we concentrate on the welfare of the "others" and ignore the welfare of the one who ceased to exist or of persons interested in his existence. Apparently this is more easily done when contemplating a potential birth than a potential death for reasons not apparent from logic of the argument itself (see [2, p. 690] for a similar point).

In any event, Usher argues that the "birth control question" is not the true "valuation-of-life question" which he says is: "How much would I pay to avoid a small probability of my death?" As an example, he states that a man who will pay $500 to avoid a 1 in 1,000 chance of death may be said to place a $500,000 value on his life. It should be emphasized that this is not the "insurance question" criticized by Mishan [2, p. 691] in which the answer to the question "What is my life worth to my wife and children?" will determine the premium the man would be willing to pay for life insurance against a 1 in 1,000 chance of his death. The $500 expenditure given in answer to the "valuation of life question" represents $500 of real resources because the man expects to avoid the 1 in 1,000 chance of death by his expenditure while a "mathematically fair" life insurance premium merely covers the risk entailed in passive acceptance of the chance of death and uses no real resources. There would be no imputation problem if all changes in mortality were the result of expenditures by individuals to change their own rates, assuming each such expenditure to be the maximum amount the individual was willing to pay for the reduction. Obviously, this is not the case; so imputation is necessary even at the risk of a fair amount of double-counting entailed by a failure to adjust conventionally measured income for expenditures designed to reduce mortality. At the end of the section "An Imputation to the Canadian Accounts," Usher gives several plausible reasons for doubting the seriousness of double-counting problems, especially when the emphasis is on measuring the growth rather than the level of income.

Usher approaches the evaluation of life question formally by assuming that an individual's utility for the rest of his life, U, can be expressed as a function of the lifetime utility, U_j, that he would receive from his current and future consumption stream if he should live exactly j years and the probability, P_j, that he lives exactly j years for all possible values of j from zero to n, the maximum length of the remaining proportion of the individual's life. In order to make this approach operational, Usher specializes this general utility function by making two assumptions. The first, which he calls the "expected utility hypothesis," is that the utility function takes the form,

$$U = \sum_{t=0}^{n} P_t U_t, \tag{1'}$$

and the second, which he calls the "separability assumption" is that

$$U_t = \sum_{i=0}^{t-1} \frac{C_1{}^\beta}{(1+r)^i}, \tag{3'}$$

where U_t is the individual's lifetime utility should he live exactly t years, β is the elasticity of annual utility with respect to consumption, and r is a discount factor which Usher argues is "different from and as a rule less than the real rate of interest on riskless assets." Given these assumptions and recognizing that the P_t are functions of the age-specific mortality rates, it is possible to find the increase in current consumption C_0 necessary to compensate the individual for a small increase in his current mortality D_0 by evaluating

$$-\frac{\partial C_0}{\partial D_0}\bigg|_U.$$

This marginal rate of substitution is considered by Usher to be the value of life, and given the schedules of future consumption and age-specific mortality rates, it will be determined by the parameters r and β.

Usher argues that national income accounts should be based upon statistics reflecting current conditions rather than forecasts of the future.

Accordingly, he assumes that $C_i = C_j = C(t)$, where $C(t)$ is the current level of NNP and that current age-specific mortality rates will continue into the future. Combining (18) and (19), these equations imply

$$U = \sum_{j=0}^{n} \frac{C_j{}^\beta S_j}{(1 + r)^j} = C(t)^\beta L(t), \qquad (18\text{–}19)$$

where the S_j are survival rates and $L(t)$ is the "discounted expectation of life." Equation (19), in turn, implies that

$$\hat{C}(t) = C(t) L(t)/L(1961)(1/\beta), \qquad (20)$$

where $\hat{C}(t)$ is "the value of net national product at which one would be as well off with mortality rates of the base year as one was in year t with actual net national product, $C(t)$, and actual mortality rates, $D_j(t)$, of that year." The difference between the growth of $\hat{C}(t)$ and $C(t)$ represents the imputation to national income for improvements in mortality.

The most remarkable implication of Usher's approach as embodied in (19) and (20) is that the growth rates of discounted life expectancy $L(t)$ and of conventionally measured income $C(t)$ cumulate rather than average out so that

$$\hat{G}_{\hat{C}} = G_C + (G_L/\beta), \qquad (21)$$

where β is assumed to be less than or equal to one. As Usher points out, "It is a consequence of the assumptions we have made about the form of the utility function and the concept of income that the effect of the imputation for increased life expectancy is necessarily to increase the rate of growth, and the increase is normally greater than the rate of growth of life expectancy itself." Since it is this implication that mainly accounts for the large empirical magnitude of the imputation, it is important to examine just what concept of income Usher is employing and how it compares to the conventional concept before we know how to react to his estimates.

I believe that it can be demonstrated that Usher's concept of income is, in one sense, the polar opposite of the conventional concept and that the meaning of the conventional concept can be greatly clarified by the use of Usher's formulation. If, to take an extreme case, an individual lived forever, we could express his "lifetime" utility in Usher's terms by suitably rewriting (18–19) to read as follows:

$$U = \sum_{i=0}^{\infty} \frac{C_j{}^\beta S_j}{(1 + r)^j} = \frac{C(t)^\beta}{r}. \qquad (18'\text{–}19')$$

If β is set equal to 1, the right hand side of (18′–19′) is equal to the present value of a perpetual continuation of consumption at its current level $C(t)$. In conventional terms, of course, this is equal to society's wealth defined as the present value of the stream of output that could be produced if the society's current stock of resources remained intact forever. Included in the stock of resources is the population from which the labor force is drawn.

It is a fact of sometimes deep significance that a population composed of mortal men may itself be immortal. In order to carry out his computations, Usher assumes "that there is a unique price $\partial C_0/\partial P_0$ corresponding to a set of mortality rates D_j and a level of permanent consumption C, as there would be if society were one individual writ large." It is now apparent that the conventional view of permanent consumption as the return from a fixed stock of resources is as it would be if the individual were immortal society writ small. In this sense, Usher's concept of income and the conventional concept are polar opposites.

It now becomes clear that Usher's rejection of Hicks's definition of income,

$$Y(t) = C(t) + W(t+1) = W(t), \tag{15}$$

was based on an erroneous supposition that a decrease in mortality rates would cause wealth to increase (see the section "Growth of What?"). If the individual is society writ small, he is immortal by definition and changes in actual mortality rates are immaterial.

It would appear that our reaction to Usher's imputations must depend on our philosophical position as to whether national income should measure the permanent output obtainable from a fixed social stock of resources or the level of a surrogate for the lifetime utility of an average individual in the population. If I were forced to make such a choice, I would find much to recommend Usher's position as against the conventional position. It seems to me, however, that the choice need not be so severe. Usher began his theoretical model with the injunction, "Ignore the fact that men live in families and that families are imbedded in communities of people who are concerned with each other's well-being." In the sense of welfare, this is an injunction to ignore sources of longevity other than one's own physical existence, especially the expectation of the existence and well-being of one's children and other heirs. In a sense, the conventional view of income implies that an individual is indifferent, after discounting, between his own and his heir's consumption; his "rate of benevolence," to use Boulding's term [1], is equal to unity. Surely, the truth is that the rate of benevolence is somewhere between zero and one. Thus, Usher's imputation—on this score, at least—probably gives us an upper bound on the value of increased life expectancy.

Following the line I have been arguing, it is parents who reveal their preference for decreasing the risk of death faced by their off-spring and to whom a change in welfare should be imputed when infant and child mortality rates change. Since parents have the power to create a new life to replace one lost while an adult cannot replace his own life, the value of a decrease in infant or child mortality using this approach would probably differ substantially from that found using Usher's approach. The magnitude of the imputation for changes in life expectancy is likely, empirically, to be quite sensitive to changes in the treatment of the mortality rates faced by the young because it is these rates that have changed the most, especially in the less developed countries.

In this paper, Usher has raised a set of issues of which many economists, including myself, were only dimly aware and he has succeeded in demonstrating that the resolution of these issues is of vast importance for our understanding of past economic growth and our evaluation of policy alternatives before us. Now that we are aware of them, I am confident that the issues raised here will be pursued much further, both empirically and conceptually.

REFERENCES

1. Boulding, K. E. "Economics as a Moral Science." *American Economic Review*, March 1969.
2. Mishan, E. J. "Evaluation of Life and Limb: A Theoretical Approach." *Journal of Political Economy*, July–August 1971, pp. 687–705.
3. Stolnitz, G. J. "A Century of International Mortality Trends—I." *Population Studies*, July 1955, pp. 24–55.

Measuring Economic Performance

in the Private Sector

LAURITS R. CHRISTENSEN

UNIVERSITY OF WISCONSIN

AND

DALE W. JORGENSON

HARVARD UNIVERSITY

1. INTRODUCTION

The problem of measuring economic performance involves comparisons. The output of an economic system is greater or less than its output at some previous point in time. The input of factors of production is greater or less in one industry than another. The standard of living in one region is greater or less than in another. Systems of economic accounts have provided a useful framework for organizing the information required for comparisons of this type.

Comparisons between the performance of two economies or the performance of an economic system at two points of time are of great interest from the scientific point of view. They are also of interest for the evaluation of economic policies. Evaluation of alternative policies involves comparison of the present state of affairs and possible alternative states associated with changes in policy.

The description of alternative states of an economic system involves the value of accounting magnitudes associated with each state. Changes from one state to another must be separated into price and quantity components. For example, the measurement of inflation involves an analysis of price changes, while the measurement of real output involves changes in quantity.

In view of the importance of the separation of changes in accounting magnitudes into price and quantity components, it is not surprising that much attention has been given to the measurement of real product. The scope of the product measure—whether and how to include activities internal to households, institutions, and governments, or services of the external environment—has been discussed in great detail.

Denison has recently drawn attention to the limitations inherent in a one-dimensional view of economic performance [17]. In comparing economic systems or alternative states of an economy it is impossible to summarize all the relevant information in a single measure of economic welfare. Real output is important, but the composition of output —by end use, industry of origin, and so on—is equally important in interpreting economic events and evaluating performance.

A complete economic system includes a production account, incorporating data on output and factor input, an income and expenditure account—giving data on factor incomes, expenditures, and saving— and an accumulation account, allocating saving to its uses in various types of capital formation.[1] In addition, a complete system contains data on national wealth from both asset and liability points of view. All of these accounting magnitudes are of interest in evaluating economic performance.

Although the separation of changes in accounting magnitudes into price and quantity components is of fundamental importance for the evaluation of economic performance, only the measurement of real product and real assets is well-established in accounting practice. For the evaluation of economic performance, measures of factor input, income, expenditures, saving, and capital formation in both current and constant prices are essential.

In this paper we present a complete accounting system in constant prices that comprehends all the aspects of economic performance we have listed above. This system is implemented in detail for the private sector of the U.S. economy. Although it would be desirable to implement the system for a detailed breakdown of the economy by sectors, our presentation is limited to national aggregates.

In measuring economic performance, our basic framework consists of a production account for the U.S. private domestic economy and a consolidated income and expenditure account for the U.S. private national economy. The income and expenditure account is consolidated with the accumulation account to provide a complete summary of the income of the private sector and its disposition in the form of consumer expenditures and capital formation.

[1] For a description of a complete accounting system, see [55].

For the production account, the fundamental accounting identity is that the value of output is equal to the value of factor input. Changes in the values of product and factor input are separated into price and quantity components. A summary measure of performance is based on the level of productivity, defined as the ratio of real product to real factor input or the ratio of the price of input to the price of output.

For the consolidated income and expenditure account the fundamental accounting identity is that the value of consumer receipts is equal to consumer outlays plus capital formation. Consumer receipts, consumer outlays, and capital formation can be separated into price and quantity components. A summary measure of performance is based on the standard of living, defined as the ratio of real expenditures to real receipts or the ratio of the price of factor services to the price of expenditures.

The interpretation of real product, real factor input, and total factor productivity requires the notion of a social production possibility frontier.[2] In each period the inputs of factors of production are transformed into outputs. In an extended description of the production possibilities, the inputs may include durable goods of various ages, inventories and financial claims, as well as the services of labor and natural agents.[3] The outputs would include used durable goods, unspent inventories, and goods and services for private or public consumption.

The interpretation of real consumer receipts and outlays and the standard of living requires the notion of a social welfare function.[4] An extended description of the determinants of social welfare must include all "goods" and "bads" relevant to social choice. Within the conventional framework the "goods" would include deliveries to final consumption in every future period and the "bads" would include deliveries of labor services in every future period. Evaluation would involve comparisons of "wealth-like" magnitudes.[5]

In this paper, we concentrate on the development of a complete accounting system in both current and constant prices. We limit the transactions included to those that can be measured or imputed from presently available primary data sources—income tax returns, population and production censuses and surveys, and so on. We present data

[2] This interpretation is developed by Solow [54], Richter [50], and Jorgenson and Griliches [40].

[3] An extended description is presented by Malinvaud [46] and Hicks [36].

[4] This interpretation is developed by Samuelson [51], [52], and many others; detailed references to the literature are given in [52, pp. 44–52].

[5] See [52, pp. 53–56].

for the period 1929–69 for each of the accounting magnitudes we discuss.

The first step in constructing an accounting system for the measurement of economic performance is to develop accounts in current prices. We present income and wealth accounts, including production, income and expenditure, accumulation and wealth accounts for the U.S. private economy for 1929–69 in Section 2 below.

In Section 3, we introduce the problem of constructing accounts in constant prices with a description of our system of index numbers for prices and quantities. In Section 4, we present an extension of the perpetual inventory method, familiar from national wealth accounting, to incorporate prices as well as quantities of capital goods. The price counterpart of the perpetual inventory method involves the estimation of prices of capital goods of every vintage at each point of time.

The presentation of a system of accounts in constant prices begins in Section 5 with the production account. The product side of the account includes consumption and investment goods output in constant prices. The factor outlay side includes labor and capital input. The ratio of output in constant prices to factor input is equal to total factor productivity. We present estimates of product, factor input, and total factor productivity for the U.S. private domestic economy for 1929–69.

In Section 6, we present income and expenditure, accumulation, and wealth accounts in constant prices for the U.S. private national economy, 1929–69. Consolidating the income and expenditure accounts we obtain a single account giving income and its disposition in constant prices.

We conclude with a discussion of possible extensions of the accounting framework in Section 7. The educational sector of the U.S. economy, which is largely governmental rather than private, could be incorporated into our accounting system by compiling data on educational investment, capital and labor input used in the educational sector, and the stock of human capital. Research and development expenditures in the private sector are treated on current account; expenditures on research should be capitalized.

Many other extensions of our accounting framework can be suggested. Activities internal to the household and government sectors could be incorporated into the accounting system by making appropriate imputations for nonmarket activities. Accounts for the educational sector could serve as a prototype for complete accounts for the household and government sectors.

A different range of extensions, not discussed in Section 7, would involve the compilation of accounts in constant prices for individual sectors of the economy. The production account could be disaggregated and complete interindustry accounts in constant prices could be incorporated into the system. The wealth account could be extended to include both assets and liabilities. Accumulation and wealth accounts could be disaggregated to incorporate complete flow of funds accounts.

As a basis for comparison we contrast our approach with two alternative accounting systems. The first is the U.S. national accounts, augmented by Denison's *Sources of Economic Growth,* which extends the framework of the U.S. accounts considerably.[6] The second is the United Nations System of National Accounts, as revised in 1968 [55]. In both systems, efforts have been made to develop accounts in both current and constant prices.

Despite the severe self-imposed limitations of our accounting system, concentrating on national aggregates of transactions that are already included in present accounting systems, our accounts differ very substantially from current practice. In comparing our system with available alternatives we focus attention on these differences. The basic similarities between our approach and current accounting practice can be recognized through the heavy reliance we have placed on data derived from the U.S. national accounts.

2. INCOME AND WEALTH

2.1. Introduction

The first problem in accounting for economic performance is the measurement of income and wealth in current prices. The solution of this problem requires a system of four accounts. First, the production account includes data on the output of the producing sector and the outlay of that sector on factor services, both expressed in current prices. Second, the income and expenditure account contains data on transfer payments and income from factor services, consumer outlays, and saving. Third, the accumulation account includes data on saving, capital formation, revaluation of existing assets, and the change in wealth from period to period. Finally, successive values of wealth are contained in the wealth account.

---

[6] All references to data from the U.S. national income and product accounts are to [49a] and [14].

2.2. Production Account

The production account contains data on the value of output and the value of input. As an accounting identity, the value of output is equal to the value of input. The two sides of the production account are linked through production of investment goods and compensation for the services of capital. Investment goods output enters the change in wealth from period to period through capital formation. Accumulated wealth generates factor incomes that arise as compensation for the services of capital. Investment goods output and property compensation must be defined in a consistent manner.

In the U.S. national income and product accounts, total output is divided among services, nondurable goods, durable goods, and structures.[7] The output of services includes the services of owner-occupied dwellings; the output of structures includes the production of new residential housing. Capital formation in the form of residential housing is a component of the change in wealth from period to period; property compensation includes the imputed value of compensation for the use of owner-occupied dwellings. The output of durables includes consumer durables and producer durables used by nonprofit institutions. However, property compensation, as defined in the U.S. national accounts, does not include the imputed value of the services of these durables.

In the U.S. national accounts, the value of the services of owner-occupied residential real estate, including structures and land, is imputed from market rental prices of renter-occupied residential real estate. The value of these services is allocated among net rent, interest, taxes, and capital consumption allowances. A similiar imputation is made for the services of real estate used by nonprofit institutions, but the imputed value excludes net rent.

To preserve consistency between the accounts for investment goods production and for property compensation we introduce imputations for the value of the services of consumer durables and durables used by nonprofit institutions and the net rent of real estate used by institutions. The value of the services of these assets is included in the output of services, together with the services of owner-occupied dwellings. Property compensation also includes the value of these services. This imputation preserves the accounting identity between the value of output and the value of input.

[7] See [49a, Tables 1.4 and 1.5].

We implement the production account for the U.S. private domestic economy, including the production activities of U.S. business and household sectors.[8] In principle, similar accounts could be constructed for government and rest of the world sectors of the economy. Wealth accounts for the government sector would be required for construction of a production account for government comparable to our production account for the private domestic sector.

We define revenue as proceeds to the sector from the sale of output, and outlay as gross outlays by the sector on purchases of input. Our concept of output is intermediate between gross output at market prices and gross output at factor cost, as these terms are usually employed. Output at market prices includes all indirect taxes in the value of output; output at factor cost excludes all indirect taxes. We distinguish between taxes charged against revenue, such as excise or sales taxes, and taxes that are part of the outlay on factor services, such as property taxes. We exclude taxes on output from the value of gross output since these taxes are not included in the proceeds to the sector. We include taxes on input since these taxes are included in the outlay of the sector.

Taxes on output reduce the proceeds of the sector and subsidies increase these proceeds; accordingly, the value of output includes production subsidies. To be more specific, we exclude excise and sales taxes, business nontax payments, and customs duties from the value of output and include other indirect business taxes plus subsidies and less current surplus of federal and state and local government enterprises. The resulting production account is given for 1958 in Table 1.

As an accounting identity, the value of gross private domestic factor outlay is equal to the value of gross private domestic product. Factor outlay is the sum of income originating in private enterprises and private households and institutions, plus the imputed value of consumer durables, producer durables utilized by institutions, and the net rent on institutional real estate, plus indirect taxes included in factor outlay. Factor outlay includes capital consumption allowances, business transfer payments, and the statistical discrepancy. Capital consumption allowances are part of the rental value of capital services. We include business transfer payments and the statistical discrepancy in factor outlay on capital. The value of gross private domestic factor outlay for the year 1958 is presented in Table 1.

[8] Our estimates are based on those of Christensen and Jorgenson [8].

TABLE 1

Production Account, Gross Private Domestic Product and Factor Outlay, United States, 1958
(billions of current dollars)

Product

1. Private gross national product (Table 1.7)	405.2
2. − Income originating in government enterprises (Table 1.13)	4.8
3. − Rest of the world gross national product (Table 1.7)	2.0
4. + Services of consumers' durables (our imputation)	40.3
5. + Services of durables held by institutions (our imputation)	0.3
6. + Net rent on institutional real estate (our imputation)	0.8
7. − Federal indirect business tax and nontax accruals (Table 3.1)	11.5
8. + Capital stock tax (Table 3.1, note 2)	−
9. − State and local indirect business tax and nontax accruals (Table 3.3)	27.0
10. + Business motor vehicle licenses (Table 3.3)	0.8
11. + Business property taxes (Table 3.3)	13.8
12. + Business other taxes (Table 3.3)	2.9
13. + Subsidies less current surplus of federal government enterprises (Table 3.1)	2.7
14. − Current surplus of state and local government enterprises (Table 3.3)	1.8
15. = Gross private domestic product	419.7

Factor Outlay

1. Capital consumption allowances (Table 1.9)	38.9
2. + Business transfer payments (Table 1.9)	1.6
3. + Statistical discrepancy (Table 1.9)	1.6
4. + Services of consumers' durables (our imputation)	40.3
5. + Services of durables held by institutions (our imputation)	0.3
6. + Net rent on institutional real estate (our imputation)	0.8
7. + Certain indirect business taxes (product account above, lines 8 + 10 + 11 + 12)	17.4
8. + Income originating in business (Table 1.13)	312.2
9. − Income originating in government enterprises (Table 1.13)	4.8
10. + Income originating in households and institutions (Table 1.13)	11.4
11. = Gross private domestic factor outlay	419.7

NOTE: All table references are to [49].

Product and income accounts are linked through capital formation and the corresponding compensation of property. To make this link explicit we must divide the total product between consumption and investment goods and total factor outlay between labor and property compensation. Investment goods production in the private domestic sector is equal to the total output of durable goods and structures included in the gross national product. Consumption goods production in the private domestic sector is equal to the output of nondurable goods and services in the gross national product, less the output of the foreign and government sectors, plus our imputation for the services of consumer durables and institutional durables and the net rent of institutional real estate. The output of the foreign and government sectors consists entirely of services.

The imputed value of the services of consumer and institutional durables and the net rent on institutional real estate is included in the value of output and the value of capital input. The value of outlay on capital services also includes the property income of self-employed persons; profits, rentals, and interest; capital consumption allowances; business transfer payments; the statistical discrepancy; and indirect taxes included in outlay on capital services, such as motor vehicle licenses, property taxes, and other taxes. The value of labor input includes the compensation of employees in private enterprises and in private households and nonprofit institutions, plus the labor compensation of the self-employed.

We estimate labor compensation of the self-employed by assuming that the compensation per full-time equivalent employee is equal to the labor compensation of proprietors and unpaid family workers.[9] This method is only one of many that have been proposed. Denison has suggested that the results are biased in the direction of allocating too large a proportion of the income of the self-employed to labor compensation.[10] However, Christensen has shown that the method produces results consistent with the assumption that rates of return to property used by the self-employed are comparable to rates of return in the corporate business sector when appropriate corrections are made for taxation and accrued capital gains or losses.[11] Gross private domestic

[9] Self-employed persons include proprietors and unpaid family workers. The method for imputation of labor compensation of the self-employed that underlies our estimates is discussed in detail by Christensen [6]. Alternative methods for imputation are reviewed in [44].

[10] See [16, p. 4].

[11] See [6].

product and factor outlay in current prices for 1929–69 are given in Table 2. Total product is divided between investment and consumption goods output. Total factor outlay is divided between labor and property compensation.

2.3. Income and Expenditure Account

The income and expenditure account includes data on transfer payments and the value of income from factor services, the value of consumer outlays, and saving. As an accounting identity, the value of consumer receipts is equal to the value of consumer outlays plus saving. The two sides of the income and expenditure account are linked through property compensation and saving. Saving results in the accumulation of tangible assets and financial claims; the accumulated wealth generates future property income. Saving must be defined in a way that is consistent with accounts for property income. Income must include all payments for factor services that result in consumption expenditures or in the accumulation of assets that result in future income.

We implement the income and expenditure account for the U.S. private national economy.[12] For this purpose we consolidate the accounts of private business with those of private households and institutions. Financial claims on the business sector by households and institutions are liabilities of the business sector; in the consolidated accounts these assets and liabilities cancel out. The assets of the private national economy include the tangible assets of the business sector. We treat social insurance funds as part of the private national economy. The claims of these funds on other governmental bodies are treated as assets of the private sector.

In the U.S. national accounts the income and expenditure account of the government sector does not include income from tangible assets owned by governmental bodies. If capital accounts were available for the government sector, we could construct income and expenditure accounts for that sector analogous to our accounts for the private sector. The income and expenditure account of the rest of the world sector of the U.S. national accounts is comparable to our account for the private sector.

We define income of the private national economy as proceeds from the sale of factor services. We define expenditure of the sector as consumer outlays plus saving. Our concept of income is closer to that underlying the concept of gross private saving in the U.S. national accounts

---

[12] Our estimates are based on those of Christensen and Jorgenson [9].

TABLE 2

Gross Private Domestic Product and Factor Outlay, 1929–69
(billions of current dollars)

Year	Gross Private Domestic Product	Investment Goods Product	Consumption Goods Product	Labor Outlay	Property Outlay
1929	104.2	28.5	75.7	60.5	43.7
1930	91.0	20.3	70.8	55.6	35.5
1931	76.6	14.1	62.5	47.3	29.3
1932	55.7	7.2	48.5	37.2	18.6
1933	54.5	7.5	47.0	34.8	19.7
1934	62.3	10.4	51.9	39.3	23.0
1935	67.9	12.7	55.2	42.6	25.3
1936	77.6	17.1	60.5	47.4	30.2
1937	85.3	19.6	65.7	53.7	31.6
1938	79.1	15.3	63.8	49.6	29.6
1939	85.4	19.3	66.1	53.0	32.4
1940	94.0	23.9	70.1	57.1	36.9
1941	115.9	36.9	79.0	69.6	46.3
1942	140.9	47.6	93.3	86.9	54.0
1943	167.8	60.5	107.3	102.3	65.5
1944	178.6	61.2	117.4	108.7	69.9
1945	177.7	52.8	124.9	108.4	69.3
1946	190.3	49.7	140.6	119.5	70.8
1947	218.3	64.1	154.2	137.8	80.6
1948	244.4	72.8	171.7	151.0	93.4
1949	235.1	72.1	162.9	148.9	86.1
1950	270.4	91.1	179.3	162.6	107.8
1951	305.8	106.0	199.8	183.8	122.0
1952	320.7	108.2	212.5	196.0	124.7
1953	340.6	115.1	225.5	210.5	130.1
1954	341.6	111.0	230.6	209.2	132.4
1955	377.7	128.5	249.2	225.0	152.7
1956	395.5	135.3	260.2	242.6	152.9
1957	413.4	140.0	273.4	254.1	159.3
1958	419.7	130.6	289.2	252.8	166.9
1959	458.1	146.8	311.3	273.6	184.5

(continued)

TABLE 2 (concluded)

Year	Gross Private Domestic Product	Invest- ment Goods Product	Consump- tion Goods Product	Labor Outlay	Property Outlay
1960	475.5	148.8	326.7	286.5	189.1
1961	488.1	147.5	340.6	292.3	195.8
1962	524.6	163.4	361.2	310.7	213.9
1963	553.4	173.2	380.2	325.0	228.4
1964	592.7	186.6	406.1	346.8	245.9
1965	640.5	204.5	436.0	371.4	269.1
1966	703.5	224.1	479.4	405.8	297.7
1967	739.8	229.3	510.4	429.9	309.8
1968	798.3	251.3	546.9	469.8	328.5
1969	863.7	270.7	593.0	514.8	348.9

than to the more commonly employed concept of personal disposable income. Accordingly, we refer to our income concept as gross private national income. Outlay on factor services by the production sector includes indirect taxes such as property taxes and motor vehicle licenses. This outlay also includes direct taxes such as corporate and personal income taxes. Our concept of gross private national income excludes both indirect and direct taxes.

To be specific, gross private national income includes labor and property income originating in the private domestic economy and the rest of the world sectors, labor income originating in the government sector, net interest paid by government, and the statistical discrepancy. Income is net of indirect taxes on factor outlay and all direct taxes on incomes. Gross private national income excludes interest paid by consumers and personal transfer payments to foreigners. Income also includes the investment income of social insurance funds, less transfers to general government by these funds. Contributions to social insurance are included and transfers from social insurance funds are excluded from income. The value of gross private national income and expenditures for the year 1958 are presented in Table 3.

Consumption is equal to personal consumption expenditures on services and nondurable goods plus our imputation for the services of consumer and institutional durables and the net rent of institutional real

TABLE 3

Gross Private National Receipts and Expenditures, 1958
(billions of current dollars)

Receipts	
1. Gross private domestic factor outlay [a]	419.7
2. + Income originating in general government (Table 1.13) [b]	42.1
3. + Income originating in government enterprises (Table 1.13)	4.8
4. + Income originating in rest of world (Table 1.13)	2.0
5. + Investment income of social insurance funds (Table 3.7)	1.8
6. − Transfers to general government from social insurance funds (Table 3.7)	0.6
7. + Net interest paid by government (Tables 3.1 and 3.3)	6.2
8. − Corporate profits tax liability (Table 1.10)	19.0
9. − Business property taxes [c]	17.4
10. − Personal tax and nontax payments (Table 2.1)	42.3
11. + Personal nontax payments (Tables 3.1 and 3.3)	2.3
12. = Gross private national income	399.5
13. + Government transfer payments to persons other than benefits from social insurance funds	8.1
14. = Gross private national consumer receipts	407.7
Expenditures	
1. Personal consumption expenditures (Table 1.1)	290.1
2. − Personal consumption expenditures, durable goods (Table 1.1)	37.9
3. + Services of consumer durables (our imputation) [d]	40.3
4. + Services of institutional durables (our imputation) [d]	0.3
5. + Opportunity cost of equity capital, institutional real estate (our imputation) [e]	0.8
6. = Private national consumption expenditure	293.6
7. + Personal transfer payments to foreigners (Table 2.1)	0.6
8. + Personal nontax payments (Tables 3.1 and 3.3)	2.3
9. = Private national consumer outlays	296.5
10. + Gross private national saving [f]	111.2
11. = Private national expenditures	407.7

[a] [8, Table 1, p. 23]. This series has been revised to include a net rent imputation to institutional structures. Our other imputations have also been slightly modified. See expenditure items 3, 4, and 5 below.

[b] All table references are to [49].

[c] [8, Table 1, p. 23, line 6, in factor outlay].

[d] [8, Section 5].

[e] We have computed an implicit rental value for institutional structures and land based on our estimate of the rate of return to owner-occupied real estate. The opportunity cost of equity capital is the difference between the implicit rental value and the net rent figure [49, Table 7.3]. This imputation was suggested to us by Edward F. Denison.

[f] See Table 5, line 10, below.

estate. Purchases of consumer durables, included in personal consumption expenditures in the U.S. national accounts, are treated as part of saving in our income and expenditure account. The value of consumption includes taxes and excludes subsidies on output; these taxes are excluded from the value of consumption goods output in the production account. Our concept of saving differs from gross private saving as defined in the U.S. national accounts in the treatment of social insurance and the statistical discrepancy. The expenditure account for the consuming sector for the year 1958 is presented in Table 3.

Our definition of income is similar to the concept of income underlying the U.S. national accounts concept of gross private saving. Our concept of income differs from the national accounts concept in the treatment of social insurance and transfer payments, the inclusion of the services of consumer and institutional durables, the net rent on institutional real estate, and the statistical discrepancy. Transfer payments are treated as a nonincome receipt of the consumer sector. The services of durables, net rent, and the statistical discrepancy are treated as part of outlays on capital services. The services of durables are included in output and capital input in order to preserve consistency between the definition of investment goods in the production account and the definition of property compensation in the factor outlay account. Net rent is included in output and factor outlay to preserve consistency between the treatment of owner-occupied residential real estate and institutional real estate. The statistical discrepancy is assigned to factor outlay so that the accounting identity between the value of output and the value of factor outlay is preserved.

Our treatment of social insurance can be compared with the treatment that underlies the U.S. national accounting concepts of personal disposable income and gross private saving. In these income concepts the social insurance funds are treated as part of the government sector rather than the private sector. Contributions to social insurance are treated as a tax, benefits paid by these funds are treated as a transfer payment, and the claims of these sectors on other governmental bodies are treated as claims on the government by itself that cancel out in a consolidated government wealth account. Our concept of income focuses on the separation of contributions to social insurance from other taxes and on the effects of a future stream of benefits on saving decisions by individuals. The national accounts treatment focuses on the involuntary nature of contributions to social insurance.

The differences between our concept of income and the national accounts concept of personal disposable income are very substantial.

In addition to the differences we have already outlined, our concept of income includes undistributed corporate profits, the corporate inventory valuation adjustment, corporate and noncorporate capital consumption allowances, and wage accruals less disbursements. All of these components of factor outlay are excluded from personal disposable income. We also exclude government transfer payments and net interest paid by consumers, which are included in personal disposable income. These differences between gross private national income, as we have defined it, and personal disposable income are primarily attributable to our consolidation of the accounts of the private business sector with those of private households and institutions. The income of the private sector includes all property compensation whether paid out in the form of dividends and interest or retained by the business sector.

Income and expenditure accounts are linked through saving and the resulting income from the services of property. To make this link explicit we must divide income between labor and property compensation and expenditure between saving and consumption. The measurement of labor and property compensation gross of taxes is straightforward. We have already described the allocation of private domestic factor outlay between the value of capital input and the value of labor input. Corresponding allocations for government and rest of the world sectors are available from the U.S. national accounts. The problem is to allocate taxes on factor services between labor services and capital services. We allocate indirect business taxes on factor services and the corporate income tax to income from capital. The problem that remains is to allocate personal income tax payments between income from labor and income from capital.

To allocate personal income tax payments between labor and property compensation we employ a method developed by Frane and Klein [21] and applied by Ando and Brown [1] to U.S. data on the personal income tax for 1929 to 1958. Personal income taxes on income from labor services are a remarkably stable proportion of total personal income tax receipts. The data for 1929 to 1958 show that the proportion of taxes on labor income in total personal taxes for the latter part of the period is .755 with negligible variation. We have extended the estimates of personal income taxes on labor income by Ando and Brown to 1969 by assuming that the proportion of these taxes in total personal income taxes is constant at 0.755. Personal income taxes not allocated to labor income are allocated to property income. Gross private national receipts and expenditures in current prices for 1929–69 are given in Table 4. Income is divided between labor and property

TABLE 4

Gross Private National Receipts and Expenditures, 1929–69
(billions of current dollars)

Year	Gross Private National Income	Labor Compensation	Property Compensation	Gross Private National Receipts and Expenditures	Consumption Expenditures	Consumer Outlays	Gross Private National Saving
1929	102.7	65.5	37.1	103.5	77.0	78.1	25.4
1930	90.1	60.8	29.3	91.0	71.4	72.4	18.6
1931	76.9	52.7	24.1	78.8	63.5	64.4	14.3
1932	56.2	42.3	13.9	57.4	50.0	50.8	6.7
1933	55.3	39.9	15.3	56.5	49.3	50.0	6.5
1934	63.8	45.4	18.4	65.1	53.9	54.6	10.5
1935	69.2	49.1	20.1	70.7	56.4	57.1	13.7
1936	79.0	55.2	23.8	81.7	62.8	63.5	18.2
1937	85.6	61.0	24.6	87.2	66.5	67.2	20.0
1938	80.6	57.6	23.1	82.3	65.4	66.0	16.3
1939	86.8	61.1	25.8	88.5	67.6	68.2	20.3
1940	94.1	65.3	28.8	95.7	70.6	71.3	24.4
1941	112.1	79.3	32.8	113.8	78.7	79.4	34.4
1942	136.7	100.7	35.9	138.4	87.1	87.8	50.6
1943	160.3	118.3	41.9	162.0	103.0	103.9	58.1
1944	178.5	130.1	48.4	180.7	111.6	112.6	68.1
1945	181.8	132.0	49.8	185.9	123.1	124.3	61.6
1946	185.2	130.7	54.5	193.4	142.8	144.1	49.4
1947	204.1	142.1	62.0	212.7	158.6	159.9	52.8
1948	230.0	156.9	73.1	238.0	171.0	172.6	65.4
1949	227.0	159.3	67.6	234.7	166.6	168.1	66.6
1950	254.0	174.1	79.9	261.8	184.8	186.3	75.5
1951	282.9	194.6	88.3	289.6	200.7	202.2	87.4
1952	299.4	206.9	92.4	306.0	215.3	216.9	89.0
1953	317.1	221.2	96.0	323.6	227.6	229.4	94.2
1954	324.3	223.6	100.7	331.0	235.2	237.2	93.8

(continued)

TABLE 4 (concluded)

Year	Gross Private National Income	Labor Compensation	Property Compensation	Gross Private National Receipts and Expenditures	Consumption Expenditures	Consumer Outlays	Gross Private National Saving
1955	354.7	239.3	115.4	361.9	252.8	254.8	107.1
1956	370.5	256.7	113.8	377.7	265.9	268.3	109.4
1957	388.6	269.2	119.5	396.2	278.7	281.4	114.9
1958	399.5	271.5	128.1	407.7	293.6	296.5	111.2
1959	431.9	292.3	139.7	440.3	315.6	318.7	121.6
1960	448.5	305.8	142.7	456.9	331.8	334.9	122.0
1961	462.0	314.7	147.3	471.0	343.0	346.4	124.6
1962	496.2	333.9	162.3	505.4	360.4	364.2	141.2
1963	522.8	350.0	172.8	532.5	380.8	385.0	147.5
1964	567.2	379.2	188.0	577.4	406.5	411.3	166.1
1965	609.9	404.9	205.0	621.1	433.9	439.1	181.9
1966	669.4	442.2	227.2	681.3	470.8	476.6	204.8
1967	708.0	470.4	237.6	721.8	499.0	505.7	216.1
1968	756.0	511.0	245.0	771.5	536.2	543.7	227.8
1969	807.8	551.8	256.0	825.7	583.5	591.9	233.8

compensation, net of taxes. Expenditure is divided between consumer outlays and saving.

2.4. Accumulation Account

The accumulation account includes data on saving, capital formation, revaluation of existing assets, and the change in wealth from period to period. Gross private national saving is reduced by depreciation to obtain saving as it enters the accumulation account. As an accounting identity, the value of saving is equal to the value of capital formation. The change in wealth from period to period is equal to saving plus the revaluation of existing assets. Although revaluations are part of the change in wealth, they are excluded from income and from saving. In measuring the return from investment in different types of assets, both returns in the form of income and returns from revaluations must be considered.

TABLE 5

Gross Private National Capital Formation, Saving,
and Revaluation, 1958
(billions of current dollars)

	Saving	
1.	Personal saving (Table 2.1)	22.3
2.	+ Undistributed corporate profits (Table 5.1)	10.8
3.	+ Corporate inventory valuation adjustment (Table 5.1)	−0.3
4.	+ Corporate capital consumption allowances (Table 5.1)	22.0
5.	+ Noncorporate capital consumption allowances (Table 5.1)	16.9
6.	+ Wage accruals less disbursements (Table 5.1)	0.0
7.	+ Personal consumption expenditures, durable goods (Table 1.1)	37.9
8.	+ Surplus, social insurance funds (Table 3.7)	0.0
9.	+ Statistical discrepancy (Table 1.9)	1.6
10.	= Gross private national saving	111.2
11.	− Depreciation (our imputation)	80.8
12.	= Net private national saving	30.4
13.	+ Revaluation (our imputation)	31.6
14.	= Change in private national wealth	62.1
	Capital Formation	
1.	Gross private domestic investment (Table 1.2)	60.9
2.	+ Personal consumption expenditures, durable goods (Table 1.1)	37.9
3.	+ Deficit of federal government (Table 3.1)	10.2
4.	+ Deficit of state and local governments (Table 3.3)	2.3
5.	− Deficit, federal social insurance funds (Table 3.7)	−1.6
6.	− Deficit, state and local social insurance funds (Table 3.7)	1.7
7.	+ Net foreign investment (Table 5.1)	−0.2
8.	= Gross private national capital formation	111.2

NOTE: Table references are to [49].

We implement the accumulation account for the U.S. private national economy.[13] Sources of saving include gross private saving, as
defined in the U.S. national accounts, the surplus of federal and state
and local social insurance funds, personal consumption expenditures on
durable goods, and the statistical discrepancy. Capital formation includes gross private domestic investment, personal consumption expenditures on durable goods, deficits of the federal, state, and local
governments excluding social insurance funds, and net foreign invest-

[13] Our estimates are based on [9].

ment. Private national saving and capital formation are given for 1958 in Table 5.

In the U.S. national accounts depreciation on tangible assets in the business sector is set equal to depreciation claimed for tax purposes. We replace this estimate of depreciation by our own imputation, described in detail in Section 4 below. No depreciation for consumer durables and durables used by institutions is included in the U.S. national accounts. Our imputed value of depreciation includes depreciation for both these classes of assets.

To estimate the change in wealth from period to period we require estimates of saving net of depreciation and estimates of the revaluation of existing assets due to price changes. Revaluations are not included in the U.S. national accounts, so that an essential link between income and expenditure accounts and wealth accounts is missing. We have estimated the revaluations for private domestic tangible assets as part of our perpetual inventory of capital goods, described in Section 4 below. Our estimates of revaluations for financial claims are based on accounts for stocks of these claims in current prices. We estimate revaluations as the difference between the period to period changes in these stocks and the deficits of the government and rest of the world sectors. Private national saving and capital formation in current prices for 1929–69 are given in Table 6.

2.5. Wealth Account

All of the accounts we have considered up to this point contain data on flows. The production account includes flows of output and input; the income and expenditure account includes the corresponding flows; the flow of saving and changes in wealth from period to period are included in the accumulation account. The wealth account contains data on the stock of wealth in successive periods. The wealth account can be presented in balance sheet form with the value of assets equal to the value of liabilities as an accounting identity. We present only the asset side of the wealth account.

We implement the wealth account for the U.S. private national economy.[14] The wealth accounts of private business are consolidated with those of private households and institutions. Our wealth account includes data on assets in the consolidated account. These assets include the tangible assets of private households and institutions and the tangible assets of private business. In addition, they include net

[14] Our estimates are based on [9].

TABLE 6

Gross Private National Capital Formation, Saving,
and Revaluation, 1929–69
(billions of current dollars)

Year	Gross Private National Saving and Capital Formation	Replace-ment and Depreci-ation	Net Private National Saving and Capital Formation	Revalu-ation	Change in Wealth
1929	25.4	19.2	6.2	3.4	9.7
1930	18.6	19.0	−0.4	−22.0	−22.4
1931	14.3	17.2	−2.8	−39.9	−42.7
1932	6.7	14.7	−8.0	−38.7	−46.7
1933	6.5	13.3	−6.7	1.7	−5.0
1934	10.5	13.5	−2.9	19.8	16.9
1935	13.7	12.9	0.7	3.4	4.2
1936	18.2	12.9	5.3	8.0	13.3
1937	20.0	14.1	5.9	17.4	23.2
1938	16.3	14.8	1.4	−2.1	−0.7
1939	20.3	14.5	5.8	−1.5	4.3
1940	24.4	15.0	9.4	6.2	15.7
1941	34.4	16.8	17.6	30.2	47.8
1942	50.6	20.3	30.3	41.7	72.0
1943	58.1	20.9	37.2	27.6	64.7
1944	68.1	21.7	46.5	21.8	68.3
1945	61.6	21.7	39.9	12.9	52.9
1946	49.4	22.9	26.4	52.5	79.0
1947	52.8	28.4	24.4	83.2	107.6
1948	65.4	33.9	31.5	46.4	77.9
1949	66.6	37.9	28.8	−10.8	17.9
1950	75.5	41.8	33.7	45.4	79.0
1951	87.4	49.6	37.8	64.9	102.7
1952	89.0	53.8	35.2	15.7	50.9
1953	94.2	56.5	37.7	5.2	42.9
1954	93.8	59.2	34.6	5.3	39.9

(continued)

TABLE 6 (concluded)

Year	Gross Private National Saving and Capital Formation	Replace- ment and Depreci- ation	Net Private National Saving and Capital Formation	Revalu- ation	Change in Wealth
1955	107.1	62.3	44.8	21.4	66.2
1956	109.4	69.8	39.6	58.1	97.8
1957	114.9	76.5	38.4	51.9	90.3
1958	111.2	80.8	30.4	32.4	62.8
1959	121.6	83.7	37.9	39.3	77.2
1960	122.0	86.7	35.3	32.1	67.4
1961	124.6	89.7	34.9	29.5	64.4
1962	141.2	92.4	48.8	40.8	89.6
1963	147.5	96.3	51.2	37.6	88.7
1964	166.1	101.5	64.6	45.7	110.4
1965	181.9	107.5	74.5	52.4	126.8
1966	204.8	115.7	89.0	64.1	153.1
1967	216.1	127.2	88.9	79.1	168.1
1968	227.8	138.5	89.3	98.6	187.9
1969	233.8	152.0	81.8	120.7	202.5

claims on the foreign and government sectors by the private sector. Social insurance funds are treated as part of the private sector rather than as part of government.

Our estimate of the stock of private domestic tangible assets is based on a perpetual inventory of capital goods, as described in Section 4. Our estimate of net claims on foreigners and governments is based on the flow of funds accounts of the Board of Governors of the Federal Reserve System and on *Studies in the National Balance Sheet of the United States* [26] and *The National Wealth of the United States in the Postwar Period* [24].[15] We distinguish between monetary and non-monetary claims on the federal government by the private sector. Monetary claims include vault cash of commercial banks, member bank reserves, and currency outside banks. Nonmonetary claims on the fed-

[15] Data on flow of funds are based on estimates of [3b], [23], [24], [25], and [26].

eral government include U.S. government total liabilities, less U.S. government financial assets, plus net liabilities of federally sponsored credit agencies and financial assets of included social insurance funds, less U.S. government liabilities to rest of world, plus U.S. government credits and claims abroad, less monetary liabilities. Private sector claims on state and local governments include state and local government total liabilities, less state and local government financial assets, plus assets of cash sickness compensation funds. Net private claims on the rest of the world include private U.S. assets and investments abroad less private U.S. liabilities to foreigners. Private national wealth in 1958 is presented in Table 7. Annual data on the components of private national wealth are presented in Table 8.

2.6. The Accounting System

The production and income and expenditure accounts are related through markets for commodities and factor services. Factor outlay by the producing sector is the most important component of income from the supply of factor services by the consuming sector. Income also includes the value of factor services supplied to the government and rest of the world sectors. The expenditure account is linked to the production account through the market for consumption goods and services. The production of consumption goods also includes goods consumed by the government and the rest of the world sectors. Expenditure on consumption goods includes goods supplied by the rest of the world sector. The expenditure account is also linked to the production indirectly through saving.

The accumulation account allocates saving among its sources and uses. The uses of saving include capital formation through investment in reproducible tangible assets. Expenditure on investment in these assets is linked to the production account through the market for investment goods output. The production of investment goods is partly consumed by government and rest of the world sectors; part of the supply of these goods originates in the rest of the world sector. The accumulation account is linked to the wealth account through the accounting identity between period to period changes in wealth and the sum of saving and revaluations of existing assets.

The structure of this accounting system can be compared with that of the U.S. national accounts. The production account is for gross national product and includes income generated in the government and rest of the world sectors. Our production account is for gross private

TABLE 7

Private National Wealth, 1958
(billions of current dollars)

1.	Private domestic tangible assets [a]		1,300.1
2.	+ Net claims on the federal, state, and local governments		280.9
	a. Federal, monetary [b]	50.6	
	(i) + Vault cash of commercial banks	3.2	
	(ii) + Member bank reserves	18.5	
	(iii) + Currency outside banks	28.9	
	b. Federal, nonmonetary	195.2	
	(i) U.S. government total liabilities [b]	256.4	
	(ii) − U.S. government financial assets [b]	50.0	
	(iii) + Net liabilities, federally sponsored credit agencies [b]	0.5	
	(iv) + Assets of included social insurance funds [c]	30.4	
	(v) − U.S. government liabilities to rest of world [d]	8.8	
	(vi) + U.S. government credits and claims abroad [d]	18.3	
	(vii) − Monetary liabilities [b]	50.6	
	c. State and local	35.1	
	(i) State and local government total liabilities [b]	62.6	
	(ii) − State and local government financial assets [b]	27.7	
	(iii) + Assets of cash sickness compensation fund	0.2	
3.	+ Net claims on rest of world [d]		13.8
	a. Private U.S. assets and investments abroad	41.1	
	b. − Private U.S. liabilities to foreigners	27.3	
4.	= Private national wealth		1,594.9

[a] [8]; see [8, pp. 294–301] for a discussion.

[b] [31].

[c] [59, February issues].

[d] [49b, "The International Investment Pattern of the United States," in October issues].

TABLE 8

Private National Wealth, 1929–69
(billions of current dollars)

Year	Corporate Tangible Assets	Non-corporate Tangible Assets	Household and Institutional Tangible Assets	Net Claims on Governments and Rest of World	Private National Wealth
1929	116.7	106.7	158.1	33.0	414.6
1930	110.3	97.9	150.0	34.0	392.2
1931	97.7	85.1	131.5	35.2	349.5
1932	84.1	73.3	108.1	37.3	302.7
1933	80.4	73.4	104.4	39.4	297.6
1934	83.1	76.3	109.5	45.2	314.2
1935	83.7	79.4	107.9	47.4	318.3
1936	86.6	82.7	112.5	50.0	331.8
1937	95.0	88.1	120.5	51.7	355.2
1938	92.2	85.6	122.2	54.4	354.3
1939	91.9	85.3	123.6	57.8	358.6
1940	96.6	88.7	129.2	59.9	374.4
1941	109.7	98.6	143.7	70.5	422.5
1942	121.1	108.6	155.1	110.3	495.0
1943	126.4	115.1	163.6	155.2	560.2
1944	130.4	121.2	173.9	202.9	628.5
1945	133.1	127.2	181.2	239.0	680.6
1946	159.6	148.5	206.7	244.6	759.4
1947	199.1	175.0	252.6	240.3	867.0
1948	224.2	192.2	291.8	236.0	944.2
1949	226.6	190.4	302.1	242.8	962.0
1950	248.2	212.7	341.8	238.8	1,041.5
1951	286.9	234.4	384.9	238.1	1,144.3
1952	303.0	237.5	408.7	245.9	1,195.0
1953	315.5	238.6	427.8	256.5	1,238.4
1954	323.1	244.4	442.9	267.6	1,278.0

(continued)

TABLE 8 (concluded)

Year	Corporate Tangible Assets	Non-corporate Tangible Assets	Household and Institutional Tangible Assets	Net Claims on Governments and Rest of World	Private National Wealth
1955	344.3	253.5	477.6	268.6	1,344.1
1956	381.8	269.7	518.8	271.6	1,441.9
1957	411.9	287.8	553.8	278.5	1,532.0
1958	422.2	303.9	574.0	294.8	1,594.9
1959	443.7	315.4	612.8	300.5	1,672.4
1960	461.9	330.6	640.7	306.4	1,739.7
1961	476.6	347.3	663.8	316.7	1,804.3
1962	500.1	367.0	698.6	328.3	1,893.9
1963	524.4	384.7	737.9	335.5	1,982.6
1964	556.4	404.8	785.1	346.9	2,093.2
1965	598.9	433.9	831.1	355.8	2,219.7
1966	660.0	464.2	880.6	367.9	2,372.7
1967	714.8	494.0	943.0	389.1	2,540.8
1968	771.4	529.5	1,022.9	404.5	2,728.3
1969	839.8	570.8	1,109.5	410.5	2,930.6

domestic product and excludes these two sectors. The income and expenditure account in the U.S. national accounts is for personal income and outlay. Factor outlay in the producing sector taking the form of undistributed corporate profits is excluded from personal income. Our concept of gross private national income is more closely related to the concept of income underlying the U.S. national accounts concept of gross private saving than to the concept of personal disposable income.

The accumulation account of the U.S. national accounts is based on national saving and investment rather than private saving and investment. However, the most serious problem with the accumulation account is the absence of two types of data that are essential in linking income and wealth accounts. The first is an estimate of economic depreciation. Estimates of capital consumption allowances in the U.S. national accounts are based on depreciation reported for tax purposes. As tax laws have evolved over time, these estimates have come to reflect widely varying depreciation formulas and lifetimes of assets for tax purposes.[16] No attempt has been made to replace estimates of depreciation for tax purposes with estimates based on an economic concept of depreciation.[17] We have attempted to remedy this deficiency. The second important omission in the accumulation account is an estimate of the revaluation of assets. Data on revaluations are essential for the construction of an integrated system of national income and wealth accounts.

The structure of our accounting system can also be compared with the United Nations *System of National Accounts* [55]. The principal difference between our system and the U.N. system is that we confine the accounts to the private sector. In the U.N. system the production account is based on the domestic economy rather than the private domestic sector; the income and expenditure account and the accumulation account are based on the national economy rather than the private sector. We have combined the accumulation and revaluation accounts of the U.N. system into a single accumulation account, which also includes period to period changes in national wealth. We have presented only the asset side of the national wealth accounts, while the U.N. system includes a balance sheet with data on both assets and liabilities.

3. INDEX NUMBERS

3.1. Introduction

The second problem in accounting for economic performance is the measurement of income and wealth in constant prices. Preliminary to the solution of this problem we must consider the selection of an appropriate system of index numbers. To express any accounting magnitude in constant prices we must separate the change in value from period to period into components associated with change in price and change in quantity. As an illustration, the change in the value of output entering the production account can be separated into a change in the quantity of output and a change in the price of output. Changes in other flows—factor outlay, income, expenditure on consumer goods, and investment—can be decomposed into price and quantity changes in the same way. As a second illustration, the change in the value of

---

[16] A detailed discussion of tax provisions affecting depreciation and amortization for tax purposes is given in [62].

[17] Estimates of replacement based on the straight-line method and estimates of depreciation and replacement based on the declining balance method for producer durables and nonresidential structures are contained in the Office of Business Economics *Capital Goods Study*. See [30].

wealth entering the wealth account can be separated into a change in the quantity of assets and a change in the price of assets. We identify the change in quantity with saving and the change in price with revaluation of assets.

3.2. Divisia Index Numbers

Our system of index numbers is based on a discrete approximation to continuous index numbers. To illustrate the construction of index numbers of prices and quantities we consider the value of output as it enters the production account. Suppose that m components of output are distinguished in the accounts; the value of output, say qY, may be written:

$$qY = q_1Y_1 + q_2Y_2 + \cdots + q_mY_m.$$

Our system of index numbers consists of an index for the price of output q and the quantity of output Y, defined in terms of the prices (q_i) and quantities (Y_i) of the m components. The first step in defining these indexes is to differentiate the value of output with respect to time, obtaining:

$$\dot{q}Y + q\dot{Y} = \Sigma\dot{q}_iY_i + \Sigma q_i\dot{Y}_i.$$

We may define the relative shares of the value of the ith output in the value of total output, say w_i, as follows:

$$w_i = \frac{q_iY_i}{\Sigma q_iY_i}.$$

Dividing both sides of the total derivative of the value of output with respect to time by the value of output, we obtain:

$$\frac{\dot{q}}{q} + \frac{\dot{Y}}{Y} = \Sigma w_i\left(\frac{\dot{q}_i}{q_i} + \frac{\dot{Y}_i}{Y_i}\right).$$

We define the price and quantity indexes for output in terms of the prices and quantities of individual components; the rates of growth of the price index q and the quantity index Y are:

$$\frac{\dot{q}}{q} = \Sigma w_i\frac{\dot{q}_i}{q_i}, \quad \frac{\dot{Y}}{Y} = \Sigma w_i\frac{\dot{Y}_i}{Y_i},$$

respectively. These index numbers are Divisia price and quantity indexes.[18] The indexes are defined in terms of rates of growth of price and

---

[18] The economic interpretation of Divisia indexes of total factor productivity has been discussed in [54], [50], and [40].

quantity components of the rate of growth of the value of output. To obtain the price and quantity indexes themselves we choose a base for the indexes and integrate the rates of growth with respect to time. For the index numbers given below we choose the base for all price indexes as 1.000 in 1958. The base for the quantity indexes is equal to the value of the corresponding accounting magnitude in 1958.

The principal advantages of Divisia index numbers for social accounting purposes are, first, that rates of growth of these indexes of prices and quantity are symmetrical and add up to the rate of growth of the value of output (factor reversal test). Second, Divisia indexes are unaffected by a change in the direction of time (time reversal test). Finally, these indexes have the important reproductive property that a Divisia index of Divisia indexes is a Divisia index of the components. As an illustration, if the quantity index of total product is a Divisia index of quantity indexes of consumption and investment goods output and if the consumption and investment goods indexes are each Divisia indexes of individual consumption and investment goods, then the total product index is a Divisia index of the individual consumption and investment goods. The Divisia index numbers provide a convenient framework for national accounting since the principles of aggregation for data from subsectors of the economy are the same as those for construction of data for the subsectors. The results for the economy as a whole are independent of the structuring of the subaggregates.

For application to data for discrete points of time an approximation to the Divisia indexes for continuous time is required. Price and quantity index numbers originally discussed by Fisher may be employed for this purpose [19]. Approximating rates of growth by the period-to-period changes in logarithms, we obtain:

$$\log q_t - \log q_{t-1} = \Sigma \bar{w}_{it}(\log q_{it} - \log q_{i,\,t-1}),$$

$$\log Y_t - \log Y_{t-1} = \Sigma \bar{w}_{it}(\log Y_{it} - \log Y_{i,\,t-1}),$$

where the weights ($\bar{w}_{it}$) are arithmetic averages of the relative shares in the two periods,

$$\bar{w}_{it} = \frac{1}{2} w_{it} + \frac{1}{2} w_{i,\,t-1}.$$

These index numbers have been suggested as a discrete approximation to the Divisia index by Tornquist [58]. Obviously, the discrete and continuous index numbers are equal if and only if relative shares are constant. If shares are not constant, the discrete approximation involves an error that depends on the variability of the relative shares and the length of the time period.

Divisia index numbers for discrete time are symmetric in data of different time periods (time reversal). They also have the basic reproductive property that a discrete Divisia index of discrete Divisia indexes is a discrete Divisia index of the components. This property implies that the indexes for the economy as a whole are independent of the structuring of subsectors from which the aggregate data are constructed. The discrete Divisia price and quantity indexes are symmetrical. Theil has demonstrated that the sum of changes in the logarithms of discrete Divisia indexes of price and quantity is approximately equal to the change in the logarithm of the corresponding value (factor reversal) [57]. The factor reversal test is satisfied exactly if relative shares are constant; the accuracy of the approximation depends on the change in relative shares.

As a practical matter the approximation of changes in value by the sum of changes in discrete Divisia price and quantity indexes is extremely accurate. For the annual rate of growth in value of personal consumption expenditures in the Netherlands for the period 1921–63, Theil shows that the error averages only 0.01 per cent of the annual growth rate. It is convenient to have the product of price and quantity indexes equal to the value of transactions so that standard accounting identities hold for variables defined as price and quantity index numbers. Accordingly, we construct discrete Divisia price indexes as the value of the corresponding accounting magnitude divided by the discrete Divisia quantity index. The resulting price indexes are approximately equal to Divisia price indexes and have the reproductive property of Divisia indexes. They also satisfy, approximately, the time reversal and factor reversal tests for index numbers.

3.3. Taxes

At a number of points in our accounting system transactions data are presented net and gross of taxes. As one illustration, consumer purchases of goods and services in the income and expenditure accounts include sales and excise taxes. Sales of the same goods and services in the production account exclude these taxes. As a second illustration, outlay on factor services in the production account includes direct taxes and certain indirect taxes such as property taxes. Income from factor services in the income and expenditure accounts excludes these taxes. We treat sales and excise taxes as part of the price paid by consumers.

We treat property taxes and income taxes as part of the price paid by producers. We can separate the change in the value of transactions into three components—change in price, change in quantity, and change in tax. The tax change is a component of the change in the price paid by the sector making an expenditure; the tax change is excluded from the change in the price received by the sector receiving income.

To illustrate the construction of price, quantity, and tax indexes we consider the value of consumer expenditure as it enters the income and expenditure account. Again, suppose that m components of consumer expenditure are distinguished in the accounts; the value of output, gross of tax, say q^+Y, may be written:

$$q^+Y = q_1{}^+Y_1 + q_2{}^+Y_2 + \cdots + q_m{}^+Y_m.$$

The prices $(q_i{}^+)$ include sales and excise taxes; the quantities (Y_i) are measured in the same way as in the production accounts. Price and quantity indexes based on these prices and quantities may be defined in the same way as before.

To introduce taxes into the system of index numbers we let the market price of output q^+ be equal to the price received by the producer, say q, multiplied by unity plus the effective tax rate, t; the value of output at market prices is:

$$q^+Y = (1 + t)qY.$$

The value of output at market prices may be expressed in terms of prices received by producers, each multiplied by unity plus the corresponding tax rate:

$$(1 + t)qY = \Sigma(1 + t_i)q_iY_i,$$

where the prices paid by the consumers $(q_i{}^+)$ are expressed in terms of prices received by producers (q_i) and tax rates (t_i).

Proceeding as before, we express the rate of growth of the value of consumer expenditure as the sum of rates of growth of taxes, prices, and quantities:

$$\frac{(1 + \dot{\imath})}{1 + t} + \frac{\dot{q}}{q} + \frac{\dot{Y}}{Y} = \Sigma w_i \left[\frac{(1 + \dot{\imath}_i)}{1 + t_i} + \frac{\dot{q}_i}{q_i} + \frac{\dot{Y}_i}{Y_i} \right].$$

The rate of growth of the tax index, $1 + t$, is:

$$\frac{(1 + \dot{\imath})}{1 + t} = \Sigma w_i \frac{(1 + \dot{\imath}_i)}{1 + t_i};$$

rates of growth of price and quantity indexes are analogous to those for the production account described above. To construct a tax index from the rate of growth we choose an appropriate base and integrate the rates of growth with respect to time. For the index numbers given below we choose the base for all tax indexes as the ratio of the corresponding accounting magnitude before taxes to this magnitude after taxes for 1958. To obtain the effective tax rate, we subtract unity from the resulting tax index.

For application to data for discrete points of time we approximate Divisia indexes for continuous time as before. It is convenient to preserve accounting identities for variables defined as price, quantity, and tax index numbers. Accordingly, we construct an index of taxes $1 + t$ by dividing the value of transactions at market prices by the value of transactions at producer prices. The resulting tax index is approximately equal to the Divisia tax index. It should be noted that Divisia price and quantity indexes at market prices differ from the corresponding indexes at producer prices since taxes enter the weights (w_i) employed in constructing the indexes.

3.4. Index Number Systems

In the U.S. national accounts only the output side of the production account is measured in current and constant prices. The index number system employed for the measurement of output in constant prices is based on a Laspeyres index number for the quantity of output and a Paasche index number for the price of output. In the Laspeyres index of output, prices of a base year are employed as weights for quantities of output. The Laspeyres index of the quantity of output, say Y^L, is defined by:

$$Y_1{}^L = \frac{\Sigma q_{i0} Y_{i1}}{\Sigma q_{i0} Y_{i0}},$$

where the base period prices (q_{i0}) are prices of 1958. Dividing the ratio of the values of transactions in period 1 to those in period 0 by the Laspeyres quantity index, we obtain the Paasche index of the price of output, q^P:

$$q_1{}^P = \frac{\Sigma q_{i1} Y_{i1}}{\Sigma q_{i0} Y_{i1}},$$

where the quantities (Y_{i1}) are quantities of the current year.

To compare the Divisia index numbers with the system of index numbers used in the U.S. national accounts we consider the rate of growth of the Laspeyres index of real product:

$$\frac{Y_1^L - Y_0^L}{Y_0^L} = \frac{\Sigma q_{i0} Y_{i1}}{\Sigma q_{i0} Y_{i0}} - \frac{\Sigma q_{i0} Y_{i0}}{\Sigma q_{i0} Y_{i0}} = \frac{\Sigma q_{i0} Y_{i1}}{\Sigma q_{i0} Y_{i0}} - 1.$$

Next we consider the Laspeyres approximation to the rate of growth of the Divisia quantity index:

$$\frac{Y_1^D - Y_0^D}{Y_0^D} = \Sigma \frac{q_{i0} Y_{i0}}{\Sigma q_{i0} Y_{i0}} \frac{Y_{i1} - Y_{i0}}{Y_{i0}} = \frac{\Sigma q_{i0} Y_{i1}}{\Sigma q_{i0} Y_{i0}} - 1.$$

The rate of growth of the Laspeyres approximation to the Divisia index is identical with the rate of growth of the usual Laspeyres quantity index.

The first difference between our system of index numbers and the system employed in the U.S. national accounts is that we approximate the underlying continuous index numbers by price and quantity indexes that satisfy the time reversal and factor reversal tests for index numbers. The Laspeyres approximation given above satisfies neither test since the corresponding price index number is a Paasche approximation to the underlying continuous price index number and since the Laspeyres and Paasche formulas are not symmetric in data of different time periods. These differences do not produce large variations in the price and quantity index numbers.

The second difference between our system of index numbers and the system of the U.S. national accounts is that our indexes are chain linked. For each year, current prices are used as weights in estimating the rate of growth of quantity to the following year and current quantities are used as weights in estimating the rate of growth of price. This process is followed for each pair of years, and the resulting indexes are chain linked. In effect the base of the index numbers is moved continually. The main advantage of a continually changing base is in the reduction of errors of approximation as the economy moves from one production or expenditure configuration to another. Chain-linked index numbers reduce the errors of approximation to a minimum. The use of a chain-linked index alters price and quantity indexes substantially for periods in which relative prices and relative quantities are shifting.

Denison has augmented the quantity and price indexes of the production account of the U.S. national accounts to provide quantity and price indexes of factor input [14]. Although he uses the quantity and price indexes of output based on the national accounts, he employs chain-linked indexes of input with weights changing every five years. The

Laspeyres approximation to the Divisia indexes of input and output is employed by Jorgenson and Griliches [40], while Christensen and Jorgenson [8] have used the approximation described above, satisfying factor and time reversal tests for index numbers. The main differences between the price and quantity indexes for these alternative systems of index numbers result from the use of chain-linked indexes. Alternative approximations to continuous indexes produce substantially similar results.

In the United Nations *System of National Accounts,* systems of index numbers like that employed in the U.S. national accounts are recommended as a basis for constructing price and quantity indexes for the output side of the production account [55]. As the base period is changed from time to time, chain linking of the resulting price and quantity indexes is recommended. Continual chain linking is not recommended for general adoption "mainly because the amount of data it requires is altogether greater than the amount required by the alternative." [19] The index numbers we employ in constructing accounts for output in constant prices are chain-linked indexes of component indexes obtained from the U.S. national accounts. They represent a mixture of chain-linked and fixed weight indexes. The index numbers we employ in constructing accounts for input, income, and expenditure are chain-linked indexes based on price and quantity data.

4. PERPETUAL INVENTORY

4.1. Introduction

Measurement of the output side of the production account and the asset side of the wealth account in constant prices is well-established in social accounting practice. Index numbers of the price and quantity of output are constructed from data on prices and quantities of individual outputs. Index numbers of the price and quantity of capital assets are constructed from data on prices and quantities of individual assets. Quantities of individual assets are estimated from data on past levels of investment, and investment goods prices by the perpetual inventory method.[20]

Our objective is to develop a complete system of accounts in constant

---

[19] See [55, p. 58].

[20] The perpetual inventory method is discussed by Goldsmith [22], and employed extensively in his *Study of Saving* [23], and more recent studies of U.S. national wealth [24], [25], [26]. This method is also used in the OBE *Capital Goods Study* and in the study of capital stock for the United States by Tice [57].

prices, linking output in constant prices to assets in constant prices. The most important obstacle to development of a complete accounting system is the lack of appropriate data on capital. To estimate the necessary data we extend the perpetual inventory method to encompass data on prices as well as quantities of capital goods by vintage. An accounting system of this type can be implemented only in a highly simplified form. However, even a simplified accounting system makes it possible to avoid inconsistencies in the treatment of capital that frequently occur in studies of total factor productivity.

4.2. Relative Efficiency

We begin the construction of a complete system of income and wealth accounts in constant prices with a description of the price and quantity data required for a single capital good. As in the perpetual inventory method, our characterization of a capital good is based on the relative efficiency of capital goods of different ages.[21] In the perpetual inventory method, the relative efficiency of a capital good depends on the age of the good and not on the time it is acquired. Replacement requirements are determined by losses in efficiency of existing capital goods as well as actual physical disappearance or retirement of capital goods. When a capital good is retired its relative efficiency drops to zero. The relative efficiency of capital goods of different ages can be described by a sequence of nonnegative numbers, $d_0, d_1, \ldots$.

We normalize the relative efficiency of a new capital good at unity and assume that relative efficiency is nonincreasing so that:

$$d_0 = 1; d_\tau - d_{\tau-1} \leqq 0; \tau = 0, 1, \ldots.$$

We also assume that every capital good is eventually retired or scrapped so that relative efficiency eventually drops to zero:

$$\lim_{\tau \to \infty} d_\tau = 0.$$

Subject to these restrictions, a wide variety of patterns of decline in efficiency may be employed in the perpetual inventory method.

For illustration we consider three patterns of decline in efficiency, "one-hoss shay," straight-line, and declining balance. In the "one-hoss shay" pattern, efficiency is constant over the lifetime of the capital good. Where T is the lifetime, relative efficiency is:

$$d_\tau = 1; \tau = 0, 1, \ldots, T - 1.$$

[21] A more detailed discussion of the economic theory of replacement and depreciation is given by Jorgenson [39].

In the straight-line pattern, efficiency declines linearly over the lifetime of the capital good:

$$d_\tau = 1 - \frac{1}{T}\tau; \tau = 0, 1, \ldots, T - 1.$$

In the declining balance pattern, efficiency declines geometrically:

$$d_\tau = (1 - \delta)^\tau; \tau = 0, 1, \ldots.$$

These patterns of decline in efficiency and many others may be treated as special cases within the framework of our extension of the perpetual inventory method.

Capital goods decline in efficiency at each point of time, giving rise to needs for replacement to maintain productive capacity. The proportion of an investment to be replaced during the τth period after its acquisition is equal to the decline in efficiency during that period. We refer to the decline in relative efficiency as the mortality distribution of a capital good, say m_τ, where:

$$m_\tau = -(d_\tau - d_{\tau-1}); \tau = 1, 2, \ldots.$$

By our assumption that relative efficiency is nonincreasing, the mortality distribution may be represented by a sequence of nonnegative numbers, $m_1, m_2, \ldots$, where:

$$\sum_{\tau=1}^{\infty} m_\tau = \sum_{\tau=1}^{\infty} (d_{\tau-1} - d_\tau) = d_0 = 1.$$

For the patterns of decline in efficiency considered above, we can derive the corresponding mortality distributions. If efficiency is constant over the lifetime of the capital good, the mortality distribution is zero except for period T: $m_T = 1$. For linear decline in efficiency, the mortality distribution is constant throughout the lifetime of the capital good:

$$m_\tau = \frac{1}{T}; \tau = 1, 2, \ldots, T.$$

For geometric decline in efficiency, the mortality distribution declines geometrically:

$$m_\tau = \delta(1 - \delta)^{\tau-1}; \tau = 0, 1, \ldots.$$

Replacement requirements can be expressed in terms of the mortality distribution for capital goods. Requirements can also be expressed in terms of the proportion of an initial investment replaced τ periods after the initial acquisition. This proportion includes replacement of the initial investment and subsequent replacements of each succeeding replacement. We refer to the sequence of these proportions as the replacement distribution of a capital good; each coefficient, say δ_τ, is the rate of replacement of an investment replaced τ periods after initial acquisition. The sequence of replacement rates (δ_τ) can be computed recursively for the sequence of mortality rates (m_τ). The proportion of an initial investment replaced at time v and again at time $\tau > v$ is $m_v\delta_{\tau-v}$. The proportion of the stock replaced in the τth period is the sum of proportions replaced first in periods 1, 2, ..., and later at period τ; hence,

$$\delta_\tau = m_1\delta_{\tau-1} + m_2\delta_{\tau-2} + \cdots + m_\tau\delta_0; \tau = 1, 2, \ldots.$$

This equation is referred to as the renewal equation.[22]

For constant relative efficiency over the lifetime of a capital good, the replacement distribution is periodic with the period equal to the lifetime of the capital good:

$$\delta_\tau = 1; \tau = T, 2T, \ldots.$$

For linear decline in efficiency, the replacement distribution may be represented in the form:

$$\delta_1 = \frac{1}{T};$$

$$\delta_2 = \frac{1}{T}\left(1 + \frac{1}{T}\right);$$

etc.

For geometric decline in efficiency, the replacement distribution is constant:

$$\delta_\tau = \delta; \tau = 1, 2, \ldots.$$

4.3. Quantities and Prices

The relative efficiency of capital goods of different ages and the derived mortality and replacement distributions are useful in estimating the data required for income and wealth accounts in constant prices. We begin our description of the required capital data with quantities estimated by the perpetual inventory method. First, capital stock at the end of each period, say K_t, is the sum of past investments, say $A_{t-\tau}$, each weighted by its relative efficiency:

[22] See [18].

$$K_t = \sum_{\tau=0}^{\infty} d_\tau A_{t-\tau}.$$

For a complete system of accounts, both capital stock and investments in every preceding period are required. For this purpose a system of vintage accounts containing data on investments of every age in every period is essential.

Taking the first difference of the expression for capital stock in terms of past investments, we obtain:

$$K_t - K_{t-1} = A_t + \sum_{\tau=1}^{\infty} (d_\tau - d_{\tau-1})A_{t-\tau};$$

$$= A_t - \sum_{\tau=1}^{\infty} m_\tau A_{t-\tau};$$

$$= A_t - R_t;$$

where:

$$R_t = \sum_{\tau=1}^{\infty} m_\tau A_{t-\tau}$$

is the level of replacement requirements in period t. The change in capital stock from period to period is equal to the acquisition of investment goods less replacement requirements.

Replacement requirements may also be expressed in terms of present and past changes in capital stock, using the replacement distribution:

$$R_t = \sum_{\tau=1}^{\infty} \delta_\tau (K_{t-\tau} - K_{t-\tau-1}).$$

The average replacement rate for capital stock at the beginning of the period,

$$\hat{\delta}_t = \frac{R_t}{K_{t-1}} = \sum_{\tau=1}^{\infty} \delta_\tau \frac{(K_{t-\tau} - K_{t-\tau-1})}{K_{t-1}},$$

is a weighted average of replacement rates with weights given by the relative proportions of changes in capital stock of each vintage in beginning-of-period capital stock.

We turn next to a description of the price data required for construction of income and wealth accounts in constant prices. These accounts require an extension of the perpetual inventory method to incorporate data on prices of capital goods of each vintage. Our extension of the perpetual inventory method is dual to the usual method in the sense that there is a one-to-one correspondence between the quantities that appear in the perpetual inventory method and the prices that appear in our extension of it.[23] To bring out this correspondence and to simplify the notation we use a system of present or discounted prices. Taking the present as time zero, the discounted price of a commodity, say p_t, is the discounted value of the future price, say q_t:

$$p_t = \prod_{s=1}^{t} \frac{1}{1 + r_s} q_t.$$

The notational convenience of present or discounted prices results from dispensing with explicit discount factors in expressing prices for different time periods.

In the correspondence between the perpetual inventory method and its dual or price counterpart, the price of acquisition of a capital good is analogous to capital stock. The price of acquisition, say $p_{A,t}$, is the sum of future rental prices of capital services, say $p_{K,t}$, weighted by the relative efficiency of the capital good in each future period:

$$p_{A,t} = \sum_{\tau=0}^{\infty} d_\tau p_{K,t+\tau+1}.$$

This expression may be compared with the corresponding expression giving capital stock as a weighted sum of past investments. The acquisition price of capital goods enters the production account through the price of investment goods output. This price also appears as the price component of capital formation in the accumulation account. Vintage accounts, containing data on the acquisition prices of capital goods of every age at every point of time, are required for a complete system of accounts.

Taking the first difference of the expression for the acquisition price of capital goods in terms of future rentals, we obtain:

$$p_{A,t} - p_{A,t-1} = -p_{K,t} - \sum_{\tau=1}^{\infty} (d_\tau - d_{\tau-1})p_{K,t+\tau}$$

$$= -p_{K,t} + \sum_{\tau=1}^{\infty} m_\tau p_{K,t+\tau}$$

$$= -p_{K,t} + p_{D,t};$$

where:

$$p_{D,t} = \sum_{\tau=1}^{\infty} m_\tau p_{K,t+\tau}$$

[23] The dual to the durable goods model was developed by Arrow [2], and Hall [32], on the basis of earlier work by Hotelling [38].

is depreciation on a capital good in period t. The period to period change in the price of acquisition of a capital good is equal to depreciation less the rental price of capital. In the correspondence between the perpetual inventory method and its price counterpart, investment corresponds to the rental price of capital and replacement corresponds to depreciation.

We can rewrite the expression for the first difference of the acquisition price of capital goods in terms of undiscounted prices:

$$q_{K,t} = q_{A,t-1} r_t + q_{D,t} - (q_{A,t} - q_{A,t-1}),$$

where $q_{A,t}$ is the undiscounted price of acquisition of capital goods, $q_{K,t}$ the price of capital services, $q_{D,t}$ depreciation, and r_t the rate of return, all in period t. The price of capital services $q_{K,t}$ is the sum of return per unit of capital $q_{A,t-1} r_t$, depreciation $q_{D,t}$, and the negative of revaluation $-(q_{A,t} - q_{A,t-1})$. The service price enters the production and the income and expenditure accounts through the price component of capital input and property compensation. Depreciation enters the accumulation account as the price component of depreciation on existing capital assets. Revaluation enters the accumulation account as the price component of revaluation of existing assets.

Depreciation may also be expressed in terms of present and future changes in the price of acquisition of investment goods, using the replacement distribution:

$$p_{D,t} = - \sum_{\tau=1}^{\infty} \delta_\tau (p_{A,t+\tau} - p_{A,t+\tau-1}).$$

The average depreciation rate on the acquisition price of a capital good,

$$\bar{\delta}_t = \frac{p_{D,t}}{p_{A,t}} = - \sum_{\tau=1}^{\infty} \delta_\tau \frac{(p_{A,t+\tau} - p_{A,t+\tau-1})}{p_{A,t}},$$

is a weighted average of replacement rates with weights given by the relative proportions of changes in futures prices in the acquisition price of investment goods in the current period. This expression may be compared with that for the average replacement rate, $\hat{\delta}_t$, given above. For a complete system of accounts, vintage data on the depreciation of capital goods of every age at every point of time are required.

In the perpetual inventory method, data on the quantity of investment goods of every vintage are used to estimate capital formation, replacement requirements, and capital stock. In the price counterpart of the perpetual inventory method, data on the acquisition prices of investment goods of every vintage are required. The price of acquisition of an investment good of age v at time t, say $p_{A,t,v}$, is the weighted sum of future rental prices of capital prices. The weights are relative efficiencies of the capital good in each future period, beginning with age v:

$$p_{A,t,v} = \sum_{\tau=0}^{\infty} d_{\tau+v} \, p_{K,t+\tau+1}.$$

A new investment good has age zero so that:

$$p_{A,t,0} = p_{A,t}.$$

Given the acquisition prices, we require estimates of depreciation and the rental price for goods of each vintage.

To calculate depreciation on capital goods of each vintage we take the first difference of the acquisition prices across vintages at a given point in time:

$$p_{A,t,v} - p_{A,t,v+1} = -\sum_{\tau=1}^{\infty} (d_{\tau+v} - d_{\tau+v-1}) p_{K,t+v+\tau}$$

$$= \sum_{\tau=1}^{\infty} m_{\tau+v} \, p_{K,t+v+\tau}$$

$$= p_{D,t,v};$$

where $p_{D,t,v}$ is depreciation on a capital good of age v at time t. Again, a new investment good has age zero so that:

$$p_{D,t,0} = p_{D,t}.$$

To obtain depreciation in terms of futures prices or undiscounted prices, we observe that acquisition prices across vintages at a given point in time and the corresponding depreciation are associated with the same discount factor, so that:

$$q_{A,t,v} - q_{A,t,v+1} = q_{D,t,v}.$$

To calculate the capital service price for goods of each vintage, we first observe that the rental of a capital good of age v at time t, say $q_{K,t,v}$, is proportional to the rental of a new capital good,

$$q_{K,t,v} = d_v q_{K,t},$$

with the constant of proportionality given by the efficiency of a capital good of age v relative to that of a new capital good. New and used capital goods are perfect substitutes in production. To calculate the service price for new capital goods, we use the formula derived above:

$$q_{K,t} = q_{A,t-1} r_t + q_{D,t} - (q_{A,t} - q_{A,t-1}).$$

To apply this formula we require a series of undiscounted acquisition prices for capital goods $(q_{A,t})$, rates of return (r_t), depreciation on new capital goods $(q_{D,t})$, and revaluation of existing capital goods $(q_{A,t} - q_{A,t-1})$.

To calculate the rate of return in each period, we set the formula for the rental price $q_{K,t}$ times the quantity of capital K_{t-1} equal to property compensation. All of the variables entering this equation—current and past acquisition prices for capital goods, depreciation, revaluation, capital stock, and property compensation—except for the rate of return, are known. Replacing these variables by the corresponding data we solve this equation for the rate of return. To obtain the capital service price itself we substitute the rate of return into the original formula along with the other data. This completes the calculation of the service price.

We conclude that acquisition prices for capital goods of each vintage at each point of time provide sufficient information to enable us to calculate depreciation and rental value for capital goods of each vintage. These data together with current investment, capital stock, replacement, and investments of all vintages at each point of time constitute the basic data on quantities and prices required for an extended perpetual inventory system. The problem that remains is to describe the role of each set of data in a complete accounting system. From this point we consider an accounting system for any number of investment goods. Price and quantity data that we have described above for a single investment good are required for each investment good in the system. The data for all investment goods are used to derive price and quantity indexes that play the role of the price and quantity data for a single investment good outlined above.

4.4. Accounting System

The quantities of investment goods (A_t) enter the production account in the period the investment is made through the quantity of investment goods output. An analogous quantity appears as part of capital formation in the accumulation account. The prices associated with investment in the production and accumulation accounts are prices of acquisition of new investment goods $(q_{A,t})$. The value of investment goods output is price times quantity, say $q_{A,t}A_t$. The value of capital formation is also equal to price times quantity; the price includes taxes on investment goods output. For several investment goods the values of investment goods output and capital formation are sums of prices times quantities for the individual investment goods. The price and quantity components of these accounts are derived by application of the Divisia index number formulas to the underlying price and quantity data for the individual investment goods.

Capital stock enters the production account through the quantities of capital service input (K_{t-1}); the quantity of capital service input also appears in the income and expenditure account as the quantity component of property compensation. The prices associated with capital services in the production and the income and expenditure accounts are rental prices $(q_{K,t})$. The value of capital input and property compensation is price times quantity, say $q_{K,t}K_{t-1}$. The service prices entering the production account are gross of taxes while the prices entering the property compensation account are net of taxes; these service prices will be discussed in more detail in sections 5 and 6 below. For several capital goods the values of capital services input and property compensation are sums of prices times quantities for each capital good. The price and quantity components of these accounts are derived by application of the Divisia index number formulas to the rental price and service quantity data for the individual capital goods.

Capital stock enters the accumulation account as the quantity component of depreciation. In the accumulation account capital stock must be distinguished by vintage so that vintage accounts containing data on investment of every age (A_{t-v-1}) may be regarded as part of the accumulation account in constant prices. The prices associated with capital stock in the accumulation account are the levels of depreciation $(q_{D,t,v})$. The value of depreciation for capital goods of age v is price times quantity, say $q_{D,t,v}A_{t-v-1}$; to obtain the total value of depreciation we sum over vintages, obtaining

$$\sum_{v=0}^{\infty} q_{D,t,v}A_{t-v-1}.$$

Even for a single capital good the separation of prices and quantities of depreciation requires application of an index number formula to the underlying vintage data. For several capital goods, the appropriate price and quantity index numbers can be constructed by applying the Divisia index number formulas to prices and quantities for each capital good derived from vintage data.

Capital stock also enters the accumulation account as the quantity component of revaluation. The prices associated with capital stock in measuring revaluation are the price changes $q_{A,t,v} - q_{A,t-1,v}$. Revaluation for capital goods of age v is price times quantity, say $(q_{A,t,v} - q_{A,t-1,v})A_{t-v-1}$; to obtain total revaluation we sum over vintages, obtaining

$$\sum_{v=0}^{\infty} (q_{A,t,v} - q_{A,t-1,v})A_{t-v-1}.$$

Separation of price and quantity components of revaluation for a single capital good or for several goods requires the application of Divisia index number formulas to prices and quantities for each vintage of each capital good, just as in the depreciation account. The prices used for depreciation and revaluation in the accumulation account must be consistent with those used for capital service prices in the production and the income and expenditure accounts.

Replacement appears in the accumulation account as part of capital formation. Gross capital formation is equal to investment. Net capital formation is equal to gross capital formation less replacement. Net capital formation is equal to the period to period change in capital stock. Replacement represents the change in the quantity of existing capital goods due to a decline in relative efficiency. Depreciation represents the change in the price of existing capital goods due to present and all future declines in efficiency. We have already described the separation of price and quantity components of gross capital formation. The methods for separation of these components of net capital formation and replacement are strictly analogous; quantities of gross capital formation or investment are replaced by quantities of net capital formation and replacement in index number formulas that also depend on prices of acquisition of investment goods.

Finally, capital stock appears in the wealth account as the quantity component of capital assets. In the wealth account, capital stock must be distinguished by vintage so that vintage accounts containing investment of every age in every time period may be regarded as part of both accumulation and wealth accounts. The prices associated with capital stock in the wealth account are the acquisition prices ($q_{A,t,v}$). The value of wealth for capital goods of age v is price times quantity, say $q_{A,t,v}A_{t-v}$; to obtain the total value of wealth we sum over vintages, obtaining

$$\sum_{v=0}^{\infty} q_{A,t,v}A_{t-v}.$$

For a single capital good or for several capital goods, price and quantity index numbers of wealth can be constructed by applying the Divisia index number formulas to prices and quantities of capital assets of each vintage at each point of time.

For capital goods with a full set of data for every time period, including investment of every vintage and the price of acquisition for every vintage, accounts can be compiled for capital input, property compensation, depreciation, capital formation, replacement, and wealth in current and constant prices. Price data corresponding to each of the accounts in constant prices can also be compiled. For capital goods with a less complete set of data, a simplified system of accounts can be constructed on the basis of the assumption that decline in efficiency is geometric. Under this assumption the rate of replacement and the rate of depreciation are constant and equal to the rate of decline in efficiency:

$$\hat{\delta}_t = \bar{\delta}_t = \delta.$$

Constant rates of replacement and depreciation lead to substantial simplifications in our system of income and wealth accounts in constant prices. Vintage accounts can be dispensed with since replacement is proportional to capital stock and depreciation is proportional to the current acquisition price of investment goods.

As a first step in construction of a simplified accounting system for income and wealth in constant prices we estimate capital stock at the end of each period as a weighted sum of past investments:

$$K_t = \sum_{\tau=0}^{\infty} (1 - \delta)^{\tau} A_{t-\tau}.$$

With a constant rate of replacement, replacement becomes:

$$R_t = \delta K_{t-1}.$$

The price of acquisition of new investment goods is a weighted sum of future rentals:

$$p_{A,t} = \sum_{\tau=0}^{\infty} (1 - \delta)^{\tau} p_{K,t+\tau+1}.$$

With a constant rate of depreciation, depreciation becomes:

$$q_{D,t} = \delta q_{A,t}.$$

The acquisition price of investment goods of age v at time t is:

$$q_{A,t,v} = (1 - \delta)^v q_{A,t}.$$

The service price for new capital goods becomes:

$$q_{K,t} = q_{A,t-1}r_t + \delta q_{A,t} - (q_{A,t} - q_{A,t-1}).$$

In the complete accounting system for income and wealth in constant prices outlined above, vintage accounts for capital are required for calculating replacement, depreciation, capital formation, revaluation, and wealth. With constant replacement rates (δ_τ) the values of replacement and depreciation are equal and depend only on the price of acquisition of new capital goods and the stock of capital:

$$q_{A,t}R_t = \delta q_{A,t}K_{t-1} = q_{D,t}K_{t-1}.$$

Similarly, the value of wealth is the product of the price of acquisition and the stock of capital, $q_{A,t}K_t$. The change in wealth from period to period,

$$q_{A,t}K_t - q_{A,t-1}K_{t-1} = q_{A,t}(K_t - K_{t-1}) + (q_{A,t} - q_{A,t-1})K_{t-1},$$

is the sum of capital formation and revaluation. No vintage accounts for capital goods are required under the assumption of constant replacement rates. For several capital goods the Divisia index number formulas must be employed to separate replacement, depreciation, capital formation, revaluation, and wealth into price and quantity components.

Geometric decline in efficiency is among the patterns most commonly employed in estimating capital stock by the perpetual inventory method.[24] For geometric decline in efficiency, depreciation is proportional to the acquisition price of new capital goods and replacement is proportional to capital stock. These properties result from the constancy of the sequence of replacement rates (δ_τ). Neither property holds for any other representation of the relative efficiency of capital goods of different ages. A fundamental result of renewal theory is that δ_τ tends to a constant value for almost any pattern of decline in efficiency.[25] Geometric decline in efficiency, resulting in a constant rate of replacement δ, may provide a useful approximation to replacement requirements and depreciation for a wide variety of patterns of decline in efficiency. Where this approxima-

---

[24] A representative study is the OBE *Capital Goods Study;* in this research straight-line and double-declining balance methods are employed. See [30].

[25] For detailed discussion of the application of renewal theory to replacement and depreciation, see [39].

tion is unsatisfactory, a complete accounting system for income and wealth in constant prices requires vintage accounts for capital goods quantities and prices.

Many different retirement distributions have been found useful in describing the retirement or physical disappearance of capital goods.[26] Considerably less evidence is available on the decline in efficiency of existing capital goods.[27] The available evidence arises from two sources— studies of replacement investment and studies of depreciation on capital goods. Geometric decline in efficiency has been employed by Hickman [37] and by Hall and Jorgenson [34], [35] in studies of investment. This assumption is tested by Meyer and Kuh, who find no effect of the age distribution of capital stock in the determination of replacement investment.[28] Geometric decline in efficiency has been employed in the study of depreciation on capital goods by Cagan, Griliches, and Wykoff.[29] This assumption has been tested by Hall, who finds no effect of the age of a capital good in the determination of the rate of depreciation as measured from prices of capital goods of different vintages.[30] The available empirical evidence supports the use of geometric decline in efficiency as a useful approximation to replacement requirements and depreciation.

4.5. Alternative Accounting Systems

We have outlined the development of a complete system of income and wealth accounts in constant prices. Only the measurement of the output side of the production account and the asset side of the wealth account in constant prices are well-established in social accounting practice. In the study of total factor productivity, attempts have been made to measure the input side of the production account in constant prices. Christensen and Jorgenson [7], [8] have applied the methods we have described for a simplified accounting system to the measurement of factor input in constant prices and the measurement of total factor productivity.

It is very useful to compare our accounting system with an alternative approach developed by Denison in his path-breaking monograph, *Sources of Economic Growth* [14]. Denison's monograph deals with output and input sides of the production account for the United States. Similar

---

[26] A relatively recent work on capital equipment lifetimes is Marston, Winfrey, and Hempstead [47]. The classic work in the field is E. B. Kurtz [45], which provides other references.

[27] When a capital good is retired, relative efficiency drops to zero.

[28] See [48, pp. 91–100].

[29] See [5, pp. 222–226], [27, pp. 197–200], and [60, pp. 171–172].

[30] See [33, pp. 19–20].

methods have been applied to data for a number of other countries in his book, *Why Growth Rates Differ* [15]. Denison takes gross national product in constant prices from the U.S. national accounts as a point of departure. He measures labor input along lines similar to those we outline below, weighting rates of growth of each type of labor input by relative shares in the values of total labor input to obtain the rate of growth of an index of labor input.[31] In comparing Denison's approach with our own, we concentrate on the measurement of capital input.

Denison points out that the construction of a capital input measure depends on the relative efficiency of capital goods of different ages:

> In principle, the selection of a capital input measure should depend on the changes that occur in the ability of a capital good to contribute to net production as the good grows older (within the span of its economic life). Use of net stock, with depreciation computed by the straight line formula, would imply that this ability drops very rapidly—that it is reduced by one-fourth when one-fourth of the service life has passed, and by nine-tenths when nine-tenths of the service life has passed. Use of gross stock would imply that this ability is constant throughout the service life of a capital good.[32]

Denison adds: "I believe that net value typically declines more rapidly than does the ability of a capital good to contribute to production. . . . On the other hand, the gross stock assumption of constant services throughout the life of an asset is extreme." [33]

Under Denison's gross stock assumption, relative efficiency is constant over the economic lifetime of the equipment:

$$d_\tau = 1; \tau = 0, 1, \ldots, T - 1;$$

where T is the economic lifetime of the capital good. Under Denison's net stock assumption, efficiency declines linearly:

$$d_\tau = 1 - \frac{1}{T} \tau; \tau = 0, 1, \ldots, T - 1.$$

In Denison's *Sources of Economic Growth* gross stock is employed as a measure of the quantity of capital input. In *Why Growth Rates Differ* an arithmetic average of gross stock and net stock is employed; [34] the

---

[31] A detailed comparison of our estimates of labor input and those of Denison is given by Jorgenson and Griliches [41]; see Section 5.2 below for further discussion.

[32] [15, p. 140].

[33] [15, p. 140].

[34] [15, p. 141].

implied relative efficiency of capital goods is an average of constant and linearly declining relative efficiency:

$$d_\tau = 1 - \frac{1}{2T}\, \tau; \; \tau = 0, 1, \ldots, T - 1.$$

Since Denison does not assume that the relative efficiency of capital goods declines geometrically, depreciation and replacement must be carefully distinguished in order to preserve consistency among production, income and expenditure, accumulation, and wealth accounts in constant prices. Depreciation is a component of the price of capital services. The value of capital services is equal to property income including depreciation. Replacement is the consequence of a decline in the efficiency of capital assets or, in Denison's language, the ability of a capital good to contribute to production. Unfortunately, a confusion between depreciation and replacement pervades Denison's treatment of the output and input sides of the production account and the measurement of capital stock. This confusion leads to a series of inconsistencies, making it impossible to incorporate Denison's measures of product and factor input in constant prices into a complete accounting system.

The first indication of confusion between depreciation and replacement is Denison's definition of net product: "Net product measures the amount a nation consumes plus the addition it makes to its capital stock. Stated another way, it is the amount of its output a nation could consume without changing its stock of capital." [35] The correct definition of net product is gross product less depreciation; this is the definition suggested by the second statement quoted above. The first statement defines net product as gross product less replacement, since the addition to capital stock or net capital formation is equal to investment less replacement. The two definitions are consistent if and only if depreciation is equal to replacement. Under any of Denison's assumptions about decline in relative efficiency, depreciation and replacement are not equal, so that his definition of net product is self-contradictory.

In *Why Growth Rates Differ* Denison measures capital consumption allowances on the basis of Bulletin F lives and the straight-line method. [36] Even under the assumption that relative efficiency or Denison's "ability to contribute to production" declines linearly, this estimate corresponds to replacement rather than depreciation. Denison reduces gross product by his estimate of capital consumption allowances to obtain his measure

[35] [15, p. 14].
[36] [15, p. 351].

of net product.[37] This procedure employs the incorrect definition of net product as gross product less replacement. A similar procedure for calculating capital consumption allowances is employed in *Sources of Economic Growth*. Denison's confusion between depreciation and replacement carries over to the input side of the production account. His measure of net product is reduced by labor compensation to obtain property compensation net of capital consumption allowances. Thus, Denison's measure of property compensation is also calculated net of replacement rather than net of depreciation. This erroneous measure is allocated among capital inputs to obtain weights employed in measuring capital input as a component of factor input in constant prices. Denison's weights for different components of capital input are measured incorrectly; these weights should reflect property compensation less depreciation rather than property compensation less replacement.

A further difficulty with Denison's estimate of capital consumption allowances in *Why Growth Rates Differ* is that in estimating capital stock Denison assumes that decline in efficiency is linear, but at half the straight-line rate. He uses the straight-line method to estimate capital consumption allowances; the resulting estimate is equal to neither depreciation nor replacement for the pattern of decline in efficiency he uses in estimating capital. In *Sources of Economic Growth* Denison assumes that relative efficiency is constant over the lifetime of a capital good.[38] Again, the straight-line estimates of capital consumption allowances are equal to neither depreciation nor replacement for the pattern of decline in efficiency underlying his estimate of capital. In both *Sources of Economic Growth* and *Why Growth Rates Differ* the price and quantity components of the input side of the production account are mutually contradictory.

In our accounting system for capital input and property compensation, the price component of the flow of capital services is the sum of return per unit of capital, depreciation, and revaluation. In estimating the rate of return Denison omits revaluations of existing capital goods and fails to measure depreciation correctly.[39] His implied estimate of return per unit of capital is erroneous. Denison omits capital gains and losses from the revaluation of assets in allocating property income among capital assets; so the weights for different components of capital input are measured incorrectly. The revaluations are required as part of the ac-

[37] [15, p. 14].
[38] [14, pp. 112–113].
[39] [16, p. 8].

cumulation account for an accounting system that includes accumulation and wealth accounts. If Denison's measure of capital input were to be incorporated into a complete accounting system, the omission of revaluations from the price component of capital services would introduce an inconsistency between the production and the income and expenditure accounts on the one hand and the accumulation and wealth accounts on the other.

Denison's assumptions about the decline in relative efficiency of capital goods can be incorporated into a complete accounting system along the lines we have suggested. Since he does not assume that efficiency declines geometrically, vintage accounts for quantities and prices of capital goods of every age at every point of time are required. Vintage data are essential even for the relatively limited objective of measuring net product; net product measurement requires an estimate of depreciation and estimation of depreciation requires vintage prices. The first step in implementing Denison's assumptions would be to assemble data on the acquisition prices of capital goods of every age at every point of time. The second step would be to estimate depreciation for goods of every vintage at every point of time from the vintage data on prices. This estimate of depreciation would replace Denison's estimate of capital consumption allowances in measuring net product and property compensation net of depreciation. The third step would be to estimate capital service prices by combining estimates of the return per unit of capital, depreciation, and revaluation of assets. These prices could be combined with Denison's estimates of capital stock to construct index numbers of the price and quantity of capital input.

We conclude that Denison's assumptions about the relative efficiency of capital goods of different ages can be incorporated into a complete accounting system for income and wealth in constant prices. A broader data base than that Denison has employed would be required. Denison's estimates of both the output and input sides of the production account would have to be revised substantially. To employ an approach that dispenses with vintage accounts for capital goods prices and quantities, like the approach Denison actually uses, it is necessary to assume that the decline in efficiency of capital goods is geometric. In the absence of vintage data the use of Denison's assumptions about relative efficiency leads to a series of inconsistencies in the construction of even a single account, the production account, in current and constant prices. If Denison's estimates of the production accounts were to be incorporated into a complete accounting system, these inconsistencies would ramify throughout the system.

In the United Nations *System of National Accounts,*[40] the construction of a production account in constant prices is discussed at some length. In the United Nations system capital stock is measured as gross stock, following Denison's practice in *Sources of Economic Growth.* Capital consumption allowances are measured by the straight-line method, again following Denison's practice. We conclude that the United Nations system of accounts in constant prices incorporates a production account similar to Denison's. We have already outlined the internal contradictions in Denison's production account; an accounting system incorporating a production account like Denison's would give rise to inconsistencies between the production and the income and expenditure accounts on the one hand and the accumulation and wealth accounts on the other. We conclude that the United Nations system provides a satisfactory solution to the problem of constructing accounts in constant prices only for the output side of the production account. Measurement of the other accounting magnitudes of the system in constant prices requires an extension of the perpetual inventory method like that we have outlined above.

5. PRODUCTION ACCOUNT

5.1. Introduction

In sections 3 and 4 our objective has been to develop methods for measuring income and wealth in constant prices. The task that remains is to present production, income and expenditure, accumulation, and wealth accounts in constant prices. To complete this task we must separate the values included in the accounts presented in Section 2 into price and quantity components. For this purpose we employ the system of price and quantity index numbers discussed in Section 3. This system is based on a discrete approximation to continuous Divisia index numbers of prices and quantities.

To construct a complete system of accounts in constant prices we must account for investment goods output, capital input, property compensation, capital formation, and wealth in a way that is internally consistent. For this purpose we have extended the perpetual inventory method to incorporate data on prices as well as quantities of capital goods by vintage. We have also presented a simplified version of the

[40] [55, pp. 52–70].

perpetual inventory method and its price counterpart, based on approximation of replacement rates for individual capital goods by a constant rate of replacement for each good. Our extension of the perpetual inventory method is presented in Section 4.

In this section we present the production account for the U.S. private domestic sector in constant prices. In the following section we present income and expenditure, accumulation, and wealth accounts for the U.S. private national economy in constant prices. In Section 7 we discuss possible extensions of our accounting system.

In constructing the production account in constant prices changes in the value of product and the value of factor outlay must be separated into price and quantity components. The ratio of the quantity of total product to the quantity of total factor input or, alternatively, the ratio of the price of total factor input to the price of total product is equal to total factor productivity. In addition to data on output and input the production account in constant prices includes data on total factor productivity.

5.2. *Output and Labor Input*

To construct a quantity index for gross product we first allocate the value of output between consumption and investment goods. Investment goods include durable goods and structures. Consumption goods include nondurable goods and services. Data for prices and quantities of both consumption and investment goods are included in the U.S. national accounts as part of gross national product. The product of the rest of the world and government sectors consists entirely of services. Price and quantity index numbers for the services of consumer and institutional durables are constructed as part of our imputation for the value of these services, described below.

The value of output from the point of view of the producing sector excludes certain indirect taxes and includes subsidies. Sales and excise taxes must be allocated between consumption and investment goods output. Since a portion of each of these taxes is levied on intermediate goods, a completely satisfactory allocation would require a detailed interindustry analysis. We have allocated these taxes in proportion to the value of consumption and investment goods output. The price index for each type of output is implicit in the value and quantity of output included in gross national product. We construct price and quantity indexes of gross output by applying Divisia index number formulas to price and quantity data for consumption and investment goods product. The results are given in Table 9.

To construct a quantity index for gross factor input we allocate the value of factor outlay between labor and capital input. The construction of a quantity index of labor input begins with data on the number of persons engaged in the private domestic sector. Persons engaged include full-time equivalent employees and proprietors. Our estimates for the nonfarm business sector are identical to those of the Office of Business Economics for full-time equivalent employees and proprietors. We add Kendrick's estimates of employment in agriculture to obtain total persons engaged.[41] To obtain a measure of labor input our next step is to estimate the number of man-hours worked. For this purpose we employ Kendrick's estimates of man-hours for the private domestic sector.[42]

Denoting the index of man-hours by L and the wage index by p_L, we first represent the value of labor input as the sum of the values of labor input for each category of labor:

$$p_L L = \Sigma p_{L,j} L_j,$$

where $p_{L,j}$ is the price of the jth type of labor, and L_j is the number of man-hours worked by workers of this type. Divisia indexes of the wage rate and man-hours worked are:

$$\frac{\dot{p}_L}{p_L} = \Sigma v_j \frac{\dot{p}_{L,j}}{p_{L,j}}, \qquad \frac{\dot{L}}{L} = \Sigma v_j \frac{\dot{L}_j}{L_j},$$

where the weights (v_j) are the relative shares of each type of labor in the value of total labor input.

For each category of labor, total man-hours is the product of persons engaged, say n_j, and hours per person, say h_j. Where N is the total number of persons engaged and H is the number of hours per man, the quantity index of labor input may be rewritten in the form:

$$\frac{\dot{L}}{L} = \Sigma v_j \left(\frac{\dot{n}_j}{n_j} - \frac{\dot{N}}{N}\right) + \Sigma v_j \left(\frac{\dot{h}_j}{h_j} - \frac{\dot{H}}{H}\right) + \left(\frac{\dot{N}}{N} + \frac{\dot{H}}{H}\right).$$

The first term in this expression represents the change in labor input per person engaged due to changes in the composition of the labor force.

[41] These data have been compiled for John W. Kendrick's forthcoming study [43]. We are indebted to Kendrick for providing us with these data in advance of publication. The conceptual basis for compilation of the data is the same as in Kendrick's [42]. The Office of Business Economics data on nonfarm proprietors and employees are from [49a, Tables 6.4 and 6.6].

[42] See note 41, above.

TABLE 9

Gross Private Domestic Product, 1929–69
(constant prices of 1958)

Year	Gross Private Domestic Product		Consumption Goods Product		Investment Goods Product		
	Price Index	Quan-tity Index	Price Index	Quan-tity Index	Price Index	Quan-tity Index	Relative Share
1929	0.556	187.5	0.566	133.7	0.508	56.1	.278
1930	0.536	169.8	0.547	129.5	0.489	41.5	.227
1931	0.489	156.6	0.497	125.8	0.453	31.2	.188
1932	0.420	132.5	0.423	114.6	0.407	17.8	.134
1933	0.418	130.3	0.421	111.6	0.403	18.6	.143
1934	0.440	141.7	0.445	116.6	0.414	25.2	.176
1935	0.447	151.8	0.453	121.8	0.418	30.5	.197
1936	0.455	170.3	0.465	130.2	0.414	41.3	.231
1937	0.471	181.1	0.476	137.8	0.441	44.5	.241
1938	0.460	171.8	0.461	138.4	0.448	34.2	.203
1939	0.458	186.4	0.460	143.7	0.441	43.8	.236
1940	0.463	202.8	0.465	150.7	0.446	53.5	.266
1941	0.503	230.6	0.497	159.1	0.504	73.2	.333
1942	0.563	250.3	0.545	171.2	0.588	80.9	.351
1943	0.626	268.3	0.625	171.7	0.617	98.1	.375
1944	0.631	283.0	0.647	181.4	0.594	103.1	.358
1945	0.636	279.5	0.667	187.4	0.569	92.7	.312
1946	0.701	271.5	0.728	193.0	0.643	77.3	.276
1947	0.787	277.5	0.807	191.2	0.748	85.8	.309
1948	0.826	295.8	0.851	201.8	0.778	93.6	.312
1949	0.796	295.3	0.800	203.6	0.791	91.2	.323
1950	0.827	326.9	0.843	212.8	0.800	114.0	.354
1951	0.876	349.1	0.884	226.0	0.862	123.0	.364
1952	0.897	357.7	0.907	234.4	0.879	123.0	.354
1953	0.906	375.9	0.922	244.6	0.878	131.1	.355
1954	0.915	373.2	0.932	247.5	0.886	125.3	.341

(continued)

TABLE 9 (concluded)

Year	Gross Private Domestic Product		Consumption Goods Product		Investment Goods Product		
	Price Index	Quan-tity Index	Price Index	Quan-tity Index	Price Index	Quan-tity Index	Relative Share
1955	0.932	405.4	0.953	261.5	0.893	144.0	.357
1956	0.951	415.8	0.956	272.3	0.943	143.4	.359
1957	0.978	422.6	0.974	280.8	0.988	141.7	.355
1958	1.000	419.7	1.000	289.2	1.000	130.6	.326
1959	1.023	447.8	1.028	302.8	1.012	145.1	.336
1960	1.034	459.8	1.046	312.5	1.009	147.4	.329
1961	1.039	469.6	1.052	323.6	1.011	145.8	.317
1962	1.051	499.3	1.066	338.9	1.018	160.5	.327
1963	1.062	521.0	1.081	351.6	1.021	169.5	.329
1964	1.074	551.6	1.096	370.6	1.029	181.3	.330
1965	1.090	587.5	1.113	391.5	1.041	196.5	.335
1966	1.121	627.4	1.149	417.1	1.062	210.9	.333
1967	1.146	645.6	1.170	436.2	1.095	209.5	.324
1968	1.177	678.2	1.202	455.1	1.125	223.4	.330
1969	1.228	703.4	1.258	471.3	1.164	232.5	.329

The second term represents the change in labor input per hour due to changes in the relative number of hours worked per man among components of the labor force. The last term is the change in total man-hours. Adjustments for changes in the composition of the labor force and the relative number of hours worked per man are required to convert an index of man-hours into an index of the quantity of labor input.

Price and quantity indexes of output require data on the prices and quantities of individual outputs. Similarly, price and quantity indexes of labor input require data on the wages and hours worked for different types of workers. It would be desirable to distinguish among hours worked by workers classified by sex, race, years of schooling, occupation, age, and so on. Price and quantity indexes of labor input would be obtained by applying Divisia index number formulas to price and quantity data for different types of workers. The data available for construction of price and quantity indexes of labor input are very limited. We distinguish among different categories of labor by years of schooling completed. We employ the data compiled by Jorgenson and Griliches and extended by Griliches to estimate the change in labor input due to changes in the educational composition of the labor force.[43]

Kendrick distinguishes among different categories of labor by industry of employment [42]. Jorgenson and Griliches distinguish among different categories by years of schooling completed [40]. Our adjustment of the index of man-hours is limited to changes in the quality of labor input due to changes in the educational composition of the labor force. Adjustments for changes in the distribution of the labor force by age and sex would require more detailed data. We have made no adjustment for changes in the relative number of hours worked by different types of workers. Estimates of the likely effect of additional adjustments of each type are given by Jorgenson and Griliches [41].

Denison has observed that the intensity of effort may vary with the number of hours worked per week [13], [14]. Correction of the quantity index of labor input to reflect changes in intensity of effort would require estimates of wages and man-hours, classified by the number of hours worked per week. Denison suggests that the stock of labor input provides an upper bound for labor input corrected for variations in intensity, while the number of man-hours provides a lower bound. He estimates effective labor input by correcting man-hours for variations in labor intensity. We have employed Denison's adjustment for the intensity of effort applied to actual hours per man rather than potential hours per man. The number of persons engaged and hours per worker, together with price and quantity indexes of labor input for 1929–69, are given for the private domestic economy in Table 10.

5.3. Capital Input

Our estimates of capital input, property compensation, depreciation, replacement, and capital assets are based on an extension of the perpetual inventory method to incorporate data on prices as well as quantities of investment goods by vintage. We estimate capital service prices, depreciation, and acquisition prices for capital goods of different vintages on the basis of the assumption that the decline in efficiency of capital goods is geometric in form. We estimate capital stock, replacement, and quantities of capital goods of different vintages on the basis of the same

---

[43] See [40] and [28]. We have extended Griliches' estimates back to 1929, using relative earnings for 1939 and estimates of the educational attainment of the labor force for 1930 and 1940 by Folger and Nam [20].

TABLE 10

Private Domestic Labor Input, 1929–69
(constant prices of 1958)

Year	Private Domestic Persons Engaged (millions)	Private Domestic Hours per Person (thousands per year)	Private Domestic Labor Input	
			Price Index	Quantity Index
1929	43.0	2.645	0.338	178.8
1930	40.8	2.600	0.326	170.6
1931	37.6	2.579	0.290	163.2
1932	34.2	2.512	0.254	146.1
1933	34.2	2.488	0.238	146.0
1934	36.7	2.281	0.257	152.6
1935	37.9	2.327	0.267	159.3
1936	39.8	2.380	0.281	168.7
1937	41.6	2.420	0.303	177.4
1938	39.1	2.350	0.298	166.6
1939	40.5	2.389	0.305	174.0
1940	42.2	2.391	0.314	182.1
1941	45.8	2.402	0.351	198.6
1942	48.1	2.458	0.411	211.6
1943	48.7	2.517	0.472	216.7
1944	47.5	2.549	0.505	215.5
1945	46.0	2.487	0.520	208.5
1946	48.6	2.372	0.543	220.1
1947	50.9	2.314	0.597	230.7
1948	52.0	2.287	0.640	236.0
1949	50.2	2.279	0.651	228.9
1950	51.7	2.250	0.689	236.0
1951	53.7	2.242	0.746	246.5
1952	54.1	2.239	0.786	249.3
1953	54.9	2.208	0.832	252.9
1954	53.2	2.185	0.854	244.9
1955	54.5	2.210	0.887	253.7
1956	55.6	2.197	0.935	259.5

(continued)

TABLE 10 (concluded)

Year	Private Domestic Persons Engaged (millions)	Private Domestic Hours per Person (thousands per year)	Private Domestic Labor Input	
			Price Index	Quantity Index
1957	55.5	2.170	0.979	259.4
1958	53.7	2.150	1.000	252.8
1959	54.8	2.175	1.040	263.0
1960	55.4	2.177	1.070	267.8
1961	54.9	2.160	1.098	266.3
1962	55.8	2.163	1.138	272.9
1963	56.3	2.160	1.173	277.0
1964	57.4	2.163	1.221	284.1
1965	59.2	2.166	1.262	294.4
1966	61.3	2.152	1.323	306.8
1967	62.3	2.154	1.366	314.7
1968	63.8	2.151	1.447	324.6
1969	65.6	2.139	1.537	334.9

assumption. Estimates of capital input, property compensation, depreciation, and capital assets in constant prices require data on both prices and quantities of capital goods by vintage. We continue our discussion of the production account for the U.S. private domestic economy in constant prices by describing the construction of prices and quantities of capital input.[44]

The starting point for a quantity index of capital input is a perpetual inventory estimate of the stock of each type of capital, based on past investments in constant prices. At each point of time the stock of each type of capital is the sum of stocks remaining from past investments of each vintage. Under the assumption that efficiency of capital goods declines geometrically, the rate of replacement, say δ, is a constant. Capital stock at the end of every period may be estimated from investment and capital stock at the beginning of the period:

$$K_t = A_t + (1 - \delta)K_{t-1},$$

where K_t is end of period capital stock, A_t the quantity of investment, and K_{t-1} the capital stock at the beginning of the period.

[44] Our estimates are based on those of [8].

For each type of capital included in our accounts we prepare perpetual inventory estimates of the stock as follows: First, we obtain a benchmark estimate of capital stock from data on national wealth in constant prices. Second, we deflate the investment series from the U.S. national accounts to obtain investment in constant prices. Third, we choose an estimate of the rate of replacement from data on the lifetimes of capital goods. Finally, we estimate capital stock in every period by applying the perpetual inventory method described above. We have prepared estimates for the stocks of consumer durables, nonresidential structures, producer durables, residential structures, nonfarm inventories, farm inventories, and land. Benchmark estimates of capital stocks in 1929, expressed in constant prices of 1958, rates of replacement, and price indexes for each type of capital are presented in Table 11.

Our price indexes for consumer and producer durables and for farm and nonfarm inventories are taken directly from the U.S. national accounts. These indexes are the implicit deflators for investment in each category from estimates of gross private domestic investment in current and constant prices. We replace the deflators from the national accounts for residential and nonresidential structures by the "constant cost 2" construction price index employed in the *Capital Stock Study* of the Office of Business Economics.[45] This index results from an attempt to correct implicit deflators for structures for changes in the quality of structures produced. In the *Capital Stock Study* the "constant cost 2" price index is employed to deflate data on investment in nonresidential structures. We employ Goldsmith's price index for land through 1958, extrapolating this index from 1958 to 1969 by assuming a constant rate of growth of the price of land at 6.9 per cent per year.[46] Our price indexes for farm and nonfarm inventory stocks [47] are based on unpublished estimates of the Office of Business Economics.[48]

Rates of replacement for inventories and land are zero by definition. To estimate rates of replacement for structures and durables we employ double declining balance replacement rates from the *Capital Stock Study*.

[45] The Office of Business Economics *Capital Stock Study* is reported in a series of articles. See [30], and the references given there. We are indebted to Robert Wasson for permission to use the underlying data on investment in current and constant prices.

[46] See [24, Tables A-40 and A-41, pp. 186–189].

[47] Asset deflators are weighted by the relative proportion of assets of each type in total assets; investment deflators are weighted by the relative proportion of investment goods of each type in total investment. See [16, p. 12]. Asset deflators are appropriate for deflating asset values and for estimating rental values of capital services.

[48] We are indebted to Shirley Loftus for providing us with these estimates.

TABLE 11

Benchmarks, Rates of Replacement, and Price Indexes
Employed in Estimating Capital

Asset Class	1929 Bench-mark (billions of 1958 dollars)	Re-place-ment Rate	Deflator
1. Consumer durables	74.9	.200	Implicit deflator, national product accounts [a]
2. Nonresidential structures	148.2	.056	Constant cost 2 deflator [b]
3. Producer durables	77.5	.138	Implicit deflator, national product accounts [a]
4. Residential structures	214.0	.039	Implicit deflator, national product accounts [a]
5. Nonfarm inventories	57.1	–	Investment: Implicit deflator, national product accounts [c] Assets: Implicit deflator, OBE [d]
6. Farm inventories	21.9	–	Investment: Implicit deflator, national product accounts [c] Assets: Implicit deflator, OBE [d]
7. Land	321.6	–	Goldsmith [e]

[a] [49a, Table 8.1].
[b] [31].
[c] [49a, Tables 1.1 and 1.2].
[d] Unpublished OBE sources.
[e] [25, Tables A-5 and A-6].

For each asset the rate of replacement is $\delta = 2/T$, where T is the mean service life for the asset given in the *Capital Stock Study*.[49] Our estimates of replacement rates incorporate both retirements of capital goods and the decline in efficiency of existing capital goods. In the *Capital Stock*

[49] These lifetimes have been compiled for the Office of Business Economics *Capital Stock Study;* we are indebted to Robert Wasson for providing us with data on service lives.

Study investment in nonresidential structures is divided into fifty-two categories. Although it would be possible to compile data on capital input for each of these categories separately, we have limited our estimates to total producer durables and total nonresidential structures. The replacement rate for each group is estimated as a weighted average of replacement rates for the individual components, using relative shares of the value of each category in the total value of capital stock as weights.

Residential structures may be divided into farm and nonfarm components. We estimate service lives for each component on the basis of Bulletin F lifetimes; the replacement rate for residential structures is a weighted average of double declining balance replacement rates with weights based on the relative shares of farm and nonfarm residential structures in the total.[50] We assume that the rate of replacement for consumer durables is 0.200; this estimate was developed by deLeeuw in estimating stocks of consumer durables [12].

We have described the measurement of capital stocks for each category of capital goods by the perpetual inventory method. Our next step is to describe the measurement of capital service prices by the price counterpart of the perpetual inventory method. For property with an active rental market the price of capital services may be observed directly as the rental price of the corresponding asset. A substantial portion of the range of capital goods employed in the U.S. private domestic sector has an active rental market; most classes of structures can be rented and a rental market exists for many types of equipment, especially large pieces of equipment such as aircraft, trucks, construction equipment, computers, and so on. Unfortunately, very little effort has been devoted to compiling data on rental rates for either structures or equipment. Data on the flow of rent payments among industrial sectors have been compiled by Creamer [11]. However, both current price and constant price flows are required for direct measurement of the price and quantity of capital services by class of asset.

Given market rental prices by class of asset, the implicit rental values paid by owners for the use of their property may be imputed by applying rental rates to capital stocks employed by owner-users. This method for imputation is used to estimate the price and quantity of capital services from owner-occupied dwellings in the U.S. national accounts. Data on rental prices of dwellings occupied by renters are employed to impute

[50] Bulletin F [4] lives have been compared with alternative lifetimes by Wasson [60].

the rental value of dwellings occupied by owners. The total rental value of owner-occupied dwellings is divided among taxes, capital consumption allowances, interest payments, and net rent. A somewhat similar but not identical method of imputation is used for the space rental value of institutional buildings. Capital consumption allowances and interest payments by institutions are estimated as components of imputed space rental value. Net rent is omitted from the imputation, but this component of space rental value could be estimated from the market rental prices of space comparable to that used by institutions. The main obstacle to broader application of this method of imputation is the lack of appropriate data on market rental prices.

An alternative method for imputation of the rental value of owner-utilized assets is included in our extension of the perpetual inventory method to incorporate data on prices of capital goods by vintage. For each type of capital included in our accounts we prepare perpetual inventory estimates of acquisition prices, service prices, depreciation, and revaluation by vintage. Under our assumption of geometrically declining relative efficiency of capital goods, perpetual inventory estimates of prices can be simplified considerably. First, beginning with acquisition prices for new capital goods of each type, the acquisition prices for goods of each vintage decline geometrically with vintage. The formula for the value of capital stock,

$$q_{A,t}K_t = \Sigma q_{A,t}(1 - \delta)^\tau A_{t-\tau} = \Sigma q_{A,t,\tau}A_{t-\tau},$$

may be regarded as the sum of past investments weighted by relative efficiency and evaluated at the acquisition price for new capital goods or, equivalently, as the sum of past investments evaluated at the acquisition price for the corresponding vintage of capital.

Second, under our assumption that replacement rates are constant, depreciation is proportional to the value of beginning of period capital stock:

$$q_{D,t}K_{t-1} = \delta q_{A,t}K_{t-1}.$$

This measure of depreciation can also be obtained by estimating depreciation separately for each vintage and summing over vintages:

$$\Sigma q_{D,t,\tau}A_{t-\tau-1} \parallel \Sigma \delta q_{A,t,\tau}A_{t-\tau-1} = \delta q_{A,t}K_{t-1}.$$

Similarly, revaluation is equal to the change in the acquisition price of new capital goods multiplied by beginning of period capital stock. This measure can also be obtained by estimating revaluation separately for each vintage and summing over vintages:

$$(q_{A,t} - q_{A,t-1})K_{t-1} = \Sigma(q_{A,t,\tau} - q_{A,t-1,\tau-1})A_{t-\tau-1}.$$

In the absence of taxation, the value of capital services is the sum of the cost of capital and depreciation, less revaluation:

$$q_{K,t}K_{t-1} = [q_{A,t-1}r_t + q_{A,t}\delta - (q_{A,t} - q_{A,t-1})]K_{t-1}.$$

We can obtain this expression by estimating the capital service price for capital goods of each vintage and summing over vintages:

$$q_{K,t}K_{t-1} = \Sigma(1 - \delta)^\tau q_{K,t}A_{t-\tau-1} = \Sigma q_{K,t,\tau}A_{t-\tau-1}.$$

Given the quantity of each type of asset held, the acquisition price, and the rate of replacement, only the rate of return remains to be determined in compiling data on the price and quantity of capital services. In measuring the rate of return, differences in the tax treatment of property compensation from different sectors must be taken into account.

For tax purposes the private domestic sector of the U.S. economy can be divided into corporate business, noncorporate business, and households and nonprofit institutions. Households and institutions are not subject to direct taxes on the flow of capital services they utilize. Noncorporate business is subject to personal income taxes on income generated from capital services, while corporate business is subject to both corporate and personal income taxes. Households and corporate and non-corporate business are subject to indirect taxes on property income through taxes levied on the value of property. In order to take these differences in taxation into account we first allocate each class of assets among the four sectors of the U.S. private domestic economy—corporations, noncorporate business, households, and institutions. The relative proportions of capital stock by asset class for each sector for 1958 are given in Table 12.

For a sector not subject to either direct or indirect taxes on property income, the value of property compensation is equal to the value of capital services, i.e., property compensation $= q_{K,t}K_{t-1}$. This formula is appropriate for a single class of assets. For several classes of assets, property compensation is the sum of price times quantity of capital services for all classes of assets. We assume that the rate of return is the same for all assets held by a given sector; rates of return can be estimated for each flow of property compensation that can be measured separately. Flows of property compensation can be separately measured for industry groups or even for individual firms.

Given property compensation, the acquisition prices of new capital

TABLE 12

Relative Proportions of Capital Stock by Asset Class and Sector, 1958

	Sector			
Asset Class	1. Corporate Business	2. Noncorporate Business	3. Households and Institutions	Total
1. Consumer durables	–	–	.138	0.138
2. Nonresidential structures	.104	.027	.014	0.145
3. Producer durables	.09	.041	.002	0.132
4. Residential structures	.019	.009	.211	0.238
5. Nonfarm inventories	.065	.013	–	0.078
6. Farm inventories	–	.021	–	0.021
7. Land	.047	.124	.077	0.247
Total	.325	.234	.442	1.000

goods ($q_{A,t}$), the rate of replacement (δ), and capital stocks estimated by the perpetual inventory method (K_{t-1}), we can solve for the rate of return by substituting the capital service price,

$$q_{K,t} = q_{A,t-1}r_t + q_{A,t}\delta - (q_{A,t} - q_{A,t-1}),$$

into the expression for property compensation. In this expression only the rate of return is unknown and we may solve for the rate of return in terms of the observed data, obtaining:

$$r_t = \frac{\text{Property compensation} - q_{A,t}\delta K_{t-1} + (q_{A,t} - q_{A,t-1})K_{t-1}}{q_{A,t-1}K_{t-1}}.$$

The rate of return is the ratio of property compensation less depreciation plus revaluation of capital assets to the value of capital stock at the beginning of the period. For more than one capital good we estimate depreciation, revaluation, and the value of capital stock by summing over all capital goods.

The formula for the rate of return given above is appropriate only with no direct or indirect taxes on property compensation. For the U.S. private domestic economy, this formula can be applied only to nonprofit institutions. We discuss the imputation of the value of the capital services utilized by these institutions below. Households hold consumer durables and owner-occupied dwellings. The property compensation associated with these assets is not taxed directly; however, part of the income is taxed indirectly through property taxes. To incorporate property taxes into our estimates of the price and quantity of capital services we add taxes to the cost of capital, depreciation, and revaluation, obtaining the capital service price:

$$q_{K,t} = q_{A,t-1} r_t + q_{A,t} \delta - (q_{A,t} - q_{A,t-1}) + q_{A,t} \tau_t,$$

where τ_t is the rate of property taxation. To estimate the rate of return we proceed as before, substituting the capital service price including property taxes into the expression for property compensation. The rate of return is the ratio of property compensation less depreciation plus revaluation of capital assets less taxes to the value of capital stock at the beginning of the period.

In measuring the capital service flow utilized by households and institutions we first estimate the value of the services of owner-occupied residential real estate, including both land and structures. This value is obtained directly from the U.S. national accounts. Using prices of acquisition for land and residential structures, the corresponding stocks in constant prices, the rate of replacement for structures, and the value of owner-occupied housing services, we estimate the implicit rate of return for the household sector. We assume that rates of return for consumer durables and for producer durables, nonresidential structures, and land utilized by institutions are the same as for owner-occupied residential real estate. This assumption results in a single rate of return for households and institutions. Adding the cost of capital and depreciation, subtracting revaluation for assets held by households and institutions, and adding property taxes for the household sector, we obtain the imputed value of property compensation, gross of taxes, for households and institutions. The imputed value of the services of owner-occupied dwellings is identical to the value of the flow of services from these dwellings from the U.S. national accounts.

Given the rate of return for households and institutions, we can construct estimates of capital service prices for each class of assets held by households and institutions—land held by households and institutions, residential structures, nonresidential structures, producer durables, and consumer durables. These estimates require acquisition prices for each capital good, rates of replacement, rates of taxation for assets held by households, and the rate of return for the sector as a whole. We employ separate effective tax rates for owner-occupied residential property, both land and structures, and for consumer durables. Corresponding to these price data we can construct estimates of capital service quantities for each class of assets. Price and quantity measures of capital input by class of asset can be combined into price and quantity index numbers of capital input by households and institutions, utilizing the Divisia index number formulas presented in Section 3 above.

Our measure of the gross output of the private domestic sector of the U.S. economy differs from that of the U.S. national accounts in the treatment of consumer and institutional durables and institutional real estate. We assign personal consumption expenditures on durables to gross investment rather than consumption. This change leaves the product of the private domestic sector unchanged. We add the service flow from consumer and institutional durables to the value of output and the value of capital input. We also add the net rent component of the services of institutional real estate to values of both output and input. The values of these service flows enter the product and factor outlay accounts given in Table 1 above and represent net additions to the value of gross product of the private domestic sector from the U.S. national accounts.

Our method for estimating the prices and quantities of capital services in the noncorporate sector is similar to the method we have described for households and institutions. For the noncorporate sector we estimate property compensation directly as the sum of income originating in business, other than income originating in corporate business and government enterprises and net rent of owner-occupied dwellings, less labor compensation in the noncorporate sector, including imputed labor compensation of proprietors and unpaid family workers, plus noncorporate capital consumption allowances, less allowances for owner-occupied dwellings and institutional structures, and plus indirect business taxes allocated to the noncorporate sector. We also allocate the statistical discrepancy to noncorporate property compensation.

To obtain an estimate of the noncorporate rate of return we deduct property taxes from noncorporate property compensation, add revaluation of assets, subtract depreciation, and divide the result by the value of noncorporate assets at the beginning of the period. The noncorporate rate of return is gross of personal income taxes on noncorporate property compensation. Property compensation of households and institutions is not subject to the personal income tax.

The value of property compensation in the noncorporate sector is equal to the value of the flow of capital services from residential and nonresidential structures, producer durable equipment, farm and non-farm inventories, and land held by the sector. All farm inventories are assigned to the noncorporate sector. Given the noncorporate rate of return, estimated from noncorporate property compensation by the method outlined above, and given data on prices of acquisition, stocks, tax rates, and replacement rates for each class of assets, we can estimate capital service prices for each class of assets held by the noncorporate sector. Quantity data on capital services for each class of assets are constructed by the perpetual inventory method. Price and quantity measures of capital input by class of asset can be combined into price and quantity index numbers of capital input by noncorporate business, using Divisia index number formulas as before.

We next consider the measurement of prices and quantities of capital services for corporate business. We measure corporate property compensation as income originating in corporate business, less compensation of employees, plus corporate capital consumption allowances, plus business transfer payments, plus the indirect business taxes allocated to the corporate sector. To obtain an estimate of the corporate rate of return we must take into account the corporate income tax. The capital service price, modified to incorporate the corporate income tax and indirect business taxes, becomes:

$$q_{K,t} = \left[\frac{1 - u_t z_t - k_t + y_t}{1 - u_t} \right] [q_{A,t-1} r_t + q_{A,t} \delta - (q_{A,t} - q_{A,t-1})] + q_{A,t} \tau_t,$$

where indirect business taxes $q_{A,t} \tau_t$ are deducted from corporate property compensation before taxes as an expense, u_t is the corporate tax rate, z_t is the present value of depreciation allowances on one dollar's worth of investment, k_t the investment tax credit, and $y_t = k_t u_t z_t$.[51] The variable y_t is set equal to zero for all years but 1962 and 1963; it is used in accounting for the fact that the investment tax credit was deducted from the value of an asset for depreciation in those years. The tax credit is different from zero only for producer durables. Depreciation allowances are different from zero only for durables and structures.

[51] A detailed derivation of prices of capital services is given by Hall and Jorgenson [34], [35] for continuous time. We have converted their formulation to discrete time, added property taxes, and introduced alternative measurements for the tax parameters. Similar formulas have been developed by Coen [10].

Our method for estimating the corporate rate of return is the same as for the noncorporate rate of return. Property compensation in the corporate sector is the sum of the value of services from residential and nonresidential structures, producer durable equipment, nonfarm inventories, and land held by that sector. To estimate the rate of return in the corporate sector we require estimates of the variables that describe the corporate tax structure—the effective corporate tax rate, the present value of depreciation allowances, and the investment tax credit. We obtain estimates of all the variables—acquisition prices and stocks of assets, rates of replacement, and variables describing the tax structure—that enter the value of capital services except, of course, for the rate of return. We then solve for the rate of return in terms of these variables and total property compensation.

Our estimate of the effective rate of the corporate income tax is obtained as the ratio of federal and state and local corporate profits tax liability plus the investment tax credit to corporate property income less taxes on corporate property and the imputed value of depreciation allowances for tax purposes. Imputed depreciation differs from depreciation for tax purposes in reflecting changes in the present value of future depreciation allowances as well as the current flow of depreciation allowances. The present value of depreciation deductions on new investment depends on depreciation formulas allowed for tax purposes, the lifetimes of assets used in calculating depreciation, and the rate of return. We assume that the rate of return used for discounting future depreciation allowances in the corporate sector is constant at 10 per cent. Our estimate of the effective rate of the investment tax credit is based on estimates of the tax credit claimed by corporations. The effective rate is the investment tax credit divided by investment in producer durable equipment by corporations.

To estimate the rate of return in the corporate sector our first step is to subtract property taxes from total property compensation before taxes. The second step is to subtract federal and state and local corporate profits tax liability. We then add revaluation of assets, subtract depreciation, and divide the result by the value of corporate assets at the beginning of the period. The corporate rate of return is gross of personal income taxes, but net of the corporate income tax. We estimate the price of capital services for each asset employed in the corporate sector by substituting the corporate rate of return into the corresponding formula for the price of capital services. These formulas also depend on acquisition prices of capital assets, rates of replacement, and variables describing the tax structure. Quantity data for each class of assets are constructed by the perpetual inventory method. Price and quantity indexes of capital input by class of asset are combined into price and quantity indexes of capital input for the corporate sector, utilizing Divisia index number formulas.

In separating changes in the value of capital input into price and quantity components we preserve the accounting identity that property compensation for each sector of the U.S. private domestic economy is equal to the value of all capital services utilized in that sector. Denoting the index of capital input by K and the capital service price index by p_K, total property compensation is the sum of values of capital input for each category of capital:

$$p_K K = \Sigma p_{K,j} K_j,$$

where $p_{K,j}$ is the price of the jth type of capital service and K_j is the quantity of capital of this type. Divisia indexes of the capital service price and capital input are:

$$\frac{\dot{p}_K}{p_K} = \Sigma v_j \frac{\dot{p}_{K,j}}{p_{K,j}}, \quad \frac{\dot{K}}{K} = \Sigma v_j \frac{\dot{K}_j}{K_j},$$

where the weights are the relative shares of each type of capital input in total property compensation.

We assume that the rate of return is the same for all assets within a given sector. This rate of return is inferred from the value of property compensation, acquisition prices and stocks of capital goods, rates of replacement, and variables describing the tax structure. To obtain price and quantity indexes of capital input for the private domestic sector as a whole we apply the Divisia index formulas to Divisia price and quantity indexes for each of the three subsectors—corporations, noncorporate business, and households and institutions. By the reproductive property of Divisia index numbers the resulting price and quantity indexes are equivalent to Divisia indexes computed from data on prices and quantities of capital goods distinguished by class of asset and sector. Price and quantity indexes of capital services for corporations, noncorporate business, households and institutions, and the U.S. private domestic sector as a whole are given for 1929–69 in Table 13.

5.4. Total Factor Productivity

We construct price and quantity index numbers for total factor input by combining Divisia indexes of labor and capital input into a Divisia

TABLE 13

Gross Private Domestic Capital Input, 1929–69
(constant prices of 1958)

Year	Corporate Capital Input		Noncorporate Capital Input		Household Capital Input		Private Domestic Capital Input	
	Price Index	Quantity Index	Price Index	Quantity Index	Price Index	Quantity Index	Price Index	Quantity Index
1929	.070	261.7	.052	204.6	.053	280.9	.057	765.8
1930	.056	268.2	.029	210.2	.050	285.1	.045	782.4
1931	.039	267.9	.025	210.9	.048	279.8	.038	776.2
1932	.026	260.0	.011	216.9	.035	270.2	.024	758.1
1933	.025	242.6	.013	211.2	.043	254.1	.028	714.3
1934	.040	228.0	.017	204.5	.044	240.5	.034	676.6
1935	.048	220.8	.025	209.6	.041	232.5	.038	661.5
1936	.059	216.8	.031	210.3	.047	231.6	.046	655.9
1937	.063	219.3	.032	213.2	.046	238.1	.047	667.6
1938	.053	224.9	.029	220.6	.046	244.6	.043	686.4
1939	.060	220.6	.034	220.3	.048	242.6	.048	678.7
1940	.076	220.7	.038	221.9	.048	247.3	.054	684.5
1941	.099	227.3	.051	225.0	.048	256.8	.066	704.0
1942	..119	239.6	.065	230.2	.040	269.5	.073	735.7
1943	.137	239.0	.074	228.5	.061	261.6	.090	728.3
1944	.139	234.5	.094	224.6	.065	250.4	.098	710.8
1945	.123	231.1	.103	223.6	.075	239.0	.099	697.4
1946	.110	234.5	.103	223.9	.094	232.0	.102	695.8
1947	.133	252.9	.095	229.3	.099	255.9	.108	744.1
1948	.155	272.1	.100	235.1	.098	285.4	.117	799.3
1949	.143	288.1	.089	245.9	.074	313.3	.101	852.4
1950	.165	295.0	.098	254.0	.101	341.6	.121	891.0
1951	.177	310.6	.117	266.2	.093	383.5	.128	955.7
1952	.163	331.0	.107	274.6	.101	408.2	.123	1,010.0
1953	.162	344.3	.101	279.4	.108	426.8	.124	1,047.1
1954	.157	357.0	.098	284.1	.108	452.8	.121	1,090.2

(continued)

TABLE 13 (concluded)

Year	Corporate Capital Input		Noncorporate Capital Input		Household Capital Input		Private Domestic Capital Input	
	Price Index	Quantity Index	Price Index	Quantity Index	Price Index	Quantity Index	Price Index	Quantity Index
1955	.184	365.3	.098	288.2	.119	476.6	.136	1,125.4
1956	.178	382.5	.089	294.7	.114	514.5	.129	1,187.1
1957	.175	402.5	.096	298.3	.112	540.2	.129	1,239.5
1958	.162	418.1	.111	302.0	.117	562.0	.130	1,282.0
1959	.187	423.7	.100	304.6	.130	574.0	.142	1,302.2
1960	.182	437.2	.096	309.1	.133	598.7	.140	1,346.1
1961	.180	452.6	.104	313.4	.132	620.9	.141	1,389.8
1962	.197	463.1	.114	316.9	.136	637.5	.150	1,421.3
1963	.202	479.7	.115	323.5	.142	663.5	.155	1,471.5
1964	.214	497.4	.115	330.8	.146	695.0	.161	1,528.8
1965	.231	520.1	.125	338.8	.146	731.2	.168	1,597.5
1966	.239	549.5	.140	349.7	.152	775.7	.177	1,684.1
1967	.224	590.0	.145	359.6	.153	819.7	.174	1,783.9˙
1968	.232	620.9	.140	368.8	.155	856.4	.176	1,864.0
1969	.230	650.2	.136	379.3	.164	903.2	.179	1,952.4

index of total factor input. The weights for labor and capital are the relative shares of labor and property compensation in the value of total factor outlay. Price and quantity index numbers for gross private domestic product may be represented in the form:

$$\frac{\dot{p}}{p} = v_L \frac{\dot{p}_L}{p_L} + v_K \frac{\dot{p}_K}{p_K},$$

$$\frac{\dot{X}}{X} = v_L \frac{\dot{L}}{L} + v_K \frac{\dot{K}}{K},$$

where p is the price index for total factor input, X is the quantity index, v_L is the relative share of labor, and v_K the relative share of capital. Discrete approximations to these continuous Divisia indexes for the price and quantity of total factor input for the U.S. private domestic economy are given for 1929–69 in Table 14.

TABLE 14

Gross Private Domestic Factor Input, 1929–69
(constant prices of 1958)

Year	Gross Private Domestic Factor Input		Property Outlay, Relative Share
	Price Index	Quantity Index	
1929	0.376	277.5	.419
1930	0.335	272.1	.389
1931	0.290	264.0	.382
1932	0.228	243.8	.333
1933	0.228	238.7	.362
1934	0.259	240.7	.370
1935	0.277	245.2	.373
1936	0.306	253.2	.389
1937	0.324	263.1	.370
1938	0.310	255.5	.374
1939	0.327	261.4	.379
1940	0.348	269.7	.392
1941	0.403	287.3	.399
1942	0.464	303.8	.383
1943	0.546	307.2	.390
1944	0.589	303.2	.391
1945	0.602	295.0	.390
1946	0.624	304.8	.372
1947	0.678	321.8	.369
1948	0.729	335.3	.382
1949	0.698	337.0	.366
1950	0.774	349.3	.399
1951	0.829	368.7	.399
1952	0.845	379.4	.389
1953	0.878	388.1	.382
1954	0.884	386.4	.388
1955	0.945	399.8	.404
1956	0.955	413.9	.387
1957	0.982	420.8	.385
1958	1.000	419.7	.398
1959	1.059	432.5	.403

(continued)

TABLE 14 (concluded)

Year	Gross Private Domestic Factor Input Price Index	Quantity Index	Property Outlay, Relative Share
1960	1.073	443.0	.398
1961	1.091	447.2	.401
1962	1.145	458.0	.408
1963	1.181	468.6	.413
1964	1.226	483.2	.415
1965	1.275	502.4	.420
1966	1.337	526.2	.423
1967	1.352	547.1	.419
1968	1.407	567.3	.412
1969	1.467	589.0	.404

Total factor productivity is defined as the ratio of real product to real factor input or, equivalently, as the ratio of the price of factor input to the product price.[52] Growth in total factor productivity may be regarded as an increase in the efficiency of the use of input to produce output or as a decline in the cost of input required to produce a given value of output. We may define a Divisia index of total factor productivity, say P, as:

$$\frac{\dot{P}}{P} = \frac{\dot{Y}}{Y} - \frac{\dot{X}}{X},$$

where Y is the quantity index of total output and X is the quantity index of total factor input. Equivalently, the index of total factor productivity may be defined as:

$$\frac{P}{P} = \frac{p}{p} - \frac{q}{q},$$

where p is the price index of total factor input and q is the price index of output. A discrete approximation to the Divisia index of total factor productivity is given in Table 15. For comparison, indexes of total factor productivity for a number of alternative conventions for the measurement of total factor input are also included in this table.

[52] For further discussion of this index of total factor productivity, see [40], especially pp. 250–254. The Divisia index of total factor productivity described in the text is a discrete approximation to the continuous Divisia index discussed by Jorgenson and Griliches.

TABLE 15

Total Factor Productivity, 1929–69
(1958 = 1.000)

Year	Labor Services and Capital Services	Labor Services and Capital Stock	Unweighted Man-hours and Capital Stock
1929	0.674	0.637	0.519
1930	0.623	0.590	0.487
1931	0.592	0.560	0.475
1932	0.543	0.512	0.438
1933	0.545	0.511	0.439
1934	0.589	0.547	0.489
1935	0.619	0.575	0.511
1936	0.673	0.624	0.549
1937	0.688	0.641	0.560
1938	0.673	0.629	0.560
1939	0.713	0.667	0.591
1940	0.752	0.704	0.625
1941	0.802	0.754	0.669
1942	0.823	0.777	0.686
1943	0.873	0.823	0.722
1944	0.933	0.878	0.773
1945	0.948	0.892	0.796
1946	0.891	0.841	0.773
1947	0.863	0.819	0.765
1948	0.882	0.847	0.798
1949	0.877	0.847	0.802
1950	0.936	0.909	0.867
1951	0.947	0.924	0.887
1952	0.943	0.924	0.890
1953	0.969	0.952	0.924
1954	0.966	0.953	0.930
1955	1.014	1.003	0.980
1956	1.005	0.998	0.980
1957	1.004	1.001	0.991
1958	1.000	1.000	1.000
1959	1.036	1.036	1.040

(continued)

TABLE 15 (concluded)

Year	Labor Services and Capital Services	Labor Services and Capital Stock	Unweighted Man-hours and Capital Stock
1960	1.038	1.042	1.050
1961	1.050	1.057	1.073
1962	1.091	1.100	1.120
1963	1.112	1.125	1.151
1964	1.142	1.160	1.191
1965	1.169	1.195	1.230
1966	1.192	1.227	1.270
1967	1.180	1.224	1.274
1968	1.196	1.247	1.305
1969	1.195	1.254	1.319

Solow uses a stock concept of capital input, omitting changes in the quantity of capital due to changes in the composition of capital input [54]. Denison distinguishes among residential real estate, farm capital, and all other capital input [14]. Since this breakdown of capital input does not coincide with sectors distinguished by a legal form of organization, Denison's measure fails to take account of differences in rates of return due to differences in the tax structure. Denison omits revaluation of assets in estimating rates of return and fails to account for the quantity of capital and depreciation in an internally consistent way. Kendrick adjusts capital input for changes in the industrial composition of capital stock [42]. This breakdown of capital input also fails to capture differences in rates of return due to the tax structure.

Solow employs unweighted man-hours as a measure of labor input, omitting the effects of changes in the composition of the labor force on the quantity of labor input. Denison weights persons engaged by an index of labor quality that incorporates the effects of growth in educational attainment, but differs in a number of details from the index we have used. Kendrick adjusts labor input for changes in the industrial composition of man-hours worked. For comparison with our index of total factor productivity we present indexes based on man-hours and capital stock and based on our index of labor input and capital stock. The first of these indexes provides an approximation to the conventions for measuring total factor productivity used by Solow. The second provides an ap-

TABLE 16

Relative Importance of Productivity Change, 1929–69
(average annual rates of growth)

	1929–49	1949–69	1929–69
Gross private domestic product			
Real product	2.28	4.34	3.31
Real factor input	0.97	2.79	1.88
Total factor productivity	1.31	1.55	1.43
Relative proportion of productivity change	0.57	0.36	0.43

proximation to the conventions employed by Denison. It is obvious from a comparison of the alternative estimates of total factor productivity given in Table 15 that the results are very sensitive to the choice of methods for measuring real factor input.

Finally, to evaluate the relative importance of growth in real factor input and growth in total factor productivity as sources of economic growth, we present the relative proportion of growth in real factor input. Geometric average annual rates of growth are given for real product and real factor input for 1929–49 and 1949–69 in Table 16. The relative proportion of growth in total factor productivity in the growth of real product is also given.

6. INCOME AND EXPENDITURE, ACCUMULATION, AND WEALTH ACCOUNTS

6.1. Introduction

In Section 5 we presented the production account for the U.S. private domestic economy in constant prices. We gave data in constant prices for both product and factor input sides of the production account. In this section we present income and expenditure, accumulation, and wealth accounts for the U.S. private national economy in constant prices. In constructing these accounts in constant prices we must separate changes in income, consumer outlays, and capital formation into price and quantity components.

The fundamental accounting identity for the income and expenditure account is that consumer receipts are equal to consumer outlays plus saving. The corresponding identity for the accumulation account is that saving is equal to capital formation. The income and expenditure account is linked directly to the production account through factor income and consumer outlays. The income and expenditure and production accounts are linked indirectly through the accumulation account. The accumulation account is linked to the production account through capital formation. Capital formation includes expenditures on investment goods. Through the accumulation account, production and income and expenditure are linked to wealth. The change in wealth from period to period is equal to capital formation less depreciation plus revaluation of assets.

The accumulation account is also linked to production through net capital formation, defined as capital formation less replacement. If the decline in efficiency of capital goods is geometric, replacement is equal to depreciation and net capital formation is equal to the change in wealth from period to period less the revaluation of assets. If decline in efficiency is not geometric, a perpetual inventory of prices and quantities of capital goods is required. Net capital formation is linked to changes in capital input, while net saving is linked to changes in wealth.

Consumption expenditures in the income and expenditure account include sales and excise taxes and customs duties on consumption goods. Taxes are excluded from the value of consumption goods output in the production account. Factor outlay in the production account includes both direct taxes on factor income and indirect taxes that form a part of outlay on factors of production. In the income and expenditure account factor incomes exclude both direct and indirect taxes. Similarly, capital formation in the accumulation account includes sales and excise taxes and customs duties on investment goods. Taxes are excluded from the value of investment goods output in the production account.

6.2. Labor Income and Consumer Outlays

We begin by presenting estimates of labor income and consumer outlays in constant prices for the U.S. private national economy. To construct price and quantity indexes of consumer outlays, we obtain data for consumption expenditures on nondurable goods and services, excluding the services of institutional real estate, in constant prices from the U.S. national accounts. We combine these data with imputed values of the services of consumer and institutional durables, and the services of institutional real estate in constant prices. Prices of services and nondurable goods are implicit in the data on personal consumption expenditures in current prices from the U.S. national accounts. Price indexes for the services of consumer and institutional durables, and institutional real estate are the capital service prices described in Section 5 above.

TABLE 17

Private National Consumption Expenditures, Consumer Outlays,
and National Labor Compensation, 1929–69
(constant prices of 1958)

Year	Consumption Expenditures and Consumer Outlays (price index)	Consumption Expenditures (quantity index)	Consumer Outlays (quantity index)	Private National Labor Compensation		
				Price Index	Quantity Index	Effective Tax Rate
1929	0.546	141.0	142.9	0.278	235.8	.001
1930	0.527	135.5	137.5	0.260	234.0	.001
1931	0.481	132.0	133.9	0.226	233.8	.001
1932	0.411	121.5	123.4	0.185	229.0	.001
1933	0.414	119.1	120.8	0.171	233.1	.004
1934	0.437	123.3	124.8	0.203	224.0	.004
1935	0.447	126.3	127.7	0.212	231.6	.005
1936	0.458	137.2	138.7	0.227	243.5	.005
1937	0.469	141.9	143.4	0.248	246.3	.007
1938	0.457	143.0	144.4	0.237	242.7	.009
1939	0.457	147.9	149.3	0.246	248.1	.008
1940	0.460	153.6	155.1	0.261	250.5	.009
1941	0.487	161.5	162.9	0.304	260.8	.011
1942	0.526	165.6	166.9	0.367	274.6	.024
1943	0.602	171.0	172.4	0.392	301.7	.086
1944	0.630	177.1	178.6	0.424	306.8	.086
1945	0.660	186.7	188.4	0.456	289.3	.090
1946	0.730	195.5	197.3	0.505	259.2	.081
1947	0.804	197.2	198.9	0.553	257.1	.092
1948	0.840	203.7	205.5	0.606	258.9	.081
1949	0.799	208.6	210.5	0.620	256.9	.068
1950	0.845	218.7	220.5	0.670	260.0	.065
1951	0.881	227.7	229.4	0.723	269.1	.092
1952	0.909	236.9	238.7	0.759	272.7	.103
1953	0.926	245.7	247.7	0.811	272.7	.101

(continued)

TABLE 17 (concluded)

Year	Consumption Expenditures and Consumer Outlays (price index)	Consumption Expenditures (quantity index)	Consumer Outlays (quantity index)	Private National Labor Compensation		
				Price Index	Quantity Index	Effective Tax Rate
1954	0.932	252.3	254.5	0.831	269.0	.089
1955	0.953	265.4	267.5	0.874	273.7	.090
1956	0.957	277.8	280.2	0.928	276.7	.094
1957	0.974	286.0	288.7	0.981	274.3	.095
1958	1.000	293.6	296.5	1.000	271.5	.094
1959	1.031	306.0	309.0	1.059	275.9	.095
1960	1.052	315.4	318.4	1.093	279.7	.099
1961	1.057	324.3	327.6	1.123	280.2	.098
1962	1.071	336.4	340.0	1.180	283.0	.101
1963	1.090	349.2	353.1	1.224	286.0	.102
1964	1.106	367.5	371.8	1.306	290.4	.090
1965	1.121	386.9	391.6	1.360	297.7	.094
1966	1.157	407.0	412.0	1.441	306.8	.099
1967	1.178	423.7	429.3	1.496	314.4	.102
1968	1.214	441.9	448.0	1.591	321.2	.111
1969	1.271	459.1	465.7	1.678	328.8	.123

The value of consumption expenditures includes customs duties, excise and sales taxes, and excludes subsidies. In Section 5 we have outlined the method for allocating excise and sales taxes between investment and consumption goods output. We construct a quantity index of consumption expenditures as a Divisia index of the quantity indexes of nondurables, services and our estimate of imputed capital services. The price index is then computed as the ratio of consumption expenditures to the quantity index. We deflate consumer outlays by the price index of consumption expenditures. We present price and quantity indexes for consumption expenditures and consumer outlays in Table 17.

Labor services offered are not identified with hours actually worked. Unemployment is a measure of the number of persons willing to offer labor at the current wage rate who do not have a demand for their labor.

We include a "normal workday" for the unemployed in working time. All nonworking time is considered to be leisure. A case could be made for including even more in working time offered on the grounds that there is an interaction between labor force participation and unemployment rates. As unemployment is reduced, people previously discouraged from entering the labor force by high unemployment are induced to enter. We include in working time offered only the time of the unemployed, assuming that the average workweek is the same as for the employed.

Our data for man-hours are from Kendrick.[53] Kendrick provides total man-hours for the farm sector, the general government sector, and the total private domestic sector. Hours for proprietors and unpaid family workers are included in his estimates. We provide our own hours estimate only for the rest of world sector. We assume that hours per man employed are equal to hours per man for the private domestic nonfarm economy. We adjust the total time endowment and the quantity of working time offered for quality change as measured by educational attainment. Both work and leisure are composed of quantities of labor services of varying qualities. Quantities of the different categories of labor services offered are combined into a Divisia quantity index of labor offered. In principle, a quantity index of labor supply could be built up from man-hours worked, classified by sex, race, years of schooling, occupation, age, and so on. Wage rates net of tax could be estimated for each class of worker. Our adjustment of the quantity of man-hours for changes in the educational composition of the labor force fails to take into account differences in taxes paid by workers at different levels of income.

Our concept of labor income is net of personal income taxes. The effective tax rate on labor income is computed as the ratio of taxes on labor income to labor income including taxes. Price, quantity, and tax indexes for labor income are presented in Table 17.

6.3. Property Income

The starting point for estimating price and quantity components of property income is a set of perpetual inventory estimates of stocks of each type of capital employed in measuring capital input in constant prices in the production account. We assume that the flow of capital services from each type of tangible asset is proportional to the stock. Real property compensation for each asset is equal to the real service

[53] See footnote 41, above.

flow. Similarly real property compensation from the government and rest of world sectors is proportional to the quantity of net claims on governments and foreigners.

Prices of capital input from the point of view of the producer include both direct and indirect taxes. To obtain prices for capital input from the point of view of the owner of the asset we exclude all taxes. Excluding both direct and indirect taxes, the price of capital services becomes:

$$q_{K,t} = q_{A,t-1}r_t + q_{A,t}\delta - (q_{A,t} - q_{A,t-1}),$$

where r_t is the after-tax rate of return. The depreciation rate δ is different from zero only for structures, equipment, and consumer durables employed in the private domestic sector. For inventories, land, and financial claims on the government and rest of world sectors the capital service price reduces to the cost of capital $q_{A,t-1}r_t$ less revaluation of assets $q_{A,t} - q_{A,t-1}$. For a financial asset the value of capital services is equal to earnings on the asset, for example, interest payments on a bond.

To construct price and quantity indexes of property compensation for the income and expenditure account our procedure is analogous to the methods we have used for the production account, except for the treatment of taxes. Property compensation before taxes includes the property share of gross private domestic factor outlay, corporate profits and net interest originating in the foreign sector, net interest paid by government, and investment income of social insurance funds net of transfers to general government. We have described effective rates of business property taxation and corporate income taxation in our presentation of the production account. We compute an effective rate of personal income taxation on property compensation net of business property taxes and the corporate income tax, and an effective rate of estate, death, and gift taxation on wealth.

We allocate federal estate and gift taxes and state and local death and gift taxes proportionally to all the components of private national wealth. Property income from assets in the household sector is not subject to personal income taxation; thus we must allocate personal income taxes attributed to property compensation among the corporate, noncorporate, government, and foreign sectors. A detailed allocation of personal income taxes to the various types of property compensation would be desirable; we simply allocate the taxes proportionately to all nonhousehold property compensation after corporate and property taxes but before personal taxes. The effective rate of personal income taxation on property compensation is estimated as the ratio of personal income taxes to property compensation before personal taxes other than household and institutional property compensation.

The after-tax return to capital in each sector includes property compensation, net of all taxes; it also includes capital gains and excludes economic depreciation. Our estimates of capital gains and economic depreciation for corporate and noncorporate tangible assets are discussed in detail in Christensen and Jorgenson [7]. Depreciation is zero for the financial assets which constitute net claims on governments and foreigners. Capital gains on net claims on foreigners are computed as the yearly increase in net claims less net private foreign investment. Capital gains on net claims on governments are computed as the yearly increase in net claims on governments less the current government deficit. These items are discussed in greater detail below.

The after-tax rate of return in each sector is computed by dividing the after-tax return to capital by the value of assets. These rates of return are nominal or money rates. We can also compute the real or own rates of return by excluding capital gains from the return to capital. Nominal and own rates of return for each sector and for the private national economy are presented in Table 18, together with effective tax rates on property compensation. We can now estimate the price of capital services for each asset from the formula above as a function of the rate of return, the depreciation rate, and the current and lagged acquisition price. Real property income for each sector and the private national economy is obtained as a Divisia quantity index of real property income from each asset. The price indexes for property income are computed as the ratios of property income to the quantity indexes. The price and quantity indexes of property income are presented in Table 19.

6.4. Accumulation Account

The fundamental accounting identity for the accumulation account is that gross private national saving, taken from the income and expenditure account, is equal to gross private national capital formation. Gross private national saving may be expressed as the sum of depreciation and net private national saving. Net private national saving is equal to the change in wealth from period to period less revaluation of assets. Gross private national capital formation can be expressed as the sum of replacement and net private national capital formation. We present data in con-

TABLE 18

Gross Private National Property Compensation, Rates of Return,
and Effective Rates of Taxation, 1929–69

Year	Corporate Sector	Non-corporate Sector	House-holds and Institutions	Net Claims on Governments and Rest of World	Private National Economy
		a. Nominal Rates of Return			
1929	.076	.056	.029	.078	.053
1930	−.008	−.067	−.031	.042	−.028
1931	−.065	−.117	−.092	−.017	−.084
1932	−.091	−.141	−.151	.036	−.113
1933	−.005	.010	.017	.043	.012
1934	.082	.062	.090	.108	.083
1935	.062	.049	.002	.032	.034
1936	.078	.071	.059	.009	.060
1937	.131	.073	.078	.034	.084
1938	.029	−.005	.032	−.001	.017
1939	.052	.027	.019	.007	.027
1940	.096	.070	.041	.002	.056
1941	.154	.159	.092	.088	.123
1942	.181	.187	.079	.109	.136
1943	.129	.156	.096	.010	.098
1944	.124	.172	.103	−.025	.087
1945	.077	.170	.080	−.017	.066
1946	.158	.265	.125	.027	.123
1947	.243	.253	.186	.008	.154
1948	.140	.141	.114	.018	.099
1949	.055	.036	−.021	.024	.020
1950	.096	.152	.074	.042	.087
1951	.136	.161	.085	.028	.100
1952	.062	.065	.040	.024	.047
1953	.048	.048	.027	.034	.038
1954	.048	.067	.017	.030	.037

(continued)

TABLE 18 (continued)

Year	Corporate Sector	Non-corporate Sector	House-holds and Institutions	Net Claims on Gov-ernments and Rest of World	Private National Economy
1955	.076	.073	.055	.029	.058
1956	.103	.092	.071	.034	.076
1957	.086	.096	.054	.032	.066
1958	.049	.097	.037	.037	.051
1959	.065	.064	.064	.041	.060
1960	.050	.069	.051	.042	.053
1961	.050	.076	.046	.031	.050
1962	.068	.082	.056	.040	.061
1963	.067	.073	.061	.034	.060
1964	.080	.075	.069	.030	.067
1965	.094	.092	.060	.039	.072
1966	.104	.100	.069	.035	.079
1967	.095	.094	.085	.023	.080
1968	.089	.092	.088	.034	.081
1969	.087	.087	.093	.041	.082
		b. Own Rates of Return			
1929	.074	.058	.012	.052	.044
1930	.050	.016	.008	.047	.025
1931	.022	.010	.014	.044	.018
1932	−.002	−.019	−.001	.035	−.002
1933	−.004	−.012	.019	.033	.007
1934	.026	−.002	.015	.036	.017
1935	.042	.017	.009	.031	.023
1936	.060	.031	.020	.027	.034
1937	.063	.027	.013	.026	.031
1938	.040	.020	.011	.026	.023
1939	.056	.033	.015	.025	.032
1940	.075	.042	.014	.027	.038
1941	.076	.069	.008	.025	.043
1942	.074	.089	−.020	.024	.037
1943	.067	.085	.011	.018	.042
1944	.075	.115	.008	.018	.048

(continued)

TABLE 18 (continued)

Year	Corporate Sector	Non-corporate Sector	House-holds and Institutions	Net Claims on Governments and Rest of World	Private National Economy
1945	.057	.119	.016	.016	.045
1946	.046	.115	.037	.018	.046
1947	.057	.086	.034	.019	.044
1948	.070	.079	.025	.021	.045
1949	.060	.061	−.003	.023	.032
1950	.054	.068	.025	.022	.040
1951	.049	.081	.010	.024	.037
1952	.042	.062	.017	.024	.034
1953	.037	.054	.024	.023	.033
1954	.040	.051	.024	.025	.033
1955	.056	.051	.036	.024	.042
1956	.045	.036	.026	.025	.033
1957	.040	.039	.019	.027	.030
1958	.034	.048	.022	.026	.031
1959	.043	.035	.033	.027	.035
1960	.039	.029	.034	.028	.033
1961	.039	.033	.032	.028	.033
1962	.050	.038	.035	.030	.039
1963	.051	.036	.039	.031	.040
1964	.059	.035	.041	.035	.044
1965	.068	.039	.040	.035	.047
1966	.070	.046	.045	.036	.050
1967	.058	.044	.043	.037	.047
1968	.052	.036	.039	.038	.042
1969	.042	.027	.042	.036	.038

(continued)

TABLE 18 (continued)

Year	Effective Corporate Income Tax Rate	Effective Personal Income Tax Rate on Property Compensation	Effective Rate of Wealth Taxation
		c. Effective Tax Rates	
1929	.108	.070	.000
1930	.083	.106	.000
1931	.074	.098	.000
1932	.113	a	.000
1933	.207	a	.000
1934	.136	.092	.000
1935	.139	.065	.001
1936	.172	.063	.001
1937	.156	.101	.001
1938	.133	.112	.001
1939	.167	.054	.001
1940	.243	.051	.001
1941	.440	.061	.001
1942	.492	.089	.001
1943	.531	.208	.001
1944	.495	.157	.001
1945	.492	.183	.001
1946	.470	.170	.001
1947	.443	.150	.001
1948	.391	.123	.001
1949	.331	.123	.001
1950	.486	.163	.000
1951	.520	.155	.000
1952	.463	.182	.000
1953	.477	.195	.001
1954	.481	.187	.001
1955	.481	.173	.001
1956	.476	.212	.001
1957	.469	.212	.001
1958	.472	.198	.001
1959	.497	.206	.001

(continued)

TABLE 18 (concluded)

Year	Effective Corporate Income Tax Rate	Effective Personal Income Tax Rate on Property Compensation	Effective Rate of Wealth Taxation
1960	.495	.230	.001
1961	.488	.222	.001
1962	.467	.200	.001
1963	.477	.201	.001
1964	.479	.173	.001
1965	.470	.165	.001
1966	.463	.169	.001
1967	.449	.186	.001
1968	.504	.222	.001
1969	.511	.282	.001

[a] Income base is zero or negligible.

stant prices for saving and capital formation, both gross and net, and for depreciation, replacement, and revaluation. Gross private national capital formation is equal to gross private domestic investment, as defined in the U.S. national accounts, plus personal consumption expenditures on durable goods, plus the current deficits of the federal and state and local social insurance funds, plus the current surpluses of federal and state and local social insurance funds, plus net foreign investment.

We divide the components of gross private national capital formation into prices and quantities using the following deflators: The implicit deflators from the U.S. National Income and Product Accounts are used for investment in producer and consumer durables, and for farm and nonfarm inventories. For residential and nonresidential structures we use the "constant cost 2" price index for structures from the Bureau of Economic Analysis (formerly the Office of Business Economics) *Capital Stock Study* for both capital formation and replacement.[54] We have constructed price indexes for claims on the government and rest of world sectors from data on changes in the value of claims from period to period and data on the corresponding components of capital formation from the U.S. national accounts. We set the price of claims of each type equal to 1.000 in 1958 and the quantity in 1958 equal to the value of

[54] See footnote 45, above.

TABLE 19

Gross Private National Property Compensation, 1929–69
(constant prices of 1958)

Year	Corporate Property Compensation		Noncorporate Property Compensation		Households and Institutions, Property Compensation		Government and Rest of World, Property Compensation		Private National Property Compensation	
	Price Index	Quantity Index	Price Index	Quantity Index	Price Index	Quantity Index	Price Index	Quantity Index	Price Index	Quantity Index
1929	.056	257.9	.039	200.9	.048	273.9	.048	35.1	.045	834.0
1930	.044	264.0	.017	212.2	.045	278.2	.044	35.0	.034	854.7
1931	.029	263.4	.013	216.0	.044	272.8	.041	36.3	.028	849.8
1932	.018	255.5	.000	214.9	.031	263.0	.031	40.0	.017	830.7
1933	.016	237.2	.003	208.6	.039	246.3	.029	42.3	.020	784.7
1934	.029	221.5	.007	202.6	.039	232.5	.032	44.2	.025	745.3
1935	.036	213.8	.015	197.6	.036	224.4	.030	47.3	.028	725.8
1936	.043	209.5	.020	197.5	.042	223.6	.025	49.5	.033	721.3
1937	.046	211.6	.020	201.8	.041	230.6	.025	53.2	.033	738.2
1938	.038	216.9	.017	211.4	.041	237.5	.024	54.6	.030	760.9
1939	.045	212.8	.022	211.3	.043	235.5	.023	59.0	.034	756.2
1940	.053	212.8	.026	213.4	.043	240.5	.024	63.8	.038	766.8
1941	.056	219.2	.038	216.7	.043	250.2	.022	67.8	.041	791.3
1942	.060	230.9	.051	221.9	.034	263.4	.023	75.1	.043	828.7
1943	.061	229.7	.053	219.5	.055	255.3	.018	108.4	.050	831.1
1944	.069	225.0	.073	215.3	.059	243.9	.018	153.7	.059	823.6

Year										
1945	.061	222.2	.079	214.2	.069	232.4	.016	209.8	.061	822.7
1946	.057	227.0	.081	214.8	.088	225.4	.017	255.8	.066	831.1
1947	.073	245.2	.073	220.6	.093	249.7	.018	259.0	.070	888.5
1948	.092	266.1	.079	227.3	.092	279.5	.020	257.2	.076	956.5
1949	.089	282.8	.069	238.6	.067	307.9	.021	253.7	.066	1,019.7
1950	.085	290.6	.074	248.0	.094	337.0	.020	260.5	.074	1,074.0
1951	.086	306.0	.090	261.4	.086	379.7	.022	250.9	.077	1,154.3
1952	.084	326.0	.079	270.6	.094	404.9	.023	249.2	.076	1,216.0
1953	.082	339.8	.072	276.1	.100	423.7	.022	257.3	.076	1,262.9
1954	.085	353.3	.070	281.4	.099	450.2	.024	265.9	.076	1,320.0
1955	.100	363.1	.071	286.2	.110	474.3	.024	275.5	.084	1,369.8
1956	.095	380.4	.061	293.6	.104	513.2	.024	275.5	.079	1,447.5
1957	.095	401.0	.066	297.9	.101	539.5	.026	276.0	.079	1,510.0
1958	.091	418.1	.078	302.0	.105	562.0	.026	282.3	.082	1,564.2
1959	.102	424.7	.068	305.0	.118	574.0	.027	294.7	.088	1,594.1
1960	.098	438.1	.062	310.3	.120	599.3	.028	296.6	.087	1,548.7
1961	.098	454.3	.067	315.7	.117	622.3	.029	298.4	.086	1,703.1
1962	.111	465.2	.074	319.9	.121	639.4	.031	307.0	.093	1,744.9
1963	.113	482.2	.073	328.1	.126	666.5	.032	315.3	.095	1,809.8
1964	.122	500.6	.073	337.4	.130	699.5	.036	321.4	.100	1,884.3
1965	.133	525.0	.080	347.8	.129	737.9	.037	333.8	.104	1,975.9
1966	.138	556.8	.090	361.5	.134	785.4	.037	340.9	.109	2,088.6
1967	.129	599.7	.092	374.3	.134	832.8	.039	353.0	.107	2,215.5
1968	.125	634.3	.084	386.3	.135	872.6	.039	378.6	.105	2,326.9
1969	.119	667.8	.076	400.9	.143	923.3	.037	395.4	.104	2,450.2

outstanding claims in that year. These price indexes are then used to deflate the government deficit and net foreign investment.

To construct an index of the quantity of gross private national capital formation we first construct a Divisia index of the quantities of investment in producer and consumer durables, residential and nonresidential structures, and the quantity indexes of net foreign investment and government deficits. Real investment in inventories of durable and nondurable goods is added to the Divisia index to obtain the quantity index of gross private national capital formation. The price index of replacement is computed as the ratio of the value of replacement to the Divisia index of replacement. A quantity index of net private national capital formation is computed as the quantity index of gross private national capital formation less the quantity index of replacement. The price of net private national capital formation is computed as the ratio of the value in current prices to the quantity index. The price and quantity indexes of gross private national capital formation, replacement, and net private national capital formation are presented in Table 20.

Net private national capital formation in constant prices is equal to the change in the quantity of capital for each type of capital utilized in the U.S. private domestic economy. Capital input and net capital formation in a given period are combined in the perpetual inventory formula to obtain capital input from each capital good in the following period. Changes in the value of capital input can be decomposed into price and quantity components. The quantity component must be carefully distinguished from the quantity of net capital formation. The quantity of capital input is weighted by capital service prices, while the quantities of gross and net capital formation are weighted by capital asset prices.

The value of gross private national saving is taken from the income and expenditure account. To construct the saving side of the accumulation account in constant prices we begin with gross private national capital formation in constant prices. The capital formation and saving sides of the accumulation account are equal in both current and constant prices. To complete the saving side of the accumulation account in constant prices we must construct accounts for depreciation and revaluation of assets in constant prices. We outline methods for constructing these accounts from a perpetual inventory of prices and quantities of capital goods; we then specialize to the case of geometric decline in efficiency of capital goods.

For a single capital good the value of wealth is the sum of values of investment goods of each vintage, summed over all vintages:

$$W_t = \sum_{v=0}^{\infty} q_{A,t,v} A_{t-v}.$$

The change in wealth from period to period may be written:

$$W_t - W_{t-1} = \sum_{v=0}^{\infty} q_{A,t,v} A_{t-v} - \sum_{v=0}^{\infty} q_{A,t-1,v} A_{t-v-1}$$

$$= q_{A,t,0} A_t + \sum_{v=0}^{\infty} q_{A,t,v-1} A_{t-v-1} - \sum_{v=0}^{\infty} q_{A,t-1,v} A_{t-v-1}$$

$$= q_{A,t} A_t + \sum_{v=0}^{\infty} (q_{A,t,v-1} - q_{A,t,v}) A_{t-v-1}$$

$$+ \sum_{v=0}^{\infty} (q_{A,t,v} - q_{A,t-1,v}) A_{t-v-1}.$$

In this expression for change in the value of wealth, the first term is the value of gross capital formation, the second is the negative of depreciation on capital goods of all vintages, and the third is the revaluation of assets of all vintages.

We have already described the construction of price and quantity index numbers for gross capital formation. Treating the change in prices across vintages, $q_{A,t,v} - q_{A,t,v-1}$, as the price component of depreciation and A_{t-v-1} as the quantity component, we may apply Divisia index number formulas to perpetual inventory data on prices and quantities of each vintage of a capital good to obtain price and quantity index numbers for depreciation on a single capital good. To obtain index numbers for several capital goods we again apply Divisia index number formulas, this time to the price and quantity indexes for each capital good. Similarly, treating the change in prices across time periods, $q_{A,t,v} - q_{A,t-1,v}$, as the price component of revaluation, we may obtain price and quantity index numbers of revaluation for any number of capital goods.

The value of gross saving is equal to change in wealth plus depreciation less revaluation of assets. We may define the quantity of gross saving as the sum of quantities of change in wealth and depreciation less the quantity of revaluation. The quantity of change in wealth itself is the sum of quantities of gross capital formation and revaluation less the

TABLE 20

Gross Private National Capital Formation, 1929–69
(constant prices of 1958)

Year	Gross Private National Capital Formation		Replacement		Effective Sales Tax Rate of Investment Goods
	Price Index	Quantity Index	Price Index	Quantity Index	
1929	0.474	53.6	0.463	41.3	.017
1930	0.473	39.3	0.449	42.3	.019
1931	0.471	30.5	0.411	41.8	.021
1932	0.441	15.2	0.365	40.2	.029
1933	0.423	15.5	0.352	37.7	.042
1934	0.483	21.8	0.379	35.5	.048
1935	0.429	31.8	0.379	34.1	.047
1936	0.436	41.8	0.381	33.8	.045
1937	0.434	46.1	0.408	34.6	.044
1938	0.490	33.2	0.416	35.7	.045
1939	0.467	43.4	0.410	35.3	.044
1940	0.460	53.2	0.418	35.8	.044
1941	0.510	67.5	0.453	37.2	.044
1942	0.765	66.1	0.516	39.2	.039
1943	0.848	68.5	0.551	38.0	.037
1944	0.861	79.1	0.595	36.4	.042
1945	0.822	75.0	0.617	35.2	.048
1946	0.661	74.6	0.655	35.0	.053
1947	0.728	72.5	0.741	38.3	.049
1948	0.798	82.0	0.792	42.9	.047
1949	0.809	82.4	0.799	47.4	.050
1950	0.803	94.1	0.817	51.2	.048
1951	0.885	98.8	0.880	56.3	.046
1952	0.906	98.3	0.898	59.9	.048
1953	0.903	104.2	0.901	62.7	.048
1954	0.906	103.6	0.895	66.2	.046

(continued)

TABLE 20 (concluded)

Year	Gross Private National Capital Formation		Replacement		Effective Sales Tax Rate of Investment Goods
	Price Index	Quantity Index	Price Index	Quantity Index	
1955	0.904	118.4	0.901	69.2	.045
1956	0.949	115.3	0.945	73.9	.046
1957	0.989	116.2	0.986	77.6	.046
1958	1.000	111.2	1.000	80.8	.045
1959	1.017	119.5	1.017	82.2	.046
1960	1.020	119.5	1.018	85.2	.048
1961	1.018	122.4	1.017	88.2	.047
1962	1.027	137.5	1.023	90.3	.047
1963	1.030	143.2	1.026	93.8	.048
1964	1.040	159.8	1.035	98.1	.047
1965	1.048	173.6	1.040	103.4	.046
1966	1.059	193.4	1.051	110.2	.043
1967	1.081	199.9	1.080	117.7	.043
1968	1.117	204.0	1.115	124.2	.046
1969	1.164	200.9	1.155	131.6	.047

quantity of depreciation. The quantity of net saving is equal to the quantity of gross saving less the quantity of depreciation. Quantities of gross saving and gross capital formation are, of course, identical.

If the decline in efficiency of capital goods is geometric the change in wealth from period to period for a single capital good may be written:

$$W_t - W_{t-1} = q_{A,t}K_t - q_{A,t-1}K_{t-1}$$
$$= q_{A,t}(K_t - K_{t-1}) + (q_{A,t} - q_{A,t-1})K_{t-1}$$
$$= q_{A,t}A_t - q_{A,t}\delta K_{t-1} + (q_{A,t} - q_{A,t-1})K_{t-1}.$$

Gross saving is represented by $q_{A,t}A_t$, which is equal to gross capital formation and has the same price and quantity components. Depreciation is represented by $q_{A,t}\delta K_{t-1}$ and is equal to replacement; the price and quantity components of depreciation differ from the price and quantity components of replacement. We construct the quantity index of depreciation as a Divisia index of the various lagged stocks, K_{t-1}, with depreciation shares as weights. The quantity index of replacement is a Divisia index of the δK_{t-1} with replacement shares as weights. The weights are, of course, the same for replacement and depreciation under geometric decline in efficiency; so the quantity indexes for depreciation and replacement are proportional. The price index of depreciation is computed as the ratio of depreciation to the quantity index of depreciation.

Revaluation is represented by $(q_{A,t} - q_{A,t-1})K_{t-1}$. We construct a quantity index of revaluation as a Divisia index of the various lagged capital stocks with revaluation shares as weights. The price index of revaluation is computed as the ratio of revaluation to the quantity index of revaluation. Price and quantity index numbers of private national saving, depreciation, and revaluation are presented in Table 21.

6.5. Standard of Living

At this point we can consolidate the receipt and expenditure account with the accumulation account to obtain a consolidated receipt and expenditure account. In the consolidated account consumer receipts are equal to the sum of consumer outlays and gross capital formation. Price and quantity index numbers for factor income can be constructed by combining Divisia index numbers of labor and property income into a Divisia index of factor income. The weights for labor and property are the relative shares of labor and property compensation in the value of total factor income. We use the price index of factor income to deflate government transfer payments to persons, except for social insurance benefits. Adding deflated transfer payments to the quantity index of factor income provides an index of total real consumer receipts. The construction of an index of total real consumer receipts is analogous to the construction of an index of total factor input in the production account; the scope of transactions covered by the two indexes is different and consumer receipts are net of both direct and indirect taxes in the consolidated consumer receipts and expenditures account.

Price and quantity index numbers for total expenditures can be constructed by combining Divisia index numbers of consumer outlays and capital formation into a Divisia index of total expenditures. The weights for consumer outlays and capital formation are the relative shares of these components of expenditure in the value of total expenditure. The price and quantity indexes of expenditures are analogous to indexes for total product in the production account; the scope of transactions is different and expenditures include sales and excise taxes, while the value of total product excludes such taxes.

TABLE 21

Gross Private National Saving, Depreciation, and Revaluation, 1929–69
(constant prices of 1958)

Year	Gross Private National Saving		Depreciation		Revaluation	
	Price Index	Quantity Index	Price Index	Quantity Index	Price Index	Quantity Index
1929	0.474	53.6	.046	418.3	.003	1,200.3
1930	0.473	39.3	.044	428.3	−.018	1,214.8
1931	0.471	30.5	.041	422.8	−.033	1,212.2
1932	0.441	15.2	.036	407.1	−.032	1,200.5
1933	0.423	15.5	.035	381.3	.001	1,293.4
1934	0.483	21.8	.037	359.2	.015	1,361.8
1935	0.429	31.8	.037	345.4	.003	1,298.2
1936	0.436	41.8	.038	342.1	.008	1,301.3
1937	0.434	46.1	.040	350.3	.013	1,299.7
1938	0.490	33.2	.041	361.3	−.002	1,384.7
1939	0.467	43.4	.041	357.6	−.001	1,445.9
1940	0.460	53.2	.041	362.6	.004	1,491.5
1941	0.510	67.5	.045	376.3	.020	1,514.1
1942	0.765	66.1	.051	396.8	.026	1,581.3
1943	0.848	68.5	.054	384.6	.017	1,598.6
1944	0.861	79.1	.059	368.4	.015	1,470.6
1945	0.822	75.0	.061	355.7	.010	1,260.3
1946	0.661	74.6	.065	354.4	.044	1,188.0
1947	0.728	72.5	.073	387.8	.067	1,235.3
1948	0.798	82.0	.078	433.9	.036	1,287.3
1949	0.809	82.4	.079	479.4	−.008	1,317.4
1950	0.803	94.1	.081	518.1	.035	1,314.2
1951	0.885	98.8	.087	570.0	.048	1,367.2
1952	0.906	98.3	.089	606.5	.011	1,411.0
1953	0.903	104.2	.089	634.2	.004	1,456.7
1954	0.906	103.6	.088	670.0	.003	1,469.6

(continued)

TABLE 21 (concluded)

Year	Gross Private National Saving		Depreciation		Revaluation	
	Price Index	Quantity Index	Price Index	Quantity Index	Price Index	Quantity Index
1955	0.904	118.4	.089	699.7	.015	1,446.6
1956	0.949	115.3	.093	747.6	.039	1,489.3
1957	0.989	116.2	.097	785.1	.034	1,534.5
1958	1.000	111.2	.099	817.7	.020	1,564.2
1959	1.017	119.5	.101	832.1	.025	1,581.2
1960	1.020	119.5	.101	862.1	.020	1,599.1
1961	1.018	122.4	.101	892.3	.018	1,603.7
1962	1.027	137.5	.101	913.9	.025	1,613.3
1963	1.030	143.2	.101	949.4	.023	1,627.5
1964	1.040	159.8	.102	992.2	.028	1,641.8
1965	1.048	173.6	.103	1,045.7	.032	1,659.1
1966	1.059	193.4	.104	1,114.7	.038	1,684.7
1967	1.081	199.9	.107	1,190.9	.046	1,721.1
1968	1.117	204.0	.110	1,256.4	.056	1,751.6
1969	1.164	200.9	.114	1,331.9	.067	1,791.3

The standard of living may be defined as the ratio of real expenditures to real receipts or, equivalently, the ratio of the price of factor income to the price of expenditures. A Divisia index of the standard of living may be defined as the ratio of Divisia indexes of the quantity of expenditures to the quantity of consumer receipts or, equivalently, the ratio of Divisia indexes of the price of factor income to the price of consumer expenditures. Divisia price and quantity indexes of consumer receipts and total expenditures and the standard of living for the U.S. private national economy are given in Table 22 for 1929–69.

6.6. Wealth Account

In Section 2 we described the asset side of the wealth account for the U.S. private national economy in current prices. Changes in the value of wealth from period to period may be separated into price and quantity components. The price component is equal to gross saving less depreciation or net saving. Capital formation is related to the change in capital input, but not to the change in capital assets, except where the decline in efficiency of capital goods is geometric. Under this assumption deprecia-

TABLE 22

Gross Private National Expenditures, Receipts,
and Standard of Living, 1929–69
(constant prices of 1958)

Year	Gross Private National Expenditures		Gross Private National Consumer Receipts		
	Price Index	Quantity Index	Price Index	Quantity Index	Standard of Living
1929	0.531	194.8	0.346	298.8	0.652
1930	0.516	176.3	0.303	300.4	0.587
1931	0.479	164.3	0.259	304.3	0.540
1932	0.416	138.1	0.193	297.1	0.465
1933	0.416	135.8	0.191	296.7	0.458
1934	0.444	146.5	0.230	283.6	0.517
1935	0.443	159.6	0.245	288.8	0.553
1936	0.453	180.4	0.271	301.9	0.598
1937	0.461	189.2	0.289	301.7	0.627
1938	0.464	177.4	0.273	301.8	0.588
1939	0.459	192.9	0.290	305.6	0.631
1940	0.459	208.5	0.310	308.6	0.676
1941	0.493	230.9	0.356	319.7	0.722
1942	0.594	233.0	0.413	335.1	0.695
1943	0.672	241.0	0.451	358.8	0.672
1944	0.695	259.9	0.498	363.0	0.716
1945	0.704	263.9	0.529	351.1	0.752
1946	0.710	272.3	0.582	332.5	0.819
1947	0.782	272.0	0.632	336.6	0.808
1948	0.827	287.7	0.693	343.5	0.837
1949	0.801	293.1	0.674	348.4	0.841
1950	0.832	314.6	0.736	355.6	0.885
1951	0.882	328.3	0.783	369.9	0.887
1952	0.908	337.1	0.808	378.9	0.890
1953	0.919	352.0	0.846	382.6	0.920
1954	0.924	358.2	0.861	384.3	0.932

(continued)

TABLE 22 (concluded)

Year	Gross Private National Expenditures		Gross Private National Consumer Receipts		
	Price Index	Quantity Index	Price Index	Quantity Index	Standard of Living
1955	0.938	385.8	0.920	393.3	0.981
1956	0.955	395.6	0.937	402.9	0.982
1957	0.978	405.0	0.977	405.7	0.998
1958	1.000	407.7	1.000	407.7	1.000
1959	1.027	428.6	1.063	414.2	1.035
1960	1.043	438.0	1.081	422.5	1.037
1961	1.047	450.0	1.101	427.6	1.052
1962	1.059	477.3	1.166	433.5	1.101
1963	1.074	496.0	1.205	441.9	1.123
1964	1.088	530.9	1.277	452.2	1.174
1965	1.101	564.3	1.329	467.2	1.208
1966	1.128	603.9	1.404	485.4	1.244
1967	1.150	627.7	1.432	504.1	1.245
1968	1.186	650.7	1.483	520.2	1.251
1969	1.240	665.9	1.534	538.2	1.237

tion is equal to replacement so that net saving is equal to net capital formation. Net capital formation, like net saving, may be interpreted as the quantity component of the change in the value of wealth, but only under the assumption of geometric decline in efficiency of capital goods.

To construct price and quantity indexes of wealth we require a perpetual inventory of prices and quantities of capital goods. We first outline methods for constructing these indexes from perpetual inventory data; we then specialize to the case of geometric decline in efficiency of capital goods. For a single capital good, the value of wealth, as given above, is the sum of values of investment goods of all vintages:

$$W_t = \sum_{v=0}^{\infty} q_{A,t,v} A_{t-v}.$$

Price and quantity indexes of wealth may be constructed from price and quantity data for each vintage, treating $q_{A,t,v}$ as the price and A_{t-v} as the quantity. Price and quantity indexes for several capital goods may be constructed by applying the Divisia index numbers to price and quantity indexes of wealth for each capital good.

With geometric decline in efficiency the expression for the value of wealth reduces to:

$$W_t = q_{A,t}K_t.$$

For several capital goods the acquisition price $q_{A,t}$ and quantity of capital K_t for each capital good can be combined into price and quantity indexes for wealth. Our wealth account for the U.S. private national economy includes tangible assets held by private households and institutions, and by corporate and noncorporate business, and net claims on the government and foreign sectors, including the claims of social insurance funds. We estimate the price and quantity of assets for each of the five sectors by applying Divisia index number formulas to price and quantity data for each class of capital assets held by the sector. We construct price and quantity index numbers for the U.S. private national economy by applying these index number formulas to Divisia price and quantity indexes for the five sectors. Price and quantity indexes of wealth for 1929–69 are given in Table 23.

7. EXTENDING THE ACCOUNTING FRAMEWORK

7.1. Introduction

As a long-term objective the basic accounting framework must be expanded to incorporate investment in human capital. Investment in human capital is primarily a product of the educational sector, which is not included in the private domestic sector of the economy. In addition to data on education already incorporated into the national accounts, data on physical investment and capital stock in the educational sector would be required for incorporation of investment in human capital into a complete accounting system.[55] We outline methods for incorporation of the educational sector into the basic accounting framework below.

A second objective for long-term research is the incorporation of research and development into a complete system of accounts.[56] At present research and development expenditures are treated as a current expenditure. Labor and capital employed in research and development activities are commingled with labor and capital used to produce marketable output. The first step in accounting for research and development is to

[55] Estimates of the stock of educational capital have been compiled by Schultz [53]; see especially pp. 123–131.

[56] The incorporation of research and development into a complete system of accounts has been discussed by Griliches [29].

TABLE 23

Private National Wealth, 1929–69
(constant prices of 1958)

Year	Corporate Tangible Assets		Noncorporate Tangible Assets		Household and Institutional Tangible Assets		Net Claims on Governments and Rest of World		Private National Wealth	
	Price Index	Quantity Index	Price Index	Quantity Index	Price Index	Quantity Index	Price Index	Quantity Index	Price Index	Quantity Index
1929	0.424	275.3	0.417	256.2	0.427	370.7	0.943	35.0	0.572	725.3
1930	0.399	276.4	0.382	256.0	0.410	366.1	0.938	36.3	0.532	736.7
1931	0.364	268.2	0.333	255.1	0.366	358.8	0.881	40.0	0.475	736.3
1932	0.332	253.5	0.293	250.4	0.312	346.7	0.882	42.3	0.414	732.0
1933	0.331	242.6	0.299	245.6	0.311	335.3	0.891	44.2	0.417	714.0
1934	0.350	237.5	0.318	240.3	0.335	327.5	0.955	47.3	0.450	698.2
1935	0.357	234.6	0.328	242.2	0.332	324.5	0.956	49.5	0.460	691.9
1936	0.363	238.6	0.341	242.5	0.345	325.9	0.940	53.2	0.478	693.6
1937	0.388	244.8	0.356	247.0	0.368	327.9	0.947	54.6	0.504	705.4
1938	0.384	240.2	0.348	246.2	0.375	325.6	0.922	59.0	0.494	717.6
1939	0.382	240.6	0.345	247.1	0.376	328.4	0.905	63.8	0.498	720.6
1940	0.390	247.7	0.355	249.7	0.387	334.3	0.883	67.8	0.511	732.8
1941	0.420	260.9	0.387	254.7	0.419	342.9	0.938	75.1	0.562	752.2
1942	0.465	260.3	0.425	255.3	0.461	336.5	1.018	108.4	0.629	787.3
1943	0.494	255.8	0.456	252.5	0.500	327.2	1.010	153.7	0.653	857.8
1944	0.518	251.6	0.482	251.6	0.547	317.7	0.967	209.8	0.669	939.4

332

1945	0.528	251.8	0.506	251.2	0.582	311.4	0.935	255.8	0.660	1,031.0
1946	0.587	271.7	0.582	255.0	0.633	326.7	0.944	259.0	0.693	1,096.0
1947	0.696	286.0	0.680	257.5	0.728	346.9	0.934	257.2	0.763	1,136.8
1948	0.746	300.8	0.722	266.2	0.793	368.1	0.931	253.7	0.806	1,171.4
1949	0.742	305.5	0.705	270.2	0.778	388.3	0.932	260.5	0.794	1,211.1
1950	0.773	321.2	0.764	278.6	0.816	418.9	0.951	250.9	0.835	1,247.9
1951	0.840	341.5	0.824	284.4	0.877	439.0	0.956	249.2	0.885	1,293.0
1952	0.857	353.4	0.827	287.2	0.897	455.4	0.956	257.3	0.893	1,337.6
1953	0.866	364.2	0.822	290.3	0.900	475.4	0.966	265.9	0.899	1,377.9
1954	0.873	370.0	0.835	292.7	0.894	495.4	0.971	275.5	0.899	1,421.6
1955	0.891	386.5	0.853	297.1	0.911	524.5	0.976	275.5	0.920	1,460.9
1956	0.942	405.2	0.901	299.2	0.952	545.0	0.984	276.0	0.954	1,512.0
1957	0.985	418.1	0.953	302.0	0.985	562.0	0.989	282.3	0.986	1,555.0
1958	1.000	422.2	1.000	303.9	1.000	574.0	1.000	294.7	1.000	1,594.7
1959	1.021	434.5	1.028	306.7	1.031	594.2	1.014	296.6	1.029	1,625.8
1960	1.033	447.4	1.069	309.2	1.049	611.0	1.028	298.4	1.046	1,664.0
1961	1.044	456.5	1.115	311.3	1.063	624.5	1.032	307.0	1.062	1,698.6
1962	1.062	470.8	1.164	315.2	1.086	643.6	1.042	315.3	1.093	1,732.5
1963	1.079	486.0	1.207	318.7	1.109	665.4	1.045	321.4	1.115	1,778.5
1964	1.101	505.3	1.255	322.4	1.140	688.7	1.039	333.8	1.146	1,825.9
1965	1.129	530.5	1.322	328.3	1.162	715.3	1.044	340.9	1.178	1,884.7
1966	1.167	565.4	1.393	333.2	1.190	739.9	1.043	353.0	1.217	1,950.4
1967	1.210	590.7	1.462	337.8	1.240	760.4	1.028	378.6	1.254	2,026.8
1968	1.255	614.5	1.545	342.7	1.300	786.9	1.023	395.4	1.299	2,100.7
1969	1.312	640.3	1.638	348.5	1.366	812.2	1.028	399.2	1.350	2,171.5

develop data on factors of production devoted to research. The second step is to develop measures of investment in research and development. The final step is to develop data on the stock of accumulated research. A similar accounting problem arises for advertising expenditures, also treated as a current expenditure.

Both education and investment in research and development are heavily subsidized in the United States, so that private costs and returns are not equal to social costs and returns. The effects of these subsidies would have to be taken into account in measuring the effects of human capital and accumulated research on productivity in the private sector. If the output of research activities is associated with external benefits in use, these externalities would not be reflected in the private cost of investment in research.

7.2. Investment in Human Capital

To illustrate the design of a system of accounts incorporating the educational sector, we suppose that the stock of human capital at any point of time, say E, can be imputed from past investment in education, say I_E:

$$I_E = \dot{E} + \delta E,$$

where δ is the rate of required replacement of human capital. Total labor compensation in the private domestic economy, $q_L L$, may be divided between the value of services of human capital, say $q_E E$, and the value of labor services, $q_{N \cdot H} N \cdot H$, where N is number of persons engaged, H is effective man-hours per person engaged, and $N \cdot H$ is the number of effective man-hours:

$$q_L L = q_E E + q_{N \cdot H} N \cdot H.$$

Our present measure of real labor input, corrected for quality change, is an estimate of the services of both labor, $N \cdot H$, and human capital, E.

Next, we suppose that the value of the product of the private domestic sector is equal to the value of factor outlay, as before:

$$p_I I + p_C C = q_K K + q_E E + q_{N \cdot H} N \cdot H.$$

The product of the educational sector consists entirely of investment in human capital, produced with physical capital, human capital, and labor in the educational sector: [57]

$$p_E I_E = q_K K_E + q_E E_E + q_{N \cdot H} N_E H_E,$$

---

[57] Labor may include the imputed value of the time of students as well as the market value of the time of teachers.

where p_E is the unit value of investment in human capital, K_E, E_E, N_E, and H_E are physical capital, human capital, persons engaged, and effective man-hours per person, all in the educational sector.[58]

An important obstacle to implementation of a consolidated system of accounts is the need to compile data on the stock of physical capital in the educational sector. In compiling data on the stock of human capital and its service flow the procedure we have followed for physical capital would be reversed. Data on the flow of services is readily available; from these data we would infer an appropriate implied rate of return on educational investment.

7.3. Research and Development

To incorporate investment in the form of research into our accounting framework, we may suppose, as in our analysis of investment in education, that accumulated research and development can be treated as a stock, say R, with a corresponding investment flow, I_R. The value of output, including research and development investment, is equal to the value of factor outlay, including the services of accumulated research:

$$p_R I_R + p_I I + p_C C = q_K K + q_R R + q_L L,$$

where p_R is the unit value of investment in research and development and q_R is the service price of accumulated research. The value of labor and capital employed in producing research are, of course, included in the value of factor outlay. The absolute contribution of productivity change is the sum of productivity changes in research and in ordinary production activities.

Now, suppose that research and development are treated, erroneously, as a current expenditure so that no investment is recorded as an output. The value of output may then be written:

$$p_I I + p_C C = q_K K + q_R R + q_L L - p_R I_R.$$

If factor outlay on capital is computed as a residual equal to the value of output less the value of outlay on labor, the service price of capital is estimated, erroneously, as:

$$q^*_K = \frac{q_K K + q_R R - p_R I_R}{K}.$$

---

[58] Educational expenditures, including student time, are not equal to private outlays, since a substantial part of total expenditures is publicly funded. Subsidies to the educational sector, like subsidies to the output of the private domestic sector, are included in the value of the output of the educational sector.

REFERENCES

1. Ando, A., and E. C. Brown. "The Impacts of Fiscal Policy." In E. C. Brown, et al., *Stabilization Policies.* Englewood Cliffs, N.J., Prentice-Hall, 1963.
2. Arrow, K. J. "Optimal Capital Policy, the Cost of Capital, and Myopic Decision Rules." *Annals of the Institute of Statistical Mathematics,* Vol. 16, 1964, pp. 21–30.
3a. Board of Governors of the Federal Reserve System. *Federal Reserve Bulletin,* August 1972.
3b. ———. *Flow of Funds Accounts, 1945–68.* Washington, D.C., 1970.
4. Bureau of Internal Revenue. *Income Tax Depreciation and Obsolescence Estimated Useful Lives and Depreciation Rates,* Bulletin F. Revised January 1942.
5. Cagan, P. "Measuring Quality Changes and the Purchasing Power of Money: An Exploratory Study of Automobiles." *National Banking Review,* Vol. 3, December 1965, pp. 217–236.
6. Christensen, L. R. "Entrepreneurial Income: How Does It Measure Up?" *American Economic Review,* Vol. 61, September 1971, pp. 575–585.
7. Christensen, L. R., and D. W. Jorgenson. "The Measurement of U.S. Real Capital Input, 1929–1967." *Review of Income and Wealth,* Series 15, December 1969, pp. 293–320.
8. ———. "U.S. Real Product and Real Factor Input, 1929–1967." *Review of Income and Wealth,* Series 16, March 1970, pp. 19–50.
9. ———. "U.S. Income, Saving, and Wealth, 1929–1969." Discussion Paper 266. Cambridge, Harvard Institute of Economic Research, 1972. To be published in *Review of Income and Wealth.*
10. Coen, R. "Effects of Tax Policy on Investment in Manufacturing." *American Economic Review,* Vol. 58, May 1968, pp. 200–211.
11. Creamer, D. "The Value of Rented Capital in the United States." Unpublished manuscript, 1971.
12. deLeeuw, Frank. Undated memorandum.
13. Denison, E. F. "Measurement of Labor Input: Some Questions of Definition and the Adequacy of Data." In *Output, Input, and Productivity Measurement.* Studies in Income and Wealth, Vol. 25, pp. 347–372. Princeton University Press for NBER, 1961.
14. ———. *The Sources of Economic Growth in the United States and the Alternatives Before Us,* Supplementary Paper No. 13. New York, Committee for Economic Development, 1962.
15. ———. *Why Growth Rates Differ: Postwar Experience in Nine Western Countries.* Washington, D.C., The Brookings Institution, 1967.
16. ———. "Some Major Issues in Productivity Analysis: An Examination of Estimates by Jorgenson and Griliches." *Survey of Current Business,* Vol. 49, May 1969, Part II, pp. 1–27.
17. ———. "Welfare Measurement and the GNP." *Survey of Current Business,* Vol. 51, January 1971, pp. 1–8.
18. Feller, W. *An Introduction to Probability Theory and Its Applications.* 2nd ed. New York, Wiley, 1957. Vol. I, pp. 290–293.
19. Fisher, I. *The Making of Index Numbers.* Boston and New York, Houghton Mifflin, 1922.
20. Folger, J. K., and C. B. Nam. "Educational Trends from Census Data," *Demography.* Vol. I, 1964, pp. 247–257.
21. Frane, L., and L. R. Klein. "The Estimation of Disposable Income by Distributive Shares." *Review of Economics and Statistics,* Vol. 35, November 1953, pp. 333–337.

22. Goldsmith, R. W. "A Perpetual Inventory of National Wealth." In *Studies in Income and Wealth,* Vol. 14, pp. 5–61. New York, National Bureau of Economic Research, 1951.

23. ———. *A Study of Saving in the United States,* Princeton, N.J., Princeton University Press, 1955.

24. ———. *The National Wealth of the United States in the Postwar Period.* New York, National Bureau of Economic Research, 1962.

25. ———. *The Flow of Capital Funds in the Postwar Economy.* New York, National Bureau of Economic Research, 1965.

26. Goldsmith, R. W., R. E. Lipsey, and M. Mendelson. *Studies in the National Balance Sheet of the United States.* Princeton University Press for NBER, 1963.

27. Griliches, Z. "The Demand for a Durable Input: U.S. Farm Tractors, 1921–1957." In A. C. Harberger, ed. *The Demand for Durable Goods,* pp. 181–210. Chicago, University of Chicago Press, 1960.

28. ———. "Notes on the Role of Education in Production Functions and Growth Accounting." In W. L. Hansen, ed. *Education, Income, and Human Capital,* Studies in Income and Wealth, Vol. 35. New York, National Bureau of Economic Research, 1970.

29. ———. "Research Expenditures and Growth Accounting." Discussion Paper 196. Cambridge, Harvard Institute of Economic Research, 1971.

30. Grose, L., T. Rottenberg, and R. Wasson. "New Estimates of Fixed Business Capital in the United States." *Survey of Current Business,* Vol. 49, February 1969, pp. 46–52.

31. Haavelmo, T. *A Study in the Theory of Investment.* Chicago, University of Chicago Press, 1960.

32. Hall, R. E. "Technical Change and Capital from the Point of View of the Dual." *Review of Economic Studies,* Vol. 35, January 1968, pp. 35–46.

33. ———. "The Measurement of Quality Change from Vintage Price Data." In Z. Griliches, ed. *Price Indexes and Quality Change.* Cambridge, Harvard University Press, 1971.

34. Hall, R. E., and D. W. Jorgenson. "Tax Policy and Investment Behavior." *American Economic Review,* Vol. 57, June 1967, pp. 391–414.

35. ———. "Application of the Theory of Optimum Capital Accumulation." In G. Fromm, ed. *Tax Incentives and Capital Spending,* pp. 9–60. Amsterdam, North-Holland, 1971.

36. Hicks, J. R. "The Measurement of Capital in Relation to the Measurement of Other Economic Aggregates." In F. A. Lutz and D. C. Hague, eds. *The Theory of Capital,* pp. 18–31. London, Macmillan, 1961.

37. Hickman, B. *Investment Demand and U.S. Economic Growth.* Washington, D.C., The Brookings Institution, 1965.

38. Hotelling, H. S. "A General Mathematical Theory of Depreciation." *Journal of the American Statistical Association,* Vol. 20, September 1925, pp. 340–353.

39. Jorgenson, D. W. "The Economic Theory of Replacement and Depreciation." Discussion Paper Number 203. Cambridge, Harvard Institute of Economic Research, 1971.

40. Jorgenson, D. W., and Z. Griliches. "The Explanation of Productivity Change." *Review of Economic Studies,* Vol. 34, July 1967, pp. 249–283.

41. ———. "Issues in Growth Accounting: A Reply to Edward F. Denison." *Survey of Current Business,* Vol. 52, May 1972, Part II, pp. 65–94.

42. Kendrick, J. W. *Productivity Trends in the United States.* Princeton University Press for NBER, 1961.

43. ———. *Postwar Productivity Trends in the United States.* New York, National Bureau of Economic Research, forthcoming.
44. Kravis, I. B. "Relative Income Shares in Fact and Theory." *American Economic Review,* Vol. 49, December 1959, pp. 917–949.
45. Kurtz, E. B. *Life Expectancy of Physical Property Based on Mortality Laws.* New York, Ronald Press, 1930.
46. Malinvaud, E. "Capital Accumulation and the Efficient Allocation of Resources." *Econometrica,* Vol. 21, April 1953, pp. 233–268.
47. Marston, A., R. Winfrey, and J. C. Hempstead. *Engineering Evaluation and Depreciation.* 2nd ed. New York, McGraw-Hill, 1953.
48. Meyer, J., and E. Kuh. *The Investment Decision.* Cambridge, Harvard University Press, 1957.
49a. Office of Business Economics. *The National Income and Product Accounts of the United States, 1929–1965, A Supplement to the Survey of Current Business.* Washington, D.C., U.S. Department of Commerce, 1966.
49b. ———. *Survey of Current Business,* various monthly issues.
50. Richter, M. K. "Invariance Axioms and Economic Indexes." *Econometrica,* Vol. 34, October 1966, pp. 739–755.
51. Samuelson, P. A. "The Evaluation of Real National Income." *Oxford Economic Papers,* N.S. 2, January 1950, pp. 1–29.
52. ———. "The Evaluation of 'Social Income': Capital Formation and Wealth." In F. A. Lutz and D. C. Hague, eds. *The Theory of Capital,* pp. 32–57. London, Macmillan, 1961.
53. Schultz, T. W. *Investment in Human Capital.* New York, The Free Press of Glencoe, 1971.
54. Solow, R. M. "Investment and Technical Progress." In K. J. Arrow, S. Karlin, and P. Suppes, eds. *Mathematical Methods in the Social Sciences, 1959,* pp. 89–104. Stanford, Stanford University Press, 1960.
55. Statistical Office of the United Nations. *A System of National Accounts.* New York, 1968.
56. Theil, H. *Economics and Information Theory.* Amsterdam, North-Holland, 1967.
57. Tice, H. S. "Depreciation, Obsolescence, and the Measurement of the Aggregate Capital Stock of the United States, 1900–1962." *Review of Income and Wealth,* Series 13, June 1967, pp. 119–154.
58. Tornquist, L. "The Bank of Finland's Consumption Price Index." *Bank of Finland Monthly Bulletin,* No. 10, 1936, pp. 1–8.
59. U.S. Department of the Treasury. *Treasury Bulletin,* various monthly issues.
60. Wasson, R. C. "Some Problems in the Estimation of Service Lives of Fixed Capital Assets." In *Measuring the Nation's Wealth,* pp. 367–374. Joint Economic Committee, 88th Cong., 2nd sess., 1964.
61. Wykoff, F. "Capital Depreciation in the Postwar Period: Automobiles." *Review of Economics and Statistics,* Vol. 52, May 1970, pp. 168–172.
62. Young, A. H. "Alternative Estimates of Corporate Depreciation and Profits: Parts I and II." *Survey of Current Business,* Vol. 48, April and May 1968, pp. 17–28, 16–28.

COMMENT

JOHN W. KENDRICK, The George Washington University

The basic vision behind Christensen and Jorgenson's opus is laudable. Their system comprises consistent sets of accounts—production, income and expenditure, accumulation, and revaluation—which link flows with stocks as of the beginning and end of each period. An integrated system of economic accounts, of course, has been one of the ultimate goals of this conference, which was wisely named, by Simon Kuznets and other founders, the Conference on Research in Income and Wealth. We have been pushed in the direction of developing a consistent system ending up with balance sheets and wealth statements by the National Accounts Review Committee, by the work of the Ruggleses, and others, and by the U.N. revised System of National Accounts which accommodates an ultimate integration of the various types of accounts.[1] The work of Christensen and Jorgenson moves us further in that direction.

I would like first to make a few comments on the basic structure of their system. It is a partial system, combined for the private domestic economy. It will be nice if ultimately they can prepare accounts for governments and the rest of the world, and include the financial flows in their capital accounts and the financial assets and liabilities for complete combined balance sheets. That is what we ultimately want, but they confined themselves to the private domestic economy because of their particular interest in productivity analysis. But even from their point of view, I think it would have been better if they could have separated their accounts into households and institutions, and business separately, because as soon as you start adding imputations in the households and institutional sector you reduce the usefulness of the productivity estimates which are a major objective of their *tour de force*. That is, they quite rightly included consumer durables in the capital account, but in imputing the rental value of those durables in real terms, I presume that the services of the durables parallel the movement of the stocks of the durables; so that their own estimates of productivity may be biased downward.

Also, one wonders why they stop with rental values of consumer durables, because one might easily add imputations for the value of the work of housewives and other unpaid household persons. At the National Bureau, Robert Eisner and I are working on these and additional imputations in the national accounts which will make them more useful for the kinds of social analysis that we are discussing at this session. What we do is to impute a value to inputs—the opportunity costs of students in school work, of housewives and others in household work, and so on. So our measures are really input measures, and later we will be comparing

[1] A recent presentation of economic accounts as a comprehensive, integrated system is contained in John W. Kendrick, *Economic Accounts and Their Uses,* New York, McGraw-Hill, 1972.

these nonmarket inputs with the market inputs, not with output, to see what has happened in the structure of the economy. Maybe in some far distant happy day we will have measures of outputs of households in terms of numbers of meals prepared, square feet of floor space cleaned, children brought up, and so on. The same thing goes for government output, and the Office of Management and Budget is pushing forward to find yet more measures of output for government agencies. For the time being, however, productivity analysis is better confined to the business economy. To the extent that Christensen and Jorgenson have imputations in their combined sector, this gives a downward bias to the productivity estimates.

In regard to structure, I approve heartily of their concept of the production account in real terms, in which they deflate final expenditure by product price indexes and factor costs by input price indexes, so that the ratio of real product to real factor costs yields a measure of changes in total factor productivity. This concept, of course, underlies my own book on productivity trends. As I indicated in the introduction to Volume 25 of the Income and Wealth series on output, input, and productivity measurement, this conception goes back at least to Morris Copeland at the first of these income and wealth conferences. He pointed out the productivity implications of real income and product accounts, although he did not follow up along these lines since his primary interest was in money flows.

Regarding Christensen and Jorgenson's execution of this useful concept, I have a few comments and exceptions that I would take to the methodology. In the case of their real labor cost, or the real value of labor services, I would prefer to weight by industry, and if possible, by occupational categories within industries instead of adjusting man-hours of labor input by a factor that reflects the effect of increasing levels of education per worker and per man-hour. If we follow the market-oriented approach of the accounts, I think we find that labor is marketed in terms of occupational categories, not in terms of years of schooling, with a few exceptions. The universities usually require Ph.D's, but that is in order to maintain the market for their output. In general, employers are not buying services according to years of education but according to skills, which of course, may be related to education. Although this is really partly a matter of taste, I also prefer to try to measure the inputs net of changes in quality or productive efficiency so that the productivity relationship brackets the whole change in productive efficiency. Now it is true that the interindustry, interoccupational shifts in part reflect an increase in quality, but only as a result of shifts, not as a result of changes in quality within the categories. This remark applies to Denison's work, too. Yet, my point is not crucial, because what we include in input or include in the residual is not so important, as long as we make clear what we are doing, and keep the effects separate so that we can identify the forces at work influencing economic growth, whether or not we include them in input or in the productivity residual.

As far as capital services are concerned, I think that Christensen and Jorgenson's method is very ingenious for obtaining service prices of capital as rental rate deflators. Yet I believe that their real net capital input would not differ much from mine because, in effect, my implicit deflators for net capital costs reflect changes in rates of return, as well as in the prices of the underlying assets. But with regard to gross capital costs, I think they are correct in taking account in their deflators of changes in depreciation or replacement rates, revaluation effects, and indirect taxes.

I have inferred that Christensen and Jorgenson have dropped their adjustment for changing rates of utilization of capital stock. I think this is good, partly because Denison has demonstrated that we do not have decent estimates of rates of utilization of capital in the economy as a whole. Also, I would argue conceptually that the real capital cost is related to the capital owned regardless of rates of utilization of capacity, and changes in those rates should show up in the change in productivity, because the capital charge goes on regardless of the rate of utilization. Many rental contracts, of course, are on an annual, weekly, or monthly basis, and the rental does not take account of hours within that period that the capital is utilized.

I think it is interesting that, as estimated using geometric depreciation rates, Christensen and Jorgenson's depreciation equals replacement, again on a somewhat peculiar definition that retirements occur piecemeal as capital goods lose their efficiency. However, there is also the rather peculiar result that their gross and net capital stocks are equal, as I see it. I would think that the traditional concept of gross capital stock which keeps the goods in until they actually disappear, defining retirement as the disappearance, or scrapping, at the end of the life, is a useful concept, particularly in looking at productivity of capital. In this connection, I think that Denison is justified in defining his stocks for purposes of productivity measurement in terms of their capacity to produce net output. Christensen and Jorgenson used the term "declining efficiency" with regard to maintaining production capacity, but without defining these terms. After working through their paper, one sees that they are really talking about "declining efficiency" in capital goods with respect to producing real net property income, not maintaining capacity intact in respect to producing either gross or net output. Presumably, with a slight decline of the capacity of capital goods for producing gross output, over their lives, there is a somewhat greater decline for producing net output, since you have to take into account increasing intermediate expenses for repair and maintenance. I think this is what Denison was trying to get at—the decline in capacity of producing net output, not in producing real net income for the capital factor. However, I do think that from a purely economic viewpoint Christensen and Jorgenson's concept is correct that depreciation is the decline in the value of a capital good as it ages, and this reflects the shortening as well as the declining stream of net income that it produces over its lifetime.

Just a few more general comments. On their income and expenditure account I am dubious about their deflating income (including net transfers), as distinguished from factor costs, by a factor price index. By this deflation procedure the identity of disposable income less outlay equaling personal saving (investment) does not obtain when the variables are expressed in constant dollars. Personally, I would confine price deflation to production accounts; but if I had to deflate income-expenditure accounts I would use consumption-price indexes for that portion of income, and investment-price indexes for the saving residual in order to maintain the basic saving-investment identities. Also, I do not find useful Christensen and Jorgenson's concept of the "standard of living" as a ratio of real expenditure to real income deflated by factor prices.

The use of Divisia indexes for factoring value changes into price and quantity components has its attractions. While not representing an ultimate solution of the index number problem,[2] Divisia index numbers have the advantage of not requiring periodic reweighting of aggregative price and/or quantity measures. But the fact that cyclical as well as secular changes in the structure of the economy affect annually chang-

---

[2] In addition to the approximation error, other problems have been discussed by Richard R. Nelson, "Recent Experiences in Growth Accounting: New Understanding or Dead End?" Yale University Economic Growth Center, Discussion Paper 18 (processed), October 1971, pp. 6–9.

ing weights introduces new problems. In particular, the relative weights of labor and property inputs can show major changes over the cycle. Nevertheless, I believe federal government statistical agencies should give serious thought to the possible use of Divisia indexes, where applicable and feasible.

Many of the details of Christensen and Jorgenson's concepts and estimating methodology deserve closer scrutiny than I have had time to give them. For example, I do not consider the use of the implicit price index for services to be the most appropriate deflator for income originating in general governments and the rest of the world. Also, I would question their method of deflating inventory stocks, when they could readily cumulate Commerce estimates of the real net change in inventories on a single stock estimate as of the end of the base period.

Finally, I am in agreement with Christensen and Jorgenson's discussion of the utility of expanding the capital accounts and balance sheets to include estimates of investments in research and development, and education, and the resulting stocks of intangible capital. I have already developed such estimates, and recently reported preliminary findings which will be of interest to economic growth accountants.[3]

In conclusion, I should like to reiterate my basically positive appraisal of Christensen and Jorgenson's contribution. We look forward to further refinements and extensions of their work in the economic accounts and growth analysis in the future.

ROBERT EISNER, Northwestern University and National Bureau of Economic Research

The handling of depreciation, replacement, and "relative efficiency" by Laurits Christensen and Dale Jorgenson merits some comment lest the reader miss critical implications of several special simplifying assumptions.

Christensen and Jorgenson distinguish usefully between changes in the current services available from a capital good, or its pattern of "efficiency" over time, and depreciation or capital consumption which, for constant prices of capital services, involves the reduction in the present value of future services as they are used up. Christensen and Jorgenson

[3] See John W. Kendrick, "The Treatment of Intangible Resources as Capital," *Review of Income and Wealth,* March 1972. The paper was presented in early September 1971, at the meetings of the International Association for Research in Income and Wealth at Ronneby, Sweden.

point out correctly the inconsistency in certain sets of assumptions regarding efficiencies and depreciation, in particular some by Edward Denison. For assumptions about the sequence of capital services or rentals or efficiencies determine, given discount rates, the value and depreciation of capital over time. Thus, both constant relative efficiency and a linear decline in efficiency, variously assumed by Denison, are inconsistent with straight-line depreciation of the value of capital. Nevertheless, Denison may be correct in his belief "that net value typically declines more rapidly than does the ability of a capital good to contribute to production" (as quoted by Christensen and Jorgenson, in Section 4.5). This would relate to a relative efficiency pattern quite different from that assumed by them, indeed a pattern which might even result in a change in value less than the change in efficiency because both are *rising* over time!

Christensen and Jorgenson's critical assumption is that of a geometric decline in efficiency over the (infinite) lifetime of capital goods. "Under this assumption," they declare, "the rate of replacement and the rate of depreciation are constant and equal to the rate of decline in efficiency." And on this basis they assume the geometric decline in value or "declining balance" depreciation which they use in their "simplified system of accounts."

In fact, however, a geometric decline in efficiency is not a sufficient condition for a geometric (and equal) decline in the value of assets. The necessary further assumption is that of a constant rate of discount. This may be demonstrated in Christensen and Jorgenson's terms as follows.

First, with $p_{A,t,v}$ the "acquisition price" or value of a capital good v years old at the beginning of the year t, d_v the efficiency or service of a capital good v years old, r_t the one-year rate of discount in the year t, r_{t+s} the one-year rate of discount for the year $t + s$ anticipated in the year t, and with the price of capital services assumed constant and equal to unity, we have for that value or acquisition price at the beginning of the year t,

$$p_{A,t,v} = \sum_{\tau=0}^{\infty} d_{v+\tau} / \prod_{s=0}^{\tau} (1 + r_{t+s}). \tag{1}$$

Then, if we assume a geometric decline in efficiency at the (constant) rate δ, we have

$$d_{v+\tau} = d_v(1 - \delta)^{\tau}. \tag{2}$$

If we add the further assumption that

$$r_{t+s} = r = \text{a constant for all } s \geq 0, \tag{3}$$

we can simplify (1) to

$$p_{A,t,v} = d_v \sum_{\tau=0}^{\infty} \left(\frac{1-\delta}{1+r}\right)^{\tau} = d_v \left(\frac{1+r}{r+\delta}\right). \tag{4}$$

But then this same capital good one year later and one year older is expected to have a value

$$p_{A,t+1,v+1} = d_v(1-\delta) \sum_{\tau=0}^{\infty} \left(\frac{1-\delta}{1+r}\right)^{\tau} \tag{5}$$

$$= d_v(1-\delta) \left(\frac{1+r}{r+\delta}\right) = (1-\delta)p_{A,t,v}$$

and the value of depreciation in the year t may be written

$$p_{D,t,v} = p_{A,t,v} - p_{A,t+1,v+1} = d_v\delta \left(\frac{1+r}{r+\delta}\right) = \delta p_{A,t,v}, \tag{6}$$

which is Christensen and Jorgenson's geometric or "declining balance" depreciation.

However, where we have a geometric decline in efficiency (2) but no constant geometric increase in the rate of discount (3), that is, where r_{t+s} does not equal a constant for all s, we can only reduce the expression for the value at the beginning of the year t of a capital good v years old to

$$p_{A,t,v} = d_v \sum_{\tau=0}^{\infty} (1-\delta)^{\tau} / \prod_{s=0}^{\tau} (1+r_{t+s}) \tag{7}$$

and the value anticipated for that good one year later is

$$p_{A,t+1,v+1} = d_v(1-\delta) \sum_{\tau=0}^{\infty} (1-\delta)^{\tau} / \prod_{s=0}^{\tau} (1+r_{t+1+s}). \tag{8}$$

Then the value of depreciation in the year t is (7) minus (8) or

$$p_{D,t,v} = d_v \sum_{\tau=0}^{\infty} \left[(1-\delta)^{\tau} / \prod_{s=0}^{\tau} (1+r_{t+s}) \right] \tag{9}$$

$$- \left[(1-\delta)^{\tau+1} / \prod_{s=0}^{\tau} (1+r_{t+1+s}) \right],$$

which, for $r_{t+1+s} = r_{t+s}$ for all s, implies

$$r_{t+s} = r, \text{ a constant for all } s \geq 0, \tag{3}$$

and, hence,

$$p_{D,t,v} = d_v \delta \left(\frac{1+r}{r+\delta} \right) = \delta p_{A,t,v}, \tag{6}$$

but not otherwise.

That this may be more than a technical curiosity may be suggested by the casual empirical judgment that, whether because of imperfection of information, increasing relative risks over time, or the finitude of life, annual rates of interest or discount tend to be greater for longer term commitments. This implies that r_{t+1+s} tends to be greater than r_{t+s}, which would in turn tend to make depreciation (or $p_{D,t,v}$) less in earlier years (for lesser v) and more in later years (for greater v) than would be the case if $r_{t+s} = r_{t+1+s}$ for all s. In nonalgebraic terms what this comes down to is that the exhaustion of early capital services does not reduce the value of a capital good as much because the component of present value due to later capital services is rising relatively sharply as these prospective services move closer in time.[1]

There are other, probably more substantial, factors that may lead one to question the correctness of geometric decline in value and declining balance depreciation. Some of these relate to the basic assumption of geometric decline in efficiency. Many capital goods, particularly plant, show little or no decline in efficiency with age. One need only compare rents by "vintage" on houses or office space, after adjustment for quality differences, to realize that in these cases declines in efficiency are minimal or nonexistent over significant portions of economic lives. Where efficiency is constant, equal say to unity, the traditional "one-hoss-shay" case, we may write the acquisition price as

$$p_{A,t,v} = \sum_{\tau=0}^{n-v} 1 / \prod_{s=0}^{\tau} (1 + r_{t+s}), \tag{10}$$

or

$$p_{A,t,v} = \sum_{\tau=0}^{n-v} (1+r)^{-\tau} = \frac{1 + r - (1+r)^{v-n}}{r}, \tag{11}$$

---

[1] Throughout we are dealing, as Christensen and Jorgenson must implicitly, with *expected* future rates of discount. To the extent that there are changes in expectations of future rates of discount, or of prices, we would recognize capital gains or losses, or "revaluations" in Christensen and Jorgenson's terminology.

for $r_{t+s} = r$ for all s where, in both cases $n =$ the expected years of life of the asset and hence $v \leq n$. Then, for $r_{t+s} = r$, the asset is expected one year later to have the value

$$p_{A,t+1,v+1} = \sum_{\tau=0}^{n-v-1} (1+r)^{-\tau} = \frac{1 + r - (1+r)^{v+1-n}}{r}, \qquad (12)$$

and depreciation is (11) minus (12) or,

$$p_{D,t,v} = \frac{(1+r)^{v+1-n} - (1+r)^{v-n}}{r} = (1+r)^{v-n}. \qquad (13)$$

Far from approximating declining balance depreciation, which implies much more rapid depreciation in early years of the asset's life, (13), derived from the one-hoss-shay or constant efficiency assumption, implies slow depreciation at first and more rapid depreciation later, as v approaches r. This may be confirmed readily by taking the derivative of (13) with respect to v whence,

$$\frac{\partial p_{D,t,v}}{\partial v} = (1+r)^{v-n} \ln (1+r) > 0 \text{ for } r > 0. \qquad (14)$$

We may further question Christensen and Jorgenson's seemingly innocuous and modest assumption "that relative efficiency is nonincreasing so that:

$$d_0 = 1; d_\tau - d_{\tau-1} \leqq 0; \tau = 0, 1, \ldots."$$

It seems probable that for many assets built to "lead" expected increases in demand or requiring substantial "break-in time," efficiency or the rate of production of capital services is initially low and rises for a significant early period. In the case of some capital goods, particularly plant and equipment, which is an integral part of new plant, there may be major capital expenditures over several years which have zero productivity or "efficiency" until construction is completed and the new plant is in operation. Thus, $d_0 = d_1 = d_2 = 0$ would prove common for substantial portions of capital additions that take three years to complete.

Some evidence that this is so can be found in work by Allan Mendelowitz [1], who estimated the time path of revenues attributable to capital expenditure by using McGraw-Hill data in regressions of profits on a distributed lag function of capital expenditures. His estimates suggest an initially rising curve of earnings. For reasonable positive rates of discounts his age profiles of earnings or efficiency actually imply initially negative rates of depreciation. This is indeed not as implausible as it may appear; as with a fruit tree, as the fruit-bearing years approach, the value of the tree rises.

And finally, further evidence that depreciation is at least less rapid than implied by a geometric decline in value is to be seen in the work of Wolfhard Ramm [2]. Ramm estimated the effect of age on value of automobiles in regressions that adjusted for quality changes. With a sample of some 8,980 observations of "Red Book" prices for specific types and models of used cars, Ramm was able to estimate year-by-year depreciation up to age six for each of the years 1961 through 1968. From his results [2, Table III, p. 156] we may calculate the mean estimates for the years 1961 to 1968 of depreciation as a ratio of value at the beginning of the years as a function of age—what might be called δ_g. These turn out to be a monotonically rising sequence, 0.209, 0.237, 0.239, 0.254, 0.294, 0.306, and 0.389, for ages 0 to 6, respectively.

This is not a marked departure from geometric depreciation and it is indeed more rapid than straight-line; the corresponding sequence of depreciation rates in terms of original cost is 0.209, 0.187, 0.145, 0.117, 0.101, 0.074, and 0.065. But it must be recalled that this kind of estimate, relating to values of used capital goods for which there are market transactions, is likely to be biased in the direction of faster rates of depreciation, since used capital goods put on the market will tend to be those whose values have declined more than the values of goods which are retained. If goods are valuable to their owners they will not be offered for sale. In the case of automobiles there is as well a substantial element of "moral hazard." A disproportionate number of cars put on the market may be offered for sale because they have proved to be "lemons." Prospective purchasers will be fearful of this and will not be willing to pay as much for "second-hand" cars as unoffered vehicles of the same vintage and specifications will be worth to their original owners. Observations of this sort, we may add, are relevant to arguments over the years by George Terborgh and others that prices of used assets indicate faster depreciation than what was (previously) accepted for tax purposes.

This note does not presume to indicate just what rates and patterns of depreciation are appropriate for our old or new income, product, and capital accounts. It should be seen clearly though that the assumption of geometric decline in value or "declining balance" depreciation, however convenient, has profound effects on our measures of income, input, output, and capital. Particularly with the *double-rate* declining balance of our tax laws, which Christensen and Jorgenson employ, we may well derive estimates of depreciation which are very much too rapid and, in an economy where capital values are generally growing, substantially high, year after year. Major empirical work to illuminate the actual path of depreciation is very much in order for all of us concerned with improving and extending our national accounts. At this point, however, if a choice has to be made, I for one would opt for the old straight-line depreciation employed by Denison as coming closest to reflecting the complex of slowly declining efficiencies and increasing rates of discounts which characterize the returns from many of our capital goods.

REFERENCES

1. Mendelowitz, A. I. "The Measurement of Economic Depreciation." American Statistical Association, 1970. Proceedings of the Business and Economic Statistics Section. Washington, D.C., 1971, pp. 140–148.
2. Ramm, W. "Measuring the Services of Household Durables: The Case of Automobiles." Ibid., pp. 149–158.

REPLY BY CHRISTENSEN AND JORGENSON

EISNER

Eisner's comment is based on an unfortunate confusion. We state that the value of assets declines geometrically if efficiency declines geometrically (middle of Section 4.4). This statement refers to a decline in value across vintages at a given point of time. Eisner misinterprets our statement as referring to a decline in value over time. This error in interpretation leads Eisner to lengthy but irrelevant deductions about conditions for geometric decline in value over time.

Geometric decline in the value of assets across vintages is the essence of the "simplified accounting system" described in our paper. Under this condition depreciation is equal to replacement, and both are proportional to the product of the price of acquisition of capital goods and the stock of capital. The geometric decline in the value of assets over time analyzed by Eisner is irrelevant to the "simplified accounting system." In general, assets will not decline in value geometrically over time in this system.

Eisner correctly points out that Denison employs inconsistent assumptions about efficiency and depreciation. He then endorses Denison's errors by stating that: "I for one would opt for the old straight-line depreciation employed by Denison . . . ." Here Eisner exhibits a personal predilection for logical inconsistency over logical consistency; this is a taste that few economic statisticians can be expected to share.

KENDRICK

Turning to the comments of John W. Kendrick, our first observation is that "real net capital input" as defined by Kendrick ignores differences in rates of return at a given point in time due to differences in direct taxes. For example, corporate returns are taxed at a rate of nearly 50 per cent while noncorporate returns are not subject to the corporate income tax. If the rate of return after taxes is the same for the two sectors, as seems likely, the before-tax rate of return should be almost twice as high in the corporate sector. Before-tax rates of return are the appropriate rates for weighting capital input. Kendrick's measure of capital input based only on capital stock fails to take account of this difference.

Deterioration of capital goods is associated with decline in efficiency as well as retirement of these goods. The concept of capital appropriate for productivity measurement is an efficiency weighted sum of past investments. Under the assumption that efficiency declines geometrically, the appropriate measure of capital is net capital stock calculated by the declining balance method. The traditional concept of gross capital stock, an unweighted sum of past investments, is not relevant to productivity measurement unless efficiency does not decline until the asset is retired. As Kendrick points out, this appears to be implausible. The accounting system developed in our paper is not limited to geometric decline in efficiency. In actual implementation other patterns are much more costly to employ consistently; it is not yet clear whether the additional expense is justified by greater realism.

The essential novelty of the complete accounting system proposed in our paper is the development of accounts in constant prices throughout. For this purpose both production accounts and income-expenditure accounts are essential. Kendrick agrees at least in principle with the methods we have developed for implementing the production account. For the income and expenditure account he prefers to deflate expenditure by price indexes for expenditure categories and to deflate income by the same price indexes. The effect of this procedure is identical to that of deflating both sides of the production account by output price indexes, which would obviously give a distorted picture of the development of real factor input.

Kendrick proposes to deflate the income side of the income and expenditure account by an expenditure price index. The correct procedure is to deflate income by an income price index, weighting the prices of individual components of factor income by their relative weight in total factor income. These factor prices differ from those that appear in the production account by direct taxes. It would not suffice to carry over the price of real factor input from the production account for deflation of the income side of the income and expenditure account. Correct deflation of the income and expenditure account gives rise to a measure of the standard of living, integrating this useful concept into a national accounting system. It is difficult for us to understand Kendrick's reservations about the usefulness of incorporating the standard of living into social accounts.

Finally, the basic justification of Divisia index numbers is that they solve the index number problem where that problem has a solution. The index number problem has a solution if and only if there exists a corresponding economic aggregate. For example, in the production function underlying total factor productivity measurement, an invariant and path-independent index number of capital exists if and only if there exists a capital aggregate; the Divisia real capital index captures the variations in the capital aggregate. No other index number formula has this property. Of course, where no aggregate exists, the index number problem has no solution, and the choice of an index number formula is completely arbitrary.

The Public Sector

Evaluating Performance in the

Public Sector

MANCUR OLSON

UNIVERSITY OF MARYLAND

I

GOVERNMENTS are not famous for efficiency. Though no one can be certain of this until the matter has been properly researched, casual observation suggests that most economists probably believe that governments are less efficient than enterprises in the market sector of society. This observation seems to be made not only about governments of different levels in the United States, but also about governments of a variety of types in many different societies. Economists are certainly not alone in associating governments with red tape, cumbersome procedures, and bureaucratic inflexibility: whatever the balance of lay opinion may be, there are certainly large numbers of laymen of assorted ideologies and nationalities who claim that governments they have observed are inefficient, by which they presumably mean less efficient than other enterprises with which they are familiar. Whether the inefficiency attributed to existing governments is believed inherent in all government activity is more doubtful, since some of those who decry the ineptitude or waste of an existing government contend that these problems would be solved if the electoral victory or social revolution they prefer were to take place. Some of the complaints about the inefficiency of government may also be focused on existing legislation which is or is thought to be ill suited to the ends it is supposed to attain, rather than with the effectiveness of public administration itself.

The empirical evidence needed to determine what degree of truth, if any, there is in these beliefs is not now available. Are there any theoretical considerations that should lead us to expect that government operations are generally less efficient than those of private enterprises? There

NOTE: The author thanks the National Science Foundation and Resources for the Future for support of his research.

are a wide variety of ad hoc explanations and obiter dicta about the causes of the alleged government inefficiency in the literature of economics, and some seminal writings devoted directly or indirectly to this subject.[1] Yet it remains true that the reasons for the exceptional inefficiency that is alleged to occur in the public sector have not been codified, nor incorporated into the body of economic theory, nor even stated in a sufficiently clear and general fashion to bring this matter (important as it obviously is) into the elementary textbooks. Some of the discussions of the causes of inefficiency in the production of public outputs are in the literature of what is, in the United States, calling the Planning-Programming-Budgeting System, or in discussions of cost-benefit analysis. But others are in the welfare economics or public finance literature on what is coming to be called the theory of public expenditure. The PPB and cost-benefit discussions and the literature on the theory of public goods or expenditure have never been properly integrated—indeed, at times it seems as though they are developing independently. Perhaps this is in part because the students of cost-benefit analysis and especially PPB are often applied economists with only a limited interest in pure theory, whereas those who write about the theory of public expenditure are often theorists with only a sporadic interest in the day to day workings of government. There is a promising and relatively well integrated set of writings on what is sometimes called "nonmarket decision making" or "public choice," but this literature has so far been mainly concerned with the constitutional, electoral, pressure group, and legislative processes that determine what public policies or purposes will be chosen, rather than with the efficiency or inefficiency with which these policies or purposes are carried out. The complaints about government inefficiency that are of interest here refer mainly to public production or administration, rather than to any stupidities or inequities in basic public policies.

II

It might seem at first glance that the explanation of the alleged government inefficiency is obvious: governments are inefficient because they do not or cannot in general use perfectly competitive markets. This is, on reflection, not an explanation at all. To be sure, if a perfectly competitive equilibrium exists, it will be efficient, in the sense that any

[1] See, for example, Charles J. Hitch and Roland N. McKean, *The Economics of Defense in the Nuclear Age,* Cambridge, Harvard University Press, 1960; and Charles Shultze, *The Politics and Economics of Public Spending,* Washington, D.C., Brookings, 1968.

rational objection to its performance must devolve into a preference for a different distribution of welfare. But it does not follow from this that governments can't also operate with Pareto-optimal efficiency. Moreover, markets in which no entity can affect the price of what it sells or buys are very much the exception, so that observations that governments are less efficient than the private sector in most cases mean that governments are supposed to be even less efficient than firms or markets with monopoly or monopsony power. What is needed is an explanation (or a refutation) of the contention that governments are even less efficient than the imperfect markets that are typical.

Another apparent explanation can likewise quickly be shown to be insufficient. Democratic systems can perhaps operationally be defined as those with an opposition party or parties that could at least in some circumstances defeat the party in power in a free election. If the party in power appoints a sufficient number of persons to public office in return for political support, or favors enough firms with government business for similar reasons, it might thereby have bought an electoral majority with public funds. This is a proximate (but as we shall later see, definitely not the ultimate) reason why some governments have civil service merit systems, rules requiring competitive bidding, and other constraints on official decision making. These constraints are understandably sometimes considered a source of government inflexibility and inefficiency. But the need to preserve the integrity of the democratic process cannot by itself explain government inefficiency, since it is only those personnel and procurement decisions which are inefficient from some national (as opposed to purely partisan) view that need to be prohibited. If we know that a government has served its announced conception of the public interest with complete efficiency, we know that it cannot at the same time have been guilty of political favoritism in its purchases of inputs. It is not in any event clear that effective controls on political favoritism in resource procurement are indispensable to continuance of the democratic process, at least when most economic activity is in the private sector. That seems to be the lesson from U.S. experience at all levels of government in the nineteenth century, and in some state and local governments (e.g., Pennsylvania) until at least very recently. Moreover, dictatorial governments that could not have this need to preserve democratic processes are often also deemed to be inefficient. The U.S. Strategic Bombing Survey and other studies have suggested that the Nazi administration of its war effort was far from efficient, and perhaps inferior to that of Great Britain and the United States. And as anyone who has traveled in the Soviet Union as well as the West is aware, many of the services provided by the Soviet government seem to be relatively inefficient.

Another possible explanation grows out of Kenneth Arrow's justly famous paradox of voting.[2] Since it is clear from Arrow's work that in certain circumstances social choices will not be stable and transitive, it might be supposed that government behavior would be too erratic and unstable to be efficient. Yet behavior of democratic governments does not often appear to be nearly as erratic or unpredictable as a naive application of Arrow's analysis might suggest. The conditions that give rise to the Arrow paradox often don't exist, and even when they do, the complex network of institutions and checks and balances in democratic governments may keep policy from changing rapidly enough to be erratic or unstable. Interestingly enough, democratic governments are often more stable and predictable than those that are dictatorial or likely to be overthrown by violence. Even if democratic governments usually reversed themselves, that would not be sufficient to explain the observations of government inefficiency: it would lead instead to charges that governments cannot make up their minds. But it is not obvious that such charges are particularly common, and when they are heard it is sometimes because the left hand of a bureaucracy has worked against the right hand for reasons that have nothing to do with the Arrow paradox. Thus, without denying the extraordinary theoretical and normative importance of the Arrow paradox, it seems that the economist must look elsewhere for an explanation (or refutation) of the commonplace observation that governments produce goods and services inefficiently.

III

The most fundamental way to approach the question of government production inefficiency versus private production inefficiency is to distinguish the demands typically placed upon governments from those placed upon private firms. Though there are many exceptions, governments (and several other types of nonprofit organizations) are most often called upon to supply public or collective goods, or to control the production of those with externalities, whereas the private sector is almost never paid (except sometimes by government) to deal with such goods. Those goods or services that in almost every country are provided mainly by government (e.g., law and order, defense, pure research, pollution control) are certainly collective goods or goods with

[2] *Social Choice and Individual Values,* 2nd ed., New York, Wiley, 1963.

more than average externalities. This paper will argue that governments are in fact as well as by reputation usually inefficient, and that this is mainly because they deal with collective goods and externalities. Though it will be necessary to amend this definition later, a collective good for the moment can be defined as a good such that, if it goes to one individual in some group, it is not possible (or at any rate economical) to exclude others in the group from the enjoyment of that good; in other words, nonpurchasers cannot practically be excluded from the consumption of the good. An externality here (and for that matter in most other discussions) is distinguished by the same defining characteristic, though it is clearly also fairly common to call a good with the nonexclusion property an externality if it is jointly produced with a private good or if the group affected by it is very small, and otherwise to call it a public or collective good.

Governments are of course also distinguished from the private sector by the fact that only they can significantly redistribute income. Questions about the efficiency of a redistributional program can also arise, especially when the program affects the incentives in the productive system. Some redistribution of income can usefully be regarded as due to the external economy a redistribution of income can have; that is, it is desired by those who give up the income because they think the transfer is in some sense in their own best interest.[3] Redistributions of this sort are covered by what will be said about collective goods and externalities. There remain some redistributions of income which are desired, or which even take place, but which are plainly not desired by the class from which the transfer is obtained. Any inefficiencies in these redistributions will here be left aside, partly on the ground that they would for the most part involve failures to anticipate the secondary effects of the redistribution in the fundamental legislation rather than any defect in public production or administration.

Though most economists no doubt realize that the problem of efficiency in government has something to do with public goods and externalities, the full implications of the relationship have not been explored. Some of the consequences of collective goods for governmental

---

[3] Even such redistributions can require coercion, because individuals in the group from which the transfer would come might believe that the benefits to them of the transfer (e.g., reduced crime) would occur only if so much income were transferred that most or all of them would have to transfer income to the poor. In such a case the individuals in the donor class would be rational to vote to force themselves to transfer income to the poor through taxes, but not rational if they gave individual and voluntary contributions.

efficiency have not been correctly explained, and others are included in one strand of the literature and ignored in another. This in turn has meant that some steps that might be taken to increase the efficiency with which collective goods are provided have not received appropriate attention.

IV

One cause of inefficiency in the provision of collective goods is familiar from the theoretical writings in welfare economics and public finance, but rarely mentioned in the PPB or cost-benefit literature. That is the difficulty of getting consumers to reveal their preferences concerning a collective good or externality, and preferences must of course be known to determine how much it is optimal to provide. It has been clear at least since Erik Lindahl developed his famous "voluntary theory of public exchange" that there can be no assurance that individuals will agree, through voting or by other means, to provide a Pareto-optimal amount of a collective good unless each individual who benefits from the collective good shares its marginal costs in the same proportion in which he shares the benefits of additional units. Otherwise, those who pay more than their share of the marginal costs will vote for a lower level of provision of the collective good than is optimal, since their own marginal benefits will be equated with the tax price they pay for each additional unit before the marginal cost to the society equals the total social benefits from another unit of the good. Conversely, those who pay a less than proportional share of the marginal costs will have an interest in a supra-optimal provision of the collective good. Thus there can be no assurance that a Pareto-optimal level of provision of a collective good will occur in a democratic system [4] unless all voters, or in any event those who cast the deciding votes, pay a tax price that is given by their marginal rate of substitution between the collective good and other goods. But if an individual's tax price will rise if he is known to place a high value on additional amounts of a collective good, he has (as Paul Samuelson has made clear) an incentive to conceal his true preferences. Since he cannot by the definition of a collective good be excluded from the consumption of it, however little he pays in taxes, he will in most cases get as much of the collective good whether he claims to want it or not. Since every consumer

[4] In a dictatorial system without any voting, inefficiency will be even more likely, since the dictator will have no direct information at all on individual preferences for the collective good.

of the collective good is in this position, it will with rational behavior normally be very difficult if not impossible to learn what preferences are and thus how much of the collective good to provide.[5]

Though the difficulty of getting preferences revealed is surely a significant part of the problem of public sector resource allocation, it is not a sufficient explanation of inefficiency in the public sector. It could by itself explain only why governments provide too little or too much in the way of public goods, not any failure of governments to attain *technical* efficiency. It is this difficulty of attaining technical efficiency —a state in which no more of one good can be produced without less of another, i.e., any position on the production possibility frontier—that this paper is about. This is probably a more important source of inefficiency than any tendency to choose the wrong mix of public and private goods. Though there are complaints in some quarters that governments provide an inefficiently large supply of public goods, there are complaints in other quarters about "public squalor midst private affluence." Though the fact that the complaints contradict one another doesn't prove anything, it may hint that the losses that result from the concealment of preferences are not of such a great magnitude that they overwhelm all other factors. Some voters will for some public goods face tax prices that are too low and vote for too much, and some voters will for some goods be in the opposite situation. Though there is nothing that would make these two errors regularly offset each other, they can often countervail each other to some extent. Then there is the fact that those politicians who succeed are likely to be those who spend a lot of time talking to constituents and have a good intuitive feel for their true preferences. These politicians also have an incentive to propose tax and expenditure packages that will command more support than those proposed by their opponents. Undoubtedly more efficient proposals, such as many of those that would reduce the extent to which tax prices are out of line with marginal rates of substitution, will often have a political advantage, for the simple reason that one or more possible distributions of the gains from a Pareto-superior policy will leave some one (if not everyone) better off and none worse off. Thus, important as the revelation of preferences problem is, there must be a good deal more to the problem of efficiency in government.

A second reason why inefficiency is particularly likely in the provision of collective goods has been neglected both in the literature of

---

[5] Ingenious schemes are being worked out to get around this problem, but there is to my knowledge no easy and universally acceptable solution.

welfare economics and in the literature of PPB and cost-benefit analysis. Writings of the latter sort are above all filled with injunctions on the importance of estimating the output of public programs. There is no doubt that these injunctions are necessary. It is perhaps the principal achievement of the PPB system that it has sensitized governments to the need to evaluate the level of public outputs. Somewhat surprisingly, there is little in the way of a parallel discussion in the welfare economics literature on public goods. Neither is there a widespread awareness in the applied or PPB literature of why the estimation of program outputs should be particularly difficult in the public sector.

It might seem at first glance that the problem of measuring outputs in the public sector is nothing more than the problem of concealment of preferences for public goods that has already been discussed. But this is not in fact the case. The concealment of preferences relates to how much an individual would pay for an additional unit of output of a collective good. It may relate to the problem a political leader would have in determining how much the citizenry would be willing to pay for additional *output* of some collective good, but it does not explain the problem a government administrator has in determining what volume of output a particular program produces. In other words, it relates to the problem of how much the output is worth, not to the prior problem of finding out how much output there is. For an individual citizen to be able to tell a public official how much value he puts on an additional expenditure on pollution control, he first has to know how much the expenditure will reduce the pollution—he has to estimate the production function for the collective good. But the individual citizen or consumer is in no position to do this, hence the need for program analysts and evaluation of output in government.

The reason that there is a special problem of measuring outputs in government is that governments typically produce collective goods or control externalities, and one of the characteristics of a collective good or externality is that, if it goes to anyone, it goes to everyone in some group. In other words, the collective good or externality is normally indivisible, in that it cannot be divided up in such a way that only those who pay their share of the costs get some of the good. In short, *the very characteristics of a collective good that make it a kind from which nonpurchasers cannot be excluded, also make it a kind of which the output is not in the form of divisible units that can be readily counted.*

It might be said that this is also true of services sold in the private sector (and all commodities ultimately produce services); the firm that sells janitorial services to individual customers also may not be able to measure its volume of output in physical terms. But this objection is insufficient, because when a good or service can be sold separately to different individuals, there is no need for a measure of the physical volume of output. All the janitorial firm needs is information on the marginal revenue it gets from providing additional service. The customer is in a position to estimate the value to himself of an additional supply of service from a firm because he can experiment with different levels of purchase. His estimate of the value of the good shows up in the marginal revenue the firm receives. By contrast, in the case of a collective good going simultaneously to many individuals, the individual consumer cannot take more or less to see how that affects his well being.

Accordingly, quite apart from the problem of concealment of preferences which makes it very difficult to know how much a given amount of a collective good is worth to those who receive it, there is the further problem that it is nearly impossible to measure what amount or volume of output a government program is in fact producing. Thus the government supplying collective goods or dealing with externalities has less of the information it needs to act efficiently than a private business (including a monopoly). A private business can in general get information about the marginal revenue it would receive if it changed its output mix or level and in most cases can measure its volume of output in physical units as well. This means that private corporations and other businesses, however much or little monopoly power they may possess, usually have a measure of physical output that allows them to calculate their technical efficiency, and often information that allows them to estimate marginal costs and marginal revenues. Governments dealing with collective goods and externalities are in a far different position. They know only their expenditures, and normally have next to no idea what impact or volume of output these expenditures bring about, if any, and if they did know what they produced, they would still have quite a problem to find out what it was worth to its consumers.

V

The inherent connection between the nonexcludability of nonpurchasers of most collective goods and the difficulty of measuring the volume of their outputs is probably even more important than the problem of concealment of preferences that is familiar from welfare economics. This is partly because it in large part explains the weakness of the forces tending to weed out inefficiency and reward efficiency in organizations providing collective goods. This weakness can best be explained by comparing a typical government agency providing a collective good with a monopoly selling an individual or private good. To make the comparison more compelling, assume that in both cases entry into the respective industry or area of responsibility of the firm or agency is forbidden. The monopoly firm without fear of new entrants still has a powerful incentive to be technically efficient. Though the monopoly may be able to survive even if it is not as efficient as it could be, it will always be able to increase its profits if it can lower its total cost curve. This will of course be true even if it has no incentive to increase output and total revenue, though it will in fact do this whenever marginal costs in the relevant range also fall. The government agency *might* also gain if it were *known* that it had reduced costs while maintaining or increasing output. But this is seldom known to have happened even when it has happened. Since the volume of output of the collective good is so difficult to measure, the agency and agency head may gain as much from *seeming* to be efficient as from being efficient. If a government administrator can persuade the powers that be that his predecessor has sent ice boxes to the Eskimo, but that he has put a stop to this waste, he may be in a strong position, even if the total volume of output he produced from a given budget in fact declined. As Charles Schultze and others have emphasized, the efficiency of an institution providing a collective good is often judged to an excessive extent by the presence or absence of obvious "mistakes," which need not be an accurate guide to its over-all degree of efficiency. It is also sometimes judged by the fashionableness of the procedures it uses (does it recruit people with advanced degrees or use a big computer), or by whether the administrator's style is in accord with current doctrine (does he run a "taut ship" or use "consultative management"), or by whether it is adept at praising itself in the right places (does it have a good press or friends on the Hill). The importance of an appearance of efficiency and usefulness naturally encourages, in spite of regulations to the contrary, considerable efforts at public relations, which from a social perspective are mainly a waste of resources.

The critic may say that this emphasis on the lack of knowledge of the physical volume of output of the relevant public goods misses the point: if it were known with absolute certainty that a given agency had increased efficiency it still might be the case that the agency head and the agency as a whole might go unrewarded, or even end up with a smaller appropriation, so the real trouble is the lack of an appropriate incentive system in government. But this criticism in turn neglects the fundamental point that an adequate incentive system cannot be established when there is no way of measuring the volume or value of output.

Whether an institution produces a divisible private good or an indivisible public good affects not only information about its over-all performance and that of its manager, but also its internal processes. The more accurate the information about the output of an institution, the greater the possibility of estimating the usefulness of its component parts. If the changes in the dependent variable are not known, there is not even the hope of estimating the contributions each dependent variable has made to its movements. But with a firm producing private goods at least the over-all result is known, and there is then often the possibility of roughly apportioning the responsibility for it among the different parts of the firm. That is not only because of the rough inferences that may sometimes be drawn from time series data or experiments, but also (and more importantly) because the contribution of each part of a firm can often be measured directly. The multiproduct or geographically dispersed firm can often set up what the accountant calls separate "profit centers" to facilitate evaluations of subordinate divisions and managers. If the firm's output is at all homogeneous, it can simply count the units or components produced or handled by each factory or work group, and relate the totals to the resources that were used. Indeed, it is often possible to tell which nut tighteners have tightened the most nuts, and to pay them accordingly—that is, to use a "piece rate" or "commission" system. The fact that a piece rate reward system is often used by firms providing private goods, but can virtually never (except at earlier stages of the productive process) be used when a collective good is being provided, is entirely consistent with the argument that is being made here, and suggests that it can have profound implications for the procedures and incentives within an institution.

The lack of readily countable outputs in jurisdictions or agencies that produce collective goods, and the resulting lack of objective bases for judging performance, has led to complicated, cumbersome, and expensive restrictions on public management. Civil service or "merit" systems, requirements for competitive bidding even in situations where that is evidently uneconomical, separate resource constraints for personnel, money, and certain classes of supplies, and "red tape" in general are the natural concomitant of unmeasured outputs. Presumably no one would care very much whether the police commissioner gave a good job to his nephew, or bought uniforms from his brother, if the police department were *demonstrably* as efficient as it could be. But since we do not know whether the police department is giving good value or not we know that the commissioner could get away with hiring his nephew, however incompetent, or buying his brother's uniforms, however costly, if we did not outlaw it directly, so we do. The civil service rules, competitive purchase provisions, and red tape requirements no doubt prevent some of the chicanery that the lack of measured output allows, since such regulations limit the extent to which resources can be diverted from public purposes; they may even sometimes increase output. But they also impose enormous costs. In some cases the labyrinth of restrictions that limits the freedom of action of public administrators is so elaborate that it prevents timely action in certain areas, at which point there is often a tendency to rely on contracts with outside suppliers (sometimes nonprofit firms) to get the job done. This can be only a temporary solution, since the lack of measured outputs allows inefficiency and corruption on the part of the contractors, and thereby leads to regulations that hem them in as well.

The fact that it is the lack of an adequately measured output, rather than any other factor, that mainly accounts for the cumbersome regulations characteristic of government bureaucracy is also demonstrated by the tendency of nationalized industries producing private goods to have fewer regulations (at least in some countries) than civil service departments providing collective goods. This in turn illustrates a point that must be emphasized: it is not that governments are inherently inefficient, but rather that the provision of collective goods and the handling of externalities, whether by government or other institution, is typically inefficient.

The difficulty of weeding out the inefficient and rewarding the efficient in institutions providing collective goods creates some problems that tend to get worse over time. The criteria for promotion, when the volume and value of output are not known, cannot by definition include productivity, so other considerations must determine who rises in the organization. These other considerations may be very diverse. Whatever they are, it seems likely that talented people will be more likely to rise than stupid ones, since they will be able to find out sooner what has to be done to get promoted and be able to do it better. One consideration that apparently often affects promotion in organizations producing collective goods is loyalty to the organization, its leadership, its ideology, and its established way of doing things. Bureaucrats with such loyalty will not "rock the boat." In military organizations, police forces, fire departments, foreign ministries, and churches, at least, it often seems to be the case that it is the consummate organization man who rises to the top. Such men, however able, tend to be conservative, in the sense that they are convinced that the organization's hierarchy and practices are basically sound. Where it is not productivity, but able and unwavering adherence to the established policy, that leads to promotion, an organization is likely to become increasingly inefficient as time goes on. The more conditions change, the farther its initial policies will be from the optimal ones.

The dynamic process just described can perhaps be illustrated most aptly by considering a well-known type of institution that provides only collective goods—the bureaucracies that handle foreign affairs, and particularly the U.S. State Department. The foreign ministries of many countries, such as France and Great Britain, have traditionally been able to recruit their professionals from the most able university graduates. Though the U.S. State Department may not be able to be quite so selective, it is still able to skim the cream. As a glance at a typical graduating class of, say, an Ivy League institution will reveal, a great many of the C and low B students go on to the business schools and then to the great corporations. But the handful that have won admission to the Foreign Service will have marks that are surpassed only by those who go on to the academic world, and in addition personality traits that have impressed references and interviewers.

The State Department, like some foreign ministries of other countries, does not, however, have a reputation for efficiency that is at all proportional to the apparent quality of its recruits, nor even as good as some of the great corporations that have had to be satisfied with the gentlemanly C students. The modest character of the State Department's reputation is illustrated by the fact that on the same day two of the best known Washington-based editorial columns carried tales of the Presidential dissatisfaction with the bureaucratic ineptitude in the State Department. The Evans-Novak column had this to say:

> At the first staff meeting of the high-level State Department officials following Henry Kissinger's secret flight to Peking last month, Secretary of State William P. Rogers announced somewhat defensively he wanted everyone to know that "the State Department has been in on this from the start."
>
> In fact, except for Rogers himself and possibly one or two of his top aids . . . State Department Far East experts were as much in the dark as everyone else.

Likewise, when President Nixon made the spectacular turnabout that killed his tattered economic game plan and floated the dollar, not one State Department economic expert had been clued in. . . .

In countless other matters involving less dramatic policy decisions, President Nixon's White House has circumvented the State Department bureaucracy, leaning not on career Foreign Service officers so often scorned by so many White House staffs in the past, but on non-career advisers, particularly the President's own national security staff in the White House.

Under Mr. Nixon, however, this effort to suffocate the professionals has been carried much farther than in the Kennedy or Johnson administration, which built the foundation of the now institutionalized foreign policy apparatus in the White House. For example, the skilled technicians on Dr. Henry Kissinger's national security staff now number about twice as many as the staffs of McGeorge Bundy or Walt Rostow in the 1960s.

. . . Rogers is under rising pressure from President Nixon to give him "non-careerist" State Department judgments on new policies. . . .

This White House aversion to careerist judgments is not new. The cautious, self-protective bureaucrat often finds 20 reasons for being against a bold shift in policy. . . .[6]

In the same newspapers Joseph Kraft pointed out that it was dangerous to exclude all those with extensive experience in foreign policy from the circle of Presidential advisers on international economic policy.[7]

Some participants in interagency meetings have compared State Department representation at these meetings unfavorably with that coming from civilian officials in the Defense Department. Yet the Defense Department has never been able to attract college graduates of comparable promise into its civilian bureaucracy. Of course, the State Department and comparable departments in some other countries may not deserve a reputation for striped pants conservatism and inflexibility. We do not and cannot if this paper is correct hope to *know* whether they are especially inefficient.

Yet the paradoxical relationship between the reputations of the new recruits of the Foreign Service and the reputation of the State Department as a bureaucracy is suggestive, and exactly what should be expected from the fact that they produce a collective good that is perhaps uniquely difficult to measure. State Department procedures and promotions have to be determined on some bases other than measured productivity. It is difficult to say what these bases are, but even critics with other perspec-

---

[6] Rowland Evans and Robert Novak, "Smothering the State Dept.," Washington *Post,* August 26, 1971, p. A-17.

[7] Joseph Kraft, "Dollar Diplomacy," Washington *Post,* August 26, 1971, p. A-17.

tives have argued that they are bureaucratic caution and fidelity to a quintessential State Department style.

The Defense Department also produces an unmeasured collective good, and it has its own well-earned reputation for waste of public funds. Yet it is possibly significant that the higher ranking *civilians* in the Defense Department, unlike most of their counterparts in the State Department, are mainly men who have been appointed from the outside in mid-career. They are often businessmen who have made money, scientists who have made discoveries, lawyers who have won cases, scholars whose books have won reputations, or politicians who have picked winners. It may be that on the average the high-ranking outsiders have proven themselves in areas where output is less badly measured. And at the very least, they know from experience that things are not everywhere done the way the Defense Department is in the habit of doing them.

It might seem that all of the above difficulties that have been ascribed to the lack of measured output are explained instead by the problem of concealment of preferences. But this is not so. As long as an organization has some measure of the volume or level of its outputs, it can produce whatever amount of each output it chooses to produce with as much efficiency as it could have attained had it known what each output was worth to its clients (i.e., had preferences been revealed). That is, it can obtain maximum technical efficiency. To be sure, an institution cannot know what mix or level of output to produce until it knows how much the outputs are worth to those who want them. But that is another matter. The problems of weeding out inefficiency, rewarding productivity, and maintaining effectiveness over time stem not so much from the familiar revelation of preferences problem as from the fact that collective goods by their very nature make it difficult to get a measure of the volume of output.

VI

How can the problem of inefficiency in the provision of collective goods be solved? Unfortunately, it cannot be completely solved, since it is an inherent consequence of a defining characteristic of collective goods. The hopes of the most optimistic advocates of cost-benefit analysis and the Planning-Programming-Budgeting System will never be realized.

But the problem can be ameliorated. Indeed, some possibilities for improving governmental efficiency grow directly out of the argument that it is the lack of a measure of the volume or level of the relevant public goods that is the largest part of the problem. In some cases it is almost certainly possible to devise arrangements that would markedly increase efficiency, and in most others possible to propose steps that would lead to modest but still significant increases in efficiency.

The possibilities of improvement are greatly augmented by the fact that the most fragmentary and approximate information on the volume of collective goods produced could bring about substantial improvements in efficiency. This is true, in any event, if the organization or official whose performance is to be judged cannot usually determine or predict which fragments of information are to be found. The fragments can of course then be assumed to be a random sample from the mass of unknown information on the output of an agency. Even if the sample of information that is assumed to be a random sample is not in fact either random or representative of the "population" of information about which inferences are made, it can nonetheless lead to substantial improvements in efficiency. This is because, if it is used to influence the incentives placed before organizations and officials, and they cannot control or predict which fragments of information will be found, it can (even when it is rather inaccurate) give agencies and bureaucrats a reason to be as efficient as they can be. It may be argued that rewards and punishments based on fragmentary information on output cannot affect incentives in more than a marginal way, since the organizations and officials being judged know that it is highly probable that their output at any given moment will be unobserved. But this is not correct. If there is neither risk aversion nor risk preference, much the same behavior can be obtained by a "one out of ten" output measurement as by a "one out of one" system if the rewards and punishments are multiplied by a factor of ten.

Societies use such systems regularly; there is statistical evidence that only a fraction of the burglaries committed are "solved," much less lead to punishment for the burglar. Nor are the burglars punished probably a random sample of the population of burglars: they are perhaps on average less intelligent and fleet of foot. Yet people often dare leave their houses, and this is partly because a convicted burglar tends to get a sentence that has a negative value several times larger than the gain from an average burglary. Nine out of ten people who park overtime can go off scot-free without loss to society, provided only that the policeman chooses the parking places to check in a way drivers cannot predict and the fine is ten times as great as it would be if every offender were caught. There are, to be sure, limits to the "economies of evaluation" that can be gained in this way; a lifetime sentence for a burglar without a prior arrest or a hundred dollar fine for a single parking violation are regarded as unjust when at the same time other offenders go unpunished (if the punishment were certain and this were known ex ante on all sides, there would usually be no offenses, except for those so rewarding that they left the offender with a net gain, and thus no injustice—except for those who "needed" to be burglars or park overtime, and that would reflect some *other* injustice). There may also be ethical objections if the rewards that are given or denied to agencies and officials are too great in relation to the intrinsic importance of the fragments of information about them. But it is surely possible to multiply rewards for fragments of favorable information to some extent, and thus to create a large incentive for efficiency with a small amount of information. This is particularly important in one important class of cases, but to identify this class it is necessary first to consider the definition of collective goods again.

The characteristic that has been used to distinguish collective goods and externalities in this paper so far is that of "nonexclusion." Though the infeasibility of excluding nonpurchasers from the consumption of some goods was sufficient to pinpoint what this paper argues is the largest source of inefficiency in the public sector, it is not sufficient for other purposes. In particular, it conceals an area in which substantial gains in government efficiency are possible.

As John Head has pointed out, there is a second condition that is also a sufficient (but again not a necessary) condition for a collective good. This is the characteristic that Paul Samuelson has emphasized in his writings on public goods, and which Head has labeled "jointness." Jointness is dramatically evident when, as Samuelson put it, increased consumption by one individual does not reduce consumption of anyone else. If one more person turns on his television set to a given channel, that does not affect the reception of those who were already enjoying the broadcast; if the minimum size of bridge which is technically feasible is such that it is never congested, an additional person can cross it without cost to anyone. In other words, there is what Head calls jointness whenever the marginal social cost of providing a collective good to another person, once it is already provided to someone, is zero. But when the marginal social cost of a good is zero, the only price for that good that is consistent with complete or Pareto-optimal efficiency is of course also zero. And if that is the socially optimal price, it follows that there is no profit to the entrepreneur who would provide that good at that price, so (at least if the number of people who would enjoy that good is large) the collective good can normally only be provided optimally by governments or other organizations with the power to pay for the good while charging a zero price for its use.

Some economists are fond of pointing out that a pure, Samuelsonian collective good is relatively rare; if new consumers are added, or some old ones take more, there will usually be at least a little reduction in the consumption of the rest. The waves from the television tower may not ever be used up, but the bridge will usually suffer some degree of congestion.

This contention illustrates the importance of making a link between two phenomena that are often considered independently, but that ought in the interests of theoretical parsimony and policy insights to be labeled with a single concept. Our profession has long been aware of the problem of the industry such that decreasing average costs make it impossible to have marginal cost pricing without running at a loss. The marginal cost pricing that Pareto-optimal efficiency demands will therefore normally require government ownership or price discrimination.

The Samuelsonian pure public good is nothing more and nothing less than a good with a positive average cost and no marginal cost—it is the extreme case of the decreasing cost industry.[8] In any industry such that, at the socially optimum level of output, the marginal cost is less than average cost, there is market failure, and thus a prima facie case for asking whether some form of government intervention could make things more efficient. All of these cases of market failure through decreasing costs, whether they involve the Samuelsonian extreme of zero marginal costs or not, should be classified together. Thus here we consider all such goods as having jointness—one of the two conditions, either of which is sufficient (but neither of which is necessary) for a collective good or externality.

Though Head has distinguished the nonexcludability and jointness characteristics of collective goods, many writers have failed to do so, perhaps because these two characteristics often go together. In the case of the classic public good of defense, for example, it is probably true both that excluding nonpaying beneficiaries would be prohibitively expensive and also that additional persons can be defended by a given military force at much less than the per capita cost for the entire population (an exception to this latter point would occur if a larger population

---

[8] That is, where the level of output is defined in terms of the number of consumers who receive a given level of service, rather than in terms of the level of service.

made a country a more appealing prize for an enemy). There is, however, a real need to distinguish the two properties that can make a good collective, because many goods have the one property and not the other, and because the two properties create very different situations for output measurement. These differences have, unfortunately, been seriously neglected, especially in much of the applied literature on output measurement in government.

When a collective good has the jointness or decreasing cost property, but the costs of excluding nonpurchasers are not great, there are promising, unexploited opportunities for output evaluation that are not present when exclusion is exceptionally costly. Though, at least where there are many customers involved, laissez faire will not provide an optimal supply of such goods, it does not follow that the government should *never* charge a price. If the marginal cost price of the good is positive, and the transactions cost of charging that price is not prohibitive, it follows that a government can determine the value of the collective good at the margin simply by charging the marginal cost price. This policy will of course be twice blessed, in that charging such a price will also lead to an optimal level of use of the service. The government activity will of course have to run at a loss (or use discriminatory pricing), but if that were not true, there would in this sort of situation be no point in government intervention in any case.

Even when the marginal cost price of a collective good is precisely zero, it is often feasible to get market evaluation of output, as long as exclusion is feasible. Admittedly, there is a fundamental conflict between the desirability of charging a zero price (which is necessary to give consumers an optimal incentive to use the good) and the desirability of a positive price (which is necessary to obtain information about what the output of the good is and what it is worth to those who bought it). But the need for output measurement and evaluation does not require that a positive price be charged to everyone all the time, or even most people most of the time. As a practical matter, it requires only price exclusion on an experimental or sampling basis. Where large numbers of people enjoy some good, we can be confident that the information about the output and valuation of a good provided by a random sample of the users will give essentially the same information as could be obtained from the entire population. And even if we cannot in practice get a sample that is random, strong incentives based on information from an imperfect sample may still induce a far more energetic, flexible, and efficient administration.

Consider the example of a bridge or highway. The prevailing practice is either to make the use of roads and bridges free at all times, or alternatively to charge tolls that are large enough (or more than large enough) to pay for the cost of the road or bridge plus the interest on the loan that was floated to build it. The former policy can be rational in those cases (which may with present practice be fairly numerous) in which the transactions cost of collecting a toll would always exceed the value of the information and the incentive provided through the toll (the main cost here is probably not the toll taker, but rather the time and other loss to the motorist of the extra stops and starts). But, as William Vickrey has argued in discussions of particular cases, it would be easy with present computer and electromagnetic technology to develop toll systems that would have only negligible transaction costs, at least when applied to certain cases (such as controlled access roads during commuter hours). The latter policy (average cost pricing) can be rational if (as J. de V. Graaff has in essence argued) average cost pricing is in some sense better than the alternative forms of taxation. This may be true in particular cases, but it is hardly conceivable that it could always be true.

Naturally, in those road and bridge cases in which marginal cost is significant (at least during some hours) but less than average cost (at least during some hours), marginal cost pricing should be considered. This might in practice mean charging tolls only during rush hours, or a tax on all day parking in the central city, or a special tax on automobile commuters who have regular working hours. If there is a lack of public understanding of the utility of such policies, or if no easy way of keeping transaction costs within bounds can be found, it is tempting to rule out the use of prices. But it must be remembered that marginal cost pricing will not only improve incentives to the user, but usually also provide better information on which to base governmental decisionmaking.

When marginal cost pricing of a general kind is for any reason infeasible for a good with a marginal cost that is less than average but positive, then experimental pricing applied to a sample of potential users can be useful. The commuters in a given representative sample of firms or residential blocks can be charged marginal cost prices and the results blown up for the population as a whole. This need not lead to injustice to those who happen to be chosen for the experiment, since they can be given a lump sum payment as large as the amount they would be required to pay in tolls. This payment can even be significantly larger than the cost of the tolls to the experimental subjects, so long as it is not so much larger that it has a substantial "income effect."

VII

The approach proposed here can more readily be illustrated by considering the important case of television. Since an additional receiver in no way damages television reception for others, and since "scramblers" that can exclude nonpurchasers already exist, this is an example which has the property that a zero marginal cost is socially optimal and the further property that exclusion of nonpayers costs very little. It is, of course, clear that television paid for by advertisers who use part of their time to advertise their products is not consistent with Pareto-optimality. If the marginal social cost of another viewer is zero, but the viewer must in fact watch commercials for X minutes out of every hour, the viewer obviously has to pay a price for watching television, and this is, of course, inefficient. The magnitude of this inefficiency is enormous. Since we know, at least for those cases in which people are able to choose how many hours of work they do, that leisure must be valued at least at the going wage rate, the value of the time lost watching television advertisements since television was introduced must amount to tens, or more probably hundreds, of billions of dollars for the United States alone. Something must be subtracted from this sum to take account of the informational and entertainment value advertisements have to consumers, and something added to take account of the positive annoyance, loss of dramatic effect, and misinformation that television advertisements sometimes cause.

Pay television or "fee vee" may well be more efficient than television paid for by sponsor advertising. Even those who would not in any event buy the advertised good must waste the time they sit through the commercial, and this is a waste. By contrast, with competitive pay television, the viewers need pay no more than the full average cost of the programs they receive. The fact that prices can readily vary from program to program and channel to channel also makes it easier for pay television to adjust to minority tastes and to obtain full rights to televise expensive events (like the right to show special sporting events on television even in the same community in which the event is held). Of course, pay television isn't optimal either, for the reason that it charges a positive price for something that has no marginal social cost.

It would seem that the best arrangement, given the considerations that have been discussed so far, is a government television system which meets its cost out of tax funds and provides programming free. This arrangement certainly can be Pareto-optimal. But in practice it may have disadvantages. One disadvantage is that a *single* government agency or corporation which has the benefit of a legal monopoly has some dangers a pluralistic arrangement need not have. The dependence of the state owned French television monopoly on the government in power has led to the use of that system for nearly naked government propaganda. The British experience with BBC has been happier, but (at least in the days before competitive private television) there were charges of some degree of subservience to the government (e.g., during the general strike). Nor is it likely that a federally owned monopoly system in the United States would have interviewed Daniel Ellsberg in a secret location about the purloined top secret papers at a time when he was alleged to have taken them, and was apparently in hiding from the authorities, but CBS did. A publicly subsidized television system in a democracy should therefore not only have great automony vis-à-vis the current government, but also many independent, competitive stations or networks, some of which would be willing to defy the government, or air a risky idea, even when the others would not.

Given that free, tax supported television is Pareto-optimal, and therefore such that it would be possible to compensate losers for changing to such a system and still leave everyone else better off, we must ask why free public television has not tended to sweep the field, or at least expand vis-à-vis private advertising television. In the United States, none of the scores of public service or educational television stations has obtained audiences that are in the same league with the commercial stations. Why hasn't even one of the public service stations been able to get a sufficient appropriation from some government to compete with the commercial stations, even, say, in the area of news? The tendency to introduce advertising in some of the continental television systems is puzzling in the same way. Most significant of all, why did the United Kingdom add commercial television after BBC television was already established, and protected by a measure of national pride and the ideology of most of the intellectual elite? And why does independent television in Britain have so many viewers, when the viewers must pay the substantial time cost of the advertisements, when they can watch equally light entertainment on BBC television for free?

One explanation is that a single state owned television or radio system, in the absence of competition from independent systems (be they public or private), may not be very effective in satisfying consumer demands. It would take a careful study, or in any event wider observation than this writer has managed, to be sure about this. But many people with relevant experience as observers have asserted that this is true. One thinks particularly of the English critic who said of the "leg shows" on BBC, in the days before independent television, that they looked as though they were put on by amateur groups from local convents.

Part of the explanation for this alleged ineptitude in meeting popular demands is surely that publicly sponsored broadcasting is not perfectly responsive to the wishes of the individuals in the electorate, at least in the short run. If it were it would be totally subservient to the politicians in office. In practice certain elites are likely to have a disproportionate influence, and certain minorities almost none; an intellectual elite may raise the intellectual level, an ecclesiastical or moralistic lobby may constrain the amount of pornography, and so on. But this surely is not the whole story. Democracy in the successful democracies surely can't be so ineffective and unrepresentative that this is a total explanation for the long run.

Probably part of the explanation is that a single, state owned television station tends to be run by a bureaucracy that has only a limited incentive to meet consumer demands efficiently. The individuals in the bureaucracy are more likely to be promoted if they fit in with the prevailing professional ethics than if they please customers. If the consumers can readily relieve them by voting, it will become the organ of the party in power. And since the consumers can't be expected to know the production function for television, they can't know whether the state system is as effective as it could be or not. In other words, a single state system will have the problems this paper has argued are characteristic when public goods are provided and there is no measure of the quantity of output.

There is surely no perfect arrangement but one measure that could be helpful in some cases would be to take advantage of the fact that exclusion would be possible on a sampling basis. A sample of potential viewers could be given a flat sum of money and in turn forced to pay for the program they watched. If there are several alternative channels, each with independent management, this system will reveal a good deal more information about what the output of each television channel is, in terms relevant to its users, than if there is only one channel. The rewards to the different program directors and channels or networks should then be related to their success in satisfying the sample consumers. Other objectives could also be pursued at the same time, by making some part of the reward to program directors and networks dependent on some "expert" evaluation of their intellectual level, artistic quality, moral standards, and so on. This approach could be used to improve noncommercial or educational stations in a country with a mainly commercial system and also to increase the efficiency of a wholly public television system.

VIII

There are several other areas in which exclusion on a sample basis (or exclusion of all nonpurchasers, if that is economic) can increase efficiency. It would take at least a substantial volume to analyze all of these appropriately, but it is possible to indicate the general nature of some of the possibilities from a brief and superficial discussion.

Though a great many, if not most, collective goods have the property that it is not feasible or economic to exclude nonpurchasers, there is in the case of every collective good nonetheless a considerable scope for the use of the exclusion principle. This is because collective goods, like other goods, are of course made with the aid of intermediate or producer goods, many of which are private goods. Thus by using markets in all but the very last stage of production of a collective good, and making this stage as small as possible, the area in which the information needed for efficiency is lacking can often be made quite narrow. This is done now whenever the private sector, rather than government factories, supplies weapons, uniforms, and the like to the military, or when a government office is built by a private contractor.

The scope for this can be expanded by close attention to the question of identifying the stage of the productive process that has outputs from which nonpurchasers can be excluded and where markets (even markets with considerable degrees of monopoly power) are possible. It may well be possible to have market-oriented enterprises (which might sometimes be government owned) provide that part of training for military pilots that imparts basic flying skills, especially those that are also in demand in the private sector. It may be the case that private companies can provide rented cars more cheaply than a government motor pool. There are a vast number of other possibilities of this sort.

Some public goods are themselves intermediate goods, from the police services that help to protect merchants from theft to the water for irrigation that comes from a reservoir created by a government. As others have pointed out before, in this case the concealment of preferences presents no great problem, because the worth of the collective good to the recipient must be given by what it adds to his profits, and this can in principle be estimated without too much difficulty. As Musgrave has emphasized, it is in cases of this sort—especially irrigation projects—that cost-benefit analysis has come closest to being successful. This is to be expected. If, however, the intermediate good is a pure collective good in the sense that nonpurchases cannot ever be excluded, the hairy problem of estimating the volume or quantity of output will still be present.

Where private goods have been gratuitously collectivized, the exclusion principle can very easily be used to increase efficiency. If there is neither any inherent difficulty of excluding nonpurchasers, nor decreasing costs such that the socially optimal output cannot be produced at a profit, then all that is needed is to replace the bureaucratic mechanisms with market mechanisms. The area of public housing is one that, in several countries, probably could be made more efficient in this way. If the argument of this paper is correct, it is the provision of collective goods rather than government per se that breeds inefficiency. Thus the point is not that government enterprise (or of course income redistribution or externality-internalizing subsidies) should necessarily have no role in housing, but rather that any government owned productive undertakings should be fully subject to the discipline of competitive markets.

For many collective goods, exclusion is not altogether impossible in a physical sense—just prohibitively costly. But costs that would be prohibitive if every nonpurchaser were excluded need not be prohibitive if borne only for a small sample of the relevant consumers. In other words, some consumers can be denied a collective good unless they pay for it, and given prior lump sum payments of similar value to avoid any injustice. The exclusion costs in these cases (unlike the television case considered earlier) will be substantial in relation to the value the good has to those excluded, but they may still be small in relation to the gain in efficiency that could result for the mass of consumers who consume the collective good but are not in the sample from which the needed information is to be obtained.

It is sometimes also feasible to exclude nonpurchasers from one level or aspect of a public good even when it is not feasible to exclude on an all or nothing basis. In the case of fire protection, for example, it may be difficult to protect a given house from burning down without putting out any fires that start next door. But in some cases, with enough fire fighting resources a given set of properties can be protected from fire without at the same time protecting all others, at least to the same degree. Thus, that degree of fire protection that is desired for property and convenience only, and is beyond that needed to protect life and widespread conflagration, can be denied to a small sample of property owners. This has been done: firemen in Missouri not long ago watched from fire trucks as the property of a noncontributor burned down across the street, having assured themselves that no lives were at stake. This particular solution seems a bit drastic, but the principle need not be applied in any drastic way. It would be perfectly possible for a sample of individuals and small neighborhoods to decide whether they would rather have a marginal decrease in fire protection and a tax rebate, or stay with things as they are. It would similarly be possible for individuals and small neighborhoods to be given the choice of more policemen passing by if they would pay the price, or fewer if they would prefer to save the money instead. Quite apart from the more general arguments for permitting consumer choice in the level of collective goods supplied, this approach would, even if applied to only small samples, provide information on the true output and value to consumers of certain collective goods.

Some collective goods or external economies are joint products with private goods. If it is impossible or very costly to change the proportions in which the private good and the externality are produced, efficiency can sometimes be increased by using some assessment of the output of the private goods as a proxy measure for the output of the externality. The ability to read and write, for example, is simultaneously a private investment good that may increase future earning and satisfactions, and also a collective good in countries with democratic procedures partly dependent on the understanding of written arguments. The elementary and secondary educational systems that attempt to teach or improve reading and writing skill are widely thought to be inefficient, at least in big central cities. The big city public school systems certainly often do have the traits that this paper argues are typical of organizations without a measure of the volume of output. They often promote on bases other than observed productivity (e.g., seniority, bureaucratic conformity, and possession of degrees), and rigidly adhere to time-honored rules and procedures.

One way to introduce a greater orientation to output and efficiency is to take advantage of the fact that the private good aspect of basic education is, like all private goods, such that nonpurchasers can be excluded. This means that a market system can often be used to supply basic education. The collective good value of education and distributional objectives can be met by giving parents vouchers that can be used only to pay for basic education. There is, to be sure, nothing new in this suggestion. It has come from many quarters, and has been particularly attractive to many advocates of laissez faire. The approach here, though, would lead to a slightly different emphasis than that which is evident in some laissez faire arguments for voucher systems. It would recommend special controls or subsidies designed to insure that the collective good part of the joint product was not slighted; it would insure that the schools at which vouchers could be spent would, so to speak, give "civics" sufficient attention in comparison with "business correspondence," racial integration in comparison with sports, and so on. This is because the parents would of course have no incentive to favor schools with a sufficient intensity of external economies.

IX

Where the exclusion of nonpurchasers is impossible even on a sample basis, it becomes again particularly important to distinguish the revelation of preferences problem from the lack of a measure of the volume or level of a collective good. When exclusion is impossible, there is no completely satisfactory way of getting consumers individually to reveal how much a further unit of a collective good is worth to them. So the preferences revealed by the political process must be used. But this process will work better, and the government agency providing the collective good will be more likely to attain technical efficiency, if there is a measure of the volume of each collective good.

The volume of many of the important collective goods—law and order, clean air and water, public health—is roughly measurable. The probability that a representative citizen will fall victim to a crime, the levels of sulphur dioxide in the air, the biological oxygen demand in the rivers, the risk of contagious disease, and the expectancy of healthy life can all be measured, and sometimes have been. The measurements sometimes cannot be at all accurate, but then neither is a businessman's estimate of the elasticity of the demand curve he faces, or even the exact level of his marginal costs, yet the private sector often works fairly well with this approximate information.

It is often possible, in other words, to get "social indicators." A social indicator, at least as this writer defines it, is a nonmonetary measure of social output or performance—a measure of welfare or illfare to which no price has yet been attached. It can be used to supplement the information about welfare in the national income and product accounts. A measure of the volume of a public good that is of direct normative interest to a society would then have to be a social indicator. Since preferences will often be concealed, and will in any event differ for people with different preference orderings or value judgments, it is utopian to expect consensus about the monetary value to be placed upon each social indicator. Rational public decisions about resource allocation will of course require that the politicians in power put some value or price on the alternative outcomes that could be obtained by using the same public funds in different ways, but there will rarely be a consensus that they have used the right values. But, to repeat, there is no reason in principle (outside the defense and international relations area) why tolerable physical or social indicator measurements cannot be obtained.

This paper has argued that volume or physical measurements of the output of public programs are all that are required to attain technical efficiency, and that this failure to reach the production possibility frontier is probably the largest source of inefficiency in government. It is also true that the art of measuring the output of public programs is in its infancy, and that there hasn't been a great deal of progress thus far. Thus the mind leaps to the possibility that the *relatively* tractable task of collecting social indicators could open up a smoother path to output measurement in government. This is a possibility which, in this writer's opinion, deserves more attention than it has so far received. It has probably been neglected in part because the PPB system got its form in the Defense Department, and it happens that this is one area where direct social indicator measurement can contribute least (it is not feasible to measure "national security," partly because it depends on a small number of other countries whose behavior is not readily predictable, either individually or in the mass; so output evaluation in defense has been based on engineers' experiments on how weapons will perform, etc.).

The problem here, as with all conceivable approaches to output measurement in government when exclusion is impossible, is that so many different variables influence the social states we are interested in. Crime rates depend not only upon policing, but also on family patterns, street lighting, income levels, the courts, the degree of urbanization, and what not; health depends not only on the public health service, but also on diet, smoking, exercise, the drug industry, nervous tension, and no doubt other factors that haven't even been specified yet. And it is presumably as complicated in other areas.

If the exclusion and even the sample exclusion possibilities set out above are infeasible, there are only two further conceivable ways in which the outputs of government programs can be measured: experimentally or statistically. We must either set up controlled experiments which keep all independent variables except the control variable essentially constant, and then calculate the effect of the control variable on output in those conditions; or alternatively we must collect a good deal of disaggregated data on the level of the variables we ultimately want to change (the social indicators) and use them along with data on resources used, and with well-specified statistical models, to estimate social production functions.

Neither approach promises striking results. Experiments are often infeasible or morally offensive. Child abuse and unhappy homes may or may not be a cause of crime, but it is out of the question to do the experiments needed to find out. Longitudinal statistical studies of criminals and noncriminals might give the answer, but for confidence they would require data we are not likely to have. To find out the value of a certain level of a collective good, someone has got to be excluded from that level of the collective good, which may be politically or morally objectionable even on an experimental basis. But "nature" may not have provided enough variety in levels of the collective good to allow statistical estimates either. In practice, cost-benefit analyses and PPB studies have often had to deal with the intermediate goods, or avoided outright efforts at output measurement, and it is easy to see why.

On the other hand, there is no telling what might be done to increase governmental efficiency if more social indicators could be collected and better experiments could be conducted. And there are many relatively obvious ways in which institutional improvements could be made. It would help, if the argument of this paper is at all correct, to prohibit inbreeding in bureaucracies: to insist that in any bureaucracy people can come in at any level from the outside, and thus sometimes from areas where productivity is better measured and where the conventional wisdom is different. If pension rights are fully vested so insiders can compete for outside jobs without handicap there is no need for this to lead to injustice. There is also, as others have pointed out, the need to be wary of the influence of organizations representing inputs used in government on the allocations chosen by the political and administrative process.

It follows from what has been said here about the lack of output measurement in government that administrators and politicians are often more likely to be judged by the extent to which they please politically organized suppliers of resources to the government than by their output. But whether through experiments, statistical estimations, or changes in institutional arrangements, general efforts to improve efficiency in government can never realize their full potential unless they start with the source of the problem: the defining characteristics of collective goods.

COMMENT
CHARLES L. SCHULTZE, The Brookings Institution

Mancur Olson's basic thesis is that government is fundamentally and incurably inefficient in much of what it undertakes. His argument has four steps: (a) government produces collective goods; (b) no particular individual can be excluded from the use or enjoyment of such goods—if they are available for one, they are available for all; (c) the output of collective goods, therefore, does not take the form of divisible physical units that can be counted; (d) since output cannot be measured, productive efficiency cannot be measured, and hence it cannot be achieved. He also argues that problems of inefficiency in the conduct of government programs do not stem from the fact of "concealed preference"—i.e., from our inability to put a value on the physical output of government. Rather they stem from the impossibility of measuring physical output itself.

In evaluating Olson's proposition it will be useful to start with a formal definition of efficiency. In the case of *private* goods there are three aspects of efficiency: first, efficiency in exchange—all marginal rates of substitution (MRS) are equal among individuals, an equality that is secured by rational consumers reacting to market prices $(p_1/p_2 = MRS_i = MRS_j$; etc.); second, efficiency in production—the ratios of the marginal products of productive factors are equal in all lines of activity and that equality is secured by rational producers minimizing costs, given factor prices $(MPL/MPK^a = MPL/MPK^b = W/p_k)$; third, joint efficiency in production and exchange—marginal rates of substitution are equal to marginal rates of transformation (MRT), and that equality is given by producers choosing a volume of output such that prices are equal to marginal costs $(MRS = MRT; p = MC)$. Because of the non-excludability property of public goods, the first and third equalities collapse into one: marginal rates of transformation are set equal to the sum of marginal rates of substitution $(\Sigma MRS = MC)$. The first and third equalities have to do with efficiency in resource allocation; the second is a requirement for efficiency in production. While Olson does not explicitly develop these various aspects of efficiency, he is clearly concerned with efficiency in production, rather than efficiency in allocation.

I shall argue (1) that our inability to measure output is indeed an important reason for the difficulty of measuring and securing efficiency in the execution of government programs; (2) that the concept of *physical* output, however, has little relevance—the major problem in measuring output is the difficulty, or indeed impossibility, of attaching *values* to various aspects of governmental activities; (3) and that another major reason for inefficiency in government program execution stems from the incentive problem which necessarily plagues bureaucracies.

In both the public and private sector we are not basically interested in measuring output in the purely physical sense. Private output is measured in terms of the values which arise in the market place. A refrigerator is five times the output of a portable TV set, not because it is five times as large or five times as heavy or has metal five times as durable or because of any other set of physical characteristics, but because consumers value it at five times a portable TV set. The problem in the public sector is not our inability to measure physical output—we can often do so. But the purely physical aspect of output is economically meaningless. The real problem of measuring performance or efficiency in the public sector is that we do not have market values to place on the goods or services produced by the government.

Let us take tanks and automobiles as examples. An "automobile," not otherwise described, is a meaningless measure of output for personal consumption, just as a tank per se is a meaningless measure of national defense output. An automobile is two tons of steel, other metals, and textiles, so assembled that it moves under its own power when fueled. But a Cadillac Eldorado with a built-in bar and all the accessories is five times the output of a Volkswagen. There are myriad things which contribute to the satisfaction of consumer desires for transportation, convenience, and status provided by an automobile. How do we measure the "output" represented by disc brakes versus shoe brakes; by hand-tooled leather upholstery versus cheap textiles; by radial steel-belted tires versus conventional tires; by electric window openers versus manual openers; by two-speed versus one-speed windshield wipers; by fuel injection versus a carburetor; etc. Because of these and many other kinds of differences, an increase in "automobile" output represented by one Cadillac has twice the weight (as measured by relative prices) of an increase in output represented by one Ford.

The relationship of the physical characteristics of automobiles to consumer satisfaction is not basically different from the relationship of the physical characteristics of a "tank" to national defense. We can count cars and we can count tanks. We can go further and provide physical measures of a host of characteristics of a car and a tank. But in the case of cars, the exceedingly complex collection of physical characteristics can be made commensurable and their contribution to output measured on the basis of the price consumers are willing to pay. And in the private sector, productive efficiency comes from minimizing the cost of producing particular collections of physical things called a car. But the "output" whose costs are minimized is meaningful only in terms of relative values assigned by consumers. In the case of a tank, however, we have no measure of value to associate with the tank. As a consequence, we must attempt to impute some kind of value to various potential physical characteristics of a tank on the basis of their presumed relationship to national defense. In any event, the problem is not the physical output represented by a car or by a tank. The problem of measuring output in the case of the tank is that we have no value to attach to it. The problem is not that it is impossible to count tanks.

Education is another example. This is a private good with public externalities, produced in part by the public sector and in part by the private sector. The externalities are most usually joint products with the private good. It is impossible to exclude particular individuals from the enjoyment of the public externalities and therefore impossible to ration this aspect of the good through the price system. But even viewed purely as a private good, a measure of the physical output of education is meaningless. The quality aspects of education are most complex and difficult to measure from an analytic standpoint. Do we measure output by the number of students educated? Are Princeton and Podunk Junior College to be counted the same? To the extent that we wanted to treat education as a private good and to accept the values which arise in the market place, the ultimate output measure of education would depend on consumer valuation. In that case, we would agree, for example, to treat an additional year at Princeton as, say, three times the year at Podunk. But the fact that one year at Princeton is three times a year at Podunk would arise from our acceptance of market values. Whether we should accept market values or not, whether education is a good which should be produced publicly because we don't want to accept market values is not at issue here. What is at stake is that in the case of education as both a private and a public good, output can only be defined in value terms. The concept of *physical* output is literally meaningless.

It might be argued that even though the concept of physical output has no economic meaning in measuring the *level* of output, physical output does take on meaning when we are measuring changes. We can construct an output index by designing indexes of each of the specific physical characteristics of a particular output, weighting each characteristic by some value. But on reflection, two things become evident. First, value weights are needed to obtain our index. The output increase represented by an additional Cadillac is not the same as the increase represented by an additional Ford; nor is one added student in the third grade the same as one added student at Harvard medical school. A measure of efficiency which assumed that the two changes were equal would surely provide misleading advice to decisionmakers. Second, only in those cases in which the nature of the physical characteristics of the good in question does not change can we unambiguously construct a component index to be weighted. To measure the economic meaning of a change in the physical nature of a product we must again rely on valuation. This is the nature of the linking procedure through which we handle changes in the physical nature of output. And, of course, precisely the same problems arise when output indexes are constructed by deflating expenditure data. In this case the quality problem rears its head in the construction of the price index where in the other it is in the construction of the output index.

In short, identifying and measuring the physical characteristics of output is neither more nor less difficult on the average in the public than in the private sector. In either case, the physical characteristics of almost all outputs are exceedingly complex. There are a few cases— usually of intermediate output—in which simple physical measures are meaningful, e.g., the Treasury check-writing process and the Veterans Administration processing of insurance premiums. But in almost all important situations, the physical characteristics of output are very complex, and the achievement of efficiency in production depends in significant part on assigning the proper weight to each of the many characteristics of output. Without such weights the attempt to minimize cost for some few arbitrary physical characteristics inevitably leads to distortion.

There is the classic case of the early Soviet nail factory in which quotas were set in terms of the *weight* of nails produced. In response to this implicit incentive a small number of very large nails was produced. When an attempt was made to correct this obvious distortion by measuring output in terms of the *number* of nails, quotas were met and Stakhanovite awards were won by producing a very large number of very small nails. A similar situation arises at the present time in attempting to measure the performance of those insurance companies who contract with the Social Security Administration as intermediaries in the payment and regulation of claims for hospital services under Medicare. One might think that the ratio of administrative costs to total benefits paid or to total business handled would be a good measure of the efficiency of "output" of these insurance intermediaries. It turns out, however, that insurance firms can easily minimize their administrative costs by doing practically no monitoring of claims, no weeding out of excessive charges, no checking on overutilization of services, and the like. As a consequence the measure of output in this case turns out again to be exceedingly complicated, and the real problem comes in assigning weights to the various possible aspects of output. There is no way of securing superior performance without carefully specifying the output to be desired, which in turn cannot be done without assigning, either explicitly or implicitly, some sort of weights to each of the aspects.

In three different places in his paper, Olson implicitly recognizes that output cannot really be measured in the absence of knowledge about relative values. In discussing the problem of output measures in the service sector, he notes that private firms producing janitorial services need not measure physical output—they simply observe the marginal revenue from supplying janitorial services and act in the light of that knowledge to minimize the cost of supplying such services. He is precisely correct. But janitorial services are not really different from automobiles or toys. The output meaning of the latter does not arise from the fact they can be touched, or seen, or broken. Rather their output meaning is imputed from the services they render. Indeed, it is impossible even to define an automobile as a physical output in anything less than a 20,000 page book of detailed specifications.

In another case Olson talks about the usefulness to decisionmakers of pricing at marginal costs the services of a bridge which has positive marginal costs. As he correctly points out, the efficiency gains from this practice would extend beyond the simple welfare rules of setting price equal to marginal costs. Pricing practices provide "better information on which to base government decisionmaking." I agree. But if one asks what kinds of information are provided to governmental decisionmakers through the price rationing device, the answer is that information is obtained about demand, and hence about values. Charging a price for a bridge-crossing, with the price moving up the slope of the marginal cost curve as congestion increases, provides information that helps to make better investment decisions about building a new bridge. It is the information on values provided by the pricing mechanism which is important. More generally, Olson's suggestions about pricing government services go not to the securing of information about physical outputs so much as to securing information about values—indeed how could we price anything unless we already had a measure of the units to be priced!

Olson also discusses the desirability of contracting out certain operations of the Defense Department. He uses as an example contracting out basic pilot training. But to do this, the Air Force would clearly have to spell out the output it wanted from the contractor. In turn, defining output could not be done simply in terms of the number of pilots turned out. The proficiency of pilots is relevant, as is the time span of the training and the auxiliary skills acquired. Somehow these and other important aspects of pilot training would have to be taken into account and weighted by Air Force "values" in order to draw up a contract.

More generally in the case of the Defense Department, there is much inefficiency in the procurement of physical weapons systems produced under private contract. This inefficiency stems from many reasons but two are most important: (1) the inability of the Department to settle on the "value" to it of the myriad physical characteristics going into a weapons system, as a consequence of which design changes, production interruptions, and redesign problems are legion and (2) the inability to devise real incentives for procurement officers and higher decisionmakers to care enough about unit costs.

In summary then, Olson is partly correct when he points out that inefficiency on the part of government is fundamental and in many cases incurable. He is also correct when he points out that these problems stem from an inability to measure output. But he is wrong, I believe, to suggest that this is not a problem of concealed preferences and therefore value, but rather a problem of measuring physical output. Considered from an economic standpoint, physical output is a meaningless concept in both the public and the private sector. Finally I would note that even when output is measured or measurable, after taking relative values into account, major efficiency problems remain because the incentives of governmental decisionmakers are often quite different from those which would tend to maximize output for a given volume of resources or minimize resource input for a given output. The molding and maintenance of a political consensus, high risk aversion to sharp changes in hiring, firing, and location policies, and the difficulty of translating analytical output measures into politically appealing terms are but a few of the reasons why the measurement of output—important as it is—represents only one aspect of the problem of improving governmental efficiency. With these last remarks I am sure Olson would agree.

GENERAL PROBLEMS OF MEASURING PERFORMANCE AND OUTPUT IN THE PUBLIC SECTOR

Performance Measures Versus Output Measures

Performance measures and output measures are not the same. In general, questions of performance go well beyond the measurement of the actual outcome of production decisions. For example, if the performance of the auto industry were at issue, a number of questions might be raised going well beyond the accuracy of our current measures of automobile output:

1. We might inquire into the status of the industry with respect to its competitive situation. From a resource allocation standpoint, the industry may be producing the wrong level of output very efficiently.
2. Even if an industry is competitive, we might ask how dynamic it is in adopting technological change. A perfectly competitive industry may still be a stagnant one.
3. We may wish to go behind consumer evaluation and look at the performance of automobiles in terms of their safety, their durability, or their economy of operation. In this case, our performance measure would implicitly question consumer evaluation on grounds of lack of information or Galbraithian manipulation of preferences.

In the context of the national accounts, it is output, not performance in the above sense, that we wish to measure. In other words, we want to measure actual outcomes which reflect collective decisions and evaluations without looking behind those decisions. The kinds of data and analytic structures which are useful for performance measurement may not be the same, and will almost always be much more complex and detailed than the data and analysis needed for output measurement.

Measurement of Public Output in the National Income Accounts

Even without raising some of the very fundamental questions about the nature and the structure of the accounts which have been brought forward in this conference, it is possible to point to several areas in which modest improvements could probably add to the usefulness and in some sense the accuracy of the accounts. One of these has to do with the way in which state and local government expenditures are deflated in the measurement of constant dollar GNP. In fiscal year 1970, state and local governments spent $132 billion. Of that amount $70 billion was compensation of employees. The deflation of this component of the state and local government sector is done by exceedingly aggregate techniques. Compensation of employees is divided into two parts: (i) the compensation of employees in education; and (ii) all other compensation. In each of these two components, changes in real output are measured by changes in employment. This is equivalent to deflating each of the two components by an index which is simply the aggregate payroll in that component divided by the aggregate number of employees. As a consequence, a shift in activity within either the "education" or the "all other" sector from a function involving low wage employees to a function involving high wage employees is washed out in the deflation. A $30,000 per year doctor and a $5,000 per year garbage worker are considered equivalent in terms of the output value of their services. A shift in employment from one to the other does not show up as a change in output. What is needed is a compensation index for state and local employees which is a true index. It should *not* simply be a measure of average compensation per man reflecting both wage increases and shifts among occupational categories. The construction of such an index would require breaking state and local employment into a number of different components, constructing wage indexes for each component, and then combining them with base period employment weights. There are several ways of accomplishing this. Edward Denison has suggested "specification pricing." Demographic, educational, and other characteristics of employees would be specified for a number of representative categories, e.g., a forty-year-old college engineering graduate. Wage and salary data would be collected for each category, weighted, and combined into an index. Another alternative would be the use of occupational specifications. Which of the two alternatives is preferable would depend principally upon data availability. In any event, the resulting wage index used as a deflator would at least allow the measure of this major component of state and local output to vary as employment was shifted from low wage to high wage categories of employees. It may turn out that in any given period the difference in the two measures (i.e., the current measure and the proposed measure) would be minimal.[1] Nevertheless,

[1] Subsequent to the conference, Charles Waite of the Office of Business Economics informed me by letter that he has calculated an alternative series of

the effort is worth pursuing because we have no a priori reason to believe that shifts in the mix of output will remain unimportant.

Other Possible Improvements in Measuring Public Sector Output

There are several major components of the public sector whose level of output and rate of change in output are probably systematically misstated in the national income accounts.

The accounts make a number of necessarily arbitrary distinctions between activities which are economic in nature and those which are not. The former are included in, the latter excluded from, gross national product. More precisely, distinctions of this nature generally turn on where and how activities are carried out rather than on the nature of the activities themselves: the household versus the business enterprise is the chief distinction. Education in the home is "noneconomic" while education carried on in a public or private institutional setting is economic; preparation of food in a restaurant is economic while preparation of food in the home is noneconomic. This distinction leads to some anomalies. The unpaid volunteer time of mothers in a cooperative kindergarten outside the home is not valued in the accounts while the wages of the maid who prepares food at home are counted. But even these anomalies are roughly consistent with concepts generally employed in the accounts. The volunteer mothers, for example, most generally are diverting time from household activities not covered in the accounts and by accounting definition their opportunity costs are zero.

But there are two major areas in the public sector where the valuations of output, by the conceptual usages of the accounts themselves, are significantly understated. One is the military budget where the wages paid draftees rather than their foregone earnings are used to measure output. The other is education where student wages foregone are excluded from the measure of output value.

deflated state and local educational output, using data on wage rate changes for five categories of employees. The increase in deflated output between 1961 and 1970 as shown by this alternative measure is only slightly different from the increase shown by the method of aggregate deflation currently in use—61.3 per cent for the former versus 60.6 per cent for the latter. This result occurred, despite the shift in employment from elementary and secondary to higher education, because the number of relatively low paid noninstructional personnel in higher education is increasing nearly as rapidly as instructional personnel. As a consequence, the difference in *average* wages paid in elementary and secondary education on the one hand and higher education on the other is nowhere near as large as the difference between the wages of teachers in the two systems.

Let us start with education. Unlike the case of the volunteer mothers in the kindergarten, the time of many students, particularly in higher education, does represent a diversion from activities otherwise included in the accounts. If the combination of public and private decisions about education roughly balances marginal costs and marginal benefits, the value of education is substantially understated in the national income accounts. The marginal product represented by foregone wages is a diversion from output which the accounts otherwise measure. More importantly, the raison d'être for including foregone earnings in measuring the value of educational output stems from the hypothesis that costs can be a surrogate for value only if all costs are included.

The current practice in constructing the accounts implies that part of the value of education is economic in nature and part is not and that the division of the value of the product into economic and noneconomic components is precisely equal to the division of costs into monetary and imputed components. But there is no warrant in the nature of education as an output to make such a distinction. None of the analysis of the impact of education on economic growth, for example, makes this distinction. This is not to suggest that the existing main structure of the accounts necessarily be altered. But a supplementary measure of educational output which included foregone earnings and which classified education as an investment outlay would be exceedingly useful for analyses of economic growth, savings, and investment. Only if we assume that education is substantially overproduced—that is, output is pushed to the point where marginal benefits are substantially below marginal costs—does the current measure of educational output in the accounts, which leaves out foregone earnings, provide an appropriate evaluation of that output.

The personnel component of the military budget provides another clear example of the same problem. The wages paid draftees have been until recently substantially less than their forgone earnings. As a consequence the resource cost of the defense budget is significantly understated. While the pay raises which have accompanied the move toward a "volunteer army" have eliminated most of the differential, it looms very large in the historical data.

In the case of education and military spending, both of which are explicitly defined to be economic activities subject to measurement in the national income accounts, a transfer of manpower resources (students or draftees) from other sectors of the economy to these activities automatically tends to reduce national output. The reduction does not stem from any explicit hypothesis that the value of output per man is necessarily less in these areas than in the sectors from which the manpower has been withdrawn. Nor does it arise because activities are being transferred from market to nonmarket sectors. Rather the reduction stems simply from the failure to impute foregone earnings to the military or educational activity in question.

Imputation of foregone earnings in the measurement of output would also require that the receipts side of the accounts be appropriately modified in order to maintain equality between receipts and expenditures in the particular activities concerned. In the case of military spending the excess of foregone earnings over the military wages paid draftees could be treated as a tax levied upon the draftees. In the case of education, the problem is not so simple. It could be handled, as is imputed rent, by treating the individual as a firm investing in education and the value of foregone earnings would be an imputed cost paid by the person as consumer to himself wearing another hat as educational entrepreneur.

ERNEST W. GROVE, U.S. Department of Agriculture

The principal theme of some papers at this conference has been a *non sequitur:* There is a tremendous need for elaboration of the national accounts in various directions; therefore it can and should be done. Olson's paper is in this by now highly respected tradition. He recognizes many obstacles in the way of his various proposals for measuring government output or the demand for government services, but he remains an incorrigible optimist nevertheless. His analysis of the problem of efficiency in government is good as far as it goes, but his suggested solutions are just another stab in the continued dark.

The much and justifiably abused PPB system provides Olson's starting point, but he concludes that "it is perhaps the principal achievement of the PPB system that it has sensitized governments to the need to evaluate the level of public outputs"—a thoroughly backhanded compliment at this late date. Defense Department origins of PPB are noted—but not the most notorious fiasco in attempting to measure "government output," the infamous "body count" in Vietnam. When first instituted, the "body count" system doubtless had much logic (of a sort) in back of it. What better measure could there be of a soldier's work performance?

But inevitably, after a while, it no longer mattered what "bodies" were being counted, and the GI and his officers were given a bad time if bodies were not produced.

This is quite typical of the way the PPB system has worked since it was forcibly and inflexibly foisted on all government departments in 1965. The result was a triumph of technique over purpose, and a tremendous burgeoning of new jobs and unnecessary work. It is impossible to disagree with the basic principles underlying the PPB system; the problem arises in their practical application, as all kinds of cooked-up statistics, fudged or invented data, and other necessary subterfuges are likely to arise when basically sound principles are indiscriminately applied to all areas of government activity. And George Jaszi was right when he said that impractical theory has to be bad theory.

Olson argues, without any substantial evidence, that even "fragmentary and approximate information" on government output could bring about substantial improvements in efficiency. And he states that such "fragments of information," even though "rather inaccurate," would "give agencies and bureaucrats a reason to be as efficient as they can be." But how would this approach differ from the present PPB system, now applied throughout government and very largely a failure? We already have things like "Operations Evaluation and Improvement Divisions" and "Offices of Management Improvement," but they are little more than window dressing and completely under the thumbs of management types now running the government.

The question must be raised, therefore, as to who would collect this fragmentary and probably inaccurate information. It would be available in many cases only in field offices of the agencies, so it should logically be collected by the agencies themselves—as is now the case! Does Olson believe that agency managements would be unable or unwilling to insure that only favorable information came to light? Or, on the other hand, does he believe that, if such information were to be collected by an outside and independent agency, there would be no danger of creating a Gestapo, USA?

Emphasizing the carrot instead of the stick, Olson further states that "it is surely possible to multiply rewards for fragments of favorable information to some extent, and thus to create a large incentive for efficiency with a small amount of information." This is not at all certain; in fact, it is most unlikely. The present incentive awards system is close to bankruptcy because of favoritism and image-building. Published dollar totals of "savings" as a result of accepted suggestions are considerably less than honest. And if Olson would choose to administer his "rewards" from somewhere outside the agency, the problems would be different but no less serious.

The proposal for "price exclusion on an experimental or sampling basis" is interesting but quite unrealistic. How long would it take to persuade the Congress to approve that kind of operation? The development of "social indicators" is a more practical proposal, but the inherent imprecision of such indicators would take administrators off the hook and negate the whole purpose. And the measurement of government output through controlled experiments or statistical model building is not considered promising even by Olson. So he winds up with the suggestion that we "prohibit inbreeding in bureaucracy!" This is a good proposal, of course, but it is comparable to support for home and mother. Much more to the point would be Ralph Nader's proposal that professional employees in government develop "an ethic of whistle-blowing" so as to keep their wrongheaded superiors in line.[1]

It is just about impossible to measure most aspects of government output, and this reckons without consideration of the many negative aspects of such output. Production may not be what was intended, but something totally different—and quite undesirable. It follows that, although measurement of government output would enable us to solve some problems, government inefficiency is actually based on something much more fundamental—the bureaucratic organization itself.

There is a growing body of opinion which argues that our burgeoning technical and organizational structures have become the main source of evil in our society, and that, to correct this situation, ordinary rank-and-file employees should be given—or should simply take on their own initiative—many more rights and much more responsibility than they now have. The whole purpose of organizational structures in government is to reduce—or even eliminate—the human element in all relations with the citizenry. So we have universal specialization, divided responsibilities—even thoroughly fragmented in some cases—an elaborate hierarchy of supervision and rigidly specified and pyramidal organization charts. The result has been that both general inefficiency in government agencies and grossly negative outputs, which are all too common, "have less to do with the malice of individuals than with unexamined and unquestioned institutional practices"—and with the universal Eichmann syndrome "wherein individual motives, consciences, or

[1] See Philip M. Boffey, "Nader and the Scientists: A Call for Responsibility," *Science,* Vol. 171, 1971, pp. 549–551.

goals become irrelevant in the context of organizational behaviors." [2]

Giving ordinary government employees more responsibility would not be likely to improve the measurement of government output, but it would almost surely guarantee that some of the more grossly negative outputs would not continue indefinitely, as they do now, and it might even improve routine efficiency as a result of greater involvement by rank-and-file employees. As Nader has pointed out, "it is difficult for outsiders to monitor" large bureaucracies, so that any significant improvement is probably dependent on insiders accepting some responsibility. Nader feels that such insiders, especially the professional employee, should feel a "duty to dissent," preferably with this duty "protected by an organization of his peers, by his professional society, and by law that requires due process and substantive justice." [3]

This is the general direction in which improvements in government efficiency must be sought. Little if any progress can be expected if efforts are confined to the scattered and narrowly technical tracks laid out by Olson.

REPLY by Olson

I

It is clear, despite his gentle and disarming style, that Charles Schultze thinks that one of the fundamental conceptual points in my paper is wrong. Though we agree on a great many questions, and seem to see the applications and practical issues in much the same way, he contends that my initial and basic argument—that there is another systematic cause of inefficiency in the provision of public goods distinct from the concealment of preferences problem—is erroneous.

I have found Schultze's comment extraordinarily helpful. It has certainly stimulated and advanced my thinking on this subject. In addition, it has allayed my initial uneasiness that my basic conceptual point, even if neglected in the literature, was already familiar to most leading specialists, and my concern that my initial point was so simple as to be obvious. If such a leader in this area of inquiry as Charles

---

[2] See Matthew P. Dumont, "Down the Bureaucracy!" *Trans-Action,* October 1970, pp. 10–14. Dumont goes on to state that inefficiency and inhumanity "can be seen in pure culture in . . . the men and women who buzz out their lives in the spaces defined by the United States government" (p. 10).

[3] Boffey, *op. cit.,* p. 549.

Schultze thinks my basic conceptual point is wrong, it is hardly likely that that point is generally taken for granted in the profession. Nor can the point be as obvious as I once thought: it is simple, certainly, but that is not the same as being obvious.

Useful and intelligent as Schultze's comment is, it is not technically correct. Nor is its critical conclusion valid. To show this, however, it is necessary to go into some important questions which I possibly should not have taken for granted in my paper.

Since this is an area in which questions have to be posed very precisely, it will be well to make clear one point that is *not* in dispute, even though that requires repetition of a point already stated in my paper, namely, that the lack of revealed preferences is indeed part of the problem of attaining efficiency in the provision of collective goods. The paper distributed to the conference said this quite explicitly, among other places, at the beginning of section IV. Since this passage (and others like it) apparently lack the prominence they should have had in the original paper, I quote it again here:

One cause of inefficiency in the provision of collective goods is familiar from the theoretical writings in welfare economics and public finance, but rarely mentioned in the PPB or cost-benefit literature. That is the difficulty of getting consumers to reveal their preferences concerning a collective good or externality, and preferences must of course be known to determine how much it is optimal to provide.

Since the problem of the revelation of preferences will normally be present only when nonpurchasers cannot be excluded, and such non-exclusion is also necessary to the additional cause of inefficiency that my paper introduced, it is often true that when preferences are revealed, both problems tend to be cleared up. As I have only lately come to realize, the fact that the possibility of exclusion will usually clear up not only the revelation of preferences problem but also the further source of inefficiency my paper explained makes that further source of inefficiency more difficult to understand. Yet, as we shall see, my further source of inefficiency can be solved in the production of certain goods when the preferences of consumers are not known, and can also remain unsolved when they are, so that the two sources of inefficiency are demonstrably distinct.

Charles Schultze and I are also in agreement, I think, about the importance of incentives—no amount of information about outputs or anything else will be sufficient to bring efficiency if the relevant actors do not have incentives to be efficient. At the same time, I see no reason to change the view expressed in my paper, that it is impossible to set up incentive systems that will reward efficiency unless there is enough information about output as well as inputs to distinguish efficiency from inefficiency; you can't reward efficiency until you can find out who deserves the rewards.

II

Part of the difficulty arises because too little attention is usually given to distinguishing the different stages of production and their different relationships to the choices of consumers or governments. Charles Schultze is probably rather typical in comparing the tank and the car as though the former were a public good and the latter a private good: The car, related to consumer satisfaction, plays the same role as the tank related to national defense. "We can count cars and we can count tanks. We can go further and provide physical measures of a host of other characteristics of a car and a tank." But in the case of the car we get a measure of output from the price consumers are willing to pay for this complex collection of characteristics.

In fact, both the tank and the car are of course private goods. There is nothing about a tank which makes it impossible, or even expensive, to exclude those who do not purchase the tank from getting it. And there is of course an international market in tanks and other armaments, albeit one in which most of the buyers and some of the sellers are governments. Defense is a collective good, but it is one which is normally produced with the aid of a wide variety of intermediate goods, most of which are private goods. In this respect, defense is like most other public goods: police departments purchase automobiles and patrolmen; public health agencies purchase doctors and vaccines, and so on. Public goods are of course sometimes also intermediate goods used in the production of private goods, as when government levees protect factories from flooding or public police protect factories from theft.

What has just been said is obvious, and does not of course tell Schultze or any other skilled economist anything he did not know before. The tendency to treat a tank as a public good is no doubt the result of a minor oversight or a casual mode of expression. There would be no need to touch upon any such oversight, but for the fact that in this case this inadvertence is intimately tied up with a far more important difficulty.

III

This more important difficulty arises from the neglect of the distinction between feasibility of prices and markets in general and the special problem of the concealment of preferences. My paper argued that there was a special problem of output measurement with public goods distinct from that due to any tendency for preference to be concealed, but never denied that prices were needed even to attain technical efficiency—which, to repeat the paper, is conventionally defined as a situation such that no more of one output can be attained without getting less of another. Prices are indeed very important to the attainment of technical efficiency. Schultze implies at diverse points in his comment that the problem of the revelation of preference is a sufficient general explanation of the difficulty of pricing public goods (and private intermediate goods used in the production of public goods). Consider the following passage from his comment:

> Olson also discusses the desirability of contracting out certain operations of the Defense Department. He uses as an example contracting out basic pilot training. But to do this, the Air Force would clearly have to spell out the output it wanted from the contractor. In turn, defining output could not be done simply in terms of the number of pilots turned out. The proficiency of pilots is relevant, as is the time span of the training and the auxiliary skills acquired. Somehow these and other important aspects of pilot training would have to be taken into account and weighted by Air Force "values" in order to draw up a contract.

> More generally in the case of the Defense Department, there is much inefficiency in the procurement of physical weapons systems produced under private contract. This inefficiency stems from many reasons but two are most important: (1) the inability of the Department to settle on the "value" to it of the myriad physical characteristics going into a weapons system, as a consequence of which design changes, production interruptions, and redesign problems are legion and (2) the inability to devise real incentives for procurement officers and higher decisionmakers to care enough about unit costs.

Much the same lumping together of the problem of revelation of preferences and the pricing problem was evident in Schultze's previous comment, paraphrased earlier, about tanks and cars.

Schultze's emphasis on the complexity of goods like pilots, tanks, and automobiles is extremely useful. A great many goods obviously have many different characteristics, and thus cannot adequately be measured in terms of any single physical quantity. But Schultze's conviction that the existence of such complexity negates or limits my argument seems to grow out of his tendency to derive the difficulty of getting market prices entirely from the concealment of consumer preferences for public goods.

In fact, the lack of a market price for output is easily distinguishable from the problems caused by the concealment of preferences: first, because it is often possible and useful to have market prices for many outputs even when consumer preferences are not known, and second, because, as my paper argued, it is sometimes impossible to get a market value or other measure of output of a good for reasons that do not derive from any concealment of preferences.

The first reason why the concealment of preferences problem and the lack of market prices problem are distinct can be demonstrated by taking a situation in which consumer preferences are not known, and demonstrating that prices could still be useful, in that they could put the individuals in the economy on a higher point on their (unknown) indifference maps. Assume an economy such as is depicted in Figure 1, which produces two private goods, x and y, subject to the constraint imposed by the production possibility frontier that is shown. Though the indifference maps are not known, I assume that they are smooth, convex to the origin, and do not intersect. Both x and y are always goods to everyone in the society: it is always better to have more of x and y than less.

Now assume a dictator in this economy who does not care about consumer preferences and thus does not bother to establish the markets

FIGURE 1

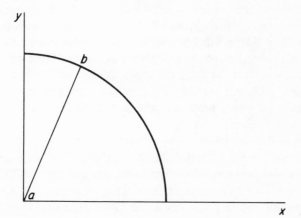

in consumer goods x and y that would reveal information about these preferences. He randomly chooses some mix of goods x and y which all consumers receive for free and are not allowed to sell or supplement. The dictator, however, shares the view that x and y are both goods and strives to organize the economy in such a way as to produce and distribute as large an output as possible. That is, he strives to attain the technical efficiency that my paper dealt with. If the capricious dictator chooses a mix of goods involving, say, two units of y for every unit of x, consumers would necessarily consume some bundle of goods along the line ab, and the dictator because of his belief that more of this mix of goods was better than less would strive to get the economy to produce at point b.

One thing that would have to be done to reach point b is that, in the absence of external effects, every firm or government enterprise that produced both x and y would have to have the same marginal private rate of transformation of x and y. The proof of this is simply that, if more x could be obtained by giving up a unit of y in one firm than in another, more output could be obtained by shifting the production of x toward the first firm and the production of y toward the second. This marginal private rate of transformation is given by the slope of the production possibility frontier at point b, and any firm which could transform x into y, but produces only x, must be able to produce more x per unit of y than this, whereas the converse must be true for enterprises that produce only y.

Another necessary condition for reaching point b, or technical efficiency, is given in Figure 2. This familiar figure assumes fixed endowments of factors of production K and L, given respectively by the lengths of the horizontal and vertical sides of the box in the figure, and the production functions for firms A and B are given by the isoquants arranged in the familiar Edgeworth box fashion. It is immediately obvious that production cannot be maximized except along the locus of points cd. This reminds us that, as even the more elementary textbooks explain, the marginal technical rate of substitution of any pair of factors must be the same for every producer who uses both factors if there is to be technical efficiency.

As long as the allocation of the bundles of x and y among the individuals in the society (i.e., the distribution of income) is not changed, and all of the x and y produced is distributed, we can be sure that welfare is higher at point b than at any point beneath it on line ab. This is true, notwithstanding the fact that consumer tastes are not revealed and did

FIGURE 2

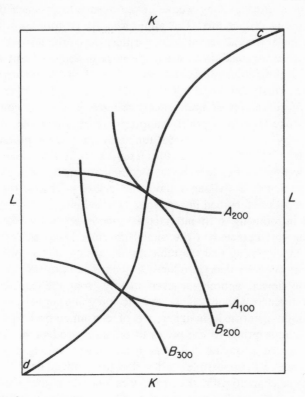

Firm B

Firm A

not influence the bundle of consumer goods chosen, because the assumption that indifference curves portray rational consumers for whom x and y are goods, and the assumption that the distribution of income is not changed, insure that every consumer is better off at point b than at any lower point along line ab.

The gains in welfare that come from attaining technical efficiency in this situation could in principle be got by using prices to guide the allocation of production and inputs among enterprises. Indeed, if a bureaucratic mechanism could somehow attain technical efficiency, it could naturally do so only by duplicating what an ideal price system for producers and inputs for this situation would do. An xy price ratio for producers given by the slope of the production possibility curve at point *b* could allocate production efficiently among maximizing enterprises and insure that they would in the aggregate produce the (arbitrarily chosen) output mix. The appropriate price for inputs could insure that they were allocated among enterprises producing *x* and *y* in such a way as to maximize output, because maximizing enterprises in the absence of external effects and monopoly will, as Schultze's comment points out, satisfy the condition that $MP_K/MP_L = W_K/W_L$. In short, the lack of revelation of preferences assumed in the foregoing model does not make the use of prices inappropriate or impossible: [1] prices of producer goods can fulfill a useful function in a society producing private goods, even when consumer preferences are not revealed.

The relevance of this to Schultze's comment can be demonstrated by considering Schultze's passages about the lack of prices for the complex of characteristics embodied in a privately trained military pilot or a tank, and then introducing such intermediate goods explicitly into a situation of the sort depicted in the model developed above. Schultze was mistaken in supposing that the difficulty of putting an appropriate price on different pilots or tanks produced by contractors for the Department of Defense flowed entirely or even mainly from the concealment of voters' preferences about defense. As the foregoing model makes clear, there is nothing intrinsic in ignorance of consumer preferences which makes it inappropriate to use prices to organize production. Schultze is of course correct in saying that some goods have a variety of characteristics that make it impossible to describe them adequately in terms of one physical characteristic. But this does *not* mean that the concealment of consumer preferences is necessarily the problem; inputs or producer goods, however complex they might be, can often usefully be priced in markets, even if consumer tastes for the final goods they are used to produce are not known. If there are two alternative intermediate goods with many different features, they can be traded in free markets for such producer goods, where they will command prices that depend particularly upon their respective marginal productivities and marginal costs (and also to some degree on the mix of final goods that we assume was arbitrarily chosen in the absence of knowledge of con-

---

[1] Critics may reasonably object that my oversimplified model leaves out the heroic administrative task of keeping consumers from buying and selling *x* and *y*, and reflects the uncertainty about the level of supply of inputs when the relation of consumer income to input supply is not specified, and abstracts from many other problems. But these difficulties have nothing to do with the point at issue with Schultze.

sumer tastes). There is nothing inherent in an ignorance of consumer preferences that makes it impossible to attain *technical* efficiency with markets in which complex intermediate goods fetch different prices. There is nothing, for example, in the Soviet neglect of the preferences of final consumers that requires that the nail factories Schultze talked about must not produce that producer good for markets in which construction enterprises would be the buyers. Such markets could readily deal with the problem of the factory that makes nails of a type that no builder can use.

We can now turn to the second difficulty with Schultze's lack of a distinction between the feasibility of prices and the concealment of preferences. This arises from the theoretical possibility that preferences could be honestly revealed, even when outputs would not be known and market prices would not be useful for the allocation of resources. This second difficulty can most simply be seen by imagining the development of a truth serum that could be used to insure that every citizen would provide honest and complete information about his marginal rate of substitution between "national security"—say, to simplify, the probability of being victim of an enemy attack—and other goods. Even with this utopian information about citizen preferences, it would not be possible to determine an optimal defense policy or defense budget, because of the argument set out in my paper for the conference. Defense is a public good and we don't know what quantity of defense results from a given defense budget; we don't know whether a larger defense budget will deter an attack or provoke an arms race, whether antiballistic missiles will be effective or not, whether it is better to use tanks or Maginot lines, to carry a big stick or to sign a nonaggression pact. We do not, in short, know the production function for the collective good of national security, so that beliefs about that production function rest as much upon ideology and fashion as upon empirical estimation. Because the production function for the public good of national security is not known, it will not, as my paper pointed out, even be possible to rely entirely on markets and contracts. When the quantity of output is not known, there is no way to determine when a contractor has appropriately fulfilled his contract, or to measure the marginal productivity of a particular input or intermediate good.

IV

The value of any good to the consumer obviously depends on two things: how much or how many units of the good he consumes; and the value or price he puts on each unit. It is not possible to say that the total value of the good to the consumer equals price times quantity, since he may value intramarginal units more than the marginal unit, but the total value of a good is plainly a function of the worth he puts on each of the units of the good he consumes and on the number of units.

Paul Samuelson argued in his famous articles on public goods that it followed from the very nature of these goods that those who received or consumed them could have an incentive to conceal the true value or price they would attach to marginal units of the good. Since the government would then be ignorant of even the relevant portions of the consumers' or citizens' utility functions, and thus of the value or price it should attribute to additional units of the collective good, it could not know how much of the collective good it was optimal to provide.

My paper for this conference accepted Samuelson's point that the government often cannot determine what *price* consumers would be able to pay for additional units of a collective good, and went on to say that it also followed from a defining characteristic of public goods that the government also could not straightforwardly determine what *quantity* or volume of output of the collective good it was supplying. The indivisibility of most collective goods—the fact that they are consumed by groups—entails that there cannot be so many experiments to test the consequences for consumers (the final output) with these goods as with private goods. This suggests that the government is not only, as Samuelson pointed out, going to know less about the utility function of consumers of public goods, but it is also going to know less about the production function for these goods than it would if it were producing private goods. This means it is more difficult to attain technical efficiency in the production of public goods.

Schultze argues in his comment that I was wrong in thinking there is any systematic tendency of the sort I put forth that makes it more difficult to measure the quantity of output of public than of private goods, and he holds that the concealment of preferences for public goods is sufficient to explain the lack of information about the output of public goods that I was writing about.

One way to test whether Samuelson's concealment of preferences is sufficient to explain the lack of information about the output of public goods is to consider real types of cases of public good production in which preferences are not concealed. If the ignorance about the level of output that I allege occurs is not then evident, Schultze is proved right and I am proved wrong, but if it is, Schultze is wrong and I am right.

Happily, the case of public intermediate goods offers a test. These are goods that facilitate production or lower costs for business firms, but which at the same time have the indivisibility or nonpurchasers-can't-be-excluded defining characteristic that I have emphasized. As Richard Musgrave and others have pointed out, the government can find out what the preferences for a public intermediate good are, because its worth to the recipients is obviously given by its effect on profits. Though there is no operational way to ascertain the consumer's utility function if he has no incentive to reveal his preferences, the estimation of the production function poses no comparable epistemological problem. The value of a given reduction in larceny to a warehouse company, for example, can readily be estimated from the dollar value of the given reduction in loss from the thefts.

Is there any special problem in determining the output of public intermediate goods that have the indivisibility property? Indeed there is. Take, for example, the value of police services to business firms. Whereas what a given reduction in the incidence of specified crimes would be worth to a business can be estimated relatively accurately, the effect of a given change in the policies or expenditures of a police department on the level of crime cannot be determined straightforwardly, if it can be determined at all. The crime rate depends not only on police policy and expenditure, but also on housing patterns, street lighting, family stability, income distribution, unemployment rates, educational policies, racial conflict, correctional policies, community attitudes, geographical migration, age distribution, and even the weather, not to mention other variables we cannot now specify with any confidence. I know of no single study that has accurately estimated the marginal productivity of police expenditures in the production function for crime control.[2] Many other examples of situations where the concealment of preferences problem does not exist, but where there are horrendous problems of output measurement, can readily be found.

The reason there is a special problem in measuring the output of public goods, even when preferences are not concealed, can best be seen by contrasting the information a consumer can get about public goods with the information he can get when deciding whether to buy a private good. The rational consumer or citizen who must decide whether to support or oppose candidates advocating a larger or smaller expenditure on a given public good must make some guess about the production

[2] See Belton M. Fleisher, *The Economics of Delinquency*, Chicago, Quadrangle, 1966, to get an impression of the difficulty of the econometric problem at issue.

function by which that public good is produced; he must estimate the impact more police or defense expenditures, for example, will have on the likelihood he will be a victim of a crime or that the country will be conquered (and then go on to decide what price he attaches to that). Though I have emphasized that very little is known about the production function for most collective goods, the citizen at issue (or those experts or officials on whose judgment he may choose to rely) has that slight degree of information that comes from comparing the history of expenditures on a given collective good with the apparent state of affairs—he can compare the crime rate or national security of high spending periods with that of low spending periods. He can also make comparisons with foreign governments or jurisdictions with different allocations, always somehow trying to allow for the many other variables that also determine the level of national security or crime rates or whatever. From this sort of judgment something may be learned (as, for example, that *extremely* militaristic nations usually perish by the sword). A government can also increase or decrease its level of spending on a collective good in the hope of getting more information in this way (e.g., in defense try either pacifism or a militarist solution), though experiments of this kind can of course be profoundly costly.

The consumer of a private service can also get more information by taking more or less of the private service over time and also by drawing on the experience of others. He can try to hire a housekeeper for a fewer or a greater number of hours to see what difference it makes and he can also get references from friends; he can try the restaurant or read what the food critic or other "consumer report" has to say. The situation at first glance seems much the same as for the public good.

But there is one profound difference affecting the information about the production function. Since a collective good by definition goes to a whole nation or group, all of whose members must take more or less of the good together, there can be only one experiment for each nation or community or catchment area for a public good. If, for example, an inoculation against a contagious disease is at issue, the question may arise whether 25, 50, or 90 per cent of the community has to be inoculated to eliminate the disease. If there is no international travel and migration, each comparable country may have a different policy, and some experimental evidence can conceivably be obtained in this way, but not much. The number of possible experiments is fewer, and the cost of each of them is greater, because the good is a public good.

But each individual can by definition take more or less of a private good or service to see what output he is in fact getting. For a nationwide service such as is offered by Avis, Hilton, or MacDonald's, there are literally millions of experiments to determine what these service firms really offer. It may even pay a "consumer reports" firm to sell the results of its experiments to the consumers. Because collective goods go by definition to a group, and because private goods can by definition be taken in greater or lesser amounts by individuals, societies systematically have more information about the quantity or volume of output of the latter than the former. This is what Charles Schultze has denied; so his comment (though unusually suggestive and helpful) is in this most fundamental respect altogether mistaken.

Measuring Performance in Education

ALICE M. RIVLIN

THE BROOKINGS INSTITUTION

THIS is supposed to be a practical conference dealing with national accounts and how to make them more useful. An early communication from the planning committee stated that the purpose of the conference was "to provide specific suggestions for changes in the existing accounts with an eye toward making the accounts more useful as measures of economic and social performance as well as increasing their analytical usefulness." In this context, my specific assignment is to discuss the measurement of performance in education.

It seems to me important to take a broad view of "national accounts" and to recognize that the present national income and product accounts are only one set of a large number of possible accounts which would be useful for various purposes. There is no point in plunging into endless wrangles about what should be included in GNP or national income (should nonmarket activities be included? what about the use of leisure time?). While some changes in the national income and product accounts may be in order, the really interesting questions relate, not to changing the present accounts, but to supplementing them. The problem is not so much to expose what is wrong with the GNP, but to decide what *other* information we need to collect on a regular and sustained basis, and how this new information can be linked to that already in the national accounts.

Similarly, it seems to me useful to take a broad view of "education" and allow for subcategories within it. Broadly speaking, education is "imparting skill and knowledge." Many different activities could come under this general heading, and there is no point in fussing over exactly what should be included (is television education? is on-the-job training education?). For some purposes, it is useful to focus on regular class-

NOTE: The views expressed in this article are those of the author and do not represent the views of other staff members, officers, or trustees of The Brookings Institution. The author is indebted to Edward Denison, Charles Schultze, and Robert Hartman for comments on an earlier draft.

room instruction. For others, it is useful to include other activities that produce skill and knowledge. What is needed is a detailed and flexible series of accounts that will allow the user to add up the various boxes as he sees fit.

OBJECTIVES OF NATIONAL ACCOUNTS

One would hope that a good set of national accounts would help to answer three types of questions: where is it going; how are we doing; and how can we do better.

Where-is-it-going questions. It is clearly useful—if one wants to understand the economy—to know where the national output is coming from and what is happening to it. How is total output allocated between consumption and investment, or among the factors of production? How much is being produced in various sectors of the economy? The income and product accounts provide a basis for examining the allocation of production and resources in the market sector of the economy. For many purposes, it is also useful to know how nonmarket production is allocated and how the nation uses its time.

Since education is now recognized not only as a major economic activity, but also as an important form of investment, one might hope for subtotals in the national accounts that would give a sense of the relative importance of education in the national productive effort. What proportion of national output is devoted to education? How much investment takes the form of education? How much education is produced in the business or government or household sectors? How much time is used for education?

How-are-we-doing questions. The second set of questions on which national accounts should shed light are those of particular interest to this conference—how the system is performing over time. It is clearly useful to correct for price changes in order to find out if total output is rising and how fast. It is useful to relate the outputs to the inputs—to measure productivity—and to determine how fast the nation is adding to its stock of capital. One might hope, in this connection, that national accounts would tell us something about performance in education. Is the real output of the education industry rising? Is it rising faster than the inputs? How rapidly is educational activity adding to the stock of human capital?

How-can-we-do-better questions. The most important use of national accounts is as input to models designed to explain how the economy works and to provide clues to improving its performance. The most obvious use is to discover relationships between aggregates, such as total income, investment, consumption, or employment. One might, however, want to use national accounts data as input to disaggregated models designed, for example, to throw light on the way the education sector interacts with the rest of the economy. One might hope to find in the national accounts information that would be useful in answering such questions as: Would national output be increased by devoting more resources (or less) to education or by shifting resources from one kind of education to another? How would shifts in the education sector affect employment or productivity or price levels?

This paper will focus on these three sets of questions in turn, examine the extent to which they can be answered by the existing income and product accounts, and explore what else might be useful.

WHERE-IS-IT-GOING QUESTIONS

Education—whether broadly or narrowly defined—is a challenge to national accountants. It is a service, not a good; it is partly consumption and partly investment; the consumption is partly immediate, and partly spread over time like consumer durables; it is produced by business enterprise and by households, as well as by government; it is partly produced outside the market altogether. At best, it takes a lot of arbitrary decisions to devise an accounting system to answer even the simplest where-is-it-going questions: How much of national product is devoted to education? How much of national income originates in the education industry?

The first thing one notices in examining the present income and product accounts to see how they treat education is that "education" is hard to find. It would be useful—now that there is such interest in the education sector—for the government to publish some regular tables breaking out both expenditures for education and income originating in the "education industry."

If one tries to do this from the currently published statistics, one encounters some anomalies of the national accounts; for example, the different treatment of public and private educational institutions that would seem to the casual observer to be doing exactly the same thing.

Suppose that a private university becomes a branch of the state university system. Even if there is no change in enrollment or expenditures, there will be changes in the national accounts. In the national income account, income originating in education will drop because interest paid by the government is excluded from the national accounts. The rationale for excluding government interest payments "stems, as a practical matter, from the fact that the bulk of government debt was created to finance

TABLE 1

Enrollment in Elementary and Secondary Schools and in
Institutions of Higher Education, Public and Private,
1950, 1970, and 1980

	Enrollment (millions)		Percentage Public
	Public	Private	
Elementary and secondary education			
1950	24.0	3.2	88.2
1970	45.6	5.7	88.9
1980 (projected)	45.6	5.4	89.4
Higher education			
1950	1.4	1.3	51.9
1970	5.3	2.0	72.6
1980 (projected)	8.7	2.4	78.4

SOURCE: U.S. Office of Education, *Digest of Educational Statistics, 1969,* 1970, 1950 data, Table 3, p. 3; U.S. Office of Education, *Projections of Educational Statistics to 1979–80,* 1971, 1970 and 1980 data, Table 3, p. 20, and Table 12, p. 29.

wars and current expenditures." [1] If one is primarily interested in the federal level, this rationale carries some weight, but at the state and local level, where almost all public education occurs, wars are not fought and debt financing bears a much closer relationship to capital outlays.

The magnitudes involved are not huge, but neither are they entirely insignificant. For example, for public elementary and secondary schools in 1968–69, interest on school debt was about $1.0 billion out of total expenditures of $35.5 billion. [2]

In recent decades, enrollment in public education has grown considerably faster than in private education, especially at the college and university level. As education has become more public, the relative importance of the excluded costs has increased and the growth of education relative to other sectors of the economy has been correspondingly understated. The projections shown in Table 1 anticipate continued growth in the proportion of students in public institutions. On the other

[1] U.S. Department of Commerce, *National Income,* 1954 edition (A Supplement to the *Survey of Current Business*), p. 35.

[2] U.S. Department of Health, Education and Welfare, *Digest of Educational Statistics,* 1969 edition, p. 52.

hand, new developments such as widespread adoption of Friedman-type voucher plans might shift large numbers of students from the public to the private sector without any change in the resources devoted to education. It clearly makes little sense to treat the costs of public and private educational institutions differently in the national accounts.

Some other possible real world events suggest some more serious questions about the completeness of the present accounts. Suppose, for example, that a corporation (or a group of corporations) induces the government to set up a public vocational school which reduces the corporation's need to engage in on-the-job training. Trainees, who were being paid—partly to work and partly to learn—now become unpaid students.

In the national accounts, such an event would show up as a decrease in factor payments by the industry in question and an increase in resources devoted to education. The increase in education, however, is likely to be less than the drop in industry factor payments because the earnings of trainees show up in the national accounts while the foregone earnings of students do not. The potential for shifts from vocational schooling to on-the-job training or vice versa is quite large and it would be useful to be able to see more clearly in the accounts what shifts are occurring.

Or suppose a group of mothers starts a cooperative nursery school, charging tuition and paying themselves salaries as part-time teachers. This event would increase the income originating in education as reported in the national accounts since the educational services of mothers show up in the accounts only if they are paid salaries. The actual amount of time the mothers spent "educating" their children, however, might not increase, indeed is likely to decrease.

The current potential for this kind of shift is very large. In 1968, only 4 million of the 12 million three- to five-year-olds in the country were enrolled in school. The current push for day care and preschool could easily put an additional 4 million children into formal programs partially financed by the government and largely staffed by their mothers. An expenditure of $1,500 per child (cheap for a full-day educational program) would increase reported educational outlays by $6 billion, perhaps half or more of which would involve substitution of paid for unpaid instruction by the same mothers.

Finally, suppose a cable television network starts a "university of the air" with a broad curriculum of courses. Some people who would ordinarily have attended regular schools and colleges begin taking these courses instead. (A procedure may be established for awarding them degrees by examination.) In this case, factor costs of education reported in the national accounts would fall and factor payments in the radio and television industry would rise, unless education became the principal activity of the establishments in the network.

If one were looking at the expenditure side of the accounts, an even odder thing would happen. The expenditures for education would fall, but the compensating increase would be spread over other products, because commercial television is treated as an intermediate product which only shows up in the prices of products made by enterprises that purchase advertising.

The potential for substituting wide varieties of nontraditional education (home courses on cable television or TV cassettes, schools without walls, external degrees, etc.) for traditional education appears to be very great, given the advance of technology and the general dissatisfaction with traditional education. The result could be a vast increase in the amount of resources, including leisure, devoted to genuine learning that would not show up in the national accounts as presently constituted.

The treatment of these rather common events in the national accounts are often regarded as "yes" or "no" decisions involving either difficult distinctions between what is or is not education (when is television "educational"?) or difficult decisions about the inclusion or exclusion of non-market costs (student time, mothers' services) or both. Those arguing against inclusion often invoke a *reductio ad absurdum* argument, alleging that the inclusion of a particular item or a particular cost, while logical for the purpose at hand, would necessarily involve—for consistency's sake—a whole series of decisions of highly questionable utility. Inclusion of mothers' time spent educating preschoolers or students' time would involve including other kinds of unpaid activities in the GNP (do-it-yourself hobbies and volunteer work), would blur the distinction between work and leisure, and might even lead to the inclusion of leisure time in the national accounts. Similarly, they argue that including educational TV in "education" would lead to including all TV and radio and books and magazines and records and all kinds of other activities that are not really educational—once one leaves the classroom there is no stopping.

But these arguments reflect the notions that (1) there must be unique classifications for each type of activity, and (2) the parts must add to a single number that accurately reflects fluctuations in economic activity over time, presumably the GNP. These notions were appropriate to an era of meager statistical information and limited computer capacity when it was hard enough to set up *one* reasonable set of classifications and fill in the boxes, and impossible to allow for multiple classifications and the possibility of adding the same item into the accounts in several alternative ways at the whim of the user. The assumptions were also appropriate when the accounts were primarily used as a measure of the fluctuation of aggregate economic activity in the market sector. Imputations and allowances for nonmarket activity just fuzzed up the numbers and masked the fluctuations of real interest to the users.

But in the 1970s, these assumptions need no longer hold. Statistical information about the economy is more plentiful and still increasing. Computers are easily able to handle multiple classifications, to show users the consequences of classifying the same activity in different ways, even to warn the user when he is double-counting or being inconsistent. Moreover, interest in national accounts no longer centers so heavily on the business cycle and aggregate activity in the market sector, but now arises partly out of interest in the way total resources are allocated among more specific market and nonmarket activities. It seems to be time for a more flexible and detailed system of accounts.

The new accounting framework proposed by the Ruggles is a step in the right direction.[3] The Ruggles divide the economy into three sectors: enterprise, households, and government. "Enterprise" includes nonprofit institutions. A consolidated income and product account would be constructed for the three sectors together and separate income and outlay accounts for each of the three sectors. Capital consumption and capital formation would be estimated for each of the three sectors in comparable terms. Moreover, "development expenditures" (education, training, research) would be estimated for each sector and shown as capital formation. To complement this change, imputed income from past development expenditures would be broken out. Subtotals for "education" could easily be shown in the income and product account (income originating in the education industry, capital consumption in the education industry) and in the income and outlay accounts for the three sectors (development expenditures on education by households, government, and enterprises; and imputed income from past development expenditures in education).

Although it would be difficult to make many of these estimates, the Ruggles system appears to provide a better framework for answering

[3] Nancy Ruggles and Richard Ruggles, *The Design of Economic Accounts*, New York, National Bureau of Economic Research, 1970.

where-is-it-going questions involving education in the economy than present accounts. It would provide a continuous series of estimates answering the questions: What part of national income originates in the education industry? How large is capital consumption in the education industry? What part of national product is devoted to capital formation in the form of education outlays by government, households, or enterprises?

The problem of defining "education" would remain. A flexible series of definitions would be possible—user's choice—under which, say, educational television or on-the-job training could be defined in or out of "education" as the interest of the user dictated. Similarly, nonmarket costs of education, such as mothers' and students' time, which the Ruggles do not include, could be estimated but included in totals only when it seemed useful to do so.

HOW-ARE-WE-DOING QUESTIONS

A one-shot or still-picture set of national accounts is useful, but even greater interest clearly attaches to changes over time, especially changes in real output.

In no sector of the economy is it easy to obtain a measure of real output. In the goods-producing sector where physical units can be counted the problem may seem easy at first glance, but becomes exceedingly difficult as soon as one begins to grapple with quality changes. The quality of almost all goods produced in the economy changes somewhat over time and for many goods the changes are rapid, continuous, and in several dimensions. Price deflators of goods as variable as toys or books or musical instruments are obviously extremely arbitrary. Measuring the output of services is also difficult, not only because quality varies, but because the unit of service is sometimes not obvious, and because, as Fuchs has pointed out, the customer himself often plays an important role in determining the quality of the service.[4]

In the case of government services which are given, not sold, to the public, the national accountant is at an even greater loss. The market does not place a value on these goods—there is no market price to deflate—so costs must be used as a measure of value. The tradition of national accounting is that costs are deflated by some measure of price changes in the input factors (wages, materials) to obtain measures of real output. Changes in productivity of the inputs are ruled out by definition.

[4] Victor Fuchs, assisted by Irving Leveson, *The Service Economy*, New York, National Bureau of Economic Research, 1968, p. 194.

In deflating the U.S. national accounts, education outlays are divided into three parts: payments to business, payments for construction, and payments to employees. Payments to business are deflated by using the most appropriate component of the wholesale price index. Payments for construction are deflated by using the Commerce Department's "building materials and construction index," adjusted for changing profit margins. Payments to employees—by far the largest education cost item—are deflated by an index of average wages in education. No attempt is made to adjust for shifts in the mix of employees—janitors, second grade teachers, and college presidents count the same—or for changes in the "quality" of specific types of employees. As Schultze points out, this highly aggregative approach could hide important shifts occurring within the education sector.[5] If colleges are expanding faster than elementary schools, average wages in education are likely to be rising because professors are paid more than elementary school teachers. A professor, however, represents "more educational input" than a second grade teacher, as valued by the market, in the same sense that a Cadillac represents "more car" than a Volkswagen. In this instance, deflating education costs by an aggregate wage index would tend to underestimate the shift in education input that was occurring. In principle, therefore, the national accounts could be improved by disaggregating education employment into more homogeneous categories, although in practice the adjustment may not make much difference.

No amount of disaggregation of inputs, however, will provide a basis for answering the how-are-we-doing questions in the education sector. As long as cost is used as a proxy for value there is no way to compare inputs with outputs or to see whether a given "amount" of education is being produced with fewer resources. It does not tell us anything about the impact of the education on the recipients and whether they are receiving more or less education than students in an earlier period. So the question arises: Are there better ways to measure output or performance in education?

Before this question is addressed, it should be noted that the difficulties of measuring the output of collective or indivisible goods, discussed at length in Mancur Olson's paper, do not seem especially important in education. There are two kinds of divisibility: divisibility of the good or service itself and divisibility of the benefits flowing from that good or service. The service "education" is not hard to divide into units—years,

---

[5] Charles L. Schultze, Comment on Mancur Olson, "Evaluating Performance in the Public Sector," in this volume.

hours, etc.—nor is it difficult to exclude potential customers from the acquisition of these units of education. Students can be excluded from Princeton or any other university by law, price, or entrance requirements. The private benefits that accrue to individuals from the acquisition of these units of education (better jobs, higher incomes, etc.) are likewise divisible. There may also, of course, be benefits of education that spill over to people who did not receive the education themselves. If education reduces crime, then the benefits of education go not only to the potential criminals who receive the education but to their potential victims as well. The size of these collective benefits relative to the private ones bears on the question of how education should be financed—to what extent potential victims should be taxed for subsidizing the education of potential criminals, for example—but the existence of collective benefits does not keep us from measuring how much of this service called education is actually being produced.

There are two principal reasons why measuring output in education is so difficult—both of which would remain if it were produced in the private market. First, the quality of education varies greatly and in many different dimensions. Second, the customer (the student) helps produce the education and the quality of the output is hard to disentangle from the customer's input.

It is not hard to think of plausible measures of output in education—the problem is choosing among them. At least six types of measures come readily to mind.

1. Body Counts

As a start, one might consider simply counting the number of customers served and using enrollment as a measure of output in education. But the customers are served in such widely different ways by various kinds and levels of education that one can only conclude there must be a better way of measuring output than simply counting the bodies passing through the system.

2. Student Exposure Measures

Part of the difficulty with body counts is that enrollees are exposed to varying amounts of education: The problem is particularly obvious in higher education where part-time students abound and even supposedly "full-time" students take different course loads. This problem can be alleviated by using a unit of student exposure, such as the credit hour, as a measure of output. This is the approach used by June O'Neill in a recent study of inputs and outputs in higher education.[6] One could conceive of extending O'Neill's approach by developing measures of student exposure at other levels of education. In elementary and secondary education, almost all students study "full-time" and for approximately the same number of hours a day, although the length of the school year varies. "Student days" might be a suitable exposure measure for grades 1 through 12. For preschool and vocational programs, one would have to adjust for varying school hours as well as varying numbers of days of exposure.

The trouble with exposure measures, of course, is that the hours or days to which students are exposed may differ greatly in quality and intensity. Students are served in larger or smaller groups (is a credit-hour in a class of 10 more valuable than a credit-hour in a class of 100?) and by teachers of varying skills and training, working with varying amounts of equipment and ancillary resources. One might, therefore, decide to derive a measure of "quality" or intensity of education which could be used to weight the exposure units. If one uses inputs as a measure of intensity of exposure, however, one is forced to derive weights for the importance of the various inputs. There is no obvious way of doing this except to use either their price or their cost. In education, price has no clear meaning because of the large subsidies, but one might construct a measure of educational output which weighted students (or credit-hours) by some measure of relative cost.

A weighted output measure in, say, higher education might classify students (or credit-hours) by the type of institution attended. The cost per student in each type would serve as weights on the assumption that relative cost roughly measures relative value.[7]

3. Student Attainment Measures

Exposure measures (whether or not weighted by cost) are still indexes of student time and other inputs to the education process, not of what the process produces or achieves. It would be preferable to have a true output measure. One possibility would be to accept the education system's own definition of output, and assume that a student who has

---

[6] June O'Neill, *Resource Use in Higher Education: Trends in Outputs and Inputs, 1930 to 1967*, Berkeley, Carnegie Commission on Higher Education, 1970, Chap. 2.

[7] For an attempt to do this, see *ibid.*, pp. 12–15 and 44–47, in which O'Neill adjusted student credit hours to reflect changes in levels of instruction (lower division, upper division, graduate) and type of institution, but found that the adjustment made little difference.

completed one level of education or has been promoted to the next level has given evidence of some kind of educational success.

Some have suggested using the proportion of students moving from one grade level to the next as a measure of output (or the proportion of students "left back" as a measure of nonsuccess). In the same spirit one might use high school graduations or college degrees as proxies for educational output.

In a country which had an elitist school system with uniformly high standards for promotion and graduation these measures might be defensible. In the United States, however, educational standards vary from high to nonexistent, and there is no reason to think that completions or graduates convey more information about output than body counts of enrollees. That the two move together may be seen in the comparison of degrees and enrollment in higher education in the 1960s presented in Table 2.

If one wants to take student intellectual achievement as the output of education, then —in the United States, at least—it will probably be more accurate to measure that achievement directly, rather than to use degrees or completions as proxies for it.

TABLE 2

A Comparison of Enrollment and Degrees in Higher Education, 1959–70

Academic Year	Enrollment (millions)	Degrees (millions)	Degrees as Percentage of Enrollment
1959–60	2.636	.389	15
1960–61	2.876	.395	14
1961–62	2.956	.414	14
1962–63	3.163	.444	15
1963–64	3.406	.494	15
1964–65	3.699	.530	14
1965–66	4.066	.551	14
1966–67	4.302	.591	14
1967–68	4.572	.667	15
1968–69	4.812	.764	16
1969–70	5.014	.784	15

SOURCE: U.S. Office of Education, *Projections of Educational Statistics to 1979–80*, 1971, Table 19, p. 36, and Table 21, p. 42.

4. Student Achievement Measures

If the purpose of education is to impart skills and knowledge to students, the most direct way to measure output is to measure those skills and knowledge. This reasoning suggests the use of test scores as proxies for output in education.

This is the age of testing. Considerable effort has gone into devising and standardizing a wide variety of tests of intellectual skills and accumulated knowledge. Billions of man-hours of student and teacher time are devoted to taking, administering, grading, analyzing, and discussing standardized tests. One might hope that all the effort would tell us something about output or performance in education.

Remarkably, almost no information presently exists which would give a basis for constructing an index of change in educational test scores over time. After shrill and sustained resistance to the idea from the school establishment, a "national assessment of education" is being undertaken for the first time this year. A battery of tests designed to reveal intellectual skills and knowledge of specific areas (science, music, etc.) is being given to a large sample of children and adults. Results are just beginning to appear. If this effort is repeated periodically in the future, there will be a basis for comparisons over time. At present, however, one would be hard put to construct an index. Some of the test-making companies have information over several years from the samples they use for standardizing.[8] A few cities have administered the same set of tests for several years, but national information about changes over time is almost nonexistent.

Two major national studies, however, have given extensive test score information for cross-sections of students. Project TALENT administered a big battery of tests to a sample of about 100,000 high school students in 1960 and collected a lot of other information about these students and the schools they attended.[9] Another survey, made pursuant to the civil rights act of 1964 and usually known as the Coleman study, tested an even larger sample of children (over 600,000) both at the elementary and high school levels and collected data on their schools.[10] These studies (and a few others in which tests were administered in a single city or

[8] U.S. Department of Health, Education and Welfare, *Toward a Social Report,* Washington, D.C., 1969, p. 67.

[9] For a discussion of the study, see John C. Flanagan et al., *Designing the Study,* Project TALENT, Monograph No. 1, Pittsburgh, University of Pittsburgh, 1960.

[10] James S. Coleman et al., *Equality of Educational Opportunity,* Washington, D.C., 1966.

other geographic area) have provided data for a series of attempts by statisticians to relate test scores (viewed as measures of outputs) to school characteristics (teacher-student ratios; age, training, or verbal aptitude of teachers; size of school; age of building; expenditures per student; etc.) and characteristics of students and their families (race, socioeconomic status, etc.).

The most general result of these statistical studies has been the finding that variables reflecting the socioeconomic characteristics of students and their families explain most of the variation in test scores, and variables reflecting school characteristics or resource inputs explain very little.[11]

These results should not be exaggerated—they do not prove that "schools don't matter"—but they certainly provide a basis for considerable skepticism about using test scores as measures of the output of the education industry as such. Test score changes may primarily reflect changes in the school population and the way it is mixed, rather than the productivity of school resources themselves. Some investigators have tried to control for the student inputs by explaining "achievement," given "ability." But serious challenges have been made to the independence of IQ tests (the usual "ability" measure) of school influences.

There are other objections to the use of standardized tests as measures of the output of education. There is the difficulty of establishing weights for different kinds of tested skills (should reading comprehension be weighted more heavily than mathematical facility?). This problem occurs in constructing tests as well as weighting different ones. There are doubts about the validity of the tests themselves (do they measure needed skills or do they mainly measure skill in taking tests?). There is the fact that some skills are clearly more measurable than others, and that some most highly prized intellectual characteristics (creativity, ingenuity, motivation) are hard to measure at all.

5. *Measures of Student Attitudes and Satisfactions*

Many people feel strongly that intellectual skills are only part, perhaps not even the most important part, of the output of education. They believe that much of the value of education, to the individual as well as to society, lies in its effect on attitudes and personality. Educated people are more likely to read newspapers (which presumably contribute to their knowledge of public issues) and more likely to vote. There is some survey evidence that educated people are happier—more satisfied with

[11] For a discussion of why these results might occur, see Alice M. Rivlin, *Systematic Thinking for Social Action,* Washington, D.C., Brookings, 1971, pp. 70–78.

themselves, their marriages, and their jobs.[12] They are less likely to be criminals (or at least less likely to be caught!) and less likely to become public dependents.

A successful educational program presumably contributes to a student's general ability to function in society, although little progress has been made in measuring this ability. Some work has been done on self-image or self-worth measures on the hypothesis that a person with a positive view of himself and his capacity is more likely to function well.

In evaluating schools or teachers, remarkably little attention has been paid to direct measures of student satisfaction. One might think that the most obvious way to measure whether a school was performing well would be to ask the students how they liked it. More sophisticated attempts might be made to develop indexes of enthusiasm or motivation of students by observing their behavior. Except at the college level, where individual professors are sometimes rated by student questionnaire, however, little serious attention has been given to student satisfaction. Such a gap is surprising—especially in view of evidence that students learn more and perform better intellectually if they are happy—and may reflect some puritan moral judgment that education ought to be painful to be good.

6. Measures of Income Increase

From an economist's point of view, the most interesting effect of education is that it increases an individual's productive capacity—a fact reflected in the higher earnings of educated people compared with less educated people with the same personal characteristics. By now, there exists a voluminous literature on the theory of human capital and ways of measuring these income differentials. Vocational education and manpower training programs are frequently evaluated by comparing groups that went through the program with supposedly similar groups that did not, measuring the difference in expected future income, and comparing this discounted income differential with the cost of the program.

There are many difficulties with using income increase as a measure of output of education: (a) It is not easy to disentangle the effects of the education from the effects of other characteristics that influence income—such as ability and family connections—many of which are highly correlated with education. This is similar to the problem that arises with the use of test scores. (b) It is difficult to know how much of the income

[12] Stephen B. Withey et al., *A Degree and What Else? Correlates and Consequences of a College Education*, A Report Prepared for the Carnegie Commission on Higher Education, New York, McGraw-Hill, 1971, Chap. 5.

differential is attributable to actual skills and knowledge acquired by education and how much to the possession of diplomas, degrees, or other educational credentials. (c) Much education is bought for other reasons than to increase income, and it is difficult to separate the amounts or kinds of education whose objectives are primarily investment. Strictly "vocational" education may be plausibly classified as primarily designed to increase income, but only a small part of the education system admits to being primarily vocational. (d) Finally, there is the practical problem that the income increase attributable to education takes a long time to show up; income differentials computed from the experience of those who have passed through the education system many years ago provide no plausible clue to the system's current productivity, especially at the younger ages.

To improve the information base for personal and social decisions about education, it would clearly be useful to have a variety of measures of the effects of education, especially the effect on intellectual skills and knowledge, attitudes and satisfaction, and productivity or income. But the question here is what measure of performance, if any, should be built into the national accounts in order to obtain better measures of the changing productivity of the education sector comparable with those for other sectors of the economy. The answer, I am afraid, is that none of these approaches now offers a procedure which would be clearly superior to the current practice of taking the value of input (deflated by changes in input prices) as a measure of output.

If one used body counts, one would be denying the possibility of qualitative change in education. Historically, one would show a sustained decline in the productivity of American education as real resources per student, and especially teacher-student ratios, have risen. This decline may, of course, be a fact, but there is no reason to assume it. Attainment measures, as pointed out above, do not differ significantly from body counts.

Exposure measures, such as credit-hours or student hours, do appear to have some appeal, especially if the exposure unit can be weighted for quality (cost) as suggested above. Such a procedure might at least make the deflation of educational expenditures more comparable to the deflation of expenditures for other types of goods produced in the private market. It would not, however, get away from the fact that one is essentially using inputs to measure outputs.

The output measures which appear independent of inputs (test scores, attitudes, income differentials) all present difficulties. Besides the primitive state of the art of measurement and doubts about the validity and reliability of individual measures, there is the overriding difficulty of weighting these measures. It is hard to believe that any set of weights that might be attached to sets of test scores, self-image measures, and income differentials would command enough consensus to be used as an output measure in national accounts. Even if it did, how would the results be used?

HOW-CAN-WE-DO-BETTER QUESTIONS

It seems useful to distinguish three rather different questions: (1) Is performance in education at least potentially measurable? (2) Would it be useful to develop better measures? (3) Would it be useful to build these measures into the present national income and product accounts, or some improved version of these accounts, in order to measure changes in education productivity? My own view is that the answer to the first two questions is a resounding "yes," and that the answer to the last question, at least for some time to come, is probably "no."

Only educational mystics persist in believing that the output of education is inherently and irrevocably unmeasurable. In practice, almost everyone (including teachers) behaves as though acquired skills and knowledge were eminently measurable. They give tests and impose education exposure requirements and base very important decisions on the results. They give more responsibility, better jobs, higher pay to people with more measurable "education" on the assumption that the performance of these individuals will justify this faith in measurement.

Of course, what is ordinarily being measured is a combination of the results of an individual's education with his inherent characteristics and other influences on his tested performance. However, there seems to be no inherent reason why these influences cannot be at least partially sorted out, especially if one is willing to make greater use of experiments than has been done in the past. Much of the difficulty in separating out the influence of education comes about because most of the data being used is retrospective and nonexperimental.

It is important to develop better performance measures in education. Indeed, it is hard to see how intelligent decisions about education can be made without them. Schools have been amazingly reluctant to provide any information on performance—no matter how it is measured—but taxpayers and parents are now demanding it. They want to know what they are buying and whether schools are getting better or worse. Test scores and other performance measures are now being used as evidence against educators. It seems likely that educators will respond by developing more comprehensive and reliable measures of their own, not only to satisfy the public, but to put their own house in order and build into the management of education some measures of what is being produced and some incentives to produce it more effectively. Several current innovations in education may hasten this process. Performance contracting is based on the idea that output is measurable. Voucher systems and community control of the schools both seem likely to lead to a greater emphasis on performance measures. The consumer with a voucher will need school output measures so that he can comparison shop on a more intelligent basis. Communities that gain control of a local school will want some basis on which to evaluate the performance of the management.

It is easy to think of decisions that would be illuminated by having better performance measures for education available to the decision makers, even if several different measures were offered at once without weights. Decisionmakers or voters could supply their own weights; at least they would have a better notion of the choices. But it is hard to think of a decision that would be improved by building such performance measures into the national accounts, even if one could agree on the weights.

In our decentralized education system, no one actually makes decisions about the aggregate resources devoted to education; but even if someone did (say, if education were federalized) he would not find average productivity or even average rate of return estimates much use. Comparisons of performance of different schools or projects or programs would be useful in channeling resources toward the most effective ones. Estimates of rates of return to particular types of vocational or professional education programs might affect decisions. Information on the distribution of educational subsidies among groups in the population would illuminate equity or distribution decisions. All of these types of information would have higher priority for decisionmaking than building performance measures for the education sector as a whole into the national accounts.

COMMENT
BURTON A. WEISBROD, University of Wisconsin

The papers by Alice Rivlin and Mancur Olson cover a wide variety of issues associated with the process of rational decisionmaking in the public sector in general and the education sector in particular. Olson directs his remarks toward two questions: why is there so much inefficiency in government, and what can be done about it? But there are two logically prior questions that must be dealt with. Are governments inefficient? And what, precisely, does "inefficient" mean?

Olson tells us, in effect, that since everyone knows that governments are inefficient, we can proceed to ask why. But surely, any serious assessment of "inefficiency" in government must begin with a definition of that term. The absence of a clear definition by Olson, and the plethora of cloudy statements, leave the reader quite unsure of what is meant by inefficiency. A sample of statements in the paper indicates that Olson includes in the term inefficiency such matters as "ineptitude or waste," and the absence of "Pareto-optimal efficiency." What does he mean when he asserts that "government production is generally less efficient *in some sense* than private production . . ." (emphasis added)? Does it make no difference in what sense, and compared to what, such inefficiency exists? Does Olson mean that governments are less efficient than (a) private sector firms "in general"; than (b) private sector firms that actually provide public-type goods; or than (c) private sector firms would be if they provided public-type goods?

Not only is the reader left uncertain as to what the "problem" is that Olson is addressing—since inefficiency is such a slippery term—but even if that were settled, another question would remain: Are governments inefficient? My own judgment is that we have little evidence to which we can refer. Olson's references to the "apparent" failures of government to reach the production frontier, or to the view that "schools are widely thought to be inefficient," and to the judgment of "anyone who has traveled in the Soviet Union as well as the West . . . [that] many of the services provided by the Soviet government seem to be relatively inefficient" are rather weak evidence.

The primary goal of his paper, as I see it, is an exploratory analysis not of the reasons for government inefficiency, but of some important differences between the goods and services governments produce and those that nongovernmental units produce. Olson regards the key difference, and hence the key problem, as "the lack of measured output" of the government sector. This, in turn, is the consequence of the government's "provision of collective goods and the handling of externalities."

Actually the problem of output assessment in the public sector is, I believe, decomposable into three subproblems: (1) defining targets or goals—that is, deciding which effects of a particular program are cared enough about to be regarded as "outputs"; (2) developing satisfactory operational measures of outputs—that is, of movement toward those targets—measures that do not affect output by the process of measurement; and (3) valuing each output.

One point to underscore, and Olson states it clearly, is that many of the problems he notes would not disappear—although they might or might not diminish—if the government turned over to the private sector the responsibility for producing and distributing many of the goods and services now in governmental hands. I suggest that this is particularly relevant to the choice between governmental production of a good and governmental provision of it via contracting-out, with or without subsidization. Since a government can ordinarily achieve its objectives of allocative efficiency or distributional equity through either its own production or through stimulation of nongovernment production, it is not clear why and under what circumstances governments opt for one or the other. There has been little attention paid to this matter in the literature; more is needed.

The first subproblem is defining goals, or What is an output? Consider a case in which consumers prefer different forms of each collective-consumption good but they agree that, given the costs of production, or the desire for equity, only one form or "quality" will be provided governmentally. When this is the case, each consumer will attempt to obtain the type or form of public service he prefers, for consumers will disagree as to what is a "relevant" output. Differences in preferences can be interpreted as differences in objectives and, hence, as differences in what each consumer regards as an output. Thus, the political struggle over the form of public service—e.g., in education, health, transit, and so forth —reflects disagreement over what is an "output," where an "output" from the viewpoint of any consumer is something which enters positively into *his* utility function. In short, some public service may produce output for you but not for me, or vice versa. Since identification of outputs thus depends on utility functions, the difficulty of defining outputs should not be surprising.

Developing operational measures of output—i.e., of progress toward goals—is the second problem associated with output valuation in the public sector. Assume that agreement has been reached on what we mean by "outputs" of any given government service, and that operational measures are being developed. A key problem at this stage is that the particular measure used to monitor (or measure) output is likely to influence the behavior of production units in unintended ways. For example, if the "output" of a school (the subject of Alice Rivlin's paper) is measured by performance of children on a standardized test, teachers will have an incentive to "teach to the test." In a recent experiment with "performance contracting" in U.S. public schools—an arrangement by which private firms are paid by government according to improvement in students' reading and mathematics achievement—an attempt was made to circumvent this problem by choosing randomly from among five or six different tests of achievement in each subject. There is, however, a dilemma: either the results of all the tests in a particular subject are highly correlated, in which case a teacher who teaches to any one test teaches to them all, or the results are not highly correlated, in which case the measured output of a teacher's or a school's efforts will depend on which of a variety of equally suitable measures were used. Of course, if we had great faith in all the tests, then we would not care if the teacher taught "to" them.

Since Olson emphasizes the importance of developing operational measures of all government outputs, it is interesting to examine further the kinds of operational measures for education that were surveyed by Alice Rivlin. Lying behind the choice of measures is the issue to which I referred above: What do we want from the government service? In other words, what do we regard as an "output"?

In general, we economists tend to think of outputs in value-added terms. In the case of education, however, most of the proposed measures of output that Alice Rivlin enumerates reflect no attempt whatsoever to distinguish between the level of a student's accomplishment and the addition to that level that results from schooling, ceteris paribus. Grades on tests and in courses, for example, measure, at best, what students know, not what the addition to their knowledge has been, and in no way do they reflect the separate influence of schooling variables as distinct from ability, motivation, etc. This suggests that tests do not generally measure "learning added" by schooling.

But by contrast, what if the objective and, hence, the "output" of schooling were in terms of certifying competence of students, as an aid to matching workers and jobs in the labor market? In that case, information about level of achievement would truly represent a value added, regardless of whether any of the achievement was attributed to schooling. It appears that the education system may be measuring its outputs in ways that imply that certification is a most significant output, while what is learned in, and because of, school is much less significant. My point is not to take a position on which output is more important—learning or certification—but to note the relationship between the measure used and the implied notion of what is an output. I agree with Alice Rivlin that an index of changes in educational output over time is needed, but I would add that the usefulness of such an index will depend critically on how satisfied we are that it measures the outputs we care about— i.e., outputs that help us to achieve our social goals.

As the problems of output measurement in the public sector are considered, it is useful to note what our measures of outputs in the private sector do and do not measure. Consider, for example, Alice Rivlin's statement that in the case of education, "some highly prized intellectual characteristics (creativity, ingenuity, motivation) are hard to measure at all." I suggest that we distinguish between the problems of measurement and of forecasting. "Creativity" and "ingenuity" of a person are extraordinarily difficult to predict, but are not nearly so difficult to measure as of a given point in time. The same is true, I believe, of private sector outputs. Durable goods prices reflect current assessments of expected outputs; how accurate the buyer's predictions turn out to be is a matter about which we seldom inquire. Need we do so in the public sector? And if we do, should it be said that the public sector is inefficient compared with the private unless we know how well the private sector predicts and how well it would predict the effects of activities in which it is not currently engaged (but has left for the government)?

Valuation of outputs is the third problem associated with output assessment in the public sector. Olson believes that the problem of inefficiency in the public sector is largely attributable to the collective-consumption nature of government services. It is surely a considerable oversimplification, however, to suggest that governmental provision of goods and services is largely limited to collective goods. Most governmental goods are rather far removed, in fact, from the pure collective-good case. And perhaps more importantly, much of what governments provide, and the manner in which such goods and services are provided, relate to distributional objectives. Zero-pricing, for example, often reflects, I believe, not the view that marginal social cost of an additional consumer-user is zero, but rather that a zero price provides equality of access to the good or service. Some recent research has raised questions about the fact of equality of access, but this does not vitiate the argument that many people believe that setting prices at zero enhances "equality of opportunity." In any case, zero-pricing of goods for which marginal social cost of a consumer is positive—perhaps because of congestion costs—is bound to pose allocative efficiency problems. Thus, it seems that governments may be trading off allocative efficiency for distributional equity. Whether the trade-offs being made are or are not efficient (in the Pareto sense) is a question worthy of further study.

The frequent use by governments of zero-pricing poses one problem, and it points up another problem in connection with our efforts to value government outputs. First, the absence of observed market prices makes it difficult to estimate output values; and second, governmental efforts to bring about greater equality of access than would occur if market demand considerations prevailed points up the distributional objective of government activities. The presence of this latter objective suggests that market-clearing prices, even if we could know them, would not be the "right" prices to use! It is for this reason that my sympathy for Mancur Olson's interesting proposal to run experiments to discover consumer demand functions is somewhat tempered.

If the relevance of distributional goals for evaluating government performance is granted, we might wish to conclude that the "same" outputs differently distributed are, in effect, different outputs or, at least, are different "values" of outputs. Then, since public and nonpublic provision of a service is likely to be distributed differently, it may not be so obviously correct that, as Alice Rivlin put it, "it clearly makes no sense to treat the costs of public and private educational institutions differently in the national accounts." Perhaps it is not entirely senseless to regard the same resources, when directed toward different consumer groups, as having different values.

One conclusion does, however, seem clear: many hurdles remain to be surmounted in the process of defining the relevant outputs of the government sector, developing operational measures of the outputs, and then valuing increments of those outputs.

ZVI GRILICHES, Harvard University

Rivlin's suggestion that different outputs in education should be weighted by relative costs is interesting and a step forward. To implement it, however, we would have to separate, among other things, the cost of university training into its undergraduate, graduate, and research components. But that would not be easy, as anyone who has thought about it a little knows. Moreover, we would have to worry about the comparability of particular completion levels over time. There are conflicting trends here that should be looked into. Structuring our estimates this way would force the "quality" question into the open and might result in our getting some additional information on it.

Olson claims that public enterprises are inefficient because they are in the business of producing output which is very hard to measure. I am not sure that this is either necessary or sufficient for the inefficiency charge. My feeling is that the problem of inefficiency is contained in the statement that they are not maximizing the right thing, that the internal incentive structure is wrong. Whether this is a consequence of the difficulty of measuring the "output" that we would want them to produce is not all that obvious. There are many private enterprises that produce hard-to-measure output in this sense but do not seem to be subject to the same inefficiency problems.

The difficulties of measurement are real, and they apply with special force to the problem of measuring the contribution of investment in research to economic growth. They can be illustrated by some recent work of my own.[1] To estimate the contribution of such expenditures to the growth in total factor productivity we need (besides the observable level of these expenditures) three numbers: (1) The fraction of such expenditures that could conceivably have an impact on productivity as currently measured; (2) the fraction of such expenditures that can be thought of as increasing the stock of relevant knowledge (i.e., what fraction of this investment is net?); and (3) the social rate of return to such investments. A careful look at the sources and uses of these funds convinces me that no more than about a half of these expenditures could affect measured total factor productivity in the United States. A large fraction of these expenditures is spent on space exploration and defense, where the achievements, if any, are valued at cost. At the same time, scattered evidence on the longevity of research results (the bulk of which is in the applied area) suggests that a depreciation rate of about 10 per cent per annum may not be out of line, particularly at a time of relatively high levels of gross investment. That would imply roughly that about half of the observed expenditures could be treated as net investment. There remains then the question of the relevant rate of return. Since we are interested in the social rate of return to such expenditures, we cannot estimate it from observed profit and loss statements. We are thus forced either to an explicit calculation of social rates of return for selected innovations or into econometric analyses of interindustry differences in productivity growth. A survey of earlier results on the

[1] Z. Griliches, "Research Expenditures and Growth Accounting," International Economic Association Conference paper, St. Anton, Austria, 1971.

former and some experimentation with the latter leads me to the use of 30 per cent as an upper bound on the average rate of return to all the relevant research and development expenditures. Since the over-all ratio of R&D expenditures to private domestic GNP was 0.03 in 1970, these numbers taken together imply a contribution of about 0.2 per cent per year to the rate of growth of total factor productivity ($0.3 \times 0.5 \times 0.5 \times 0.03 \simeq 0.002$). This is not negligible but neither is it overwhelming.

While each of these numbers is based on some evidence and quite a bit of scrutiny on my part, I hope that I have conveyed implicitly the wide uncertainty surrounding each one of them. While they are about as good as I can make them at the moment, I would not urge the OBE to take over their routine production and to award them their explicit Good National Accounting Seal. I think such exercises are interesting and worthwhile but are based on too sparse a data base and too weak a theoretical framework to warrant their incorporation into the official accounts as they are currently constituted.

NESTOR E. TERLECKYJ, National Planning Association

I would like to discuss the measurement of output which would reflect the use and usefulness of goods and services *after* they have entered the household sector. Such measurements are important for an understanding of a number of current issues in that they may make it possible to judge the "cost-effectiveness" of consumer expenditures in terms of the capacity of consumer goods (and public programs) to satisfy specific wants—e.g., for shelter, health, or mobility—as represented by specific criteria or indicators in a manner similar to the methods employed in analyzing the effectiveness of public expenditures.

Measurement at this level of utility is much more difficult than the measurement of the public sector output alone as discussed by Schultze, but the nature of problems encountered is similar in both cases. He pointed out that in the private sector valuations of commodities are given by the market, but that in the public sector comparable decision relevant valuations are not available and that the measurement of physical units is not likely to reflect the really important performance characteristics. These are more likely to be the functional characteristics of goods and services measured by their capacity to contribute to the output of a "consumer production" process.

But, in attempting to evaluate the prevailing effectiveness of the satisfaction of consumer wants, one necessarily must consider a much wider set of data than that generated by the operation of the markets because both market and nonmarket goods enter as inputs into their satisfaction and there is no reason to expect that optimizations occur between the market and the nonmarket components. For this reason there is much less of a basis than in some other contexts to rely on the valuations produced by the existing markets as necessarily applicable to the more fundamental and in a large measure nonmarket concerns.

In dealing with what Olson calls "things that people really care about," the really important indicators of performance may be quite different from the usually measured physical units or the factor cost and price, mainly because of the nonlinearities in the production of consumer satisfactions and the nonexistence of the equimarginal optimization in the large (over the given system of inputs).

It is important to attempt to define output of the final demand sectors in terms better related to welfare concepts than the amount of resources used in its production. The units of measurement of performance characteristics that people care about may be defined by specific indicators for the consumer units to reflect actual objectives of consumption. It may be an interesting question for future research to find out whether and to what extent those performance elements can be aggregated into some kind of social indicators representing national totals. Perhaps the work that Hartle described can suggest some possibilities.

The joint relationships among various inputs and outputs, both public and private, can perhaps best be seen as an incremental input-output matrix, with the input dimensions representing specific goods, services, and public programs and the output dimensions representing indicators of satisfaction of specific wants and with interaction effects among the inputs. For example, the output of an automobile in terms of mobility and access without the public complements of roads and highways is negligible by itself, and in many cases may approach zero. Its value, in a consumer decision sense, also depends on the extent and quality of the existing and prospective (over the lifetime of the commitment made) alternative systems.

Thus, the "performance output" of a given consumer or public program is contingent on the level of the complementary inputs. The "success" of a highway will depend on what type of industrial or residential development will occur; the extent to which a given public health program may be successful will depend on how the public and the medical professions will respond to it; an educational innovation at the elementary level may critically depend for its success on the response of the parents, etc.

In the sense of utility generating consumer activities then, any government program, like any private product, is only a partial input, and almost any nontrivial level of performance output and any efficient mode of its production requires complementary "inputs" from both sectors. This suggests that the magnitude of the "performance product" (total product) of a single governmental program per se is inherently indeterminant, because of the jointness in production of the higher order output within the final demand. All we can really determine ex ante is the range in which the output of a public program can fall, when measured from the given initial conditions and as contingent on the complementary inputs, or ex post what has been the joint result of a combination of events, in particular periods and circumstances, and what range of magnitude of effects of particular factors is suggested by the evidence.

Finally, performance measurement has to be selective and relativistic. It cannot and probably should not be definitive. To the extent that a given public program or a given market good or a combination of market goods and public programs has multiple outputs, the conflict about defining *the* correct measure of output can be reduced, if not resolved, by measuring more than one important performance characteristic where there is more than one. A matrix representation is quite helpful in this respect. This would also reduce the risk of bias in policy making, which would automatically follow from selecting a single performance characteristic for attention.

Measuring the Amenities and Disamenities of Economic Growth

Measuring Social and Economic Change:

Benefits and Costs of Environmental

Pollution

ORRIS C. HERFINDAHL

AND

ALLEN V. KNEESE

RESOURCES FOR THE FUTURE, INC.

INTRODUCTION

Benefits and costs associated with the environment involve not only pollutants and their effects in the usual sense but psychic responses to features of the environment some of which may not even be describable in relevant quantitative terms. Our focus is on pollution in the narrow sense, however, not because the wider and less tractable issues are unimportant, but because of considerations of comparative advantage.

Of the many possible approaches to the measurement of benefits and costs connected with the environment, two are selected for examination here. One possibility is to approach the measurement problem within the framework of the national income accounts. Flows of environmental benefits or costs or responses to them are already partially reflected in the national accounts, and there is a possibility that present deficiencies in their treatment could be remedied. We consider this at some length, with results that are rather negative. Although change in the official definitions does not seem to be warranted, it probably would be useful to prepare some auxiliary series reflecting response to environmental change and control that users could combine with the official series.

NOTE: We are indebted to Henry Peskin, Robert A. Kelly, Clifford S. Russell, and Walter O. Spofford, Jr., for comments on an earlier draft.

Orris Herfindahl died on December 16, 1972, in Nepal, while on a hiking expedition in the Himalayas. This paper reflects the keen interest and concern he had for the natural environment.

Apart from the national accounts approach, a thoroughgoing application of which would involve estimates for the environment of various aggregates corresponding to the series already included—value of service flows, maintenance, environmental capital formation and depreciation (depletion?)—it may be possible to measure environmental benefits and costs on a more limited basis, say, in marginal terms, and this is the approach we have taken. We do not attempt any estimates of benefits and costs as such, but confine ourselves to some general observations on how such estimates might be made and what the data and information requirements are for some of the possible methods.

It is of central importance to any method being used to throw light on environmental benefits and costs that important real external effects are involved with no counterpart money flow. This is in strong contrast to the treatment of ordinary goods for which benefits and costs can be estimated on the basis of market prices. Similar estimates of the changes in environmental benefits and costs that would result from a specified change in pollutant output require the explicit use of a model which can take account of these real repercussions not reflected in market prices or costs or that would be reflected only under some different institutional arrangement.

Several models that can go some distance toward tracing the repercussions of control actions or that can contribute to decisions on the proper control action are discussed. Among these are the adaptation of the input-output scheme to the analysis of pollution problems and a conceptually more elaborate model containing an activity analysis model and other components designed to portray certain physical and biological events accompanying a change in pollution outputs.

The final question to be considered is the kinds of data and information needed for the design and administration of pollution control schemes. The data of the specific models examined in some detail provide substantial guidance here, but since our discussion is necessarily rather general, it has a wider applicability. In effect, the question considered is this: Given that there is to be a pollution control system, what kinds of data and information are needed to make it work? First, it is essential to have baseline or indicator data to know when things have changed for the worse or to get some indication of the possibility that it might be possible to improve things in city A in view of the fact that conditions are better in a similar city B. Second, control requires accurate and comprehensive information on pollutant flows. The possibility of assembling this information as a part of a comprehensive accounting for materials flows is examined. Finally, pollution control requires some change in the way things are now done, but what options are there? What parts of the production function would provide the best compromise between the demands standing behind pollution production and the demands of those who are injured by it, assuming that institutional arrangements permitted the change? The need for systematic information on production possibilities is often neglected, but in fact it is of strategic importance to the design of control schemes that pay at least some attention to the relevant benefits and costs.

I. SOCIAL ACCOUNTS AND ENVIRONMENTAL BENEFITS AND COSTS

The Nature of Social Accounts

An accounting system is a way of systematically describing what has happened between two points in time to the state of a certain group of objects in a system. Ordinarily what happens to the state of the different objects in the system will be associated with various types of flows during the period in question.

We speak of an accounting *system* because the entities involved in the state descriptions and the flows accounted for are members of a proper classification. There is no overlapping of entities or flows, there is some principle of closure which definitely circumscribes the group of entities and flows, and the flows and objects are related in a definite manner. Flows always come from and go to members of the group of entities, and in doing so they behave in accordance with certain relationships that can be specified.

The design of an accounting system requires a selection of the "objects of interest." What phenomena are we trying to account for? The answer to this question determines the nature of the classification of entities and flows. In any practical application of the system, there must be a determination of the boundaries of the system, and this will depend on the phenomena of interest.

One property of an accounting system with boundaries defined in spatial terms is that totals can be broken down by area, as with the income payments series, wealth estimates, and so on. This property is extremely useful if environmental resources are incorporated into an accounting framework, because our interest in these resources usually has a very strong locational component. Unlike, say, the monetary system, there are few aspects of any environmental resource the proper management of which is connected with national totals or any of their national physical aspects. Much of our later discussion stresses the locational aspect.

Weight of flows of physical objects, like money flows between economic units, could form a suitable basis for an accounting system because its components add up to a definite total. While there is merit in an accounting system based on flows of mass—simply to provide an exhaustive means for tracing the flow of different substances—weight in fact may not be very closely connected with the true objects of our interest in connection with the natural environment. We would emphasize, however, the great importance of this exhaustive accounting device, at least for certain areas.

There is a possibility that many of the objects of interest may be such that a system of accounts—defined as above—could make only an indirect contribution to our understanding. For example, one of the things we are interested in is the effects of air pollutants on health—that is, effects on the feeling of well-being a person enjoys, on his performance, on sickness objectively viewed, and on age at death. To study these questions, we need to know the spatial and temporal distributions of concentrations of the different types of air pollutants and the temporal exposures of individuals to the various concentrations. It seems entirely possible, even likely, that the systematic series that we should like to see collected over time to facilitate study of the effects of air pollutants for the most part could not be combined in an accounting system apart from the aspect of mass. There is no point in adding concentrations at different locations, although their comparison in various ways may be of interest. Certain statistical operations can be viewed as the equivalent of adding together the exposures of different individuals at the same location, but there is little point in adding together the exposures of persons at different locations if exposures are different.

Considerations like these lead us to examine the possibility of thinking of social accounts in a looser way. We might, for example, think of social accounts as a systematic series of records over time that will aid us in "accounting" for what has gone on in a certain sphere of interest. Here we are thinking of "accounting" in the sense of describing or explaining rather than in the sense of identifying the numerical components of a total. In the case of the accounting system narrowly viewed, there is an additive unit of measurement which opens the possibility of forming a proper classification and specifying the boundaries of system and subsystem. With the looser system it is still possible to think of system and subsystem, but perhaps with less precision, and the publicly additive property is not present. A weighted sum may be conceivable in certain cases, but the weights usually will be private and more or less subjective.

Series of this kind can be thought of as serving several purposes. They may provide summary indicators of tendencies, they may provide baseline information for future studies, or they may provide important inputs to research studies on specific problems. A major part of our discussion in part III concerns these matters.

Should GNP and NNP Be Modified to Account for Environmental Pollution and Its Control?

The question whether the aggregate output accounts—GNP and NNP—should be modified to reflect the growing generation, treatment, and discharge of residuals from production and consumption activities can be interpreted in two ways. First, should the official definitions be changed, and, second, should auxiliary modified series be presented along with the official series based on unchanged definitions? As a general matter, we feel that the official series should be continued on the basis of the present definitions, both because of the desirability of avoiding breaks in the series and because the advantages and significance of some of the changes that might be made are not yet completely clear. The discussion applies, then, to the second interpretation. Whenever we speak of the desirability of modifying GNP or NNP,[1] we refer not to the official series but to modified auxiliary series. Of course, experience with such series might later be thought to indicate the desirability of a change in the official definitions.

GNP is intended to measure the production of "final" goods and services in the economy. The final "consumers" of these goods and services are taken to be individuals and households (consumers in the traditional sense), government, and nonprofit institutions. It is assumed that these economic agents do not usually use inputs to provide intermediate services (such as, for example, a trucking company would), but rather that they "use up" the utility embodied in the goods and services which the economy produces. This is a working assumption which, in numerous particular instances, is highly debatable.

At any given time there exists a list of goods and services which is officially regarded as final. These goods and services are exchanged

[1] The discussion always refers to deflated, or "real," gross national product or net national product.

in markets [2] and therefore have market exchange determined prices attached to them in some base year as well as in the current period. As time passes, new goods and services are often "wedged in" to help keep the list more nearly complete. To calculate price-corrected or "real" GNP, the changing amounts of physical units of the final goods and services produced are multiplied by the unchanged base-period set of prices—currently, 1958 prices are used. The system of accounts is of the double entry type. In current prices the total of GNP calculated from the product side must balance GNP calculated as the sum of values added of all activities contributing to GNP. This is not true of real GNP, however, because no deflator has been devised with which the value-added side could be price corrected. [3] Thus, since we are here interested in real GNP, we will refer exclusively to the product-side calculations.

If it were true that all salient goods and services were exchanged in markets; that the degree of competition in these markets did not change; that the programs of government and nonprofit institutions did not change in such a way that they produced substantially altered welfare relative to the final goods and services that they absorbed; that population stayed constant; and that the distribution of income did not change; then alterations in real NNP (GNP minus capital consumption) could be regarded as a good indicator of changes in the economic welfare of the population.

This is an imposing string of assumptions, none of which is ever exactly met in reality. To the extent that they are not met, NNP diminishes in usefulness as a welfare measure. In fact, the distance between reality and these assumptions is large and significant in some cases, thus seriously reducing the practical usefulness of NNP as a welfare measure.

Of course the national accounts, which include much more than total NNP, have been designed to serve a number of purposes. They are intended to provide information useful for economic stabilization policies and programs, and they are meant to provide an estimate of the production of goods and services which the society has available to meet alternative ends. The designers of the accounts thought that at best they would serve to provide only a rough indicator of one dimension of welfare.

But to divorce completely discussion of the accounts from broader questions of welfare, as some would do, would be a serious mistake.

---

[2] In fact, some of these transactions are virtual or imputed. For example, the value of owner-occupied housing is estimated by imputation.

[3] Deflated gross national product by industry is calculated by deflating industry outputs and purchases separately and subtracting.

Whether originally intended or not, total NNP or GNP is often explicitly or implicitly viewed as an index of welfare change. Moreover, it is important to recognize explicitly that there are enormous flows of services and disservices, valued by people, which do not enter into the exchange system and therefore are not in the list of final goods and services. Unless care is taken to observe and analyze these flows, the real NNP may become grossly misleading even as to what is happening to production of potentially marketable goods and services in the economy. For example, should there be a large-scale shift from purchases of services (e.g., house painting, grass cutting, construction, household services) to self-provision of these services, the NNP would tend to fall although it would not necessarily be true that production had decreased. The reason that NNP would tend to fall is that the labor going into these self-provided services is not in the list of final products; consequently, working time shifted toward them "disappears" from the account. The reason they are not in the list is that the accountants have found them too difficult and costly to identify and evaluate—although there may be good reason to reconsider this position in view of contemporary techniques of data collection and handling.

It is highly illuminating to view objections of the "environmentalist" to the accounts as involving a question of what is or is not in the list of final products. When the environmentalist contends that GNP overstates growth, he implicitly incorporates in his list of final products many service flows which do not enter into market exchange and consequently are not in the official list. Moreover, he believes that the net effect of including the omissions would be to reduce real product. His list would include the life support, aesthetic, and convenience services of clean air, clean water, and spacious surroundings—all of which in some of their aspects are *common property* resources unsuited to private exchange. The only way a change in these service flows could influence the GNP and NNP as presently measured is if their changed quality or quantity made the production of items which are included in the list easier or more difficult. In reality, such feedbacks on the national accounts from altered quality of the common property resources are probably trivial, up to now, compared with alteration of service flows from these resources direct to final consumers. These are nowhere reflected as such in the list of final products, although they may affect some items that are. It is the marked deterioration of the environmental services not on the list that mainly concerns the environmentalist.

The exclusion of the services of clean air, clean water, space, etc., from the list of final goods probably is not the result of disagreement that the services provided by nature are a factor in true welfare but rather of the judgment on the part of the income accountant that obtaining acceptable estimates for these values would be too difficult and costly. It is clear, however, that any reduction in the service flows of common property resources that is viewed as a loss in real product by consumers means that NNP overstates any increase in final product as compared with the total flow from the truly relevant and larger list of final goods and services. In the extreme case the "true" service flow could actually decrease while NNP rises. Some writers, like E. J. Mishan, believe that this is happening now.[4] This view seems a bit extreme, but whether it is or not is an empirical question.

That burdens on the service flows of common property assets tend to rise with increasing production unless effective, collectively imposed controls are undertaken is obvious from observation. There are also some reasons to believe that this rise will tend to be more than proportional to production growth in developed economies. Conservation of mass requires that all material resources used as inputs to the extractive, productive, and consumptive activities of the economy must appear as residuals which in some manner are returned to the environment—except for changes in the inventory of mass. If the use of material rises faster than production of final goods and services, so must the production of residuals. There are counteracting trends affecting materials use in the economy. However, as lower-quality ores are used greater quantities of unwanted material must be processed to get a given quantity of wanted material; as a result there appears a tendency for residuals to rise faster than final production of goods *and* services "embodying" materials. Also, energy usage recently has been rising faster than real NNP, and so long as it is obtained primarily from conversion of fossil fuels this implies a rapidly rising flow of residual materials and gases. In the absence of effective collective restriction on the use of common property resources like air and water they tend to become the receptacles into which residuals are discharged. Other sources of nonlinearities can be readily identified. Indeed, sometimes discontinuities or thresholds are encountered, as when a water body becomes anaerobic and its functioning changes dramatically for the worse so far as services like recreation and fishing are concerned.

There seems to be considerable agreement among those who have studied the matter that if it were practical to extend the list of final goods and services to include service flows from the natural environment

[4] See E. J. Mishan, *The Costs of Economic Growth,* London, Staples Press Ltd., 1967.

this should be done. But there also seems to be near universal hopelessness about the feasibility of doing it—at least for a long time to come. Accordingly it is often concluded that the best we can do in this respect is to supplement the real NNP with physical, chemical, or biological indicators of the state of the environment. We discuss this possibility in part III.

But are there any less ambitious adjustments that should be made? One possibility is to deduct consumer "defensive" expenditures from NNP. If environmental service flows remained constant, then "defensive" expenditures made voluntarily by consumers would be on the same footing as any other, being carried to the point where utility gained is equated with alternative cost in utility lost. It would make no difference if environmental service flows are included in the list of final products so far as indication of welfare changes over time is concerned.

If environmental service flows change, however, then it is clear that a list of final products that omits either these or the defensive consumer expenditures may give an incorrect indication of welfare change over time. If defensive expenditures were simply deducted from the present GNP, the necessary implicit assumption would be—if welfare change is to be correctly indicated—that the defensive expenditures exactly offset the decline in value of the environmental services that "ought" to but do not now affect the GNP. Even so, it probably would be of interest to try to estimate consumer defensive expenditures.

Defensive expenditures by industry are already appropriately treated from this point of view since they never appear in real NNP. We will not develop the rationale for these points here since it is quite analogous to that developed in some detail for residuals control expenditures, below.

Costs of meeting environmental standards. Up to this point we have been discussing common property environmental resources as though their use were completely unrestricted. In the United States, this was a fairly good approximation of reality until recently, but public policy development is now proceeding rapidly to regulate their use for residuals disposal. The policy path we are taking seems to be leading toward ambient *environmental* standards which are to be achieved by enforcement of *emission* standards or, in a few cases, through the incentives provided by emission charges or taxes. If these policies become effective they should give rise to large expenditures for the control of residuals generation and discharge. The time pattern these will follow is uncertain, but probably they will "hump" in the next five to ten years during a clean-up phase, possibly then declining slightly for a time, following which they may tend to rise nonlinearly with increasing input. Table 1 gives some idea of the outlays which might be involved in the period 1970–75 if objectives are pursued very vigorously, although actual expenditures probably will be much less. The question arises, How should these expenditures be treated in the NNP?

Before trying to answer, we should review how such expenditures would be treated under present procedures. The fact is that they would be handled differently depending on whether they are incurred by consumers or government on the one hand or by industry on the other. In the following discussion we will neglect direct expenditures for pollution control by consumers, because we think they will be small (with one major exception which we discuss later), and in any case no different principles are involved.

The differential effect of industrial and governmental expenditures can easily be illustrated by a very simple example. Assume an economy in which only two commodities are produced in the base period, haircuts and bread (the citizens will be nude but well clipped). Accordingly the list of final products will consist of haircuts and bread (see Table 2). Let us assume that the production of haircuts generates no significant amount of residuals but that the production of bread does. Suppose also that barbers can be diverted to control residuals if that is desired (the bread can be produced with less waste if more labor is used).

In the base period there is a standard for the discharge of residuals, but the production of bread is just low enough to avoid violating it. In period 1, a change in family composition causes a shift in demand from haircuts to bread together with an increase in residuals. If there were no standard for discharge of residuals, the situation would be that labeled 1a. That is, $500 of productive services would have been diverted from the production of haircuts to bread, and residuals discharge would have increased.

There is a standard for residuals discharge, however, and it is not being met in situation 1a. If it is met by a diversion *within the industry* of barbers to residuals control, NNP will register a decline as compared with period 0, as shown by 1b. The decline in the flow of residuals is not recorded, of course. In contrast, if the government hires these same men to limit the discharge of residuals to the standard level, NNP will show no decline, as in 1c. The reason is that there is nothing in the list of final products corresponding to residual controls, and so the activities directed toward that end cannot be reflected in NNP evaluated

TABLE 1

A Collection of Rough Estimates of Increase in Costs to Achieve
"Substantial" Reductions in Environmental Pollution, 1970–75

	Billions of Dollars [a]
Water	
Treating municipal sewage	12
Reducing nonthermal industrial wastes	6
Reducing thermal discharges	3
Sediment and acid mine drainage control	3
Reducing oil spills, water craft discharges, and other miscellaneous items	1
Added reservoir storage for low flow regulation	1
Separating storm and sanitary sewers	40
Total	66
Total without last item	26
Air	
Controls on stationary sources	5
Mobile sources	
To modify refining and distribution of gasoline	2
Engine modifications	2
Added fuel costs	1
Total	10
Solids	
Increased coverage of collection	1
Increased operating cost, including environmental protection costs	3
Total	4
Other	
Control of heavy metals (mercury, cadmium, etc.), stopping use of persistent pesticides, improving water treatment, control of pollutant-bearing soil runoff, control of feed-lot operations, etc.[b]	15
Grand total	
With storm-sewer separators (about 35 per cent increase of GNP)	95
Without storm-sewer separators (about 20 per cent increase of GNP)	55

SOURCE: Allen V. Kneese, "The Economics of Environmental Pollution in the United States," in Allen V. Kneese, Sidney E. Rolfe, and Joseph W. Harned, eds., *International Environmental Management: The Political Economy of Pollution,* Proceedings of Atlantic Council–Battelle Memorial Institute Conference of January 1971, Washington, D.C., forthcoming.

[a] Estimates include investment and operating costs.

[b] A sheer guess.

TABLE 2
The Haircuts and Bread Economy

		Q	P_0	NNP
Period 0	H	100	$10	$1,000
	B	100	10	1,000
				2,000
Period 1a	H	50	10	500
(as it would be without resid-	B	150	10	1,500
uals control)				2,000
Period 1b	H	25	10	250
(as it would be if industry	B	150	10	1,500
had to control residuals by				1,750
diverting 25 extra barbers)				
Period 1c	H	25	10	250
(as it would be if govern-	B	150	10	1,500
ment hired the extra bakers	G	25	10	250
and set them to controlling				2,000
residuals)				

H = haircuts.
B = bread.
G = government.

at base-year prices. However, since government is in effect regarded as a final consumer, its expenditure for the barbers (or rather residuals controllers) is included in NNP.[5]

Observations on Treating the Costs of Environmental Standards. If we visualize a situation in which the government establishes effective environmental standards which must be continuously met, the present NNP treatment of industry outlays to comply with them would seem to indicate welfare change more appropriately than the present treatment of similar governmental outlays. The reason is that the outlays made for residuals control can be viewed as simply being necessary to maintain, at some specified level, the service flow naturally provided by the common property assets. In that sense they are expenditures necessary to

[5] A more formal justification of these points is included in a forthcoming study by Karl-Göran Mäler of the Stockholm School of Economics.

maintain the unproduced capital stock. Failure to treat them this way could result in an anomalous situation in which a progressively larger share of production would have to be devoted simply to environmental quality maintenance with NNP continuing to rise. It would be hard to claim that this rise could in any way be regarded as indicating increased welfare. Viewed this way the appropriate procedure would be to treat industry outlays for control as at present and to change procedures so that government outlays for control could be treated similarly.[6] This would require identification of government expenditures for residuals control, which we think would not be too difficult, and their subtraction from the present NNP for presentation as an auxiliary series.

The one major exception to the view that consumer expenditures to control residuals will be small is in the control of emissions from automobiles. The approach adopted in the official series is essentially to add items called control devices to the list of final products. If this were not done, the price deflator would tend to indicate a reduced real production of automobiles.

The better approach, it seems to us, is to treat this case—again in an auxiliary series—symmetrically with the way industry is now treated. The consumer would be regarded as producing a service for himself, the production of which generates residuals. He is required in the interest of maintaining the service flow from common property assets to incur a cost. To add such costs to NNP over time would have the same anomalous results as already described in the case of industry.

As we have already indicated, our view appears to be contrary to the views of some experts in national income accounting. Their position apparently rests on two major considerations. The first reflects the special problem of dealing with a catch-up phase such as we are now experiencing in connection with the control of environmental pollution. When effective standards of higher than prevailing quality are first set, some of the expenditures made will result in actual improvements in environmental quality. Thus, the anomalous situation would arise that the population actually experiences an improvement in welfare while the associated influence on NNP is downward. To avoid this situation it has been proposed that the list of final products be expanded to include industrial outlays for residuals control. For reasons already explained we do not think this is the appropriate approach for the longer term welfare indicator. It would be preferable not to add the outlays but to

[6] We are still assuming, we think correctly, that consumer expenditures for residuals discharge control will be minor.

prorate them over a longer period of time, especially from earlier periods when NNP tended to be understated as an indicator of welfare.

The second argument relates to the accounts as measures of production. If it is argued that the GNP is an important measure of the production that might be diverted in periods of national emergency (wartime, for example) for overriding national ends, then the production going into residuals control should be included in GNP. This is because it could be diverted at the cost of permitting deterioration of the service flows from common property assets. In this sense it is quite analogous to running down private capital during such periods. But this does not argue that these expenditures should ever be included in NNP.

The argument is also made that not including production directed toward residuals control would distort labor productivity series which are obtained by dividing NNP by man-hours worked. One's point of view on this seems to be highly contingent on what one regards as measured by labor productivity. If one regards it as the output per man-hour net of the output needed to maintain the service flows of all assets—private and common—then it is wholly appropriate that productivity should tend to fall if a larger proportion of total effort has to go for meeting environmental standards. On the other hand if one regards productivity as pertaining only to conventional production processes, then one would wish activities devoted to environmental maintenance to be in the list of final goods.

Conclusions on national accounts. Since the character of the national product and income accounts is not directed very closely to the single objective of measuring changes in social welfare and uncertainty surrounds some of the changes that have been discussed—both as to implications and practicality—we feel that the official definitions should not be changed. However, series should be prepared that reflect, at least in part, the growth of activities that would indicate decreases in an idealized list of final products or that offset, at least to some degree, the apparent increases registered in, say, NNP.

To this end, we suggest the regular preparation and publication of the following series:

1. Industrial expenditures for residuals control;
2. Government expenditures for residuals control;
3. Consumer expenditures for residuals control;
4. Consumer, industry, and government defensive expenditures.

None of these is prepared currently, and all offer considerable difficulty. If they can be put together, however, the accounts could be adjusted to reflect various preferences and points of view. It probably would be desirable to publish auxiliary series modifying the official series. The following are some of the possibilities, with all series assumed to be price corrected:

1. GNP—including all residuals control in the list of final products;
2. NNP₁—GNP minus net depreciation of private assets;
3. NNP₂—GNP minus net depreciation of private assets and minus the nonindustry cost of residuals control and defensive expenditures (and in principle all other costs which may be induced by the growth process itself).

In no case, however, should the mistake be made of thinking that adjustments of these types can come very close to indicating changes in "true" welfare so far as flows of environmental services are concerned. The essential ingredient that is lacking is a valuation for the environmental services themselves and, on capital account, an expression for decreases or increases in the value of the corresponding natural assets.

Apart from this general caveat, the definition of some of the series is not very precise. This is especially true of industrial outlays made for pollution control to meet standards of environmental quality. This is evident immediately merely by considering the possible responses of industry to an increase in these standards. True, it may make some outlays, both capital and operating, which would be designated as pollution control outlays. These might include equipment for extracting substances from stack gases or fluid effluent, for example. There are other responses, however. A material may be substituted which is not regarded as a pollutant when emitted in gaseous, fluid, or solid waste. A basic process may be changed which cuts emission of pollutants. Total emission of pollutants may be cut by a combination of ordinary pollution control equipment which in turn causes a reduction in consumption of the article in question by increasing cost and price. There is little hope for estimating the latter types of response on any comprehensive basis.

Thus the whole problem cannot be solved. Even though the suggested adjustments are partial, however, they ought to be made, for they may permit some sharpening of conclusions on what has happened to real product.

II. MODELS FOR ACCOUNTING AND ANALYSIS

To go beyond the rather simpleminded compilation of series on expenditures made in connection with pollution change or control and estimate the net benefits associated with changes in pollutants emitted requires the use of a model that will simulate, at least in part, the real repercussions that result from a change that is imposed. There are many models of widely varying degrees of complexity and adequacy that might be and are used for this task.[7] Several models have been presented in recent literature which lend themselves to rather detailed forecasting and policy analysis. They include rather straightforward extensions of open input-output models, analytical-type accounting models which balance materials flows as well as money flows, and activity analysis models embodying important features of natural environmental systems. In discussing them we will proceed from the simpler ones which are relatively easy to implement to those which encompass more significant elements of reality but are harder to implement. We discuss three, a national input-output model, models to account for all materials flows, and a linear programming model adapted to the analysis of regional pollution problems.

The National I-O Model

In recent papers, W. Leontief has proposed an extension of the basic national open I-O model which would permit forecasting of residuals emissons and of the effects of certain types of policy measures. The following exposition of his proposal is based on the mathematical appendix of Leontief's article in the *Review of Economics and Statistics*.[8] Although interpretation of the mathematics is rather straightforward, we shall describe the system in some detail because pollutants are handled somewhat differently from ordinary commodities and also because some readers may not be familiar with matrix representation of a system of equations.

The physical input-output balance with pollutants included in the system is shown by matrix equation (1) in Exhibit 1. We have m ordinary goods and $n - m$ pollutants, making a total of n inputs and outputs.

Each of the A matrices is a matrix of input-output coefficients. For example; a_{ij} is the amount of ith ordinary input required per unit of jth ordinary output (submatrix A_{11}); a_{ik} is the amount of ith ordinary input required to produce a unit of the kth pollutant reduction output (submatrix A_{12}); a_{ki} is the amount of the kth pollutant resulting from producing a unit of ith ordinary output (submatrix A_{21}); a_{kl} is the

---

[7] It is an interesting exercise to try to specify the model that is implicit in some of the current "analyses" of pollution problems.

[8] Wassily Leontief, "Environmental Repercussions of the Economic Structure: An Input-Output Approach," *Review of Economics and Statistics,* August 1970, pp. 262–271.

EXHIBIT 1

Physical Input-Output Balance

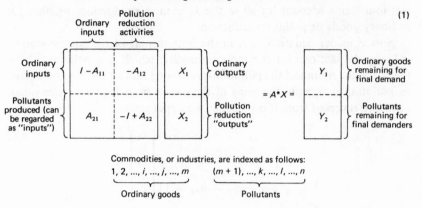

Commodities, or industries, are indexed as follows:

$1, 2, ..., i, ..., j, ..., m$ $(m + 1), ..., k, ..., l, ..., n$

Ordinary goods   Pollutants

amount of the kth pollutant produced as a result of a unit reduction in the lth pollutant (submatrix A_{22}).

To see what is involved in this system of equations, let us separate out one of them and write it out in full. Assume that we have three ordinary commodities and two pollutant reduction activities,[9] a total of five outputs, or "inputs," in all. Take, for example, the first equation, (2), which is formed by multiplying each member of the first row of A^* by the corresponding members of the X vector of industry outputs and adding these products together, thereby obtaining the first member, y_1, of the vector of final outputs, Y:

$$[1 - a_{12} - a_{13} - a_{14} - a_{15}]\begin{bmatrix} x_1 \\ x_2 \\ x_3 \\ x_4 \\ x_5 \end{bmatrix} = y_1 \tag{2}$$

or,

$$x_1 - a_{12}x_2 - a_{13}x_3 - a_{14}x_4 - a_{15}x_5 = y_1.$$

Note that in the matrices of input-output coefficients we have regarded a_{ii} and a_{kk} as zero so that industry output is always net of its own output that *it* uses.

[9] We speak of pollutant reduction activities rather than industries because in any application the pollutant reduction activities often will be a part of an ordinary industry. In some cases it may be desirable to account for these separately.

This equation simply says that the total output of the first commodity minus the amount used in the production of x_2, x_3, x_4, and x_5 is equal to the amount of the first commodity, y_1, going to final demanders. The last four terms account for all of the x_1 used in production, whether for ordinary goods or pollution reduction.

Now consider equation (3), in the bottom part of the square matrix, A^*, say the last one for the nth commodity, which is a pollutant. Note that since the output of the pollution-processing industry is here measured as pollution reduction, the signs of the elements of the two lower quadrants are reversed from those of the two upper ones:

$$[a_{51} + a_{52} + a_{53} + a_{54} - 1] \begin{bmatrix} x_1 \\ x_2 \\ x_3 \\ x_4 \\ x_5 \end{bmatrix} = y_5 \tag{3}$$

or,

$$a_{51}x_1 + a_{52}x_2 + a_{53}x_3 + a_{54}x_4 - x_5 = y_5.$$

This says that the pollutant, which is commodity number five, that is generated in the production of x_1, x_2, x_3, and x_4 *minus* the amount by which this pollutant is reduced equals the amount which goes to final demanders.

Thus, in abbreviated matrix form, the physical input-output balance is $A^*X = Y$, where X and Y are vectors of industry outputs and deliveries of final goods, respectively. Industry outputs include pollutant reduction, and final goods include pollutants received.[10]

---

[10] So far, no account has been taken of pollutants generated by the final demand sector. To do so, form a "household" pollution generation matrix, A_y, of the coefficients a_{gy_i}, showing the amount of pollutant g generated per unit of commodity y_i consumed.

Then the vector of pollutants generated by household consumption will be, say, $Y_H = A_y Y_1$.

If Y_E is the vector of pollutants reaching the "environment," we have:

$$Y_E = \boxed{A_{21} \;\vert -I + A_{22}} \begin{bmatrix} X_1 \\ X_2 \end{bmatrix} + Y_H$$

$$= [A_{21} \qquad A_{22}] \begin{bmatrix} X_1 \\ X_2 \end{bmatrix} + Y_H \qquad - X_2$$

$$\underbrace{\phantom{= [A_{21} \qquad A_{22}] \begin{bmatrix} X_1 \\ X_2 \end{bmatrix} + Y_H}}_{\substack{\text{Total generated by industry} \\ \text{and households}}} \underbrace{}_{\substack{\text{Pollutants} \\ \text{processed}}}$$

$$= Y_2 + Y_H.$$

[Cont. on p. 459]

EXHIBIT 2

Input-Output Balance Between Prices and Values Added

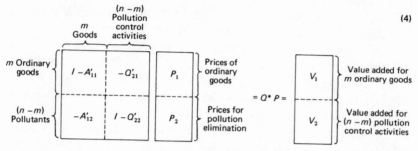

The system of equations, $A*X = Y$, can be solved for the vector X, industry outputs, by premultiplying each side by the inverse of the matrix, $(A*)^{-1}$, obtaining $X = (A*)^{-1}Y$. Thus, if $(A*)^{-1}$ has been calculated for a given industrial structure, the industry outputs, X, that would be associated with any specified bill of final goods, Y, can be calculated very easily, given, of course, the peculiar assumptions of the input-output scheme as commonly formulated. The main one is that the input coefficients, the a's, are fixed no matter what the size of an industry's output. That is, there is only one way to produce an output, a way that is completely described by one column of a coefficients. It is this assumption that facilitates calculation of economy-wide effects of certain policy changes or changes in final demands.

If the value added in the production of a unit of a commodity is known,[11] this schema can be used to calculate the prices of the commodities that will rule under certain specified conditions. First we express the input-output balance between prices and values added, as in equation (4) in Exhibit 2. P is a vector of prices of outputs, partitioned into ordinary goods and pollutants, as before, and V is a vector of values added, partitioned in the same way. The square matrix is different, however, in

[Cont. from p. 458]

Thus, if (1) is to hold, the lower part of the Y vector must be net of household pollution since these equations express relations between pollutants generated by industry, processed by industry, and delivered by industry to households:

$$\begin{array}{|c|} \hline Y_1 \\ \hline Y_E - Y_H \\ \hline \end{array}$$

If $Y_H = 0$, this reduces to the original formulation with $Y_E = Y_2$.

[11] For example, if labor is the only factor input and the labor input coefficients, analogous to the input-output coefficients, a_{ij}, are known and a wage rate is specified, value added can be calculated for each good.

that A^* has been transposed, that is, its columns and rows have been interchanged so that, for example, element a_{ki} is now where element a_{ik} used to be.

In addition, the coefficients involving pollution generation [those in A_{21} and in $(-I + A_{22})$] have been modified. They have been reduced by a factor which reflects the proportion of pollutant generated by an industry the elimination of which is paid for by it. Thus, if industry i generates a_{ki} pollutant per unit of output (a_{ki} is in A_{ki}) and pays for the elimination of $100r_{ki}$ per cent of it, we replace a_{ki} by $q_{ki} = r_{ki}a_{ki}$. A similar modification is made for pollutants produced by the pollutant control industries, that is, of the a_{kl} found in the quadrant $(-I + A_{22})$.

After these modifications, A_{21} becomes $-Q_{21}$ and $(-I + A_{22})$ becomes $(I - Q_{22})$. Note that signs are changed in order to have the price of the product minus the sum of required inputs times their prices be equal to value added for each industry.[12]

In matrix form, the price–value-added balance is expressed as $Q^*P = V$. As before, we can premultiply both sides by $(Q^*)^{-1}$ and in this way determine the prices that must rule for a given set of values added *and* q's: $P = (Q^*)^{-1}V$. Note that if each industry pays for the

[12] Consider now an equation involving the top portion of the large square matrix, Q^*, in Exhibit 2, say the first. Assume a five-commodity economy as before.

Since A^* has been transposed (as indicated by the prime to the upper right of A_{11}, etc.), the first column of A^* is now the first row of Q^*, with the coefficients a_{ki} and a_{kl} modified as just explained. Thus the first equation, using *original* subscripts, is:

$$[1 - a_{21} - a_{31} - q_{41} - q_{51}] \begin{bmatrix} p_1 \\ p_2 \\ p_3 \\ p_4 \\ p_5 \end{bmatrix} = v_1$$

or,

$$p_1 - a_{21}p_2 - a_{31}p_3 - q_{41}p_4 - q_{51}p_5 = v_1.$$

This says that the price of commodity number one minus the cost of ordinary inputs numbers two and three minus that *portion* of the per unit cost of eliminating pollutants four and five generated in the production of good number one to be borne by industry number one is equal to the value added of industry number one.

Similarly, the equation involving the last line of Q^* is:

$$-a_{1n}p_1 - a_{2n}p_2 - a_{3n}p_3 - q_{4n}p_4 + p_5 = v_n.$$

This says the same thing, with the industry in question a pollution control industry.

whole per unit cost of pollutants eliminated that it has produced (i.e., if r_{ki} and r_{kl} equal 1), then $Q_{21} = A_{21}$ and $Q_{22} = A_{22}$.

By using the relationships established in these equations, various interesting analyses can be performed. For example, calculations can now be made of changes in residuals resulting directly and indirectly from a change in final demand [13] or of the net increase in production needed to achieve a specified reduction in residuals while holding final goods production constant. This analysis accounts not only for the resources needed by the residuals control sector but the resources used indirectly to control residuals from the supplying industries.

Equation (4) and those derived from it balance the system in value terms and admit the possibility of some residuals being controlled by the manufacturing industries themselves (but still in activities separable from their normal production process) rather than only by the residuals control sector.

The appeal of the I-O approach as extended to include residuals generation and control lies in the ease with which it can be implemented. At least two efforts are already underway. Leontief reports on one in this volume, and at our own organization, Resources for the Future, an effort is being made to project resource use and residuals generation several decades into the future by means of a mathematical model which embodies a national input-output matrix.[14] This model contains techniques for projecting the "exogenous" final demands in the I-O model and also techniques for projecting the technical coefficients based on technological change and substitutions induced by relative price shifts. The model also projects residuals from government activities and final consumption.

The economy-wide I-O approach is best suited for residuals problems where location of discharge does not matter, or at least is not a dominant consideration, either for natural or policy reasons. For example, should the increase in atmospheric CO_2 become a problem of real concern, the I-O approach would permit testing the influence of different patterns of final demand on CO_2 discharge, given that the production technology of the economy did not change or changed in accordance with the projections of technical and residual coefficients. In this case the specific loca-

---

[13] When the change in final demand is a unit increase in the ith good or service, ordinary inputs required and residuals generated are the elements of the ith column of $(A^*)^{-1}$.

[14] This work is being conducted by Ronald G. Ridker and Robert U. Ayres.

tion of the discharge does not matter, because more or less uniform dilution occurs globally—at least in a given hemisphere.

In those cases where concentration, exposure, and assimilative capacity do vary with location, an "ideal" policy would take account of these differences, but certain considerations, cost of implementation, for example, may point to the desirability of national emission standards even in these cases. In this circumstance, the national I-O model will still be of some use. For example, the implications for residuals and industry outputs of alternative patterns of final demand and levels of residuals control can be played out, although the linkage with environmental effects must then be extremely loose.

As of September 1970, performance standards for new facilities had been established by the Environmental Protection Agency (EPA) for nitric acid plants, contact sulfuric acid plants, portland cement plants, large incinerators, and fossil fuel steam plants. In addition, emission standards applicable to all sources will shortly be established for asbestos, mercury, and beryllium.[15] The national I-O approach would be of considerable help in analyzing these and similar cases.

Another calculation that can be made is one in which patterns of final demand are projected under the assumption of no residuals control and with present or projected production technologies, including residuals generation coefficients, going into the future. One can get an impression of alternative possible futures by means of these "projections," as will be possible with the Ridker-Ayres model already mentioned.

The I-O approach as we have described it so far has some notable shortcomings, however:

1. The system as suggested up to this point is on a national scale whereas pollution "problem sheds" tend to be on a regional scale, and sometimes the region is quite small.

2. It has not accounted in a logically complete manner for the residuals generated in production and consumption in the initial attempts at application. In principle, however, the pollutant categories could be expanded to include *all* residuals. If the classification were rather detailed, there would be many pollution "control" industries with zero output.

3. It is usually not correct to think of residuals control as taking place in a separate residual control sector or even in separate residual control activities—especially in the case of industrial activities. In most indus-

[15] *Environmental Quality,* second annual report of the Council on Environmental Quality, August 1971, p. 9.

tries, process changes resulting in residual control and greater production of usable products are important alternatives to separate residual control activities either outside or within the industry. The only way such changes resulting either from new application of existing technology or development of new technology can be inserted into the I-O approach is by changing coefficients relating residuals generation to output. There is no internal optimizing method for selecting industrial processes in view of their residual generation characteristics and other economic attributes—unless I-O analysis is abandoned for activity analysis, its close relative.

4. The model focuses on residuals generation and discharge. It does not analyze what happens to residuals once they enter into the environment, nor does it incorporate any consideration of damages. The processes of transportation and transformation in the environment, as affected by hydrological, meteorological, biological, and other natural system conditions have a significant bearing on the damaging effects of a given amount of residuals discharge.

5. The model focuses on residuals control costs but gives no attention to the value of the loss in function of common property resources when their quality deteriorates due to the effects of residuals discharge.

Some of the deficiencies of the I-O approach as just described can be remedied within its framework, but only at the cost of considerable complication. For example, the limitation of national scale of the model immediately suggests regional I-O models. However, even this extension would leave two important limitations: the linearity of the system, which limits the extent of the changes with which it can deal, and the one-to-one relationship between process and product.

Regional and Interregional I-O Models

National boundaries seldom describe a satisfactory area for the analysis of pollution problems. They tend to conform more nearly to natural regions ranging from the entire globe (as with CO_2 and DDT) to small stretches of river or highly localized airsheds. In principle this fact could be accommodated in the I-O approach by developing a set of linked interregional models for the nation. There is not much logical or mathematical difficulty in converting the national to an interregional model. The extensions are straightforward, and consist primarily of adding rows and columns specifying imports to and exports from the various regions. The problem lies rather in data requirements.

There are many reasons for wishing to have a set of coherent I-O models for subnational regions. Many tables have been constructed for individual states and regions, but no consistent set exists for the nation as a whole. The pollution issue adds another argument for developing such a system. We propose that discussions be initiated leading to the design of a national system of regional I-O models for analysis of various problems, including residuals generation and discharge.[16]

Accounting for Residuals in a Logically Complete Manner

The residuals generation aspect of the present I-O models does not completely account for all materials flows, including residuals, that are generated by the various parts of the real-world system. There is no environmental sector, and all residuals not processed are viewed as ending up in the final demand sector. Moreover, interdependencies among solid, liquid, and gaseous residuals in production, consumption, and transformation (treatment) processes are not identified or accounted for.

In a recent study by Ayres, d'Arge, and Kneese,[17] models have been explored which provide for a logically complete accounting of materials flowing into production and consumption processes in the economy and thence to the environment. The approach proceeds by specifying a set of equations representing materials balances in conjunction with the equations representing an interdependent economic system. We will treat it only briefly because so far it has had little empirical application. It has called attention to the importance of the conservation of mass in considering residuals processes—both as to the amounts produced and the limitations of treatment processes with respect to them. Essentially all raw materials (in terms of mass) which enter the extractive and materials-processing activities of the economy must be returned to the environment as residuals. This fact is not controverted by the application

[16] A substantial amount of work has already been done on regional environmental problems involving the I-O approach. See John H. Cumberland, "A Regional Interindustry Model for Analysis of Development Objectives," *Regional Science Association Papers,* 1966, pp. 65–94; Cumberland, "Application of Input-Output Technique to the Analysis of Environmental Problems," prepared for the Fifth International Conference on Input-Output Techniques, Geneva, January 11–19, 1971; and Walter Isard et al., "On the Linkage of Socio-Economic and Ecologic Systems," in *Regional Science Association Papers,* 1968, pp. 79–100.

[17] Allen V. Kneese, Robert U. Ayres, and Ralph C. d'Arge, *Economics and the Environment: A Materials Balance Approach,* Washington, D.C., Resources for the Future, Inc., 1971. For later comments on this approach, see Roger G. Noll and John Trijonis, "Mass Balance, General Equilibrium, and Environmental Externalities," *American Economic Review,* September 1971, pp. 730–735; and A. O. Converse, "On the Extension of Input-Output Analysis to Account for Environmental Externalities," *American Economic Review,* March 1971, pp. 197–198.

of treatment processes, since they only transform materials and do not destroy them. Some estimates of residuals generated in the U.S. economy have been made based on materials balance concepts, and other applications in analysis and forecasting are being explored.

The model developed by the above-mentioned authors is essentially an extension of the Walras-Cassel-Leontief general interdependency analysis with explicit introduction of the concept of mass balance. Theoretical welfare economic aspects of the model have also been examined, but these are of no particular interest to us here. Extensions of a model comparable to the one presented here have also been examined from a welfare economics point of view by Karl-Göran Mäler.[18]

There are a number of ways in which a comprehensive materials balance might be illustrated. Perhaps the simplest and most direct would be an adaptation of the activity analysis format, as in Exhibit 3. Row headings indicate particular goods or services. Activities (which could be industries but do not have to be) are indicated by column headings. Final consumption activities (here combined into one column) are also included in the format.

A negative entry in a cell indicates the quantity of the good (measured by weight except for services, which must be measured in conventional units) in that row that is used as an input by the corresponding activity. A positive entry in a cell indicates the amount of the good in that row that is produced by the corresponding activity.[19] For example, suppose that on row 3 a -22 appears in column 6 and a $+37$ in column 9. This would mean that 22 units of good 3 are used as an input to activity 6 and that 37 units of good 3 are produced by activity 9.

Resources coming from the environment are always inputs; hence the negative signs as indicated. Purely intermediate goods and services are used only within the industrial sector. Hence, all rows sum to zero for this sector.

Final goods and services have net positive balances for the industrial sector, but the totals for all economic units are zero, since goods and services going to the final consumption sector are regarded as inputs into the consumption activity.

Residuals may go into an activity that transforms them, perhaps producing some salable product (reclamation) along with other residuals or they may go to the environment. The destination might be indicated by a subscript, say A for atmosphere or W for water. In the case of

[18] *Op. cit.*
[19] All entries are per unit of time.

EXHIBIT 3

Format for Materials Balance

Outputs and/or Inputs	Industrial Activities 1	Industrial Activities 2	Industrial Activities ...	Total	Final Consumption Activities (e.g., households)	Total for All Economic Units	Total to Environment from: Industry	Total to Environment from: Final Consumption	Total from Environment to: Industry	Total from Environment to: Final Consumption
Resources 1. 2. .	−	+	−	−	−	−	0	0	−	−
Intermediate goods and services 1. 2. .	−	+		0	0	0	0	0	0	0
Final goods and services 1. 2. .	−	+	+	+	−	0	0	0	0	0
Residuals (including pollutants) 1. 2. .	-5 0	0 -2	$+3I$ $+2I+4A$	0 or ± -2 $+4$	0 or + $+2I+3W$ $+3A$	0 if all is processed; + if not (some goes to environment) 7	4	$3H$ 3		
Column total (excluding services)	0	0	0	0	0	0	} B		} C	

residual 1, for example, five units are "processed" by activity 1, of which three come from industry and two from households. These units contribute to the production of the outputs of activity 1, which may include other residuals. Households also discharge three units of residual 1 to water bodies.

In the case of residual 2, two units are used as input by activity 2, all of them coming from industrial activities. Industrial activities also discharge four units to the atmosphere along with three discharged by households.

Residual row totals for all activities will be zero if all of a given residual produced is processed. If not, the row total will be positive, with some of the residual going to the environment.

Neglecting inventory changes, column totals of tangibles should be zero for each activity, as should also the totals coming from and going to the environment ($B = C$).

Needless to say, the practical implementation of a materials balance accounting system would encounter a host of difficulties that have not been touched on here. This format is useful for thinking about pollution problems, however, since it provides the basis for viewing the choice of production and consumption activities and their levels as a programming problem that treats the production and processing of residuals as an integral part of the whole.

An interesting extension of the economic-materials balance model has been made by James E. Wilen.[20] The connecting link between Wilen's model and the economic-materials balance model is the r vector of resources inputs. In broadest overview, the linkage is as follows: via fixed coefficients, a Y vector of final demands determines the vector of resource materials (r) needed for their production. Next, a matrix D is defined such that $D^{-1}r$ yields a vector, m, of the mass and energy inputs necessary to produce r in nature. The use of these inputs to produce ecosystem products going to the economy (r) results in a reduction of ecosystem products available as production inputs into the ecosystem. This reduction is given by Cm, where C is a matrix converting mass and energy inputs into ecoproduct. The return of mass and energy from the economy to the ecosystems can be handled in an analogous fashion and a net impact on the ecoproduct derived.

This formulation is an interesting extension of the model in a highly

[20] James E. Wilen, "Economic Systems and Ecological Systems: An Attempt at Synthesis," paper presented at the Symposium on Economic Growth and the Natural Environment, April 26–28, 1971, University of California, Riverside.

desirable direction—the incorporation of the ecological impacts of production and consumption activities. However, the formulation does suffer from extreme abstraction and neglects the nonlinearities and interactions that are of central importance in ecological systems—as Wilen recognizes. The problem of linking ecological systems to economic systems will be pursued further in the discussion, below, of the Russell-Spofford model, which exhibits a somewhat greater concreteness and realism.

The Russell-Spofford Model

We have seen that in principle the interindustry-type models can be regionalized, made to account for materials flows to the environment in a logically complete fashion, and, at least in a rough way, to incorporate ecological impacts of production and consumption. We turn now to an operational model of quantitative residuals management devised by Russell and Spofford [21] which to some extent meets all five of the criteria implied by our above discussion:

1. It is regional and location-specific within the region. Its results can be translated into an accounting entity such as gross regional product. In this, it is similar to the I-O models.

2. It can account for residuals in a logically complete manner and does so in some of its submodels.

3. It can treat process, input, and product changes as well as residuals treatment in an integral manner.

4. It traces residuals discharged to the environment through processes of diffusion and degradation and specified concentrations of them at receptor locations. It incorporates an ecological model which translates these concentrations into impacts on higher organisms of direct interest to man.

5. It explicitly considers economic damages to receptors resulting from residuals discharge. In contrast to the I-O type models, it is an optimizing model which can be used to analyze a wide range of policy alternatives.

The Russell-Spofford model deals simultaneously with the three major general types of residuals—airborne, waterborne, and solid—and reflects the physical links among them. It "recognizes," for example, that the decision to remove waterborne organic wastes by standard sew-

[21] Clifford S. Russell and Walter O. Spofford, Jr., are the authors' associates at Resources for the Future, Inc.

age treatment processes creates a sludge which, in turn, represents a solid residuals problem; the sludge must either be disposed of on the land or burned, the latter alternative creating airborne particulates and gaseous residuals. Second, it can incorporate the nontreatment alternatives available (especially to industrial firms) for reducing the level of residuals generation. These include input substitution (as of natural gas for coal); change in basic production methods (as in the conversion of beet sugar refineries from the batch to continuous diffusion process —see Chart 1, below); recirculation or residual-bearing streams (as in recirculation of condenser cooling water in thermal-electric generating plants); and by-product recovery (as in the recovery and reuse of fiber, clay, and titanium from the white water "waste" of papermaking machines). Third, the model incorporates and can handle environmental simulation models if necessary, as well as analytical transformation functions which translate quantities of discharge (mass and energy— for example, heat) at particular (source) locations into concentrations at other (receptor) locations. Moreover, it incorporates an ecological model which translates residuals concentrations into impacts upon various species.

The model containing these features is shown schematically in Exhibit 4. The four main components of the over-all framework may be described as follows:

1. A linear programming interindustry model that relates inputs and outputs of selected production processes and consumption activities at specified locations within a region, including the unit amounts and types of residuals generated by the production of each product; the costs of transforming these residuals from one form to another (as of gaseous to liquid in the scrubbing of stack gases); the costs of transporting the residuals from one place to another; and the cost of any final discharge-related activity such as landfill operations.

The interindustry model permits choices among production processes, raw material input mixes, by-product production, recycling of residuals, and in-plant adjustments and improvement, all of which can reduce the total quantity of residuals generated; that is, the residuals generated are not assumed fixed either in form or in quantity. This model also allows for choices among treatment processes and hence among the possible forms of the residual to be disposed of in the natural environment and, to a limited extent, among the locations at which discharge is accomplished.

EXHIBIT 4

Schematic Diagram of Residuals—Environmental
Quality Planning Model

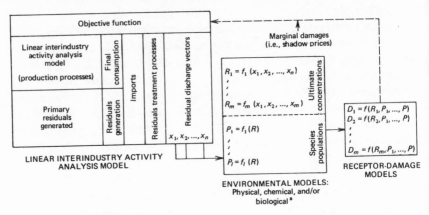

a Linear and nonlinear analytical expressions as well as simulation models are implied by these expressions. For simplicity, the functions in the figure reflect only one type of pollutant.

2. Environmental diffusion models which describe the end of various residuals after their discharge into the physical environment. Essentially, these models may be thought of as transformation functions operating on the vector of residuals discharges and yielding another vector of ambient concentrations at specific locations throughout the environment. Between discharge point and receptor locations, the residual may be diluted in the relatively large volume of air or water in the natural world, transformed from one form to another (as in the decay of oxygen-demanding organics), accumulated or stored (as in the accumulation of organics in benthal deposits) and, of course, transported to another place. Fortunately, for many situations the equations characterizing the transformation of residuals between discharge and receptor locations reduce to simple linear forms for steady-state deterministic conditions so that the linkage sometimes can be made via a coefficient.[22]

3. Ecological models analogous to the more familiar physical diffusion models are models of ecological systems which reflect the changes (as through a food chain) following on the introduction of a particular

[22] It should be noted, however, that physical, chemical, and/or biological interactions among residuals in the environment cannot be handled quite so easily.

residual discharge or on moving to a different set of ambient concentrations. Instead of residuals concentrations as the end products of this type of model, we might obtain estimates of the populations of species of direct interest to man, such as sport fish or rare and endangered animals.

4. Ideally, a set of receptor-damage functions relating the concentration of residuals in the environment and the impact on species to the resulting damages, whether these are sustained directly by humans or indirectly through impacts on material objects or the medium of such receptors as plants or animals in which man has a commercial, scientific, or aesthetic interest. Ideally, the functions relating concentrations and impacts on species to receptor damage should be in monetary terms. Actually, adequate damage functions have not been estimated for any phase of the residuals problem. Consequently, in the computations so far, which have been aimed at testing the whole framework, it has been necessary to use arbitrary functions.

As an alternative to the use of damage functions in the analysis (or in their absence), constraints, or standards, could be specified for emissions or for concentrations at points where receptors are exposed to the pollutant. In practice, this will be a very important type of analysis because of the many difficulties in estimating damage functions.

The linkage between the components and the method of optimum-seeking may be explained in an illustrative way as follows. Solve the linear programming model initially [23] with no restrictions or prices on the discharge of residuals. Using the resulting initial set of discharges as inputs to the diffusion models and the resulting ambient concentrations as the arguments of the damage functions, the marginal damages can be determined (damage associated with a unit change in discharge). These marginal damages may then be applied as interim effluent charges on the discharge activities in the linear model, and that model solved again for a new set of production, consumption, treatment, and discharge activities. The procedure is repeated until the optimum is found.

This procedure can be looked at as a steepest ascent technique for solving a nonlinear programming problem. The objective function is linearized locally, using the provisional marginal damages as "fixed" residuals discharge prices. Because the constraint set is also linear, the resulting problem may be solved using standard linear programming

[23] There are a number of different ways in which the objective function and constraints might be formulated.

methods. This linearized subproblem is solved subject to suitable bounds on the allowable distance that a decision variable may move in a single iteration. The objective function is then linearized again around the new temporary solution point, and so on until a local optimum is reached.

The problem for which the model is intended to provide an approximate solution could also be stated in a completely general manner not suitable to numerical solution, as the above described version is, but perhaps easier to understand. The objective is to maximize, for a region, a complicated economic criterion function reflecting the costs of regional production, the benefits from regional consumption, the costs of residuals treatment, and the external damages resulting from residuals discharges, with allowance for the "assimilative" capabilities of the regional environment.[24] In this form, the regional residuals management problem is a general nonlinear programming problem, with both objective function and some constraints being nonlinear. But since the solution of a nonlinear problem as complicated as this one may be very difficult, if not impossible, it is useful to make the changes required to get rid of the nonlinearities. The problem then appears as sketched earlier.

The Russell-Spofford model was designed for the analysis of residuals management in regions where the scale and severity of the problems justify a considerable investment in data and analysis. The model is now in the process of being applied to the lower Delaware River basin. As a result, we shall know a good deal more about the precise form the model should take and about the volume and nature of the data required to provide a useful tool.

The model does not completely portray all aspects of the simultaneous economic production of goods and services and the handling of residuals. As it now stands, it does not incorporate adaptations at the consumer or household level. In principle, the consumer can be viewed as choosing among "consumption processes" to maximize utility in a manner entirely analogous to the choice among production processes that is an integral part of the solution of the linear programming part of the R-S model.[25] Specification of the consumption processes would

[24] For more detailed explanations of the model, see Clifford S. Russell and Walter O. Spofford, Jr., "A Quantitative Framework for Residuals Management Decisions," in Allen V. Kneese and Blair T. Bower, eds., *Environmental Quality Analysis: Theory and Method in the Social Sciences*, Baltimore, Johns Hopkins Press, 1971; and Clifford S. Russell, "Regional Environmental Quality Management: A Quantitative Approach," paper presented at the California Institute of Technology Conference on Technological Change and the Human Environment, October 19–21, 1970.

[25] See Kelvin Lancaster, "A New Approach to Consumer Theory," *Journal of Political Economy*, April 1966, pp. 132–157.

be enormously difficult, but the omission no doubt is quantitatively important for some problems. The cheapest way to reduce exposure to some pollutants is by substitution in the consumer budget.

Another partial limitation is the way in which the locational aspects of the problem are handled. As pointed out above, the model is location-specific in that locations of emission sources and receptors play an essential role in determining the concentrations to which receptors are exposed. The model does not optimize for location, however. That is to say, the effects of different specified locational configurations must be compared by successively solving models incorporating them. Apart from these limitations, the R-S model presents a pattern for considering analysis of environmental pollution problems that provides valuable guidance for the collection and organization of pertinent data.

III. DATA NEEDS SUGGESTED BY THE MODELS FOR ANALYSIS OF ENVIRONMENTAL POLLUTION

The models for analysis of environmental pollution discussed above could be implemented in various degrees of complexity and detail. They could be complicated or extended, as, for example, by a more elaborate treatment of the location factor or by giving direct attention to consumer response to changed conditions (including price changes) resulting from pollution controls.

Clearly, the types and depth of data that will be needed are going to depend on the particular forms of these and other possible models that will be found to be useful in grappling with pollution problems. Useful guidance for practical data decisions will be provided by efforts under way to implement the national I-O model, the Russell-Spofford model, and possibly others. Without waiting for substantial progress on these efforts, however, it is possible to make a few detailed suggestions for data on the basis of what we already know and to make a number of more general suggestions on types of data whose compilation should be initiated or expanded.

Our suggestions on needs for continuing data will be considered under two categories. First, baselines need to be established and maintained, the general idea being that departures from baselines serve as warning signals. Two types of baseline data will be considered: first, measures of a summary or indicator nature which will be useful for the general public, and, second, more detailed or sophisticated baselines useful to technicians. The second general category consists of data more directly needed for the design, analysis, and administration of pollution control schemes.

The idea behind use of the term "baseline" seems to be that in the absence of interference the system under examination—for example, an ecological system—continues to function in a manner approximating a steady state. This must be understood to include the case of nonexplosive oscillatory behavior, too. A definite departure from this baseline situation indicates that a new element has been introduced into the operation of the system. The resulting change may or may not be desirable with respect to human objectives. In any case, departure from the baseline calls for investigation. If the effect of the intrusion is benign, it would be good to know what has happened, for we might be able to turn the mechanism involved to our account. If the effect has been undesirable, we ought to understand what has happened, for the observed deterioration may presage more serious effects unless the disturbing factor is properly dealt with.

Baseline and Indicator Data for the Citizen

It is unlikely that any problem involving deterioration of the "environment" can be handled by public action unless a substantial part of the public understands that a particular type of deterioration actually has taken place. This is necessary if there is to be any consideration at all of the desirability of remedial action by members of the public and its elected representatives.

The general characteristics of baseline measures that might fill this need are suggested and limited by the level of technical understanding of the general public of the various physical and biological systems. Although the level of comprehension no doubt is rising gradually, the types of measures needed can best be characterized as indicators. The indicator itself may not be a part of the group of variables that are significant for control or manipulation of the system, although it will be closely associated with the variables that the expert might view as expressing best the state of the system in question.

With this in mind, it is possible to suggest some of the characteristics that a system of indicators useful to the general public should have. First, and very important, the number of indicators should be limited, for there is no useful result to be expected from asking the ordinary citizen to take the time to determine the significance of several hundred series even if he could. Indeed, even for the expert the very idea of changes in the state of a system that have significance for man seems to imply the view that there are some variables that perform the function of summarization. This function should be the main basis for choosing the limited number of indicators. In systems with living organisms, the measure should be chosen with a view to its properties as an integrator of effects over time and over a variety of intrusions. This suggests that indicators probably should be chosen from the higher trophic levels of the various types of ecosystems in which we are interested, since in many cases substances are concentrated as the successive members of the food chain eat each other, thereby revealing adverse effects or intrusions more clearly.

To give concreteness to these general considerations, a few candidates for general indicators are suggested here. Our purpose is only to provide illustrations and not to suggest that these ought to be among the indicators that should be adopted, this determination being one that we gladly leave to the experts in these matters.

In the case of water bodies, changes in the various types of fish populations are a good summary indicator of changes in many aspects of the aquatic environment. The complete disappearance of certain types of fish is easily understood to signify a major change in the condition of the water body, perhaps a large change in dissolved oxygen content or the introduction of substances incompatible with the species in question.

In water bodies of various types, especially estuaries, changes in the distribution of the populations of different types of shellfish or in their density at particular locations can serve as summary indicators of effects flowing from a variety of sources.

A physical aspect of water bodies that is of direct concern to the nonexpert is turbidity, a quality that is measured in an easily understood standard way. Changes in turbidity—on the average, seasonal, after rains, etc.—may be caused by a variety of factors, which is the same as saying that this is an integrative indicator, a property we believe to be desirable. Note that the emphasis here is on changes in turbidity. In some cases natural conditions produce a permanently high but harmless level of turbidity.

Changes in bird populations are indicative of changes in soil and vegetation. That these changes can register effectively the introduction of pesticides into the soil and other parts of the environment (as, for example, with the introduction of the poison compound 1080 into carrion eaten by birds) is widely understood. The whole web of relations involved is very complex, of course, but the summarization of the effects on birds is just the kind of indicator that is needed to lead the nontechnician to an awareness that something important may be happening which will affect other things that may be more important to him than the birds themselves.[26]

In the case of the atmosphere, some of the pollutants that may have adverse effects on health are not visible nor do they have a distinctive odor. Still, because the presence of this type of pollutant is associated with the presence of other pollutants that are directly detectable by persons, an indicator of detectable pollutants can serve the double purpose of warning of the perceptible changes as well as those not directly accessible to human perception. What types of measure might qualify? There are various ways to measure haze, but many of the methods have no immediate significance for the nonexpert. Again, merely to indicate the *type* of measure needed, one possibility easily understood by the nonexpert would be an adaptation of a procedure used to test the quality of a camera lens. In this test a standard test card with various numbers of lines per inch on it is photographed under standard conditions (distance, light, etc.). Perhaps it would be possible to use a somewhat similar test to measure haze, for example, by photographing a test card under standard conditions at rather long distances. Whatever the method of measurement the technical expert might finally recommend, it is desirable that the procedure and the way in which the results of the test are expressed have a ready meaning for the ordinary person.[27]

The particulate content of the air is of rather direct significance for the nonexpert and would qualify as a suitable measure if translated into a form or forms with simple meaning, perhaps by a simple model of the respiration process or as calculated deposition per year under standard conditions.

Is the miner's canary the prototype of an indicator of the general severity of air pollution for health? Ideally several types of indicator, which might be insects, plants, or animals, would be useful. Some indicators are especially sensitive to particular pollutants, and the same indicator may not serve equally well to register acute episodes and longer-

[26] Leaving aside aesthetic or recreational interest in a wild animal or bird, the view of some—that extinction of a species is nothing very significant since extinctions have been occurring throughout all natural history—begs the question. This question is whether the observed imminent or actual extinction is the result of a change that will produce adverse effects in addition to the observed extinction.

[27] One of the authors was told of a similar and even simpler test conducted in Tokyo, Japan, over a period of many years. It appears that one gentleman kept a record each day of whether Mount Fuji could be seen or not. Over the period of rapid industrialization, the number of days per year on which it could be seen declined from about 90 to less than 1. What more dramatic indicator of air pollution for a Tokyo resident could be found?

term changes in pollutant levels. In any case, the desideratum is that a change in pollutant level increase mortality or produce other easily observable and quantifiable changes in appearance or function. Colonies of indicator plants, insects, or animals could be maintained in various cities and other environments with the members having a standard genetic composition and receiving standard care. The resulting data would serve as indicators of differences in pollution in time and space, thus suggesting when and where additional investigation should be undertaken.

Note that there is a locational aspect to all of the baseline indicators discussed to this point. Although some of them probably could be combined into state, regional, or national measures, there is little reason to do so. The effects are not national as are those, for example, of so many economic phenomena whose effects are dispersed and homogenized by the market mechanism. The appropriate remedies often appear to be mainly local, granted that it is possible and in some cases may be desirable to apply measures that require uniform action across the nation regardless of variation between locations in the damages produced and in the cost of reducing pollutants to reduce damages by a given amount.

Baseline and Indicator Data for the Experts

The rationale for baseline data useful to technical experts on various aspects of the physical environment is the same as that for indicators useful to the nonexpert. Movement of a measure outside the range of values it has taken in the past serves as a warning that something important may have happened. If the causative factor can be identified and its effect was adverse, it may be possible to develop corrective measures.

There is no need that data collected on a regular basis for possible use by experts have an immediate or obvious significance for the nontechnical person. Nor is it necessary that all of them should be rather summary and/or integrative. Detail is no bar to data being useful to the expert, for if he truly is expert he will know how to use it and put it to work, but it is important to realize that he, too, can be overwhelmed by the enormously high rate at which some types of data can now be generated. This category of data should include a number of "basic" physical, chemical, and biological characteristics of the various environments.

Physical and chemical data. A good illustration of a data system for basic physical characteristics of an environment is provided by the present data system for water quality in the United States. The label "water quality" is somewhat misleading, of course, since what is involved are characteristics which do not indicate generalized quality in and of themselves. This depends on the values attached to physical qualities by water users.

The water data system includes a large number of variables, generally expressed as concentrations, including several families of chemicals (e.g., phenols, chlorinated hydrocarbons), pH, individual metals (e.g., mercury, chrome, cobalt, lead), temperature, various aspects of flow behavior, and so on.

The system of baseline measurements for air pollution is far less well developed, reflecting in part the much shorter period over which interest has been strong enough to lead to formation of a measuring system. Pollutants are but part of a desirable system of atmospheric baselines; others include elemental and basic compound measurements and various meteorological characteristics such as cloud cover—a complex phenomenon in itself.

Baseline measures are needed for all the major natural systems, and in many areas systematic measures have been collected for a long time. What is needed at this time is to examine the scope and adequacy of the various systems of measurement to insure that important areas are not neglected and that the measurement programs meet proper sampling requirements.

Of what use are these seemingly isolated series, multiplied in number to a point that must seem otiose to the nontechnician? If a control system already exists or if the need for one should arise, these series very often will have a direct relevance for design or administration of the control system. More fundamental than this, research on the large-scale behavior of these systems cannot be very productive without data.

It ought to be possible to characterize the major changes in ways that would be meaningful to the nonexpert. Some small beginnings are made in the 1971 report to the Congress of the Council on Environmental Quality, but a larger effort is warranted. One essential is that the summary presentations contain references that will direct the interested person to the basic data sources for continuing series.

Biological data. Biological or ecological baseline data for expert use are needed, too. By and large, the detailed series that ought to be collected for different types of situations must be left to the experts for decision, just as in the case of the physical and chemical series on water quality and in other areas of interest. However, we venture to suggest discussion of one type of more general series, namely, studies of ecosystems. The results of these studies should perhaps be included eventually in an augmented system of social accounts.

Studies of ecosystems. Every location in and bordering the country is a part of an ecosystem of one type or another. How can we get some indication that something important may have gone wrong with the way one of them functions, something that may have serious consequences for humans directly or indirectly? A possible method is a systematic program of repeated studies of different ecosystems at different locations in all parts of the country, including the study of populations of the different species and changes in their characteristics such as size, function, appearance, chemical composition, and so on. The discussion proceeds in terms of populations, since that is an aspect of the studies that is easily understood by the nonexpert.

By population study of an ecosystem we mean a study of the levels or densities of the populations (which could be measured by biomass) of the different species (or larger groups) of living beings in the system. We discuss first the general rationale of such a system and then the factors constraining its implementation.

The rationale of population studies of this type is simple. The basic ideas of ecology tell us that the size of an ecosystem—as expressed, say, by biomass—will depend on the energy and nutrients available to the system, other characteristics of the physical environment, and the species constituents. Ecology can be viewed as the study of the relations among energy, nutrients, and living things that determine the size of the system as measured by the rate of biomass production and the relative numbers (or masses) of the different species.

A fundamental concept here is that of the steady state. That is, if the system is subjected to a temporary disturbance, it will (usually) return to its original equilibrium position after a time. The equilibrium position might actually be one of nonexplosive continual oscillation, and these oscillations might be very complex. If the disturbance is permanent rather than temporary (for example, as with the continued inflow of a degradable pesticide into the system), the system will move to a *different* steady state characterized by a different total biomass and different relations among the numbers (or masses) of the various species originally present. Some may disappear altogether. In the larger and longer view, of course, the idea of a steady state to which ecosystems tend to return is bound to be erroneous because of the presence of natural forces producing progressive alteration of the system. Over

decades, ecological succession is a major changing force. On the evolu-
tionary time scale, mutations are an important source of change. Our
concern, however, is with shorter periods of time to which the concept
of steady state has more relevance. Even from a shorter perspective,
an "ecosystem" that is so small that it is not well separated from the
influences of surrounding systems (that is, a system that is not large
relative to the forces coming from the neighboring systems) is likely
to evolve progressively, as may be the case, for example, with some of
our national parks.

The steady state concept suggests that periodically collected population data for an ecosystem possibly could provide a comprehensive and
sensitive indicator of the introduction of foreign substances and also
of damage to some of the species therein, thereby indicating possible
damage of significance to humans if we eat things related to the ecosystem, if we value it for its beauty or other qualities, or if we ingest
things which, although not from this particular ecosystem, have been
exposed to or contain the same substance. If the population census were
quite detailed, it would direct our attention automatically to the most
sensitive parts of the ecosystem, thereby increasing the probability of
early warning. Whatever may be the species or group most susceptible
to damage by, say, a pesticide, or whatever species that rapidly increases to fill the gap thus created, it would be forcefully brought to
our attention by the change in its numbers. Furthermore, low concentrations of the foreign substance would in some cases be brought to our
attention by being concentrated in organisms as it passes up the food
chain. Some of these organisms near the end of the chain will be affected
adversely. For example, reproduction may be impaired or death rates
may rise. In other cases, however, the foreign substance may be concentrated in certain tissues without evident adverse effect.

Ideally, a system of population censuses like this would embrace all
types of living things in the particular ecosystem including microorganisms, ranging from those on the surface, such as plants, mammals, or
birds, those in the soil, those in water bodies, and those in the sediments
underlying water bodies. In general, more frequent censuses would seem
to be desirable where there already is a large flow of pollutants to an
ecosystem, because the composition and quantity of the effluents could
change over a comparatively short period of time. In certain cases where
man's activities greatly simplify the "natural" ecosystem, as with agriculture, stability of the system is often diminished. It would be desirable
that the censuses be more frequent in these cases, too. The period be-

tween studies would not have to be the same for every location, although a study ought to be made at the same time of year for a given location and probably should be made at the same time of year for the same type of ecosystem at different locations.

The difficulties. All of the above is a rather idealized version of how a system of studies of ecological systems might work. Unfortunately, there are many difficulties that prevent its realization, not the least of which is cost, which would rise rapidly as the attempt is made to cover each ecosystem site more completely and in more detail. After all, there are critters on critters, some critters have others inside them, and these have others on and in them—not ad infinitum, as a well-known limerick has it, but far enough in that direction to make the complex world of man-made objects seem simple by comparison.

The layman may believe that it is a simple matter to count the numbers of each species, but the unfortunate fact is that the biological world is not so simple nor is species identification or classification into higher groups an easy thing. Perhaps some 10,000 new species are found each year. Among large creatures that are abroad during the day, the number discovered each year is much less. Perhaps only some two or three are added to the list of birds (now about 8,600), but six to seven thousand insects are added each year to the present list of three-quarters of a million. Nor are species easy to identify. Some groups of organisms have no specialists currently studying them, for example.[28]

Having recognized the cost difficulty and the impossibility of taking a complete count by species, we encounter the fact that there is far from a consensus on classification or on what ought to be measured if budgets are limited. This has an important bearing on the effectiveness with which the diagnostic scheme outlined in the discussion of the idealized system can operate. In this case the detection of changes in the functioning of ecosystems depends on changes in relative populations, not of species—which would be too costly—but of larger groups. But the changes that are observed will depend on the type of measures and the classification used, and classification cannot be said to be the object of a very strong consensus. The difficulty is closely related to the problem of inferring changes in the stability of an ecosystem from changes in species diversity. As is so often pointed out, however, measures of species diversity are very sensitive to the particular scheme of classification that is used.

[28] See Philip Handler, ed., *Biology and the Future of Man,* New York, Oxford, 1970, p. 518ff.

Classification difficulties are but one of many in determining when a permanent change has taken place in the system. Populations of ecosystems do fluctuate. As one investigator states, "All populations of organisms fluctuate in size. For any population the only assertion that can be made about it with certainty is that its size will not remain constant." [29] For example, variations in weather affecting vegetal food supply are sufficient to induce changes in populations which will reverberate throughout the whole system, and these will be not only seasonal in nature but very likely annual, too, and of a rather complicated pattern.

In short, how is the usual noise of the system, consisting of fluctuations of populations within the range of past experience, to be distinguished from changes in populations that are associated with a genuine change in the structure of the system that determines its mode of functioning? Clearly there is a distinct possibility that a genuine change—perhaps one with ultimately important consequences—may be evidenced by population movements well within the range of fluctuations that have occurred in the past and that perhaps have been observed. More accurate interpretation of such fluctuations in populations will require much additional research on many aspects of the behavior of pertinent types of ecosystems.

These several difficulties diminish considerably the value that a system of ecosystem studies might at first sight appear to have, but they are far from sufficient to warrant an easy conclusion that a useful system cannot be formulated. What can be done?

One possibility would be to concentrate on some of the many known sensitive indicators.[30] Egg shells, for example, appear to be rather sensitive to the presence of certain pesticides in the environment. In addition, measurement might concentrate on those species or groups of species that are cheaper to identify, count, and/or weigh. Census efforts might be concentrated, for example, on the higher species. Birds would be preferred to mammals, the former being cheaper to count for various reasons. The principal species of fish, shellfish, and insects in an

[29] E. C. Pielou, *An Introduction to Mathematical Ecology*, New York, Wiley-Interscience, 1969, p. 7. Of course the sentences quoted were not intended to deny the existence of forces producing strong tendencies to equilibria.
This excellent work would be quite accessible to the economist with a modest preparation in mathematical statistics and matrix algebra.

[30] Dale Jenkins, director of the ecology program of the Smithsonian Institution, has provided a discussion of a possible biological environmental monitoring system in a paper entitled, "Biological Monitoring of the Global Chemical Environment," June 1, 1971 (processed). Many of the potential monitors are plants.

area might be included in the count. And of course in some cases important change may be reflected by an easily observable characteristic other than numbers or mass.

Every act of economy has its cost, of course, and a decision to concentrate on higher species or classes is no exception. It *is* possible that effects of the greatest significance to man would first and most clearly be evident in the detailed functioning of systems of microorganisms. Perhaps a suitable compromise in view of our great ignorance would be to make the censuses of a small number of systems rather complete, extending down to the important microorganisms of the system.

We advocate intense discussion looking forward to a larger, more systematic, and better integrated program of ecosystem studies. It would be extremely useful to have a more adequate system of biological indicators of a number of types in many different locations to give us warning of possible adverse changes that would be detected in other ways only with costly delay.

These suggestions—made very diffidently by nonspecialists—are put forward only to give other nonspecialists a sense of the potential usefulness that we feel such a system may have. Actually, the monitoring systems already in operation, both physical and biological, go a substantial distance in the directions suggested. Apart from the water and air quality systems mentioned earlier, a multiagency pesticide monitoring program has been in operation for a number of years under which residues in foods, feed, people, birds, animals, water, and soil have been measured. Many important changes—and decisions not to change—have been effected through these programs.

There is, of course, a multiplicity of monitoring programs. In the federal government alone, there are some 56 in sixteen agencies, costing about $40 million per year.[31] The mere multiplicity of programs raises the problem of coordination. While there may be good reasons for this multiplicity, it seems clear that the enormous quantity of data being generated is not being distilled into a form that will tell the interested layman what is happening. It ought to be possible for a citizen of, say, Washington, D.C., to find out what has happened to any of the various aspects of the environment in the area around his city over the last one, five, or ten years. At present he cannot possibly do this without calling on the services of not one but several specialists and even then will find many lacunae. To get out of the impasse will require an expanded monitoring effort on many fronts and a much

31 Kneese and Bower, eds., *Environmental Quality*, p. 210.

stronger effort to convert the technical data into series that will speak to the nontechnician. The annual report of the Council on Environmental Quality would certainly seem to be the first point of reference. It does give some signs of eventually fulfilling this role.

Data for the Design, Analysis, and Administration of Control Schemes

When it becomes evident through the baseline-monitoring system or other means that something has gone wrong in the environment, the next question is whether remedial action is possible and should be taken. In short, what is needed to design a control scheme and to predict its operation in a way that will facilitate the decision to put it into operation? Three types of data are essential to this task: first, materials balance data; second, production function information—what types of action are possible; and, third, information on the benefits associated with the possible courses of action.

Materials balance accounts. One thing that seems to us to emerge rather clearly from the experience to date is the desirability of a genuinely complete accounting for material inputs and outputs of all economic units, including households, governmental units, and nonprofit institutions, measured in weight, and including those that are sold or paid for as well as those that are not. We discuss first the desirable characteristics of these data without reference to the current status of data collection efforts along these lines.

A materials balance accounting system certainly merits being called basic. These data are essential to almost any approach to the management of unsold residuals flowing from economic units. At a minimum, they permit the identification of sources and locations of emissions and provide the fundamental basis for estimates of transfer and ultimately of exposure. In those cases where a substance is suddenly recognized as an important and perhaps dangerous pollutant, the system would be of immense aid in tracking down the sources of emissions. Finally, if we do find it possible and desirable to move in the direction of models of the sort that have been discussed earlier, the process of implementing them could make very good use of such data. They would be essential for any calculations involving the national input-output system or regional systems that may be constructed in the future. This materials balance accounting system, therefore, should be integrable with the present I-O system, although in some cases a more detailed industrial classification would be desirable.

Classification of the noneconomic output (the residuals or effluents) poses a very difficult problem, and here there is no escape from trying to anticipate later data needs. A considerable body of experience and thought on these matters is reflected in the current classifications of water and air pollution data that are now being collected on a regular basis. An important general question with respect to the classifications now used is whether in certain cases data should be gathered in more detail, as, for example, where one member of a family of pollutants is thought or known to have more serious effects than its relatives.

The products of economic units that are not sold include many things not included in the categories presently regarded as pollutants. One consideration relevant to their classification is the possibility that in the future the substance may be treated in some way (including reclamation) or that it may come to be recognized as a pollutant.

The materials balance accounting system would be more detailed than the I-O system in that discharge data would be for industry *by location*. A location tag for the discharges is an absolutely essential part of the system, although the degree of precision in the location designation need not be the same for all effluents. For those now regarded as important pollutants, the degree of required precision is very high, however. It would be advisable to record initial destination of the effluent in question—whether to an effluent-processing industry or to another disposal site such as atmosphere, water body, or land. In some cases it would be useful to have data not only on final discharges of effluents but also on certain pollutants produced in a plant and processed in that plant.

The data for such an accounting system would be organized by some type of geographical unit. The designation of geographical units should be such that county totals could be formed which could then be related to all the other data presently available on this basis. Probably the geographical unit should not be larger than the county in any case, but where an industrial complex is concentrated in an area, the basic geographical unit should be quite small.

The various censuses will be helpful in developing these balances, but where there are many similar firms in operation, sample coverage would be adequate. The required totals could be estimated on the basis of sample relations between the various materials flows and other variables which are already collected on a comprehensive basis.

Since so many other data with which materials balance data may be associated in the future are available on an annual basis, the calendar year seems to be the appropriate time unit for which the data should be prepared for the system as a whole. In the case of many pollutants, however, there are strong seasonal, weekly, daily, or even hourly variations that carry important implications for measurement by control authorities and for the production of damages. Where sample inquiries are made, presumably of firms that emit important quantities of pollutants, it would be convenient simultaneously to collect more detailed data on the temporal variation in these flows. Existing knowledge is probably sufficient to allow a proper determination of firms falling in this category.

Use of a materials balance accounting system does not mean that every economic unit will literally have to weigh every transaction and split it into the various components dictated by the classification scheme. Although the system is an accounting system which in principle implies complete balance for each economic unit, for all subunits of the system, and for the system as a whole (just as is implied by the national income system), the basic data for the system could be built up from a variety of sources.

Emissions of residuals are currently the target of data collection programs of at least three federal agencies: the Water Quality Office and the Air Pollution Control Office of the Environmental Protection Agency [32] and the U.S. Army Corps of Engineers. The first two are using questionnaires and other means to assemble data on quantities and patterns of pollutant emissions. The Corps of Engineers is using the Refuse Act of 1899 (33 U.S. Code 407) as authorization to collect a quite elaborate body of data on industrial and various other discharges to navigable water bodies.

It is not yet clear just how extensive a body of data will result from these efforts, which are of course closely tied in with the current content of control programs in the case of the two EPA agencies. In any case, it seems clear that the existing programs will fall short of providing data by industry (i.e., all sectors of the economy) by location of pollutants emitted, let alone sufficient data to permit construction of a materials balance system of accounts.

It seems to us that the appropriate first step is to assign some statistical agency of the government the task of attempting to construct a system of materials flows on an annual basis. Only by making the attempt will it be possible to coordinate the pollution emission data activities already underway and to identify the gaps that must be filled

[32] Formerly Federal Water Quality Administration and National Air Pollution Control Administration.

before a complete set of accounts can be constructed. That the system of accounts be complete is not of importance in and of itself. The overwhelmingly important reason is that the possible repercussions of changes in residuals flows in one part of the system can be traced only if complete materials flow data are available on a rather detailed basis. This is true whether sufficiently detailed I-O systems are available for use or not. Any simpler procedures, such as catch-as-catch-can tracing of principal materials impacts, will require the same sort of data.

A possible result of the attempt to construct the complete system may be the integration of data-gathering activities directed principally at substances presently designated as pollutants. The cost of amplifying the body of basic data that will be available shortly to the point where a periodic accounting of the *whole* materials flow can be made may not be very great if the collection of the additional data needed is integrated with data generation activities already in existence.

Information on control techniques and costs. Historical I-O data, baseline data, and information on materials flows all have an important role to play in the comprehension and analysis of pollution problems, but they provide little direct help in deciding what, if anything, should be done. To make headway on this question, we need to know what options are open. For example, we need to know what the possibilities are for processing an effluent containing pollutants or for changing processes so as to alter the composition of effluents together with the costs associated with these different options. The question of what technical options are available arises not only in connection with industrial effluents, but also in connection with residuals coming from households. Similarly, we need also to know what technical options are available for intervention in a given type of environment to raise its assimilative capacity or to improve its condition and thereby the flow of service coming from it.

Assembly of information of this type does not necessarily entail going far beyond the range of experience. As is well-known, industrial processes often exhibit sizable geographical variations. The fact that processes are changing through time means that at any one time there will be processes recently adopted that may not be widely known. In many cases, it is possible to transfer or adapt processes from one industry or function to another, earlier conditions simply not having been such as to encourage the transfer. Thus there is often a rather wide range of choice simply from among already existing and quite well-known options.

Techniques and costs of controlling industrial residuals. Control of residuals may take a number of different forms. One possibility, perhaps the most obvious to the nontechnician, is to process the present flow of effluent, that is, to alter the composition of the final effluent so that it is less harmful. Additional inputs will be required, but whether the new effluent will be larger in mass than the old will depend on the extent to which salable products are recovered as a result of the new effluent treatment. In any case the main objective of effluent processing is to change the form of residuals so that they are less harmful or more concentrated and therefore more readily disposed of in comparatively harmless ways. Removal of sludge from sewage and putting it in land-fill is a good example.

Most of the estimates of the cost of pollution control one finds in official documents like *Clean Water* and *Clean Air* are based solely on the processing alternative and therefore tend, as we shall see below, to be too high. On the other hand they also tend to be low because they neglect the interrelations among liquid, solid, and gaseous residuals. A more integrated approach embracing a wider range of options is needed. This is illustrated below with a study of the beet sugar industry.

As just indicated, tacking on additional processes is only one of the possibilities. The composition and size of the effluent stream can also be changed by changing inputs (e.g., by substituting a nonpersistent for a persistent pesticide or by substituting low- for high-sulfur fuel) or by changing basic processes before the stage at which the present effluent is emitted. In addition, it may be possible to change the location of processes so that the concentration of the pollutant-reaching receptors is reduced. Finally, the quality characteristics of the final product can have a large bearing on the amount of residuals generated. For example, production of high brightness paper creates far more chemical residuals than that of low brightness paper.

The type of information on technical options and cost that is needed can be illustrated very forcefully by an examination of the operations of the beet sugar industry in the United States.[33] Here, as in many other industries, the most important of the possible responses to emissions control is not the adding on of separable effluent-processing devices, the technology conventionally considered by engineers and policy makers, but rather process change which results in fuller use of materials either

[33] The discussion in this section is based primarily on George O. G. Löf and Allen V. Kneese, *The Economics of Water Utilization in the Beet Sugar Industry*, Baltimore, Johns Hopkins Press for Resources for the Future, 1968. The materials balance described in later pages was calculated by George Löf.

by producing more of the primary product or by generating salable by-products.

As shown in Table 3, one of the major residuals causing water quality deterioration—the organic materials residuals load expressed in pounds of BOD (biochemical oxygen demand) per ton of beets processed—has been reduced greatly in the beet sugar industry as a whole in the last two decades by comparatively simple and economical alterations in processes. The main changes have been substituting beet pulp drying for storage of wet beet pulp in silos and the use of Steffens waste for the production of by-products. These changes reduce BOD generation by about 60 per cent. The other process change, i.e., a shift from cell type to continuous diffusers, is integrally related to recirculation of screen and press water. This further reduces the BOD generated by about 10 per cent.

Chart 1 indicates the main processing and waste water residuals streams in representative beet sugar plants. Chart 2 shows residuals streams in a plant practicing no material or by-product recovery and discharging all of its liquid residuals into a watercourse. A few cases approaching this still exist. Chart 3 shows a plant in which all water is fully recirculated, and there is no external discharge of waterborne residuals. There is one plant in the United States which uses basically this system; the others fall into intermediate positions. Charts 2 and 3 are not only helpful for understanding Table 3, but also the materials balance for a beet sugar plant, presented below.

It should be noted that the "closed" plant requires treatment (in the form of clarification) for its recirculating water stream, even though materials recovery and by-product production have greatly reduced water-borne residuals. Even where opportunities to utilize process changes and increase recovery are favorable, some residual material usually remains. The stream containing this residual may be treated, thus producing a solid or gaseous residual or changing the chemical composition of the waterborne residual. However, the treatment in this case is different from the usual add-on devices in the sense that it is an integral part of a re-circulating water stream which permits the external discharge of waste water to be closed off completely. Admittedly this is an extreme situation, but note that in this instance cost information about add-on devices would yield *no* information about what has been done to control residuals. On the other hand, attributing the cost of all process changes to residuals reduction would be erroneous because many valuable salable products have been generated as a result.

TABLE 3

Estimated Reduction of Biochemical Oxygen Demand (BOD) in Beet Sugar Processing, 1949 and 1962
(1,000 pounds per day)

Type of Waste	1949					1962				
	BOD Generated [a]	BOD Removed by Process Changes [b]	BOD Removed by Waste Treatment	Total BOD Removal	BOD Discharged	BOD Generated [a]	BOD Removed by Process Changes [b]	BOD Removed by Waste Treatment	Total BOD Removal	BOD Discharged
Flume and washer water	510	–	–	100	410	710	–	–	270	440
Cooling water and condensate	80	–	–	10[c]	70[c]	110	–	–	30	80
Pulp screen and press water	550	50	70	120	430	840	630	60	690	150
Silo drainage	1,390[d]	660[e]	140	800	590	1,940[d]	1,920[e]	10	1,930	10
Lime cake slurry	730	0	350	350	380	1,030	0	960	960	70
Steffens filtrate	610	160[f]	80	240	370	770	560[f]	160	720	50
Total BOD	3,870			1,620	2,250	5,400			4,600	800

490

Notes to Table 3

NOTE: Based on 158,000 tons of beets per day processed by 58 plants operating in 1962. In 1949, 113,000 tons per day were processed. To enable direct comparison, the data for 1949 were extrapolated to production of 158,000 tons per day, assuming constant proportions.

SOURCE: George O. G. Löf and Allen V. Kneese, *The Economics of Water Utilization in the Beet Sugar Industry,* Baltimore, Johns Hopkins Press for Resources for the Future, 1968.

[a] Based on BOD per ton of beets sliced in an "unimproved" plant, from U.S. Public Health Service, "Industrial Waste Guide to the Beet Industry," December 1950.

[b] By process changes and recirculation.

[c] Based on estimated 10 per cent reuse as diffuser make-up water.

[d] BOD which would be generated if all spent pulp were handled in silos, i.e., no pulp drying.

[e] BOD not generated because of use of pulp driers.

[f] By recycle-to-production process and production of concentrated Steffens filtrate.

To conclude this section we present a detailed materials balance calculation for two beet sugar production processes. One of these we term "high residual" and the other "low residual." Charts 4 and 5, showing the materials flow and residual materials, correspond to Charts 2 and 3 above, which show the water circulation streams. In a wet-process industry like beet sugar the two are closely related. Table 4 summarizes a few salient figures from the materials balance.

It will be noted from the table that a large reduction in organic residuals was purchased at the expense of a comparatively small increase in potentially harmful gas and inert solids. The interdependence among the residual waste streams going to different environmental media is revealed by these calculations. Considering the environmental circumstances in which most beet sugar factories operate—away from large cities but near small streams with very limited capacity to assimilate organic wastes—the trade-off shown is probably favorable, a conclusion that would not be evident if emission control policies for different media are considered in isolation, as has been the conventional practice.

To sum up, this example illustrates that control of emissions to one environmental medium may come at the expense of increased discharges to another. Consequently, an adequate study of the technology and costs of residuals control must consider the *sets* of emissions levels of interest as being simultaneously imposed for each type of stream. In this case, as probably in others, adjustment to emissions control would also result in greater production of salable output, and the value of this output must be subtracted from the expenditure to get a net cost of control.

Several studies of industrial residuals control taking these factors into account are now in process at Resources for the Future.

CHART 1

Main Processes in a Beet Sugar Plant

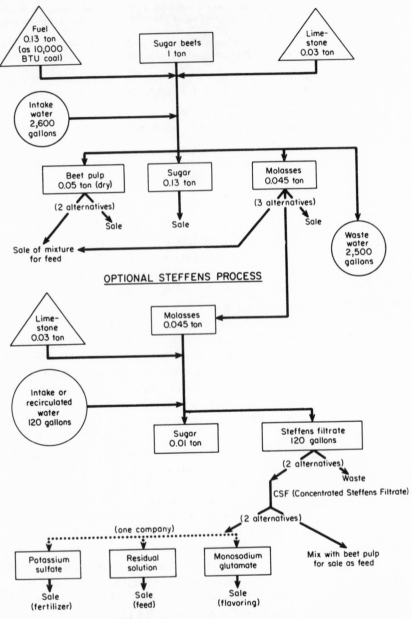

Source: Allen V. Kneese, Robert U. Ayres, and Ralph d'Arge, *Economics and the Environment: A Materials Balance Approach,* Baltimore, Johns Hopkins Press for Resources for the Future, 1970.

CHART 2

High Residual Beet Sugar Production Process

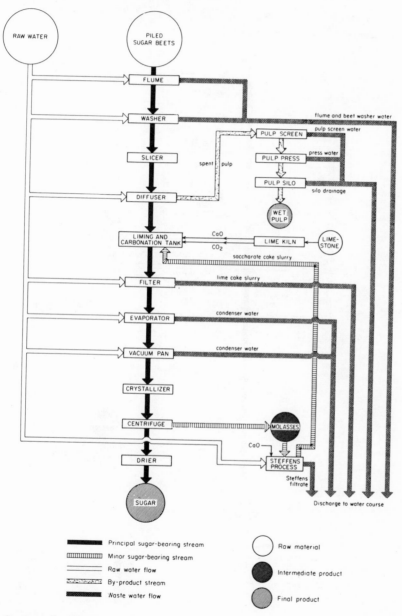

Principal sugar-bearing stream
Minor sugar-bearing stream
Raw water flow
By-product stream
Waste water flow

Raw material

Intermediate product

Final product

SOURCE: See Chart 1.

CHART 3

Low Residual Beet Sugar Production Process

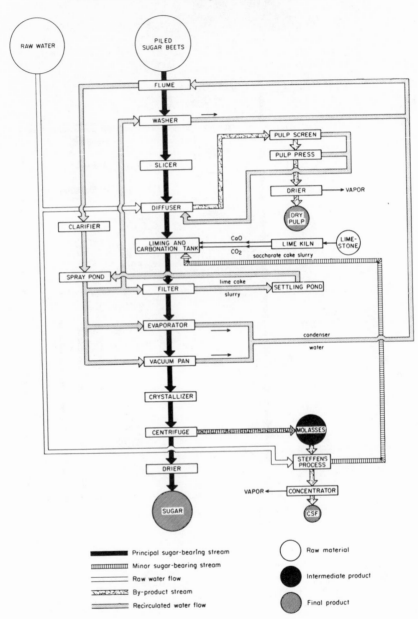

SOURCE: See Chart 1.

CHART 4

High Residual Beet Sugar Production Process Without Recirculation (in pounds per ton of beets processed except where otherwise stated)

Intake: 5,250 gallons per ton of sliced beets—regular; 175 gallons per ton of sliced beets—Steffens additional.

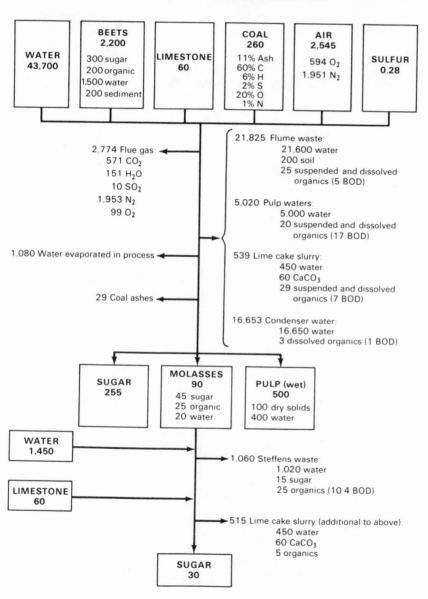

CHART 5

Low Residual Beet Sugar Production Process with Extensive Recycling (in pounds per ton of beets processed except where otherwise stated)

Intake: 270 gallons per ton of sliced beets—regular; 128 gallons per ton of sliced beets—Steffens.

Coal quantity based on 200 for simple plant plus 60 for pulp drying plus 25 for CSF production (evaporation). Coal assumed 10,000 Btu per pound, 11 per cent ash, 60 per cent carbon, 6 per cent hydrogen, 20 per cent oxygen, 2 per cent sulphur, 1 per cent nitrogen. Coal assumed to provide all the plant heat requirements, including pulp drying.

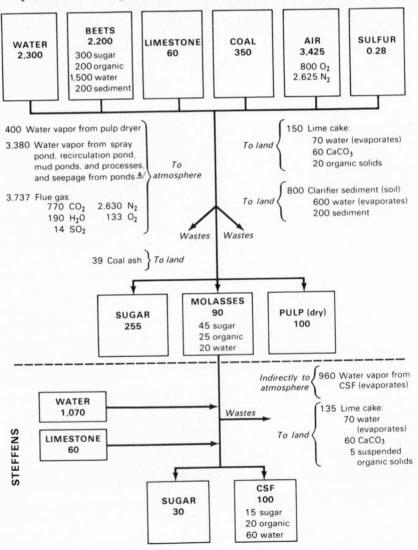

TABLE 4

Selected Figures from Materials Balance for
Two Beet Sugar Processes
(pounds per ton of beets processed)

Inputs and Outputs	High Residual Process	Low Residual Process
Raw material inputs		
Beets	2,200	2,200
Limestone	60	60
Coal	260	350
Sulfur	0.28	0.28
Product outputs		
Sugar	285	285
Pulp	100 [a]	100 [b]
Concentrated Steffens filtrate [c]	0	100
Waste residuals		
SO$_2$	10	14
CaCO$_3$	120	120
Coal ashes	29	39
Organics	122	25
Soil	200	200

SOURCE: Allen V. Kneese, Robert U. Ayres, and Ralph C. d'Arge, *Economics and the Environment: A Materials Balance Approach*, Johns Hopkins Press for Resources for the Future, 1970.
[a] Dry weight of wet pulp.
[b] Dry.
[c] Used for stock feed to recover monosodium glutamate and potassium sulfate.

It seems clear that information on alternative processes is a *sine qua non* for evaluating the implementation of any control scheme, whether this involves effluent charges, emission standards, or outright prohibitions.

Technical options and costs: household residuals and alteration of environmental states. Household residuals are on a par with industrial wastes as regards the need to know the technical options for management. The quantities of such residuals moving into sewers and into present channels of solid waste disposal are very large. Household consumption activities are an important direct contributor to air pollution since transportation, consisting primarily of passenger automobiles, is

the main source of carbon monoxide, hydrocarbons, and nitrous oxides
sent to the atmosphere (71, 53, and 47 per cent, respectively).[34] Large
quantities of waste heat are discharged in connection with home heating and cooling. A variety of effluents not entering the usual disposal
channels comes from numerous consumption activities, an especially
important one for water bodies being oil from motor boats with two
stroke motors.

In general terms, the options available for the control and management of household effluents are similar to those for industrial effluents.
It is possible to add on treatment devices at the effluent end, as is usually done with domestic sewage and solid waste. Other options are just
as important, however, as in the case of industrial effluents. That is,
"consumption processes" can be altered and inputs can be changed in
ways that will alter the composition of effluents in a less harmful
direction and perhaps reduce their quantity. Changes of this type are
well illustrated by those already introduced for automobile motors,
including closed crankcase ventilation circuits, which result in a more
complete burning of hydrocarbons, elimination of atmospheric venting
of gasoline tanks and carburetors, the use of unleaded gas with associated changes in motors (such as fuel injection), and alteration of
timing in the tuning of motors.

A more fundamental process change would be to abandon the internal
combustion engine altogether and substitute for it an inherently low
emission engine type like the Rankine cycle. This looks like an option
that should be taken very seriously.[35]

Another shift of inputs is exemplified by the changes that have taken
place in the last few years in the types of household detergents used.

Clearly there is a need for a large body of up-to-date information on
the options available for the management and processing of household
discharges to sewers, for gathering, transporting, and processing or dis-
posing of solid wastes, and for discharges going directly to the atmosphere from consumption activities.

Almost needless to say, this type of information on technical options
and costs at both the levels of the firm and household is also essential
for the effective application of analytical models such as those discussed in part II above. In fact, the building of these models and efforts

[34] Kneese and Bower, eds., *Environmental Quality*, p. 212.
[35] See Robert U. Ayres and Richard P. McKenna, *Alternatives to the Internal
Combustion Engine: Impacts on Environmental Quality*, Baltimore, Johns Hopkins Press, forthcoming.

to bring them to empirical application has probably been the chief stimulus and guidance for structuring the proper approaches to information gathering. The research and information-gathering efforts in this area are, however, tiny in relation to our need to know. Leaving aside scientific and engineering work on details, they amount to no more than a few hundred man-years per year.

The "environment," or particular environments, are the final place for disposal of effluents. Here, too, there are options for control that should be available for consideration. In some cases it may be possible to alter the state of a particular environment so as to increase its assimilative capacity or to reduce adverse effects flowing from it to receptors. Perhaps the most familiar example is the augmentation of low-stream flows through releases from reservoir storage to increase the assimilative capacity of streams. Artificial stream aeration has a similar objective and has proved to be practical in some cases. Another example—not yet brought to fruition—is provided by the schemes that have been proposed to break up temperature inversions in the Los Angeles basin. Sometimes ecological systems can be altered in favorable ways as with the introduction of the coho salmon in the Great Lakes.

Amount and value of damages from different levels of residuals in the environment. It is not enough to know that a pollution control scheme will produce certain physical results at a specified cost. The decision to adopt it or reject it ought to be based on a more or less definite answer to the further question of what difference the change makes to the people concerned. The question we should like to have answered is: How much would the beneficiaries be willing to pay for the change (with what income constraint?) if they understood its nature and significance and if they had the opportunity to buy it? Failing estimates of the value of the change to them, it would be desirable to describe the impact of the change on humans in quantitative or otherwise communicable terms so that some judgment can be made on the desirability of the change. In many cases, it will be found that some of the effects of the change can be quantified and perhaps that values can be attached to them, but some of the effects will not permit this, in which case reliance must be had on a reaction to the proposal based on experience with similar conditions in other areas.

Note that a serious complicating factor is that the damage (or benefit) functions are often not linear, that is, the value of a marginal unit of reduction in a pollutant is not constant, since the initial reductions from a very undesirable situation are more significant than similar changes initiated from an already favorable situation. While this characteristic of damage functions means that there will be many cases in which it can be demonstrated that a certain proposed change should be made since it may be possible to establish that the benefits are likely to be much greater than the costs, the question of the extent to which pollution control should be carried requires more precise estimates of the damage functions.

This is in full recognition of the fact that the final decisions concerning the use of common property resources must and should be made through our processes of collective choice, i.e., political processes. The effectiveness with which these work to aggregate preferences is itself an important topic for research and data collection.[36] The collective choice-making process cannot proceed rationally unless usable information about benefits and costs can be made available to it.

Of all the types of information required for formulation of a rational control scheme, the benefit functions are probably in the worst state. Without at least rough estimates of them, there is danger that control measures costing substantial sums will be introduced with little or no benefit, or, on the other side, that we will fail to take relatively cheap steps that could produce benefits far in excess of cost.

The work of Lave and Seskin provides an indication of the state of affairs in one sphere, namely, air pollution.[37] Limiting themselves to the effects of air pollution on human health, they surveyed a large number of studies attempting to relate air pollution to health (mainly epidemiological studies), reworked some of these, and also did a cross-sectional study of mortality, air pollution, and certain socioeconomic factors in 114 standard metropolitan statistical areas. Their summary conclusions are that the evidence is extremely good for association between air pollution and bronchitis and lung cancer but only suggestive for other ailments such as cardiovascular diseases and nonrespiratory tract cancers. They estimate that a 50 per cent reduction in air pollution might produce a 25 to 50 per cent reduction in morbidity and mortality from bronchitis at a saving in cost (direct earnings forgone) of $250 million to $500 million per year; lung cancer mortality would be reduced by 25 per cent with a saving of $33 million per year; all respiratory disease would be reduced by 25 per cent with a saving of $1,222 million per year. In sum, a 50 per cent reduction in air pollution levels in

[36] See Edwin T. Haefele, "Environmental Quality as a Problem of Social Choice," in Kneese and Bower, eds., *Environmental Quality.*

[37] Lester B. Lave and Eugene P. Seskin, "Air Pollution and Human Health," *Science,* August 21, 1970, pp. 723–733.

major urban areas might save about $2 billion per year. Whatever the particular costs assigned, they estimate that 4.5 per cent of the morbidity and mortality associated with air pollution would be saved by a 50 per cent reduction.

Their estimates are significant in indicating the importance of the air pollution problem, and if one believes the coefficients they have estimated, the equations can be applied to local and regional areas, but what is mainly of interest here are the limitations of the estimates. While two major classes of pollutants are distinguished in the Lave-Seskin study (particulates and sulfates), more detailed information would be very useful. A general difficulty afflicting most of the studies examined is the approximate nature of the exposure assigned to the individuals in the samples, the major weakness generally being the implicit assumption that the residents of an area have experienced the current levels of air pollution—as measured—for a long period of time. In fact, even within a city there are often significant variations in exposure. Finally, the availability of data for making such studies is revealed by the fact that they had to limit their own estimates to mortality, although morbidity and other loss of function are probably even more important. There is a great need for a program to generate health statistics that are truly usable for this type of problem.

While we are far from being completely at sea about the costs of air pollution, a great deal more work is warranted to provide more precision, greater detail, and a larger body of evidence. The need is fully as great for other types of pollution control.

IV. CONCLUSIONS

The national accounts approach for measuring benefits and costs resulting from environmental pollution was the first to be considered. While the treatment of industrial outlays for pollution control or defensive expenditures in the present official series is reasonably satisfactory, the consumer end of the problem is not. The difficulty lies in our inability to provide estimates of the value of environmental service flows, positive or negative, not reflected in ordinary transactions, and until this is done, any attempts to doctor the official series are likely to produce new errors to replace those corrected. However, outlays for pollution control and defensive expenditures are of interest in their own right and should be assembled. It can do no harm to see what the official series would look like if they were modified by these series in various ways.

If benefits and costs from environmental pollution cannot be estimated in the national accounts framework, it is possible to get at them in a marginal sense. Indeed, estimates of this sort are needed to determine when, where, and how pollution should be controlled.

This line of investigation requires the use of some sort of model to portray the effects that would result from the institution of different types of control measures. Several models designed to aid in the analysis of these problems were examined, among them the national I-O model and the Russell-Spofford model, which is a linear programming model that can go some distance toward optimizing while taking into account process options available, transport of pollutants, exposures of receptors, damages suffered or avoided, and also prediction of changes in some aspects of the environments involved.

We then examined briefly some of the data and information needed to apply these models (or any model) to the design of pollution control schemes. Comprehensive information on materials flows is essential, and it must be linked with location. A serious problem in the implementation of a materials balance accounting system which we have only pointed out is that of classification. On the one hand, great detail is needed because of the specific effects and sources of many pollutants, but the same degree of detail cannot be carried into all parts of the accounting system. Detail is most important for the flows from economic units to the environment.

The need for a large body of information on alternative processes bearing on pollution reduction was emphasized. This is required for three areas: industrial processes, handling and processing of final consumer effluents, and alteration of environmental states.

Finally, pollution control can come close to its target only if usable estimates of effects on receptors are available. These should be expressed in money terms if possible. The need for information of this kind in a form useful to the design of pollution control measures is pressing.

In sum, progress in measuring the benefits and costs from environmental pollution will depend on the efforts of a very large group of people with diverse skills. The problem is rendered complex not only by the physical and biological aspects of the systems involved but also because pollution problems generally are location-specific. An emission that has no adverse effects in one area may be a great danger in another.

We have been able only to allude to the pressing need for estimates of damages suffered from various levels of pollutants in the environment. The desirability of expressing these damages in monetary form, if possible, has been emphasized, although many effects of environmental polution are psychic. This does not mean that they cannot be related to sums of money, but in many cases this will be very difficult.

The fact that many features of the environment which do not lend themselves very readily to quantitative description may nevertheless be of great importance to many persons greatly complicates the task of comprehensive estimation of benefits and costs from environmental pollution.

COMMENT
WILLIAM VICKREY, Columbia University

I find myself in such close general agreement with what Herfindahl and Kneese present in their paper that I hope I may be forgiven for taking this opportunity to make a few remarks prompted primarily by some of the preceding papers.

Mancur Olson's characterization of governments as generally inefficient has, I think, to be considered in the light of the fact that the activities involved are of a type which, when they are carried on by private enterprise, are to varying degrees carried on by a monopoly, and that these monopolies themselves are often considered to be less efficient than their competitive counterparts. There is a considerable body of opinion, for example, holding that the pricing policies, at least, of publicly owned electric power distribution systems have been more conducive to efficiency than those of privately owned systems. In the case of telephone service, again, many major innovations, among them the combination hand set, direct distance dialing, and free emergency calls from public telephones, were common practice in publicly operated services considerably before they were general in private systems. And while some claims have been made that the quality of service offered tended to be higher in private systems, it is at least arguable that this quality of service might well have been excessive in consideration of its greater cost, motivated by the closer association of private telephone managements with business and higher-income consumers whose preferences for a higher grade of service, even at a higher cost, may have been given rather more weight than might be considered appropriate on an over-all basis. In the field of pricing, especially, public enterprise seems to have been more daring than private monopoly: witness the off-peak passenger fare schemes of the Canadian National Railways, the promotional electricity rates of the Tennessee Valley Authority, and the low prices offered by many public telephone systems for very brief long-distance calls. It is at least dangerous to attempt to judge performance of public enterprise by the financial standards used in the competitive areas of the economy. To the extent that the New Jersey Turnpike is a financial success, for example, it is an economic failure in that such success necessarily entails an impaired performance in relieving congestion on U.S. 1.

There is, to be sure, a "succession problem" that is more severe in government, especially where political parties alternate frequently in power, than in private industry. Private management tends to be judged rather critically in terms of the future prospects of the firm as viewed, at the time the management leaves office, by fairly sophisticated investors. This judgment tends to be reflected fairly conspicuously in the quoted prices of the shares of the company. Government administrations are under a much greater temptation to resolve current issues in an atmosphere of *après moi le déluge* by planting time bombs under the desks of their successors, for example, in the form of labor dispute settlements by which government officials, in collusion with the older and more influential members of the labor unions, provide for large benefits in the form of liberal pension provisions which will constitute substantial windfalls to the older union members, while meaning relatively little in terms of discounted present value to the younger union members and which will constitute a relatively small immediate burden on the public budget, especially if the benefits are unvested or unfunded or both. If bonds can be floated for the financing of non-self-liquidating public works, and sometimes even for current operating expenses that can be capitalized by relabeling as capital improvements what should properly be called maintenance or replacement, there is a grave temptation for incumbents to try to claim the credit for such expenditures, while leaving to their successors the onus of levying the taxes. In extreme cases the resulting policy of "billions for construction, but not one cent for operations" can lead to serious inefficiency, as happened, for example, with the New York Transit Authority, where this general tendency was reinforced, for the period 1951 to 1967, by a legislative mandate that required fares to be raised to cover operating expenses but not capital charges. When to this is added the temptation to favor the construction of enduring monuments to which commemorative plaques and names can be attached, the cumulative bias can be substantial.

I find I am intrigued by Olson's discussion of measurement possibilities in the field of broadcasting. Some aspects of the quantity of the product consumed are measured, at considerable expense, by the Nielson and other ratings, and the price, in terms of involuntary attention to commercials, can be expressed in terms of the ratio of programming to commercial time. As Olson indicates, this is a very high price indeed, the high price being a reflection of the fact that broadcast advertising is intrusive in a way that the classified ads, or even the display ads, in printed media are not. While the price thus exacted is subject to some degree of downward pressure from vague threats of license withdrawal by the FCC, and there is some degree of competition among stations and networks, "price" competition in terms of reducing the proportion of advertising seems to be minimal, with the result tending toward the shared monopoly solution of maximizing total "revenue," interpreted as prices times quantity, or in this case, the aggregate amount of man-hours spent by the the audience listening to or watching commercials. While there may be a modicum of information conveyed in this way, it seems to be far outweighed by misinformation, contained especially in advertisements for drugs of various kinds ranging from caffeine and aspirin to alcohol, the nicotine complex, and narcotics ("sleeping pills") (and then we wonder why we have a drug problem!).

There are interesting ramifications in Olson's suggestion for investigating the more directly monetary aspects of relating demand to a money measure by picking out a sample who would be required to pay a cash price for the reception of each program. It is worth noting that he deems it necessary that those picked out for the sample be compensated by some form of lump sum payment, in contrast to the procedure of drafting men for military service according to their dates of birth without any compensations. It may be hoped that arrangements would be made for appropriately reduced payments if the listener turns the program off in disgust halfway through. It is interesting to consider the application of this technique in another context, that of attempting to evaluate the benefits from an increased frequency of bus service. For example, in a small town the optimal long-run fare for a bus service may well be clearly zero, but whether a 10-minute or a 20-minute service should be operated may be less obvious. One could, experimentally, operate a 10-minute service with alternate buses designated "red" and "green" and similarly alternate bus stops designated "red" and "green." Then a suitable sample, say those who cannot show evidence that they were not born on the day of some month corresponding to the current dates would be required to pay an extra fare for boarding a bus of a color not corresponding to the stop they board at. By varying the extra fare and observing how many wait for the succeeding bus rather than pay the extra fare, the value of the more frequent service can be estimated.

Of course, any evaluation of this kind has a cost in that during the evaluation the members of the sample, at least, will not be making optimal use of the service being provided. Moreover, to the extent that the individuals concerned are aware that the results of the measurement will be used to determine whether or not they will get the improved bus service, they may be tempted to bias their behavior according to whether or not they individually prefer the better service, together with whatever share of the added tax burden they expect to have to bear in order to finance it. This bias, moreover, will be the greater the smaller the sample. This can, perhaps, be considered an instance of what might be termed the Acton-Heisenberg principle: "Every use of a measure for a socially important purpose corrupts the measurement, and the worse the measure to begin with or the more important the use, the greater the corruption."

Turning to the Herfindahl-Kneese paper, my chief concern is with the concept that in the long run it is appropriate as a first approximation to assume that environmental services are constant, and that hence a correct welfare concept requires that outlays to control pollution or defend against its presence are not to be considered a part of the final product. While this is a convenient convention that at least reduces a part of the bias inherent in treating as final product outlays that merely preserve the status quo, it introduces an awkward distinction between the accounting procedure deemed appropriate for long-term purposes and that obviously required to account for the impact of short-run variations in antipollution efforts, not related to variations in pollution-producing activity. But although some such convention does represent a compromise, albeit arbitrary, between considering that environment has improved and that it has deteriorated, it does not in principle solve the problem inherent in this appraisal. Impact on the environment is only one of the many aspects of the problem of dividing the product of government activity between final product and intermediate product. If air pollution is a negative, final by-product of industry, to the extent that it is not controlled, do we not also have to consider jails as a negative, final by-product of the government's production of security? It is difficult enough to determine whether even over past history the environment has improved or worsened, considering, for example the impact of DDT on malaria on the one hand and on the peregrine falcon on the other, or the increased pollution of streams vis-à-vis the reduced incidence of typhoid fever on the other; determining what is currently happening, on balance, to the environment, or what environmental trend might be considered optimal is even harder. We have already for a long time been guilty of ignoring the fact that much government output is intermediate product on any reasonable definition. Perhaps in the course of trying to deal with the problem of environmental change we can be brought to face the entire problem of the welfare impact of the government sector more realistically, even at the expense of some accuracy of computation.

In any case it seems a natural extension of the idea of incorporating environmental impacts in an input-output model, whether in terms of economic values or materials balances, that the dynamic aspects not be overlooked, and that distinctions be made between the treatment accorded short-lived pollution, such as that of streams, and of sulphur and nitrogen compounds in the air, and that accorded long-term and in some cases irreversible changes such as the dispersion of heavy metals, the accumulation of carbon dioxide in the atmosphere, or the extinction of species or the introduction of new predators.

Finally, it is perhaps worthwhile pointing out that while when considered in isolation the control of pollution at the household level through effluent charges may appear to involve disproportionately high costs, if such control is considered in conjunction with other costs, such as, in the case of the automobile, congestion and accident costs, the prospects may be considerably brighter. Indeed, if a system of congestion charges were to be instituted, the superposition of charges reflecting marginal pollution costs would be a fairly simple matter, involving chiefly a periodic rating of the individual automobiles, following which charges could be imposed that would take into account such factors as the time and place at which the vehicles are operated, and even, if desired, weather conditions. Such charges would have a salutary role to play especially during periods of transition from more to less pollution-prone vehicles, providing an equitable sharing of the burden between those using the new and those retaining the old vehicles, as well as providing appropriate incentives for the relegation of the pollution-prone vehicles to types of use where the pollution produced would have less impact. The required mechanism consists merely of some optical or electronic identifier device on each vehicle which will enable it to be identified each time it passes scanning stations located along various screen lines. From the records thus generated and the recorded characteristics of the car, the appropriate charge could be computed and billed to the owner, and would represent the contribution that operation of the vehicle makes to congestion costs, pollution costs, and possibly accident hazard. A cost of assessing and collecting the charge which might be considered excessive for one of these elements separately may become a relatively minor drawback when applied to all three purposes at once.

Is Growth Obsolete?

WILLIAM D. NORDHAUS AND JAMES TOBIN

YALE UNIVERSITY

A long decade ago economic growth was the reigning fashion of political economy. It was simultaneously the hottest subject of economic theory and research, a slogan eagerly claimed by politicians of all stripes, and a serious objective of the policies of governments. The climate of opinion has changed dramatically. Disillusioned critics indict both economic science and economic policy for blind obeisance to aggregate material "progress," and for neglect of its costly side effects. Growth, it is charged, distorts national priorities, worsens the distribution of income, and irreparably damages the environment. Paul Erlich speaks for a multitude when he says, "We must acquire a life style which has as its goal maximum freedom and happiness for the individual, not a maximum Gross National Product."

Growth was in an important sense a discovery of economics after the Second World War. Of course economic development has always been the grand theme of historically minded scholars of large mind and bold concept, notably Marx, Schumpeter, Kuznets. But the mainstream of economic analysis was not comfortable with phenomena of change and progress. The stationary state was the long-run equilibrium of classical and neoclassical theory, and comparison of alternative static equilibriums was the most powerful theoretical tool. Technological change and population increase were most readily accommodated as one-time exogenous shocks; comparative static analysis could be used to tell how they altered the equilibrium of the system. The obvious fact that these "shocks" were occurring continuously, never allowing the

NOTE: The research described in this paper was carried out under grants from the National Science Foundation and the Ford Foundation. The paper and its appendixes were originally published in *Economic Growth,* Fiftieth Anniversary Colloquium V, New York, National Bureau of Economic Research, 1972; the paper is reproduced here as it appeared in the colloquium volume. All references to the appendixes pertain to that publication.

The paper is published in this volume upon recommendation of the Executive Committee and approval by the National Bureau of Economic Research because it stimulated considerable discussion at the conference, some of which is reproduced here. It was invited for presentation when an earlier paper by another author was not forthcoming, and most importantly because of its special relevance to the subject of this conference.

We would like to express our appreciation to Walter Dolde, James Pugash, Geoffrey Woglom, Hugh Tobin, and especially Laura Harrison, for assistance in the preparation of this paper. We are grateful to Robin Matthews for pointing out some problems in our treatment of leisure in the first draft.

system to reach its equilibrium, was a considerable embarrassment. Keynesian theory fell in the same tradition, attempting rather awkwardly, though nonetheless fruitfully, to apply static equilibrium theory to the essentially dynamic problem of saving and capital accumulation.

Sir Roy Harrod in 1940 began the process, brought to fruition by many theorists in the 1950s, of putting the stationary state into motion. The long-run equilibrium of the system became a path of steady growth, and the tools of comparative statics could then be applied to alternative growth paths rather than to alternative stationary states. Neo-Keynesian macroeconomics began to fall into place as a description of departures from equilibrium growth, although this task of reinterpretation and integration is still far from a satisfactory completion.

By now modern neoclassical growth theory is well enough formulated to have made its way into textbooks. It is a theory of the growth of potential output, or output at a uniform standard rate of utilization of capacity. The theory relates potential output to three determinants: the labor force, the state of technology, and the stock of human and tangible capital. The first two are usually assumed to grow smoothly at rates determined exogenously by noneconomic factors. The accumulation of capital is governed by the thrift of the population, and in equilibrium the growth of the capital stock matches the growth of labor-*cum*-technology and the growth of output. Simple as it is, the model fits the observed trends of economic growth reasonably well.

The steady equilibrium growth of modern neoclassical theory is, it must be acknowledged, a routine process of replication. It is a dull story compared to the convulsive structural, technological, and social changes described by the historically oriented scholars of development mentioned above. The theory conceals, either in aggregation or in the abstract generality of multisector models, all the drama of the events — the rise and fall of products, technologies, and industries, and the accompanying transformations of the spatial and occupational distribution of the population. Many economists agree with the broad outlines of Schumpeter's vision of capitalist development, which is a far cry from growth models made nowadays in either Cambridge, Massachusetts, or Cambridge, England. But visions of that kind have yet to be transformed into a theory that can be applied in everyday analytic and empirical work.

In any case, growth of some kind is now the recognized economic norm. A symptom of the change in outlook can be found in business cycle semantics. A National Bureau *recession* was essentially a period in which aggregate productive activity was declining. Since 1960 it has become increasingly customary to describe the state of the economy by the gap between its actual output and its growing potential. Although the word recession is still a source of confusion and controversy, almost everyone recognizes that the economy is losing ground —which will have to be recaptured eventually—whenever its actual rate of expansion is below the rate of growth of potential output.

In the early 1960s growth became a proclaimed objective of government policy, in this country as elsewhere. Who could be against it? But like most value-laden words, growth has meant different things to different people and at different times. Often growth policy was simply identified with measures to expand aggregate demand in order to bring or keep actual output in line with potential output. In this sense it is simply stabilization policy, only more gap-conscious and growth-conscious than the cycle-smoothing policies of the past.

To economists schooled in postwar neoclassical growth theory, growth policy proper meant something more than this, and more debatable. It meant deliberate effort to speed up the growth of potential output itself, specifically to accelerate the productivity of labor. Growth policy in this meaning was not widely understood or accepted. The neoclassical model outlined above suggested two kinds of policies to foster growth, possibly interrelated: measures that advanced technological knowledge and measures that increased the share of potential output devoted to accumulation of physical or human capital.[1] Another implication of the standard model was that, unless someone could find a way to accelerate technological progress permanently, policy could not raise the rate of growth permanently. One-shot measures would speed up growth temporarily, for years or decades. But once the economy had absorbed these measures, its future growth rate would be limited once again by constraints of labor and technology. The level of its path, however, would be permanently higher than if the policies had not been undertaken.

Growth measures nearly always involve diversions of current resources from other uses, sacrifices of current consumption for the benefit of succeeding generations of consumers. Enthusiasts for faster

---

[1] The variety of possible measures, and the difficulty of raising the growth rate by more than one or two percentage points, have been explored by Edward Denison in his influential study, *The Sources of Economic Growth in the United States and the Alternatives Before Us*, New York, Committee for Economic Development, January 1962, Supplementary Paper No. 13.

growth are advocates of the future against the present. Their case rests on the view that in a market economy left to itself, the future would be shortchanged because too small a fraction of current output would be saved. We mention this point now because we shall return later to the ironical fact that the antigrowth men of the 1970s believe that it is they who represent the claims of a fragile future against a voracious present.

Like the enthusiasts to whom they are a reaction, current critics of growth are disenchanted with both theory and policy, with both the descriptive and the normative implications of the doctrines of the previous decade. The sources of disenchantment are worth considering today, because they indicate agenda for future theoretical and empirical research.

We have chosen to direct our attention to three important problems raised by those who question the desirability and possibility of future growth: (a) How good are measures of output currently used for evaluating the growth of economic welfare? (b) Does the growth process inevitably waste our natural resources? (c) How does the rate of population growth affect economic welfare? In particular, what would be the effect of zero population growth?

MEASURES OF ECONOMIC WELFARE

A major question raised by critics of economic growth is whether we have been growing at all in any meaningful sense. Gross national product statistics cannot give the answers, for GNP is not a measure of economic welfare. Erlich is right in claiming that maximization of GNP is not a proper objective of policy. Economists all know that, and yet their everyday use of GNP as the standard measure of economic performance apparently conveys the impression that they are evangelistic workshipers of GNP.

An obvious shortcoming of GNP is that it is an index of production, not consumption. The goal of economic activity, after all, is consumption. Although this is the central premise of economics, the profession has been slow to develop, either conceptually or statistically, a measure of economic performance oriented to consumption, broadly defined and carefully calculated. We have constructed a primitive and experimental "measure of economic welfare" (MEW), in which we attempt to allow for the more obvious discrepancies between GNP and economic welfare. A complete account is given in Appendix A. The main results will be discussed here and summarized in Tables 1 and 2.

In proposing a welfare measure, we in no way deny the importance of the conventional national income accounts or of the output measures based upon them. Our MEW is largely a rearrangement of items of the national accounts. Gross and net national product statistics are the economists' chief tools for short-run analysis, forecasting, and policy and are also indispensable for many other purposes.

Our adjustments to GNP fall into three general categories: reclassification of GNP expenditures as consumption, investment, and intermediate; imputation for the services of consumer capital, for leisure, and for the product of household work; correction for some of the disamenities of urbanization.

1. Reclassification of GNP Final Expenditures

Our purposes are first, to subtract some items that are better regarded as instrumental and intermediate than as final output, and second, to allocate all remaining items between consumption and net investment. Since the national accounts do not differentiate among government purchases of goods and services, one of our major tasks will be to split them among the three categories: intermediate, consumption, and net investment. We will also reclassify some private expenditures.

Intermediate products are goods and services whose contributions to present or future consumer welfare are completely counted in the values of other goods and services. To avoid double counting they should not be included in reckoning the net yield of economic activity. Thus all national income accounts reckon as final consumption the bread but not the flour and as capital formation the finished house but not the lumber. The more difficult and controversial issues in assigning items to intermediate or final categories are the following:

Capital Consumption. The depreciation of capital stocks is a cost of production, and output required to offset the depreciation is intermediate as surely as materials consumed in the productive process. For most purposes, including welfare indexes, NNP is preferable to GNP. Only the difficulties and lags in estimating capital consumption have made GNP the popular statistic.

However, NNP itself fails to treat many durable goods as capital, and counts as final their entire output whether for replacement or accumulation. These elementary points are worth repeating because some of our colleagues are telling the public that economists glorify wasteful "through-put" for its own sake. Focusing on NNP, and accounting for all durables as capital goods, would avoid such foolish paradoxes as the implication that deliberate efforts to make goods more perishable raise national output. We estimate, however, that proper treatment of consumer durables has little quantitative effect (see Table 1, lines 3 and 5).

The other capital consumption adjustments we have made arise from allowing for government capital and for the educational and medical capital embodied in human beings. In effect, we have reclassified education and health expenditures, both public and private, as capital investments.

Growth Requirements.   In principle net national product tells how much consumption the economy could indefinitely sustain. GNP does not tell that; consuming the whole GNP in any year would impair future consumption prospects. But *per capita* rather than aggregate consumption is the welfare objective; neither economists nor other observers would as a rule regard sheer increase in the numbers of people enjoying the same average standard of living as a gain in welfare. Even NNP exaggerates sustainable *per capita* consumption, except in a society with stationary population—another example of the pervasiveness of the "stationary" assumption in the past. Per capita consumption cannot be sustained with zero net investment; the capital stock must be growing at the same rate as population and the labor force. This capital-widening requirement is as truly a cost of staying in the same position as outright capital consumption.[2]

This principle is clear enough when growth is simply increase in population and the labor force. Its application to an economy with technological progress is by no means clear. Indeed, the very concept of national income becomes fuzzy. Should the capital-widening requirement then be interpreted to mean that capital should keep pace with output and technology, not just with the labor force? If so, the implied sustainable consumption per capita grows with the rate of technological progress. This is the point of view which we have taken in what follows. On the other hand, a given level of consumption per capita could be

---

[2] Consider the neoclassical model without technological change. When labor force is growing at rate g, the capital-labor ratio is k, gross product per worker is $f(k)$, net product per worker is $f(k) - \delta k$, then the net investment requirement is gk, and sustainable consumption per worker is $f(k) - \delta k - gk$. Denoting the capital-output ratio as $\mu = [k/f(k)]$, sustainable consumption per worker can also be written as $f(k)[1 - \mu(\delta + g)]$. Although NNP embodies in principle the depreciation deduction δk, it does not take account of the capital-widening requirement gk.

sustained with a steady decline in the capital-output ratio, thanks to technological progress.[3]

The growth requirement is shown on line 7 of Table 2. This is clearly a significant correction, measuring about 16 per cent of GNP in 1965.

Our calculations distinguish between actual and sustainable per capita consumption. *Actual MEW* may exceed or fall short of *sustainable MEW*, the amount that could be consumed while meeting both capital consumption and growth requirements. If these requirements are met, per capita consumption can grow at the trend rate of increase in labor productivity. When actual MEW is less than sustainable MEW, the economy is making even better provision for future consumers; when actual MEW exceeds sustainable MEW, current consumption in effect includes some of the fruits of future progress.

Instrumental Expenditures. Since GNP and NNP are measures of production rather than of welfare, they count many activities that are evidently not directly sources of utility themselves but are regrettably necessary inputs to activities that may yield utility. Some consumer outlays are only instrumental, for example, the costs of commuting to work. Some government "purchases" are also of this nature—for example, police services, sanitation services, road maintenance, national defense. Expenditures on these items are among the necessary overhead costs of a complex industrial nation-state, although there is plenty of room for disagreement as to the necessary amounts. We are making no judgments on such issues in classifying these outlays as intermediate rather than final uses of resources. Nevertheless, these decisions are difficult and controversial. The issues are clearly illustrated in the important case of national defense.

We exclude defense expenditures for two reasons. First, we see no direct effect of defense expenditures on household economic welfare. No reasonable country (or household) buys "national defense" for its own sake. If there were no war or risk of war, there would be no need

---

[3] As is well known, the whole concept of equilibrium growth collapses unless progress is purely labor-augmenting, "Harrod-neutral." In that case the rate g above is $n + \gamma$, where n is the natural rate of increase and γ is the rate of technological progress, and "labor force" means effective or augmented labor force. In equilibrium, output and consumption per natural worker grow at the rate γ, and "sustainable" consumption per capita means consumption growing steadily at this rate. Clearly, level consumption per capita can be sustained with smaller net investment than $g\mu f(k)$; so μ and k steadily decline. See section A.2.3, below.

for defense expenditures and no one would be the worse without them. Conceptually, then, defense expenditures are gross but not net output.

The second reason is that defense expenditures are input rather than output data. Measurable output is especially elusive in the case of defense. Conceptually, the output of the defense effort is national security. Has the value of the nation's security risen from $0.5 billion to $50 billion over the period from 1929 to 1965? Obviously not. It is patently more reasonable to assume that the rise in expenditure was due to deterioration in international relations and to changes in military technology. The cost of providing a given level of security has risen enormously. If there has been no corresponding gain in security since 1929, the defense cost series is a very misleading indicator of improvements in welfare.

The economy's ability to meet increased defense costs speaks well for its productive performance. But the diversion of productive capacity to this purpose cannot be regarded simply as a shift of national preferences and the product mix. Just as we count technological progress, managerial innovation, and environmental change when they work in our favor (consider new business machines or mineral discoveries) so we must count a deterioration in the environment when it works against us (consider bad weather and war). From the point of view of economic welfare, an arms control or disarmament agreement which would free resources and raise consumption by 10 per cent would be just as significant as new industrial processes yielding the same gains.

In classifying defense costs—or police protection or public health expenditures—as regrettable and instrumental, we certainly do not deny the possibility that given the unfavorable circumstances that prompt these expenditures consumers will ultimately be better off with them than without them. This may or may not be the case. The only judgment we make is that these expenditures yield no direct satisfactions. Even if the "regrettable" outlays are rational responses to unfavorable shifts in the environment of economic activity, we believe that a welfare measure, perhaps unlike a production measure, should record such environmental change.

We must admit, however, that the line between final and instrumental outlays is very hard to draw. For example, the philosophical problems raised by the malleability of consumer wants are too deep to be resolved in economic accounting. Consumers are susceptible to influence by the examples and tastes of other consumers and by the sales efforts of producers. Maybe all our wants are just regrettable necessities; maybe productive activity does no better than to satisfy the wants which it generates; maybe our net welfare product is tautologically zero. More seriously, we cannot measure welfare exclusively by the quantitative flows of goods and services. We need other gauges of the health of individuals and societies. These, too, will be relative to the value systems which determine whether given symptoms indicate health or disease. But the "social indicators" movement of recent years still lacks a coherent, integrative conceptual and statistical framework.

We estimate that overhead and regrettable expenses, so far as we have been able to define and measure them, rose from 8 per cent to 16 per cent of GNP over the period 1929–65 (Table 2, line 4).

2. Imputations for Capital Services, Leisure, and Nonmarket Work

In the national income accounts, rent is imputed on owner-occupied homes and counted as consumption and income. We must make similar imputations in other cases to which we have applied capital accounting. Like owner-occupied homes, other consumer durables and public investments yield consumption directly, without market transactions. In the case of educational and health capital, we have assumed the yields to be intermediate services rather than direct consumption; that is, we expect to see the fruits of investments in education and health realized in labor productivity and earnings, and we do not count them twice. Our measure understates economic welfare and its growth to the extent that education and medical care are direct rather than indirect sources of consumer satisfaction.

The omission of leisure and of nonmarket productive activity from measures of production conveys the impression that economists are blindly materialistic. Economic theory teaches that welfare could rise, even while NNP falls, as the result of voluntary choices to work for pay fewer hours per week, weeks per year, years per lifetime.

These imputations unfortunately raise serious conceptual questions, discussed at some length in section A.3, below. Suppose that in calculating aggregate dollar consumption the hours devoted to leisure and nonmarket productive activity are valued at their presumed opportunity cost, the money wage rate. In converting current dollar consumption to constant dollars, what assumption should be made about the unobservable price indexes for the goods and services consumed during those hours? The wage rate? The price index for marketed con-

TABLE 1

Measures of Economic Welfare, Actual and
Sustainable, Various Years, 1929–65

(*billions of dollars, 1958 prices, except lines 14–19, as noted*)

	1929	1935	1945	1947	1954	1958	1965
1 Personal consumption, national income and product accounts	139.6	125.5	183.0	206.3	255.7	290.1	397.7
2 Private instrumental expenditures	−10.3	−9.2	−9.2	−10.9	−16.4	−19.9	−30.9
3 Durable goods purchases	−16.7	−11.5	−12.3	−26.2	−35.5	−37.9	−60.9
4 Other household investment	−6.5	−6.3	−9.1	−10.4	−15.3	−19.6	−30.1
5 Services of consumer capital imputation	24.9	17.8	22.1	26.7	37.2	40.8	62.3
6 Imputation for leisure							
B	339.5	401.3	450.7	466.9	523.2	554.9	626.9
A	339.5	401.3	450.7	466.9	523.2	554.9	626.9
C	162.9	231.3	331.8	345.6	477.2	554.9	712.8
7 Imputation for nonmarket activities							
B	85.7	109.2	152.4	159.6	211.5	239.7	295.4
A	178.6	189.5	207.1	215.5	231.9	239.7	259.8
C	85.7	109.2	152.4	159.6	211.5	239.7	295.4
8 Disamenity correction	−12.5	−14.1	−18.1	−19.1	−24.3	−27.6	−34.6
9 Government consumption	0.3	0.3	0.4	0.5	0.5	0.8	1.2
10 Services of government capital imputation	4.8	6.4	8.9	10.0	11.7	14.0	16.6
11 Total consumption = actual MEW							
B	548.8	619.4	768.8	803.4	948.3	1,035.3	1,243.6
A	641.7	699.7	823.5	859.3	968.7	1,035.3	1,208.0
C	372.2	449.4	649.9	682.1	902.3	1,035.3	1,329.5
12 MEW net investment	−5.3	−46.0	−52.5	55.3	13.0	12.5	−2.5
13 Sustainable MEW							
B	543.5	573.4	716.3	858.7	961.3	1,047.8	1,241.1
A	636.4	653.7	771.0	914.6	981.7	1,047.8	1,205.5
C	366.9	403.4	597.4	737.4	915.3	1,047.8	1,327.0
14 Population (no. of mill.)	121.8	127.3	140.5	144.7	163.0	174.9	194.6

(continued)

Table 1 (concluded)

		1929	1935	1945	1947	1954	1958	1965
	Actual MEW per capita							
15	Dollars							
	B	4,506	4,866	5,472	5,552	5,818	5,919	6,391
	A	5,268	5,496	5,861	5,938	5,943	5,919	6,208
	C	3,056	3,530	4,626	4,714	5,536	5,919	6,832
16	Index (1929 = 100)							
	B	100.0	108.0	121.4	123.2	129.1	131.4	141.8
	A	100.0	104.3	111.3	112.7	112.8	112.4	117.8
	C	100.0	115.5	151.4	154.3	181.2	193.7	223.6
	Sustainable MEW per capita							
17	Dollars							
	B	4,462	4,504	5,098	5,934	5,898	5,991	6,378
	A	5,225	5,135	5,488	6,321	6,023	5,991	6,195
	C	3,012	3,169	4,252	5,096	5,615	5,991	6,819
18	Index (1929 = 100)							
	B	100.0	100.9	114.3	133.0	132.2	134.3	142.9
	A	100.0	98.3	105.0	121.0	115.3	114.7	118.6
	C	100.0	105.2	141.2	169.2	186.4	198.9	226.4
19	Per capita NNP							
	Dollars	1,545	1,205	2,401	2,038	2,305	2,335	2,897
	1929 = 100	100.0	78.0	155.4	131.9	149.2	151.1	187.5

Note: Variants A, B, C in the table correspond to different assumptions about the bearing of technological progress on leisure and nonmarket activities. See section A.3.2, below, for explanation.

Source: Appendix Table A.16.

sumption goods? Over a period of forty years the two diverge substantially; the choice between them makes a big difference in estimates of the growth of MEW. As explained in Appendix A, the market consumption "deflator" should be used if technological progress has augmented nonmarketed uses of time to the same degree as marketed labor. The wage rate should be the deflator if no such progress has occurred in the effectiveness of unpaid time.

In Tables 1 and 2 we provide calculations for three conceptual alternatives. Our own choice is variant B of MEW, in which the value of leisure is deflated by the wage rate; and the value of nonmarket activity, by the consumption deflator.

TABLE 2

Gross National Product and MEW, Various Years, 1929–65

(*billions of dollars, 1958 prices*)

	1929	1935	1945	1947	1954	1958	1965
1. Gross national product	203.6	169.5	355.2	309.9	407.0	447.3	617.8
2. Capital consumption, NIPA	−20.0	−20.0	−21.9	−18.3	−32.5	−38.9	−54.7
3. Net national product, NIPA	183.6	149.5	333.3	291.6	374.5	408.4	563.1
4. NIPA final output reclassified as regrettables and intermediates							
a. Government	−6.7	−7.4	−146.3	−20.8	−57.8	−56.4	−63.2
b. Private	−10.3	−9.2	−9.2	−10.9	−16.4	−19.9	−30.9
5. Imputations for items not included in NIPA							
a. Leisure	339.5	401.3	450.7	466.9	523.2	554.9	626.9
b. Nonmarket activity	85.7	109.2	152.4	159.6	211.5	239.7	295.4
c. Disamenities	−12.5	−14.1	−18.1	−19.1	−24.3	−27.6	−34.6
d. Services of public and private capital	29.7	24.2	31.0	36.7	48.9	54.8	78.9
6. Additional capital consumption	−19.3	−33.4	−11.7	−50.8	−35.2	−27.3	−92.7
7. Growth requirement	−46.1	−46.7	−65.8	+5.4	−63.1	−78.9	−101.8
8. Sustainable MEW	543.6	573.4	716.3	858.6	961.3	1,047.7	1,241.1

NIPA = national income and product accounts.

Note: Variants A, B, C in the table correspond to different assumptions about the bearing of technological progress on leisure and nonmarket activities. Variant A assumes that neither has benefited from technological progress at the rate of increase of real wages; variant C assumes that both have so benefited; variant B assumes that leisure has not been augmented by technological progress but other nonmarket activities have benefited. See section A.3.2, below, for explanation.

Source: Appendix Table A.17.

3. Disamenities of Urbanization

The national income accounts largely ignore the many sources of utility or disutility that are not associated with market transactions or measured by the market value of goods and services. If one of my neighbors cultivates a garden of ever-increasing beauty, and another makes more and more noise, neither my increasing appreciation of the one nor my growing annoyance with the other comes to the attention of the Department of Commerce.

Likewise there are some socially productive assets (for example, the environment) that do not appear in any balance sheets. Their services to producers and consumers are not valued in calculating national income. By the same token no allowance is made for depletion of their capacity to yield services in the future.

Many of the negative "externalities" of economic growth are connected with urbanization and congestion. The secular advances recorded in NNP figures have accompanied a vast migration from rural agriculture to urban industry. Without this occupational and residential revolution we could not have enjoyed the fruits of technological progress. But some portion of the higher earnings of urban residents may simply be compensation for the disamenities of urban life and work. If so we should not count as a gain of welfare the full increments of NNP that result from moving a man from farm or small town to city. The persistent association of higher wages with higher population densities offers one method of estimating the costs of urban life as they are valued by people making residential and occupational decisions.

As explained in section A.4, below, we have tried to estimate by cross-sectional regressions the income differentials necessary to hold people in localities with greater population densities. The resulting estimates of the disamenity costs of urbanization are shown in Table 1, line 8. As can be seen, the estimated disamenity premium is quite substantial, running about 5 per cent of GNP. Nevertheless, the urbanization of the population has not been so rapid that charging it with this cost significantly reduces the estimated rate of growth of the economy.

The adjustments leading from national accounts "personal consumption" to MEW consumption are shown in Table 1, and the relations of GNP, NNP, and MEW are summarized in Table 2. For reasons previously indicated, we believe that a welfare measure should have the dimension *per capita*. We would stress the per capita MEW figures shown in Tables 1 and 2.

Although the numbers presented here are very tentative, they do suggest the following observations. First, MEW is quite different from conventional output measures. Some consumption items omitted from GNP are of substantial quantitative importance. Second, our preferred variant of per capita MEW has been growing more slowly than per capita NNP (1.1 per cent for MEW as against 1.7 per cent for NNP, at annual rates over the period 1929–65). Yet MEW has been growing. The progress indicated by conventional national accounts is not just a myth that evaporates when a welfare-oriented measure is substituted.

GROWTH AND NATURAL RESOURCES

Calculations like the foregoing are unlikely to satisfy critics who believe that economic growth per se piles up immense social costs ignored in even the most careful national income calculations. Faced with the finiteness of our earth and the exponential growth of economy and population, the environmentalist sees inevitable starvation. The specter of Malthus is haunting even the affluent society.

There is a familiar ring to these criticisms. Ever since the industrial revolution pessimistic scientists and economists have warned that the possibilities of economic expansion are ultimately limited by the availability of natural resources and that society only makes the eventual future reckoning more painful by ignoring resource limitations now.

In important part, this is a warning about population growth, which we consider below. Taking population developments as given, will natural resources become an increasingly severe drag on economic growth? We have not found evidence to support this fear. Indeed, the opposite appears to be more likely: Growth of output per capita will accelerate ever so slightly even as stocks of natural resources decline.

The prevailing standard model of growth assumes that there are no limits on the feasibility of expanding the supplies of nonhuman agents of production. It is basically a two-factor model in which production depends only on labor and reproducible capital. Land and resources, the third member of the classical triad, have generally been dropped. The simplifications of theory carry over into empirical work. The thousands of aggregate production functions estimated by econometricians in the last decade are labor-capital functions. Presumably the tacit justification has been that reproducible capital is a near-perfect substitute for land and other exhaustible resources, at least in the perspective of heroic aggregation customary in macroeconomics. If substitution for natural resources is not possible in any given technology, or if a particular resource is exhausted, we tacitly assume that "land-augmenting" innovations will overcome the scarcity.

These optimistic assumptions about technology stand in contrast to the tacit assumption of environmentalists that no substitutes are available for natural resources. Under this condition, it is easily seen that output will indeed stop growing or will decline. It thus appears that the substitutability (or technically, the elasticity of substitution) between the neoclassical factors, capital and labor, and natural resources is of crucial importance to future growth. This is an area needing extensive further research, but we have made two forays to see what the evidence is. Details are given in Appendix B, below.

First we ran several simulations of the process of economic growth in order to see which assumptions about substitution and technology fit the "stylized" facts. The important facts are: growing income per capita and growing capital per capita; relatively declining inputs and income shares of natural resources; and a slowly declining capital-output ratio. Among the various forms of production function considered, the following assumptions come closest to reproducing these stylized facts: (a) Either the elasticity of substitution between natural resources and other factors is high—significantly greater than unity—or resource-augmenting technological change has proceeded faster than overall productivity; (b) the elasticity of substitution between labor and capital is close to unity.

After these simulations were run, it appeared possible to estimate directly the parameters of the preferred form of production function. Econometric estimates confirm proposition (a) and seem to support the alternative of high elasticity of substitution between resources and the neoclassical factors.

Of course it is always possible that the future will be discontinuously different from the past. But if our estimates are accepted, then continuation of substitution during the next fifty years, during which many environmentalists foresee the end to growth, will result in a small increase—perhaps about 0.1 per cent per annum—in the growth of per capita income.

Is our economy, with its mixture of market processes and governmental controls, biased in favor of wasteful and shortsighted exploitation of natural resources? In considering this charge, two archetypical cases must be distinguished, although many actual cases fall between them. First, there are appropriable resources for which buyers pay market values and users market rentals. Second, there are inappropriable resources, "public goods," whose use appears free to individual producers and consumers but is costly in aggregate to society.

If the past is any guide for the future, there seems to be little reason to worry about the exhaustion of resources which the market already treats as economic goods. We have already commented on the irony that both growth men and antigrowth men invoke the interests of future generations. The issue between them is not whether and how much provision must be made for future generations, but in what form it should be made. The growth man emphasizes reproducible capital and education. The conservationist emphasizes exhaustible resources —minerals in the ground, open space, virgin land. The economist's initial presumption is that the market will decide in what forms to transmit wealth by the requirement that all kinds of wealth bear a comparable rate of return. Now stocks of natural resources—for example, mineral deposits—are essentially sterile. Their return to their owners is the increase in their prices relative to prices of other goods. In a properly functioning market economy, resources will be exploited at such a pace that their rate of relative price appreciation is competitive with rates of return on other kinds of capital. Many conservationists have noted such price appreciation with horror, but if the prices of these resources accurately reflect the scarcities of the future, they must rise in order to prevent too rapid exploitation. Natural resources *should* grow in relative scarcity—otherwise they are an inefficient way for society to hold and transmit wealth compared to productive physical and human capital. Price appreciation protects resources from premature exploitation.

How would an excessive rate of exploitation show up? We would see rates of relative price increase that are above the general real rate of return on wealth. This would indicate that society had in the past used precious resources too profligately, relative to the tastes and technologies later revealed. The scattered evidence we have indicates little excessive price rise. For some resources, indeed, prices seem to have risen more slowly than efficient use would indicate ex post.

If this reasoning is correct, the nightmare of a day of reckoning and economic collapse when, for example, all fossil fuels are forever gone seems to be based on failure to recognize the existing and future possibilities of substitute materials and processes. As the day of reckoning approaches, fuel prices will provide—as they do not now—strong incentives for such substitutions, as well as for the conservation of remaining supplies. On the other hand, the warnings of the conservationists and scientists do underscore the importance of continuous monitoring of the national and world outlook for energy and other resources. Substitutability might disappear. Conceivably both the market and public agencies might be too complacent about the prospects for new and safe substitutes for fossil fuels. The opportunity and need for fruitful collaboration between economists and physical scientists has never been greater.

Possible abuse of public natural resources is a much more serious problem. It is useful to distinguish between *local* and *global* ecological disturbances. The former include transient air pollution, water pollution, noise pollution, visual disamenities. It is certainly true that we have not charged automobile users and electricity consumers for their pollution of the skies, or farmers and housewives for the pollution of lakes by the runoff of fertilizers and detergents. In that degree our national product series have overestimated the advance of welfare. Our urban disamenity estimates given above indicate a current overestimate of about 5 per cent of total consumption.

There are other serious consequences of treating as free things which are not really free. This practice gives the wrong signals for the directions of economic growth. The producers of automobiles and of electricity should be given incentives to develop and to utilize "cleaner" technologies. The consumers of automobiles and electricity should pay in higher prices for the pollution they cause, or for the higher costs of low-pollution processes. If recognition of these costs causes consumers to shift their purchases to other goods and services, that is only efficient. At present overproduction of these goods is uneconomically subsidized as truly as if the producers received cash subsidies from the Treasury.

The mistake of the antigrowth men is to blame economic growth per se for the misdirection of economic growth. The misdirection is due to a defect of the pricing system—a serious but by no means irreparable defect and one which would in any case be present in a stationary economy. Pollutants have multiplied much faster than the population or the economy during the last thirty years. Although general economic growth has intensified the problem, it seems to originate in particular technologies. The proper remedy is to correct the price system so as to discourage these technologies. Zero economic growth is a blunt instrument for cleaner air, prodigiously expensive and probably ineffectual.

As for the danger of global ecological catastrophes, there is probably very little that economics alone can say. Maybe we are pouring pollutants into the atmosphere at such a rate that we will melt the polar icecaps and flood all the world's seaports. Unfortunately, there seems to be great uncertainty about the causes and the likelihood of such occurrences. These catastrophic global disturbances warrant a higher priority for research than the local disturbances to which so much attention has been given.

POPULATION GROWTH

Like the role of natural resources, the role of population in the standard neoclassical model is ripe for re-examination. The assumption is that population and labor force grow exogenously, like compound interest. Objections arise on both descriptive and normative grounds. We know that population growth cannot continue forever. Some day there will be stable or declining population, either with high birth and death rates and short life expectancies, or with low birth and death rates and long life expectancies. As Richard Easterlin argues in his National Bureau book,[4] there surely is some adaptation of human fertility and mortality to economic circumstances. Alas, neither economists nor other social scientists have been notably successful in developing a theory of fertility that corresponds even roughly to the facts. The subject deserves much more attention from economists and econometricians than it has received.

On the normative side, the complaint is that economists should not fatalistically acquiesce in whatever population growth happens. They should instead help to frame a population policy. Since the costs to society of additional children may exceed the costs to the parents, childbearing decisions are a signal example of market failure. How to internalize the full social costs of reproduction is an even more challenging problem than internalizing the social costs of pollution.

During the past ten years, the fertility of the United States population has declined dramatically. If continued, this trend would soon diminish fertility to a level ultimately consistent with zero population growth. But such trends have been reversed in the past, and in the absence of any real understanding of the determinants of fertility, predictions are extremely hazardous.

The decline may be illustrated by comparing the 1960 and 1967 net reproduction rates and intrinsic (economists would say "equilibrium") rates of growth of the United States population. The calculations of Table 3 refer to the asymptotic steady-state implications of indefinite continuation of the age-specific fertility and mortality rates of the year 1960 or 1967. Should the trend of the 1960s continue, the intrinsic growth rate would become zero, and the net reproduction rate 1.000, in the 1970s. Supposing that the decline in fertility then stopped. The actual population would grow slowly for another forty or fifty

[4] *Population, Labor Force, and Long Swings in Economic Growth: The American Experience,* New York, NBER, 1968.

TABLE 3

U.S. Population Characteristics in Equilibrium

	Intrinsic Growth Rate (per cent per year)	Net Reproduction Rate	Median Age
1960 fertility-mortality	2.1362	1.750	21–22
1967 fertility-mortality	0.7370	1.221	28
Hypothetical ZPG	0.0000	1.000	32

years while the inherited bulge in the age distribution at the more fertile years gradually disappeared. The asymptotic size of the population would be between 250 million and 300 million.

One consequence of slowing down the rate of population growth by diminished fertility is, of course, a substantial increase in the age of the equilibrium population, as indicated in the third column of Table 3. It is hard to judge to what degree qualitative change and innovation have in the past been dependent on quantitative growth. When our institutions are expanding in size and in number, deadwood can be gracefully bypassed and the young can guide the new. In a stationary population, institutional change will either be slower or more painful.

The current trend in fertility in the United States suggests that, contrary to the pessimistic warnings of some of the more extreme anti-growth men, it seems quite possible that ZPG can be reached while childbearing remains a voluntary private decision. Government policy can concentrate on making it completely voluntary by extending the availability of birth control knowledge and technique and of legal abortion. Since some 20 per cent of current births are estimated to be unintended, it may well be that intended births at present are insufficient to sustain the population.

Once the rate of population growth is regarded as a variable, perhaps one subject to conscious social control, the neoclassical growth model can tell some of the consequences of its variation. As explained above, sustainable per capita consumption (growing at the rate of technological progress) requires enough net investment to increase the capital stock at the natural rate of growth of the economy (the sum of the rate of increase of population and productivity). Given the capital-output ratio, sustainable consumption per capita will be larger the lower the rate of population increase; at the same time, the capital-widening requirement is diminished.

This is, however, not the only effect of a reduction of the rate of population growth. The equilibrium capital-output ratio itself is altered. The average wealth of a population is a weighted average of the wealth positions of people of different ages. Over its life cycle the typical family, starting from low or negative net worth, accumulates wealth to spend in old age, and perhaps in middle years when children are most costly. Now a stationary or slow-growing population has a characteristic age distribution much different from that of a rapidly growing population. The stationary population will have relatively fewer people in the early low-wealth years, but relatively more in the late low-wealth

TABLE 4

Illustrative Relationship of Sustainable Per Capita Consumption to Marginal Productivity of Capital and to Capital-Output Ratio

Marginal Productivity of Capital					Index of Consumption Per Capita (c)		
Gross (R) (1)	Net of Depreciation ($R - \delta$) (2)	Ratio of Capital to GNP (μ') (3)	Ratio of Capital to NNP (μ) (4)	Index of NNP per Capita (y) (5)	1960 Pop. Growth (6)	1967 Pop. Growth (7)	ZPG (8)
.09	.05	3.703	4.346	1.639	1.265	1.372	1.426
.105	.065	3.175	3.637	1.556	1.265	1.344	1.386
.12	.08	2.778	3.125	1.482	1.245	1.309	1.343
.15	.11	2.222	2.439	1.356	1.187	1.233	1.257

Note: A Cobb-Douglas production function is assumed for GNP, with constant returns to scale, with an elasticity of output with respect to capital (α) of $\frac{1}{3}$, and with the rate (γ) of labor-augmenting technological progress 3 per cent per year. The depreciation rate (δ) is assumed to be 4 per cent per year. GNP per capita (Y) is $ae^{\gamma t}k^\alpha$ and NNP per capita (y) is $Y - \delta k$, where k is the capital-labor ratio.
Column 3: Since $Rk = \alpha Y$, $\mu' = k/Y = \alpha/R$.
Column 4: $\mu = \mu'/(1 - \delta\mu')$.
Column 5: $y = (1 - \delta\mu')Y$. For the index, $ae^{\gamma t}$ is set equal to 1.
Columns 6, 7, and 8: $c = [1 - (n + \gamma)\mu]y$. Given $\gamma = 0.03$, $n + \gamma$ is 0.0513 for 1960, 0.0374 for 1967, 0.0300 for ZPG.

TABLE 5
Desired Wealth-Income Ratios Estimated for Different Rates of Population Growth (and for Different Equivalent Adult Scales and Subjective Discount Rates [a])

Net Interest Rate $(R - \delta)$	Desired Wealth-Income Ratio (μ)		
	1960 Pop. Growth (.021)	1967 Pop. Growth (.007)	ZPG
Teenagers, 1.0; Children, 1.0; Discount, 0.02			
.05	−1.70	−1.46	−1.24
.065	0.59	0.91	1.16
.08	2.31	2.70	2.90
.11	4.31	4.71	4.95
Teenagers, 0.8; Children, 0.6; Discount, 0.01			
.05	0.41	0.74	0.97
.065	2.36	2.75	3.00
.08	3.74	4.16	4.41
.11	5.17	5.55	5.75
Teenagers, 0.8; Children, 0.6; Discount, 0.02			
.05	−1.17	−0.95	−0.75
.065	1.08	1.38	1.60
.08	2.74	3.11	3.34
.11	4.61	4.98	5.18
Teenagers, 0.0; Children, 0.0; Discount, 0.02			
.05	−0.40	−0.15	0.02
.065	1.93	2.20	2.36
.08	3.56	3.85	4.01
.11	5.20	5.47	5.61

Note: The desired wealth-income ratio is calculated for a given steady state of population increase and the corresponding equilibrium age distribution. It is an aggregation of the wealth and income positions of households of different ages. As explained in Appendix C it also depends on the interest rate, the typical age-income profile and the expected growth of incomes ($\gamma = 0.03$), the rate of subjective discount of future utility of consumption, and the weights given to teenagers (boys 14–20 and girls 14–18) and other children in household allocations of lifetime incomes to consumption in different years. See Appendix C for further explanation.

[a] Shown in boldface.

TABLE 6
Estimated Equilibrium Capital-Output Ratios
and Per Capita Consumption Rates [a]

Population Growth Rate	Interest Rate $(R - \delta)$	Capital-Output Ratio (μ)	Consumption Index (c)	Per Cent Increase in c over 1960
	Teenagers, 1.0; Children, 1.0; Discount, 0.02			
1960	.089	2.88	1.23	
1967	.085	2.99	1.30	5.62
ZPG	.082	3.07	1.34	9.04
	Teenagers, 0.8; Children, 0.6; Discount, 0.01			
1960	.074	3.28	1.25	
1967	.071	3.38	1.33	6.23
ZPG	.069	3.47	1.37	9.74
	Teenagers, 0.8; Children, 0.6; Discount, 0.02			
1960	.084	3.00	1.24	
1967	.080	3.11	1.31	5.82
ZPG	.078	3.16	1.35	8.97
	Teenagers, 0.0; Children, 0.0; Discount, 0.02			
1960	.077	3.22	1.25	
1967	.074	3.28	1.32	6.42
ZPG	.073	3.33	1.36	9.99

Note: Estimated by interpolation from Tables 4 and 5. See Figure 1.
[a] Equivalent adult scales and subjective discount rate are shown in boldface.

years. So it is not obvious in which direction the shift of weights moves the average.

We have, however, estimated the shift by a series of calculations described in Appendix C. Illustrative results are shown in Tables 4–6 and Figure 1. Evidently, reduction in the rate of growth increases the society's desired wealth-income ratio. This means an increase in the capital-output ratio which increases the society's sustainable consumption per capita.[5]

On both counts, therefore, a reduction in population increase

[5] Provided only that the change is made from an initial situation in which the net marginal productivity of capital exceeds the economy's natural rate of growth. Otherwise the increased capital-widening requirements exceed the gains in output.

FIGURE 1

Determination of Equilibrium Capital-Output Ratio and Interest Rate
(*equivalent adult scale for teenagers and children* = *1.0; subjective
discount rate* = *0.02*)

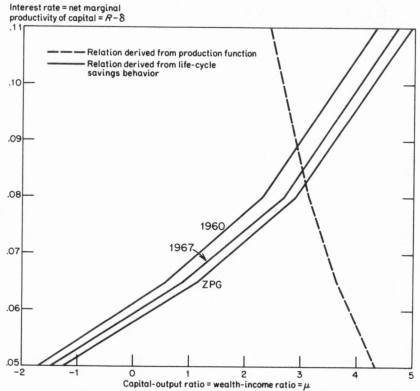

Interest rate = net marginal
productivity of capital = $R-\delta$

—————— Relation derived from production function
—————— Relation derived from life-cycle
savings behavior

1960
1967
ZPG

Capital-output ratio = wealth-income ratio = μ

Source: Tables 4 and 5.

should raise sustainable consumption. We have essayed an estimate
of the magnitude of this gain. In a ZPG equilibrium sustainable consumption per capita would be 9–10 per cent higher than in a steady
state of 2.1 per cent growth corresponding to 1960 fertility and mortality, and somewhat more than 3 per cent higher than in a steady state
of 0.7 per cent growth corresponding to 1967 fertility and mortality.

These neoclassical calculations do not take account of the lower
pressure of population growth on natural resources. As between the
1960 equilibrium and ZPG, the diminished drag of resource limitations
is worth about one-tenth of 1 per cent per annum in growth of per cap-

ita consumption. Moreover, if our optimistic estimates of the ease of substitution of other factors of production for natural resources are wrong, a slowdown of population growth will have much more important effects in postponing the day of reckoning.

Is growth obsolete? We think not. Although GNP and other national income aggregates are imperfect measures of welfare, the broad picture of secular progress which they convey remains after correction of their most obvious deficiencies. At present there is no reason to arrest general economic growth to conserve natural resources, although there is good reason to provide proper economic incentives to conserve resources which currently cost their users less than true social cost. Population growth cannot continue indefinitely, and evidently it is already slowing down in the United States. This slowdown will significantly increase sustainable per capita consumption. But even with ZPG there is no reason to shut off technological progress. The classical stationary state need not become our utopian norm.

COMMENT

S. FRED SINGER, University of Virginia

1. In December 1970, I was asked to give my reaction to an earlier version of the Nordhaus-Tobin paper. I quote from my letter: [1]

It is an outstanding, pioneering paper. It sets out to do something that we have long wanted to do (see, for example, the express remarks by Preston Cloud and Garrett Hardin at the AAAS Symposium on Optimum Population), namely, to transform the GNP into an index which measures more directly what would correspond to quality of life. This paper is an admirable effort in that direction and combines sound and original thinking with a very fine style of writing. There are six different kinds of corrections that are made to the GNP, or rather to the NNP (Net National Product). I have to withhold judgment on how well they have succeeded until I have a chance to study the appendices in detail. It is clear that what they have done is much more than just a bookkeeping job, i.e., pushing items from one category to another. They have incorporated a good deal of judgment, some educated guesses, and some interesting and original analyses.

Their most striking conclusion is that MEW (Measure of Economic Wel-

[1] The symposium of the American Association for the Advancement of Science that is mentioned in the letter was held in 1969. The papers and discussion are contained in S. F. Singer, ed., *Is There an Optimum Level of Population?*, New York, McGraw-Hill, 1971.

fare) has grown faster than the NNP. One word of caution, though; their corrections to the NNP are not small. In many cases they are larger than the NNP itself so that their final result is very sensitive to the goodness of the correction.

An area in which their analysis is weak is the exhaustion of natural resources and the evaluation of the diseconomies of pollution. . . .

Although I would take issue with many points in detail, and perhaps some other major points, the study is immensely valuable and breaks new ground. It is of particular value to me because it complements what I am trying to do and therefore helps me very directly. Even the title of their paper "Is Growth Obsolete?" resembles mine, which is "When Does Growth Become Too Expensive?" The factors which they have not handled or handled well are precisely the ones that I am covering. . . .

I have now given it one reasonably careful reading; it deserves at least three more. . . .

2. I have now done my three readings and have no reason to change my mind. It is indeed an "outstanding, pioneering" paper. However, I will take issue in detail, in the expectation that constructive criticism will help us arrive at a better approximation to an index of economic welfare. If I am a little diffident in putting forth my views on the paper, it is because of John Meyer's admonition to "let a hundred flowers bloom." Perhaps he recalls that this pronouncement was made by Chairman Mao who then promptly chopped off the heads of all those flowers.

George Jaszi has admonished us not to construct indexes on a wholesale basis. One should have a particular purpose in mind, because this in turn conditions the index. Another important thing to keep in mind is the time scale of our examination. We are definitely interested in time scales of ten to twenty years rather than one to two years. This allows important simplifications for the determination of an index.

My own purpose is to answer a very simple-sounding question, namely: Would we be better off or worse off in the future if we had more people or fewer people? [2] This requires a rather different kind of

---

[2] This problem, however, is not addressed by Nordhaus and Tobin, although it may appear so on a superficial reading of their Appendix C (the appendixes may be found in *Economic Growth,* Fiftieth Anniversary Colloquium V, New York, National Bureau of Economic Research, 1972). Instead they address a second-order effect, namely, how does age distribution of a population (or rate of growth, which is equivalent) affect welfare. Although they show that zero population growth rate, i.e., a specific age distribution corresponding to a net reproduction ratio of one, gives a higher index than a growing population, I would hazard that a negative population growth rate may give an even larger value to the quality index MEW.

examination than that in the Nordhaus-Tobin paper. In particular, I believe that the exhaustion of natural resources and the increasing use of "free" goods, such as air and water, have to be closely examined because they may play a primary role.

3. In their Appendix B, Nordhaus-Tobin arrive at the surprising conclusion that welfare will increase as growth continues in spite of the exhaustion of natural resources. Closer analysis shows that they assume the ready substitution of one resource for another. This of course is the key problem, and I rather doubt whether this assumption will be valid. The word *ready* has to be emphasized; and an appreciable time lag in substitution will affect growth through price increases. To gain some perspective on this problem, we should note that currently about 3 to 4 per cent of the GNP is spent on fossil fuels, and that fossil fuel prices have been rising rather steeply. Increased fuel costs will reflect themselves in increased costs of all goods and most services. In particular, the necessities of life, including food, will become more costly and thus affect the welfare of the poorer section of the population even more strongly. (I purposely choose fossil fuels because they play such an important role in our economy. Nonrenewable fuel resources are not easily replaceable, and they certainly cannot be exchanged for land, as in neoclassical growth analysis. Computer simulations, as in Appendix B, do nothing to support the correctness of Nordhaus and Tobin's basic assumptions.)

It can of course be argued that exhaustion of natural resources will raise the price of manufactured goods, leading to a reduced emphasis on growth in that direction and more emphasis on services. This is a current trend, but it cannot continue all the way and is not caused by resource shortages. On the other hand, costs associated with manufactured goods may rise even more steeply, because of the associated environmental costs. This matter is discussed in more detail below.

4. Most of the Nordhaus-Tobin paper (Appendix A) is of course given over to the calculation of a new welfare index. There is a great deal of room for subjective views on both the imputations and amputations which they perform. I will review my known predilections rather briefly, but then spend more time on a major omission, i.e., the one dealing with environmental externalities and social costs.

Before starting on a detailed discussion, I need to explain the difference between what I call intrinsic and extrinsic items. Intrinsic items are those directly connected with and traceable to economic growth: items such as exhaustion of natural resources, pollution control costs, disamenities due to crowding, etc. Extrinsic items are not necessarily related, or at least not strongly related, to economic growth, and include expenditures for defense, space research, and science generally. Since relative (rather than absolute) welfare measures are of real importance in relation to governmental policies, i.e., would we be better off or worse off if we do something and follow a certain path, we can in many cases neglect or sidestep extrinsic factors and the corrections which they produce to the GNP.

The big Nordhaus-Tobin corrections are for leisure (on the order of 200 per cent of market consumption) and for nonmarket activities, on the order of 100 per cent. On the other hand, their disamenity correction for urban congestion and all other urban problems is less than 5 per cent, which is surprisingly small; and they have no correction at all for pollution control. Since leisure and nonmarket activities are so large, this means that the corrections have to be done with great care: a small difference can distort the over-all result. Unfortunately, these corrections are rather arbitrary. With respect to the Nordhaus-Tobin discussion on leisure, three points could be made. One is that eating is a necessity; it should not be counted as a leisure-time activity. Another is that leisure-time value might be established by observing what people actually do. After all, working involves not only a benefit, i.e., wages, but also disutility. How much of a premium are people willing to pay, say, to save travel time and have more leisure? And finally, their key assumption is that leisure time can in fact be traded for working hours and additional wages. This may not be true; perhaps the economy cannot accommodate increased working hours without increasing unemployment. In that case, the basis for using opportunity costs for leisure disappears.

The urban disamenity correction calculated by Nordhaus and Tobin on the basis of higher urban incomes is interesting but it may be an underestimate.[3] The reason is that many urban diseconomies are subsidized by nonurban residents, i.e., by the general taxpayer. One would like to see additional analyses, using as a basis the costs for urban services or the urban cost-of-living index. It would be interesting to see if these methods arrive at the same result as Nordhaus-Tobin.[4]

[3] On the other hand, the increased urban salaries may be closely tied in to the increased costs and time of commuting to work which they subtracted under "regrettables." Also, to what extent are urban salaries higher just because there are more job opportunities in urban areas for people of higher education?

[4] It is necessary to subtract here all costs, direct or indirect, that are based on the higher value of land in the city. Unlike the real costs of traffic snarls and

5. The correction for environmental protection is a major one, I believe. Pollution control costs should rise more rapidly even than GNP. This nonlinear relationship is easy to explain if we consider that the natural environment has a limited but finite assimilative capacity.[5] Once the effluent level exceeds this capacity, then expenditures must be provided. In order to maintain a fixed level of environmental quality, the degree of clean-up has to increase, and unfortunately, the costs rise steeply with the degree of clean-up. This is the approach that I have taken in my work: by holding environmental quality fixed I do not have to consider the benefits or damages of environmental quality or pollution. Most of the costs are connected with the production or use of various forms of energy, but through the input-output table, these costs will reflect themselves also in the costs of intermediate and consumer goods, principally, aluminum, fertilizers, paper, etc. In the final analysis, the prices of food and other items that play an important part in the cost of living index will rise and diminish welfare.

6. In conclusion, it is possible to apply various corrections to the GNP to arrive at a better measure of welfare, including some imputations and some amputations. There is one item, however, which deserves more careful attention and that is the distribution of welfare. Intuitively, one would think that a narrow distribution leads to a more stable society, and therefore contributes greatly to societal welfare. It would be important to know how to assign a welfare value to changes in income *distribution* as well as to changes in the *average* income.

IMRE BERNOLAK, Canada Department of Industry, Trade, and Commerce

In my view it is very significant that the major adjustments Nordhaus and Tobin have made in the national accounts in order to allow for welfare considerations did *not* lead them to the conclusion that growth was obsolete, or that the progress indicated by conventional national accounts was just a myth. However, I cannot see why they take the defensive attitude about growth which is indicated by their remarks: "at

other impediments to intra-urban transportation, land rents (and the price increases they cause) are transfer payments. For the same reason, urban salaries are subject to a large correction when used to measure urban disamenities.

[5] As a matter of interest, it should be noted that if people were perfectly distributed, according to the available surface water, then the United States could accommodate 250 million people without requiring any sewage treatment.

present there is no reason to arrest general economic growth . . . ," or "even with zero population growth there is no reason to shut off technological progress." I believe that economic growth and technological progress are not only *possible* but also *necessary* for the betterment of human welfare.

The disagreement is probably due to the general confusion about the meaning of growth, and an attempt to clarify it might serve a useful purpose. Why is it that the same policymakers who are the staunchest advocates of the protection of the environment and who often criticize economic growth on the basis that it might be detrimental to our natural resources and to the quality of life take the strongest measures to stimulate expansion as soon as the growth of the gross national product tends to slow down? What leads to this apparent *growth dilemma?*

I think the explanation of the problem is historical. It was observed that over the centuries the might and wealth of nations was associated with the size of their populations, and even today we see that those nations and industries prosper which find large numbers of customers for their products and services. These observations have led to the widespread, and erroneous, assumption that growth necessarily means population growth, together with the environmental problems it may cause.

To find the true meaning of economic growth, we must look at what the economy is all about: people producing goods and services to satisfy their wants. The wants are individual wants, even if they are satisfied collectively. As Nordhaus and Tobin themselves emphasized it correctly, it is "per capita rather than aggregate consumption [that] is the welfare objective." Progress in welfare is, therefore, growing in per capita consumption and, in order to provide for this increasing per capita consumption, economic growth must mean increasing per capita production (unless it comes from self-generating free resources).

The latter is determined by the productivity of the labor force engaged in production, and economic growth cannot originate from any other source than increased over-all labor productivity (whatever the factors may be that bring about this productivity increase). It is true that society may choose increased leisure time as a preferred welfare objective but this is then proportionately traded off against economic growth in the per capita production (and consumption) of goods and services. It may also be chosen as a welfare objective to divide at least part of the national real output among all members of the society rather than in accordance with the contribution of the individual to total output, as is in the case of many public services and of the various forms of guaranteed annual income or similar income-sharing plans. This is only a question of income distribution and all must come out of the productivity of the employed labor force.

As our real income increases, it is just human nature to want more and/or a better quality of goods and services. In addition, it takes only simple arithmetic to show that if we can produce the goods and services we want at a lower environmental cost or from fewer resources than before through better technology, it is also economic growth. If we can produce a nonpolluting car tomorrow instead of today's polluting car, that is economic as well as welfare growth.

Summing up this point, I see the true chance for economic growth in the increasing per capita demand for (and production of) goods and services and in the improving quality of these, rather than in population growth. And I believe that this per capita growth potential is much greater than estimated by Nordhaus and Tobin.

The second point I wish to make refers to the contribution of national accounts to the measurement of welfare growth.

Although gross national product is not a welfare measure, the Nordhaus-Tobin paper supports the view that, in spite of its shortcomings, it does correctly indicate the direction of progress. How could it be otherwise? We cannot have better health without doctors and medicines, hospitals, and modern equipment; enjoy outdoor life without roads, transport equipment, skis, boats, proper clothing, or prepared foods; concerts without musicians or musical instruments (and nowadays without amplifiers); or arts without artists, metals, or paints; and so on. All of these *are* measured in the national accounts. Although GNP does not measure welfare, many if not most elements of welfare are, in fact, measured by it.

At this conference numerous suggestions were made toward the development of an integrated framework of social indicators which would be distinct from the national accounts. With these I agree. I also believe, however, that the national accounts can be improved further, particularly in the measurement of quality change and in the sectors where output is now measured by inputs. I think that through detailed studies of principal characteristics of a carefully selected sample of products and services, productivity indicators can be developed, through which progress can be made toward better output measures in these areas.

In the field of quality measurement I think there is scope in cross-sectional analyses because it is easier to measure the differences between a $3 steak served in one restaurant and an $8 steak served in another at the same time, than changes over time. Other useful suggestions about the direction such studies could take have been presented in Jaszi's note in the August 1962 issue of the *Review of Economics and Statistics,* and still apply.

In the field of government output, two approaches toward improvement appear to be particularly feasible. Impact or output measures, which are usually very complex, can be subdivided into measurable elements. For instance, instead of "industrial development" we can strive toward measuring the elements of this over-all objective, such as progress in productivity, profitability, wage level, employment, distribution of employment, industrial structure and concentration, the ratio of technically trained labor force, etc. At the performance level, specific productivity indexes can be developed, which can be applied through careful analysis, to adjust governmental output. In the United States, John Kendrick has clearly illustrated the feasibility of such measures, while in Canada some successful experiments have been made in this direction by the National Output and Productivity Division of Statistics Canada (formerly Dominion Bureau of Statistics). Since productivity does not just happen but is brought about by various factors, and since these factors, including better management, better education, better methods and equipment, are more or less keeping pace in the public service with the private sector, it just does not make sense to keep the productivity measure constant in the public sector. Furthermore, ignoring productivity changes in the public sector leads to noncomparability of national accounts on an international basis.

With the growing importance of *quality* in the production of both goods and services, and with the rapid growth of the *public sector,* I believe that improvements in these areas are much more promising avenues toward a better measurement of economic, or even welfare, progress then imaginative (but for the time being unworkable) attempts at turning the national accounts into social welfare measures. I think that a number of points raised by George Jaszi in his comments on the Juster paper apply equally to the Nordhaus-Tobin study too.

In conclusion, I would like to make two brief observations concerning the Nordhaus-Tobin paper. First, I do not understand why the authors exclude defense services from national output (or more precisely, from their measure of economic welfare) when these can hardly be considered as anything else but *freedom* as output, measured by the relevant inputs. Freedom is, as the authors pointed out, one of the basic welfare goals even according to Paul Erlich. Secondly, I tend to disagree with the authors when they consider health services as intermediate output and exclude them from national output. I realize that good health contributes to one's productivity but I cannot help taking medical services as final output because when I buy them I do so, and I believe that there are others who share my views, because I simply enjoy living and being healthy.

DAN USHER, Queen's University

The effect of Nordhaus and Tobin's imputation for leisure is to reduce the rate of economic growth despite the fact that consumption of leisure is increasing over time. I would like to contrast their imputation with an alternative according to which more leisure implies more growth, not less.

There are three variants of Nordhaus and Tobin's imputation for leisure and nonmarket activity. Variant A is based on the assumption that there is no change over time in labor productivity of leisure and nonmarket activity. Variant B is based on the assumption that there is no change over time in labor productivity of leisure but that productivity of labor in nonmarket activity increases along with and to the same extent as labor productivity in creating ordinary goods and services. Variant C is based on the assumption that the growth over time in the productivity of labor is the same for leisure, nonmarket activity, and ordinary goods and services. In this comment I shall consider only variant A, but the points I raise are relevant with modification to variants B and C as well.

Nordhaus and Tobin impute for leisure by treating leisure over and above an assumed minimum of seven hours a day as an extra commodity which they evaluate at the wage in the base year. Suppose that output is produced with labor alone, that the wage rate is $9 per hour in 1961 and $36 per hour in 1971, that the consumer price index is the same in 1961 and 1971, and that people work an eight-hour day in 1961 and a six-hour day in 1971. Income as conventionally measured grows by a factor of 3.0 from $72 per day to $216 per day. Leisure increases from 9 hours per day $(24 - 8 - 7)$ to 11 hours per day $(24 - 6 - 7)$, its value at 1961 prices and wages is $81 in 1961 and $99 in 1971, income inclusive of the imputation for leisure is $153 in 1961 and $315 in 1971, and income inclusive of the imputation grows by a factor of 2.1. Notice that the ratio of incomes in 1961 and 1971 and the implied growth rate between these dates are reduced by the imputation despite the fact that the number of hours of leisure has increased.

An alternative method of imputation would treat the reduction in hours as an extra bit of growth. To the conventional measure of income is added or subtracted each year a sum of money sufficient to compensate the representative consumer for the difference in hours worked between that year and the base year. The rationale of the alternative method is based on an analogy between real incomes in different years and the spectrum of money incomes in some given base year. If in 1961, Mr. A earns $72 per day and Mr. B earns $216 per day, we would say the Mr. B has 3 times the income of Mr. A. We might even be prepared to say that the ratio of their incomes is larger than 3 if Mr. B works less than Mr. A, but we would certainly not say that it is only 2.1 because both parties enjoy a substantial amount of leisure. We make a distinction among good things between those like cars, food, and clothing that we treat as part of income and those like leisure, friendship, or the love of God that we exclude from income. Normally when we speak of growth, we consider only the growth of what we choose to call income and we suppose that good things not included in income remain invariant, thus preserving the analogy between real incomes over time and the spectrum of income at a moment of time. The alternative imputation adjusts incomes to what they would have to be if existing levels of utility were preserved and if the ceterus paribus assumptions were true.

Formally, we may impute for changes in amounts of leisure in the same way that I have imputed for changes in life expectancy in my essay in this volume. The representative consumer is assumed to have a utility function $U[C(t), L(t)]$, where $C(t)$ is the value in the year t of real income as conventionally measured, and $L(t)$ is the amount of leisure in the year t. Define $\hat{C}(t)$, real income inclusive of an imputation for leisure, by means of the equation

$$U[\hat{C}(t), L(1961)] = U[C(t), L(t)], \qquad (1)$$

where 1961 is the base year. We can solve for $\hat{C}(t)$ explicitly if we know the exact form of the utility function; otherwise we can use the evidence about wage rates to approximate $C(t)$. Expand $U[\hat{C}(t), L(1961)]$ in a Taylor series around $U[\hat{C}(t), L(t)]$ and ignore all but the first three terms:

$$U[\hat{C}(t), L(1961)] = \qquad (2)$$

$$U[C(t), L(t)] + U_c[\hat{C}(t) - C(t)] + U_L[L(1961) - L(t)].$$

Since $U[\hat{C}(v), L(1961)] = U[C(t), L(t)]$ by definition, and since U_L/U_C is the real wage, we have

$$\hat{C}(t) \simeq C(t) + \text{wage }(t)[L(t) - L(1961)], \tag{3}$$

all terms of which may be estimated from market data. This formula may be contrasted with Nordhaus and Tobin's formula variant A which is

$$\hat{C}(t)_{N.T.} = C(t) + \text{wage}(1961) [17 - L(t)]. \tag{4}$$

The contrast between the imputations represented by formulas (3) and (4) may be seen in an extension of the example used above. Suppose we are measuring economic growth between 1951 and 1971 using 1961 as the base year. Real wages per hour were $4 in 1951, $9 in 1961, and $36 in 1971, hours worked were 10, 8, and 6 and incomes per day were $40, $72, and $216.

Without any imputation for leisure the ratio of incomes in 1971 and 1951 is about five ($216 \div 40$). Nordhaus and Tobin's imputation reduces the ratio to about three $[216 + (9 \times 11)] \div [40 + (9 \times 7)]$. The alternative imputation of equation (3) increases the ratio of incomes to nine $[216 + (2 \times 36)] \div [40 - (2 \times 4)]$.

The Nordhaus and Tobin imputation, the exact form of the alternative imputation, and the approximate form of the alternative imputations are illustrated in Figure 1. The figure shows the representative consumer's choice between income (without the imputation) and leisure. Through the point on the leisure axis representing 0 hours of work are drawn three straight lines the slopes of which are equal to the real wages in 1951, 1961, and 1971. The representative consumer, three of whose indifference curves are illustrated, chooses points A, B, and C in 1951, 1961, and 1971. Nordhaus and Tobin's imputation amounts to projecting A, B, and C onto a line representing an assumed minimum of seven hours of leisure or an assumed maximum of 17 hours of work. Their measure of the ratio of incomes in 1951 and 1971 is J/H, where each letter stands for the distance of the corresponding point from the horizontal axis. The exact form of the alternative measure is G/D, where G is indifferent to C and D is indifferent to A, and G and D correspond to 8 hours of work. The approximate form of the alternative measure is F/E, where F and E are incomes that the representative consumer would have had in 1951 and 1971 if he worked eight hours in both years. One cannot say a priori which of the ratios G/D and F/E is the larger, but F/E is necessarily larger than J/H.

The effect of the alternative imputation on Nordhaus and Tobin's re-

FIGURE 1

Imputations for Leisure

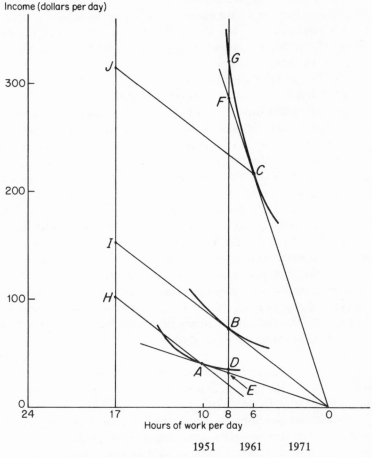

Income (dollars per day)

Hours of work per day

	1951	1961	1971
Wage ($ per hour)	4	9	36
Work (hrs. per day)	10	8	6
Income ($ per day)	40	72	216

(All sums of money are corrected for changes in the price level.)
Estimates of the ratio of incomes per head in 1971 and 1951:

a. According to Nordhaus and Tobin,

$$J/H = [216 + (9 \times 11)] \div [40 + (9 \times 7)] = 3.06.$$

b. According to the approximate form of the alternative imputation,

$$F/E = [216 + (2 \times 36)] \div [40 - (2 \times 4)] = 9.00.$$

c. According to the exact form of the alternative imputation,

$$G/D = (\text{as indicated by the diagram}) \ 320/35 = 9.15.$$

sults is shown in Table 1, which is intended as an addition to their Table 1. The alternative imputation should be read into Table 1 as variant D of lines 6 and 16. As I have made no distinction between leisure and non-market work, Table 1, line 7, variant D would be zero in all years. All of the data in the accompanying table are from Nordhaus and Tobin's paper, as explained in the notes on sources. No imputation is required in variant D for housekeeping or for schoolwork because it has been assumed that hours of work of people engaged in these occupations have remained constant over time. The table itself should be self-explanatory, and the point to emphasize is the contrast in the growth rates of MEW between variants A and D, which are directly comparable in their assumptions about the productivity of labor in nonmarket activity and leisure. Variant A of Nordhaus and Tobin, Table 1, line 16a, entails a ratio of real incomes per head in 1965 and 1929 of only 1.14 while variant D in the accompanying table entails a ratio of 1.98. A comparable difference would be found between the alternative imputation and the Nordhaus and Tobin imputations variant B or C if an alternative were constructed embodying the assumptions of variant B or C about labor productivity in nonmarket activity and leisure.

To sum up, we have contrasted two ways of imputing for leisure in a measure of economic growth. One way is to treat leisure as an additional commodity, and the other is to say the leisure itself is not part of income but that there should be imputed to income each year a sum sufficient to compensate the representative consumer for changes in leisure since the base year. The latter method requires no imputation if hours of work have remained unchanged, that is, if the ceteris paribus assumption we make in ignoring leisure is true.

The alternative imputation preserves the analogy between real incomes of the representative consumer at different periods of time and the spectrum of personal incomes at a moment of time. In abandoning that analogy, the Nordhaus and Tobin imputation opens the measure of economic growth to more speculation than most of us would find acceptable. For, if new commodities are to be introduced, why stop at leisure? Why not reduce the growth rate still further by imputing for friendship, or the love of God? The alternative measure gets around this problem by lumping all these intangibles into the ceteris paribus of utility analysis and by supposing that the love of God, for instance, is about the same in each year in the income comparison. Only if God has come to love us more (or less) would an imputation be in order.

TABLE 1

Adjustments to Nordhaus and Tobin Table 1

	1929	1935	1945	1947	1954	1958	1965
1. Labor force (millions)	49.4	53.1	65.3	62.0	67.9	71.2	78.1
2. Extra hours of leisure per worker per year (over and above hours of leisure in 1958)	−478.1	−161.2	−286.0	−150.8	−52.0	0	−26.0
3. Real wage per hour in 1958 dollars	1.01	1.21	1.55	1.56	1.92	2.11	2.40
4. Value of extra leisure (Table 1, line 6, variant D), billions of dollars, 1958 prices	−23.8	−10.4	−28.9	−14.6	−6.8	0	−4.9
5. Index of per capita MEW (Table 1, line 15, variant D), 1929 = 100	100	94.4	118.8	136.9	154.8	168.0	198.4

NOTE: Tables A-9, A-10, A-11, and A-12 are appendix tables to the Nordhaus-Tobin paper. For availability of these tables, see the note on the first page of the Nordhaus-Tobin paper.

SOURCE: Line 1 – Table A-9, employed and unemployed. Line 2 – Table A-10, employed and unemployed. From each year's figure is subtracted the hours of leisure and nonmarket work in 1958, and the resulting figure is multiplied by 52. Line 3 – Tables A-11 and A-12. The wage in 1958 was 2.11 per hour. Real wages in other years were estimated by multiplying the figure of 2.11 by the ratio of the wage deflator and the consumption deflator [A-12, (2) divided by A-12, (3)]. Line 4 = line 1 × line 2 × line 3. Line 5 – From Table 1, line 15B, subtract the sum of line 6B and line 7B, and add the value of extra leisure (this table, line 4). Divide the result by the population (Table 1, line 14) to obtain Table 1, line 15, variant D.

545

EDWARD F. DENISON, The Brookings Institution

Nordhaus and Tobin introduce leisure into their measure of economic welfare (MEW) but make no explicit allowance for the real cost of work. They introduce leisure by adding its value in 1958 prices to net national product valued in 1958 prices. They provide two alternative measures of the value of leisure in 1958 prices.

Variant A is relatively straightforward. It regards the value of an hour of leisure in 1958 prices as always equal to the hourly wage in 1958. This value is multiplied by the number of hours of leisure each year to obtain the total value of leisure in 1958 prices. Once the 1958 value is established, leisure is thus treated as an output component just like loaves of bread or numbers of haircuts. Since the per capita quantity of leisure has scarcely changed, the effect is to add a large constant value to per capita NNP, which reduces the growth rate of an index of per capita welfare.

Variant C uses the same procedure for 1958, but in every other year the value of an hour of leisure in 1958 prices is different. It is the amount of goods valued in 1958 prices that could have been bought each year by the hourly wage (in current prices) that year. This seems analogous to measuring the bread component of NNP in, say, 1929 not by the number of loaves of bread purchased in 1929 but by the number of haircuts that could have been purchased in 1929 by the expenditure that was made for loaves of bread in 1929. Nordhaus and Tobin prefer this variant, justifying its use by introducing the assumption that efficiency in the enjoyment of leisure has risen at the same rate as efficiency in the production of marketable goods and services as a whole. The basis for such an assumption is flimsy, and I prefer a method, such as their method A, that assigns the same value to an hour of leisure every year. When leisure is valued as in variant C, its addition to marketed output scarcely changes the growth rate.

The point of this comment is not to express a preference for variant A. Rather it is to ask whether the approach adopted even in variant A does not start from a wrong premise and yield the wrong results. To pose the question in its bluntest terms, have not Nordhaus and Tobin added when they should have subtracted or divided?

Their calculation assumes that the hourly wage measures the price that was required to induce an individual to give up one hour of leisure and to work one hour instead. But if this is so, the wage cannot measure the value of an hour of leisure. Rather, it is the sum of the values of two amounts. One is the utility of one hour passed in any way except working in gainful employment—not just any hour, but the nonwork hour with the smallest utility of all such hours, since that is the hour that would rationally be given up. The second is the disutility of one hour passed in gainful work—not just any hour, but the work hour with the greatest disutility. It is the last hour of work, which our nineteenth century predecessors aptly called "the most onerous hour" because fatigue and boredom have reached their peak.

Suppose we find a man working for pay 45 hours of the week, and consequently not so working the remaining 123 hours. We might ask him two questions. (1) "Suppose we could shorten the week from 168 to 167 hours and cut your nonworking hours from 123 to 122 while leaving your work time unchanged at 45 hours. You are free to take the lost hour from time you spend sleeping, doing housework, playing, or anything you like, or to subtract a few minutes from each activity. What would you pay us not to do this?" (2) "Suppose we could shorten the week by one hour and cut one hour from your work time, reducing it from 45 to 44. What would you pay us to do so?" The answer to the first question would value the marginal utility of an hour of nonworking time while the answer to the second question would value the marginal disutility of one hour of working time. The sum of the man's answers to the two questions should equal his hourly wage if he were in equilibrium (and if, in addition, he were free to choose his hours, and if his output per hour were unaffected by the number of hours he works).

The value of the utility of the marginal nonworking hour so obtained in 1958 could then be multiplied by the number of nonworking hours to obtain the value of nonworking hours in 1958 prices, a calculation similar to the Nordhaus-Tobin variant A calculation for leisure. But it is probable that this value, per hour, is small and that the addition would be only a small fraction of the variant A addition. It is my impression that the bulk if not all of the wage rate has traditionally, and rightly, been regarded as recompense for the disutility of the most onerous hour.

MEW must take account of the disutility of work, or more generally, of real costs, in addition to the value of leisure. The total value of the disutility of work in 1958 prices is the product of its 1958 value per hour and the number of hours worked each year. To complete a calculation of real costs, we might follow Jevons and add the cost of abstinence from consumption, perhaps obtained as the product of the capital stock and the 1958 rate of return. We might then proceed to obtain MEW by subtracting real costs from positive welfare items.[1] But this is not very convenient because total real costs in 1958 would approximate the value of marketable output so that MEW in the base year would approximate zero, except for values placed on nonmarketed output. In later years, to be sure, we would obtain a positive number (because of rising productivity) and in earlier years a negative number, so this procedure is not nonsensical. But the results do not lend themselves to transformation into index form and are difficult to interpret. A more interesting procedure would be to divide real costs into output, rather than to subtract them, in order to obtain a measure of output in constant prices per unit of real cost. Either procedure would yield results very different from those Nordhaus and Tobin obtain.

This comment refers, of course, only to the starting point for a calculation. I have ignored all the real problems, such as those associated with the fact that switching an hour from work to nonwork involves different values when working hours are 44 than when they are 45, and that most people do not work at all in gainful employment and hence have no wage to subdivide as a starting point for a calculation.

JOHN R. MEYER, National Bureau of Economic Research and Yale University

In many ways it is difficult to play the role of constructive critic or discussant of these papers. Among other difficulties—as this conference has amply shown—the topics do tend to generate emotions. And to be only critical would be to miss what is basic in these papers: posing extremely important questions and, even more to their credit, providing at least partial answers to some.

There is, moreover, more than a little element of boldness, or even courage and heroism, in these undertakings. In recent years our profession often has tended to address its professional talents more to questions that were fairly easily answered by the existing or established tools, rather than addressing those which seemed most relevant. Even more disturbingly, certain of our numbers have come dangerously close of late to suggesting that even to be intellectually curious about certain difficult

---

[1] Most of this subtraction, representing the real cost of labor, would correspond to the amount which Nordhaus and Tobin now *add*, because per capita hours of work are not far from a constant.

questions, in particular measurement, constitutes a grave disservice to economics as a science.

These worries, I feel, represent a gross misunderstanding of what the real issues are. For example, the issue has sometimes been posed as: "Should GNP measure social welfare?" To my knowledge, no responsible professional has even suggested anything of the kind. Insofar as determining the potential contribution of GNP to improved social measurement, the usual issue, rather, has been whether we can derive from GNP certain indexes or concepts that might better measure economic welfare. Accordingly, Nordhaus and Tobin do not speak about constructing a measure of social welfare but rather of the possibility of constructing one of macroeconomic welfare.

Once posed properly, certain other false issues also quickly disappear. For example, I again know of no competent professional who seriously advocates early, prompt, or, in most cases, even long-term abandonment of GNP measures. Nor do many competent professionals even suggest ignoring GNP! Rather, the prevailing or almost unanimous opinion, as Nordhaus and Tobin take great pains to point out, is that GNP clearly has an established position and is a useful measure "for short-run stabilization policy and for assessing the economy's long-run progress as a productive machine." As I read this, this is a strong appeal to keep the GNP accounts, more or less as now constituted, separate and available. Or, another way of putting much the same point is to observe that a multiplicity of measures may well be needed to meet modern policy requirements. And why should that surprise us as our economy and policy concerns become ever more complex?

Indeed, about the closest that any professional critics have come to suggesting some major alteration in GNP for traditional purposes is to point out (as do also those insisting that GNP should not be changed) that the really strong aspect of GNP is its use as a measure of market-oriented activity. Accordingly, some critics have suggested that certain GNP imputations now made for nonmarket sectors might be usefully excluded. Certainly it is a suggestion worth consideration. Among other possibilities it might reduce the confusion about the meaning and intent of GNP as a measure. On the other hand, I can see strong arguments for not undertaking this kind of a "purification" quickly or lightly since GNP as now measured, even with all of its acknowledged imperfections or even minor inconsistencies, is a measure that is well-established and reasonably well-understood. Furthermore, GNP is often the only reasonably good aggregate number "in town" and as such certainly has a claim to an important or even paramount role for macroeconomic policy decisions.

Indeed, it is these very qualities—of availability, reliability, and acceptance—that lead Nordhaus and Tobin to an analysis of how these numbers might be rearranged, modified, or augmented so as to provide better insights on other (i.e., nonstabilization) issues of considerable concern to society, specifically whether and to what extent the *economic* welfare of our society has been improving or deteriorating over recent years. Certainly, this is not a question without considerable interest. Furthermore, it does not take a seer of unusual talents to predict that it is likely to be an issue of increasing concern.

The essential question, therefore, to pose about the Nordhaus-Tobin effort is: Have they succeeded in constructing a measure of macroeconomic welfare that is superior to those implicit or explicit in existing accounts, particularly that of net national product per capita? My own view would be that the jury should still be out. Following the lead of the authors and using admittedly quite subjective considerations, I would suggest focusing on periods when MEW per capita and NNP per capita go in opposite directions. I thus find it encouraging that their index (using actual MEW per capita and their "preferred" variant B) rose (from 121.4 to 123.2) between 1945 and 1947 even though per capita NNP declined (on an index basis from 155.4 to 131.9) in those years. On the other hand, I find it somewhat disconcerting by my lights that their measure of per capita economic welfare remains very stable or even rises between 1929 and 1935 (the index of MEW variant B actually goes from 100.0 to 108.0) while the NNP per capita index declined by roughly one-quarter (from 100.0 to 78.0) during those same years.

As for the years since 1947, which are recent and therefore also of special interest, I am not quite sure which measure is better, per capita MEW or per capita NNP. The differences are actually slight (at least between NNP and most of the MEW series). My subjective guess would be that NNP is slightly the better welfare index over this period. The actual MEW variant B index rises from 123.2 in 1947 to 141.8 in 1965 while the NNP per capita index goes from 131.9 to 187.5. My "feel" or intuition would be that the truth is somewhere in between, i.e., that the postwar years were rather better than suggested by the MEW index.

Quite obviously, the next question to ask is why the Nordhaus-Tobin MEW fails when it does (at least by my subjective valuations). For the thirties I suspect that the answer is fairly obvious. In those depression years, MEW overvalues leisure or undervalues the deterioration in human capital. Much of the leisure of the thirties perhaps merited a negative entry. A considerable improvement in MEW might be achieved by incorporating current research aimed at better measuring human capital, say along lines being pursued by Jacob Mincer or the Ruggleses. In short, Nordhaus and Tobin have focused the issue well, but a good deal still needs to be done on refining the actual measures.

As for my suspicion that MEW per capita may have been a slightly inferior measure to NNP of economic welfare after 1947, one might attribute this to increased defense expenditures. On defense, the Nordhaus-Tobin argument is that these are regrettables because increased outlays over the years have not clearly bought us more security. If true, this argument would seem to hold best for the post-1947 years. Certainly, it seems easier to accept the argument for the years after 1947 than for the years between 1929 and 1947.

Alternatively, I would suggest that the explanation for the post-1947 "softness" in MEW may reside in the treatment of disamenities. Specifically, the Nordhaus-Tobin regressions may overestimate any post-1947 increase in disamenities of urban life, mainly because of structural misspecification. For one thing the selection processes of migration normally result in younger, more energetic, and more intelligent members of the work force drifting from rural to urban areas. Thus, a potentially important missing variable from their county income regressions may be a measure of IQ or intelligence qualities. To very crudely check for this possibility I reran some very simple, but quite standard, income determination equations using the NBER-Thorndike-Air Force sample, which is the only one that I know of which provides an opportunity to control for intelligence differentials by geographic area. My preliminary results show that those in this sample who *originated* in large (over 1 million) cities do have significantly higher incomes than those who did not. (The t-ratio for the city size dummy is 2.8.) I also hope to check for the relationship between *current* place of residence and income using this same sample, but time was not sufficient to do the necessary coding. Actually, place of origin may be a better control for quality of education or of opportunity than a measure or proxy of the urban disamenity effects that Nordhaus-Tobin seek; thus, without a size measure for current residence, it probably measures both disamenity and opportunity influences. I should add that the intelligence measure variable is indeed significant as a determinant of income (the highest t-ratio of any included variable) and is positively correlated with the large city dummy; accordingly, some room for improvement in the Nordhaus-Tobin specification almost surely exists.

In general, my own hypothesis about the so-called disamenities of urban living would be rather different from that implicit in Nordhaus and Tobin. Specifically, I would guess that the relationship between urban density or population to well-being is nonlinear. Specifically, people may prefer living in urban centers of small to medium size and density rather than living at either extreme, e.g., very small towns, farms, or very large cities. Also, as a first approximation, I would hypothesize that substantial disamenities of urban living do not appear sharply until relatively high net densities and a total conurbation population of more than 2 or 3 million is achieved. This, in turn, suggests that some measure of maximum "point" (e.g., a census tract) density in a county might be a useful additional variable in the Nordhaus-Tobin regressions. Actually, there is some accumulating evidence that Americans seem to prefer living in cities of approximately 50,000 to 500,000 population and, correspondingly, some recent trend for new work opportunities to locate in such cities.

In addition, one might hypothesize that suburban living and working are deemed more attractive than doing either in the central city. Certainly, suburban wages are commonly somewhat lower than in the central cities of many SMSA's, thus suggesting less disamenity by the Nordhaus-Tobin test. Accordingly, the substantial increase in suburban work opportunities during the 1950's and 1960's could have led to some decrease in total disamenities experienced if Nordhaus and Tobin had differentiated between suburbs and central cities as well as, more grossly, between rural and urban areas. Furthermore, the rise in suburban living opportunities may have made the rural-urban disamenity premium less in 1960 than in earlier years so that the Nordhaus-Tobin assumption of a constant disamenity premium over the period could well misstate the changes over time, particularly from 1947 on.

Indeed, my guess would be that there may have been an over-all decrease in urban disamenities during the postwar period. This would mean that the urban "disamenities" correction (line 5c in Table A-17) should well have been less in 1965 and rather more in 1947. The disamenities correction is, of course, relatively small (about − $19.1 billion in 1947 and − $34.6 billion in 1965) but it is not trivial. For example, if these disamenities corrections were simply reversed for these years, the actual MEW variant B index per capita would have been more expansive and thus behaved more like NNP in the postwar period.

The Leontief paper deals with some of the same issues as Nordhaus and Tobin but is less concerned with valuation as such. Leontief concentrates instead on constructing a tool to better characterize and analyze relationships between ordinary or regular market activities and pollution. However, he does suggest a highly imaginative interindustry framework for evaluating or attaching costs to antipollution efforts at the margin. As such, he provides us with at least a primitive tool for attaching "shadow prices" to antipollution programs. The major limitation, as recognized by Leontief, is not uncommon to interindustry tables: their implicit technological rigidity. In the particular case of pollution this is somewhat disturbing since there is much to suggest that various kinds of antipollution policies, such as effluent charges or more rigid regulation of permissible levels of pollution, would induce industry to use production techniques that result in less pollution per unit of product or service rendered.

There are, of course, some fairly straightforward means of meeting these difficulties. As Leontief points out, one would be to add alternative columns of input-output coefficients to represent alternative production possibilities. This, in turn, suggests mathematical programming to investigate the relative efficiency of these alternatives. Indeed, a programming approach would seem to be potentially quite useful in investigating the implications of such basic policy alternatives for dealing with pollution as those of subsidy vs. effluent charges or regulatory standards. These alternatives, moreover, should be readily representable in a programming approach, e.g., effluent charges would suggest different prices or costs associated with different activities while the regulatory standard might be represented by different constraints.

In sum, these papers focus on important questions and even if they do not give us all the answers, they certainly suggest some of the research that will be needed to achieve better answers. As such, they represent a very considerable improvement over much previous public or even professional discourse. Certainly, professional economists should not be tolerant of misguided public criticism of GNP because GNP does not do what it was never intended to do, i.e., measure social welfare. On the other hand, I also believe that our tolerance should not be terribly high for those who suggest, even by implication, that we should not investigate, as intensively and open-mindedly as our resources and intellectual qualities permit, the extent to which the tools of economics might be applicable or inapplicable to questions of welfare measurement. We should not be concerned, moreover, that this curiosity may sometimes challenge long-established traditions or measures, though we surely should not abandon these lightly either.

REPLY BY NORDHAUS AND TOBIN

DENISON AND USHER

Both Denison and Usher direct their comments to the valuation of leisure. Their emphasis is natural, because difficult conceptual issues are involved and substantial quantitative differences are at stake.

We regard all our quantitative estimates as extremely tentative, and especially the leisure components. To begin with, the data on allocation of time are inadequate. We derived them from a single benchmark survey. What is needed is a periodic sample survey of household uses of time. What is happening to hours spent in preparing meals, laundering, and cleaning; in do-it-yourself repair and construction; in child care; in commuting? Is it really true, as we assumed, that the number of hours in nonmarket productive activity, as distinguished from recreational leisure, has remained constant? Or has the increase in the household capital-labor ratio released time for leisure activities? A careful survey might enable us to distinguish better among leisure, home production, and uses of time that do not contribute to household utility either directly or indirectly.

Even with improved data, difficult conceptual issues will remain. In discussing them here, we will ignore the distinction of our paper between household work and leisure proper and refer to both as "leisure." Incidentally, Denison is incorrect in attributing to us a preference for variant C, our most optimistic procedure. Our expressed preference was for variant B, which assumes that the productivity of work at home has increased with the real wage while the yield of leisure proper has remained constant.

One conceptual issue is how to count leisure in estimating the *absolute* increments of total consumption between two dates. The contribution of leisure is obviously greater if technical progress is assumed to have augmented leisure time (variant C) than if an hour of leisure time is assumed always to be the same hour, no more, no less (variant A). Denison seems to believe it is more likely less than more. Unfortunately no one can marshal arguments much above the level of anecdote and casual empiricism on either side of this debate. Perhaps careful detailed surveys of time allocation, repeated periodically, could enable us to do better.

An even more difficult conceptual issue arises in estimating the *relative* growth of total consumption between two dates. Once we agree on how to estimate the absolute increment in total consumption, we have the numerator. But what is the right denominator? What is the proper estimate of total consumption in the base period? Both Usher and Denison think that the procedures of our paper overstate base-period consumption and therefore understate the rate of growth.

Usher objects to the fact that if, as in variant A, the value of an hour of leisure is assumed not to have increased, inclusion of leisure in a consumption index is almost bound to diminish the estimated rate of increase. This will happen whenever the percentage increase in leisure is smaller than the percentage increase in consumption. The greater the amount of nonwork time assigned to leisure, rather than to maintenance items such as sleep, the more likely is this result. Usher correctly points out that this assignment is arbitrary. His solution is extreme—do not count leisure in base-period income. On the other hand, our estimates of percentage growth in leisure, and in consumption inclusive of leisure, would have been even smaller if we had used 24 hours instead of 18 hours as the day to allocate among welfare-generating activities. We chose 18 hours as the available time simply because this was the way the sample study was designed.

Usher's preferred procedure is to add to the increment in market consumption the value—imputed at the wage rate—of any increase in leisure at the expense of work. We have no quarrel with this estimate of the *absolute increase* in total consumption. But Usher uses only the base-year value of market consumption as the denominator in calculating the *percentage increase* in total consumption. His exclusion of leisure from base-period income is not a procedure that could logically be repeated in successive calculations. Once the year 1950 has been credited with leisure equal to reduction in hours of work since 1929, it is hardly possible to pretend that there was no leisure in 1950 in calculating the relative gain of 1965 over 1950.

Denison also regards our base-period consumption as too large, but for a different reason. He raises the interesting and difficult question of the disutility of work itself, a question we explicitly finessed. The real wage measures the sum of the marginal disutility of work and the marginal utility of leisure, both relative to the marginal utility of market consumption. There is no observed variable that enables us to decompose the real wage into these two components. We explicitly assumed the marginal disutility of work was zero. If it is really positive, then at least part of the market consumption purchased from wages simply offsets the unpleasantness of work, and the net contribution to welfare from working is smaller than wage income. The procedure of our paper, therefore, by exaggerating the value of base-period consumption, understates the percentage growth of welfare.

Denison comes close to asserting that the wage rate represents exclusively the marginal disutility of work, or at least did so in some base year, like 1958. We do not see the empirical basis for this assertion, or for Denison's evident belief that traditional economic theory regards the wage wholly as compensation for the unpleasantness of work rather than for leisure foregone.[1]

We now realize that the estimation of percentage gains and rates of growth is even more arbitrary than we originally understood. We have two unobservable strategic quantities—the rate of augmentation of leisure time, and the marginal disutility of work. Here is the algebra of the problem:

Let R_t, L_t, and W_t be total hours, leisure hours, and work hours, all during period t. Let v_t be the wage rate, and λ_t the leisure-augmentation factor. Take $\lambda_0 = 1$. Note that $R_t = R_0 = R$. In each period the consumer is to maximize, with respect to W_t, his utility $V(v_tW_t, L_t, W_t) = U(v_tW_t, R - W_t, W_t)$. The condition for the maximum at time 0 is:

$$v_0U_1 - U_2 + U_3 = 0, \text{ or } v_0 = \frac{U_2}{U_1} - \frac{U_3}{U_1}, \tag{1}$$

where U_2/U_1 is the marginal utility of leisure in terms of goods and $-U_3/U_1$ the marginal disutility of work in terms of goods. Here is the linear approximation of the gain in utility, time t compared to base-period 0:

$$\Delta U = U[v_tW_t, (R - W_t)\lambda_t, W_t] - U[v_0W_0, (R - W_0), W_0]$$

$$= U_1(v_tW_t - v_0W_0) + U_2[(R - W_t)\lambda_t - (R - W_0)]$$

$$+ U_3(W_t - W_0).$$

[1] Denison goes even further—or one might say further backward in the history of economic thought toward "real cost" doctrine—in suggesting a symmetrical proposition for capital incomes, that they represent compensation for the pain of abstinence, rather than the opportunity cost of current consumption. In this way Denison reaches the conclusion that the net utility value of all production and exchange is zero. Wages just pay for the pain of work, property incomes for the pain of waiting. At least this was so in 1958. Denison intimates that productivity gains may have made positive contributions since then, though he does not discuss the implication that net welfare was negative before 1958.

Some manipulation shows that:

$$\Delta U = U_1 W_t (v_t - v_0) + U_2 (R - W_t)(\lambda_t - 1)$$
$$+ v_0 U_1 (W_t - W_0) - U_2 (W_t - W_0) + U_3 (W_t - W_0).$$

By (1) the last three terms sum to zero. Hence the gain in utility is

$$\Delta U = U_1 W_t (v_t - v_0) + U_2 (R - W_t)(\lambda_t - 1). \qquad (2)$$

To convert this into an equivalent amount of market consumption we divide by the marginal utility of such consumption, U_1, and we obtain

$$\frac{\Delta U}{U_1} = W_t (v_t - v_0) + \frac{U_2}{U_1} (R - W_t)(\lambda_t - 1) \qquad (3)$$

$$= W_t (v_t - v_0) + \left(v_0 + \frac{U_3}{U_1} \right) (R - W_t)(\lambda_t - 1).$$

Now we have several cases:

a. No Augmentation of Leisure; No Marginal Disutility of Work. Then (3) becomes:

$$\frac{\Delta U}{U_1} = W_t (v_t - v_0). \qquad (3a)$$

The denominator, base-period consumption, inclusive of leisure, is unambiguously the equivalent of Rv_0 of market consumption. Therefore the proportionate gain is, as in our variant A:

$$\frac{W_t}{R} \cdot \frac{v_t - v_0}{v_0}. \qquad (4a)$$

b. Augmentation of Leisure; No Marginal Disutility of Work.

$$\frac{\Delta U}{U_1} = W_t (v_t - v_0) + v_0 (R - W_t)(\lambda_t - 1), \qquad (3b)$$

and the proportionate gain is:

$$\frac{W_t}{R} \cdot \frac{(v_t - v_0)}{v_0} + \frac{(R - W_t)}{R} (\lambda_t - 1). \qquad (4b)$$

If $\lambda_t - 1 = (v_t - v_0)/v_0$, we have the result of variant C of our paper. The proportionate increase in welfare is equal to the increase in the real wage rate.

c. No Augmentation of Leisure; Positive Marginal Disutility of Work. The absolute gain, measured in market consumption, is the same as (3a):

$$\frac{\Delta U}{U_1} = W_t (v_t - v_0). \qquad (3c)$$

But now it is not obvious what the denominator should be. One candidate, as before, is Rv_0. But another candidate is the "net" consumption:

$$W_0 v_0 + (R - W_0)\frac{U_2}{U_1} + W_0\frac{U_3}{U_1}$$

$$= W_0 v_0 + (R - W_0)\left(v_0 + \frac{U_3}{U_1}\right) + W_0\frac{U_3}{U_1} = R\left(v_0 + \frac{U_3}{U_1}\right).$$

The first candidate values all the time available at the market wage of the base period. The second candidate values the time at the *net* wage, i.e., the market wage minus the marginal disutility of work. The first procedure gives the result (4a). The second procedure gives a larger relative gain:

$$\frac{W_t(v_t - v_0)}{R\left(v_0 + \dfrac{U_3}{U_1}\right)}. \tag{4c}$$

d. Augmentation of Leisure, Positive Marginal Disutility of Work.

$$\frac{\Delta U}{U_1} = W_t(v_t - v_0) + \left(v_0 + \frac{U_3}{U_1}\right)(R - W_t)(\lambda_t - 1). \tag{3d}$$

This is smaller than (3b). Thus the assumption of our paper that marginal disutility of work is zero may exaggerate the absolute increment of welfare. Technological progress has the effect of giving the representative consumer additional leisure. He gets it even if he does not reduce his hours of work. How should this extra leisure be valued? The wage rate, used in (3b), overvalues the gift to the extent that the wage is compensation for disutility of work. Indeed, if that is *all* the wage represents, the augmentation of leisure has no value at all.

Moreover, we have the same ambiguity about the denominator as in the previous case. If Rv_0 is used, relative gain is greater than (4a), smaller than (4b). If $R[v_0 + (U_3/U_1)]$ is used, relative gain is

$$\frac{W_t}{R}\left(\frac{v_t - v_0}{v_0 + \dfrac{U_3}{U_1}}\right) + \frac{(R - W_t)}{R}(\lambda_t - 1). \tag{4d}$$

This is the largest of the several estimates. Although the marginal disutility of work scales down the value of the incremental leisure, it scales down the value of base-period time even more.

A summary comparison of alternatives is shown in Table 1. The table shows the value of the growth of welfare for the different assumptions

TABLE 1

Summary of Alternative Measures of Growth
of Consumption Including Leisure

Assumption [a]	Rate of Growth of Welfare	Rank
(4a) ⎫ (variant A) (4c-I) ⎭	$\dfrac{(v_t - v_0)}{v_0} \dfrac{W_t}{R}$	5
(4b) [b] (variant C)	$\dfrac{v_t - v_0}{v_0}$	2 or 3
(4c) II	$\dfrac{v_t - v_0}{v_0} \left\{ \dfrac{W_t v_0}{R[v_0 + (U_3/U_1)]} \right\}$	2 or 3
(4d) [b] I	$\dfrac{v_t - v_0}{v_0} \left[\dfrac{W_t}{R} + \dfrac{v_0 + (U_3/U_1)}{v_0} \cdot \dfrac{R - W_t}{R} \right]$	4
(4d) II	$\dfrac{v_t - v_0}{v_0} \left\{ \dfrac{R - W}{R} + \dfrac{W}{R} \left[\dfrac{v_0}{v_0 + (U_3/U_1)} \right] \right\}$	1

[a] Assumption I used the gross wage, thus setting initial consumption at $v_0 R$. Assumption II uses the net wage, with consumption being $R[v_0 + (U_3/U_1)]$.

[b] Assumes rate of augmentation, λ, is equal to rate of growth of real wage rate, v.

discussed above and shows how the magnitudes are ranked (1 showing the most rapid growth, and so forth). Our preferred variant was variant A for leisure, which is indeed the most pessimistic, and variant C for home production. It should be noted that all other variants require knowledge of the marginal disutility of work.

It will be helpful to visualize the two candidates for denominator. Imagine indifference surfaces in three-dimensional space with axes representing work, leisure, and market consumption. Given the constraint on time, the consumer is confined to the plane Work + Leisure = Total hours available. Within this plane he is further constrained by the relationship: Work $\times$ Wage = Market consumption. We would like to obtain the market consumption equivalent of the indifference surface he reaches. One procedure is to stay within both constraining planes, and follow the tangent line to the maximum market consumption, obtained by setting leisure equal to zero and work equal to R. This gives the conventional measure, Rv_0. The other procedure is as follows: There is a plane tangent to the attained indifference surface at the chosen point. The plane does not represent choices effectively open to the consumer, since it departs from the clock constraint on leisure and work. Nevertheless we can follow this tangent plane to the market consumption axis, where both work and leisure are hypothetically zero, and read off the height of the intersection. This gives to the denominator the value $R[v_0 + (U_3/U_1)]$. Measuring along an axis which the consumer cannot reach may seem farfetched. But we see no compelling logic in favor of one approximation over the other.

In Figures 1 to 4 we illustrate graphically the four measures just discussed. In Figure 1, E_0 and E_t are the chosen work, leisure, and consumption points in the two periods. N_a is the estimate of the increment of consumption, or the numerator. D_a is the estimate of the equivalent market value of the base-period consumption, the denominator.

In Figure 2, the augmentation of leisure is represented by shifting

FIGURE 1

No Disutility of Work; No Time Augmentation

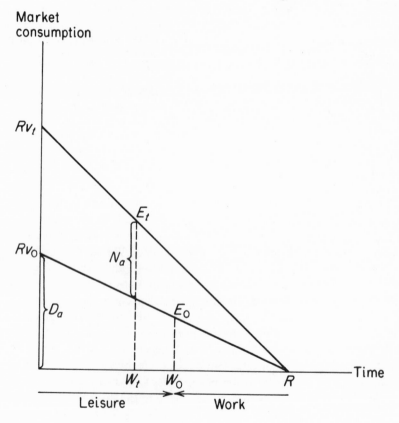

FIGURE 2

No Disutility of Work; Positive Time Augmentation

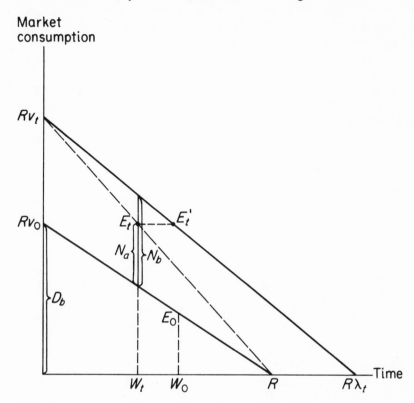

Market
consumption

point R out to $R\lambda_t$. The observed point E_t is the equivalent of E'_t in base-period hours. The market consumption value of this augmentation is added to N_a. Therefore, the numerator, N_b, is larger than in Figure 1, while the denominator is the same.

In Figure 3 the dashed curve RA represents the marginal disutility of work (in market consumption units) times the hours of work, $-W(U_3/U_1)$. The slope of a line from R to the dashed curve at $W = W_0$ is the marginal disutility of work in the base period. Subtracting an allowance for this disutility reduces the denominator to D_c.

In Figure 4, the calculation of the denominator follows Figure 3. The augmentation of leisure from point E_t to E'_t is the same as in Figure 2, but in the valuation of this leisure the wage rate used in Figure 2 is diminished by the marginal disutility of labor.

FIGURE 3

Positive Disutility of Work; No Time Augmentation

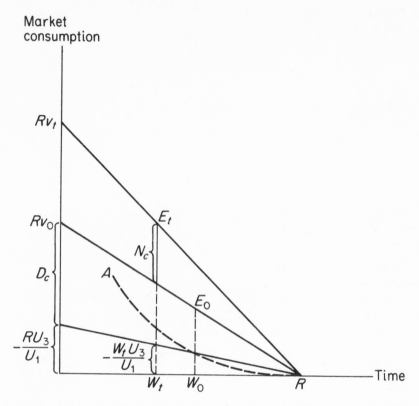

The upshot of this is that many alternative measures of welfare are plausible, and that there is no unambiguous answer to the question, how fast has welfare grown? Nevertheless, until some reasonable method for measuring utility or the disutility of work has been devised, we see no plausible alternative to the variants we presented in the original paper.

FIGURE 4

Positive Disutility of Work; Positive Time Augmentation

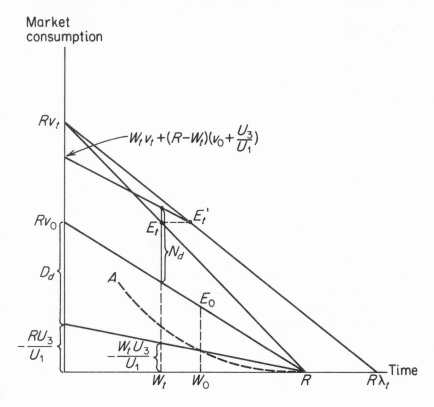

MEYER

John Meyer's comments refer mainly to other aspects of our paper, and call for a separate response. We certainly concur with the main thrust of his remarks, that much remains to be done.

Meyer does make one point on the valuation of leisure, namely, that overvaluation of leisure is responsible for our finding that MEW (variant B) was 8 per cent higher in 1935 than in 1929, a finding which Meyer regards as counter-intuitive. The 22 per cent decline in NNP per capita corresponds better to his impression. We did not, of course, count unemployment as leisure. But we did attribute positive value to time outside normal working hours, for the unemployed as well as the employed. It might be argued that the opportunity cost of time is effectively zero for people who cannot find jobs. We thought it more reasonable to assume that the unemployed would have chosen the normal amounts of work and leisure if they could have found jobs at the prevailing wages. But we stressed in the original paper, and we stress again now, that MEW is designed for secular rather than cyclical comparisons.

Meyer also suggests that allowance should be made for depreciation of human capital during the Depression, nonuser cost, so to speak. We accept in general the point that experience as well as education should be reckoned in human capital. But this cannot affect the NNP-MEW comparison, because neither concept makes such an allowance.

As Meyer points out, the disamenity calculations need to be refined in a number of directions: (1) Cross-sectional regressions should be run for various census dates; the disamenity premium of urban living may have changed. (2) At least some of the variables in the regressions should refer to finer geographical areas than our counties. (3) Nonlinear relationships and threshold effects should be examined. Meyer also suggests that higher incomes in cities may reflect the higher intelligence of urban residents rather than any compensation for disamenities. It would indeed be desirable to add intelligence to the variables we used to control for nongeographical sources of income differentials. The calculations Meyer reports do not tell us whether controlling for intelligence would increase or decrease our disamenity estimates.

National Income, Economic Structure, and Environmental Externalities

WASSILY LEONTIEF

HARVARD UNIVERSITY

I. NATIONAL INCOME AS A WELFARE INDEX

The per capita net national income used as a measure of the level of welfare is a typical index number. The computation of an index number involves application of some well-defined but essentially arbitrary conventional procedures to direct or indirect measurements of observed, or at least in principle observable, phenomena.

The conventional interpretation of net national income valued in some constant prices can be conveniently rationalized in terms of the ad hoc assumption that preferences of a representative average consumer can be described by a social utility function or a fixed set of well-behaving social indifference curves.

At this point observed or at least observable facts come in. The bundle of goods actually consumed by a representative individual has been obviously preferred—so goes the argument—to all the other alternative bundles that were accessible to him.

Under the special conditions of a market economy the set of all alternative bundles accessible to a representative consumer is uniquely determined by (a) the amounts of various goods that he has actually consumed and (b) the relative prices of these goods. The relative prices represent the marginal opportunity costs of each good in terms of every other good as seen from the point of their actual or potential consumer.

This factual information, combined with the before-mentioned ad hoc assumption concerning the existence of a "well-behaved" set of collective indifference lines, permits us to identify *some* of the bundles of goods that the representative consumer apparently judges to be *less desirable* than the particular bundle that he actually chose to use.

This analytical proposition constitutes the basic, not to say the sole, theoretical justification for interpreting the *differences* in per capita net national income—valued in fixed prices—as an index of changes in the level of average per capita welfare attained by a particular society in different years.

Goods acquired through other means than purchases at given prices on a free market can still be taken into account in computation of the conventional welfare index provided their opportunities costs—as perceived by the representative consumer—can be ascertained in some other way.

Much of the work aimed at inclusion of various nonmarketable components into the measure of natural income is centered on devising plausible methods of determining the imputed prices or more generally the opportunity costs of such goods.

In the light of what has been said above, the inclusion of pollutants and other kinds of environmental repercussions of economic activities into the measurement of the per capita national income as a welfare index requires answers to two sets of questions. One concerns the establishment of acceptable conventions pertaining to the inclusion of environmental repercussions into the conceptual framework of an all embracing social utility function and a corresponding set of representative indifference curves. The other pertains to the actual physical description and measurement of the generation and elimination of pollutants by the economic system and the empirical determination of their opportunity costs in terms of ordinary goods and of each other.

The answer that one can give to these questions is critically influenced by the typically external nature of most environmental repercussions of economic activities and also by the fact that because of that measures aimed at abatement of their undesirable effects must in most instances be promulgated by the government.

Speaking in this context of collective indifference lines or preferences of a representative individual one must interpret such preference —at least so far as the environmental effects of economic activities are concerned—as being revealed not through private but rather through collective choice reflected in specific actions of the government.

Moreover, in case the conjectured opportunity costs reflected in the level of antipollution actions actually observed differ from the true opportunity costs, it is the former rather than the latter that would have to provide the base for proper weighing of pollution components to be included in a revised, more comprehensive, national income index.

Who would pretend to know what opportunity costs (if any) are being taken into account in the design of antipollution measures now actually being carried out in the United States?

Many of the contributors to the present symposium when touching upon problems of social valuation abandon the difficult revealed preference criteria in favor of a strictly axiomatic approach.

That solves the problem of welfare measurement as simply as Columbus solved his problem with the egg. One chooses ad hoc a social utility function which for some ethical or mathematical reason is appealing, inserts into it the levels of consumption of ordinary goods and net output of pollutants as they actually are and then compares the index of welfare thus attained with the highest number of points that could be reached if the society were to move to the optimal point along the empirically given opportunity costs frontier.

Who can decide, however, what social utility function one should finally choose? Certainly not the economists in their professional capacity!

II. ENLARGED INPUT-OUTPUT TABLE, STRUCTURAL COEFFICIENT, AND INTERSECTORAL DEPENDENCE

Exhibit 1 presents a schematic outline of an expanded input-output table that traces not only the intersectoral flows of ordinary commodities and services, but also the generation and elimination of pollutants. The conventional classification of economic activities and goods is accordingly expanded to include the names of various pollutants and activities aimed at their elimination.

The entries are organized in such a way as to have each column contain inputs and outputs controlled by the same autonomous set of structural relationships (i.e., by the same "cooking recipe"). The table is subdivided into rows and corresponding column strips. Each strip can be thought of as containing many rows and columns of figures not shown in this schematic presentation. Each of the rectangular intersections on a row and a column can be conveniently identified by two numbers.

All entries can be interpreted as representing physical quantities measured in appropriate physical units or indices of physical amounts. All dollar figures appearing in the table can be interpreted as such indices (with a defined or undefined base). Hence, the usual *column* sums are pointedly omitted.

EXHIBIT 1

Interindustrial Flows Expanded to Include the Generation and Elimination of Pollutants

	Industries 1	Pollution-eliminating Activities 2	Final Demand Sector 3		Totals 4
			(3A)	(3B)	
Industries 1	(1,1) Inputs of goods into industries (+) $[a_{ij}]$	(1,2) Inputs of goods into pollution eliminating activities (+) Output of goods by pollution eliminating activities (−) $[a_{ig}]$	(1,3A) Delivery of goods to final demand sector (+)	(1,3B) (Empty)	(1,4) Total outputs of goods excluding the amounts generated by the pollution eliminating activities
Pollutants 2	(2,1) Outputs of pollutants by industries (+) $[a_{gi}]$	(2,2) Elimination of pollutants by pollution eliminating activities (−) Output of pollutants by pollution eliminating activities (+) $[a_{gk}]$	(2,3A) Outputs of pollutants by final demand sector (connected with the consumption of goods) (+) $[c_{gi}]$	(2,3B) Outputs of pollutants by the final demand sector (connected with the consumption of primary factors) (+) $[c_{gf}]$	(2,4) *Net* outputs of pollutants (+)
Primary Inputs 3	(3,1) Inputs of primary factors into industries (+) $[v_{fi}]$	(3,2) Inputs of primary factors into pollution eliminating activities (+) $[v_{fg}]$	(3,3A) (Empty)	(3,3B) Delivery of primary factors to final demand sector (+)	(3,4) Total inputs of primary factors (+)

(1,1) Inputs of (ordinary) goods into industries. Most of these goods are produced by industries listed on the left, but some might originate as the "by-product" in pollution-eliminating activities. See (1,3).

(1,2) Inputs of ordinary goods into various pollution-eliminating activities and outputs of ordinary goods (entered with a negative sign) generated as by-products of pollution-eliminating activities. Reprocessed materials, for example, are entered here.

(1,3A) Goods delivered to the final demand sector are entered along the main diagonal of this square. See (3,3B).

(1,4) These totals do not include amounts of ordinary goods (as their by-products) originating in the pollution-eliminating activities and thus represent the activity levels of ordinary industries.

(2,1) Each row shows the amounts of one particular pollutant generated by industries listed at the heads of different columns. In other words, pollutants are treated here the way by-products are treated in ordinary input-output tables.

(2,2) Along each row are entered—as negative numbers—the amounts of one particular pollutant eliminated by activities named at the heads of different columns. The amounts of a pollutant generated, as is often the case, in the process of elimination of some other pollutants are entered along its appropriate row as positive numbers.

(2,3A), (2,3B) For purely descriptive purposes the total amounts of various pollutants generated in the final demand sector can be presented in a single column. For purposes of structural analyses, however, these totals should be distributed among as many separate columns as there are different inputs, i.e., industrial product inputs and primary factor inputs, absorbed by the final demand sector. In the process of final consumption each of these inputs is liable to generate its own "column" of pollutants. The inputs of ordinary goods into the final demand sector are entered in rows along the main diagonal of the square formed by (1,2) and (2,2) considered together. It sounds rather complicated, but that is the price one has to pay for orderly bookkeeping.

(2,4) Each figure in this column is obtained by subtracting the sum of all negative from the sum of all positive entries appearing to the left along the entire length of the row. These are the undesirable *net* outputs of various pollutants delivered by the economic system to the final users alongside the desirable ordinary goods and primary factors entered in (1,3A) and (3,3B). Together they make up the final results of economic activities upon which the welfare of the society supposedly depends.

(3,1), (3,2), (3,3B), (3,4) These contain a single row of aggregated value-added figures or several rows of physical or dollar figures depending on the amount of detail one wants to present.

III. STRUCTURAL RELATIONSHIPS AND OPPORTUNITY COSTS

The figures entered in each one of the separate columns of the first three vertical strips of the enlarged flow table can be interpreted as representing the inputs absorbed and outputs generated by one particular process carried on side by side with many other structurally different processes within the framework of the given economic system.

Assuming that the structure of each such process can be described in terms of a linear or at least linearized "cooking recipe," the actual level of each output and each input as entered in the flow table can be interpreted as a product of two numbers: a technical coefficient and a number describing the level at which the process that absorbs that particular input or generates that particular output actually operates.

The levels of operation of ordinary industries are usually measured in terms of their principal output, while the level of operation of a pollution-eliminating activity can be conveniently described by the number of units of the specific pollutant that it eliminates. The levels of consumption activities that might generate pollution are described by the number of units of a particular good or primary factor delivered to the final demand sector.

The structural matrix of the economy—corresponding to the enlarged flow table described above—can be written in the following partitioned form:

	1	2	3 A	B
1	$[a_{ij}]$	$[a_{ig}]$		
2	$[a_{gi}]$	$[a_{gk}]$	$[c_{gi}]$	$[c_{gf}]$
3	$[v_{fi}]$	$[v_{fg}]$		

The elements of each submatrix are technical input or output coefficients; they are defined concisely in the Mathematical Appendix, below.

While the input coefficient of ordinary goods can usually be derived from the observed flows, information on the magnitude of the structural coefficient describing the generation and elimination of pollutants has in most instances to be obtained directly from technological sources. Combined with appropriate figures of the outputs of all pollution-generating activities, these coefficients provide a basis for estimation of the pollution flows.

In many, not to say in most, instances pollution is being combated not through the operation of separate elimination processes, but rather through the use of less polluting alternative techniques for production of ordinary goods. To incorporate such additional information the structural matrix would have to describe the input structure of some industrial and possibly even of some final demand sectors in terms of several alternative columns of input and output coefficients. The corresponding flow tables would, and actually do already in many instances, show for some sector two or more columns of input-output flows.

Without explaining in detail the mathematical formulation and solution of the system of input-output equations involved [1] it suffices here to say that on the basis of the information contained in an enlarged structural matrix of a given economy it would be possible to compute (and some such computations have already been made) the total factor inputs (measured in physical amounts or more or less aggregated "value added" dollars) required directly and indirectly: (a) to deliver to final users one additional unit of any particular good while keeping the deliveries of all the other goods and the net outputs of all pollutants constant; (b) to reduce by one unit the *net* output of any particular pollutant while keeping constant the net outputs of all the other pollutants and final deliveries of all goods.

This means that factual information contained in an enlarged structural matrix of a particular economy would permit us to compute in a rough and ready fashion the opportunity costs of an additional unit of any good and of an eliminated unit of the "net output" of each pollutant. The basic matrix of structural coefficients that governs the physical flows presented on the enlarged input-output table determines also a corresponding set of price-cost relationships.

The elimination of pollutants originating in various sectors can be paid for either directly by the final users or by the producing sectors

[1] See Mathematical Appendix; see also Wassily Leontief, "Environmental Repercussions and the Economic Structure: An Input-Output Approach," *Review of Economics and Statistics,* August 1970; and Wassily Leontief and Daniel Ford, "Air Pollution and the Economic Structure: Empirical Results of Input-Output Computations," *Proceedings,* Fifth International Input-Output Conference, forthcoming.

in which they are being generated. In the latter case the cost of doing so will obviously be included in the price of the finished product. I have explained elsewhere [2] how these institutionally determined parameters can be introduced in standard input-output formulation of balanced price-cost equations.

If the prices are expected to reflect the true opportunity costs of various goods (including the "products" of pollution-eliminating activities) to final users, they must cover the costs of eliminating all additional pollution generated in the process of their production. Otherwise in purchasing a useful good the consumer would receive, probably unwittingly, an additional delivery of undesirable pollutants. Hence, the system of prices to be used for purposes of welfare decisions should be computed on the assumption that each industry and each pollution-eliminating process bears the full cost of eliminating all pollutants generated by it. This of course does not imply that the actual institutional arrangement and consequently the actual pricing should necessarily be governed by the same principle, the more so that the distributional effect of such "pure" opportunity cost pricing might turn out to be undesirable.

Once the prices of all outputs (including those of all antipollution activities) have been determined, all entries in the expanded tables of interindustrial flows can be valued in dollars. Marginal totals can be entered not only at the end of each row but also at the bottom of each column. The outputs of all pollutants will be represented by negative dollar figures; the amounts of pollutants eliminated by positive dollar figures. In particular the net outputs of pollutants delivered to final users (2,4) will add up to a negative dollar figure. It can be interpreted as representing the upper limit of the amount that would have to be spent (but in fact was not spent) for this particular purpose if the final users decided to eliminate all pollution actually delivered to them.

MATHEMATICAL APPENDIX

The Numbering of Goods, Pollutants, and Primary Factors

$1, 2, \ldots, i, \ldots, j, \ldots, n$
    n goods.

$n + 1, n + 2, \ldots, g, \ldots, k, \ldots, n + m$
    m pollutants.

$n + m + 1, n + m + 2, \ldots, f, \ldots, n + m + h$
    h primary factors.

[2] *Ibid.*

Technical Coefficients

a_{ij}—input of good i per unit of output of good j (produced by industry j).

a_{ig}—if > 0, input of good i per unit of eliminated pollutant g; if < 0, output of good i per unit of eliminated pollutant g.

a_{gi}—if > 0, output of pollutant g per unit of output of good i (produced by industry i); if < 0, input (productive use) of pollutant g per unit of output of good i (produced by industry i).

a_{gk}—output of pollutant g per unit of eliminated pollutant k.

c_{gi}—output of pollutant g generated in the final demand sector in the process of consuming one unit of good i.

c_{gf}—output of pollutant g generated in the final demand sector in the process of consuming one unit of the primary factor f.

v_{fi}—input of factor f per unit output of good i (produced by industry i),

v_{fg}—input of factor f per unit of eliminated pollutant g.

v_i —"value added" paid out by industry i per unit of its output.

v_g —"value added" paid out by the pollution-eliminating sector g per unit of pollution eliminated.

Vectors of Technical Coefficients

$[a_{ij}]$, $[a_{ig}]$, etc.

Variables

x_i—total output of good i by industry i.

x_g—total amount of pollutant g eliminated by pollutant-eliminating activity g.

x_f—total amount of factor f used in all sectors.

y_i—total amount of good i delivered to final demand.

y_g—*net* output of pollutant (delivered to final demand).

y_f—total amount of factor f delivered to final demand.

p_i—price of one unit of good produced by industry i.

p_g—price of eliminating one unit of pollution g by sector g.

Vectors of Variables

$$X_1 = \begin{bmatrix} x_1 \\ x_2 \\ \cdot \\ \cdot \\ x_i \\ \cdot \\ \cdot \\ x_j \\ \cdot \\ \cdot \\ x_n \end{bmatrix} \qquad X_2 = \begin{bmatrix} x_{n+1} \\ x_{n+2} \\ \cdot \\ \cdot \\ x_g \\ \cdot \\ \cdot \\ x_k \\ x_{n+m} \end{bmatrix} \qquad X_3 = \begin{bmatrix} x_{n+m+1} \\ x_{n+m+2} \\ \cdot \\ \cdot \\ x_f \\ \cdot \\ \cdot \\ x_{n+m+h} \end{bmatrix}$$

$$Y_1 = \begin{bmatrix} y_1 \\ y_2 \\ \cdot \\ y_i \\ \cdot \\ \cdot \\ y_j \\ \cdot \\ \cdot \\ y_n \end{bmatrix} \qquad Y_2 = \begin{bmatrix} y_{n+1} \\ y_{n+2} \\ \cdot \\ y_g \\ \cdot \\ \cdot \\ y_k \\ \cdot \\ y_{n+m} \end{bmatrix} \qquad Y_3 = \begin{bmatrix} y_{n+m+1} \\ y_{n+m+2} \\ \cdot \\ \cdot \\ y_f \\ \cdot \\ y_{n+m+h} \end{bmatrix}$$

$$V_1 = \begin{bmatrix} v_1 \\ v_2 \\ \cdot \\ v_i \\ \cdot \\ v_j \\ \cdot \\ v_n \end{bmatrix} \quad V_2 = \begin{bmatrix} v_{n+1} \\ v_{n+2} \\ \cdot \\ v_g \\ \cdot \\ v_k \\ \cdot \\ v_{n+m} \end{bmatrix} \quad P_1 = \begin{bmatrix} p_1 \\ p_2 \\ \cdot \\ p_i \\ \cdot \\ p_j \\ \cdot \\ p_n \end{bmatrix} \quad P_2 = \begin{bmatrix} p_{n+1} \\ p_{n+2} \\ \cdot \\ p_g \\ \cdot \\ p_k \\ \cdot \\ p_{n+m} \end{bmatrix}$$

Balance Equations

Each of the following matrix equations describes the balance between the outputs and the inputs entered in one of the three row strips of the enlarged input-output table.

Goods $[I - a_{ij}]X_1 - [a_{ig}]X_2 \qquad = Y_2$

Pollutants $-[a_{gi}]X_1 + [I - a_{gk}]X_2 = [c_{gi}]Y_1 - Y_2 + [c_{gf}]Y_3$ (1)

Factors $-[v_{fi}]X_1 - [v_{fg}]X_2 + X_3 = \qquad\qquad Y_3$

The general solution of that system for the unknown x's in terms of given y's is

$$
\begin{bmatrix} X_1 \\ X_2 \\ X_3 \end{bmatrix} = \begin{bmatrix} [I - a_{ij}] & -[a_{ig}] & 0 \\ -[a_{gi}] & [I - a_{gk}] & 0 \\ -[v_{fi}] & -[v_{fg}] & [I] \end{bmatrix}^{-1} \begin{bmatrix} Y_1 \\ [c_{gi}]Y_1 - Y_g + [c_{gf}]Y_3 \\ Y_3 \end{bmatrix}
$$
(2)

Separating the effects of the three kinds of outputs delivered to the final demand sector and expressing the relationship (2) in incremental terms:

$$
\begin{bmatrix} \Delta X_1 \\ \Delta X_2 \\ \Delta X_3 \end{bmatrix} = M^{-1} \begin{bmatrix} \Delta Y_1 \\ [c_{gi}]\Delta Y_1 \\ 0 \end{bmatrix} + M^{-1} \begin{bmatrix} 0 \\ -\Delta Y_2 \\ 0 \end{bmatrix} + M^{-1} \begin{bmatrix} 0 \\ [c_{gf}]\Delta Y_3 \\ \Delta Y_3 \end{bmatrix}
$$
(3)

The inverse of the enlarged structural matrix of the economy appearing on the right-hand side is the same that appears in (2) above.

The first and the third terms on the right-hand side describe the effect —on the output of goods (ΔX_1), the level of antipollution activities (ΔX_2) and on total factor inputs (ΔX_3)—of a given change in the final demand for goods (ΔY_1) and, respectively, final demand for primary factors (ΔY_2). These effects are computed on the assumption that the level of pollution-eliminating activities will be adjusted in such a way as to leave the net delivery of pollutants to final users unchanged (i.e., $\Delta Y_2 = 0$).

The second right-hand term shows what it would take—in total outputs of goods and total primary factor inputs—to *reduce* the delivery of (un-eliminated) pollution to final users by the amount ΔY_2, while holding the deliveries of goods and factor services constant ($\Delta Y_1 = 0$, $\Delta Y_3 = 0$).

For purposes of price-cost computations, all primary factor flows entered along the second row-strip of the expanded input-output table can be valued in dollars and consolidated into a single row of "value-added" figures. Accordingly the two coefficient matrices $-[v_{fi}]$ and $[v_{fg}]$ can be reduced to row vectors V_1 and V_2 of value-added coefficients.

If each industry and each antipollution activity were to pay—and include in the price of its product—the costs of eliminating all pollution directly generated by it,[3] the balance between revenues and outlays in all goods-producing and pollution-eliminating sectors could be described by the following matrix equations.

Goods $\qquad\qquad [I - a'_{ij}]P_1 - [a'_{gi}]P_2 = V_1$

Pollutant elimination $[a'_{ig}]P_1 + [I - a'_{gk}]P_2 = V_2$ $\qquad\qquad$ (4)

The general solution of that system for unknown p's in terms of given v's is

$$
\begin{bmatrix} P_1 \\ -- \\ P_2 \end{bmatrix} = \begin{bmatrix} [I - a'_{ij}] & -[a'_{gi}] \\ \hline -[a'_{ig}] & [I - a'_{gk}] \end{bmatrix}^{-1} \begin{bmatrix} V_1 \\ -- \\ V_2 \end{bmatrix} \qquad (5)
$$

[3] For price computations based on different assumptions see the article cited in notes 1 and 2.

Concluding Remarks

Concluding Remarks

SIMON KUZNETS

HARVARD UNIVERSITY

1. THE PROBLEMS

To summarize the long and complex papers presented and the lively discussion to which they gave rise is a task beyond my capacity; and may not provide a useful substitute for a careful study of the full record. My choice is rather to reflect on the broad issues that are central to most of the papers and much of the discussion. These issues relate to significant and meaningful measurement of economic performance and change—excluding here the measurement of *social* performance, as distinct from economic. Measuring social performance raises many additional, and somewhat different, problems. Except for Dan Usher's interesting treatment of the economic value of the long-term gain in life and health, a gain too wide to be comprised under economic, all papers dwelt on measuring economic performance—and even so perhaps too narrowly: little attention was paid to distributive aspects of economic performance, and to questions of international comparability of economic aggregates and of their significant components—a point to be touched upon below.

The various issues, many of them covered in the Juster paper, but discussed also, separately and with more emphasis and detailed analysis, in most of the other papers, stem from the difficulties of attaining a measure of net output of the economy that would reflect properly the full range of returns and costs—both viewed not merely as monetary receipts and outlays in a defined institutional setting, but as positive and negative entries with respect to what may be regarded as final goals of, and constraints on, economic activity. For the present purpose, we may agree that the final goals are provision of goods to ultimate consumers, the living members of society, and net additions to capital stock relevant to ultimate consumption, current and future; and that the major basic constraints are the limited time and knowledge at the disposal of the current generation, with responsibility to both the current and the future generations. It is with reference to these goals and constraints that the problems in the measurement of net product arise, reflecting the limitations of the current measures. These limitations should not be viewed as a matter of intellectual willfulness, but as results of deeply rooted measurement problems, and of the difficulty of agreement on underlying concepts and on assumed analytical relations.

If we start with the measurement of "pure" consumption, implicit in the definition of final goals of economic activity, the major issues relating to presently included components can be listed as follows: (i) The separation of outlays, within the present totals of household purchases of commodities and services, that are the results of changed conditions of production and are required for the changed role of the consumer as producer, distinguishing them from those that are in response to needs not governed by the requirements of production. The illustration that easily comes to mind are the larger consumer expenditures in dense urban communities, the latter called for by the increasing scale of modern production, for satisfying the same level of wants that were so much more cheaply satisfied in the countryside. (ii) Another important category is the outlays on education, and possibly on other items relevant to raising the quality of individuals as workers, which suggests that there is a component of investment, in addition to pure consumption. (iii) When collective final consumption is examined, as now represented by government current outlays on goods, there is the possibility that much of the flow is a "regrettable necessity" and does not add directly to the flow of goods into consumption by the living members of society; nor does it add to the relevant stock of capital. These three sets of questions about the character of several important components now included under "final" consumption may be supplemented by a fourth (iv), relating to the difficulty of measuring the net output of some activities, whose product is clearly relevant either to final consumption or to net capital formation, but the market mechanism for which yields inadequate gauges of their appropriate value. This difficulty arises either because the activities may refer to public goods, or because the goods may have quality aspects which the market is not in a position to evaluate properly (or perhaps no one is now able to evaluate, say many educational services). The reference to these four questions in the papers and in the discussion is widespread, and the papers by Olson and Rivlin are particularly to be noted.

While the present estimates of final household and collective consumption may be viewed as including sizable components that are either offsets to production-induced costs, or intermediate products, being costs of running the machinery of society and the state, or investment in human capital, there are also omissions of components that are properly part of a pure consumption total. This refers not only to (i) tangible products of household activity which, for many comparative purposes, should be included, even though there is no orientation to the market or easily available market counterparts; and possibly (ii) returns on household capital (besides housing), with consequent modification of the treatment of purchases of durable consumer goods. There is, also, the major topic of (iii) greater leisure and other intangible benefits of the lesser demand that work and economic activity make upon the time and limited capacities of human beings—a topic conspicuously raised in the Nordhaus-Tobin paper and the discussion that followed. There is finally (iv) the problem of measuring negative correlates of both production and final consumption in the way of *current* injection of ill-elements into conditions of life—whether they be pollution of the air, congestion, and the like. These are to be distinguished from increases in negative capital stock, just as we distinguish positive returns from capital from the relevant positive capital stock.

The list of problems, or questions of inclusion and omission, for the second component of net product—net capital formation—is different from that just suggested with respect to household and collective consumption. In particular, the questions of inclusion of nonrelevant components are far more limited, while those of omission are many and weighty. This tilt of the problems when we deal with net capital formation, as compared with consumption, is significant: it suggests that, limited as the scope of net product in conventional accounting is, with emphasis on market-oriented activities for which proper weights can be secured, the tendency has been to define consumption widely, including a number of components whose inclusion is of doubtful legitimacy; and net capital formation too narrowly, limiting it to reproducible material capital. As will be suggested below, this reflected a theory of production and of economic growth in which the requirements for output and growth were far too narrowly defined.

To be sure, even net reproducible capital formation may include components (i) which, in their strict relevance to "regrettable necessities" and in their nontransferability to serve the ends of pure consumption, should not be viewed as adding to real net product (no matter how well they may reflect the capacity of society to produce more of real goods *if* the resources can be turned to alternative uses. The point is that they cannot be so turned so long as regrettable necessities persist, and the reference to *"necessities"* is not accidental). But it is the omissions that are far more important. To begin with, there are (ii) stocks of consumer durable goods within the household (other than housing), the changes in which, on an alternative treatment of this component, would be recorded—to be combined with current returns from use, as part of current consumption. Then there are (iii) stocks of intangible capital representing the investment in education and other means of raising the quality of human beings as economic producers, these recorded for the given level of current useful knowledge that such education transmits. Of most interest, and indeed of importance dominating any concern with education as capital investment, are (iv) the intangible stock of knowledge, of material technology, and related processes and (v) the stock of social knowledge and institutions employed in translating the existing stock of technological and other useful knowledge into greater output and productivity. Considering that accretions to the stock of knowledge were the major dynamic element in modern economic growth in the developed countries, and that the succession of social inventions and institutional changes shaped the major channels for transforming the potential of growing knowledge into the reality of growth of output and productivity, it is frustrating to note that little effort or progress has been made toward measuring, or devising some reasonable gauge for, the changing volume of the stock of knowledge. Such approximations would have permitted us to observe the changing difference between movements in the stock of knowledge and those in output and in material reproducible capital formation. The same comments apply to the stock of social inventions and institutions—an even more complex problem of measurement. It is hardly a surprise that the relations between net capital formation, narrowly defined, and changes in output have been found so puzzlingly variable over time and different in space.

There is finally (vi) the exclusion of changes in the stock of natural, "irreproducible resources"—in quotes because both resources and reproducibility are functions of the existing state of knowledge and technology; and will change as the latter change. Indeed, it is this dependence that may explain the omission from national accounts of depletion of even observable natural resources. If the depletion were to be counted, so would additions to resources produced by new discovery and knowledge—and the latter measured not by the small inputs of labor and capital into the process but by the much bigger addition to capacity. Given the difficulties of estimating resource-significance of new technological knowledge and the omission of the latter in measuring net capital formation, it would have been illogical and misleading to deduct depletion of existing known resources. The same reasoning applies to depletion by pollution, etc. Since the original contribution of natural resources, and particularly of improvements in their use (of air, water, etc.), when represented by new technology, had not been included in the estimate of changes in stock, it is illogical and biased to enter a minus sign for pollution or deterioration. This does not preclude the value of undertaking a separate analysis of stocks and changes in stocks of natural resources, under conditions of a given technology—dealing with a range of problems raised in the Herfindahl-Kneese and Leontief papers—but they should not be included in net balances for estimating net capital formation. The point is simply that the propriety of doing the latter, i.e., including negative changes, is contingent upon including the positive changes in the stock of useful knowledge relating to material or social technology, which presently is not being done and probably cannot be done in the near future.

2. EFFECTS OF CONCERN WITH ECONOMIC GROWTH

The list of problems above may have omitted some of the issues raised in the papers and the discussion; or, what is more likely, may not have stated them in the form that seems most appropriate and revealing to the participants. But my hope is that, with some qualifications, the list formulates adequately the major issues that dominated most of the papers and much of the discussion.

The list suggests two reflections. The first is that the problems are numerous, and recalcitrant; and would require a variety of sustained experimental and imaginative research before acceptable answers and measures are established. Second, in their character and recalcitrance, these are all questions of long standing in the national income literature, belonging to the problems of inclusion or drawing the dividing line between economic and noneconomic, on the one hand, and productive and unproductive, on the other; of netness and grossness—of distinguishing between costs and returns, between intermediate and final products; and of valuation, i.e., of a meaningful weighting system by which to combine the diverse costs and net economic products into acceptable and articulated totals. These are the groups of questions that have occupied the Income and Wealth conference from its very start, some thirty-six years ago. And in somewhat different form and language, these questions were the foci of repeated discussions in the economic literature going back now some two centuries, or longer. While I cannot document this statement by an adequate exercise in bibliography and history of doctrines, a reference to the long controversy about productive and unproductive services in the classical and Marxian schools (still affecting the national income accounting in the communist countries today) should remind us that the distinction between final and intermediate products, and that between economic transaction and economic production, were at issue then. In general, the problems under the three heads above are perennial, because they deal, essentially, with the separation between economic activity and life in general, and with theories of production and valuation which, however elaborated, would tend to lag behind rapidly changing reality and the rapidly shifting focus of observation of economic research; and thus always be present, if in changing variants.

If these be old questions, although in somewhat new guise, one may ask why the sudden rise in interest in them—a recent trend, of which this conference is only one illustration. The answer seems to me to lie in the effects of recent concern with, and an accelerated study of, economic growth, combined with some recent products of such growth—all of which raise questions about its quality as distinct from quantity—or better, questions about its real or *true* quantity as distinct from that yielded by conventional measures.

Thus, the quantitative study of economic growth, in which the *conventional* measures of gross and net product and its components, that are now subjected to various criticisms, were used to gauge the rate and reflect the structure of growth and the relations of growing output to the inputs, revealed the productivity gap. This was an unexplained residual, left after allowance for inputs of labor and capital, on the definitions of these inputs that were implicit in the conceptual framework of national product accounts. The gap suggested that either the production factors implied in the conventional national product framework were incompletely formulated; or that the relations between input and output were incorrectly perceived—and, in either case, more had to be learned about the characteristics of the factors or about the determinants of the shape of the relations between input and output. The singling out of quality of labor, reflective of differences in education and perhaps of other investments in quality of human beings as producers, was a clear response to this explanatory gap. While we may be uneasy about the emphasis placed on this source of quality differences in labor, and particularly bothered by the difficulty of establishing the specific component of outlays on education, etc., that represents investment rather than consumption, it is clearly the emphasis on economic growth that resulted in the emergence of this concern with investment in human capital—and of a host of issues that would lead to fairly far-reaching modification of the current economic accounts if they were to be consistently followed through.

Likewise, the demonstration that the high rate of modern economic growth is necessarily accompanied by a high rate of shift among production sectors, in the scale of productive enterprise, and in conditions of life required by active participation in the production process, leads to emphasis on changes in conditions of the life of individuals, as both ultimate consumers and workers, that were *required* by the changes in the production system. This called attention to the components in the changing structure of household expenditures that were clearly imposed by the changing conditions of work, in addition to education and other investment in human capital; and raised questions about these components as regrettable necessities, this time within the household rather than within the government collective.

Furthermore, the increasing complexity of economic structure resulting from economic growth, the large monopolistic scale of some of the production units, and the necessity of controlling the continuous, incipient conflicts generated by structural shifts in the course of modern economic growth called for a greatly augmented governmental apparatus—for economic regulation, for responding to pressures for greater equality of economic opportunity, and later for greater economic equality, and finally for assuring the international position of an economic society organized under a sovereign state in an age of intensified nationalism. The relevance of the resulting government output to the final goals of economic activity was brought sharply into question by the great rise not merely in the absolute, but in the proportional, magnitudes of resources devoted to government consumption in the rapidly growing developed countries.

Finally, pollution, depletion, and other negative by-products of economic production were greatly accelerated because of the very rapid rise of total output, in the conventional measurement—the growth of both output and pollution reflecting the rapid rise in the technological power of the modern production system, particularly with rising population. Economic production, and the technology that it employs, may be viewed as interference with the natural course of events, in order to shape the outcome to provide economic goods to man. All such interference has potential negative ecological consequences—pollution and the like—the more lasting, the higher the level of production technology as measured by its capacity to produce goods. After all, wooden products decay and plastic and rustless steel do not; and the economic advantage of salvaging the latter, once discarded, is, in many cases, absent. Likewise, the pollution potential of a modern power or chemical plant far exceeds anything observed with the more traditional technology of the ox and bullock. If one adds that modern economic growth feeds on a succession of technological innovations, the eventual consequences of the mass spread of which, positive and negative, cannot easily be forecast, then the inevitability of unexpected, unforestalled, negative consequences of economic growth is practically assured.

To put the arguments above simply, the concern with, and the process of rapid learning about, modern economic growth revealed that the production theory implicit in conventional national product measurement, based on simple relations between labor viewed as a kind of homogeneous substance and reproducible material capital, on the one hand, and output on the other, was too bare—overlooking many of the additional requirements of production, a variety of sources of productivity other than material reproducible capital, and the high probability that, in addition to positive output, increased production yielded also negative output, in the way of pollution, congestion, and the like. It suggested that the theory of valuation, in its reliance on prices observed in the markets, was also subject to severe limitations—in that the role of public goods was increasingly large, and the changing quality of goods not adequately reflected in the market because proper judgment of quality became increasingly difficult. This is not to deny the value of the conventional measures (with the theories implicit in them) as useful, if crude, approximations. One had to begin with those, as well-established in the conceptual structure of the discipline and as yielding articulated aggregates that would be relatively easily obtainable, and use them to derive the first approximations. Without the use of the latter, we could hardly have been able to learn as much as we did. But it is this learning that resulted in reemphasizing the various questions of improper inclusion and omission, the large magnitudes of which were suggested in the course of applying conventional measures to the quantitative analysis of economic growth. It is clearly the long-term aspect of the latter, the use of a period long enough for productivity residuals, structural changes, changes in conditions of life, and the sources of the large advances in both positive output and negative by-products to be observed; with the observations serving to emphasize the gaps in the conventional measurement, gaps that would not look as large in dealing with the more limited perspective of short-term changes.

The shift to the long-term viewpoint of economic growth suggests other problematic aspects of the current measures of economic performance—aspects not covered in the papers and discussion here, and probably meriting a brief note. First, increased emphasis on investment in human capital, on the household, and, in general, on the human factor in economic growth—as distinct from material capital and impersonal-seeming organizations and institutions—calls also for much greater attention to the distributive aspects of economic performance than appears to have been paid in the recent past. With rapid structural changes and dependence of high levels of economic performance on continuous reconciliation of conflicts incipient in the shifts of economic position of various social and economic groups implicit in structural changes, the distributive questions—who gets how much of the growing product—emerge to key importance. It is curious that properly formulated allocations of total product among significantly distinct groups in the population are *not* an integral part of the dominant systems of national economic accounts. And the aggregation that takes place automatically treats total product as an undifferentiated mass in which the high product of the upper income groups and the low product of the poor form one pool—the divisions of which are by industrial origin, or type of factor return, or type of use, or by region, but not by meaningful class and other economic groups within the population. Yet the sharing of these groups in economic growth is an important prerequisite of maintenance of economic productivity and high level of economic performance. The increasing stress on the household, and on the human factor, suggests that distributive allocations will have to be integrated into the measurement of economic performance much more closely than they have been so far.

The second aspect relates to international comparability. Many of the issues raised in the papers and in the discussion would assume an even clearer form, and perhaps different weights, if discussed in the context of meaningful comparisons in the level, or changes in the level, of economic performance among countries at different levels of economic development, or characterized by different patterns of social and economic organization. Perhaps it was wise, in organizing the present conference, to limit the discussion to measurement of economic performance in a single country (or a group of countries similar in their level of development and character of their social and political organization). As it was, the authors and discussants had to grapple with a wide variety of far-reaching and difficult problems. But it should be recognized that however the issues are resolved for the case of a single country or a given group of countries at specified levels of development and with a given sociopolitical structure, they will have to be reexamined when the goal is set of establishing comparability *beyond* the assumedly narrow range of differentials in levels of development or in the conditioning sociopolitical structure. There is a clear parallel in the effects on the various issues raised above between those of concern with the longer run of economic growth, and those resulting from attempts at international comparison of economic performance across a wide span of differences in levels of development and in the character of the social structure of the countries.

3. THE SHORT- AND THE LONG-TERM PERSPECTIVES

Every measure of economic performance, particularly an aggregate for a large entity like a country, reflects some basic assumptions and theories —assumptions about the distinction between economic activity and life in general, and about final goals of economic activity; and theories of production (inputs and outputs, and the relations between them) and of valuation (ways of combining inputs and outputs of different description). There are inevitably compromises in the extent to which the agreed-upon underlying assumptions and theoretically grounded concepts are faithfully and fully implemented in measurement—for the cost of complete conformity may be extremely high and yet yield only trivial adjustments as compared with a reasonable compromise. But the concepts and theories may differ depending upon the orientation and analytical uses that the measures are intended to serve—and they are relevant only to such uses. After all, we do not estimate, and use the national product estimate, of a country in order to measure its attainment in pure science, or in the arts, or in the increased supply of specimens of the New Communist Man; nor even to gauge levels of happiness, or changes therein, as reflected in responses of a representative sample of a country's population.

Clearly, the current set of measures of aggregative economic performance in the developed countries are better designed to reflect changes in the short rather than the long period, and may have been meant largely for that use. In the short run, structural changes and changes in conditions of life may be assumed to be small; changes in technology and pollution may be taken to be limited; and so would changes in quality of labor and capital, in the quality of complex goods, in the relative magnitude of public goods and in the duplication introduced by the intermediate character of much government activity. This assumption of relative fixity in the "questionable" components in the economic accounts is, of course, with reference to the magnitude of the possible short-term changes in those inputs and outputs about which there is little question— and it is particularly plausible when we are concerned with the kind of fluctuation that is involved in business cycles. Furthermore, if we are guided by the Keynesian notion of the possible insufficiency of final demand as the major short-term problem, we may be justified in classifying all household purchases and all purchases of goods by government as final consumption, since they do represent demand not for resale in the near future (with or without fabrication or processing); and demand for business capital formation is classified as final because the resale through use is extended into the much longer future. In short, in the concern with short-term changes, particularly fluctuations, it is possible to set aside many of the issues raised so sharply by the long-term perspective, and derive measures that are tolerable, and agreed-upon, gauges of the short-term movements in the economy and in its major component parts—of the type provided by the U.S. Department of Commerce or embodied in the international set of accounts of the United Nations.

The value of such acceptable measures of short-term changes and fluctuations, for orientation and analysis of short-term policies, should not be underestimated. So long as it is clearly understood that they are not adequately meaningful measures of economic growth [1]—not even of the short-term path of the long-term trend—and so long as they are used in full recognition that they are measures of total short-term change of which growth is one, but still to be determined, component, no harm and much gain can be derived. After all, a full record is provided of the outputs and inputs in many sectors of the economy; and the fact that there are elements of duplication and omission, when the change is viewed as

[1] A semantic confusion is introduced by the double connotation of the term "growth" and the verb "grows": they may mean merely an increase (and it is to be noted that a decline is rarely referred to as "decay" or "senescence" which would be the proper opposite of growth); or they may mean movement along the long-term secular path, which is the quantitative counterpart of a properly defined growth process, connoting much more than mere increase. When a statement is made in an economic report that the country *grew* in a given year, it is, literally taken, true only in the sense of an increase in some specific aggregative total; and much more analysis and knowledge would be required to establish that the country moved along the path of meaningful growth, involving backward and forward implications. The demands posed by a true measure of growth for resolution of the issues listed in the discussion lie in the reasonably assumed importance of the costs and returns defined differently from the conventional for both measuring and analyzing growth conceived as a movement along the secular growth path. In our discussion of economic growth here, it is the second of the two connotations of the term that is meant.

part of a growth trend, may be seen only as a partial qualification, still leaving the record useful as a gauge of current fluctuations, either in the absolute totals or in the apparent rate of change. Furthermore, considering the variety of conceptual and measurement problems that would have to be resolved before a fully adequate measure of growth is secured, and considering how much more will have to be learned about varying patterns of growth over time, one will have to wait long before reliable measures of the ongoing process of growth over short periods can be designed. Meanwhile, it may be useful to have crude measures of short-term movements, even if they are only uncertain approximations to current growth.

One should note that the remarkably rapid spread of the Department of Commerce gross national product estimates in this country into wide use in the recent two decades appears to have been accompanied by an effort to make these measures more timely, i.e., available for increasingly shorter intervals; to impound the major debatable and complex measurement problems, because of the danger that they would make the estimates less rather than more serviceable as acceptable gauges of short-term changes; and to strive to preserve and improve the accuracy of the estimates within the limits of the agreed-upon conventional concepts. The bias of the measures toward their use as short-term indicators has thus increased—and naturally so, since it is in this use that they found their increasingly widespread application, by business firms, by government, and for purposes of general orientation by the periodical press.

It would not be easy to argue that, given the limited resources (financial and intellectual), and the difficulty of establishing acceptable measures of economic growth that would take sufficient cognizance of still largely unknown aspects of the issues raised above, the choices in the development of national income accounting by the Department of Commerce over the last two decades were not optimal. This does not mean that more could not have been done, within a narrower scope than that suggested by the issues listed, to remove at least some of the limiting conventions. For example, possibly more could have been done in moving toward a replacement basis of fixed capital depreciation charges; or even in an attempt at adjustment for price changes, at least for household expenditures, that would reflect the changing weights of urban communities with their different price levels. But it would be improper to press even these points, without adequate knowledge of the constraints and of the alternatives that had to be weighed.

Two reflections are suggested by the comments just made. The first, already noted, is that the magnitude and difficulty of the measurement problems raised in the papers and in the discussion in this conference are great; and that an extensive program of experimental work, using the present data, calling for further and different data, and then using the latter, is required, before some of the components can be so defined that approximations in quantitative terms would be derivable continuously in sufficiently acceptable form to assure their usefulness in some set of national accounts—perhaps a set geared to measurement of growth, although still linkable with, and translatable into, the short-term accounts. While exploratory forays may be, and should be, made within the proximate future, it will take a number of years before the results of continuous research will cumulate into an acceptable new measurement framework. Second, we cannot expect that such experimental work will be carried through within the government. The decisions of government with respect to economic measurement have to be based upon a sufficiently agreed-upon framework to warrant expectation of wide acceptance, a sufficient consensus of confidence, so as to provide an adequate basis for use in broad orientation and in policy decisions within the government. It remains to be seen whether the experimental and imaginative work by economists and other social science analysts will succeed in formulating the concepts and in devising acceptable measures of economic growth that could serve as proper guides to the government in its commitment, through various policy instruments, to assist and promote the desired economic growth as defined and measured.

The problems raised in the papers and discussion set the task largely for experimental, scholarly research, and are not fitted for coverage by the type of consensus reporting that is done so well under government auspices, with the use of large resources and adequate coverage—once the basic consensus on concepts and meaning is given. The work exemplified by the Nordhaus-Tobin paper is clearly in this experimental and imaginative category; and one looks forward with great expectations to the results of work at the National Bureau by Kendrick, Eisner, and the Ruggleses reported on in the *51st Annual Report,* September 1971 (pp. 77–81). Such work has been rather limited so far, and perhaps it is not surprising—given the emphasis on the major issue provided by concern with, and learning about, economic growth. After all, the outburst of work on economic growth is a matter of the last twenty-five years; and the time for the evaluation and absorption of the problems raised by it, in the way of limitations of the traditional framework of economic measurement, has been rather short.

It would not help to underestimate the difficulties of research which these problems call for, and cast our discussion in terms that might suggest that the conventional system of national product accounting could be easily modified to accommodate the issues. Nor would it help to underestimate the importance of systematic, exploratory, and continuous work on the issues just raised by scholars outside the constraints of government, within academic and research institutions, for gradually building up a set of concepts and measures more appropriate for gauging long-term changes in economic performance. No mere improvement in the conventional accounts is likely to be sufficient to provide adequate answers and solutions to the complex issues that the rapidly changing structure and pattern of modern economic growth raise in approximating meaningful measures of unduplicated net product for significant components and groups. But the cumulative contribution of the continuous and detailed conventional accounts do provide us with an invaluable quarry, a base from which the radical revisions, substitutions, and supplementation can start.

Index

Abraham, C., 209–212
Accountability in education, 427–428
Accounting systems, 39, 234–237, 278–283, 443–444. *See also* National accounts
Accumulation accounts, 309, 314, 322–325, 326–328
Acton-Heisenberg principle, 506
Advertising business, 50
Age and income, 135
Aidenoff, Abraham, 9
Air: as asset, 5; and health, 500–501; quality of, 37–38, 444, 476–477, 478. *See also* Automobiles; Environment; Pollution control
Air conditioning expenditures, 74–76, 94–95, 157
Air Pollution Quality Office, 486
Ando, A., 247
Annual Survey of Manufacturers, 123, 129
Aquatic environment, 475
Arrow, Kenneth J., 270n, 358
Asset deflators, 291–292
Assets, evaluation of, 349. *See also* Capital assets
Aukrust, Odd, 119–120
Automobiles: depreciation of, 348; low emission, 498, 507–508, 538; and pollution, 525; value of, 385–386, 399, 436
Ayres, Robert U., 461, 464, 498n

Balance tables and social accounts, 118
"Baseline," 474

Becker, G. S., 32n, 33n, 34–35, 56, 169
Beet sugar industry, 488–497
Ben-Porath, Y., 171n
Berry, Charles, 130
Boffey, Philip M., 396n, 397n
Boulding, K. E., 232
Bowen, W., 32n
Bower, Blair T., 472n, 483n, 498n, 500n
Broadcasting. *See* News media; Television
Brookings Institution: microdata sets, 127, 128; Tax Model, 126, 134
Brown, E. C., 247
Budd, Edward C., 7n, 125
Budget constraint, and consumer valuation, 96–97
Bundy, McGeorge, 368
Bureau of Labor Statistics. *See* United States Department of Labor
Bureau of the Census. *See* United States Department of Commerce
Business sector. *See* Enterprise sector

Canadian National Railways, 503–504
Capital. *See* Capital accounts; Capital assets; Capital formation; Capital goods; Human capital
Capital accounts, 84–85
Capital assets: and capital stock, 275–276; index of, 265; intangible, 51–55, 106; as part of income, 100; tangible, 54, 85–86, 106, 251–254
Capital consumption allowances, 101